Mysterium & Medulla Bibliorum
THE
Mystery and Marrow of the B I B L E
NAMELY:

God's Covenants

WITH MAN

In the *First Adam* before the Fall, and in the *Last Adam*, JESUS CHRIST, after the fall, From the beginning to the end of the world:

Unfolded & Illustrated

In positive *aphorisms* & their *explanations*.

WHEREIN

The general nature, several kinds, gradual discoveries, sanctions and administrations of all God's *holy COVENANTS*, from first to last, throughout the whole *Scriptures*: together with their peculiar terms, occasions, author, federates, matter, end, properties, agreements, disagreements, and many other their noted excellencies are largely and familiarly expounded: the blessed person and office of *JESUS CHRIST*, the *soul of all the Covenant of Faith*, and sole *Mediator* of the *NEW COVENANT*, is described: many choice fundamental points of Christianity, are explained, sundry practical questions, or cases of conscience are resolved; various puzzling controversies about the present occasionally elucidated; and in all, the great supernatural MYSTERY of the whole Sacred BIBLE, touching God's most wise, gracious, merciful, righteous, plenary, wonderful, and eternal salvation of sinners by *JESUS CHRIST through faith*, sweetly couched and gradually revealed in his *covenant-expressions* in all ages of the church, is disclosed and unveiled.

---

by F R A N C I S   R O B E R T S, *M. A.*
Pastor of the Church at Wrington, in the County of Somerset

Berith Press
P.O. Box 861, Kansas, OK 74347
(918) 896-2055
www.berithpress.com

God's Covenants: The Mystery & Marrow of the Bible was first published in 1657. This Berith Press reprint, in which spelling, grammar, and formatting changes have been made, is 2024 by Berith Press, is a public domain work, as are now considered all volumes published by Berith Press.
Printed in the U.S.A.

ISBN 978-1-963516-06-7

But ye are come unto Mount Sion,—and to JESUS the Mediator of the NEW COVENANT, Hebrews 12:22-24

"I will be, says God, their God, and they shall be my people. What is better than this good, what is happier than this happiness?!" Augustine, On The Spirit and Letter, Chapter 22, Tome 3

London, Printed by R.W. for George Calvert, and are to be sold at his shop at the sign of the half-moon in Paul's Church-yard. 1657.

THIS is THE COVENANT that I will make with the House of Israel after those days, saith the LORD; I will give my Laws into their mind, and write them in their hearts. And I will be to them a God; and they shall be to me a people, etc.
Hebrews 8:10-12, Jeremiah 31:33-34

4

Volume 4

The Covenant of Faith under the David and Babylonian-exilic administrations

(Book III, chapters 5 & 6)

OF God's Covenant OF PERFORMANCE, Made and Confirmed in JESUS CHRIST actually Performed and Exhibited in our flesh, according to the Covenants of Promise: namely: the New Covenant, being the last and most excellent covenant expressure, which shall continue New, from Christ's death, until the world's end.

(Book IV)

Editor's Note

In preparing this work, I have placed most Scripture references as footnotes rather than within the body of the text. This is because (a) this follows the pattern presented by Roberts in early publication of this work, and (b) because there are simply so many Scripture references that Roberts gives.

The numbering system may take some getting used to. Roberts makes points within points, and sub-points within these, and so on. If you do not follow his numbering system closely, it is easy to feel lost quite quickly. To remedy this issue, I have listed the points from which each further sub-point derives. The sequence of parentheses appears usually in this manner: (1) [1] {1} (i) (a) - and then back to (1).

Footnotes are generally as they appear in the original work, rather than following a standardized modern format. Missing words are mostly eliminated, although in some places I have issued an explanatory footnote.

Latin quotations have been preserved, although some translations have been provided where convenient.

I pray that this work will be a blessing to you, dear reader.

Joseph Weissman, Oklahoma, 2024

Contents

~~~

BOOK THREE - Of God's Covenant of Faith in Christ, in particular, namely: of the Covenants of Promise before Christ, in six remarkable expressions of it.

Chapter 5 – Of the discovery, nature and administration of God's Covenants of Promise in the fifth observable period of time, from David until the Babylonian captivity, namely: of God's Covenant with David and his seed. *15*

A general introduction to this and the next covenant explanation. *16*

Aphorism 1: The author and nature of the Covenant with David. The covenant which God made with David and his seed was a Covenant of Faith in Jesus Christ promised. *26*

Aphorism 2: The federate parties to this Covenant. *41*

Aphorism 3: The impulsive cause and occasion of this Covenant. *51*

Aphorism 4: The substance, or subject matter of this Covenant with David. *59*

Section 1: The covenant mercies or blessings herein graciously promised on God's part to David and his seed. *61*

> First, the covenant mercies or blessings more especially concerning David himself were these: [etc] *61*
>
> Secondly, the covenant mercies or blessings more especially concerning David's seed were chiefly these, namely: God promised: [etc] *88*
>
> Thirdly and lastly, the covenant blessing or mercies touching the people Israel, the subjects of King David and his royal seed, were especially these; namely: [etc] *108*

Section 2: The covenant duties conditioned, required, and restipulated on the part of David and his seed in this Covenant, may be reduced chiefly to these two heads. *122*

Aphorism 5: The form of this Covenant with David and his seed. *141*

Aphorism 6: The End or Scope of God's Covenant with David. *147*

Aphorism 7: Seventhly, General Inferences from the whole of this Covenant with David. *151*

Chapter 6 – Of the Discovery, Nature and Administration of God's Covenants of Promise, in the sixth and last noted Period of Time, namely: From the Babylonian Captivity, Until the Death of the Blessed Messiah **Jesus Christ**. *173*

The preface to this Covenant's explanation, namely, of this Covenant's: (1) duration, (2) difference from David's, and (3) order of handling it. *174*

Aphorism 1: The Author, Occasion, Impulsive Cause, Federates & Nature of this Covenant. *179*

Aphorism 2: The Subject Matter or Substance Of God's Covenant with the Captive Jews. *204*

Section 1: The Subject Matter of this Covenant on God's Part. *206*
    [1] His raising up the Messiah, namely: Jesus Christ unto them. *206*
    [2] His redeeming them out of Babylon's captivity, and bringing them into their own land. *215*
    [3] God's cleansing of his people the Jews, when redeemed out of Babylon from all their spiritual defilements, from all their idols, from all their detestable things, and from all their transgressions. *238*
    [4] God's putting his Spirit within them, for new framing and spiritualizing their heart. *244*
        (Influence & Effect 1): Newness of heart and spirit. *248*
        (Influence & Effect 2): A heart knowing the LORD. *268*
        (Influence & Effect 3): Fleshiness or tenderness of heart, instead of stoniness of heart. *273*
        (Influence & Effect 4): Penientialness of heart. *292*
        (Influence & Effect 5): Oneness of heart and way. *296*
        (Influence & Effect 6): The constant fear of God. *347*
        (Influence & Effect 7): Obedience towards God. *351*
    [5] God's presence and residence in his sanctuary and tabernacle among his people, by his Spirit, Word, and public ministry forever. *353*
    [6] God's greatest covenant relation between himself and them, namely: that he would be their God, and they should be his people. *361*
    [7] Finally, the seventh and last covenant blessing, which the Lord in this Covenant promised to his captives, was: the mutual covenant

constancy between God and them in this everlasting Covenant – He would not turn from them, and they should not depart from him. *363*

Section 2: The subject matter or substance of this Covenant, on the part of God's captive people, consisted in sundry covenant duties required and restipulated from them to God. *366*

Section 3: Inferences from the whole matter of this Covenant. *375*

Aphorism 3: The Form of God's Covenant with his captive people. *385*

Aphorism 4: The End or Scope of God's Covenant with his captive people in Babylon. *392*

Aphorism 5: Fifthly, General Inferences from the whole of this Covenant with the captive Jews. *399*

BOOK FOUR – OF God's Covenant of Performance, made and confirmed in Jesus Christ actually performed and exhibited in our flesh, according to the Covenants of Promise, namely: the New Covenant: being the last and most excellent covenant expressure, which shall continue New, from Christ's death, until the world's end. *409*

Chapter 1 – Of the discovery and administration of the New Covenant, in the seventh and last period of time most remarkable, namely: from the death of Jesus Christ, until the end of the world. *411*

Aphorism 1: The terms, bounds, or limits of time for and during which the New Covenant became and remains of force, are especially from the death of our Lord and only Savior Jesus Christ, until the end of the world. *415*

Aphorism 2: The interval, space, or revolution of time, from the death of Jesus Christ until the end of the world, during which the New Covenant administration continues, is of all other revolutions or intervals of time, during which any other fore-going covenant administration continued, most considerable and remarkable. *433*

Chapter 2 – Of the Names and General Nature of the New Covenant. *449*

Aphorism 1: In various respects and considerations, this Covenant is represented to us in holy Scriptures under a variety of names. *450*

Aphorism 2: Having thus considered the names, next we consider briefly the nature of this New Covenant more generally, in this aphorism. *471*

Chapter 3 – Of the Author or Efficient; the Occasion, and Impulsive Causes of this New Covenant. *475*

Aphorism 1: The LORD God – namely: God the Father, in the Son Jesus Christ, by the Holy Spirit – is the sole efficient Cause or Author of this New Covenant: promising it of old, establishing it in fullness of time, and applying it in due time to his called people. *476*

Aphorism 2: The LORD God, Father, Son and Holy Spirit, took occasion, From his own people's afflicted condition, the Old Testament's insufficiency, and the greatness of man's misery, to promise, establish, and apply this New Covenant to them that are called of his mere grace, in and for the merit of Jesus Christ. *484*

Chapter 4 – Of the federates, or parties to this New Covenant. *509*

Aphorism 1: The confederates, or federate parties to the New Covenant, are, on the one hand, God the LORD, or God as Jehovah, the principal party; on the other hand, the house of Israel, and the house of Judah, in Christ, the less principal party; that is, the Jews, Israel, and Judah united, and their seed; as also the Gentiles that shall be called and their seed. *511*

Position 1: That Israel and Judah, or the house of Israel and Judah, that is, the whole body of the Jews, or Jewish church, united in Christ, were first and immediately intended to be federates with God in this New Covenant: is evident upon these grounds. *515*

Position 2: That the Gentiles, whom afterwards God should call and incorporate into one church body with the Jews by Christ, were next intended to be joint federates with the Jews in this New Covenant with God. *522*

Position 3: The posterity, seed, or children both of believing Jews and called Gentiles, are – with their parents – federates in this New Covenant. *531*

Aphorism 2: Hence, (1) the New Covenant is most sure and faithful; (2) most complete and comprehensive; (3) most uniting and consolidating to the church and people of God; (4) and is, beyond all other Covenant dispensations, greatest matter of consolation, joy, and thankfulness to the Gentiles. (5) In and under which, All the infant children of New Covenant federates, being in Covenant with their parents, ought to be signed and marked with the first New Covenant token, baptism, as well as their parents. *559*

> [Argument 1] All sorts of persons that are federates with God in the New Covenant, ought to be initiated, signed, marked, and distinguished by baptism: the first token of the New Covenant. *566*
>
> [Argument 2] All sorts of persons for whom Christ's enlarged New Covenant commission in Matthew 28:19-20 was intended, ought to be baptized. *571*
>
> [Argument 3] All sorts of persons to whom the promise is (which was anciently made to Abraham, Isaac, Jacob and to their seed, etc. and afterwards confirmed by Jesus Christ in his New Covenant) ought to be baptized. *576*

[Argument 4] All sorts of persons that were once admitted by God to the initiating sacrament or first Covenant token of the Covenant of Faith, and were never since by him debarred, ought still to be admitted to the first token of the Covenant of Faith, what ever it be, under all sorts of ensuing federal administrations. *578*

[Argument 5] All sorts of persons that were Circumcised before and under the Old Covenant administration even until the days of Christ, ought to be baptized under the New Covenant Administration since the days of Christ. *583*

[Argument 6] All sorts of persons to whom the mercies, benefits, and blessings promised in the New Covenant and signified in this first New Covenant token of baptism, appertain, and are communicated, ought to be baptized. *587*

[Argument 7] All sorts of persons, whom God has expressly or virtually commanded to be baptized, ought to be baptized. *590*

Chapter 5

Of the discovery, nature and administration of God's Covenants of Promise in the fifth observable period of time, from David until the Babylonian captivity, namely: of God's Covenant with David and his seed.

A general introduction to this and the next covenant explanation.

The fifth considerable period of time, wherein God renewed and much enlarged the **Covenant of Faith** in reference to **Christ promised** for sinners' recovery and salvation, was from David until the Babylonian captivity. And the sixth period (of which afterwards in chapter 6) from the captivity until the Death of Christ.

The administration of the Sinai Covenant or Old Testament (as I have formerly shown)[1] continued from the giving of the law on Mount Sinai until the death of Jesus Christ – even from God's typical redeeming of Israel a little before that from corporal bondage in Egypt, until God's true redeeming of all his elect from spiritual bondage under sin and Satan by the death of Jesus Christ.

Now under this Old Testament administration, and even during the same, these two subsequent Covenants were revealed and superadded: not to annul or abrogate this Old Testament administration at all, but rather to enlarge, amplify, and expound the same in some particulars, especially with reference to the sacred line of Jesus Christ, both by law, and by nature.

Hence as Ezekiel saw in his vision, as it were, a wheel in the middle of a wheel;[2] so methinks I see here a covenant in the middle of a covenant, yea these two covenants in the bosom of the Sinai Covenant. Or rather, the Sinai Covenant – big with child – having these twin Covenants in its womb. For clearing this particular yet more distinctly, I offer this thesis or position, namely:

When God was pleased to change Israel's civil rulers from judges to kings, and from kings to governors (the Old Testament administration

---

[1] In Book 3 Chapter 4, in the Introduction, etc
[2] Ezekiel 1:16

still standing in force), he notably amplified this Sinai Covenant, or Old Testament, by other two Covenants of Promise in Christ; namely: (1) his Covenant with David and his seed. (2) His Covenant with the Jews under the Babylonian captivity.

This position I resolve into parts, and explain as follows: (1) That under this Sinai Covenant, God revealed two other Covenants: the one to David, and the other to the captive Jews. (2) That both these were Covenants of Promise in Christ. (3) That notwithstanding, these two Covenants were not disannulled, but rather, this Sinai Covenant, or Old Covenant still stood in force. (4) That by these two Covenants, the Sinai Covenant was notably enlarged. (5) That God, by these two Covenants, then enlarged the Sinai Covenant, when he made those two great changes of Israel's civil rulers from judges to kings, and from kings to governors.

(1) That under this Sinai Covenant, God revealed two other Covenants – the one to David and his seed; the other to the Captive Jews – is evident: [1] by Scripture testimonies, and [2] By computation of times.

[1] By Scripture testimonies, declaring:

{1} *That God revealed and made a Covenant with David and his seed.* For: (i) the occasion and substance of this Covenant was revealed in vision to Nathan, and by Nathan to David.[3] (ii) The recital or repetition of this Covenant is also made, with some enlargements and expositions thereupon.[4] (iii) And this Covenant was the great consolation of David against all the afflictions upon his family, with this he supported himself in his old age, as he declares in his last words.[5]

---

[3] 2 Samuel 7:4-18; 1 Chronicles 17:3-16
[4] Psalm 89 & 132
[5] 2 Samuel 23:1-6

{2} *That God revealed and made a Covenant also with his people the Jews in their Babylonian captivity*; is evident both by the words of Jeremiah,[6] Ezekiel,[7] and of other prophets,[8] speaking of his people's redemption out of Babylon, especially of their spiritual redemption by Christ.

[2] By computation of times. For all the times of David, and all the times of the Jews' captivity in Babylon, did fully fall in, under this Old Testament dispensation – the Sinai Covenant administration continuing still in force from the establishment of it at Mount Sinai until the death of Jesus Christ; even from the typical redemption out of Egypt, until the true redemption out of sin and misery by Christ.

(2) That both of these Covenants (namely: with David and the captive Jews) were Covenants of Promise – in *Christ* promised – is plain.

For: [1] Under them both, Christ is promised. To David, Christ is promised as his primary seed in that Covenant which God made with him and his seed, that *his throne should be established forever*, etc.,[9] to the captive Jews also, Christ is promised as *the LORD their righteousness*, as *the righteous branch*, as he that *by the blood of the Covenant should send forth his prisoners out of the pit wherein was no water*, that should *finish transgression after seventy weeks*, etc., so that Christ is singularly revealed in them both.[10]

[2] Christ is revealed and promised in them both, as *to come afterwards*, not as come already; as future, not as past or present; as hoped for *in fullness of time*, not as already actually enjoyed. Now as the New Covenant alone, representing Christ as performed and exhibited already, is (in propriety of speaking) the only Covenant of Performance, so all other Covenants of Faith

---

[6] Jeremiah 32:36 to the end & chapter 33
[7] Ezekiel 11:14-22 & 36:22 to the end
[8] Isaiah 48:20-21, 46:3-4, Zechariah 9:12, Daniel 9:24, Micah 5:2
[9] Psalm 89:3-4; 2 Samuel 7:11-12, Luk. 1:32-33, 69, Acts 2:30-31
[10] Jeremiah 23:5-6, 33:14-15, Zechariah 9:12, Daniel 9:24, Micah 5:2

foregoing, representing Christ only as promised, for future, are properly mere Covenants of Promise in Christ.[11]

(3) That notwithstanding these two Covenants of God with David and the captive Jews, the Sinai Covenant, or Old Testament was not hereby abrogated, but still stood in force and use; is apparent, for:

[1] David lived in obedience and subjection to God according to this Covenant. He made use of the Levitical priesthood;[12] he took care of God's tabernacle and ark, and of God's worship there with greatest delight, enquiring at his holy oracle;[13] he provided most liberally for the building of the temple[14] (a blessing promised in this Sinai Covenant),[15] delivering the pattern of it to his son Solomon, with instructions about it, etc.

[2] The captive Jews also were under this Sinai Covenant administration. For they lamented sadly the ruins of Zion in a strange land.[16] They – as soon as God vouchsafed them deliverance from Babylon – returned to Jerusalem to rebuild the temple and city, and restore the worship of God according to the Sinai Covenant, and accordingly effected it.[17] And they continued this way of worship (though defiled with many mixtures of their own) until the coming of Christ.[18]

[3] Jesus Christ himself, who according to this Sinai Covenant came from them according to the flesh, he lived in obedience and subjection to his heavenly Father under this Covenant, until his dying hour. He was circumcised the eighth day;[19] he was presented in the temple according to the

---

[11] Ephesians 2:12
[12] 1 Samuel 23:9-13
[13] 2 Samuel 6 throughout, Psalm 5:7; Psalm 42, 63 & 84
[14] 2 Samuel 7:1-3; 1 Chronicles 22-26 & 28-29
[15] Deuteronomy 12:5-6, 10-12, 14
[16] Psalm 137:1, etc.
[17] Ezra 1:5, etc; 2:1, etc/
[18] Daniel 9:26-27, Luke 1:5, 8-9 & 2:21-24
[19] Luke 2:21

law at the time of his mother's purification;[20] he went up to Jerusalem to worship at the solemn appointed feasts;[21] he did offer the sacrifice of the passover in his season;[22] until at last he offered up himself (as the passover, as the sacrifice of all sacrifices, the body of all those shadows, the truth of all those types) once for all for his elect, accomplishing and so abolishing all those Levitical sacrifices, together with that covenant administration.[23]

(4) That by these two Covenants, the Sinai Covenant administration was notably enlarged. This enlargement of the Sinai Covenant by these two Covenants was especially: [1] by many mercies promised,[24] and [2] by the line of Jesus Christ according to the flesh drawn down by David[25] and Zerubbabel;[26] and [3] by the particular designation of the time for the Messiah's suffering[27] – of all which afterwards in the further opening of these two Covenants.

(5) That by these two Covenants, God then enlarged this Sinai Covenant, when he made those two great changes of his people's civil rulers: from judges to kings, and from kings to governors.

[1] God changed Israel's judges into kings, namely: when he chose David to be his king, and caused him to be anointed for that regal office. As for Saul, he was the people's king rather than God's king.[28] God *gave him in anger, and took him away in wrath.*[29]

---

[20] Luke 2:22-24
[21] John 5:1, 7:10 & 12:1
[22] Matthew 26:17-20
[23] 1 Corinthians 5:7, Hebrews 10:9-14
[24] Isaiah 55:3, Acts 13:34
[25] Psalm 132:12-13, Acts 2:30
[26] Haggai 2:23 with Matthew 1:1, 6, 12, Luke 3:21, 31
[27] Daniel 9:24-27
[28] 1 Samuel 8:5-7
[29] Hosea 13:11

From Moses until David, the Lord himself was their king, and they were God's theocracy – God's commonwealth more immediately under his government; over whom he from time to time raised up extraordinary persons, calling judges to rule them as his substitutes.

But in David's days, God changed these judges into kings. And with David, (God's first beloved and approved king), he makes a covenant:[30] peculiarly to assure him that Christ should descend from him in particular, according to the flesh; and should succeed him, sitting upon his throne, and ruling the church of God (typified by David's kingdom) forevermore. So that by this Covenant with David, the glory and royal dignity of Christ's kingdom, typed out in David's kingdom, is set forth most resplendently.

[2] God changed his people's kings again into princely governors under the Babylonian power that captivated them. So that after the captivity, when they were released and returned into their own land, we read no more of their kings, but only of their rulers or governors.[31] Hereby the regal glory was greatly eclipsed, though not totally extinguished, until the coming of Jesus Christ, so that the prophecy of Jacob might be fulfilled: *The sceptre shall not depart from Judah, nor a lawgiver from between his feet, till Shiloh come.*[32]

In their captivity, when this great eclipse was coming upon their regal government, God makes a covenant with them: partly, to comfort them in hopes of their redemption from Babylon and restoration to Canaan, though their royal glory was much dimmed and obscured; partly to assure them of the near approach of the Desire of all Nations,[33] the King of Kings and Lord of Lords,[34] Jesus Christ, in whom all the authority, power, and glory of judges, kings and governors should be swallowed up, and by whom all the four grand

---

[30] 2 Samuel 7:3-4, etc., Acts 13:22-23
[31] Ezra 6:7, Nehemiah 6:7, 5:14 & 12:26
[32] Genesis 49:10
[33] Haggai 2:7
[34] Revelation 19:16

empires and opposite kingdoms of the world should be broken, and brought as small as the dust of the summer threshing floor.[35]

Inferences hence:

---

(1) **This Sinai Covenant, or Old Testament, was an eminent and comprehensive covenant.**

[1] *Comprehensive*: In that it formally comprised within itself and under its own administration, God's Covenant with David, and with the captive Jews, together with all the accomplishments and perfections of them both. This was a pregnant and fruitful Covenant, having two Covenants in its bowels: covenants within a covenant. This Sinai Covenant was as the mother; these two as the twin daughters.

[2] *Eminent*: In that no other expression of the Covenant of Faith, besides this, has another covenant or covenants formally, but only virtually within itself. In this comprehensiveness, it excels them all.

(2) **These Covenants with David and with the captive Jews, though sweetly furnished with their peculiar mercies and advantages, yet were but as parts and branches of the Sinai Covenant, or Old Testament.**

They were as two grand branches of the same tree, or as two greater limbs of the same body. For the Sinai Covenant comprised them both, and all in them. Though therefore there are in these two covenants sundry things requiring a peculiar consideration; yet all of them are, in their general notion, of the same nature with the Old Testament. And hereupon a short and compendious explanation of these two Covenants may be sufficient: the Old Testament being already expounded, and that at large.

---

[35] Daniel 2:34-35, 44-45

(3) All the mercies promised and duties restipulated – together with other properties and perfections of these two Covenants – may be fitly ascribed to the Sinai Covenant, or Old Testament. For, they and these Covenants themselves are all within and under this Old Testament. As whatsoever is in the limb or branch may be fitly ascribed to the body or tree.

(4) Behold here the wisdom and goodness of God, who in the grand and noted alterations of his people's outward condition, is pleased to revive and renew afresh his Covenant of Faith in Christ unto them. Renewing his Covenant upon such alterations of his people's outward state:

[1] Makes his Covenant more notably observed by his people.

[2] Imprints it more deeply upon their hearts, inclining them to close with it.

[3] Assures them that such outward changes do not befall them without the hand of their gracious God, ordering all for his people's greatest good.

[4] And encourages them with hope and comfort to go on under such changes, having them thus sweetened and sanctified by renewed covenants and promises. Therefore, when God was about to turn lapsed Adam out of paradise into the wide world, he covenanted and promised that the seed of the woman should bruise the serpent's head, etc.[36] When God was about to drown the whole world with water, he covenanted with Noah to save him and his family in the ark by water.

When God called Abraham from his country, kindred and father's house, which was a great change to him.[37] He covenanted to give him Canaan for an inheritance, and a numerous seed to inherit it.[38] When God brought Israel from Egypt into the wilderness, from bondage to liberty, from a land wherein they were strangers, to go towards a land which they should inherit as their

---

[36] Genesis 3:15
[37] Genesis 6:18, etc.
[38] Genesis 12:1-3, 13:14-17, 15:18-21 & 17:4, 8

own, which was a great change, he entered into Covenant with them at Mount Sinai, according to the tenor of the Old Testament.

When he changed their judges into kings;[39] he made a covenant with David and his seed, his first approved king.[40] When he had brought his people the Jews into Babylon's captivity, and was about to deliver them thence, changing their kings into governors, he renewed his Covenant with those of the captivity.[41]

And when the fullness of time was come, that Christ should be actually exhibited and sacrificed for his elect – his church being grown up from minority to maturity, from non-age to full-age, which was her greatest change of condition beyond all others – he revealed his New Covenant in Christ performed, which is to continue until the world's end.[42]

Thus God – renewing his Covenant of Faith with his people – was still in some eminent change or alteration of their condition, for the greater discovery of his wisdom and goodness unto them: and tended singularly to satisfy, quiet and comfort them in all such great changes and alterations of their condition, as came upon them.

(5) **Finally, as the Sinai Covenant, or Old Testament itself, so these two Covenants comprised therein, remain of force and virtue from their several and respective manifestations, until the very death of Jesus Christ.** Their substance remains still, though their administrations then expired altogether. And so far as the mercies promised and duties restipulated in all three of them concern the very substance of the Covenant of Faith, and are not restrained or peculiarly limited by some particular circumstances of time, place, persons, etc. so far they concern us, and are applicable to us and to God's people in all succeeding ages for edification and consolation. But so far as they

---

[39] Exodus 24 with Deuteronomy 5:1-5, etc.
[40] 2 Samuel 7
[41] Jeremiah 32 & Ezekiel 37
[42] Hebrews 8:8 to the end

had peculiar restrictions and appropriations to times, places, persons, or other Circumstances, so far they were dissolved and expired at the death of Jesus Christ.

But this may suffice in general for an introduction to the opening of these two covenants, namely: (1) of the Covenant with David and his seed, and (2) of the Covenant with the captive Jews in Babylon.

Come we now More particularly to consider and look into God's Covenant with David and his seed, according to the former method in opening the other covenant expressures. And here: [1] the author and nature of this Covenant with David and his seed, [2] the federate parties to it, [3] the impulsive cause and occasion of it, [4[the substance or subject matter of it, [5] the form of it, [6] the end or scope of it, and [7] the corollaries or inferences resulting from the whole: shall be especially unfolded and explained in so many distinct aphorisms.

These things I shall expedite with all possible brevity and perspicuity so that this volume may not swell too big, and that I may hasten to the explanation of the New Covenant, the last and most complete expression of all God's Covenants of Faith from the beginning to the end of the world.

Aphorism 1

The author and nature of the covenant with David. The covenant which God made with David and his seed was a Covenant of Faith in Jesus Christ promised.

For clearing of this aphorism, three things are especially to be explained: (1) Who this David was, with whom this covenant was made. (2) That God made a covenant with this David and his seed. (3) That the Covenant made by God with David and his seed, was a Covenant of Faith in Jesus Christ promised.

(1) **Who this David was, with whom this Covenant was made.** Here I shall briefly describe him by his [1] name, [2] descent, [3] qualifications, [4] offices regal and prophetical, [5] renowned acts, [6] failings or miscarriages, [7] penitential recoveries, [8] afflictions, and [9] death.

[1] His *name* is thought to be at first imposed by God's special providence, as by the signification and event thereof may be collected. דָּוִד *David*, a Hebrew name, derived from דּוֹד *Dod*: {*Beloved*}. Whence {*David*} signifies *beloved*. He was so beloved of God, that God counted him *a man after his own heart.*[43] God calls him: *my chosen, my servant, my king, my firstborn, higher than the kings of the earth.*[44] He is styled *the man who was raised upon high, the anointed of the God of Jacob*, and *the sweet psalmist of Israel.*[45]

[2] His *descent* or *pedigree* was immediately from Jesse of the tribe of Judah; mediately from Abraham, in the fourteenth generation.[46] He was Jesse's

---

[43] 1 Samuel 13:14, Acts 13:22
[44] Psalm 89:3, 27 & 2:6
[45] 2 Samuel 23:1
[46] 1 Chronicles 34, verse 2 [and] throughout, Matthew 1:1-18

seventh and youngest son.⁴⁷ He was born in Bethlehem, a town in the tribe of Judah within the land of Canaan: whereupon it is called *the city of David* and *the town of Bethlehem where David was*.⁴⁸ His birth was in about the 2915th or 2917th year of the world, and 366 years after Israel's entering into Canaan.⁴⁹ And being the youngest, and least esteemed of his brethren, he was set to keep his father's sheep, and follow the ewes: great with young.⁵⁰

[3] His *qualifications* were eminent: whether natural, artificial, or spiritual. He was ruddy, and also *of a beautiful countenance, and goodly to look to*.⁵¹ He was *cunning in playing the harp, a mighty valiant man, a man of war, and prudent in matters* (or *in speech*), *and a comely person, and the LORD was with him*.⁵²

But above all, his spiritual endowments and qualifications excelled. He was effectually acquainted with God in his youth.⁵³ He had much knowledge of Jesus Christ's incarnation, of the fruit of his loins, offices – prophetic, priestly and kingly, sufferings and afflictions, death, burial, resurrection ascension into heaven, and session at God's right hand in highest majesty, until all his foes become his footstool.⁵⁴

He had much sweet fellowship with the Holy Spirit raising up his spirit to such sweet contemplations about spirituals, heavenly [expressions], fervent prayers, seraphical praises and ravished affections, towards his God and all his ways.⁵⁵ His faith was victorious over all worldly difficulties and oppositions.⁵⁶ His love to his God was wholly transcendent, prizing nothing in earth, no, nor

---

[47] 1 Chronicles 2:13-15
[48] Luke 2:4, John 7:42
[49] *Sacred Chronology* by Roger Drake, pp.52-53, Answer: pre, a, to Psal.
[50] 1 Samuel 16:10, Psalm 78:70-71
[51] 1 Samuel 16:12
[52] 1 Samuel 16:18
[53] 1 Samuel 16:7, 13, 18 & 17:32-38, 45-47
[54] Acts 2:30, Psalm 45:2, 7, 110:4, 2:6, 110:1-3, 6, Psalm 22 throughout, 110:1, 7, 22:16-18, 16:10-11; Psalm 68:18 with Ephesians 4:8 & Psalm 110:1
[55] 2 Samuel 23:2
[56] 1 Samuel 17:30-38, 45-47, Psalm 3:6, 27:1, 3, Psalm 116:10

in heaven like unto him alone.[57] His panting desires, thirstings, and longings after him were restless and unsatisfied.[58] His zeal to him, his house, to his word and law, to his worship and ordinances, to his church's prosperity, and to the whole welfare of true religion, was most ardent and intensive.[59] His affection to all of God's people and sincere servants was very large and lively.[60]

In the saints, the excellent upon earth was all his delight, though he was a mighty king, yet was he a companion of all them that feared the Lord and kept his statutes. His obediential disposition was such towards God and all his commands, that God counted him a man after his own heart, who should fulfill all his will.[61] His integrity and uprightness such before the Lord, in the whole course of his life, that God gives this testimony of him: *David did that which was right in the eyes of the LORD, and turned not aside from anything that he commanded him all the days of his life, save only in the matter of Uriah the Hittite* (1 Kings 15:5).[62] He was upright in his personal, domestic, ecclesiastical and political capacity. He was a sincere lover of his very enemies,[63] though a vehement hater of the enemies of God.[64] In a word, he was of a holy, heavenly disposition in his whole conversation; having heaven in his heart, and his heart in heaven.[65]

[4] His *offices*, which God cast upon him, were two high offices:

{1} He was a holy prophet in the church, a penman of most of those sweet heart-ravishing Psalms by the inscription of the Holy Spirit. He said: *The Spirit of the LORD spake by me, and his word was in my tongue.*[66] He

---

[57] Psalm 18:1, 4:6-7, 73:25-26
[58] Psalm 63:1-3, 8 & 42 & 84 & 27:4
[59] 2 Samuel 6:16, 21-22 & 7:2; 1 Chronicles 15 & 29:1-5, Psalm 132. etc., 96:3, 119:20, 67, 136, 139; Psalm 122:1-4, 6-9
[60] Psalm 16:3, 101:6 & 119:63
[61] Psalm 119:5-8, 10-11, 32, 106, etc., Acts 13:21
[62] Psalm 18, 20-23 & 101 throughout
[63] Psalm 35:12-13 & 119:139
[64] Psalm 23:5, 110:3, 101:21-22
[65] Psalm 26:6-8 & 25 throughout & 16; [Psalms] 65 to the end – yea, the whole book of Psalms eminently discovers the holy, spiritual, and heavenly frame of the soul.
[66] 2 Samuel 23:12

prophetically foretold many things very punctually touching Jesus Christ as has been shown.

{2} He was a godly king in the commonwealth. *Yet have I set* (or *anointed*) *my king upon my holy hill of Zion.*[67] God anointed him king by Samuel the prophet,[68] more privately in the presence of his father and brethren at Bethlehem, when he was about twenty three years old, and the Spirit of the LORD came upon David from that day forward. The men of Judah, upon the death of King Saul, came and anointed him king the second time over Judah in Hebron, when he was thirty years old: and he reigned over Judah seven years and six months.[69] All the elders of Israel anointed him the third time king over all Israel in Hebron, over whom he reigned in Jerusalem thirty three years. In all, forty years.[70] David in this his kingly office was a singular type of Christ: as after, will appear.

[5] His *renowned acts* are most observable after his royal unction, when the Spirit of God came eminently upon him:

{1} After his first and more private anointing by Samuel: (i) He appeared and repelled the evil spirit from Saul.[71] (ii) He slew Goliath of Gath with a sling and a stone, so discomfiting [embarrassing] the whole host of the Philistines.[72] Whereupon, Jonathan's heart was knit to him, and he made a league with him.[73] But King Saul, his father, though he advanced him, yet secretly hated him, because the Lord was with him, and because the woman of Israel sang of him: *Saul hath slain his thousands, and David his ten thousands.*[74] So that Saul persecuted the life of David, who was forced to fly and escape from him for his life nine or ten times.[75] (iii) He (being by singular

---

[67] Psalm 2:6
[68] 1 Samuel 16:1-14
[69] 2 Samuel 2:3-4 with [5:4-5]
[70] 2 Samuel 5:1-11
[71] 1 Samuel 16:14 to the end
[72] 1 Samuel 17 throughout
[73] 1 Samuel 18:1, 3-4
[74] 1 Samuel 18:2, 5-10, etc.
[75] 1 Samuel 21-28

providence preserved from assisting the Philistines against Israel in the battle wherein Saul and Jonathan were slain) rescued Ziklag, the captives and spoil thereof from the Amalekites.[76] (iv) He lamented for Israel's overthrow, and for the death of Saul and Jonathan.[77]

{2} After his second anointing, he prevailed against Abner's opposition, who set up Ishbosheth Saul's son as king over Israel for two years.[78]

{3} After his third anointing: (i) He took the stronghold of Zion from the Jebusites, and called it {*the city of David*}.[79] (ii) He subdued the Philistines, and other enemies.[80] (iii) He brought up the ark of God, first to the house of Obed-Edom, and afterwards into the city of David.[81] (iv) He purposed to build God a house, acquainting Nathan the prophet therewith: upon which God took occasion to reveal his Covenant to him and to his seed by Nathan, telling him, that not he but his son should build the house of the LORD, yea that the LORD would build David's house.[82] (v) He prepared abundantly all sorts of materials for the temple.[83] (vi) He instructed Solomon about the building.[84] (vii) He commanded all the princes of Israel to assist Solomon herein.[85] (viii) He ordered all the sorts of officers for the house of the Lord.[86] (ix) He gave Solomon the pattern of the house, encouraging him to the work, and charging him sincerely to serve the Lord.[87] (x) He invited the princes and people to offer willingly towards the building, greatly blessing God for their

---

[76] 1 Samuel 28-31
[77] 2 Samuel 1:11 to the end
[78] 2 Samuel 2:8 to chapter 5:6
[79] 2 Samuel 5:6
[80] 2 Samuel 5:17, etc., & 8:1-15; 1 Chronicles chapters 18-22
[81] 2 Samuel 6:1, etc.
[82] 2 Samuel 9:1, etc.
[83] 1 Chronicles 22:1-5
[84] 1 Chronicles 22:5-17
[85] 1 Chronicles 22:17-19
[86] 1 Chronicles chapters 23-27
[87] 1 Chronicles 28

readiness and liberalness therein.[88] (xi) He appointed Solomon his son to sit on his throne after him.[89]

[6] Sundry his *failings and miscarriages* are notwithstanding recorded very impartially, which were great blemishes to his renowned acts, both civil, military, and sacred. As: {1} He feigned himself mad before Achish King of Gath, changing his behavior before him, being surprised with base slavish fears.[90] {2} He easily vowed the destruction of Nabal's house, because of his churlish unkindness in denying some food to his soldiers.[91] {3} He distrusted God's providence and promises touching the throne, even despairing of life, because of Saul's uncessant persecuting of him.[92] *And David said in his heart, I shall now perish one day by the hand of Saul*. And elsewhere: *I said in my haste, All men are liars*. All – that have promised me the crown – are liars, etc.[93] {4} He lied to Achish, pretending that he and his men had made a [rod] against the south of Judah, etc, when they had been slaying the Amalekites, etc.[94] {5} He was too prone to go with Achish and the Philistines to battle against King Saul and Israel, in which battle Saul and Jonathan fell, and Israel was worsted. But God, by special providence, disengaged him.[95] {6} He defiled Bathsheba, and murdered Uriah, her husband, by the sword of the children of Ammon.[96] By these two great sins, he gave great occasion to the enemies of the LORD to blaspheme, and hereby also his uprightness was most shaken, and his obedience most shattered.[97] {7} He was too indulgent to his son Absalom though a murderer of his brother Amnon, and a traitor against his own father, David himself.[98] {8} He too hastily gave credit to Ziba's slander of

---

[88] 1 Chronicles 29
[89] 1 Kings 1:32-41; 1 Chronicles 29
[90] 1 Samuel 21:14-15
[91] 1 Samuel 25:21-22
[92] 1 Samuel 27:1
[93] Psalm 116:11
[94] 1 Samuel 27:8 to the end
[95] 1 Samuel 28:1-2 & 29 throughout
[96] 2 Samuel 12:9, 14
[97] 1 Kings 15:3-5
[98] 2 Samuel 18:5, 33 with 13:38 & 15:10-11

Mephibosheth, giving Ziba half his land, but very injuriously.[99] {9} He – hearkening too much to Satan's provocation – caused Jacob to number the people, placing too much carnal confidence in the arm of flesh, whereupon God broke the reed of carnal trust, slaying with the pestilence 70,000 men.[100] {10} Finally, he was too fondly indulgent to Adonijah, for *he had not displeased him at any time, in saying, why hast thou done so?*[101]

[7] His *penitential recoveries* nevertheless out of these failings, yea out of the grossest miscarriages, are storied [celebrated]. His failings are written for our caution and admonition, that we fall not: His recoveries for our instruction and consolation, that if we fall, we may rise again. But, as Augustine has well noted: "Many will fall with David, but they will not rise again with David," etc.[102] He acknowledged his base fears, and error in changing his behavior before Achish in Psalm 34 title and verse 4. He blessed God, blessed Abigail, Nabal's wife, and blessed her advice, whereby he was kept from shedding of blood and avenging himself with his own hand (1 Samuel 25:32-34). He acknowledged it was in his haste, that he said all men are liars, questioning God's promises, (Psalm 116:11). He habitually hated and abhorred lying, resolving that he that tells lies should not tarry in his sight (Psalm 119:163 & 101:7). He lamented the worsting of Israel by the Philistines and the death of Saul and Jonathan – mourning, weeping, and fasting (2 Samuel 1:11-12, etc.) He deeply repented of his murder and adultery, witnessing the same to all Israel and all succeeding ages of the church of God, by Psalm 51 purposely penned upon that occasion. His heart smote

---

[99] 2 Samuel 19:24-31
[100] 1 Chronicles 21:1; 2 Samuel 24:1-2, 15
[101] 1 Kings 1:5-6
[102] "For many men will to fall with David, and will not to rise with David. Not then for falling is the example set forth, but if you shall have fallen for rising again. Take heed lest you fall. Not the delight of the younger be the lapse of the elder, but be the fall of the elder the dread of the younger. For this it was set forth, for this was written, for this in the Church often read and chanted: let them hear that have not fallen, lest they fall; let them hear that have fallen, that they may rise." Augustine on Psalm 51
Site: <https://www.newadvent.org/fathers/1801051.htm>
[Accessed 2/26/2024]

him for numbering the people, so that he acknowledged his sin, begged pardon, accepted the punishment, and offered burnt offerings and peace offerings (2 Samuel 24:10, 17, 25). Thus David falling, is a caution against relapsing; David rising again, is a pattern of repenting.

[8] His *afflictions and chastisements* wherewith the Lord exercised him (notwithstanding his repentance) for his failings were very many. Besides the persecutions of Saul probably ordered to him upon some other account, he had many troubles: {1} in his family, {2} in his kingdom, and {3} with foreign adversaries of several sorts.

{1} *In his own family*: (i) The child begotten in adultery was smitten with death.[103] (ii) Tamar was incestuously forced and defiled by Amnon her brother.[104] (iii) Amnon was bloodily murdered thereupon by the command of his brother Absalom.[105] (iv) Absalom treasonably rebelled against his father David, seeking his crown, defiling his father's concubines.[106] At this time, Achithophel fell from David to Absalom. And Shimei reviled and cursed David, being forced to flee from Jerusalem to escape the conspiracy, upon which flight he penned Psalm 3. (v) Adonijah also mutually sought his father's crown contrary to David's appointment of it to Solomon.[107]

{2} *In his kingdom and without, he was exercised with many troubles*. As: (i) With the insurrection of Sheba the son of Bichri, a wicked Benjamite.[108] (ii) With the three-year famine in the land for Saul and his bloody house.[109] (iii) With several battles against the Philistines and other enemies in one of which, David's life was in extreme hazard. (iv) With three days of pestilence for his numbering the people, by which stroke of God, he lost 70,000 men, thus God breaking the staff or reed of his carnal confidence.[110] By these and like

---

[103] 2 Samuel 12:14-24
[104] 2 Samuel 13:1-23
[105] 2 Samuel 13:28-29
[106] 2 Samuel 15:1-19
[107] 2 Kings 1:5, etc.
[108] 2 Samuel 20
[109] 2 Samuel 21
[110] 2 Samuel 24:15

afflictions his sorrows grew so great, that his life was spent with grief, his years with sighing, his strength failed, and his bones were consumed.[111] The pangs of death compassed him about, the floods of Belial (ungodly, yokeless men) made him afraid, the cords of hell compassed him, the snares of death prevented him. His heart was sore-pained within him, and the terror of death fell upon him. Fearfulness and trembling came upon him, and horror overwhelmed him.[112] But what time he was afraid, he trusted in God; his shield about him his glory, and the uplifter of his head.[113] In his distress, he called upon the Lord, and he delivered him from all his fears, drew him out of many waters, rescued and freed him from all his enemies, and brought him forth into a large place.[114] So that he loved the Lord his strength most dearly; awakened up himself, his glory, his psaltery and harp, and all within him, to bless the Lord and triumph in his praises, resolving to call upon him as long as he lived, etc.

[9] Finally, when he had served the will of God in his generation, and the time of *his departure* approached,[115] in his last words he singularly comforted himself, by the everlasting covenant, ordered in all things and sure, which the Lord had made with him, although his house were not so with God.[116] And after he had settled his kingdom in the hand of Solomon his son, and given him godly instructions about his conversation and the structure of the temple;[117] *He fell asleep and was gathered to his fathers, dying in a good old age, full of days, riches and honor.*[118]

This was that renowned David, with whom the Covenant was made.

---

[111] Psalm 31:11
[112] Psalm 55:4-5
[113] Psalm 56:3-4 & 3:3
[114] 2 Samuel 22:7, 17-18, etc., 50; Psalm 34 & 18 throughout & 57:8 & 103 & 116
[115] Acts 13:36
[116] 2 Samuel 2:3-5
[117] 1 Chronicles 28 & 29
[118] Acts 13:36; 1 Chronicles 29:28

(2) That God made a Covenant with this David and his seed, is evident in several ways, as:

[1] By the vision which Nathan the Prophet had from God, and imparted unto David, when he entertained that pious resolution in his heart of building God a house, when the Lord had given him rest from all his enemies round about.[119] In this vision, the occasion and substance of God's Covenant with David and his seed, touching the establishment of his throne and kingdom forever, etc., is expressed, which elsewhere is styled {*a covenant*}.[120]

[2] By the express testimony of God himself, in the recital, exposition, and enlargement of his Covenant with David and his seed, saying: *I have made a* **covenant** *with my chosen: I have sworn unto David my servant. Thy seed will I establish forever, and build up thy throne to all generations, Selah. My mercy will I keep for him forever: and my* **covenant** *shall stand fast with him. His seed also will I make to endure forever*, etc. *My* **covenant** *will I not break: nor alter the thing that is gone out of my lips*, etc.[121] Here, God calls his promises to David his {*covenant*}, three several times, and those promises {*that covenant*}. extended to David and to his seed. And elsewhere – further reciting and explaining this covenant – he said: *The LORD hath sworn in truth unto David, he will not turn from it: of the fruit of thy body will I set upon thy throne. If thy children will keep my* **covenant** *and my testimony, that I shall teach them: their children also shall sit upon thy throne for evermore.*[122]

[3] By David's own acknowledgement in express terms; when in his last words he comforted himself in God's faithful promises, saying: *Although my house be not so with God; yet he hath made with me an everlasting* **covenant**, *ordered in all things, and sure*: for (or therefore) *this is all my salvation, and all my desire, although he make it not to grow.*[123]

---

[119] 2 Samuel 7:1-18; 1 Chronicles 17:3-16
[120] Compare Psalm 89:3-4, 28, 34-37 & 132:11-12 with 2 Samuel 7:11, 16
[121] Psalm 89:3-4, 28-29, 34, etc.
[122] Psalm 132:11-12
[123] 2 Samuel 25:5

By these three particulars, it is clear that God made a covenant with David and his seed, and that God was the sole efficient cause and author of this Covenant.

(3) That this Covenant made by God with David and his seed, was a Covenant of Faith in Jesus Christ promised.

This Covenant, for the nature and kind of it, was not a Covenant of Works holding forth righteousness and life upon condition of perfect and exact doing, but a Covenant of Faith in Christ tendering righteousness and life upon terms of sincere believing in Christ. And that believing in Christ, as promised, and to be performed afterwards in fullness of time, not as performed and exhibited already. That this is the nature and kind of God's Covenant with David and his seed, may be thus evinced, namely:

[1] Because David remained still under the duty, obligation, and authority of the Sinai Covenant, after this present Covenant was made with him, as well as before.

{1} Before this Covenant was made with David, he was under the duty and obligation of the Sinai Covenant. This is plain: (i) By David's enquiring of the Lord by the Levitical ephod and Abiathar the priest, and the Lord's answer.[124] (ii) By his zeal and diligence in bringing up the ark of God (the chiefest of the holy things in the tabernacle) into its place prepared for it in the City of David.[125] (iii) By his offering of Levitical sacrifices, namely: burnt offerings and peace offerings, etc.[126] (iv) By his zealous purposes for building a house to the LORD, even a habitation for him to put his name there, as God had promised by Moses.[127]

{2} After God had made this Covenant with David, he was also under the obligation and authority of the Sinai Covenant. For: (i) As soon as Nathan had

---

[124] 1 Samuel 30:7-8
[125] 2 Samuel 6:1-17, Psalm 132:1-10
[126] 2 Samuel 6:17-18
[127] 2 Samuel 7:2, etc., with Deuteronomy 13:5-7

revealed God's Covenant to David and his house, David immediately went to the tabernacle before the ark to perform his praise and prayer before the Lord.[128] (ii) After his sin in the matter of Uriah the Hittite, he went into the Levitical house of the Lord and worshiped.[129] He begged pardon of his sin in that phrase: *Purge me with hyssop and I shall be clean, wash me and I shall be whiter than snow*, alluding to the ceremonial purgations and washings.[130] And he promised burnt offerings, whole burnt offerings, and bullocks to be offered on God's altar. (iii) In his flight from Absalom his son, David had Zadok the priest and all the Levites with him bearing the ark of the Covenant of God, etc.[131] (iv) When he had carnally numbered the people, trusting in the arm of flesh, whereupon the Lord slew in three days 70,000 men with the pestilence, he built an altar, and offered burnt offerings and peace offerings, as the Lord commanded him, for the staying of the plague.[132] (v) Finally, before his death, he made great preparations for the building of the temple, received the pattern of it from God, gave it to Solomon, instructing and encouraging him unto the work.[133]

{3} Both before and after this Covenant, David was under the full obligation and authority of the Sinai Covenant, because the Sinai Covenant remained in full force from the giving of it at Mount Sinai until the death of Christ at Jerusalem, as has formerly been manifested. Now David – both before and after this Covenant was made with him, remaining still under the duty and force of the Sinai Covenant – this Covenant with David must needs be symbolical to, and of like nature with, the Sinai Covenant, namely: a Covenant of Faith in Christ promised, and not as then performed. For David could not at one and the same time be under the duty and obligation of two such opposite Covenants, as of Works and Faith.

---

[128] 2 Samuel 7:18, etc.
[129] 2 Samuel 12:20
[130] Psalm 51:7
[131] 2 Samuel 15:24, 25-30
[132] 2 Samuel 24:1, 10, 15, 18-19, 25
[133] 1 Chronicles 28 & 29

[2] Because Jesus Christ *to be performed and exhibited long after the times of David* was one of the great covenant-blessings promised to David in this Covenant. The perpetuity of David's seed, and of his kingdom to his seed, having its fullest accomplishment in Jesus Christ and his everlasting kingdom.[134] And Jesus Christ was never revealed or tendered in the Covenant of Works, wherein is no need of a mediator, but only in the Covenant of Faith. And that Covenant of Faith, which reveals and promises Christ as to be performed afterwards, is properly to be referred to the **Covenants of Promise**.[135]

[3] Because David, even under this Covenant which God made with him, describes and sets forth the righteousness of faith without our own works of the law, as Paul shows.[136] Therefore this Covenant with David was a Covenant of Faith, not of Works: the righteousness of faith without works being the peculiar terms, condition, and tenor of the Covenant of Faith.

[4] Because, David and his seed (with whom this Covenant was made,) were (as has been shown)[137] special types of Jesus Christ the true David and of his seed, principally intended in this Covenant.[138] Consequently, this Covenant was a Covenant of Faith in Christ promised, the very foundation of this Covenant.

Inferences

(1) **Hence the authority of this Covenant with David was wholly divine**: an immediate vision from God to Nathan the prophet, and by Nathan

---

[134] Compare 2 Samuel 7:12-13, Psalm 89:3-4 with Luke 1:31-33 & Acts 2:30
[135] Ephesians 2:12
[136] Romans 4:1-9 & Psalm 32:1-2
[137] In Aphorism 7 of this chapter
[138] Acts 2:30

to David.[139] Hence Nathan thus began the narrative thereof to David: *Thus saith the LORD*, and went on therein with these words: *Thus saith the LORD of Hosts* (2 Samuel 7:5, 8). And therefore, all the promises therein propounded were most infallible, sure, well-ordered, and comfortable to David, as he himself testifies in his last words most emphatically.[140] And all the conditions required on the part of David and his seed were their unquestionable duties towards God.

(2) **Hence God's Covenant with David was his gospel to David.** For, this was a Covenant of Faith, preaching the glad-tidings of life and salvation by Jesus Christ to all that believe in him, and particularly to David and all his believing seed – and this is pure gospel. Oh how sweet was this Gospel Covenant to blessed David, saying of it: *This is all my salvation, and all my delight!*[141] As it was said of Jacob that his life was bound up in his son's life,[142] so it might be much more said of David that his life, salvation, and delight were bound up in this Covenant, and in Jesus Christ his chief promised seed that should sit upon his throne forever. When therefore we read God's Covenant with David, or the explanation thereof, in Old or New Testament, we should still remember we are reading the gospel of God in Jesus Christ – and that should allure us to read on, and meditate therein with great delight.

(3) **Hence God's Covenant with David was one of the Covenants of Promise.**[143] The Covenant of Faith (as has been already shown)[144] comprises in it:

{1} The Covenants of Promise, in Christ promised from the foundation of the world, and to be performed in human flesh in the fullness of time.

---

[139] 2 Samuel 7:1-18; 1 Chronicles 17:3-16
[140] 2 Samuel 23:1-7
[141] 2 Samuel 23:5
[142] Genesis 44:30
[143] Ephesians 2:12
[144] In Book 1 Chapter 2 Aphorism 3

{2} The Covenant of Performance, in Christ actually performed and manifested in the flesh already. And this is only the New Covenant. Now this Covenant with David had reference to Christ that should be performed in the flesh afterwards; of the house and lineage of David, and therefore it was not the Covenant of Performance, but only one of the Covenants of Promise; yet an eminent Covenant of Promise, in some regards surpassing all that went before, as after will appear.

Therefore David, his house, and the whole church of the Jews, had their hopes and expectations sweetly raised towards Christ, and their longing desires exceedingly inflamed and incited after Christ, by this Covenant. So that in King Solomon's days, the church thus expressed her panting desires after Christ's incarnation, *Let him kiss me with the kisses of his mouth; for thy love is better than wine.*[145] As if she had said: "The kisses of Christ in the patriarchs mouths by their doctrines of Christ, are sweet to me." The kisses of Christ in the prophets' mouths by their fuller doctrines of Christ, are much sweeter. But oh, the kisses of Christ's own mouth manifested in the flesh, by his own personal doctrines and consolations, will be far sweetest of all. *Oh let him kiss me with the kisses of his mouth* – his own mouth. And again: *Oh that thou wert as my brother, that sucked the breasts of my mother* – (that is, "Oh that you were as mine own natural brother in the flesh! Oh that you were incarnate already!" The words are a periphrasis of a natural brother) – *When I should find thee without, I would kiss thee, yet I should not be despised. I would lead thee, and bring thee into my mother's house, who would instruct me: I would cause thee to drink of spiced wine, of the juice of my pomegranate. His left hand should be under my head, and his right hand should embrace me.*[146]

---

[145] Song of Solomon 1:2
[146] Song of Solomon 8:1-3

Aphorism 2

The federate parties to this Covenant

The federates or parties to this Covenant were: on the one hand **God**, as the LORD of Hosts, the God of Israel, the Rock of Israel, a father to David and his seed, his God, and the rock of his salvation. On the other hand **David** and his **seed**. David, as one that was mighty, God's chosen, God's servant, God's anointed king, God's firstborn, higher than the kings of the earth, David's seed, as God's son, and king forever.

For evidencing and explaining of this aphorism, consider especially these two particulars:

(1) That God, on the one hand, and David and his seed on the other, were parties to this Covenant.

(2) In what peculiar notions, God, David, and his seed, were such federate parties. Both of these are briefly comprised in this aphorism.

(1) **That God, on the one hand, and David and his seed on the other, were parties to this Covenant**, is evident sufficiently: [1] by God's vision to Nathan, [2] by God's own testimony, and [3] by David's acknowledgement – all opened in the former aphorism.

(2) In what notions and considerations, God, David, and his seed, were such federate parties to this Covenant, I thus further explain:

[1] First, **God** was the chief federate party to and author of this Covenant in these notions and respects especially, namely:

{1} As the Lord of Hosts. When God first revealed this Covenant to David by Nathan's vision, God commanded Nathan to speak unto David in this style: *Thus shalt thou say unto my servant David, Thus saith the LORD of*

Hosts, etc.¹⁴⁷ God is Lord of Hosts, partly, because all creatures in heaven and earth are his hosts or armies, to execute his will at his command as angels, sun, moon, and stars; fire, hail, snow, wind, dragons and all deeps; mountains, trees, beasts, creeping things, flying fowl; kings of the earth and all people. He is sole supreme Lord and absolute commander of them all. Partly, because his providence is eminently interested in all matters of war in the world. As:

(i) In raising and stirring up war (Jeremiah 25:29, Isaiah 5:26 & 7:18 & 13:14, Jeremiah 50:25). (ii) In giving instruction and encouragement to the battle (2 Samuel 22:55, Psalm 144:1). (iii) In assisting his people in battle by his presence and power, etc. (Deuteronomy 20:4, Zechariah 10:5, Joshua 5:13, etc.) (iv) In prospering armies with success, or dashing them with disappointment, (Zechariah 10:3, 5, Ecclesiastes 9:11, Psalm 33:17, Isaiah 54:17, Psalm 76:5, 12; Isaiah 19:16). (v) In continuing wars for as long as he pleases (Jeremiah 47:6-7, Hosea 11:6). (vi) In making wars to cease when he lists (Psalm 46:9).

Thus God had manifested himself singularly a Lord of Hosts to David, by his peculiar providence to him in all his expeditions, having brought all his enemies under his feet, and cut them off from before him.¹⁴⁸ And in this notion, As the Lord of Hosts, he revealed his Covenant to David, a man of war: intimating his presence, providence, power and all-sufficiency for David against all his enemies for future, as for time past; so that no enemies, nor difficulties could hinder the accomplishment of his Covenant to David and his seed.

{2} As the God of Israel, and the Rock of Israel. When David in his last words comforted himself with the mention of God's Covenant the ground of his faith and hope, he thus prefaced to it: *The God of Israel said, the Rock of Israel spake to me* – that is, Israel's Covenant-God, who has accepted them as his peculiar treasure, as his special people, who dwelt in the midst of them, and

---

[147] 2 Samuel 7:8, etc.; 1 Chronicles 17:7, etc.
[148] 1 Chronicles 17:8

walked amongst them, and is nigh unto them in all things that they call upon him for, etc.[149] This God of Israel became David's Covenant-God, and spoke to him many things by inspiration, and this Covenant in vision. Again, *the Rock of Israel*;[150] that is, the Rock, κατ' ἐξοχήν, the only Rock in the world.[151] *For who is God save the LORD? Or who is a Rock save our God?* (Psalm 18:31). He is the only sure immovable, immutable, everlasting and all-sufficient foundation, fortress, and refuge of his people flying to him and trusting in him. He is their Rock of salvation (Deuteronomy 32:15), rock and salvation (Psalm 62:7), rock and redeemer (Psalm 19:15), Rock of refuge (Psalm 94:22), Rock of their strength (Psalm 62:7-8. & 31:3, Isaiah 17). He became the Rock of David's heart, and his portion forever (Psalm 73:26).

{3} As a Father to David and his seed. The Lord said touching David: *I have found David my servant; He shall cry unto me, Thou art my Father.*[152] This is spoken in reference to God's Covenant with David there explained, yea this is one clause of the Covenant. {*Father*} is a term of most loving, sweet, comfortable and familiar relation. And no father in the world is such a father in whom alone all fatherly perfections and properties are all-sufficient, immutable, eternal, and infinite.[153] This heavenly Father, this matchless Father, became David's Covenant-Father. How confidently, comfortably, prevailingly, might David look up by faith and prayer to this Father! The Lord also said touching his seed: *And when thy days be fulfilled, and thou shalt sleep with thy fathers, I will set up thy seed after thee, which shall proceed out of thy bowels, – I will be his Father.*[154] David's seed was: (i) Mediate and less principal, as Solomon, and others of his race. (ii) Mediate and most principal, as Christ Jesus who according to the flesh came from David's loins. God was a Covenant-Father to both these sorts of seeds: To his *immediate seed*, a Father

---

[149] 2 Samuel 23:3-5
[150] 2 Samuel 7:17, Psalm 89:19
[151] Deuteronomy 32:4
[152] Psalm 89:20, 26
[153] Nullus pater tam pater.
[154] 2 Samuel 7:12-14

by adoption; to his *mediate seed*, Christ, a Father by peculiar creation and generation of his human nature. Christ said: *I go to my Father, and your Father; to my God, and your God.*[155]

{4} As a God to David. *He shall cry unto me, Thou art my Father, my God,* said the Lord in his recital of his Covenant with David.[156] By this Covenant, God intended to enable David to plead his interest in God as his God. To have the Lord for our Covenant-God in Christ, and to be able in assurance of faith to say, *Thou art our God*; is a high degree of happiness: yea, this is the highest Covenant-blessing, as has been at large expounded.[157]

{5} As the Rock of David's salvation. In the Lord's recital of his Covenant with David, he represents himself to David in this consideration: *He shall cry unto me, Thou art my Father, my God, and the Rock of my salvation.*[158] Of what salvation? Of all salvation: temporal, spiritual, and eternal. The whole stress of all his salvation should rest and be founded on God alone, as the Rock thereof, and upon him David's salvation should be strong, sure, unshaken, and constant. Hence David – casting his eye upon God's Covenant with him – comforted himself against all the adversaries of his family, saying: *Therefore this is all my salvation, and all my desire, although he make it not to grow.*[159]

But of these things more hereafter, in opening the matter of this Covenant.

[2] Secondly, **David** and **his seed** were the other federate party to this Covenant, with whom God made this Covenant in these respects and notions, namely:

{1} With **David** himself:

(i) As one that was mighty. *Then thou spakest in vision to thy holy one* (namely: to Nathan the prophet, 2 Samuel 7:4-18), *and saidst, I have laid help*

---

[155] John 20:17
[156] Psalm 89:20, 26
[157] Book 3 Chapter 3
[158] Psalm 89:20, 26
[159] 2 Samuel 23:5

upon a mighty one.[160] A worthy, a champion, namely: David, who was a mighty man of war, and who helped God's people Israel in fighting the Lord's battles against their enemies, with mighty resolution and mighty success.[161] In this Covenant also, God promised to David: *His enemies will I clothe with shame, but upon himself shall his crown flourish.*[162]

(ii) As God's elect or chosen one. *I have made a Covenant with my chosen. I have exalted one chosen out of the people.*[163] David was *electus*: chosen; consequently *dilectus*: beloved. As Christ is called God's elect in whom his soul delighted. Matthew has it: *My servant whom I have chosen, my beloved in whom my soul is well-pleased.*[164] David was *chosen of God, to the inheritance incorruptible, undefiled, and that fadeth not away, reserved in heaven for us,*[165] as also, to the throne of Israel.[166] This latter is here specially intended. As David was chosen, he was designed to the kingly office. As he was a mighty one, he was qualified for that office.

(iii) As God's servant. *I have sworn unto David my servant, I have found David my servant, with whom my hand shall be established,* etc.[167] God covenanted with David as his servant: yea by his Covenant he encouraged and established him in his service. David is often styled {*God's servant*}, and he was God's servant, not only *generally* as all are his servants (Psalm 119:91),[168] nor only *specially*, as all true believers and godly persons are his servants, improving his talents to his glory (Matthew 25:14, etc., Luke 19:13, etc., Revelation 22:3), but also *particularly* by his peculiar office, in church as a prophet, in commonwealth as a king, wherein he did singularly serve the Lord:

---

[160] Psalm 89:19
[161] 1 Samuel 18:13-14, 32
[162] Psalm 132:11, 17-18
[163] Psalm 89:3, 19
[164] Isaiah 42:1 with Matthew 12:18
[165] 1 Peter 1:3-4
[166] Psalm 78:70-72; 2 Samuel 6:21
[167] Psalm 89:3, 20; 1 Samuel 16:12
[168] 2 Samuel 3:18 & 7:5, 8; 1 Kings 8:24-26, 66 & 11:31, 13 & 14:8; 2 Kings 8:9, 19:34 & 20:6; 1 Chronicles 17:4, 7; 2 Chronicles 6:15-17, 42, Psalm 18:1, 36:1, 78:70, 89:4, 21, 144:10, Luke 2:69, Acts 4:25

and in which respect he is frequently styled {*the servant of the Lord*}, as Psalm 18:1 & 78:70-72, 2 Samuel 7:8, etc. And in this notion, God had particular respect unto him in this Covenant:

(iv) As God's anointed king. *I have found David my servant, with mine holy oil have I anointed him, with whom my hand shall be established*, etc.[169] In this Covenant, God had special respect to David's kingdom, to settle, establish, and perpetuate it by his Covenant, as afterwards will appear in the matter of this Covenant.

(v) As God's firstborn, higher than the kings of the earth. Also *I will make him my firstborn, higher than the kings of the earth. My mercy will I keep for him for evermore, and my covenant shall stand fast with him.*[170] The Chaldee adds: *The firstborn of the kings of the house of Judah*. Firstborn, or First-begotten, namely: the chief or principal king, as the following phrase exegetically explains it. The firstborn had a fourfold prerogative, as: (a) the prophecy, for instructing the family,[171] (b) the priesthood, for sacrificing,[172] (c) the kingship, for government, as chieftains and principal rulers thereof,[173] and (d) the double portion for bearing up their dignity, and encouraging them in all.[174]

Now in all these particulars, Jesus Christ is primarily intended and shadowed out. For: (i) Christ is a mighty one indeed, on whom our help and salvation is laid. *The mighty God, having all power, able to save to the uttermost*, etc.[175] (ii) Christ is God's chosen and beloved one above all others: they being accepted by God only in the beloved.[176] (iii) Christ is God's most eminent and faithful servant in the great work and service of sinners'

---

[169] Psalm 89:20-21, etc.; 1 Samuel 16:12
[170] Psalm 89:27-28
[171] Numbers 8:13-20, Matthew 2:4-7
[172] Numbers 8:14-17, Malachi 2:5-7 & 3:2
[173] 2 Chronicles 21:3
[174] Deuteronomy 21:17
[175] Isaiah 9:6, Psalm 45:3, Matthew 28:18, Hebrews 7:25
[176] Isaiah 42:1, Matthew 12:18, Colossians 1:13, Ephesians 1:6

redemption, for the salvation of both Jews and Gentiles.[177] (iv) Christ is God's anointed king[178] – anointed, not with material oil from the tabernacle, but with the oil of gladness above his fellows, even with the Spirit of God from heaven above measure. (v) Finally, Christ is God's firstborn, higher than the kings of the earth. For, Christ is the firstborn of every creature, and the firstborn of the dead, that in all things he might have the preeminence;[179] the prince of the kings of the earth,[180] Lord of Lords and King of Kings,[181] whom all the kings of the earth, and angels of God in heaven, are to fear, serve, and worship.[182] This Covenant therefore God made with David in Christ. Christ was the prime foundation and intention of it; Christ with David and his seed was the other federate party to it.

{2} With David's **seed**:

(i) As God's son. *and when thy days shall be fulfilled, – I will set up thy seed after thee, which shall proceed out of thy bowels, – I will be his father and he shall be my son.*[183] This was immediately intended of Solomon, who should build the material and typical temple at Jerusalem, who was God's son by gratuitous adoption; but mediately and primarily of him that was greater than Solomon, Jesus Christ, who should build the true living temple of God, the church, of living stones from among both Jews and Gentiles, who was God's Son by eternal generation, according to his Godhead, by miraculous creation and procreation according to his manhood.

(ii) As God's king forevermore. *I will raise up thy seed after thee, which shall proceed out of thy bowels, and I will establish his kingdom. He shall build an house for my name, and I will establish the throne of his kingdom forever.*[184] This had its immediate and secondary accomplishment in Solomon and the

---

[177] Psalm 42:1, etc. & 49:3, 5-6
[178] Psalm 2:6, etc., 11-12 & 45:1, 3-4, 6-8, John 3:[34], Colossians 1:19
[179] Colossians 1:15, 18
[180] Revelation 1:5
[181] Revelation 19:16
[182] Psalm 2:11-12, Hebrews 1:6
[183] 2 Samuel 7:12, 14; 1 Chronicles 17:11, 13
[184] 2 Samuel 7:12-13; 1 Chronicles 17:11-12, 14, Psalm 89:3-4, 34-36 & 132:11-12

successive seed of David which continued forever, that is, for a long time, until the great year of jubilee, the time of Jesus Christ; but its mediate and primary accomplishment in the person of Christ Jesus of the seed of David, who should reign over the Israel of God, the church, forever and ever.[185]

Inferences by way of application

(1) Hence God's condescension to David was wonderful, in becoming a covenant party under such notions and considerations, in this Covenant with David.

God stooped to David exceedingly in making Covenant with him; and therein he dealt familiarly with him, as man with man, as a man with his familiar friend. For between God and David was as great disparity, as between light and darkness, life and deadness, the creator and the creature, and finite and infinite. And yet God stooped and condescended to David in this Covenant so much more, so that he would be a covenant-party herein with David, as the LORD of Hosts, as the God and Rock of Israel, as a Father to David and his seed, as his God, and as the Rock of his salvation.

Well might David hereupon burst out: *Who am I O LORD God, and what is mine house, that thou hast brought me hitherto?*[186] (namely: that you have brought me from the sheepcote to the throne and scepter; have cut of all my enemies; have made me a name like the name of the great men of the earth; and have been with me whithersoever I went; as 1 Chronicles 17:7-8): *And yet this was a small thing in thine eyes O God, for thou hast also spoken of thy servant's house for a great while to come, and hast regarded me according to the estate of a man of high degree O LORD God.* Or as the parallel place expresses

---

[185] Luke 1:31-33, Acts 2:30-32, etc.
[186] 1 Chronicles 17:16-17

it: *And is this the manner* (or *law*) *of man O LORD God*. Or as Junius reads it: *And that after the manner of men, O LORD God*.[187] That is (says one): "You deal familiarly with me as a man deals with man)."[188]

Now in these former expressions, David intimates that though God's former kindnesses were so admirable that he was astonished at them, yet this familiar covenant-kindness as it were struck him dumb. *And what can David say more unto thee?*[189] As if all the former mercies had been a small thing in God's sight, he superadded this familiar Covenant, and herein made known all these greatnesses. *O LORD there is none like, neither is there any God besides thee.*[190]

(2) **Hence the privilege of David and his seed was exceedingly great, to be the other covenant party with God – and that under such notions and considerations.** In this Covenant, God descended and condescended to David; but David and his seed ascended towards God. God stooped below himself, but David is herein lifted up above himself. What? Shall David, the youngest and most despised of Jesse's sons, the late keeper of his fathers sheep – shall he be particularly taken into a special Covenant with God? And this under such advantageous and comfortable notions? As a mighty one, as God's chosen, as God's servant, as God's anointed king, as God's firstborn, higher than the kings of the earth? What manner of privileges are these – and how many privileges? Surely all the notions under which the Lord became a covenant-party with him and his seed, and all the notions under which he and his seed became a covenant-party with God, are so many eminent privileges and covenant-advantages devolved upon David and his seed.

(3) **Hence David and his seed in this Covenant typically sustained and represented the person of the Lord Jesus Christ.** Especially David and his son Solomon were eminent types of Christ, the true David most entirely

---

[187] 2 Samuel 7:19
[188] Mr. John Ball in his *Treatise of the Covenant*, chapter 9
[189] 2 Samuel 7:20
[190] 1 Chronicles 17:19-20

beloved of God,[191] and the true Solomon and Prince of Peace to his church and people.[192] They were the types; Christ the antitype. They were the shadows; Christ the substance. All the notions and considerations under which David and his seed, were federate parties with God in this Covenant had a more special tendency to and accomplishment in Jesus Christ then either in David or in Solomon. But in what regards David and his seed Solomon were such types of Christ shall more particularly be unfolded in the general inferences from consideration of this whole Covenant.[193]

Thus of the federates to this Covenant, namely: God, David and his seed.

---

[191] Ezekiel 34:23-24 & 37:24-25, Jeremiah 30:9, Hosea 3:5, John 3:16, Colossians 1:13
[192] Psalm 72 throughout, Isaiah 9:6
[193] In Aphorism 7 Inference 2 of this chapter

Aphorism 3

The impulsive cause and occasion of this Covenant.

The impulsive cause moving God to make this Covenant with David and his seed was his rich grace and mercy in Jesus Christ, upon occasion of God's changing Israel's governors from judges to kings and of King David's holy purposes of building a house or temple for the Lord his God at Jerusalem. In this aphorism are two things chiefly to be opened and cleared: (1) the impulsive cause, and (2) the occasion of this Covenant. Of both briefly.

(1) The **impulsive** or **moving cause** inclining the Lord to make this Covenant with David and his seed, and therein to condescend so familiarly unto them in such liberal and bountiful promises, is twofold: [1] inward, and [2] outward.

[1] The inward moving cause of this Covenant was only God's own rich grace and mercy. As appears:

{1} By David's thankful acknowledgements presently upon God's revealing of this Covenant to David by Nathan, saying: *According to thine own heart* (of thy mere grace, not of any merit of mine) *hast thou done all these great things* (namely: these great things of this Covenant now revealed by Nathan), *to make thy servant know them.*[194] Or, as it is elsewhere: *According to thine own heart hast thou done all this greatness, in making known all these greatnesses.*[195] That is: "According to the mere good pleasure of your own will, have you revealed this Covenant to me. You have fetched all motives and impulsives from within yourself only, from your own mere grace, goodness,

---

[194] 2 Samuel 7:21 *Iuxta cor tuum. Nullo meo merico; sed ex mera gratia.* Lavater in 1 Chronicles 17:19
[195] 1 Chronicles 17:19

and mercy. Hence Peter Martyr: "According to your heart."[196] For God is so good, that he expects not our merits, but is moved by his own sole will and mere mercy. Therefore Paul to the Ephesians says, God *worketh all things according to the counsel of his own will* (Ephesians 1:11).

{2} By God's own testimony, styling the substance of this Covenant {*mercy*}: Not only materially, because the blessings covenanted therein were mercies, a compound of mercy; nor only formally, because they were promised and performed as mercies; But also efficiently, originally, and fundamentally, because they were the peculiar fruits and effects of divine mercy and grace. *My faithfulness and my mercy shall be with him* (namely: with David), *and in my name shall his horn be exalted. – My mercy will I keep for him for evermore: and my covenant shall stand fast with him.*[197] Ethan also the Ezrahite, speaking of this Covenant, styles it by way of emphasis, {*mercy*}: *for I have said mercy shall be built up forever: thy faithfulness shalt thou establish in the very heavens.*[198]

[2] The outward moving cause of this Covenant, was only Christ Jesus the Messiah and his merit, in whom alone the Lord so accepted David as to make this excellent Covenant with him; not anything at all in David's person or family.

Hence David, in his thankful return to God for this Covenant, first devolves all causality of it from himself, then casts it all upon the Messiah. He acknowledges self-denyingly that nothing in him could move or incline God to dignify him with such favor. *Then went King David in, and sat before the LORD, and he said; who am I, O Lord GOD? And what is my house, that thou hast brought me hitherto?*[199] As if he had said "O Lord, I am even astonished at this transcendent covenant-mercy! For there's nothing in me nor in my house,

---

[196] See Peter Martyr on 2 Samuel 7:21
[197] Psalm 89:24, 28
[198] Psalm 89:1-2, etc.
[199] 2 Samuel 7:18; 1 Chronicles 17:16

that might in the least measure incite thee thereunto." This was his great humility, self-denial, and self-abhorrence before the Lord.

He seems also on the other hand to attribute all to Christ (the Word and Servant of God) as the only outward impulsive cause and motive: *For thy Word's sake and according to thine own heart, hast thou done all these things,* etc.,[200] which elsewhere is thus expressed: *O LORD for thy servant's sake, and according to thine own heart hast thou done all this greatness, in making known all these greatnesses*[201] – both passages having peculiar and principal reference to this Covenant.

What's this **Word** of God? Who's this **servant**? By {*word*}, some understand the truth and promise of God. But how can that be? For what word or promise did God make to David of any such Covenant formerly? And by {*servant*}, we cannot well understand Nathan the prophet, by whom God revealed this Covenant to David; for though he did reveal it by Nathan, yet not for Nathan's sake. Nor can we understand David himself. for David utterly disclaims all his own worth, saying: *Who am I O Lord GOD? And what is my house, that thou hast brought me hitherto?* Nor is it as much as if he had said: "For thy promise's sake, which thou hast made to thy servant David," as some think: for the former doubt still occurs; where did God make any such Promise?

Some, by {*word*} understand God's decree, thus: "This admirable revelation of thy grace towards me and my posterity is grounded upon nothing but only upon the decree which thou hast set down of thine own mere free will." But {*word*} here cannot be expounded, {*God's decree*}, for that will not agree with the parallel word, {*servant*}: *for thy servant's sake*, that is, "for your decree's sake," which would be a harsh and unusual exposition.

I therefore rather incline to their exposition who by {*word*} understand {*Christ*}, the essential Word of God (John 1:14, Revelation 19:13) – Christ

---

[200] 2 Samuel 7:21
[201] 1 Chronicles 17:19

also being called {*God's servant*} in regard to his office (Isaiah 42:1 with Matthew 12:18). And then the sense is: "For thy word's sake," *For thy servant's sake*, namely: "For the merit and mediation of your Christ (who is thy eternal Word, and thy servant in the mediatory office), you have graciously done all this greatness. You have inclined hereunto, according to the mere good pleasure of your will, within yourself; for the mediation and merit of your Christ without yourself." And this interpretation (as some think) is yet further strengthened by those words: *And hast regarded me according to the estate of a man of high degree, O LORD God. What can David speak more to thee for the honor of thy servant.*[202] That {*according to the estate of a man of high degree* or *of excellency*}, may more rightly be referred to Christ, for he is truly the most excellent, and as Paul speaks, the second Adam. So the sense shall be, "Thou givest me these things, not according to my merits and my virtues, but for Christ that high and excellent man." Thus Peter Martyr.[203] And he further says, "Rabbi Solomo reads this sentence by way of interrogation, as a sentence of admiration, and as if David should say thus: "Is this the condition of man, that you should embrace him with such love?" And this well agrees if it is transferred to Christ in this manner: "Is this my condition, that Christ should be born of my stock, and I should be the father of the Son of God?" And this agrees most fitly with that which follows. "*What can David speak more to thee?* etc." For as Paul says, *Since God hath given us his Son, how shall he not with him also freely give us all things?*" Thus he.

(2) The **occasion** of this Covenant was: [1] more mediate, and [2] more immediate.

[1] More *mediate* and *remote*, was God's changing Israel's governors and chief rulers from judges to kings. Judges were governors more extraordinarily

---

[202] 1 Chronicles 17:17-18
[203] Peter Martyr commentary on 2 Samuel 7:19-20

raised up by God during Israel's more unsettled condition in Canaan, by whom God as their king ruled them. They were not so full of outward majesty as kings, nor did their posterity succeed them. Instead of these, God set up kings as more ordinary fixed rulers, fuller of awful majesty. The first king of God's approbation was David (Saul being given in anger and taken away in wrath),[204] in whose days the Lord brought Israel to a more settled condition in Canaan,[205] and God annexed the regal succession peculiarly unto David and his natural seed, until Jesus Christ, the chief natural seed of David, and chief king of Israel, should come to rule his church forever, in whose kingdom, the whole government of that people should be swallowed up, and David's throne perpetuated forevermore. God – intending this honor and happiness peculiarly to David and his house – reveals this Covenant to David by Nathan, the chief new clause whereof superadded to the Sinai Covenant, was the promise of the Messiah to descend from David according to the flesh, and of the kingdom to be perpetuated in him forevermore.

[2] More *immediate* and *near*, was David's holy purpose to build a house or temple for the Lord at Jerusalem. This purpose, David probably entertained in his heart from consideration of God's promise by Moses to Israel, that when they should be possessed of Canaan and have rest from their enemies round about. *There should be a place which the LORD their God should choose out of all their tribes to cause his name to dwell there,* etc.[206] This his purpose, David imparted to Nathan the prophet,[207] when the LORD had given him rest round about from all his enemies.[208] Nathan encouraged him, but God by vision revealed to Nathan forbids David to build, upon various grounds. Nevertheless, God was so well-pleased with David's holy intendments herein that he made a special Covenant with David; therein assuring him, that he

---

[204] Hosea 13:11
[205] 1 Chronicles 23:5
[206] Deuteronomy 12:5-6, 9-11
[207] 2 Samuel 7:1-3
[208] Compare 2 Samuel 7:2-18 with 1 Chronicles 17:1-16

would build David a house, raise up his seed after him (which should build God a house), and would establish his throne forevermore. These promises had their peculiar and principal accomplishment in the Messiah, Jesus Christ the Son of David.

How acceptable to God, was David's zeal for God! He purposed to build God a house; God thereupon promised to build him a house – yea to set up his seed upon his throne after him forever, which seed should be Christ especially.[209] Oh how was David enlarged in thankfulness, and his Spirit wrapped up with astonishing admiration hereupon, so that he wanted words to express his thoughts![210] Who would not be zealous for the house, worship, ordinances, and church of God, which is so well pleasing to God and so abundantly rewarded?

Inferences by way of application

(1) Hence admire the riches of God's free grace in this covenant discovery to David. God made and revealed all these covenant greatnesses to David according to his own heart, according to the good pleasure of his own will. Nothing in David, nothing in his father's house, could incline or move God hereunto. Herein God manifested to David both his *gratiam favoris*, his grace of free favor, which he freely expresses towards his creature without any merit on the part of the creature; and *gratiam commiserationis*, his grace of free pity and commiseration, which he expresses towards his sinful creature contrary to merit. For, David had no merit, to deserve any good from God. David had many sins and frailties to deserve all evil from him.

---

[209] Luke 1:31-33, Acts 2:30-31, etc.
[210] 2 Samuel 7:18 to the end; 1 Chronicles 17:16 to the end

(2) **Hence Jesus Christ – the essential word of God and the grand servant of God in his mediatory office – was not only one primary blessing promised and a principal end intended in this Covenant; but also the only outward impulsive cause inclining God thereunto.** Christ was the matter, end, and foundation of this Covenant. Christ was the center, the lines, and the circumference of this Covenant. Jesus Christ was the very life and soul of this, as of all other Covenants of Faith: *the same yesterday, and today, and forever.*[211] You cannot study this Covenant, but therein you shall learn Christ. He is the jewel in this cabinet. Oh, delight to open and look into this cabinet, for the jewel's sake laid up therein!

(3) **Hence true zeal to build God a house is the ready way to engage the Lord to build our house.** David had it in his heart (and but in his heart) to build a house for God; As yet not one stone of the foundation was laid, nor any materials at all prepared for the building. And yet God was so exceedingly pleased with his religious purposes of heart to build God a house, that God presently rewards this his zeal with a Covenant and rich promises to build David a house, by raising up his seed and establishing his throne forevermore. David but purposed to build God's house, and God promised to build David's house. Did his religious intent of building the material temple so please God? How much more will our religious intents, endeavors, and actings for building his spiritual temple the church (one special antitype of that type) please God abundantly? We have in this land entertained purposes of building the spiritual house of God. Otherwise why did we in the days of our distress so solemnly covenant with God to endeavor in our places a thorough reformation in doctrine, worship, discipline, and government, according to the word of God?[212] And has God not built our house, since we covenanted to build his house? Has he not subdued our enemies, and crowned us with peace by sea and land? From that day, did the Lord not bless us? Oh then, why have we not

---

[211] Hebrews 13:8
[212] In the year 1643. See the Solemn League & Covenant, Article 1

pursued our pious purposes, and performed our Covenant, which remains still upon record in heaven and earth against us? Shall we ever lose, by our zeal towards the house of God? Nay, since the Lord has begun to build our houses, Have we not neglected to build God's house? Have we not said: *The time is not yet come, the time that the house of the Lord should be built?*[213] Have we not pulled down God's house, and built the devil's house, by blasphemies, heresies, errors, divisions, profaneness, confusion, and a sinful toleration of evils intolerable? Thus did not David. Yea, when God suffered him not to build the temple, yet he prepared for it with all his might. So if we cannot build, as we desire, yet where are our preparations?

Thus of the impulsive causes and occasions of this Covenant.

---

[213] Haggai 1:2

Aphorism 4

The substance, or subject matter of this Covenant with David.

The substance or subject matter of God's Covenant with **David** and his **seed** consisted:

(1) On God's part, in many eminent mercies and blessings promised, namely:

[1] Touching David himself: {1} the subduing of all his enemies, {2} strengthening and establishing him, {3} the increase and enlargement of his glory, prosperity, power and dominion, {4} his sweet Covenant relations to him, {5} fulfilling of his days, {6} building him an house, especially by raising up his seed after him to sit upon his throne forever, and {7} perpetuating this Covenant.

[2] Touching his seed: {1} the like fatherly relation to it, {2} the honor to build God a house, {3} the establishment of his seed in his kingdom and throne forever, and {4} the constancy of God's loving kindness and faithfulness thereunto but with exception of chastisements in case of miscarriages.

[3] Touching Israel, the subjects of David and his seed: {1} God's habitation in Zion forever, {2} their peaceable and secure establishment in Canaan, and {3} their singular prosperity in temporals and spirituals.

(2) On the part of David and his seed, In the covenant duties conditioned and restipulated, which are comprised in: {1} their keeping God's Covenant and testimony walking in his commandments, statutes, and judgments, and {2} their being just, ruling in the fear of God.

The main body and substance of God's Covenant with David and his seed, may be easily reduced to these particulars in this aphorism. And these mercies promised on God's part, with this duty conditioned on the part of David and his seed, are evidently the subject matter of this Covenant, they being collected: [1] Partly, out of the vision of Nathan wherein God first revealed this his Covenant to David;[214] [2] partly, out of the recitals and expositions of this Covenant, especially in two eminent Psalms;[215] and [3] partly, out of David's last words, wherein he comforts himself against all the discomforts of his house, by this excellent Covenant which God had made with him. And this I shall yet further clear, by this brief ensuing explanation of this aphorism according to the several branches of it, in two sections.[216]

---

[214] 2 Samuel 7:4-18; 1 Chronicles 17:3-16
[215] Psalm 89 & 132
[216] 2 Samuel 23:1-8

Section 1

The covenant mercies or blessings herein graciously promised on God's part to David and his seed.

These are namely: (1) some concerning David, (2) some concerning David's seed, and (3) some concerning the subjects of King David and his seed.

---

(1)   First, the covenant mercies or blessings more especially concerning David himself were these:

[1] **God's subduing of all his enemies; clothing them with shame and confusion.** This is one clause in Nathan's vision, revealing this Covenant: *Moreover, I will subdue all thine enemies.*[217] This the explanatory recital of the Covenant confirms: *I have found David my servant – The enemy shall not exact upon him: nor the son of wickedness afflict him. And I will beat down his foes before his face, and plague them that hate him.*[218] And elsewhere: *His enemies will I clothe with shame.*[219]

And this is yet further ratified in David's prophecy or last words touching this Covenant: *But the sons of Belial shall be all of them as thorns thrust away, because they cannot be taken with hands. But the man that shall touch them must be fenced with iron and the staff of a spear: and they shall be utterly burnt with fire in the place* (Hebrew: *in the mansion*).[220] Here the enemies of the kingdom of David and his seed are described and threatened. *Described*, by

---

[217] 1 Chronicles 17:10
[218] Psalm 89:20, 22-23
[219] Psalm 132:18
[220] 2 Samuel 23:6-7

their dissoluteness – they are styled {*sons of Belial*}: yokeless, profane wretches.[221] By their mischievousness; being compared to thorns, that prick or wound those that touch them or have anything to do with them, unless they are fenced with iron and spear against them. *Threatened*, partly to be moved or thrust away as thorns, which are stubbed up by the roots because of the mischief they do to grass or corn, etc. Partly, to be utterly burnt with fire in the mansion or place of their abode. This promise of subduing all David's enemies had reference, immediately and literally to the enemies of David and his seed in the kingdom of Israel; mediately, typically and spiritually to the enemies of Jesus Christ in the kingdom of his church: Satan, Antichrist, and all the yokeless wicked ones of the world, whose utter extirpation and destruction is here foretold for the comfort of David's house.[222]

This mercy promised was performed and accomplished two ways:

{1} **Literally and immediately to David himself.** David fought the battles of the LORD:[223] And *he went on and grew great, and the LORD God of Hosts was with him: yea he was with him whithersoever he went and cut off all his enemies out of his sight, and made him a great name like unto the name of the great men that are in the earth.*[224] And David himself thankfully confessed thus much in that triumphant psalm penned to that purpose,[225] namely: that he might triumph in God's praises who had trodden down all his enemies under his feet. To which psalm, this title is prefixed: *And David spake unto the LORD the words of this song, in the day that the LORD had delivered him out of the hand of all his enemies, and out of the hand of Saul. And he said*: etc.[226] This psalm also may be very properly sung by the church and people of God, for his subduing the enemies of Christ and his church: David herein being a

---

[221] בְּלִיַּעַל "Nequina, Nequam. quasi בלי-עיל ab{que}-jugo. qui jugum laboris pictatis ac legis Dei Excussit, ac proinde nihil boni agit vel [quasi] בלי-ווּעיל Qui nihil protest, Qui nullius frugis & utilitatis est." Buxtorf. in *Lexic* ad verb. עלל
[222] Peter Martyr, commentary in this place.
[223] 1 Samuel 25:28
[224] 2 Samuel 5:10 & 7:9; 1 Chronicles 17:8
[225] 2 Samuel 22 throughout, Psalm 18
[226] 2 Samuel 22:1-2

special type of Christ, and David's enemies, of the enemies of Christ and his Church.

{2} *Spiritually, mystically and mediately, this promise is, and shall be performed to Jesus Christ the true David, typified by David.* Christ:

(i) *Inchoately* has conquered, judged, and condemned all his and his members' spiritual enemies, as sin, death, hell, Satan, Antichrist, the world, etc.[227] He has already stabbed them to the heart: has given them such a death's wound as they shall never be able to recover. And he is riding on still most victoriously, conquering and to conquer.

(ii) *Completely* – he will subdue them all, before, or at, his second Coming. For he sits on God's right hand and there must reign till all his foes become his footstool.[228] This stone cut out without hands shall break in pieces the whole image of gold, silver, brass, iron and clay – even all the grand empires and kingdoms of the world, that are enemies to the kingdom of Christ.[229] Great Babylon – Rome – shall be utterly burnt with fire, and shall be found no more at all.[230] The beast and false prophet shall both of them be taken by him that sits on the white horse, and shall be cast alive into a lake of fire burning with brimstone.[231] The last enemy – death – shall be destroyed, when the devil and death and hell and all the wicked shall be cast into the lake of fire.[232]

[2] **God's establishing and strengthening David in his kingdom, that his foes might be brought under.** *Then thou spakest in vision to thine holy one, – I have found David my servant; with my holy oil have I anointed him. With whom my hand shall be established: mine arm also shall strengthen him.*[233] *The enemy shall not exact upon him,* etc. As God was the anointer of

---

[227] Romans 8:3, Hebrews 2:14-15, Colossians 2:13-15, Ephesians 4:8; 2 Thessalonians 2:8, John 16:11, 33
[228] Psalm 110:1; 1 Corinthians 15:24-26
[229] Daniel 2:32-46
[230] Revelation 18:2, 8, 21
[231] Revelation 19:11, 20
[232] 1 Corinthians 15:24-26, 54-55, Revelation 20:9 to the end
[233] Psalm 89:19-23

David, and so the author of his kingdom, so he covenanted to be the strengthener and keeper of him and his kingdom against all adverse power. God (as Calvin notes well) does not forsake his works begun, but by a continual progress, carries them on to their end and perfection.[234] Except the Lord strengthens and establishes, what king or kingdom can be established? And if he strengthens and establishes, who shall weaken or abolish?

This promised establishment and strengthening had its accomplishment also:

{1} *In David himself.* For after David had taken the stronghold of Zion and had enjoyed so much peace as to build himself a house, *David perceived that the LORD had established him king over Israel, and that he had exalted his kingdom for his people Israel's sake.*[235] And after that, he twice conquered the Philistines and at last subdued them, as also Syria, Moab, Ammon, Amalek, etc, so that David grew greater and greater, and got himself a mighty name.[236]

{2} *In Jesus Christ, the primary seed of David.* For God established and strengthened him and his mediatory kingdom so that no enemies can shake it, but it shakes and destroys all enemies and opposers, and subdues people unto Christ, that he rules in the midst of his enemies.[237]

[3] **God's increasing and enlargement of David's glory, prosperity, power, and dominion.** In the recital and explanation of this Covenant, God said: *But my faithfulness and my mercy shall be with him, and in my name shall his horn be exalted. I will set his hand also in the sea: and his right hand*

---

[234] "It is afterwards added, that he will be the guardian and protector of this kingdom of which he was the founder; for it is not his usual way to abandon his works after having commenced them, but, on the contrary, to carry them forward by a continued process of improvement to their completion."
John Calvin's commentary on Psalm 89:21
[https://sacred-texts.com/chr/calvin/cc10/cc10023.htm]
<Accessed 4/15/2024>
[235] 2 Samuel 5:7, 9-12
[236] Verse 17 to the end of the chapter; 2 Samuel 8:1, 11-13
[237] Psalm 2 throughout & 45 & 110:1-2, Isaiah 49:7-13

in the rivers. Also: *I will make him my firstborn, higher than the kings of the earth.*[238] Here, besides other blessings, these royal favors are promised to David, namely:

{1} ***Exalted glory***: *In my name shall his horn be exalted.* Here and often elsewhere, "the horn of David," says Calvin, "is taken for his glory, dignity, power," etc.[239] Therefore the sense is, through God's goodness, the state of his kingdom should be always prosperous and flourishing. It's an elegant metaphor from brute beasts, whose ornament and power is in their horns, thence translated to signify sometimes divine glory and power;[240] sometimes human royal glory and power, as here.[241]

{2} ***Enlarged dominion***. The hand, the right-hand, whereby the sword and scepter are held, and power is put forth, denotes *dominion*. {*His hand in the sea and rivers*} imports the extent of his dominion from the sea to the rivers. By {*sea*}, here understand, the great sea, namely: the Mediterranean Sea, which was the border of the promised land in the West.[242] By {*rivers*}, Calvin understands the River Euphrates, which was divided into many channels, and the neighboring rivers on the part of Syria.[243] But forasmuch as God had mentioned sundry rivers as part of the borders of the promised land, namely: the great River Euphrates (Genesis 15:18, Deuteronomy 11:24), the River Jordan (Numbers 34:12), and the River of Egypt (Numbers 34:5, Joshua 15:4). I see not any reason why any of them should here be excluded, but that David's dominion should be extended to them all according to God's promises of old to Abraham[244] and to Israel.[245] The people by their many sins had deprived themselves of some part of their promised inheritance, and straightened their borders, but now God assures them that under David and

---

[238] Psalm 89:24-25, 27
[239] John Calvin in this place
[240] 2 Samuel 22:3, Hebrews 3:4
[241] Daniel 7:7-8, 24, Revelation 13:1 & 17:12
[242] Numbers 34:6, Joshua 1:4
[243] John Calvin, commentary on Psalm 89:26
[244] Genesis 15:18
[245] Exodus 23:31, Numbers 34:1-16, Deuteronomy 11:24, Joshua [1:4]

his seed, there should be an enlargement of the borders according to the ancient promises.

{3} ***Eminency of sovereignty and rule.*** That he should be higher than the kings of the earth; or, kings of the land, namely: higher than all the kings within the bounds of the promised land, which David should subdue, and higher in royal dignity, excellency, authority, prosperity, than all the neighboring kings round about him. And elsewhere, God says: *There* (namely: in Zion) *will I make the horn of David to bud: I have ordained a lamp for mine anointed. His enemies will I clothe with shame: but upon himself shall his crown flourish.*[246] This Psalm also recites and explains God's Covenant with David, and in these words, God promised the increase of David's glory, prosperity, and dominion, under three metaphors, namely:

(i) **Of a horn budding.** *There will I make the horn of David to bud.* {*Horn*} sometimes denotes the royal glory and power of David and his house, as was noted formerly; sometimes the budding posterity of David, full of honor and power. So Christ is called {*an horn of salvation in the house of David*}.[247] The budding of the horn of David may denote partly, the small and contemptible origin of David's kingdom: he being taken out of a mean family, and from one of the meanest employments, keeping of sheep, to the greatest dignity of feeding Jacob God's people, and Israel his inheritance – from the shepherd's crook and sling to the scepter, and from the sheepfolds to the throne.[248] So that the first budding of his royalty was from a very small and despised beginning – partly, the wonderful restitutions of David's shattered and decayed kingdom, Rehoboam's losing ten tribes, the residue being often times brought extremely low by potent adversaries, especially when they were held captive in Babylon 70 years. In such cases, how was the horn of David bruised and broken! Whereupon Christ springing of David is called {*a rod* (not out of the tree, but) *out of the stem of Jesse*}, and {*a branch out of his*

---

[246] Psalm 132:17-18
[247] Luke 1:69
[248] 1 Samuel 16:11; 2 Samuel 7:8, Psalm 78:6, 70-72

roots},[249] and {*the man whose name is the branch*},[250] alluding perhaps to this prophecy. But still God did wonderfully preserve his kingdom from rain, and made it often bud again afresh, until Christ came.

(ii) **Of a lamp**. *I have ordained a lamp for mine anointed*. Or, *I have prepared a candle*, etc. This metaphor of a lamp or candle is used in Scripture to signify many and several things, but all with allusion to the light, comfort, and benefit of a lamp or candle in darkness.[251] As sometimes it signifies man's soul, spirit, or mind, which is the candle of the LORD within a man; sometimes the corporal eye, which is the candle of the body;[252] sometimes, the word of God, which is a lamp to our feet, and light to our path;[253] sometimes, the lightsome and comfortable presence and favor of God to Israel in deepest troubles – Abraham had this represented to him in vision of a smoking furnace and burning lamp;[254] sometimes the lightsome joy, comfort, prosperity, and brightly-shining glory of a kingdom or royal family, breaking forth in midst of darksome troubles and afflictions, and especially resplendent in a comfortable succession continued.

Thus God said touching Solomon: *And unto his son will I give one tribe, that David my servant may have a light* (or *candle*) *always before me in Jerusalem*.[255] And touching Abijam, King of Judah, though wicked, God said: *Nevertheless for David's sake did the LORD his God give a lamp* (or *candle*) *in Jerusalem, to set up his son after him, and to establish Jerusalem*.[256] In this last sense here, understand this clause of the Covenant. Contrariwise, the dashing of wicked men's prosperity, joy, comfort, glory, etc., is often threatened under the metaphor of putting out their candle.[257]

---

[249] Isaiah 11:1
[250] Zechariah 6:12
[251] Proverbs 20:27
[252] Matthew 6:22
[253] Psalm 119:105
[254] Genesis 15:17-18
[255] 1 Kings 11:36
[256] 1 Kings 15:4
[257] Job 18:6, 21:7, Proverbs 13:9, 20:20, 24:20

(iii) **Of a flourishing crown but upon himself shall his crown flourish.** His crown and kingdom shall be prosperous like a flourishing flower full of beauty and glory. Contrariwise, the glorious beauty of the crown of pride, the drunkards of Ephraim, is compared to a fading or withering flower.[258]

This promise had its accomplishment: much in David, more in Solomon, and most of all in Jesus Christ, the chief Son of David.

(1) **In David.** For, God preserved David whithersoever he went, and David by his victorious successes got himself a name.[259] *David also smote Hadadezer King of Zobah, as he went to recover his border at the River Euphrates.* Whether Hadadezer or David is understood here to go to recover his border at Euphrates.[260] David, by smiting Hadadezer, enlarged his dominion towards Euphrates, which was his promised border. And so God set his hand, or power in the rivers. The Moabites and Syrians and their kings became servants to David and brought gifts;[261] so David was higher than the kings of the earth or of the land. David's horn budded, from a sheepfold to a royal throne. And though ofttimes it seemed quite broken, and his light in Israel extinguished, yet it again still budded afresh, and his candle was again lighted in Jerusalem until the coming of the Messiah.[262]

(2) **In Solomon his son.** For, *he was strengthened in his kingdom, and the LORD his God was with him, and magnified him exceedingly.*[263] He had riches wealth, and honor, such as none before or after him had the like, and he made silver and gold at Jerusalem as plenteous as stones, etc.[264] And *all the kings of the earth sought the presence of Solomon, to hear his wisdom, etc, and they brought every man his present, vessels of silver, and vessels of gold, etc., a rate year by year;*[265] And Solomon *reigned over all kingdoms from the River unto*

---

[258] Isaiah 28:1
[259] 2 Samuel 8:2, 5, 13-14
[260] 2 Samuel 8:3
[261] 2 Samuel 8:2, 6 & 10:19
[262] 1 Kings 15:4
[263] 2 Chronicles 1:1
[264] 2 Chronicles 1:12, 15
[265] 2 Chronicles 6:23-24

the land of the Philistines, and unto the border of Egypt: they brought presents and served Solomon all the days of his life, etc.[266]

(3) In Jesus Christ this promise was most eminently accomplished. He was *raised up as a horn of salvation for us in the house of David.*[267] He is *a light to lighten the Gentiles, and the glory of his people Israel.*[268] He had the throne of his father David to *reign over the house of Jacob forever;*[269] yea he had given him *the heathen for his inheritance, and the uttermost parts of the earth for his possession;*[270] all nations being brought into subjection to him by the scepter of his Spirit and gospel; and the kingdoms of this world becoming our Lord's and his Christ's, who is therefore Lord of Lords, and King of Kings, and shall reign forevermore.

(4) God's sweet covenant relations to him. In the recital of this Covenant, God promised to David: *He shall cry unto me, Thou art my Father, My God, and the Rock of my salvation. Also I will make him my firstborn, higher than the kings of the earth.*[271] In these words, God assures David of three excellent and most comfortable relations between himself and David, which David should acknowledge, and upon all occasions make use of by faith and prayer,[272] flying and cleaving still to him as to [1] his Father, [2] his God, and [3] his Savior. Oh how sweetly might David's faith and prayer fix upon the Lord in all temptations, troubles, discomforts, straits, etc., who thus made himself David's by these endeared relations! Namely: God covenanted to be:

[1] ***David's Father.*** *He shall cry unto me, Thou art my Father.* God here promised to be a Father to David, not generally, as he is Father of all his creatures, Father of lights (James 1:17), and Father of spirits (Hebrews 12:9),

---

[266] 1 Kings 4:21; 2 Chronicles 9:26
[267] Luke 1:69
[268] Luke 2:32
[269] Luke 1:32-33
[270] Psalm 2:8-9, Matthew 28:18-19, Acts 1:8, Colossians 1:5-6, Revelation 11:15 & 19:16
[271] Psalm 89:26-27
[272] Ipse invocabit me, quoniam mihi adhaerebit, & cognoscet fibi a me dignitatem & omne robur conti gisse; adeo{que} ad me semper consuglet; Me quasi [via] trem acDeum & Servatorem suum semper Inclamabir. Sim. de Muis n Psalm 89:27

nor only especially, as he is father of rulers and magistrates: *I have said ye are gods, and all of you are children of the most high* (Psalm 82:6). But more peculiarly and eminently, as he is Father of his adopted in Christ (Luke 11:2; 2 Corinthians 6:18, Romans 8:15). And as he intended a peculiar dearness between himself and David, as his firstborn, higher than the kings of the earth, as Calvin well observes.[273]

This promise was really performed to David himself: *When my father and my mother forsake me, then the LORD will take me up* (Hebrew: *will gather me*).[274] The LORD will not only be a father, but both father and mother to David; yea more than both father and mother: They may forsake, but God will gather me. There's more fatherliness in this Father, than in all the fathers in the world. But this promise primarily intended, and had its fullest accomplishment in the antitype Jesus Christ, who was indeed God's firstborn higher than all kings of the earth. And therefore the apostle applies this promise to Christ, and thereby proves him to be above all the angels in heaven.[275]

So then, the Lord covenanted that he himself would be a Father to David, and that David should be his son, yea his firstborn, his choice son. What blessings does this imply from God to David, and what duties from David to God!

{1} **What blessings and mercies hence flowed from God to David, that God would be his Father!** As:

(i) ***Fatherly procreation.*** A father begets his child of his own substance. *Hearken to thy father, that begat thee.*[276] This is the very foundation of fatherhood. The Lord begat David, partly by regeneration, as he begets all his spiritual children by his Spirit and word;[277] partly by royal unction, whereby

---

[273] John Calvin's commentary on Psalm 89:27
[274] Psalm 27:10
[275] Hebrews 1:4-5
[276] Proverbs 23:22
[277] John 3:3, 5, James 1:17-18; 1 John 5:1

he begat him to the throne. *Thou art my son this day have I begotten thee.*[278] By regeneration, he begat him a saint; by unction, he begat him a king.

(ii) **Fatherly communication.** A father imparts and communicates himself peculiarly to his child, his nature, his image, his properties, his perfections, etc. God – this heavenly Father – communicates to his children, and so to David his nature and his Spirit. (a) His nature. They partake of the divine, or godly nature;[279] and the image of God, in knowledge, righteousness and true holiness.[280] (b) His Spirit: partly as a Spirit of adoption, witnessing their sonship, etc.; partly as a Spirit of supplication, enabling them with groans unutterable to cry "Abba Father" with childlike boldness and confidence.[281]

(iii) **Household relation to all the children of the household of God.** They that have God their father, are of God's family or household; some of which family are in heaven, some on earth, yet all but one and the same family.[282] Herein Jesus Christ, the firstborn, is their elder brother: *nor is he ashamed to call them brethren* – and in him also his members are holy brethren and a holy brotherhood.[283]

(iv) **Fatherly affections, as love.** A father naturally loves his children, and usually more than children love a father. Love rather descends than ascends. God's love to his children is admirable and incomparable. *Behold, what manner of love the Father hath bestowed upon us, that we should be called the sons of God!*[284] John stands amazed at this compassion. A father's bowels melt upon his children, yea though unkind and unnatural, as David's upon Absalom.[285] But God's fatherly compassions to his children transcend: *Like as a Father pitieth his children, so the LORD pitieth them that fear him*, etc.[286]

---

[278] Psalm 2:7
[279] 2 Peter 1:4
[280] Colossians 3:10, Ephesians 4:24
[281] Galatians 4:6, Romans 8:15-16, 26
[282] Ephesians 2:19 & 3:15
[283] Romans 8:19, Hebrews 2:11, 22, etc.; 1 Peter 2:17
[284] 1 John 3:1
[285] 2 Samuel 18:5, 32-33
[286] Psalm 103:13

Hence God is represented like a tender father conflicting within himself about the chastisement of his Israel: *How shall I give thee up Ephraim? How shall I deliver thee, Israel: How shall I make thee as Admah? How shall I set thee as Zeboim? Mine heart is turned within me; My repentings are kindled together. I will not execute the fierceness of mine anger, I will not return to destroy Ephraim; for I am God, and not man, the holy one in the midst of thee.*[287]

(v) **Fatherly education.** Natural parents have a natural instinct to bring up their children naturally. Christian and godly parents have supernatural principles inciting them to educate them Christianly. But God's own fatherly education of his children is most fatherly. For: (a) He feeds them with heavenly food, hidden manna, the bread and water of life, making them live for evermore: even with Jesus Christ the true bread that came down from heaven.[288] (b) He clothes them with the best robe; even with the righteousness of Jesus Christ and the sanctifying graces of the Spirit, enabling them to put on the Lord Jesus Christ and the new man, so that they become all glorious within, and their clothing of wrought gold.[289] (c) He instructs them in the best lessons, in the deep things of God, Jesus Christ, and the mysteries of salvation – and this by his Spirit and Scriptures, able to make them wise unto salvation, and to furnish them thoroughly unto every good work.[290] (d) He also as a tender Father, corrects them discreetly and faithfully – not as earthly parents for their own pleasure or passion, but for their profit, that they may be partakers of the peaceable fruit of righteousness, may know he loves them, and that they are not bastards, but sons.[291]

(vi) **Fatherly protection.** Fathers – according to their ability – defend their children from harms and injuries. They will *fight for their sons, and their*

---

[287] Hosea 11:8-9. See also that emphatic expression: Isaiah 49:14-16.
[288] John 6:32, 33-59, Revelation 2:17.
[289] Luke 15:22, Matthew 22:12, Revelation 19:8, Romans 13:14, Ephesians 4:22, 24, Psalm 45:13
[290] 1 Corinthians 2:9-12; 2 Timothy 4:15-17
[291] Hebrews 12:5-12

daughters, and their wives, as Nehemiah encouraged.[292] But this heavenly Father will be to his people and children a wall of fire round about them, and their glory in the midst of them: yea *as the mountains round about Jerusalem, so the LORD is round about his people from henceforth and forever. And he that toucheth them toucheth the apple of his eye*, etc.[293]

(vii) **Fatherly provision.** *The children lay not up for the parents, but the parents for the children.*[294] This heavenly Father makes the best provision for his children, both here in this world, and hereafter in the world to come. They are heirs of earth and heaven, of two whole worlds, all things are theirs, and *eye hath not seen, ear hath not heard, nor hath the heart of carnal man conceived what he hath prepared for them that love him.*[295] These, and like paternal favors God assured to David in this Covenant, whilst he promised to be a Father to him.

{2} **What duties hence were to be returned from David to God: the Lord accepting him as his son, his firstborn.** Mutual relations, have in them mutual obligations. The duties of a child to a natural father, much more to God the heavenly Father, are such as these, as:

(i) Conformity to the heavenly Father. A child of God is to be holy, as he is holy; merciful, as he is merciful; etc.[296]

(ii) Love and childlike affection; primarily to the heavenly Father himself in Jesus Christ, with all the heart, soul, mind and might.[297] Secondarily, to all God's children bearing the image of this heavenly Father. *Everyone that loveth him that begat, loveth him also that is begotten of him*,[298] namely: the heavenly child, for the heavenly Father's sake.

---

[292] Nehemiah 4:14
[293] Zechariah 2:5, 8, Psalm 125:1-2
[294] 2 Corinthians 12:14
[295] 1 Timothy [4:8], Romans 4:13; 1 Corinthians 3:21-23, Psalm 31:19; 1 Corinthians 2:9-10
[296] 1 Peter 1:14-18, Matthew 5:44 to the end
[297] Deuteronomy 6:5, Matthew 22:27; 1 John 4:19
[298] 1 John 5:1

(iii) Honoring him. The child ought to honor his father.[299] Hence the Lord of Hosts says: *A son honoreth his father and a servant his master: If then I be a father, where is mine honor?* etc.[300]

(iv) Fearing him with filial reverence, not with slavish fear. *If ye call on the Father, who without respect of persons judgeth according to every man's work, pass the time of your sojourning here in fear.*[301] If you profess God to be your Father, and pray to him as to your Father, fear him in your whole course of life.

(v) Obeying him. *As obedient children, not fashioning yourselves according to the former lusts in your ignorance.*[302] Jesus Christ counted it his meat and drink to do the will of his Father that sent him, and to finish his work, yea he became obedient to him to the death, even the death of the cross, laying down his life rather than laying aside his obedience.[303] Herein all his members should follow him in like obedience.

(vi) Trusting in him, and depending upon him, as children upon a loving and faithful father, for all necessary supplies, comforts, etc., as Christ did in death.[304]

(vii) Praying to him, as a child to a Father. *By the Spirit of adoption we cry, Abba, Father.*[305] Christ prayed to him as to his Father often,[306] and Christ has taught us to pray to him as to our Father every day.[307] Now as David was obliged to perform these and like filial duties to God, as to his Father, so the Scriptures, and especially the Psalms, abundantly testify such his performance.

[2] **David's God.** *He shall cry unto me, thou art my Father, my God*, etc. This is the highest mercy promiseable: that the Lord would be a God to David by covenant, and consequently, that David should be one of his covenant

---

[299] Ephesians 6:2-3
[300] Malachi 1:6
[301] 1 Peter 1:7
[302] 1 Peter 1:14-17
[303] Vitam petuidit, ne obedientiam perderet.
[304] Psalm 22:1, 4, 8, Luke 23:46
[305] Romans 8:15, 26
[306] John 17 throughout, Matthew 26:39, 42, 44
[307] Matthew 6:9, etc., Luke 11:2, etc.

people, is implied.[308] But of this supreme sweetest and most comprehensive promise, has been spoken heretofore abundantly, especially in opening God's Covenant with Abraham. Thus David experimentally had the Lord for his God: and gave up himself to God as one of his people.

[3] **David's Rock of salvation.** *He shall cry unto me, Thou art my Father, my God, and the Rock of my salvation.*[309] How emphatically! Not only *a savior*, but *my savior*; not only *my savior*, but *my salvation*; Not only *my salvation*, but *the Rock of my salvation*. My strong, my impregnable, my immovable, my everlasting salvation. Such a salvation, God here covenants to be to David, even his all-sufficient Savior. God saves, or is a Savior in various ways, and in every way he became David's Savior. As: (i) By sustaining and preserving by his common providence. Thus, he saves man and beast.[310] Thus he is *the Saviour of all men*.[311] (ii) By lending help and assistance. *Save LORD, let the king hear us when we call* (Psalm 20:9; 2 Kings 6:27, Psalm 118:25). (iii) By delivering: (a) From temporal evils, afflictions, enemies, etc. (Psalm 3:7 & 7:1 & 118:14). (b) From spiritual evils, sins, miseries, etc., and from eternal wrath, death, and condemnation. So *God is the Saviour especially of them that believe*.[312] And thus salvation is often ascribed to God (Titus 3:4, Jeremiah 17:14, Ezekiel 36:29, Luke 1:72, Hebrews 5:7; 2 Timothy 1:8-9).

Now David, being in every one of these ways saved by this Rock of his salvation, as in his Psalms is plentifully evident: David was obliged to demean himself towards God, as the saved of the Lord. Accordingly, upon this ground, David: (i) loved the Lord his Savior exceedingly;[313] (ii) praised God his Savior with much enlarged thankfulness – *What shall I render unto the LORD for all his benefits towards me? I will take the cup of salvation*, etc. *I will praise*

---

[308] Psalm 22:1-2, 25:2, 16:2, 42:6, 43:4 & 119:94
[309] Psalm 89:26
[310] Psalm 36:6
[311] 1 Timothy 4:10
[312] 1 Timothy 4:10
[313] Psalm 18:1, etc. & 116:1, etc.

thee, for thou hast heard me, and art become my salvation;[314] (iii) trusted in the Lord the more confidently for the future;[315] and (iv) devoted himself to the service of the Lord his Savior, the more cheerfully: *O LORD, truly I am thy servant, I am thy servant, and the son of thy handmaid: thou hast loosed my bonds.*[316]

(5) **God's fulfilling of David's days.** *And when thy days be fulfilled that thou shalt sleep with thy fathers.*[317] This has in it an implicit promise of long life to David, that his days should not untimely be cut off, but be fulfilled and come to maturity. Peter Martyr thus expounds it: "Thou shalt not be taken away with a violent or immature death, for thou shalt fulfill thy days."[318] All do fulfill their days in regard to God's predestination in whatsoever age they die. But they are said to *fulfill their days*, who live so long, until the humor which they call *radical* is dried up. Long life is ofttimes promised as a great blessing to God's people, as to Abraham,[319] to Job,[320] to Israel,[321] etc. And long life becomes an eminent mercy to God's people in several regards. namely: [1] As long life is a continual testimony and evidence of God's constant care and fatherly providence over his people: supplying them with all necessaries, preserving and delivering them from many dangers and deaths, ordering and overruling all things for good, etc. [2] As long life is the evident fruit and experimental performance of many sweet promises made to that effect.[322] [3] As long life is the godly man's longer seedtime for eternity, he has the larger opportunity of good (Proverbs 16:31); to advance God's glory to advantage his own spiritual and eternal good; to promote the heavenly welfare of God's people, or of nearest relations: there being no work, nor device, nor

---

[314] Psalm 116:12, etc. & 118:14-22
[315] 1 Samuel 17:37
[316] Psalm 116:16, 18-19
[317] 2 Samuel 7:12
[318] Peter Martyr's commentary on 2 Samuel 7:12
[319] Genesis 15:15
[320] Job 2:26
[321] Exodus 20:12, Ephesians 6:1-3
[322] Genesis 15:15, Exodus 20:12, Psalm 34:12 & 128:4-6, Proverbs 3:2 & 9-11

knowledge, nor wisdom in the grave.[323] [4] As long life affords a larger opportunity of furthering and beholding the public good and prosperity of the church of God.[324] Paul upon this account was contented to live longer upon earth, though in regard to his own peculiar personal happiness, he desired to be dissolved and be with Christ, which was far best of all.[325] This blessing was accomplished eminently in David according to the very letter, For, *he reigned over Israel forty years; seven years reigned he in Hebron, and thirty three years reigned he in Jerusalem. And he died in a good old age, full of days, riches, and honor.*[326]

(6) **God's building David a house, making it powerful and prosperous, especially by raising up his seed to sit upon his throne forever.** This is a grand and eminent promise, much insisted upon by God in this Covenant. When David had it in his heart to build God a house, God returned him this covenant promise: *Also the LORD telleth thee, that he will make thee an house.*[327] Thai elsewhere is thus expressed furthermore: *I tell thee, that the LORD will build thee an house.*[328] As if God had said, "David, will you build me a house? Nay rather, I will build you a house."

If God that built the world, that built all things, will build David a house;[329] then David's house shall be built – most [1] skilfully, [2] magnificently, [3] strongly, and [4] durably.

But if God does not build it, all other building is to little purpose: *Except the LORD build an house, they labor in vain that build it.*[330] God's building of David a house, did primarily imply God's raising up of David's seed from his own loins to sit upon his throne and succeed in his kingdom forever. Posterity are the pillars of the house or family; when they fail, the house is ruined,

---

[323] Ecclesiastes 8:10
[324] Psalm 128:4-5
[325] Philippians 1:22-27
[326] 1 Chronicles 29:27-28
[327] 2 Samuel 7:11
[328] 1 Chronicles 17:10
[329] Hebrews 3:4
[330] Psalm 127:1

pulled down, and destroyed. By these, the glory, prosperity, power, and dominion of David's house was increased and continued. Therefore, after God had promised to build David a house, he presently by way of exegetical explanation adds: *And it shall come to pass, when thy days be expired, that thou must go to be with thy fathers, that I will raise up thy seed after thee, which shall be of thy sons, and I will establish his kingdom. He shall build me an house, and I will stablish his throne forever.*[331] And elsewhere: *The LORD hath sworn in truth unto David, he will not turn from it. Of the fruit of thy body will I set upon thy throne.*[332] And in another explanation of this Covenant: *I have made a covenant with my chosen, I have sworn unto David my servant: thy seed will I establish forever, and build up thy throne all generations. Selah.*[333]

This building up of David's house, by raising up unto David a successive seed that should sit upon his throne forever, was an high and excellent mercy. Princes that die childless know what a blessing posterity is. Among the Roman emperors (as Peter Martyr notes)[334] from Julius Caesar to Antoninus, none of them (except Vespasian) could leave a son behind them succeeding in the empire. The Turk has detained the empire in one family for over 250 years, but by force, violence, tyranny, patricide, fratricide, etc. Yea, in the kingdom of Israel, the kings over the ten tribes were chosen from others, and other tribes continued not in a line of natural succession; their house was not firmly built, nor their throne established. But here God assures David of a natural lineal succession forever.

This covenanted blessing was accomplished:

[1] More immediately and less principally, in David's ordinary natural seed. For, his natural posterity did in lawful government sit upon his kingly throne until the Babylonian captivity, which was about 430 years. And

---

[331] 1 Chronicles 17:11-13; 2 Samuel 7:12-13
[332] Psalm 132:11
[333] Psalm 89:3-4
[334] Peter Martyr's commentary on 2 Samuel 7:11

afterwards the Jews had princely governors of David's line, or at least rightful heirs of the government until Christ was born.

[2] More mediately and principally, this is fulfilled in David's extraordinary natural seed according to the flesh, **Jesus Christ** – and this in two ways. Partly, by Christ's propagation according to the flesh from David's loins. Whence Paul says: *Jesus Christ our Lord was made of the seed of David according to the flesh.*[335] And Matthew styles him: *Jesus Christ the son of David, the son of Abraham.*[336] And to put all out of question, the natural line of Christ is brought down by rule from David to the virgin Mary, the real mother of Christ,[337] and the legal line of Christ is drawn down by Matthew from David to Joseph, the supposed father of Christ.[338] This was a great honor and favor to David to be the grandfather of Jesus Christ our Savior. Partly, by Christ's royal succession of David in the throne, who reigns over the house of David, the church of God, forever and ever, of whose dominion there shall be no end.[339] His kingdom shall (as Daniel has foretold) never be destroyed, nor left to other people, but it shall break in pieces and consume all these four great kingdoms, and it shall stand forever.[340] By the glory of his seed, and perpetuity of this kingdom, chiefly accomplished in Christ, David in his last words comforted himself against all the weaknesses and discomforts of his family, from the everlasting nature of his Covenant in Christ.[341] *Now these be the last words of David*, etc. Let the reader diligently observe David's last words. They are very short but sweet, few but weighty, wherein we may notably discover how God's Covenant of building David a house chiefly intended Christ, and had its fullest accomplishment in him.

---

[335] Romans 1:3
[336] Matthew 1:1
[337] Luke 3:23 to the end
[338] Matthew 1:1-18
[339] Luke 1:31-33, Acts 2:30, 37
[340] Daniel 2:34-35, 44
[341] 1 Samuel 23:1-8

The last words of dying saints, of dying prophets, tend to be ponderous, holy, heavenly, serious, and challenge special consideration.

Touching **David's last words**, consider briefly: [1] their nature, [2] scope, and [3] principal branches.

[1] *Their nature.* They are called {*David's last words*}: *Now these the last words of David*, namely: his last words, not touching civils, but touching spirituals.[342] Or, his last words, because they contain that which David had in his mouth to his last, and dying day. These last words are, for the general nature of them, a Psalm: **David's** last Psalm, David's comfortable covenant-Psalm, his swan-like song. It's made up of prophecy, doctrine, and comfort, and therefore is a mixed Psalm: partly prophetic, partly doctrinal, and partly consolatory. Wherein David sweetly comforts himself, by the doctrine and nature of God's Covenant with him in Christ, which prophetically promises God's building of David's house and kingdom in Jesus Christ most gloriously and perpetually.

[2] *Their scope and intent is*: prophetically to promise and declare, for David's singular consolation, the righteousness, holiness, glory, prosperity, and perpetuity of his house and kingdom, in Jesus Christ his seed, according to God's Covenant; but the utter confusion of all his kingdom's enemies.

[3] Their *principal parts* to this end are:

{1} **Firstly, a preface to this comfortable covenant-Psalm**, describing:

(i) The instrumental cause of it, David: (a) By his natural descent: *David the son of Jesse said*. (b) By his royal dignity: *And the man who was raised up on high*. (c) By his divine unction to his kingship: *the anointed of the God of Jacob*. (d) By his pleasantness and sweetness in the Psalms which he penned and left upon record for Israel, for the church of God: *And the sweet Psalmist of Israel said* (Hebrew: *And the pleasant one in the Psalms of Israel said*: verse 1).

(ii) The efficient cause, or principal author of it, God the Father, Son, and Holy Spirit, who seem to be set forth in three expressions. (a) The Spirit of the

---

[342] 2 Samuel 23:2

LORD not only inspired his heart with matter but also furnished his tongue with words: *The Spirit of the LORD spake by me, and his word was in my tongue* (verse 3). (b) The Father. *The God of Israel said.* He was Israel's primarily by covenant, by profession, by worship, etc. (c) The Son: *The Rock of Israel spake to me* (verse 3). That is the Son, Christ. *For, Israel drank of that spiritual rock that followed them, and that rock was* **Christ**.[343] Thus of the preface.

{2} Secondly, the substance of this sweet covenant Psalm, prophetically promising and delineating partly the happiness of David's house and kingdom in Christ; partly the misery and confusion of all his kingdom's enemies.

(i) **The happiness of David's house and kingdom in Christ** is federally described and set forth in many ways, as:

(a) By the righteousness of the king that shall rule therein: *He that ruleth over men must be just*, or, *shall be just*. The verb is omitted in the Hebrew, and therefore we may supply the imperfect sentence with a word of promise, as well as with a word of command. If the words be taken as a command, they impose a duty upon David and on all his royal posterity to be just and righteous in their government, so that they might be fit types of Christ. If as a word of promise, they prophetically disclose the righteousness of Christ the primary seed and son of David that should sit upon his throne.[344]

(b) By the holiness of him that should rule in David's kingdom: *Ruling in the fear of God* (verse 3). These words as a *command* require David and his seed to rule religiously, to make holiness the basis of their righteousness; to take care of the church and spirituals, as well as of the commonwealth and civils, but as *promise*, they foretell the holiness of Christ's dominion. Though David and his ordinary seed were many of them righteous and holy rulers, yet both in their holiness and righteousness there were many failings. But Jesus Christ, David's extraordinary seed, was a most holy and righteous ruler in all

---

[343] 1 Corinthians 10:4
[344] Psalm 45:4, 6-7

exactness.[345] He was not only holy and righteous in himself, but is *made of God to us righteousness, sanctification, etc., the LORD our Righteousness.*[346] He not only commands, but makes, all his subjects to be righteous and fearers of the Lord.

(c) By the royal glory and prosperity of this just and holy ruler, elegantly illustrated by two lively similitudes, namely: of clearest morning light. *And he shall be as the light of the morning when the sun ariseth, even a morning without clouds.* Of grass growing and flourishing by virtue of sun and rain: *as the tender grass springing out of the earth by clear shining after rain* (verse 4). This clear morning light without clouds, this budding and flourishing of David's house and kingdom, was not so verified and made good in David or his ordinary posterity; his house was not so with God, in his morning there were many clouds; to his budding and flourishing there were many stops and impediments. But it was abundantly accomplished in the kingdom of Jesus Christ, among the Jews, but especially among the Gentiles, in a visible or invisible manner.

(d) By the foundation of all this happiness of David's house and kingdom, namely: God's everlasting, well-ordered and sure Covenant with David, whereupon he abundantly supports and comforts himself in hope of future performance in Christ, though the present condition of his house came far short of these promises: *Although my house be not so with God, yet he hath made with me an everlasting covenant, ordered in all things and sure: Therefore, this is all my salvation, and all my delight, although he make it not to grow* (verse 5).

Thus the Hebrew may well be translated, and so the sense is more full and clear. As if David had said: "This righteousness, holiness, royal splendor, and prosperity promised to me and my family are most sweet and precious mercies; but alas my house hitherto comes very short in all these blessings, my house,

---

[345] Psalm 45:4, 6-7, Isaiah 11:1-6
[346] 1 Corinthians 1:30, Jeremiah 23:6

and kingdom are not so with God, they do not yet shine so clearly, not yet bud and grow so prosperously. Yet God's Covenant with me touching all these and like mercies is sure, ordered in all things, and everlasting, therefore what ever be the present infirm low mean afflicted cloudy condition of my house, I lay the whole stress of all my salvation and delight upon this his Covenant and this is my great stay and comfort now in my old age when I am going to my grave: that according to this Covenant at last my house shall be fully built and every way prosper and flourish in and through the promised Messiah, Jesus Christ, that is to descend out of my loins according to the flesh."

(ii) **The misery and confusion of all his kingdom's enemies**, those sons of Belial; yokeless, dissolute, ungodly persons; those intolerable mischievous piercing and wounding thorns – they shall be thrust away from hurting David, house and kingdom, and quite consumed in their place: *But the sons of Belial shall be all of them as thorns thrust away, because they cannot be taken with hands: but the man that shall touch them must be fenced with iron, and the staff of a spear, and they shall be utterly burnt with fire in the same place* (verses 6-7), wherein the enemies of his kingdom are described and threatened.

(a) Described and characterized, partly by their yokelessness, dissoluteness, and ungodliness: *sons of Belial*: that will not submit to the laws of his – especially of Christ's kingdom. Partly by their perniciousness and mischievousness; hence compared to thorns – piercing, wounding, intractable thorns – that cannot be taken with hands without iron and staff of a spear. These enemies literally were the ungodly and pernicious enemies opposing the kingdom of David and his ordinary seed as Zenacherib, Nebuchadnezzar, etc; *mystically*, the spiritual enemies of Christ's kingdom, as Satan, Antichrist, all cruel persecutors and all the wicked of the world.

(b) Threatened, partly to be thrust away as thorns: partly, to be utterly burnt with fire in the same place. This was literally accomplished when the enemies of David's kingdom were thrust away from annoying his kingdom and destroyed, as God put his hook in the nose of Sennacherib and turned him away, yea destroyed 185,000 of his army about Jerusalem;[347] destroyed Belshazzar and the Babylonian kingdom; giving it to the Persians, etc.[348] Spiritually, this shall be fulfilled most completely upon the enemies of Christ's kingdom, both in this world, when Christ shall break in pieces all opposite empires and powers on earth, the gold, the silver, the brass, the iron, and the clay, etc.[349] shall destroy the great whore, the beast, and false prophet, Gog and Magog, etc.[350] But especially at the day of judgment, *when the Son of Man shall send forth his angels and they shall gather out of his kingdom all things that offend, and them which do iniquity: and shall cast them into a furnace of fire. There shall be wailing and gnashing of teeth.*[351] Then also he shall separate the goats from the sheep, and shall thrust the goats away from his presence with that dreadful sentence: *Depart from me ye cursed into everlasting fire prepared for the devil and his angels. And these shall go away into everlasting punishment.*[352]

Thus, in this great promise of building David an house, by raising up a royal seed to sit upon his throne forever, God principally intended the building of David's house and kingdom in Jesus Christ for evermore, as these last words of David rightly understood do notably declare, many passages therein being completely applicable to none but to Jesus Christ alone.

(7) Finally, the perpetuity and stability of God's Covenant and federal mercy to David. This is the last covenant mercy, more especially directed to David which I shall mention: the chief effect and accomplishment whereof notwithstanding was upon his seed, especially upon Christ. *My mercy will I keep for him for evermore: and my covenant shall stand fast with him. His seed also will I make forever, and his throne as the days of heaven.*[353] – *My*

---

[347] 2 Kings 19:28 to the end
[348] Daniel 5:30-31
[349] Daniel 2:34-35, 44-45
[350] Revelation 19:1-2, 20-21 & 20:8-9, 15
[351] Matthew 13:41-42
[352] Matthew 25:32-33, 41, 46
[353] Psalm 89:28-29, 33-35

loving-kindness will I not utterly take from him, nor suffer my faithfulness to fail. My covenant will I not break nor alter the thing that is gone out of my lips. Once have I sworn by mine holiness, that I will not lie unto David.

O what variety, vehemence, and emphaticalness of divine expressions are here, to ascertain the unalterableness and utter irrevocableness of God's Covenant with David and his seed! In these expressions God confirms the immovable perpetuity of this Covenant with David, as of old he had established his Covenant with Abraham, by two immutable things by which it was impossible for God to lie, for the strengthening of David's consolation, namely: by his promise and by his oath.[354]

[1] By his promise. Yea, by his promises; yea, by a heap of promises. Here are nine promises: five whereof do evidently, and the other four consequentially, confirm the unchangeableness of this Covenant. God's single word and promise is unchangeably sure. How sure then are his many promises to the same purpose? If God promises his Covenant's stability and perpetuity but once, there is ground enough for believing it; but if he promises the same thing often, if five times, if nine times, and all so pathetically, then there's no place for doubting.

[2] By his own sacred oath. *Once have I sworn by mine holiness, that I will not lie unto David.* If yet God's promises make not the Covenant sure enough, here's his oath. And God, having no greater to swear by, swears by himself, by his holiness, that he will not deceive David, or deal falsely with him in this Covenant. But why is it said, *Once have I sworn?* Muis notes out of R. Ezra, that {once} may here imply as if God never swore by his holiness, but only at this time to David.[355] But that is a gross mistake: God elsewhere swore by his holiness.[356] Rather, {once} implies the sufficiency, peremptoriness, and irrevocableness of God's oath. Once for all, immutably, irrevocably,

---

[354] Hebrews 6:13 to the end
[355] Simone De Muis' commentary on Psalm 89:36
[356] Amos 4:2

unalterably, etc. as Calvin[357] and Muis[358] do well explain the emphasis of the word and phrase. Thus God promised and swore the perpetuity of his Covenant with David. And David, hereupon in his last words, greatly comforts himself by this, among other properties of this Covenant: *Although mine house be not so with God, yet hath he made with me an everlasting covenant, ordered in all things, and sure*, etc.[359]

This promised perpetuity of God's Covenant with David, was made good and fulfilled: partly, to David's posterity, successively raised up to sit upon his throne, for a long time together. Principally to Jesus Christ, his primary seed, to whom the Lord God gave the throne of his father David.[360] *And he shall reign over the house of Jacob forever, and of his kingdom there shall be no end.* But remove Christ from David's house, where is the eternity of his kingdom, or of this Covenant? For Rehoboam, David's second successor, of twelve tribes lost ten, retaining scarce one and a half. And that small remainder, how sadly was it vexed, torn, and weakened with frequent wars and afflictions, until at last both king and people were most disgracefully carried captives to Babylon, there remaining seventy years together? Whereupon probably, Ethan laments thus: *Thou hast made void the covenant of thy servant* (namely: of David), *Thou hast profaned his crown to the ground*, etc.[361] By Ezekiel also, God thrice-over threatens the overthrowing of King Zedekiah's crown: *I will overturn, overturn, overturn it, and it shall be no more, until he come, whose right it is, and I will give it him.*[362] That is, the kingdom of David over Judah

---

[357] John Calvin's commentary on Psalm 89:35: "The adverb {once} denotes that the oath is irrevocable, and that therefore we have not the least reason to be apprehensive of any inconstancy."
<https://sacred-texts.com/chr/calvin/cc10/cc10023.htm>
[Accessed 2/28/2024]

[358] Semel, hoc est, irrevocabiliter & immutabiliter. Hoc sensu hanc particulam accipit Kimchi; Nec non Ezra, qui explicat Semel, id quod Satis est. Simone de Muis Com. in. Psalm 89. 36.

[359] 2 Samuel 23:5

[360] Luke 1:31-33, Acts 13:30, 34-36

[361] Psalm 89:38-39, etc.

[362] Ezekiel 21:25-27

shall be eclipsed, for after their return from Babylon it was low, mean, despicable and full of miseries (as is clear by Ezra, Nehemiah, Esther, Daniel 11, the books of Maccabees, etc.), and it shall never be restored to its native luster and glory until Jesus Christ the Messiah come, to whom of right it belongs: he being David's successor according to the flesh, and constituted by God, the spiritual and eternal king of the church.

These are the covenant mercies, which God on his part promised, touching David himself. Most of these are chiefly intended of Christ, and accomplished in Christ the true David, whose person David did typically sustain and shadow out in this Covenant, as in the general inferences will after appear.[363]

---

[363] In this chapter, Aphorism 7, Inference 2

(2) Secondly, the covenant mercies or blessings more especially concerning David's seed were chiefly these, namely: God promised:

[1] *That he would be a father to the seed of David, and he should be his son*. This sweet relation is once and again promised to David's seed in the vision of Nathan revealing this Covenant: *I will set up thy seed after thee, which shall proceed out of thy bowels and I will establish his kingdom. – I will be his Father: and he shall be my son.*[364] How much paternal mercy this relation imports from God to David's seed, and how much filial duty from David's seed reciprocally to God, may be easily collected from what has been already said touching the like fatherly relation to David – there see.

This promise of paternal relation to David's seed was accomplished and fulfilled:

{1} More immediately and less principally, upon David's ordinary seed. As upon Solomon, David himself being witness: *And he said unto me, Solomon thy son he shall build my house and my courts: for I have chosen him to be my son and I will be his Father.*[365]

{2} More mediately and principally, upon David's extraordinary seed Jesus Christ. For the apostle in his epistle to the Hebrews testifies that this is the more excellent name than that of angels, which Christ has by inheritance obtained: *For unto which of the angels said he at any time, Thou art my son, this day have I begotten thee? And again I will be to him a Father, and he shall be to me a son?*[366] This last alleged testimony seems peculiarly to be taken from God's promise in this Covenant of this paternal relation both to David and to Solomon his son: both of them being counted God's sons here, as they typically sustained the person of Christ, who is the Son of Sons. Though the terms of this testimony here alleged seem more exactly to agree to this promise made to David's seed, Solomon. Besides, when the angel promised Christ to be

---

[364] 2 Samuel 7:12, 14; 1 Chronicles 17:11, 13
[365] 1 Chronicles 28:6
[366] Hebrews 1:4-5

born of the virgin Mary, he said: *Thou shalt conceive in thy womb, and bring forth a son, and call his name Jesus. He shall be great, and shall be called the Son of the Highest*, etc. And indeed, Jesus Christ did most fully receive all the privileges and mercies of this relation from his Father, and did most exactly return all the duties of this relation to his Father.

[2] **That David's seed should build God a house.** God had told Israel by Moses in the wilderness that when they should be possessed of Canaan, having rest from their enemies round about, that then there should be a place which the LORD should choose out of all their tribes to put his name there and thither they should bring all that God commanded them, etc.[367] Hereupon, when the LORD had given David rest round about from all his enemies, David had it in his heart, to build a house of rest for the Ark of the Covenant of the LORD, and for the footstool of our God, and had made ready for the building.[368] But God said unto him, *Thou shalt not build an house for my name, – Solomon thy son he shall build my house and my courts. – He shall build me an house: and I will stablish his throne forever.*[369]

This house was the fixed temple at Jerusalem, called for the excellency and dignity of it: the temple of the LORD (Jeremiah 7:4), his temple at Jerusalem (Psalm 68:29), the house of the LORD (Nehemiah 6:10, Ecclesiastes 5:1), the holy and beautiful house, where the fathers praised him (Isaiah 64:11), the house of prayer (Mark 11:17), the house whereupon God's name was called (Jeremiah 7:11), the palace of the LORD (1 Chronicles 29:1), the sanctuary (Psalm 20:2), the beauty of holiness (Psalm 29:2), the holy place of the habitacles of the Most High (Psalm 46:4), the courts of his holiness (Isaiah 62:9), the place of his feet (Isaiah 60:13), a house of rest for the ark of the Covenant of the LORD, and for the footstool of our God (1 Chronicles 28:23). By these and many such like synonymous denominations, the eminence of God's house is abundantly intimated.

---

[367] Deuteronomy 12:5-11
[368] 2 Samuel 7:1, etc., with 1 Chronicles 28:2-3, 6
[369] 1 Chronicles 17:12; 2 Samuel 7:13

Now that God should choose from among all Israel only the seed of David to build this holy and magnificent house to God, and assure David hereof by covenant and promise, this was a high honor cast upon David and his seed, especially considering that this house was to be: (a) a special habitation for God, wherein he would dwell and vouchsafe his presence to his people;[370] (b) the fixed place of God's public worship for all the people Israel: where all their sacrifices were to be offered; wherein or towards which, all their prayers and praises were to be presented to God;[371] (c) a singular type: (1) of Christ in whom the fullness of the Godhead dwelt personally;[372] (2) of the church, that mystical body of Christ, where God dwells by the Spirit;[373] (3) of every particular believer and member of Christ, wherein Christ dwells by faith.[374] This promise was fulfilled:

{1} Literally and typically in David's immediate seed, Solomon. David found favor before God, and desired to find a tabernacle for the God of Jacob.[375] But Solomon built him a house. The history of the temple structure refers it to King Solomon. He prepared materials for the building (1 Kings 5). He – in seven years' space – set up the fabric and finished it, at Jerusalem in Mount Moriah (1 Kings 6, 2 Chronicles 3:1, etc). He also when the building was completed, dedicated it (1 Kings 8:1, etc.) And in all this, King Solomon had a special eye to the accomplishment of God's promise to David thereby, as appears partly in his letters to Hiram King of Tyre: *I purpose to build an house unto the name of the LORD my God, as the LORD spake unto David my father saying: Thy son, whom I will set upon thy throne in thy room, he shall build an house unto my name, etc.;*[376] partly, at the dedication of the temple: *Then spake Solomon, The LORD said, That he would dwell in the thick darkness. I have*

---

[370] Psalm 46:4; 1 Chronicles 28:2-3
[371] Deuteronomy 12:5-12, Mark 11:17, Isaiah 64:11
[372] Colossians 2:9, John 2:21
[373] 1 Corinthians 3:16, Ephesians 2:21
[374] 1 Corinthians 3:19, Ephesians 3:17
[375] Acts 7:45-47
[376] 1 Kings 5:5

surely built thee an house to dwell in, a settled place for thee to abide in forever. – Blessed be the LORD God of Israel which spake with his mouth unto David my Father, and hath with his hand fulfilled it. – And the LORD said to David my father, whereas it was in thine heart to build an house to my Name, thou didst well that it was in thy heart. Nevertheless thou shalt not build the house, but thy son that shall come forth out of thy loins, he shall build the house unto my name. And the LORD hath performed his word that he spake, and I am risen up in the room of David my Father, and sit on the Throne of Israel, as the LORD promised, and have built an house for the LORD God of Israel.[377]

{2} Spiritually and anti-typically in David's mediate seed Jesus Christ, greater than Solomon. For he built, not the material and typical temple, but the spiritual and true temple, the church, which is the temple and house of the living God.[378] This the apostle shows evidently in his epistle to the Hebrews, saying: *Jesus Christ was counted worthy of more glory than Moses, inasmuch as he who hath built the house, hath more honor than the house. – And Moses verily was faithful in all his house as a servant, – But Christ as a son over his own house, whose house are we if we hold fast the confidence and the rejoicing of the hope firm unto the end.*[379] In which words these things are plain: (1) that believers are the house of Christ; (2) that this house of Christ is built by Christ. Christ is the chief architect or builder of his Church, his house; (3) that Christ has more honor, in that he is builder of this house, than Moses himself, who was only a part of this house a living stone in this building. Moses built the tabernacle: that was much honor; King Solomon built the material temple at Jerusalem: that was more honor; but Jesus Christ builds the spiritual temple, the church of the faithful; this was most honor of all.

---

[377] 1 Kings 8:12-13, 15-22
[378] Ephesians 2:20-22; 1 Peter 2:4-5
[379] Hebrews 3:2-6

The temple and tabernacle were types of the church of God and of particular believers, who are therefore called the temples of God and of the Holy Spirit frequently.[380] Herein the type and antitype agree:

{1} The temple was a very magnificent building, full of outward beauty and glory, especially within the temple – see 2 Chronicles 3 & 4 throughout – hence called {*a beautiful house*}.[381] And David said: *The house that is to be built for the LORD, must be exceedingly magnifial, of fame and of glory throughout all countries.*[382] Thus, the king's daughter, the church, is all glorious within. Her clothing is of wrought gold; her visible beauty is great; her invisible and inward glory is transcendent.[383]

{2} The temple was the settled house for all God's solemn and public worship. There all the sacrifices, oblations, and incense were to be offered to God. There God was solemnly prayed to and praised. There the word of God was preached, etc.[384] So the Church of God is the spiritual house wherein all spiritual sacrifices are offered unto God by his royal priesthood, and all the ordinances of Christ publicly managed for the perfecting of the saints for the edifying of the body of Christ.[385]

{3} The temple was the place of God's special presence and residence among his people.[386] There he dwelt symbolically, the ark being a peculiar symbol or token of his presence. So the church of Christ and all the true members thereof, are a habitation of God by his Spirit, and of Christ through faith. His presence, residence, and abode is with them. *Know ye not that ye are the temple of God? and that the Spirit of God dwelleth in you?*[387] – *In whom all the building fitly framed, groweth unto an holy temple in the Lord: In whom*

---

[380] 1 Corinthians 3:16-17, 6:19; 2 Corinthians 6:16, Ephesians 2:20-22; 1 Peter 2:5
[381] Isaiah 64:11
[382] 1 Chronicles 22:5
[383] Psalm 45:13
[384] Deuteronomy 12:5-15, Hebrews 9:6-7, Mark 11:17, Isaiah 64:11, Matthew 26:55, Acts 5:25
[385] 1 Peter 2:5; 1 Timothy 3:15, Ephesians 4:11-13
[386] Psalm 46:4
[387] 1 Corinthians 3:16-17 & 6:19

you also are built together for an habitation of God through the Spirit.[388] *– For, ye are the temple of the living God, As God hath said, I will dwell in them, and walk in them, and I will be their God and they shall be my people.*[389]

{4} Hereupon the temple of God was holy.[390] God's solemn worship and presence there made it holy. So the church, this spiritual temple of God, is holy. *If any man defile the temple of God, him shall God destroy: for the temple of God is holy, which temple ye are.*[391] *– An holy nation.*[392] The church and people of God are holy: (i) By separation from the unholy corrupt mass of the world (2 Corinthians 6:16-17). (ii) By dedication to God and his holy service (2 Corinthians 8:5). (iii) By sanctification and inherent holiness (1 Corinthians 6:11).

{5} The temple was made up of many sorts of choice and costly materials, whereof some were taken from the land of Canaan, some from the countries of the Gentiles, as from Tyre, Ophir, etc. So this spiritual house and temple is made up of many sorts of lively stones, purchased by the invaluable price of Christ's blood: partly, taken out from among the Jews;[393] partly from among the Gentiles, all which are reconciled unto God in one body by the cross, and are made one household and temple of God.

{6} The temple had three principal partitions, namely: the outward court, for the people; the sanctuary, for the priests; and the holy of holies into which the high priest only entered once every year, and that not without blood of sacrifices.[394] So in this spiritual temple the church, these are the three like partitions, namely: the outer court, of the visible church;[395] the sanctuary, of the church invisible peculiar to the holy priesthood, all true believers, militant

---

[388] Ephesians 2:21-22 & 3:17
[389] 2 Corinthians 6:16
[390] Psalm 46:4, 29:2, Isaiah 64:11
[391] 1 Corinthians 3:17
[392] 1 Peter 2:9
[393] 1 Peter 1:4-5, Ephesians 2:14 to the end
[394] Exodus 26:31-32, etc.
[395] 1 Corinthians 12:13, 27-28

here on earth;[396] and the holy of holies, heaven itself, wherein the spirits of just men made perfect are triumphant in the presence of God and of the lamb forevermore.[397] Thus the temple (as also the tabernacle of old) was a type of the church of God, and of believers, the embers thereof.

Now, as the temple which King Solomon built was a type of the church and people of God. So Solomon himself in building this material temple was a special type of Jesus Christ the only master-builder of the spiritual temple of his church, as hereafter in the general inferences shall further appear.[398]

[3] *That God would establish his seed after him in his kingdom and throne forever.* This blessing is much insisted upon, and often promised in this Covenant and the explanations thereof.

{1} In this Covenant: *I will raise up thy seed after thee, which shall be of thy sons, and I will establish his kingdom. He shall build me an house: and I will establish his throne forever. I will be his Father: and he shall be my son: and I will not take my mercy away from him, as I took it from him that was before thee.* (that is, *I will not utterly take away the kingdom from his house, as from Saul*). *For I will settle him in mine house, and in my kingdom forever, and his throne shall be established for evermore.*[399] *– Moreover I will establish his kingdom forever: if he be constant* (Hebrew: *strong*) *to do my commandments and my judgments as at this day.*[400]

{2} In the explanations also of this Covenant: *I have made a covenant with my chosen: I have sworn unto David my servant. Thy seed will I establish forever, and build up thy throne to all generations. Selah. – His seed also will I make to endure forever, and his throne as the days of heaven. – His seed shall endure forever, and his throne as the sun before me. It shall be established forever as the moon, and as a faithful witness in heaven. Selah.*[401] And

---

[396] Ephesians 5:23-27, 29-32
[397] Hebrews 9:24, 10:19-20 & 12:23
[398] In this chapter, Aphorism 7, Inference 2
[399] 1 Chronicles 17:11-14; 2 Samuel 7:12-17
[400] 1 Chronicles 28:7
[401] Psalm 89:3-4

elsewhere: *If thy children will keep my covenant and my testimony, that I shall teach them: their children also shall sit upon thy throne for evermore.*[402]

In these testimonies, note:

(i) That this **blessing** of his seed's established throne and kingdom forever, is here frequently promised, namely: nine or ten times over, to show how certainly and fully this thing was determined by God.

(ii) That these **promises of this blessing** are notably illustrated, partly from the dissimilitude or disparity of God's dealing with King Saul that was before David. From him and his seed, the kingdom was quite taken away, but God would not so take away his mercy from David and his seed forever. Partly, from similitudes of things permanent and perpetual, as:

(a) Of heaven itself. All earthly things are mutable, fading and vanishing: but heaven abides still the same: *His throne as the days of heaven.*

(b) Of the sun: *And his throne as the sun before me.* The sun is sometimes beclouded, sometimes eclipsed, every night sets, but yet still keeps his place and course in the heavens; so though his seed's throne and kingdom should sometimes be obscured by the clouds and eclipses of great afflictions, and sometimes the darkness thereof should be so extreme that the sun thereof should seem to set, yet should it rise again, shine forth again, and have still a permanency notwithstanding all seeming alterations.

(c) Of the moon: *It* (that is, David's seed, and his throne) *shall be established forever as the moon, and as a faithful witness in heaven. Selah.* The moon also is liable to be often beclouded and eclipsed, and every day sets, and besides this it is still in a posture of alteration waning or increasing, it never appears to us twice together exactly with the same face: So though the throne of David's seed should be exposed to increasings, decreasings, and manifold alterations, yet the substance of it shall still remain. The latter clause {*as a faithful witness in heaven*} is by some made a fourth similitude, and interpreted to be the rainbow (Genesis 9:8-18). But by others such as Rashi,

---

[402] Psalm 132:12

and it is referred to the moon, or to both sun and moon, which though liable to the fore-mentioned alterations, yet shall be constant and faithful witnesses of God's Covenant with David, that as long as they shall endure, so long David's kingdom shall endure in his seed.[403]

(d) Of the day and night. This similitude is added by the prophet Jeremiah: *Thus saith the LORD, If you can break my covenant of the day, and my covenant of the night; that there should not be day and night in their season: then may also my covenant be broken with David my servant, that he should not have a son to reign upon his throne.*[404]

(iii) The **condition of all these promises** is expressed, which God expects from David's seed, namely: *If he be constant to do my commandments and my judgments, as at this day.*[405] And elsewhere: *If thy children will keep my covenant and my testimony that I shall teach them.*[406] This condition is constant obedience to God, and covenant-keeping with God. This condition, David's seed must perform to God, if they expected God should perform his promises unto them. This promised mercy of the perpetuity of David's seed and kingdom, was performed:

(a) More immediately and literally to the seed of David, from Solomon until the Babylonian captivity, in the succession of twenty kings of David's race that sat upon his throne in Jerusalem.[407] And after the captivity, in the succession of governors, having the principality and supremacy of rule, such as Zerubbabel, etc., after the kingdom was taken away. And after that, in the supreme authority of their great council or senate, as Peter Martyr has observed: "It is credible that David perceived this promise belonged to his posterity, which should not only have the kingdom, but should continue even until Christ. For it endured so long, not always in the kingdom, but partly in a

---

[403] Simone De Muis, commentary on Psalm 89:38; Larger London Annotations on the place.
[404] Jeremiah 33:20-21 with Genesis 8:21-22
[405] 1 Chronicles 28:7
[406] Psalm 132:12
[407] See 1 Chronicles 3:1, 5, 10-17, Matthew 1:6-12

principality when the kingdom was now taken away, partly in the senate, for thus it was by little and little diminished even until Herod. For he wholly dissipated and took away the public council and senatory order. And thus the prophecy of Jacob was accomplished: *The sceptre shall not depart from Judah, nor a lawgiver from between his feet, till Shiloh come.*"[408] So he.[409] It's true that the sins of David's seed brought many clouds and eclipses upon David's house, as will appear in the next particular, but still more or less, God continued this promised mercy to David's seed.

(b) More mediately and spiritually to Jesus Christ, of the seed of David according to the flesh, whose spiritual and everlasting Kingdom over the Church swallowed up the earthly kingdom of David.[410] Of Christ, the angel said to the virgin Mary his mother: *The Lord God shall give unto him the throne of his father David, and he shall reign over the house of Jacob forever, and of his kingdom there shall be no end.*[411]

(iv) Finally, that **God would not utterly take away his covenant faithfulness and loving-kindness from his seed, no not in case of their iniquity, but chastise their sinful miscarriages with the rod of men**. God was so resolved upon the perpetuity of David's seed and kingdom, that he resolved, their very sins should not disannul his Covenant in this particular, though they should not escape without due chastisement in David's offending seed. *I will be his father and he shall be my son: If he commit iniquity, I will chasten him with the rod of men, and with the stripes of the children of men. But my mercy shall not depart away from him, as I took it from Saul, whom I put away before thee.*[412] This is yet more fully expressed in the explanation of this Covenant: *If his children forsake my law, and walk not in my judgments; if they break my statutes and keep not my commandments: Then will I visit*

---

[408] Genesis 49:10
[409] "Credibile est, Davidem sensisse, hanc promissionem pertinere ad poste ritatem suam" – Peter Martyr commentary on 2 Samuel 7:19
[410] Romans 1:3
[411] Luke 1:31-33
[412] 2 Samuel 7:14-15

their transgression with the rod, and their iniquity with stripes. Nevertheless, my loving-kindness will I not utterly take from him, nor suffer my faithfulness to fail.[413] *My covenant will I not break nor alter the thing that is gone out of my lips,* etc. God will not break covenant with David's seed until first they break with him. Yea though they become unfaithful to him, yet will he remain faithful to them, for his covenant sake with David, yet will he chastise them with the rod and stripes of men, for their iniquities. By {*the rod of men*} and {*stripes of the children of men*}, understand: *either* the instrumental means of correcting them, which God will make use of, making men a rod and scourge to David's seed offending, as it often came to pass; *or* the moderation, lenity, and gentleness of his fatherly chastisements (Jeremiah 30:10-11, Isaiah 27:8-9 & 28:23 to the end).

In this branch of the Covenant, note how the iniquity of David's seed is presupposed, described, threatened, and the threatening qualified.

(a) **The iniquity of David's seed is presupposed by God, as possible.** *If he commit iniquity.*[414] This passage in Samuel seems peculiarly to be intended of Solomon, who would build God's house, but the Psalm shows it is also to be extended indefinitely to any of David's seed. *If his children forsake my law.*[415]

(b) **This iniquity is described and characterized more generally by forsaking God's law, and more especially:** (1) By not walking in God's judgments, namely: his judicial laws. (2) By breaking his statutes, namely: his ceremonial laws. (3) By not keeping his commandments, namely: his moral laws. If they should transgress any sort of God's laws, this would be their iniquity in the sight of God.

(c) **This iniquity is threatened to be visited with the rod and stripes of men.** If David's seed will sin, even David's seed shall smart. God's Covenant with them, exempts them not from afflictions in case of iniquity, but rather assures them of afflictions to their transgressions. This clause seems to have the

---

[413] Psalm 89:30-38
[414] 2 Samuel 7:13-15
[415] Psalm 89:30

nature both of a threatening, and of a promise. Of a threatening: in regard to sin, in order to its destruction. Of a promise: in regard to the sinners, in order to reformation and salvation. It is a great discovery of God's fatherly affection and fidelity to his children, that he will chastise them for their sins, and not suffer them to die under these diseases without remedy.[416] If sinners escape without chastisements, it's a dangerous sign they are bastards, not children.

Now the Lord visits the iniquity and transgression of his covenant people with the rod and stripes of chastisement, for their manifold advantage. As:

(1) **To awaken them to a true sense of their iniquities**, by discovering and aggravating their sins, unto them. *And if they be bound in fetters; and be holden in cords of affliction, then he showeth them their work, and their transgressions that they have exceeded.*[417] The bitterness of affliction convinceth of the greater bitterness of corruption the cause thereof. Some writings may be best read at the fire, and some in the water: so the blurs of sin are best discovered in the fire and water of distresses. The furnace and fining pot discovers how much dross is mixed with the gold, and blots run most abroad in wet paper; so the dross and blots of sin are best discovered in the fining pot and wet paper of tribulation.

(2) **To humble them for their iniquities discovered**. God aims at his people's humiliation for sin, when he visits them with castigation upon that account.[418] The fire melts the very stones into fluid metal; so afflictions the most stony heart. Manasseh himself – that monster for wickedness – when the king of Assyria took him among the thorns, and bound him with fetters, and carried him to Babylon, and when he was in affliction, *he besought the LORD his God, and humbled himself greatly.*[419] The Lord loves our tears and sorrows, rather than our sins: yea and those sorrows most, that are for sin.

---

[416] Proverbs 3:11-12, Hebrews 12:5-12
[417] Job 36:8-9
[418] 2 Chronicles 7:13-14
[419] 2 Chronicles 33:11-12

(3) ***To provoke them unto prayer and supplication to that God that visits them with castigation.*** *If I shut up heaven that there be no rain or if I command the locusts to drown the land, or if I send pestilence among my people: If my people which are called by my name shall humble themselves and pray and seek my face,* etc.[420] So that, this God intends and expects when his people are chastised, that they come down upon their knees and cry to him for favor, Manasseh himself falls to praying, when God had brought him into chains; when he was in affliction he besought the LORD his God, *and prayed unto him, and he was entreated of him.*[421] The rod makes us find prayer, and prayer makes us find God. This effect, affliction usually has upon God's people, it stirs up the spirit of prayer: *LORD in trouble have they visited thee, they poured out a prayer* (Hebrew: *a secret-speech*) *when thy chastening was upon them.*[422] And, as the musical instrument makes the sweetest melody when you strike the strings, and not until then, so our hearts make no such spiritual melody to God in supplications, until he smite our heartstrings with his castigations. David prayed most fervently, when afflictions lay upon him most heavily. As in the spring, the birds tune most sweetly when it rains most sadly.

(4) ***To instruct them unto repentance, and purge them from their iniquities.*** *If they are bound in fetters, and held in cords of affliction, he openeth their ear to discipline, and commandeth that they return from iniquity.*[423] Repentance and reformation are the grand lesson which God would have his children learn by the rod. *By this shall the iniquity of Jacob be purged, and this is all the fruit to take away his sin.*[424] David acknowledged: *Before I was afflicted I went astray: but now have I kept thy word.* Ephraim thus bemoaned himself: *Thou hast chastised me, and I was chastised as a bullock unaccustomed to the yoke: Turn thou me, and I shall be turned; for thou*

---

[420] 2 Chronicles 7:13-14
[421] 2 Chronicles 33:12-13
[422] Isaiah 26:16
[423] Job 36:8-10
[424] Isaiah 27:6

art the LORD my God. Surely after that I was turned, I repented; and after that I was instructed, I smote upon my thigh: I was ashamed, yea even confounded, because I did bear the reproach of my youth.[425] Afflictions are God's Jordan to heal our spiritual leprosy. They are his fuller's soap to wash out our spots and stains of sin. They are his fan to blow away our chaff. They are his fining pot and furnace to burn up our dross out of us. A gracious heart shall lose nothing but his dross and rubbish in his afflictions.

(5) *To preserve them from like sinning for time to come.* Afflictions are not only restorative from sin past, but also preservatives against sin to come. They are like sea-marks to warn them continually against such mischiefs. They are as a wall or an hedge of thorns to keep his flock from straying and wandering in the by paths of iniquity. As Hosea makes the allusion: *Therefore behold, I will hedge up thy way with thorns, and wall a wall, that she shall not find her paths.*[426] Afflictions are to sin, as the banks or sea-walls to the sea: restraints and preventions of their overflowing. By all this, it is apparent that this clause in David's Covenant of chastising the iniquity of his seed with the rod and stripes, was a covenant favor to David and his seed, and deservedly to be reckoned up among the rest of his covenant mercies. God's fatherly rod preserves his children from spiritual ruin.

(d) **This threatened chastisement is notwithstanding sweetly allayed and mitigated with that sweet promise of God's covenant faithfulness, and not taking his mercy and loving-kindness utterly from his seed in reference to the kingdom, as he took it from Saul.** This promised blessing had its accomplishment:

(1) **Upon David's ordinary seed and posterity, especially in two ways:**

[1] *The conditioned chastisements* in case of the iniquity of his seed (which were threatened and promised) were often actually inflicted upon his seed for their transgressions, and sometimes very sadly. As:

---

[425] Psalm 119:67, 71
[426] Hosea 2:6

{1} **Upon Solomon himself,** for his Paganish idolatries, wherewith he gratified all his strange wives.[427] Whereupon, God threatened to rend all the kingdom save one tribe, out of his son's hand and to give it to Jeroboam the servant of Solomon. Also God stirred up adversaries against Solomon, as Hadad the Edomite and Roezen the son of Eliadah.

{2} **Upon Rehoboam, son of Solomon.** For upon his tyrannical answer to Jeroboam and Israel, God rent ten tribes from him, and gave them to Jeroboam.[428] And afterwards, upon his forsaking of the Lord when he had strengthened the kingdom of Judah, the Lord forsook him and gave Jerusalem so far into the hand of Shishak king of Egypt, that he took away all the treasures of the house of the LORD and of the king's house; as also the shields of gold which King Solomon had made. And the people of Judah were Shishacks servants for a time.[429]

{3} **Upon Asa.** For he, relying upon the help of Benhadad King of Syria against Baasha King of Israel, rather than upon the Lord, was thenceforth afflicted with wars, and at last being diseased in his feet, he sought not to the Lord but to the physicians, and died of his disease.[430]

{4} **Upon Jehoshaphat.** For he, helping wicked Ahab who sold himself to work wickedness,[431] Jehu the seer said to him: *Shouldst thou help the ungodly, and love them that hate the LORD? Therefore is wrath upon thee from before the LORD.* And afterwards, joining himself with Ahaziah, king of Israel, who did very wickedly to make ships to go to Tarshish, *the LORD broke his ships that they were not able to go thither.*[432]

{5} **Upon Jehoram son of Jehoshaphat.** For he slew his brethren with the sword, and walked in the ways of Ahab, having his daughter to wife. Therefore God stirred up the Philistines and Arabians so that they broke into the king's

---

[427] See 1 Kings 11 throughout
[428] 2 Chronicles 10 throughout
[429] 2 Chronicles 12:1-13
[430] 2 Chronicles 16 throughout
[431] 2 Chronicles 18 with 19:2
[432] 2 Chronicles 20:35-37

house, and carried away his wives, sons and all his substance. And at last, God smote him in his bowels with an incurable disease, and after two years, his bowels fell out, and so he died of sore diseases.[433]

{6} **Upon Ahaziah son of Jehoram, King of Judah.** For he, walking in the wicked ways of the House of Ahab after his mother's counsel, and joining in war with Jehoram son of Ahab against Hazael King of Syria, was slain by Jehu, as he was executing judgment upon the House of Ahab.[434]

{7} **Upon Joash son of Ahaziah.** For, when Jehoiadah the godly priest, his guardian, was dead, he with Judah and Jerusalem forsook the Lord, and served groves and idols, and stoned Zechariah son of Jehoiada for reproving their wickedness. Therefore the Syrians came with a small company, and destroyed a very great host, and all the princes of the people, and sent their spoil to Damascus, and left Joash in great diseases who afterwards was slain in his bed by his own servants, for the blood of Zechariah.[435]

{8} **Upon Amaziah son of Joash.** For he, having conquered the Edomites, set up their idols to be his gods, and threatened to smite the prophet that reproved him. God gave him and his army into the hand of Joash King of Israel and his army, who broke down 400 cubits of the wall of Jerusalem, took all the gold and silver, and all the vessels in the house of God with Obed Edom, and the treasures of the king's house.[436]

{9} **Upon Uzziah son of Amaziah,** for when he was strong, his heart was strong, his heart was lifted up to his destruction. He invaded the priest's office, and went into the temple to burn incense, therefore the Lord presently smote him with leprosy, so that he was cut off from the house of the Lord, remaining a leper till the day of his death.[437]

---

[433] 2 Chronicles 21
[434] 2 Chronicles 22:1-10
[435] 2 Chronicles 24:15-27
[436] 2 Chronicles 25:14-25
[437] 2 Chronicles 26:16-22

{10} **Upon Ahaz**, for he was very wicked: served Baalim, burnt incense in the valley of the son of Himnom, burnt his children in the fire after the heathenish abominations, sacrificed and burnt incense in high places, on hills, and under every green tree. Therefore God delivered him and his people into the hands of the king of Syria, and of the king of Israel, so that in one day, Pekah slew 120,000 valiant men, and Israel carried away captive 200,000 women, sons, and daughters, besides all the spoil. The Edomites also and the Philistines brought Judah low for their sins. And yet this Ahaz in the day of his distress trespassed more against the Lord.[438]

{11} **Upon Hezekiah**, for after his recovery from his mortal sickness, his heart was lifted up, and he rendered not again unto the Lord according to the benefit done unto him: therefore there was wrath upon Judah and Jerusalem.[439]

{12} **Upon Manasseh son of Hezekiah**, for he was a monster for all manner of idolatry and wickedness. *Wherefore the LORD brought upon them the captains of the host of the king of Assyria, which took Manasseh among the thorns, and bound him with fetters and carried him to Babylon.*[440]

{13} **Upon Josiah**, for he – fighting with Pharaoh Necho in the valley of Megiddo, contrary to the words of Necho from the mouth of God – was slain by the archers, to the extreme grief of all Judah and Jerusalem. And for a season, the kingdom of Judah was in some thralldom under Necho.[441]

{14} **Upon Jehoiakim**. He wrought evil in the sight of the Lord. Therefore Nebuchadnezzar came up, bound him in fetters, carried him to Babylon with vessels of the house of the Lord.[442]

{15} **Upon Jehoiachin**. *He did that which was evil also in the sight of the Lord.* So that Nebuchadnezzar sent and brought him to Babylon with the

---

[438] 2 Chronicles 28:1-26
[439] 2 Chronicles 32:24-26 with Isaiah 39 throughout
[440] 2 Chronicles 33:2-12
[441] 2 Chronicles 35:20-26
[442] 2 Chronicles 36:5-7

goodly vessels of the house of the Lord, and made his brother Zedekiah King over Judah, etc.[443]

{16} **Upon Zedekiah.** *For he did evil in the sight of the Lord, and humbled not himself before Jeremiah the prophet speaking from the mouth of the LORD,* broke his oath and covenant with Nebuchadnezzar, the priests and people grew notoriously wicked, defiled the temple, and despised all God's messages for their reformation. Therefore God sent upon them the king of the Chaldees who destroyed temple, city, and people, carrying the residue of them shamefully captives into Babylon, where they remained seventy years together as people buried in their graves. Thus God visited the iniquity of David's seed with the rod of men, and with the stripes of the children of men. And so the clause of the Covenant touching their castigation for their transgressions was abundantly performed.[444]

[2] The promised qualification and mitigation of this chastisement was also accomplished as truly. In that, God – in midst of all his judgments upon them for their sins – yet still reserved the kingdom of Judah to David's seed, and raised him up a seed as a lamp or a light to sit upon the throne in Jerusalem, as the story several times observes, and the series thereof plainly evidences.[445] Yea and under and after the captivity until the coming of Christ, God raised up governors and rulers of David's race over Judah and Jerusalem; either single persons, as Zerubbabel, etc., or societies as the sanhedrin (wherein they of the tribe of Judah had greatest share) in which was the supreme power more or less until the destruction of Jerusalem after Jesus Christ, or at least until Christ's incarnation.[446] Thus, the scepter did not depart from Judah, nor a lawgiver from between his feet, until Shiloh came – until Jesus Christ the prosperer or Savior, of Judah's race, came.[447] This point is well cleared by

---

[443] 2 Chronicles 36:9-10
[444] 2 Chronicles 36:11-22, Ezekiel 37:11-14
[445] Under Solomon: 1 Kings 11:12-13, 31, 36; under Abijah: 1 Kings 15:45; under Jehoram: 2 Chronicles 21:7; 2 Kings 8:16-23
[446] Luke 3:23-32, Matthew 1:12, etc.
[447] Genesis 49:10

several of our modern writers, to the diligent perusal of whose elaborate determinations therein I refer the learned reader, for brevity's sake; namely: Andre Rivet in Genesis 49, Exercitations 178 & 179, and after him, Frederick Spanheim in *Dubia Evangelica Part 2, Dub. xviii*, And after them both, the late, large London Annotations on Genesis 49:10, who (although they have some difference in their explanations of this point, yet) give great light thereunto. Thus this promised mercy had its accomplishment upon David's ordinary seed.

(2) Upon David's extraordinary seed, Jesus Christ, was accomplished also in two ways, namely:

[1] The chastisement threatened in case of the iniquity of David's seed was deeply inflicted upon Jesus Christ. For *He bore our sins upon his own body on the tree;*[448] *He was made sin for us, who knew no sin;*[449] *God laid upon him* (or *made meet on him*) *the iniquities of us all* – even of all the elect from the beginning to the end of the world.[450] So that, by imputation, Jesus Christ became one of the greatest sinners that ever was in the world. Hereupon consequently, God visited our iniquities upon him with the rod and stripes of men: *He was wounded for our transgressions; he was bruised for our iniquities, the chastisement of our peace was upon him, and by his stripes we are healed,* etc.[451] He was chastised for our sins, that had none of his own to be chastised for. Whence Augustine pathetically: "O wonderful condition of the censure! O ineffable disposal of the mystery! The unjust sins, and the just is punished; the guilty does the fault, and the guiltless is beaten; the impious offends, and the pious is condemned; what the evil deserves, the good endures; what the

---

[448] 1 Peter 2:24
[449] 2 Corinthians 5:21
[450] Isaiah 53:5-6
[451] Isaiah 53:4

servant perpetrates, the master pays; what man commits, God undergoes," etc.[452]

[2] The qualification also of this threatening was made good upon Christ. For in his deepest sufferings and humiliation God did not take away his mercy and loving-kindness from him, nor suffer his faithfulness to fail. God did not forsake him, though upon the cross, when he seemed most to forsake him. For then God was his God and Father;[453] then by divine power, he converted the thief most miraculously;[454] then he commended his spirit into his Father's hands, and that day went to paradise;[455] then heaven and earth did homage to him, the sun withdrawing his light, the veil of the temple tearing, the earth quaking, the rocks rending, the graves opening, all the dead rising.[456] Yea when he was in grave, in his lowest degree of humiliation; *God did not leave his soul in hell, nor suffer his holy one to see corruption, but showed him the path of life*, and after set him at his own right hand, to reign forever and forever.[457]

These are the covenant mercies promised more especially to David's seed, having their primary accomplishment in Jesus Christ his primary seed.

---

[452] "O ineffabilis mysterij dispositio, peccat iniquus & punitur iustus, delinquit reus, & vapulat innocens, offendit impius & damnatur pius, quod meretur malus patitur bonus, quod committit homo sustinet Deus." – Augustine, *Lib. Meditat.* C.7, Tom 9
[453] Matthew 27:46, Luke 23:46
[454] Luke 23:39-44
[455] Luke 23:43, 46
[456] Matthew 27:45, 51-55
[457] Acts 2:25-37

(3) Thirdly and lastly, the covenant blessing or mercies touching the people Israel, the subjects of King David and his royal seed, were especially these; namely:

[1] God's habitation in Zion forever, [2] their peaceable and secure establishment in Canaan, and [3] their singular prosperity both in temporals and spirituals. The second flows from the first, as a proper fruit and effect thereof; the third results from both the former, as a consequent thereof; so the first is the root and foundation of them all.

[1] **God's habitation in Zion forever.** This is plain in that exposition of God's Covenant with David: *If thy children will keep my covenant and my Testimony, that I shall teach them, their children also shall sit upon thy throne for evermore. For the LORD hath chosen Zion: he hath desired it for his habitation. This is my rest forever: Here will I dwell, for I have desired it.*[458] This promise is very emphatic, and yet sufficiently obscure. For the clearing whereof, these particulars are a little to be explained, namely: {1} What is the connection of this promise with that before? {2} What place is intended by {*Zion*}? {3} How did God dwell in Zion? {4} Why would God dwell there? {5} In what sense God said of Zion {*This is my rest forever*}, having long since removed his resting place and habitation thence, for the sins of the Jews?

{1} *The connection of this promise with the promise foregoing*, is in the word' כִּי *Ki*: {*for*} or {*because*}.[459] So that in this promise, God gives a reason for the perpetuity of David's throne and kingdom to his seed: because God himself had chosen Zion for his own perpetual rest, where he would clothe his priests with salvation. Upon this, Calvin has a good note: "This connection," (says he) "is to be noted, because the stability of that kingdom was nowhere else to be sought but in Christ; but the kingdom of Christ is

---

[458] Psalm 132:11-14
[459] Psalm 132:12-17

inseparable from his priesthood. Hence we see why he mentions Zion chosen, because God ordains nothing touching the kingdom separately, but brings in the sanctuary also, that it might be a true image of the mediator that was to come, who after the order of Melchizedek, was not only a king, but also a priest. Whence, the state of the kingdom and tabernacle were undivided."[460] So he.

{2} *The place here intended by* {Zion}, was:

(i) Literally that double-topped hill in Jerusalem, whereof, the one top was called {*Zion*} and the other {*Moriah*}, whereupon Solomon built the temple,[461] and whereupon also Abraham had of old offered up Isaac in a figure.[462] Of Zion it cannot precisely be understood, the holy place of the habitacles of the Most High, being built, not upon Zion, but upon Mount Moriah: the city of David the royal seat being built on Mount Zion, which was on the northside of Moriah.[463] Therefore under the term {*Zion*} we must understand *Moriah* also; as Muis has here well observed.[464]

(ii) Mystically and spiritually, the church of God, typified and notably shadowed out by Mount Zion, and the temple there. To this effect, the church of God is often in the Prophets called {*Zion*}. Thus that prophecy of Christ must be understood: *Yet have I set my king upon mine holy hill of Zion*; that is, in the church.[465] And in the New Testament, {*Mount Sion*} is put for {*the church*} also: *But ye are come unto Mount Sion*, etc.[466] And *I looked, and lo, a lamb stood on the Mount Sion, and with him 144,000, having his Father's name written on their foreheads.*[467]

{3} ***In Zion, God did promise to dwell in a peculiar sort, so as he would dwell nowhere else.*** *The LORD loved the gates of Zion, more than all*

---

[460] John Calvin, commentary on Psalm 132:14
[461] 2 Chronicles 3:1
[462] Genesis 22:2 & Hebrews 11:17-19
[463] Psalm 48:2
[464] Simone De Muis, commentary on Psalm 132:13
[465] Psalm 2:6
[466] Hebrews 12:22-23
[467] Revelation 14:1, etc.

the dwellings of Jacob (Psalm 87:1-2 & 76:1-2). For clearing this note, that God's presence and habitation is:

(i) General, everywhere (Psalm 139:7, etc.): (a) By immensity of his essence (Jeremiah 23:24), (b) by extent of his power and dominion, (Job 42:21, Psalm 135:6), (3) by efficacy of his providence (Jeremiah 23:24, Acts 17:28).

(ii) Special, in some special places. So God is and dwells: (a) gloriously in heaven (Matthew 6:9), and (b) graciously in Zion, in his church. And this: (1) by peculiarity of his fatherly providence (Isaiah 63:9). (2) By visible symbols, signs, or tokens of his presence, such as by his fiery and cloudy pillar, tabernacle and ark he dwelt in his church in the wilderness: By his temple and ark and other Levitical ordinances he dwelt on Mount Zion, on Mount Moriah at Jerusalem, and in his Jewish church; and by his New Testament ordinances, he dwells now in all the churches of the Gentiles, which are the spiritual Zion. (3) By inhabitation of his Spirit and efficacy of his grace. So he dwelt and dwells in the true invisible church among both Jews and Gentiles, and in the hearts of all true believers (1 Corinthians 3:16-17, Ephesians 2:22 & 3:17). (c) Wrathfully, by acts of wrath, justice and indignation God dwells even in midst of his enemies (Psalm 110:2).

So that God promised to dwell in the literal and spiritual Zion, the church, graciously, in all those fore-mentioned ways. And this was a very high and eminent mercy, for where God pitches such his special and gracious habitation, there these sweet privileges attend and ensue upon his presence and residence. namely:

(i) Enjoyment of the special tokens of his presence and residence. While God dwelt in the midst of Israel, they still had the signs and tokens of his inhabitation continued to them, as his pillar of cloud and fire, his tabernacle, ark of his presence, temple, etc. And while God dwells in any church, he continues his oracles and ordinances as signs of his presence there.[468] Now such tokens of his presence are great privileges.

---

[468] Romans 3:1-2 & 9:4-5

(ii) Mutual nearness between God and that people. They that dwell together are near to one another. God is near to them, and not afar off (Deuteronomy 4:7). And they are a people near to God (Psalm 148:14). They who *sometimes were afar off, are made nigh by the blood of Christ.*[469]

(iii) Peculiar manifestation of God and Christ to them, so as not to the world (John 14:21-23). They that dwell together, are more intimately and familiarly acquainted one with another.

(iv) Reciprocal love and dearness between God and them, Christ and them. *He that loveth me* (said Christ) *shall be loved of my Father, and I will love him, and will manifest myself unto him. – And we will come unto him, and make our abode with him.*[470] Father and Son make their abode with him that loves Christ, and he that loves Christ is beloved of Father and Son. There's two loves for one; and both infinite.

(v) Sweet relations between God and them. *Ye are the temple of the living God; as God hath said, I will dwell in them, and walk in them: and I will be their God, and they shall be my people. – And I will receive you, and will be a Father unto you, and ye shall be my sons and daughters, saith the Lord Almighty.*[471] Here's a family relation between Father and his children; here's a covenant relation between God and his people: both accompanying God's indwelling in a people. How sweet, how glorious are these relations!

(vi) Dear communion and intimate heavenly fellowship between God and them. *As God hath said, I will dwell in them* (there's God"s habitation in them) *and walk in them* (there's his communion with them thereupon).[472] And elsewhere, Christ says: *If any man will open unto me, I will come in unto him* (there is his habitation) *and sup with him and he with me*, (there is the

---

[469] Ephesians 2:13
[470] John 14:21, 23
[471] 2 Corinthians 6:16-18
[472] 2 Corinthians 6:16

dear communion between them: they spiritually feasting and rejoicing one with another).[473]

(vii) Safe and secure protection against all evils and enemies, and seasonable relief in all dangers and difficulties. Where God dwells, safety dwells. See Psalm 46:5 and 76:2-3. and 23:4.

(viii) Satisfying refreshments and consolations. Where God dwells, there love, peace, joy, comfort, holiness, happiness, yea heaven dwells. *God is love: and he that dwelleth in love, dwelleth in God, and God in him.*[474] And he that dwelleth in God, having God to dwell in him, dwells in the midst of the paradise of God.

{4} *Why would God dwell in Zion: in literal Zion, at Jerusalem, or in spiritual and mystical Zion the church?* Here are three reasons given, but all for substance one and the same, and all drawn from God only, none from Zion. *The LORD hath chosen Zion; He hath desired it for his habitation; Here will I dwell, for I have desired it.* God promised his presence and residence there, not for any merit or worthiness in Zion, but of his own mere election, grace, and affection to Zion. God fetches all arguments and motives from himself, for his favors to his church. He will dwell in her, because he loves her; and he loves her, because he has chosen her and set his love upon her.[475]

{5} *In what sense did God say of Zion* {This is my rest forever}: *he having long since removed his habitation thence for the sins of the Jews?* Answer: this particular may be thus cleared.

(i) The phrase {*forever*} in the Hebrew language:

(a) Sometimes is used indeterminately, for absolute continuance to all eternity without end, as Psalm 9:7. and 29:10. and 33:11.

(b) Sometimes it's used determinately, for a long continuance of time, yet which shall at last determine and end: as at a man's death, or at the year of jubilee, etc. which is the *ever* of life, the *ever* of Jubilee, etc (1 Samuel 1:22,

---

[473] Revelation 3:20
[474] 1 John 4:16
[475] Deuteronomy 7:7-8

Exodus 21:6 with Leviticus 25:13, 28, 40-41). In this later sense, we must needs understand this phrase here, though Zion should have been God's rest until the world's end, for then at least it should have [been] determined. But it was determined sooner: even at the great jubilee of jubilees when Christ came, and the worship of God should no more be affixed to any particular place, but be managed anywhere purely and spiritually.[476]

(ii) The blessings of this Covenant were promised:

(a) Some of them absolutely: as the raising up of Christ of the seed of David, and the perpetuity of his kingdom, etc. which, notwithstanding all intervening failings in David himself or in his posterity, were exactly in their season performed.[477] (b) Some of them conditionally: as a succession of rulers in Israel of David's race continually, upon condition of their obedience, covenant-keeping, etc.[478] – God's presence and residence in the temple forever, upon the same condition.[479] And therefore he afterwards adds: *But if ye turn away and forsake my statutes and my commandments which I have set before you, and shall go and serve other gods and worship them, then will I pluck them up by the roots out of my land which I have given them: and this house which I have sanctified for my name, will I cast out of my sight, and will make it to be a proverb and a by-word amongst all nations. And this house which is high, shall be an astonishment to everyone that passeth by it; so that he shall say, why hath the LORD done thus unto this land, and unto this house? And it shall be answered, Because they forsook the LORD God of their fathers, which brought them forth out of the land of Egypt, and laid hold on other gods, and worshipped them, and served them therefore hath he brought all this evil upon them.*[480] So that Israel, failing in the condition of this promise, the promised

---

[476] John 4:21-23; 1 Timothy 2:8
[477] Psalm 132:11 with Luke 1:69, Acts 2:30
[478] 2 Chronicles 7:17-18, etc., Psalm 132:12
[479] 2 Chronicles 7:16
[480] Verses 19-22. See also Deuteronomy 29:22 to the end; Jeremiah 22:8-9

blessing failed. God removed his presence from them, and yet his promise was fully performed.

(iii) The sins which provoked God to forsake his habitation, to take away his presence and the tokens of his presence from his people the Jews, and so consequently from any other people, are especially these:

(a) Unbelief in Jesus Christ, and being hardened therein (Romans 11:7-8, 20), stumbling at Christ that stumbling stone (Romans 9:31-33), rejecting Christ and murdering him (Matthew 21:38-39, 42-43). (b) Forsaking the Lord, his law, and Covenant (2 Chronicles 12:1-2, 5 & 15:2; 1 Chronicles 28:9, Jeremiah 22:8-9). (c) Leaving first love and first works (Revelation 2:4-6). (d) Lukewarmness in religion (Revelation 3:15-17, 19) (e) Unsoundness in doctrine, when the prophets are fools and spiritual men (namely: they that pretend to the Spirit) are mad (Hosea 9:7-13) when the truth and gospel of Christ is contradicted and blasphemed (Acts 13:45-46). (f) Extreme and general barrenness, unfruitfulness, etc., under God's ordinances and means of spiritual fruit-bearing (Matthew 21:34-53, Isaiah 5:1-8). (g) Idolatry, in laying hold of, worshiping and serving other gods, etc. (2 Chronicles 7:19-22, Deuteronomy 29:22, etc. and 31:16-17, etc, and 32:16-17, etc., Psalm 6:39-40 and 78:58, etc., Jeremiah 7:29, etc. & 22:8-9, Ezekiel 8:5-6, etc., Hosea 9:9, etc.) What sin more speedily drives God away than idolatry? (h) The using of sorcery and like curious diabolical arts like pagans (Isaiah 2:6). This one of Manasseh's sins, for which among others God forsook his people (2 Kings 21:6, 14). When the gospel comes in power, the diabolical arts go down (Acts 19:18-20). When such devilish arts are re-embraced, proportionably the Gospel goes down. (i) General profaneness and wickedness in all sorts: magistrates, ministers, and people; especially when aggravated, with contempt of reformation, and persecution of God's faithful messengers that would reform them. Then there is no remedy (2 Chronicles 36:11-21, Matthew 21:34-36, 43). (j) Finally, a long continued perseverance in all manner of wickedness from time to time under God's mercies, deliverances, judgments, ordinances, and all manner of his dispensations (2 Kings 21:14-15). For these sins, God is wont to withdraw his presence and residence from a people; and for most of these he forsook Zion and Jerusalem, that once was his delightful rest and habitation.

[2] The peaceable and secure establishment of Israel, the subjects of King David and of his royal seed, in the land of Canaan.

This blessing results from the former most eminently. Israel could never have a better foundation of peaceable and secure settlement in Canaan, than God's rest and residence in the midst of them. According to that – *God is in the midst of her, she shall not be moved; God shall help her at the peering of the morning.*[481] This blessing is thus expressed and promised in the body of the Covenant in Nathan's vision: *Moreover, I will appoint a place for my people Israel, and will plant them, that they may dwell in a place of their own, and move no more; neither shall the children of wickedness afflict them anymore, as before time, And as since the time that I commanded judges to be over my people Israel, and have caused thee to rest from all thine enemies.*[482]

In this promise, God assures David of the good condition of his subjects; the flourishing happiness, prosperity, and security of subjects, being the honor and glory of their princes. This blessing has in it many branches. For herein God promises, touching his people Israel:

{1} *To appoint (or ordain) a place for them.*

Objection: But had not God done this already, Promising Canaan to Abraham and his seed (Genesis 12:7 & 15:18-21 & 13:14-17), and giving them possession thereof in the days of Joshua? (Joshua 15:1, etc.)

Answer: True, but "here" (says Kimchi), "God promises more plentiful influences of heaven, and more ample blessings, both in regard to the fruitfulness of the fields and firmness of the kingdom, than formerly." So that

---

[481] Psalm 46:5
[482] 2 Samuel 7:10-11; 1 Chronicles 17:9-10

the words are to be taken comparatively: not absolutely. Besides, until David's days, Canaan was not in the complete possession of Israel, for until then, the Jebusites possessed the fort or castle of Zion, which David took, and called it the city of David; but afterwards they should have the complete possession of it.[483]

{2} *To plant Israel, that they may dwell in a place of their own, and move no more.*

This metaphor of planting them, imports their firm and secure settlement in Canaan. "What is planted" (says Peter Martyr), "is not easily plucked up by the roots."[484] This planting was also formerly promised by Moses.[485] Trees planted dwell in their own place, and are not soon moved thence: they alone possess the ground wherein they are planted; other trees grow not on their roots. Israel in Egypt were in a strange land, none of their own;[486] and in the wilderness they were in their pilgrimage, not in their heritage; and in Canaan itself they were scarce yet thoroughly rooted, being often disturbed with many sorts of enemies – but they should now take deeper roots, and move no more.

Objection: But how did they move no more, when after this the ten tribes were carried away captive into Assyria, and the tribes of Judah and Benjamin were ofttimes grievously shaken by sundry enemies, and at last shamefully carried captive into Babylon for 70 years together?

Answer: Two things may be replied to this objection, namely:

(i) This phrase of {*their moving no more*} may be taken conditionally. They should move no more out of Canaan, upon condition they kept God's Covenant, obeyed his commandments, and avoided God-provoking sins in Canaan. Temporal mercies are still promised upon such conditions, expressed or implied, such as 1 Samuel 2:30 and Jeremiah 10:9-10. They therefore –

---

[483] 2 Samuel 5:6-11; 1 Chronicles 17:4-11
[484] "Quae plantata sunt, non facile a radicibus auferantur" – Peter Martyr, commentary on 2 Samuel 7:10
[485] Exodus 15:17
[486] Genesis 15:13

performing the conditions of this promise – were not removed out of their land, as in the days of their godly kings, Asa, Jehoshaphat, Hezekiah, Josiah, etc. is evident. But when they failed in these conditions, themselves evacuated and voided the promises of God, and were removed out of their Land, yea plucked up by the roots, as God had threatened, the ten tribes being carried away captive into Assyria, and Judah afterwards carried away into Babylon.

(ii) The phrase being taken absolutely and simply, as without condition, so this promise was fulfilled *literally*, in the days of David and Solomon, the two chief royal types of Christ, for in their days, Israel moved no more out of Canaan their inheritance. *Mystically*, this promise had and has its chief accomplishment in the everlasting kingdom of Jesus Christ, who shall reign upon the throne of his father David over the house of Jacob forever; and of his kingdom there shall be no end, it shall never be destroyed, removed or shaken. Whereupon the apostle styles it {ἀσάλευτον βασιλείαν}: *an unshaken kingdom, an unmoved kingdom*.[487] The word properly signifies a freedom from such motion as is in the sea. The sea is restless, always in motion, by ebbings and flowings, or by stormy winds and tempests. But Christ's kingdom shall never be moved from within itself, or from without itself, until Christ, having destroyed all his enemies, and put down all rule, and all authority and power, shall surrender up his mediatory kingdom to the Father, not in regard of the substance, but the circumstance and manner of the administration thereof, that God may be all in all.[488]

(iii) Finally, that *the children of wickedness should not afflict them* (or *waste them*) *anymore, as before-time*, (or *from the beginning*) and as since the time of the judges. By {*children of wickedness*}, understand the Paganish idolaters and persecutors, who lived without God in the world, in all wickedness, such as Egyptians, Idumeans, Philistines, Amalekites, etc. These should no more afflict and waste them in their persons and states, as formerly

---

[487] Hebrews 12:28
[488] 1 Corinthians 15:24-29

from the beginning. namely: as Egyptians afflicted them in Egypt; as the Amalekites, Edomites, Amorites, Moabites, etc. afflicted them in their journey towards Canaan; as the Canaanites, Philistines, and other enemies wasted them in time of the judges, and under the reign of King Saul. God had now given rest to David from all his enemies, and in comparison with former times, his subjects Israel should not be under anymore such afflictions. Israel henceforth should have his *quietus est*,[489] etc. This promise must be understood, (a) not simply but comparatively: in comparison of former afflictions by the wicked, they should not afterwards be afflicted by them. (b) Not absolutely, but conditionally: upon condition of Israel's keeping covenant with God. Otherwise, God would chastise them with the rods of men, as afterwards upon the sins of kings and people it fell out, as I have already abundantly manifested. In all temporal promises, God still reserves this latitude to himself: to shorten or remove promised mercies, and to chastise his people with contrary judgments in case of their miscarriages.

{3} *Finally, touching Israel the subjects of David, God in this Covenant promised their singular prosperity, both in temporals and Spirituals.*

(i) Israel's prosperity in temporals is promised in that explanatory recital of this Covenant in Psalm 132, where God said of Zion: *I will abundantly bless her provision: I will satisfy her poor with bread.* By {provision} and {bread}, understand a confluence of all necessary temporals good for Zion. She should have them not only with God's leave, but with his love; not only by his permission, but by his benediction; she shall have provision; God will bless her provision; God will bless her abundantly. This is one happy fruit and effect of God's habitation in Zion. *Godliness hath the promise of the life that now is.*[490] Yea the poor in Zion, the meanest members of the church, have part in this

---

[489] *Quietus est*: "A release or discharge from debt; a receipt." Middle English Compendium <https://quod.lib.umich.edu/m/middle-english-dictionary/dictionary/MED35615> [Accessed 2/28/2024]

[490] 1 Timothy 4:8, Matthew 6:33

promise. God will sufficiently provide for them, and their comfortable subsistence, he will satisfy her poor with bread. This is a sweet promise for Zion's poor to rest upon.

(ii) Israel's prosperity in spirituals, in the same explanation of this Covenant that God promised: *I will also clothe her priests with salvation: and her saints shall shout aloud for joy.*[491] The blessings here promised are also mentioned by Solomon in his prayer at the dedication of the temple: *Now therefore arise O LORD God into thy resting place, Thou and the ark of thy strength: Let thy priests O LORD God, be clothed with salvation, and let thy saints rejoice in goodness.*[492]

In this promise are mercies:

(a) **More peculiar to the priests.** *I will clothe her priests with salvation.* In the former petitory part of this Psalm, the words are: *Let thy priests be clothed with righteousness: and let thy gracious saints shout aloud.*[493] Interpreters here somewhat differ about the sense. By {*salvation*} here, Calvin understands only God's protection, under which God's priests should be safe and happy.[494] And by {*righteousness*}, God's righteousness, that is, the fruit of God's righteousness, in defending, protecting, and taking care of his priests. Simeon de Muis interprets this their {*clothing with salvation*}, of God's open and visible help and salvation to Zion's priests, as evident to all as the garments wherewith they are clothed.[495] Or rather as if God had said: "I will wholly encompass Zion's priests with salvation, as with a garment, and I will never forsake them." But in the former verse he understands by {*righteousness*} the priests' constant righteousness, as evident to all, as their very garments wherewith they were clothed.

---

[491] Psalm 132:16
[492] 2 Chronicles 6:41
[493] Psalm 132:9
[494] John Calvin, commentary on Psalm 132:9, 16
[495] Simon De Muis, commentary on Psalm 132:16, 9

Lavater thinks here is an allusion to the priests' garments, which shadowed out many virtues, that they should be evidently clothed and adorned with true virtues and holiness of life.[496] But none of these satisfy: nor (in my judgment) do they fully reach the sense and intent of the Holy Spirit herein. The phrase {*clothing Zion's priests with salvation*}, is comprehensive and seems to me to import these three things namely:

(1) The safe conservation and continuation of the public ministry in Zion. Her priests should not be destroyed, nor driven into corners, but Zion should still see her teachers before her eyes.

(2) The eminent decking and adorning of Zion's priests with the spiritual ornaments of righteousness and salvation which should be as visible and evident in their functions and conversations: as their priestly robes (types of such spiritual ornaments) were eminent and visible in their ministrations.

(3) The efficacy and prevalent success of the ministry of Zion's priests, upon the people for salvation and righteousness. Their ministration should be salvifical to the church and people, full of saving efficacy. The word {*salvation*} is in Scripture used in such latitude and variety of acceptations, as it may easily comprise all this. And the sense of words or phrases in Scripture are not to be restrained without just and apparent necessity. That learned and judicious writer Mr. John Ball expounds them much to this effect.[497]

(b) **More common to all the holy people and saints in Zion.** *And her saints shall shout aloud for joy* (Psalm 132:16). This Eminent joy of Zion's saints, seem to have reference: to the Lord's peculiar affection to, and

---

[496] Ludwig Lavater, commentary on 2 Chronicles 6:41

[497] "*That the priests should be clothed with salvation*, etc. – That is, the ministration of the priests should be profitable and saving to the people, which should be an ornament to them, as a garment of honor: and the people should sing cheerfully. The salvation of the person only is not here meant, but the conservation of the ministry. As if it should be said "I will cause that the ministry of the priests be safe, that it shall not be troubled with ungodly men, nor defiled with the filth of error: and that it shall be effectual in the minds of the godly, and many by the blessing of this ministry may obtain eternal happiness." It may also be applied to the private salvation of the priests, because they should be defended and protected from above, and adorned with blessings of all kinds."

Mr. John Ball in his *Treatise of the Covenant*. Chapter 9, page 148, London 1645.

habitation in Zion; to God's blessing of Zion with a confluence of outward accomplishments; and to his clothing of Zion's priests with salvation. These fore-promised mercies shall be singular matter of Zion's saints rejoicing, yea, of their triumphant shouting for gladness (Psalm 132:13-16). For what greater cause can there be of rejoicing to God's saints than to enjoy their God resident in the midst of them, and with God, a confluence of temporal and spiritual blessings in his saving ordinances?

These now are the covenant blessings or mercies which on God's part were promised to King David and his seed in this Covenant.

Section 2

The covenant duties conditioned, required, and restipulated on the part of David and his seed in this Covenant, may be reduced chiefly to these two heads.

Namely: (1) their keeping God's Covenant and testimony, walking in his commandments, statutes, and judgments; (2) their being just in their kingdom, ruling in the fear of God. That, they were to perform, as good men; this, as good kings and rulers over men. That was common to them with all Israel; this was peculiar to the house of David in Israel.

(1) **Their keeping of God's Covenant and testimony**, etc. As God would keep covenant with David and his seed, so they must keep covenant with him. He will not be federally bound and they set at liberty. As he performs Covenant mercy, so they must perform covenant duty. This condition on their part is notably expressed in several recitals and expositions of this Covenant, such as: *The LORD hath sworn in truth unto David, he will not turn from it; of the fruit of thy body will I set upon thy throne. If thy children will keep my covenant and my testimony that I shall teach them: their children also shall sit upon thy throne for evermore.*[498] But contrariwise, he adds elsewhere: *If his children forsake my law, and walk not in my judgments; If they break* (Hebrew: *profane*) *my statutes, and keep not my commandments: Then will I visit their transgression with the rod, and their iniquity with stripes. Nevertheless my loving-kindness will I not utterly take from him: nor suffer my faithfulness to fail,* etc.[499]

---

[498] Psalm 132:11-12
[499] Psalm 89:30-33

Here's God's law, as the genus or general; and in his judgments, statutes, and commandments, namely: judicial, ceremonial, and moral laws, as the species, or specials. The breach or violation of any of these by David's seed is threatened to be visited with God's rod and stripes. Consequently, the observance of them all is required from them. And David, having reference to this Covenant, particularly applies this condition to his son Solomon, in his speech to the solemn assembly of Israel: *And he said unto me, Solomon thy son, he shall build my house and my courts: for I have chosen him to be my son, and I will be his Father. Moreover I will establish his kingdom forever, if he be constant* (Hebrew: *strong*) *to do my commandments and my judgments, as at this day.*[500] And hereupon David presently applies this by way of exhortation: first to all Israel, inciting them to keep and seek for all the commandments of the LORD their God, that they might possess Canaan and leave it for an inheritance to their children forever; then to his son Solomon, enjoining him to know the God of his Father, to seek him, and to serve him with a perfect heart and a willing mind, that thus, both David's seed, and the subjects of David and his seed, might perform the conditions of this Covenant with God.[501]

From all these passages, we may thus determine and conclude touching the covenant duties and conditions imposed upon David and his seed, namely:

More generally, that the covenant duties and conditions required of David and his seed in this Covenant, are the same with those imposed upon Israel and their posterity in the Sinai Covenant, for:

[1] God, in imposing these conditions upon David and his seed, plainly has reference to the duties of the Sinai Covenant, as the phrases of keeping his Covenant and testimony, of doing his commandments and his judgments, namely: his judicial, ceremonial, and moral laws (the body of the Sinai Covenant) do abundantly evidence.[502]

---

[500] 1 Chronicles 28:9, 7
[501] Verses 8-9
[502] Psalm 132:11-12; 1 Chronicles 28:7, Psalm 89:30-31

[2] This Covenant with David did not void or annul the Sinai Covenant or the duties thereof. It continued in force until the death of Jesus Christ, when it had its general accomplishment. David therefore – and all his seed – remained still under the obligation and duties of the Old Testament or Sinai Covenant. This Covenant with David was not destructive but cumulative, to that with Israel. Look back therefore upon the covenant duties of the Sinai Covenant, and the explanations of them,[503] and there you shall also, as in a glass, behold the covenant duties of this Covenant at large unfolded.

More particularly, the covenant duties and conditions imposed upon David and his seed under this general are these, namely:

[1] Their being God's saved, God's people, God's sons and firstborn by covenant – see Psalm 89:26-27; 2 Samuel 7:24; 1 Chronicles 17:13 & 28:6. These covenant relations have in them both a dignity from God, and a duty to God. The duties thereof have been formerly laid open, both in this, and in the Sinai Covenant.[504] How can any persons keep God's Covenant faithfully and acceptably, until they themselves first become God's covenant people effectually? They must first have covenant principles and abilities before they can truly put forth those abilities in covenant performances.

[2] Their true knowledge of God and of his Covenant, and seeking for all his commandments (1 Chronicles 28:7-9). Such knowledge is the necessary inlet to all sincere covenant-keeping by faith and obedience.

[3] Their keeping covenant by true faith in Jesus Christ, the great mercy and mystery promised both in this and the Sinai Covenant. That Christ was revealed, and faith in Christ required and conditioned, in the Sinai Covenant, I have abundantly proven.[505] That Jesus Christ was also revealed and chiefly intended in this Covenant, I have in this chapter evinced. Compare also, Luke 1:31-33, Acts 2:29-31, etc., and Hebrews 1:5 with the tenor of this Covenant. Therefore, true faith in this Christ, is necessary to the keeping of this

---

[503] In Book 3, Chapter 4, Aphorism 4, Section 2
[504] See Book 3, Chapter 4, Aphorism 4, Section 2 & Chapter 5, Aphorism 4, Section 1
[505] Book 3, Chapter 4

Covenant: For: {1} without true faith, Christ herein revealed could not be apprehended by David or his seed. {2} And without true faith, neither their persons nor performances could be accepted. For, *without faith it is impossible to please God.*[506]

[4] Their keeping covenant, by {1} willing, {2} perfect, {3} entire, and {4} constant obedience – see 1 Chronicles 28:7-9, Psalm 132:11-12 & 89:30-31. What such obedience is; in what notion it is required in the Sinai Covenant, and so in this; and what is the rule of such obedience; I have sufficiently elsewhere unfolded.[507] That the Lord intended the keeping of this his Covenant by such obedience, King Solomon intimates in his blessing of the people at the dedication of the temple, saying: *The LORD our God, be with us, as he was with our fathers: Let him not leave us nor forsake us: that he may incline our hearts unto him, to walk in all his ways, and to keep his commandments and his statutes and his judgments which he commanded our fathers, – Let your heart therefore be perfect with the LORD our God, to walk in his Statutes and keep his commandments as at this day.*[508] God himself confirms the same in his answer then returned to King Solomon's prayer: *And the LORD said unto him, I have heard thy prayer and thy supplication that thou hast made before me: – And if thou wilt walk before me as David thy father walked, in integrity of heart and in uprightness, to do according to all that I have commanded thee, and wilt keep my statutes and my judgments: Then I will establish the throne of thy kingdom upon Israel forever, as I promised to David thy father, saying, There shall not fail thee a man upon the throne of Israel*, etc.[509]

[5] Their repentance and returning to the Lord unfeignedly in case of any of their covenant failings and miscarriages. This covenant duty in all the people of Israel (and therefore consequently in David's seed, rulers over Israel),

---

[506] Hebrews 11:6
[507] In Book 3, Chapter 4, Aphorism 4, Section 2
[508] 1 Kings 8:57-58, 61
[509] 1 Kings 9:3-9; 2 Chronicles 7:17 to the end

King Solomon intimates in his prayer at the dedication of the temple, and God confirms, in the accepting and granting of his prayer.[510] What true repentance is – That such repentance was required and conditioned in the Sinai Covenant, and so also by consequence in this, with inferences hereupon, I have explained in the Sinai Covenant; see Book 3 Chapter 4 Aphorism 4 Section 2.[511]

These were the covenant duties and conditions imposed here upon David and his seed, which did in common belong to David's house and to all the house of Israel. The covenant duties more peculiar and appropriate to David and his house follow.

(2) **Their being just in their dominion and royal government, ruling also piously and religiously.** This is laid down notably in David's last words: *He that ruleth over men must be just, ruling in the fear of God.*[512] In the Hebrew phrase (which studies brevity), the sentence is imperfect; some word or words being omitted which should perfect the sense. The words are exactly thus to be translated: *A ruler over-earthly-man just, ruling the fear of God.* And they may be interpreted two ways, namely:

[1] Mandatorily, as requiring a covenant duty from David and his seed. Thus: *A ruler over-earthly-man must be just, ruling in the fear of God.* Or thus: *Be thou a just ruler over-earthly-man, ruling in the fear of God.* So it is a command or divine injunction to David and his royal seed, to rule righteously and religiously.

[2] Promissorily, as foretelling the covenant-dignity and excellency of Christ and his kingdom, that was to come of David according to the flesh, thus: *The ruler over-earthly-man, shall be just, ruling in the fear of God.* That is: *The Messiah that shall descend of David shall be a just ruler*, etc. In my judgment, these words are here so laid down on purpose by the Holy Spirit, so

---

[510] See 1 Kings 8:33-54 & 9:3; 2 Chronicles 6:26-40 & 7:12-14
[511] This is Volume 3 of *God's Covenants* as published by Berith Press in 2023
[512] 2 Samuel 23:3

that they may be taken in full latitude, both as commanding a duty from David and his seed, as types of Christ; and as promising an excellency in Christ, the antitype of David. Christ should succeed David as a king (Psalm 2:7-9 & 110:2 & 72:1, 8-11, Zechariah 9:9-10, Hosea 3:5). And Christ should reign and rule in his kingdom most righteously and religiously. See Psalm 45:3-7 & 72:1-4, 7, 12-14, Isaiah 11:1-10, Jeremiah 23:5-6, and Zechariah 9:9-10. He is the true Melchizedek, or King of Righteousness (Hebrews 7:1-3, etc.) But here I shall consider the words only in the first notion, as commanding a covenant duty from David and his seed, because I am speaking of them as imposing a covenant duty upon them, in reference to the throne and kingdom, which by covenant, God settled upon David and his seed.

{1} ***David and his seed must rule over Israel, righteously.*** A *ruler* (or *he that ruleth over-earthly-man*) *must be just.*[513] The ruler here spoken of is the royal or kingly ruler, who in his dominions is supreme, the supreme ruler, or governor of a people, or styled by some other denomination, namely: David and his seed.[514] The subjects here particularly intended by men or earthly man were Israel, which was the commonwealth of God, of his peculiar institution. And they were at that time the only church of God on earth. The qualification of this ruler and of his rule is righteousness and religiousness. First of his justice or righteousness. David and every of his successive seed sitting on the throne must be just. How? (i) Just in their person. (ii) Just in their office.

(i) **Just in their persons.** Having due qualifications of justice and principles of righteousness inwardly; without which, their office and administrations could never be righteous outwardly. The fruit resembles the nature of the tree. Such is the fountain; such are the streams. Justice of the person of a ruler, is that habit of righteousness whereby he is disposed duly to administer both mercy and judgment to all his subjects indifferently without respect of persons, fear, or rewards. He must be inclined both to mercy and

---

[513] 2 Samuel 23:3
[514] 1 Peter 2:13

judgment (Psalm 101:1, Proverbs 20:28 with Proverbs 29:4). And this to all without respect of persons (Proverbs 24:23 & 28:21, Psalm 82:2, Deuteronomy 1:16-17). As also without fear of men, or taking rewards from them to pervert justice (Deuteronomy 1:17, Isaiah 1:23, Proverbs 29:4). Unto such a habit and qualification of righteousness, several subservient endowments are very necessary. As: (a) Knowledge and judicious understanding in every cause, etc. (Psalm 2:10, Proverbs 28:16, Ecclesiastes 10:16, Isaiah 3:3-4). (b) Clemency, gentleness, mercifulness (Proverbs 20:28), that he may lay to heart every good cause, even of the poor, widow, fatherless and oppressed (Isaiah 1:17, 23). (c) Fortitude and courage, not to fear men's faces, but rather to be a terror to evildoers (Proverbs 20:2, Deuteronomy 1:17, Romans 13:3). (d) Humility, that his heart be not proudly lifted up above his brethren, and he oppress them, or turn tyrant (Deuteronomy 17:19-20). Rehoboam's fault and ruin (1 Kings 12:14, etc., Psalm 131:1). (e) Chastity, that his heart be not turned away from right judgment (Deuteronomy 17:17), Proverbs 31:3). Lust destroys kings. (f) Temperance and sobriety, that the judgment be not darkened in discerning things that differ. *It is not for kings to drink wine*, etc. (that is, intemperately) *lest they drink, and forget the law, and pervert the judgment of the afflicted* (Proverbs 31:4-5, Ecclesiastes 10:13-14). (g) Contentedness, hating covetousness (Deuteronomy 1:16-17 & 17:17, Proverbs 28:16).

(ii) **Just in their office of ruling**. It was not enough that David and his seed had just principles, they must also perform just practices and do just things. This justice of their office comprises in it two things, namely:

(a) Firstly, a just advocation to, or acquisition of, their office; that they come not to their rule and government by unlawful usurpation, without any just right or title. This was the fault of usurping Athaliah (2 Kings 11:1-3).

(b) Secondly, a just execution and discharge of their office, in the impartial and due administration of mercy and judgment to all their subjects for their good, without respect to men's persons, fear of men's faces, or expectation of their corrupting gifts and rewards, as has been formerly proved. Now this actual execution or exercise of their just rule, has in it a twofold act, namely: protection and gubernation.

(1) **Protection.** The supreme ruler or governor ought to improve his utmost authority and power, for the protecting, preserving and defending of his subjects and commonwealth in safety, peace and prosperity. *Behold a king shall reign in righteousness, and princes shall rule in judgment. And a man* (namely: such a king or princes) *shall be as a hiding-place from the winds: and a covert from the tempest; as rivers of water in a dry place; as the shadow of a great rock in a weary land.*[515] This king is very generally interpreted to be King Hezekiah, yet as a type of Jesus Christ; these princes, the princes of Hezekiah, as Shebna, etc. employed under him in the government. His protection of his subjects from all sorts of evils and injuries is elegantly described by four notable metaphors or similitudes. Such protection is due from all supreme rulers to their subjects. And this especially against three sorts of evils. namely:

[1] Against all enemies foreign or domestic; from without, or from within the commonwealth, so that they may be powerfully resisted, prevented and suppressed, and the subjects defended.

[2] Against all injuries, wrongs, oppression, violence, etc. that the subjects, (especially the poor, the friendless, the widow, and the fatherless, which of all other are most exposed to injuries and oppressions without remedy), may be defended, rescued, and relieved (Psalm 82:3-4, Isaiah 1:17) – and this by a righteous current and course of judgment.[516]

[3] Against public wants and necessities, prejudicial and destructive to their commonwealth's public welfare and prosperity. As want of bread in a time of famine, want of trade with foreign nations, without which they cannot well subsist within their own territories, etc. Rulers must be like rivers

---

[515] Isaiah 32:1-2
[516] Job 24:3-4, 9-10

of water in a dry place, as well as a hiding place from wind and covert, from tempest (Isaiah 33:1-2).

(2) **Gubernation**, or **actual governing**. The supreme ruler ought to exercise his power and authority in the upright guiding and governing of all his subjects according to mercy and judgment, as the cause shall require, for their good and benefit (Romans 13:3-4; 1 Timothy 2:2). This actual governing hath in it two principal branches:

[1] Direction of the subjects in all good ways of righteousness, by making, enacting and publishing righteous good and equal laws for the Common-wealth, subservient, not opposite, to true religion. *Establish judgment in the gate* (Amos 5:15), such the good decrees even of Pagan rulers sometimes, as of Cyrus (Ezra 1:1), etc. Darius (Ezra 6:1-3), etc., (Daniel 6:25-27), Nebuchadnezzar (Daniel 3:29). Opposite thereunto are: the decreeing of unrighteous decrees (Isaiah 10:1-3), the framing mischief by a law (Psalm 94:20), the statutes of Omri (Micah 6:16), ungodly, unrighteous, ensnaring and bloody decrees (Esther 3:8 to the end, Daniel 3:10, etc., and 6:7, etc.)

[2] Remuneration, by compensating the subject's observation or violation of such directions or laws, according to the right rules of distributive and emendative justice. This remuneration ought to have respect:

{1} To all welldoers and good subjects, that they may be praised for, countenanced, and encouraged in their well-doing and in all virtuous ways (Romans 13:3-4). Such government makes the righteous flourish (Psalm 72:7).

{2} To all evildoers and wicked subjects, that, by just execution of vengeance and wrath upon them for their evil-doing (Romans 13:4), and that they may be put to exemplary shame before others (Judges 18:7), and may be terrified for, and restrained from evil-doing, hence rulers are called *possessors* or *heirs of restraint* (Judges 18:7). Or if the cause so requires, they may be cut off and destroyed out of the commonwealth by banishment (Ezra 7:26) or death (Psalm 101:8), *that all Israel may hear and fear, and do no more so wickedly*

(Deuteronomy 13:11, 17:13 & 21:21). Thus *he that ruleth over man, must be just*: in person and in office.

{2} ***David and his seed must rule over Israel religiously as well as righteously, ruling in the fear of God.***[517] They must not – Gallio-like – cast off all care of the affairs of God and religion, but rather make these things their primary scope and intendment, and all politicals subordinate and subservient thereunto.

{*The fear of God*} is used in Scripture in various acceptations. Especially, as to our present purpose, it denotes: (i) The object feared, namely: God himself. *Bring presents to the fear* (Psalm 76:11) – so God is styled {*the fear of Isaac*} (Genesis 31:42, 53:2). (ii) The rule or law prescribing and directing in the true fear of God, (Psalm 19:9). (iii) The whole course and way of God's true religion and service (Ecclesiastes 12:13, Job 1:9, Acts 9:31). In this sense, it is used very frequently. And these are the proper fruits, effects, and acts of the true fear of God implanted in man. (iv) The inward habit or principle of God's fear engraven upon the sanctified heart, whereby the heart is inclined and disposed to have an awful reverential respect to God, to his whole will and all his ways: to forbear what he forbids, to perform what he prescribes, etc. *I will put my fear in their hearts, that they shall not depart from me.*[518] (v) The affection of fear in the heart, whereby a man is disposed to be afraid of God's dreadful or terrible manifestation of his majesty and greatness. As Moses at Mount Sinai said: *I exceedingly fear and quake, so terrible was the sight.*[519] Most of these acceptations, especially the first four, are of use here.

To rule in the fear of God therefore principally comprises in it these things, namely:

(i) To have the heart and spirit graciously and effectually principled with the fear of God, whereby rulers are inclined to have an awful eye and respect to God, his will, and ways in all their government, and this with a good

---

[517] 2 Samuel 23:3
[518] Jeremiah 32:40
[519] Hebrews 12:20-21

conscience (Genesis 42:18). This fear makes the persons of rulers religious, and consequently their government religious (2 Chronicles 17:3-6; 2 Chronicles 34:3, etc).

(ii) To manage the whole rule and government according to the word of God, the rule and measure of God's fear: not according to carnal rules of policy inconsistent with God's word. Hence God appointed all the kings of Israel to have a copy of God's law by them, to read therein continually, so that they might manage their government in God's fear accordingly (Deuteronomy 17:18-20).

(iii) To make it the primary scope, intent, and end of all their ruling, to advance the glory of God, and of Jesus Christ, to advantage the spiritual welfare of his church, and to further every way the prosperity of the gospel and true religion (Romans 13:3-4, Isaiah 60:10, 16; 1 Timothy 2:2). The authors of the *Magdeburg Centuries* observe well: "Seeing as magistrates are in holy Scriptures called {*gods*}, their first and chiefest care of all should be, in such sort to serve God, as that his kingdom may appear, grow, and be preserved in their dominions."[520] Commonwealths are for the church, not the church for commonwealths; they are but *hospitia ecclesiae*: the church's inns. Rulers are for God, not God for rulers. Rulers usually prosper no longer in their civils than they take care for the prosperity of religion and spirituals. I remember not that any kings in Israel or Judah are commended by God in Scripture for ruling righteously, but only those who ruled religiously. Their chief zeal and all their prime endeavors should run out this way: as Jehoshaphat's *heart was lifted up in the ways of the LORD.*[521] Oh! How many ways may, yea ought, the supreme ruler to improve his authority for advancing the interest of God, of Jesus Christ, of his church, of his gospel, and of

---

[520] Cum Magistratus in Sacris literis Dii nominantur, prima & potissima ipsorum cura esse Debet, tali pacto Deo servire, ut regnum ejus in imperiis suis innotescat, crescat, conservetur. Cent. Magd. in Prefat. Cant. 7.
[521] 2 Chronicles 17:6

Christian religion, by ruling in the fear of God as a nursing father of the church (Isaiah 49:23)! As:

(a) By encouraging and countenancing the public use of all God's ordinances and public exercise of all duties of religion within his dominions (2 Chronicles 15:9-16, 20:7-9, and chapters 29-31 and 34-35; Deuteronomy 17:18-20).

(b) By removing all external impediments to true religion in doctrine, worship, discipline, etc., such as heresy, idolatry, profaneness, persecution, etc (Deuteronomy 13:1-6, Zechariah 13:3; 1 Kings 15:14 with 2 Chronicles 19:17; 1 Kings 22:24; 2 kings 12:3; 2 Chronicles 15:8, chapter 16, 17:3-4, 6-10; 2 Kings 23:8, 13, 19-20, 24-25).

(c) By reforming the church, when the truth, worship, or ordinances of Jesus Christ are contemned, corrupted, polluted, etc (Exodus 32, Joshua 24; 2 Chronicles 15 & 17; 2 Kings 18 & 23), as did Zerubbabel and Nehemiah in their days.

(d) By calling together councils and synods to consult and conclude according to the Word, how the church should be reformed, and all the affairs of religion duly managed (1 Chronicles 13:1-2, 23:1-2; 1 Kings 8:1; 2 Chronicles 29:4; 2 Kings 23:1-2, Romans 13:1-3; 1 Timothy 2:2), which persons so convocated must be such as the Scriptures allow to consult and conclude in like cases.

(e) By strengthening the laws and ordinances of God and Jesus Christ with his civil sanction, commanding them under civil penalties to be duly observed (2 Chronicles 34:33, Nehemiah 12:13, etc., Daniel 3:28-29 & 6:26-27), as Hezekiah took care that priests, Levites, and people should respectively perform their duties (2 Chronicles 29:5, 24 & 30:1).

(f) By furnishing and supplying the church of Christ with all outward necessaries and helps to the greater prosperity of religion, as convenient places for public worship, honorable maintenance for the ministers of the gospel, etc

(1 Chronicles 22; 2 Chronicles 3:1, etc. and 34; 1 Timothy 5:17-18; 1 Corinthians 9:6-15 with 2 Chronicles 31:4-9).

(g) Finally, by punishing offenders, as well against the first, as against the second table, with civil mulcts [fines] or penalties, so that the sacred ordinances and ways of God may be vindicated from contempt and profanation (Deuteronomy 13:1-61, Zechariah 13:3, Deuteronomy 21:18-21, Genesis 9:6 with Numbers 35:30-34 & Deuteronomy 10:11-13, Leviticus 20:11-12, 14, 17, 19-25, Exodus 22:1-15, Deuteronomy 19:16, etc).

Now David and his seed were to rule over Israel righteously and religiously, as has been described, for these reasons especially:

{1} Because David and his seed, in their rule over Israel, were God's kings, deputies, and vicegerents over God's peculiar commonwealth.[522] {2} Because the righteous and religious rule of supreme governors or rulers is most pleasing to God. How exceedingly has God commended the pious and religious government of David, Asa, Jehoshaphat, Hezekiah, Josiah, etc., but condemned the contrary wicked reign of others! And how abundantly has the Lord testified his approbation of righteous judgment (Isaiah 1:17-20, Jeremiah 5:1)! Hence Solomon said: *To do justice and judgment is more acceptable to the LORD than sacrifice.*[523] {3} Because David and his seed in their religious and righteous ruling were to be special and eminent types of Jesus Christ the most godly and righteous ruler in his spiritual kingdom.[524]

This covenant duty of ruling Israel righteously and religiously was performed:

{1} By David himself, who *fed Israel according to the integrity of his heart, and guided them by the skilfulness of his hands.*[525] He ruled them religiously. This was his primary design and scope in his government to advance God's true religion. Hence:

---

[522] Psalm 2:6 & 82:1-7.
[523] Proverbs 21:3
[524] Isaiah 11:1-10, Psalm 72 throughout, Psalm 45
[525] Psalm 78:71-72

(i) He was most zealously affected to the ark of God's Covenant, the eminent token of God's presence, to prepare a place for it, and to bring it and settle it in his place (Psalm 132:1-11; 1 Chronicles 15 throughout and 16 throughout).

(ii) He appointed certain Levites and priests to minister before the ark continually, and delivered into the hand of Asaph on that day an excellent psalm wherewith to thank the Lord (1 Chronicles 16:4 to the end).

(iii) He had it in his heart to build a resting-place for the ark, a temple for the Lord, with which the Lord was so pleased, that thereupon he revealed this Covenant by Nathan to David (1 Chronicles 17:1, etc.), although he would not suffer David to build the house.

(iv) He notwithstanding so set his heart to the house and worship of his God, that he prepared abundantly for the building of the temple (1 Chronicles 22).

(v) He appointed the courses and divisions of the Levites, of the priests, of the singers, and of the porters, for the service of God in the temple when it should be built (1 Chronicles chapter 23-26). (vi) He instructed and encouraged Solomon to the building of the Temple, giving him the pattern thereof which he had from the Lord (1 Chronicles 28).

(vii) And finally, he by his own example notably excited the princes of Israel to offer liberally towards the building of God's house, blessing God that had inclined him and them to offer so willingly, and praying for Solomon that he might be upright and perfect, and that he might build the house for which David had prepared (1 Chronicles 29 throughout). Thus David ruled religiously. He ruled also the people Israel righteously (Psalm 101 throughout).

{2} By Solomon, and other godly kings of Judah after him, as Asa, Jehoshaphat, Hezekiah, Josiah, etc., who ruled righteously and religiously in the fear of God. King Solomon ruled religiously, for: (i) He built the temple on Mount Moriah at Jerusalem, most magnificently according to the pattern given him, 2 Chronicles 3:1, etc. and chapter 4 throughout. (ii) He most solemnly dedicated the temple built, with praises, prayers and sacrifices before all Israel: the Lord most graciously answering his prayers and accepting his sacrifices (2 Chronicles 5-7 throughout).

He ruled also righteously, for: (i) he caused Adonijah to be put to death, Abiather the priest to be deposed and turned out of the priesthood, and Joab to be slain at the horns of the altar, for their combination in sedition and treason against the crown, and other offenses.[526] (ii) He confined Shimei for cursing and reviling his father King David, and afterwards put him to death being found without the bounds of his confinement.[527] (iii) He wisely as well as justly decided the controversy between the two harlots about the living child, and gave it to the right mother.[528]

{3} By Jesus Christ especially, the conditioned duties of this Covenant had their fullest and most exact accomplishment. David and his seed, even the most religious and righteous of them had their failings and miscarriages, as their histories abundantly declare. But Jesus Christ, the primary seed of David, fully kept God's Covenant and all his charge, walked most religiously and righteously in his spiritual kingdom over the house of Jacob, as the prophets under the Old Testament promised, and the apostles with other holy penmen of the New Testament declare to be performed by him.

This aphorism, touching the matter and substance of this Covenant, I close up briefly with these ensuing inferences.

Inferences

(1) **Hence, the goodness and bounty of God was singularly discovered and testified in this Covenant to David and his seed.** What variety and

---

[526] 1 Kings 2:22-36
[527] 1 Kings 2:36 to the end
[528] 1 Kings 3:16 to the end

excellency of covenant mercies and blessings are herein assured to David, to his seed, and to their subjects with respect unto them: [1] God's subduing of all his enemies, [2] his strengthening and establishing him, [3] his enlargement of his glory and dominion, [4] God's sweet covenant relations to him, [5] his fulfilling of his days, [6] God's building him a house, by perpetuating and enthroning of his seed forever, [7] God's fatherly relation unto his seed, [8] he honor cast upon his seed to build God a house, [9] God's establishment of his seed in his kingdom forever, [10] God's constancy of lovingkindness and faithfulness to his seed, yet with chastisements for their miscarriages, [11]. God's habitation in Zion forever, [12] Israel's secure establishment in Canaan thereupon, and [13] their singular prosperity both in temporals and spirituals. These, these are the covenant mercies promised to David and his seed in this Covenant. Any one, even the least of these, was a great fruit and evidence of God's bounty to them; how much more this whole bundle and heap of blessings together.

Hereupon, when Nathan first revealed this Covenant from God to David, how was David affected and transported with joy and admiration of God's goodness and his grace! *He presently went, and sat before the LORD, and said, Who am I O Lord GOD? and what is my house, that thou hast brought me hitherto? And this was yet a small thing in thy sight O Lord GOD: but thou hast spoken also of thy servant's house for a great while to come. And is this the manner of man, O Lord GOD? And what can David say more unto thee! For thou Lord GOD knowest thy servant. For thy Word's sake, and according to thine own heart hast thou done all these great things, to make thy servant know them*, etc.[529] Oh, how pathetically, zealously, and thankfully does David herein express himself to God for all his covenant goodness! With what raised, ravished, and astonished affections!

More particularly, in this his address to God, note:

[1] His praise. He praises God for his goodness, partly to himself, and this:

---

[529] 2 Samuel 7:18

{1} For time past. That God had brought him hitherto; to such victories, to such preference, to such a throne and kingdom. and this notwithstanding the extreme unworthiness both of David and his house (2 Samuel 7:18).

{2} For time present and to come; that God had superadded this excellent Covenant over and above all former favors (as if they had been small matters), therein assuring David of the happiness of his house for all time to come. This is amplified: (i) By the superabounding bountifulness of God therein. (ii) By the familiarity of God's dealing with David in such a covenant way (verse 19). (iii) By the unutterableness of this mercy, silencing David himself (verse 20). (iv) By the moving causes inclining God both to do these great things for David, and to make them known in this sort to David, namely: his Word Christ and his own heart; his meet grace and good-pleasure of his will (verse 21). (v) By his thankful acknowledgment of God's matchless greatness (verse 22) – partly, to his people Israel, in redeeming them out of Egypt, and making them his people (verses 23-24).

[2] His prayer. He prays that God would perform all his covenanted goodness to him and to his house forever (verses 25-29). Thus David admired and extolled the rich bounty and goodness of the Lord to him and his seed in this Covenant.

(2) Hence the privileges of David and his seed were greatly heightened and advanced by this Covenant. By the Sinai Covenant or Old Testament, The people of Israel – and with them David and his house – were eminently privileged above all the people and nations of the world, as the Scriptures often testify.[530] But by this present Covenant, David and his house were peculiarly privileged above all the house of Israel itself. To them it was peculiarly directed; upon them it was peculiarly fulfilled, and in reference unto them some promises therein are extended to Israel their subjects. In this regard, Israel was as the jewel of God, his *segullah*;[531] David and his seed, were

---

[530] Deuteronomy 4:7-9, 13, Psalm 147:19–20, Romans 3:1-2, 9:4-5, Ephesians 2:12
[531] Exodus 19:5

as the orient sparks and precious garnish of this jewel. And Christ the primary seed of David was the great and peerless gem in that garnish.

(3) Hence by this Covenant, God settled and established royal favors and dignities upon David and his seed. So by this Covenant, he expected and required royal returns of duty and homage to himself from David and his seed. God hereby made them great kings over men, but yet they must still remain subjects to himself, the king of kings. They shall rule over men: but so, as God will still rule over them; they must remain still subject to his covenant commandments, statutes and judgments. They must so rule as yet to be ruled. They must so be kings as yet to remain subjects. They must so be in authority as yet to be under authority. When this loyalty and covenant duty to God was forgotten by David or any of his seed, how sadly and severely did God chastise those miscarriages?

(4) Hence the nature of this Covenant with David and his seed was partly absolute and partly conditional. *Absolute* in regard to the perpetuity of the Covenant, the perpetuity of his seed upon his throne, and some other promises as having only their full accomplishment in Jesus Christ;[532] but *conditional* in regard to other promises more immediately applicable to David's ordinary seed, which were to be performed if they kept God's Covenant and commandments.[533] Therefore hence it came to pass, that David and his seed – sundry ways failing in their covenant duty – God chastised them severely, and eclipsed the glory of their kingdom often and sometimes extremely, as in a case of the ten tribes' revolt, and Judah's captivity in Babylon, which seemed to be a sad violation of God's Covenant. But the Lord was still righteous and faithful in his promises of absolute nature.[534] The substance of the Covenant remained still inviolable, until at last it had its entire accomplishment in Jesus Christ. In what sense we are to understand

---

[532] Psalm 89:33-38
[533] Psalm 132:12 & 89:29-32; 2 Samuel 23:3-4
[534] Psalm 89:38 to the end

covenant conditions, and how such conditions are in no way inconsistent with God's free grace, has been elsewhere already expounded.[535]

(5) Hence the grand and most observable occurrences under this Covenant with David were: God's establishing and continuing of the royal government over Israel, his appropriating of the throne to David's seed of whom Christ should descend according to the flesh, the glory of that kingdom in the days of Solomon, and the most magnifical building of the temple by Solomon at Jerusalem, on Mount Moriah.

(6) Hence, the fidelity of God to David and his seed according to this Covenant was very conspicuous. For how notably did God (as has been shown) perform all covenanted blessings, either upon David or his ordinary Seed, or his extraordinary seed Christ, or upon the subjects of his kingdom. Not one promise failed, or fell to the ground.

(7) Hence, the primary scope and intent of this Covenant was to reveal Jesus Christ as the chief Seed of David, and the perpetuity of his kingdom over the church of God for evermore. This is the sea, whither all the streams of the Covenant flow: This is the center where all the promise lines of the Covenant meet. Christ is the marrow and soul of this, as of all the Covenants of Faith. Those who do not intentively fix their eye upon Christ in this Covenant, they utterly miss the scope, and mistake the mystery of this Covenant.

Thus of the subject, matter, or substance of this Covenant, namely: the covenant mercies promised on the part of God, and the covenant duties re-promised on the part of David and his seed.

---

[535] Book 2, Chapter 2, Aphorism 2, Section 5, Corollary 4 throughout

Aphorism 5

The form of this Covenant with David and his seed.

The form of God's Covenant with David and his seed was either inward and essential, in the mutual obligation between the federates, or outward and accidental, in the manifestation, confirmation, and administration of this Covenant. This aphorism I briefly thus explain:

(1) **The more inward, essential, and constitutive form of this Covenant with David consisted in the reciprocal covenant obligation between the federates,** namely: between God on the one hand, by his promises of sundry federal mercies, and David and his seed on the other hand, by their restipulating of several covenant duties. These mercies promised, and duties re-promised, have been at large unfolded in the last foregoing aphorism. Without such reciprocal covenant obligation, plainly expressed, or at least necessarily implied, there can be properly no covenant. This is that which makes the specific difference between covenants and bare naked promises. The obligation of a bare promise is single and personal, but the obligation of a covenant is double and reciprocal.

(2) **The more outward and accidental form of this Covenant consisted in the [1] manifestation, [2] confirmation, and [3] administration thereof.**

[1] The **manifestation** of this Covenant to David from God was not immediate, but mediate. God revealed it to the prophet Nathan by vision, which vision is there at large recorded;[536] and Nathan accordingly declared it unto David, upon occasion of David's purpose to build God an house. *According to all these words, and according to all this vision, so did Nathan*

---

[536] 2 Samuel 7:1-18; 1 Chronicles 17:1-16, Psalm 89:19, etc.

speak unto David – Then thou spakest in vision to thine holy one, etc. A vision or sight is often mentioned in Scripture, It is of several sorts, namely:

(i) An afflicting vision – one sort of Job's afflictions: *Thou scarest me with Dreams, and terrifiest me with night visions*.[537] Not here meant.

(ii) An instructing, consolatory, or prophetic vision. This was one of God's ways whereby he was wont both before and since Christ to reveal unto men things secret or future, affecting their senses and intellectuals with certain outward objects and sensible species to that end. And such visions are usually represented to men in a trance, rapture, deep sleep, etc. They usually fall down upon their faces to the ground, as stupid, senseless, and dead men. So, a *trance or deep sleep fell upon Abraham*;[538] Daniel was afraid, and fell on his face, and was in a deep sleep with his face towards the ground;[539] Ezekiel fell on his face (Ezekiel 1:28 & 3:23 & 43:3 & 44:4). Thus, Peter fell into a trance when he had that vision of a sheet from heaven, teaching him to go and preach to the Gentiles.[540] John was ravished in spirit when he received his revelation from Christ, who when he saw him fell at his feet, as dead.[541] Such this vision of Nathan here, wherein God revealed to him this Covenant. In this sense vision is taken: (a) properly, for the act of seeing that which God thus reveals; or God's way of visional manifestation of his will (Psalm 89:19). (b) Metonymically for the instruction, prophecy, or mystery thus revealed and seen (Isaiah 1:1; 2 Chronicles 32:32; 2 Samuel 7:17). (c) Synecdochically, for all manner of ways whereby God makes known his will; as 1 Samuel 3:1, Lamentations 2:9; 2 Kings 17:3, and Joel 2:28 with Acts 2:17. (d) Catachrestically, or abusively for false and counterfeit pretenses of visions in Zechariah 13:4; *vision of falsehood*: Jeremiah 14:14; *vision of vanity*: Ezekiel 12:24. and 13:6-7: *vision of their own heart* (Jeremiah 23:16). But this vision

---

[537] Job 7:14
[538] Genesis 15:12
[539] Daniel 8:17-18
[540] Acts 10:10, etc.
[541] Revelation 1:10, 17

of Nathan was a real and purely divine vision; and consequently, this Covenant of infallible divine authority.[542]

[2] The **confirmation** of this Covenant by God to David and his seed, was various, especially fourfold, namely: [1] by ratifying promises, [2] by God's sacred oath, [3] by explanatory repetitions thereof, and [4] by actual accomplishments thereof in part.

[1] *By ratifying promises*. Some Promises, appertaining to this Covenant, lead peculiarly to assure David of the infallibility and perpetuity of this Covenant: which may therefore be justly styled {*ratifying promises*}. They are comprised in Psalm 89:28-29, 33-35, and have been formerly opened in the seventh promised mercy to David. Thus God adds promise to promise, and binds one promise with another.

[2] *By God's sacred oath*. God's promise and oath are *two immutable things in which it is impossible for God to lie*;[543] and God willing more abundantly to show to David and his seed, the immutability of his counsel, he confirmed this Covenant by these two, that David and his seed might have strong consolation thereby.[544] *I have sworn to David my servant, Once have I sworn by mine holiness, that I will not lie unto David. The LORD hath sworn in truth unto David, he will not turn from it.*[545] But of this oath, I have spoken in the former aphorism.

[3] *By explanatory repetitions of this Covenant*. God caused this Covenant not only to be twice recorded in terms at large,[546] but also several times recites and explains the same in other Scriptures both of Old and New Testament;[547] especially in those three observable places, which are a threefold

---

[542] 2 Samuel 7:4, 17, Psalm 89:19
[543] Hebrews 6:16-18
[544] Hebrews 6:16-18
[545] Psalm 89:3, 35 & 132:11
[546] 2 Samuel 7:1-18; 1 Chronicles 17:1-16
[547] 1 Kings 5:5, 8:15-27; 1 Chronicles 28:2-11, Jeremiah 33:19 to the end, Ezekiel 34:23-24 & 37:24-25, Hosea 3:5, Luke 1:30-33, Acts 2:29-31. As also in those Scriptures that testify, how God, in case of the miscarriages of some of David's seed, did not utterly destroy his kingdom, nor root out his seed, but still reserved a light for David of his seed in Israel,

commentary upon this Covenant, namely: Psalm 89 throughout, Psalm 132:11 to the end, and 2 Samuel 23:1-8. Now in all such places as either cite, recite, or expound this Covenant, it is notably confirmed and established. The Covenant is doubled, trebled, etc., for the greater certainty and unquestionable stability. These Scriptures have been opened in the matter of this Covenant. See Aphorism 4.

[4] ***Finally, by God's actual accomplishments of the promises of this Covenant by degrees.*** Some were fulfilled in David's days, such as God's subduing all his enemies, strengthening and establishing him, his enlarging his glory and dominion, His sweet covenant relation, fulfilling of his days, and building up his house after him in raising up his seed. Some were fulfilled in the days of his seed, as: God's fatherly relation to his seed, the building God a house, establishment of his seed upon his throne, constancy of his faithfulness to them, etc. All of this, I have formerly unfolded.[548] Now all these gradual accomplishments of this Covenant upon David and his seed, were as so many infallible seals to the truth and faithfulness thereof, and as so many earnests, handsels and firstfruits, assuring the like performances of all promises for the future, till they all should have their grand and highest accomplishment in **Jesus Christ** the chief Son and Seed of **David**.

[3] The **administration** of this Covenant with David and his seed, was in effect the same with that of the Sinai Covenant (which remained in force till the death of Jesus Christ), namely: {1} by the Levitical priesthood as the fixed and standing ministry of the Old Testament. {2} By the Levitical sacrifices and all others, the ceremonial and typical ordinances of God. {3} By the typical and worldly sanctuary, as also: {4} By the ordinary covenant tokens, circumcision and the passover, instituted under God's Covenant with Abraham, but continued under the Sinai Covenant even until the death of Jesus Christ.

---

according to his Covenant. As 1 Kings 11:12-13, 31, 36 & 14:4-5; 2 Chronicles 21:7; 2 Kings 8:16-20.

[548] In Aphorism 4 of this chapter, Section 1

Notwithstanding in some respects, this administration admitted some perfective alterations under this Covenant with David. For, {1} the public place of God's solemn worship, which was formerly an ambulatory and moving tabernacle, during Israel's moving and unsettled condition, was now a fixed and most magnificent temple at Jerusalem, suitable to the fixed condition of Israel now peaceably possessing their promised rest. {2} The priests, Levites, singers, and porters – even all the Levitical ministry – were more completely settled in their fixed courses of ministration. {3} The promises of this Covenant run in a more royal strain, touching the kingdom and kingly seed of David, having more peculiar tendency to Jesus Christ the Son of David, that should be Lord of Lords and King of Kings. {4} The political government of the commonwealth of Israel was now changed from that by judges to that by kings.

Inferences

(1) **Hence when David or his seed failed in their covenant-duty towards God, they sinned against the very constitutive form and essence of this Covenant, namely: the mutual obligation between God and them.** And offending against the very life and being of the Covenant, it was just with God to chastise them, and cut them short in such Covenant blessings as were only Conditional.

(2) **Hence the unquestionable divine authority of this Covenant is evident.** For it was first revealed by divine vision unto Nathan the prophet, and by him to David; and afterwards confirmed by God in sundry passages of Scripture, as has been shown.[549] So that the faith, hope, and comfort of David

---

[549] 2 Samuel 7:4-18, Psalm 89:19

might securely rest and repose themselves upon the promises of this Covenant, as upon an authentic divine foundation.[550]

(3) **Hence the immutability of God's counsel touching the everlasting kingdom of David's seed (that absolute promise of this Covenant, as relating to Christ) was clearly demonstrated:** in that he established this Covenant by those two immutable things, his promises and oath, in which it was impossible for God to lie, or fail.[551] Hereupon David and his seed might have strong consolation, especially in reference to the Messiah promised.

(4) **Hence the fidelity of God to David and his seed in this Covenant, was very conspicuous.** The gradual accomplishments of the promises thereof being daily discovered upon David and his seed in their successive generations.

Thus of the form of God's Covenant with David and his seed.

---

[550] 2 Samuel 23:4-5
[551] Psalm 89:33-38 & 132:11 & 89:35 with Hebrews 6:16-18

Aphorism 6

The End or Scope of God's Covenant with David.

The end, or intended scope, of God in this Covenant was immediately, some more peculiar revelation of Jesus Christ, and mediately, the furtherance of the happiness of David, of his seed, and of their subjects in Christ, as also the singular advancement of the glory of God. This aphorism I thus briefly explain:

(1) **The immediate end or scope herein intended was: a more peculiar revealing of Jesus Christ.**

In all the foregoing covenant expressures, the revealing of Jesus Christ still more and more was immediately intended. So in this. A more peculiar revelation of Christ in this Covenant than in any of the former, was intended in two respects, namely: [1] in regard to his descent, and [2] in regard to his office.

[1] *In regard to his descent.* In the Covenant with Adam, Christ's descent is revealed most generally, that he should be the seed of the woman. In the following Covenants, his descent is still more and more particularly revealed, such as, that he should be the seed of Noah in Noah's Covenant, the seed of Abraham in Abraham's Covenant, and the seed of Israel in the Sinai Covenant. But in this Covenant with David, Christ's descent is yet more peculiarly Revealed, and appropriated to one family of Israel; namely: To the House of David. That Christ should descend from David, and be the seed of David, there being sundry promises made in this Covenant, which (as has been abundantly shown in the fourth aphorism) can have their proper and plenary accomplishment in none but only in Jesus Christ. So that the time of Christ is now more peculiarly limited, restrained, reduced and appropriated, then ever formerly, namely: to the house or family of David.

[2] ***In regard to his office.*** In this Covenant, there is a more peculiar display of Christ's office than in the former. Christ's office was described in former Covenants variously, namely: more generally, under the three first Covenants, such as: a bruiser of the serpent's head under Adam's Covenant, as a Savior of an elect seed and remnant in Noah's Covenant, and as a blesser of all the kindreds of the earth in Abraham's Covenant. More especially and particularly, under the Sinai Covenant: as a prophet like unto Moses, to be hearkened to in all things; and as a priest like Aaron, Christ's priesthood being many ways typified in Aaron's priesthood, as formerly it was shadowed out in Abraham's Covenant also by Melchizedek's more excellent priesthood. And now under this Covenant, as an everlasting king that should sit upon the throne of his father David, and rule the house of Jacob, the church, forevermore.[552] I grant this kingly office of Christ was somewhat dimly and briefly pointed at in Abraham's time, under that Covenant's dispensation to Abraham in the type of Melchizedek, *King of Salem, first being, by interpretation King of Righteousness; and after that also King of Salem, which is, King of Peace.*[553] But the everlasting kingdom of David's seed, Christ, is the very burden and main business of this Covenant with David, which is insisted upon again and again.

(2) The mediate end or scope herein intended, is twofold: subordinate and ultimate.

[1] ***Subordinate***, to further the happiness of David, of his seed, and of his subjects in Christ. The three sorts of covenant blessings promised to David, his seed, and subjects, as has been evidenced, eminently tend to advance their happiness, and that in Christ, in whom most of them had their chief accomplishment. Judiciously consider those covenanted mercies, and therein you may palpably read God's intention of furthering their happiness in Christ.

---

[552] 2 Samuel 7:12-14, Psalm 89:36-37, 132:11 with Luke 1:31-33, Hebrews 1:4-5, Acts 2:30-32, etc.

[553] Hebrews 7:1-3, etc.

[2] ***Ultimate***, to advance singularly the glory of God. God intends primarily his own glory in all his acts, and consequently, in all his covenant discoveries. In this Covenant, the glory of God is variously intended, such as: {1} The glory of his free-grace and rich mercy in Jesus Christ. *Mercy shall be built up*[554] – *for his **Word's** sake* (namely: his essential *Word* Christ, called in the parallel place, his *servant*), *and according to his own heart*,[555] God revealed this Covenant. {2} The glory of his bounty, in promising such plenty of great blessings, called {*greatnesses*}. David was astonished thereat (1 Chronicles. 17:16, etc).[556] {3} The glory of his justice and severity against sin. That he would visit the iniquities even of David's seed with rod and stripes.[557] {4} The glory of his truth and faithfulness. That his Covenant should not be broken, nor his loving kindness should utterly be taken from him, nor his faithfulness fail, etc.[558] Nay, their sins should not disannul his Covenant. {5} The glory of his holiness, in imposing such covenant duties of holiness and righteousness upon David and his seed. {6} The glory of his power, in perpetuating the seed and throne of David against all evils and enemies forevermore.

Inferences

(1) Hence, as Christ in regard to his descent and royal office was more peculiarly revealed in this Covenant, so David had answerably a more peculiar knowledge of Jesus Christ by this, than by former Covenants. And this was a fundamental addition to David's happiness: to know Jesus Christ is life eternal in the foundation and inchoation thereof. David and his seed would have missed the end of this Covenant, if therein they had not eyed Christ.[559]

---

[554] Psalm 89:2.
[555] 1 Chronicles 17:19; 2 Samuel 7:21
[556] 1 Chronicles 17:19
[557] Psalm 89:30-32
[558] Psalm 89:2-3, 30-38
[559] John 17:3

(2) Hence, how great cause had David to place all his salvation and delight upon this Covenant; the happiness of him, his seed, and subjects being so eminently intended and provided for in this Covenant in Christ.[560]

(3) Hence, no wonder that David so thankfully magnified and glorified God, for revealing this Covenant, in which God so exceedingly manifested the riches of his glory towards David and his seed.[561]

Thus of the end of this Covenant.

---

[560] 2 Samuel 23:5
[561] 1 Chronicles 17 & 2 Samuel 7

Aphorism 7

Seventhly, General Inferences from the whole of this Covenant with David.

The mystery of God's Covenant with David (notably amplifying the Sinai Covenant) being thus at large unfolded and described, according to: (1) the author and nature of it, (2) the federate parties of it, (3) the impulsive cause and occasion, (4) the substance or subject matter, (5) the form, and (6) the end thereof. It now remains, that I should close up this whole discourse with some general corollaries or inferences clearly resulting from the whole, and I shall comprise them all in this concluding aphorism, namely:

From this whole discourse about God's Covenant with David and his Seed, we may plainly see: (1) that this Covenant was a very princely and royal Covenant; (2) that David and his seed, especially Solomon, were eminent types of Jesus Christ; (3) what the properties of this Covenant are; (4) what agreement and disagreement this Covenant has with or from all foregoing covenants; and (5) that so much of Christ was revealed to David and his seed in this Covenant, that he and Solomon knew and spake much of Christ in their writings.

(1) **First, hence it's plain that God's Covenant with David and his seed was a very princely and royal Covenant.** For the chief stream of covenant mercies herein promised did run in the royal channel, and singularly tended to advance the royal dignity and authority of David and his seed in Israel, especially the spiritual and everlasting kingdom of **Jesus Christ**, the primary seed of David, in and over the church. In their temporal kingdom over the literal Israel, Christ's spiritual and everlasting kingdom over the spiritual *Israel of God* was shadowed out. Under the Sinai Covenant, Christ's prophecy was shadowed out by Moses' prophecy; and Christ's priesthood by the Levitical

priesthood. But under this enlargement and amplification of the Sinai Covenant, Christ's kingdom was represented in the type of David's kingdom. Under this Covenant, only the kingly government over Israel, was settled and flourished. And under this Covenant chiefly, the spiritual kingdom of Christ was typified and adumbrated.

How wisely has God contrived to reveal Christ's person and office in his covenant expressures!

[1] ***His person***, to be God and man, by his Covenant with Adam: {1} *Man*, as the seed of the woman; {2} *God*, as the bruiser of the serpent's head, which mere man could never have done.

[2] ***His office***, {1} in general, to be a Savior of God's elect remnant and family from the midst of the perishing world, in his Covenant with Noah, and to be a blesser of all the families of the earth in his Covenant with Abraham. {2} But his mediatory office in particular, namely: his prophecy under the type of Moses, and priesthood under the type of Aaron, were set forth in the Sinai-Covenant with Israel; his kingship and royalty under the type of David and his seed in this Covenant with David. David's Covenant may therefore be deservedly styled {*the Royal Covenant*}. This is an excellent covenant mystery.

(2) Secondly, hence it's evident that King David and his royal seed, especially Solomon, were eminent types of Jesus Christ.

These kings were notable types of this king of kings: their kingdom of his kingdom, and their subjects of his subjects. View a little the correspondence between the types and antitype: [1] in David and [2] in Solomon.

David was so eminent a type of Christ, and especially in reference to his kingdom, that after David's decease, Christ is oftentimes promised to be the king and ruler of his church, under the very name of {*David*}. *Afterward shall the children of Israel return, and seek the LORD their God, and David their king.*[562] – *They shall serve the LORD their God, and David their king, whom I*

---

[562] Hosea 3:5

*will raise up unto them.*⁵⁶³ – *And I will set up one shepherd over them, and he shall feed them, my servant David: he shall feed them, and he shall be their shepherd. And I the LORD will be their God, and my servant David a prince among them*⁵⁶⁴ – *And David my servant shall be king over them, and they all shall have one shepherd, etc. – And my servant David shall be their prince forever.*⁵⁶⁵ In these and like promises of Christ, Christ is called David, because he is God's true **David** indeed, typified by King David of old. And the whole series of this Covenant implies thus much.

[1] Now **David** was a type of Christ. In regard to his {1} person, {2} office, {3} condition, and {4} acts done, or effects wrought by him.

{1} *In his person*. David was a type of Christ three ways: For:

(i) He was (not without special providence) called **David** which in Hebrew is the same with דוד {*dod: beloved*}, beloved, of God, a man after his own heart.⁵⁶⁶ Christ also is called **David** (Jeremiah 30:9, Hosea 3:5, Ezekiel 34:23-24, 37:24-25), being his *beloved Son* (Matthew 3:17), the beloved (Ephesians 1:6), *the Son of his love* (Colossians 1:13), so both of them are, Davids: both beloved.

(ii) Both of them sons of Jesse: David in 2 Samuel 23:1-2; Christ a rod out of the stem of Jesse, and a branch out of his roots.⁵⁶⁷ Both of them out of dry and despised roots, having low and obscure parentage.⁵⁶⁸

(iii) Both of them sons of God; yea, God's firstborn David (Psalm 89:26-27), and Christ (Hebrews 1:1, 6, Matthew 1:25). Christ is so God's first begotten, that he is his only begotten Son (John 1:14 and 3:16); David so by supernatural adoption. Christ so by eternal Generation, according to his

---

⁵⁶³ Jeremiah 30:9
⁵⁶⁴ Ezekiel 34:23-24
⁵⁶⁵ Ezekiel 37:24-25
⁵⁶⁶ 1 Samuel 13:14, Acts 13:22
⁵⁶⁷ Hosea 11:1
⁵⁶⁸ 2 Samuel 7:18, Isaiah 53:2

divine person (Psalm 2:7, John 1:1) by extraordinary conception by the Holy Spirit, according to his human nature (Luke 1:34-36).

{2} *In his office.* For David was;

(i) *A prophet* (Acts 2:30). He penned by the inspiration of God's Spirit, that sweet part of holy Scripture, the Psalms, for the greatest part of them at least. Hence styled {*the sweet Psalmist of Israel*}.[569] So Christ is the great prophet (Acts 7:37 and 3:32, Luke 24:19). David did but pen the Scripture, but Christ indited it by his Spirit (2 Timothy 3:16; 2 Peter 1:21). Hence the Scripture is called {*the word of Christ*}.[570]

(ii) *A priest.* David was a priest somewhat extraordinarily, in his building an altar in the threshing floor of Araunah the Jebusite, a Gentile,[571] (the place where Isaac was offered in a figure, and where afterwards Solomon built the temple, 1 Chronicles 3:1 – both types of Christ),[572] and in his offering a sacrifice there for the land to stay the plague of pestilence, which God accepted, and the plague was stayed. So Jesus Christ was our great and most extraordinary high priest, who upon the altar of his Godhead offered himself a sacrifice at Jerusalem for the sins of Jews and Gentiles that God's wrath might be stayed which sacrifice was most acceptable as an odor of a sweet smell to God (Hebrews 10:5-19, Ephesians 5:2).[573]

(iii) A *king*. This was David's primary and ordinary office, wherein he was a most singular type of Christ, the King of kings, for: (i) Both of them were kings (Matthew 1:6, John 18:37). (ii) Both of them were kings of Israel (2 Samuel 6:20, Psalm 78:70-71, John 1:49 & 12:13). (iii) Both of them {*messiahs*}, that is, {*anointed*}, yea both the anointed of God unto their kingly office, hence called {*God's kings*} (Psalm 2:2, 6 & 18:15). David anointed with material oil by Samuel (1 Samuel 16:13). Christ anointed with immaterial oil,

---

[569] 2 Samuel 23:1-2
[570] Colossians 3:16
[571] 2 Samuel 24:18 to the end
[572] Genesis 22:1-2 with Hebrews 11:17-19
[573] Hebrews 8:1, 9:11-14, Luke 9:31, Hebrews 9:26, 28

the *oil of gladness above all his fellows* (Psalm 45:7), God having anointed him with the Holy Spirit and with power (Acts 10:38). (iv) Both of them furnished with the Spirit of God for their royal government, upon their anointing David (1 Samuel 16:13); Christ (Acts 10:38, Matthew 3:16).

{3} ***In his condition and state.*** Herein David notably typified Christ: see the agreement herein between David the type, and Christ the antitype.

(i) Both of them were born of obscure and mean parents in Bethlehem (John 7: 42, Matthew 2:5-6).

(ii) Both of them were advanced from a low and despicable state to their royal dignity. David, *a caula ad aulam,* from a mean family to the kingdom (2 Samuel 7:18 and 23:1-2), from the shepherd's staff to the scepter (Psalm 78:70-71; 1 Samuel 16:11-12); so Christ from a mean parentage to kingly dignity, born king of the Jews, from the manger to the throne, (Isaiah 53:2, Luke 2:4-7, Matthew 2:2).

(iii) Both of them met with grievous opposition when once it was known that they were ordained and appointed of God for the kingdom. David was so persecuted by King Saul, that he fled to heathenish nations (2 Samuel 21:40, 22:3 & 27:2); Christ as soon as it was noised that he was born King of the Jews, was cruelly persecuted by King Herod, so that he fled to the heathen country Egypt.[574]

(iv) Both of them, having obtained the kingdom, were deeply afflicted by a variety of adversaries (Psalm 2:1-2, etc. Acts 4:24-28) For:

(a) David was oppugned by the Philistines (2 Samuel 5:17. & 8:1-3, 5 & 10:6) exiled from his kingdom by Absalom (2 Samuel 15:12, 14, Psalm 3:1), betrayed by Achitophel his familiar counselor (2 Samuel 16:21 & 17:1), cursed by Shimei (2 Samuel 16:5-7), forsaken and mortally pursued by his own people (2 Samuel 18:6), and had as it were gall and vinegar given him to drink (Psalm 69:21).

---

[574] Matthew 2:20-22

(b) Christ in like manner was rejected of his own (John 1:11 & 9:21), traduced with horrid and blasphemous reproaches (Matthew 10:25 & 12:24, John 9:24), betrayed by Judas, one of his own familiar disciples (Psalm 14:10 & 55:14, John 13:18), cast out of his vineyard and kingdom by the scribes, priests, and elders (Psalm 118:22, Matthew 21:42-43), persecuted by the Jews, his own people, even to the death upon the cross (John 19:15, Acts 2:23, 36 and 3:13-14), and delivered to death at last by Pilate, etc. (Psalm 2:1-2, Acts 4:24-27), having gall and vinegar given him to drink (Psalm 69:22, Matthew 27:34, John 19:28-29).

(v) Both of them at last were exalted to a high and glorious state. David after all his afflictions retained his kingdom in peace and honor, having rest from his enemies roundabout (2 Samuel 7:1 & 22:31; 1 Kings 1:17), and at last was full of days; riches, and honor (1 Chronicles 29:28); so Christ after all his conflicts and sufferings, having conquered his enemies on every side, and led captivity captive, entered into his heavenly glory (Romans 8:3, Colossians 2:14-15, Hebrews 2:9, 14-15, Philippians 1:8, etc, Luke 24:26).

(vi) Both of them had their kingdom enlarged even over strangers. David became head of the heathens about him, so that strangers unknown served him, and he was higher than the kings of the earth (Psalm 18:44 & 89:27). Christ also became head not only of Jews but of Gentiles also, having all power over them, being Lord of lords and King of kings (Ephesians 2:12, Psalm 2:8, Matthew 28:18-19, Revelation 19:16).

(vii) Both of them had an everlasting kingdom established upon them: David in some respects only (Psalm 89:3-4, 36-37); Christ absolutely (Psalm 45:6, Isaiah 9:6-7, Daniel 2:44).

{4} *Finally, in his acts or works done by him.*

Herein also David notably resembled and typified Jesus Christ in sundry ways, for:

(i) Both of them believed and hoped in God, rolling themselves upon him by faith and prayer in their distresses, David (Psalm 3:4, 7 & 22:1-5, etc., and

17:6, 13). So also Christ (Psalm 22:17, 2; John 11:42, Matthew 27:46, Hebrews 5:7).

(ii) Both of them walked holily and religiously before God. David, though he had many frailties, yet walked sincerely (Psalm 18:21-22, 1 Kings 15:5). But Christ walked without all spot of sin (Isaiah 53:9, Hebrews 7:26).

(iii) Both of them were zealous for God, for his worship, laws, and ordinances: David (Psalm 119:72, 103, 84:11, 122:1, 69:10 & 101:7-8); much more Christ (John 4:34, Matthew 6:42, Psalm 69:10. John 2:15, 17).

(iv) Both of them were universally obedient to God their heavenly Father. David obeyed him sincerely (1 Kings 9:4, Acts 13:22; 1 Kings 15:3, 5), but Christ obeyed him exactly in all things, doing always those things that pleased him, yea he was obedient to the death, even the cursed, and shameful, and painful death of the cross (John 8:29, Philippians 2:8).

(v) Both of them walked very wisely and prudently. David was wise in matters (1 Samuel 16:18), and behaved himself wisely in all his ways (1 Samuel 18:14), Christ had in him all treasures of wisdom and knowledge (Colossians 2:2-3, Isaiah 11:1-2), made men astonished at his understanding and answers (Luke 2:47) by his Word and Spirit makes wise unto salvation (2 Timothy 3:15-16, Colossians 3:16; 1 Corinthians 2:9-10, etc.)

(vi) Both of them excelled in fortitude and valor: (i) In conquering and subduing their enemies. David subdued Goliath of Gath (1 Samuel 17). slew Philistines and others, so that they sang of him: *David hath slain his ten thousands* (1 Samuel 18:10). But Christ subdued greater enemies: spiritual enemies, sin, Satan, the world, etc. (Romans 8:3, John 16:11, Colossians 2:14-15, Hebrews 2:14-15, John 16:33, Psalm 110:1-2). (ii) In protecting and defending their subjects: David (Psalm 101:4-6, 8); Christ (Isaiah 11:4), he protected his saints and subjects against Saul's persecution.[575]

(vii) Both of them ruled and governed righteously in the fear of God. David (2 Samuel 23:3, Psalm 101 throughout), yet with some intermixture of

---

[575] Acts 9 throughout

failings; Christ without all failings and miscarriages (Isaiah 11:1-5, etc., Psalm 45:7, etc.)

Finally, both of them were loving and tender to their parents: David in his trouble requests the king of Moab that his father and mother might dwell by him (1 Samuel 22:3); Christ upon the cross commends his mother to the care of John, his beloved disciple (John 19:26-27).

In these and many like respects David was an eminent type of Christ.

[2] **Solomon** the immediate seed of David was also a notable type of Jesus Christ, who was greater than Solomon (Matthew 12:42, Luke 11:31). And this in his {1} person, {2} office, {3} state, and {4} acts.

{1} *In his person*. For (i) both of them were sons of David by nature: Solomon in an ordinary way of generation (Matthew 1:6); Christ in an extraordinary way of propagation (Matthew 1:1 with Luke 1:32, 35). (ii) Both of them, beloved of God. Solomon named *Jedidiah*, that is, *Beloved-of-the-LORD*, and this by God's appointment (2 Samuel 12:24-25). Christ was called God's *beloved Son*, in whom he was *well-pleased* (Matthew 3:17) and *the Son of his love* (Colossians 1:13). (iii) Both of them Sons of God (2 Samuel 7:14 with Hebrews 1:5).

{2} *In his office*. For:

(i) Both of them were **prophets**. (a) Solomon was a preacher in Jerusalem (Ecclesiastes 1:1, 12), and a holy penman of those three eminent books of Scripture: Proverbs, Ecclesiastes, and Song of Songs.[576] Thus he was a prophet; (b) but Christ a greater prophet: *that prophet* (John 6:14, Acts 3:23). The spirit of prophecy is from him (Revelation 19:10, Ephesians 4:11). He also was preacher in Jerusalem (John 18:19-21), And he indicted all the Holy Scriptures (Colossians 3:16) by his Spirit (2 Peter 1:20-21).

(ii) Both of them were **kings**, namely: (a) both kings of Israel (Proverbs 1:1, John 1:49 and 12:13). (b) Both kings in Jerusalem (Ecclesiastes 1:1, Luke

---

[576] Proverbs 1:1, Ecclesiastes 1:1, Song of Solomon 1:1

19:37-38, Matthew 21:5, 9). (c) Both kings of peace. *Solomon*, that is, *peaceable, prosperous*, etc. His very name had peace engraven upon it by God himself (1 Chronicles 22:9).[577] He was a man of rest: God gave him *rest from all his enemies round about*. And by this means, *Israel and Judah dwelt peaceably without fear under their vine and fig-tree*; yea, God gave *peace and quietness to Israel in his days* (1 Chronicles 22:9, 1 Kings 4:25). But Jesus Christ procures his subjects an inward, spiritual, heavenly, everlasting peace with God passing all understanding (Romans 5:1, John 14:27, 16:33, Philippians 4:7). So that he is our peace (Ephesians 2:14) and the prince of peace (Isaiah 9:6). His scepter is the gospel of peace (Psalm 110:2, Isaiah 2:3, Ephesians 6:15). His kingdom consists in righteousness and peace (Romans 14:17). His subjects are subjects of peace (Luke 1:79). His birth and coming into the world was with a song of peace by the angels (Luke 2:14), and his death and going out of the world was with a blessing of peace left with his disciples (John 16:33, 14:27). He makes the wolf dwell with the lamb, the leopard lie down with the kid, the calf, the young lion, and the fatling together, that a little child may lead them, the cow and the bear to feed, and their young ones to lie down together, the sucking child to play on the hole of the asp, and the weaned child to put his hand on the cocatrice den. (d) Both kings of incomparable wisdom (1 Kings 3:9, 12, Colossians 2:2-3, 1 Corinthians 1:30, Isaiah 9:6).[578]

{3} *In his state and condition*. For:

(i) Both of them were exceedingly rich. Solomon made silver and gold at Jerusalem as plenteous as stones, and the cedar trees as the sycamore trees that are in the vale for abundance.[579] But Christ, the true Solomon, is infinitely higher. He is heir of all things (Hebrews 1:2), has unsearchable riches (Ephesians 3:8), and all that the Father has is his (John 16:15). His riches are spiritual and heavenly, far transcending all Solomon's outward wealth: riches

---

[577] 1 Chronicles 17:19; 2 Samuel 7:21
[578] Isaiah 11:6-9
[579] 2 Chronicles 2:1, 15 & 9:21-22

of righteousness and pardons (Romans 1:17, 1 John 1:7, 2:1-2), riches of grace (John 1:14, 16), riches of truth (John 1:14), riches of life (John 15:10), and all fullness (Colossians 1:17).

(ii) Both of them were full of princely glory and royalty. Solomon surpassed in princely glory all that were before and after him (2 Chronicles 9 throughout and Ecclesiastes 2 throughout). The daughters of Zion admire his crown and royalty (Song of Solomon 3:11), and the Queen of Sheba was so astonished at it that there was no more spirit in her (2 Chronicles 9:3-4). Yet Solomon in all his royalty and glory was not clothed like one of the lilies (Matthew 6:29). But Christ is the brightness of his Father's glory, and the express image of his person (Hebrews 1:3). having not one, but many crowns upon his head, and the armies following him upon white horses, and on his thigh and vestures a name written *King of kings and Lord of lords* (Revelation 19:11-17).

(iii) Both of them were of great and large dominions, not only over Jews, but also over Gentiles. That of the psalmist concerns them both, but especially is true of Christ in whom it is primarily accomplished (Psalm 72. 8-11; see also 2 Chronicles 9:24, 26, and Matthew 28:18-19).

{4} *In his acts, Solomon was a singular type of Jesus Christ.* For:

(i) Both of them were builders of the house and temple of God. Solomon built the material [and now] dead temple at Jerusalem of materials fetched from both the holy land and [foreign] nations, and that very magnificently – see 2 Chronicles chapters 2, 3, and 4 throughout. After which, he solemnly dedicated it by prayer and sacrifices (2 Chronicles chapters 5 and 6). And set in order the service of the temple (2 Chronicles 8:14-16). But Jesus Christ builds the mystical, spiritual, and living temple, the house and church of God, of people both from among Jews and Gentiles (Hebrews 3:1-6, etc., Ephesians 2:13 to the end). He also consecrated and solemnly dedicated his spiritual temple, both by prayer (John 17 throughout), and by the sacrifice of himself (John 17:19, Hebrews 10:14). And set in order most faithfully all the worship, ordinances, and officers of his house (Hebrews 3:1-2, etc. Acts 1:2-3, Matthew 28:18-20, 26:26-31, 18:15-21; 1 Corinthians 5 throughout; 2 Corinthians 2:6, etc., Ephesians 4:8-17).

(ii) Both of them ruled righteously (Psalm 72:1-8, 12-14). As Solomon in punishing offenders after David's death (1 Kings 2 throughout), and in giving the child to the right mother (1 Kings 3:16 to the end). But Christ is *the LORD our Righteousness* (Jeremiah 33:15-16). He rules so righteously that he makes all his subjects righteous (1 Corinthians 1:30).

(iii) Both of them enriched their subjects abundantly. Solomon enriched his subjects with outward temporal wealth (2 Chronicles 1:15). But Jesus Christ enriches his subjects both with outward and inward, temporal, spiritual and eternal wealth. He alone gives the true and chief riches (2 Corinthians 8:9; 1 Corinthians 1:5, Ephesians 1:3; 1 Corinthians 2:9-10; 1 Timothy 4:8; 1 Corinthians 3:20-22). Christ is heir of all things (Hebrews 1:2), and all true believers are heirs, co-heirs with Christ (Romans 8:15-17). Thus Jesus Christ is **the David**, and **the Solomon**.

(3) Thirdly, hence we may clearly take notice, what the properties of this Covenant are. It is: [1] gratuitous, [2] evangelical, [3] mixed, [4] ordered in all things, [5] sure and faithful, [6] everlasting, and [7] comfortable. Of these briefly.

[1] Gratuitous. Of mere free grace to David and his seed. And that, not only *ex gratia favis*, from the grace of free favor,, for so God's Covenant and promise to, and blessings upon man in innocence, were all of grace, undeserved by man from his maker: But also *ex gratia [commiserationis]*, from his grace of commiseration, whereby he in bowels of compassion heaps good upon his sinful creatures, deserving all contrary evil.[580] Thus, of free favor without any desert of David, yea, of free commiseration contrary to his desert [merit], this Covenant was made with David. Hence David – wholly excluding himself and

---

[580] 2 Samuel 7:18-20

his house from being any motive ground or cause of this Covenant. *Who am I, and what's my house*, etc. ascribes God's grace, as the inward Impulsive cause; and to Jesus Christ the essential Word and servant of God, as the outward impulsive cause thereof.[581] *For thy Word's sake, for thy servants sake, and according to thine own heart, hast thou done all this greatness, in making known all these greatnesses.*[582]

[2] **Evangelical.** This is a pure evangelical Covenant: mere gospel. For: {1} This Covenant is an additional enlargement to the Sinai Covenant, which is purely evangelical, as has been proven in chapter 4. {2} The moving cause of this Covenant was the mere commiserating grace of God in Jesus Christ. And all Covenants which have their origin in such grace, are purely evangelical. {3} The foundation of this Covenant is evangelical. namely: Jesus Christ the Word, and servant of God.[583] {4} The matter and substance of this Covenant is wholly evangelical, namely: covenant mercies in Christ promised on God's part, and covenant duties in Christ re-promised on David's part. This has at large been unfolded.[584] {5} The scope and intended end of this Covenant was evangelical also: namely: The further revealing of Jesus Christ more peculiarly, for advancing the true happiness of David and his seed. Thus, God's Covenant with David, was God's gospel preached to David and his seed: setting forth the sweet tidings of their restitution from the kingdom of sin, Satan and death by the prevailing and everlasting kingdom of Jesus Christ, shadowed out in the kingdom of David and his seed.

[3] **Mixed.** This Covenant was a mixed Covenant. How? {1} Not only mixed of covenant blessings promised by God, and covenant duties re-promised by David – as all Covenants are proportionably in reference to the federates; {2} but mixed and made up of promises and threats. Many eminent blessings are promised to covenant keepers. And on the other hand, sundry

---

[581] 1 Chronicles 17:19 with 2 Samuel 7:21
[582] 1 Chronicles 17:19 with 2 Samuel 7:21
[583] 2 Samuel 7:21; 1 Chronicles 17:19
[584] In this 5th Chapter, Aphorism 4

chastisements by stripes and rods of men, are threatened in case of iniquities and sinful miscarriages against the Covenant.[585] {3} And mixed also even in regard of covenant blessings themselves, some of them being absolutely promised, and which should notwithstanding the very sins of David's seed be certainly and infallibly performed, as the descent of Christ of David and his seed according to the flesh. And the everlasting kingdom and throne of Christ, etc. – some of them being only promised conditionally, upon condition of their covenant keeping with God, etc., such as, the sitting of his seed upon his throne forever,[586] his making Zion his habitation and rest forever, etc.[587] The condition is as the sinew of the promise. Those failing in the condition, cut asunder the sinews of all such conditional promises, and (if I may so speak) disoblige God.

[4] **Ordered in all things**. This property, David notes in his last words, saying: *yet he hath made with me an everlasting Covenant, ordered in all things*.[588] That is, orderly-disposed, orderly-set, prepared, settled, etc., as the Hebrew word properly implies. Of this, I have spoken generally in opening the properties of the Covenant of Faith in general: Most of the particulars there are applicable to this Covenant in particular. There see.[589] This Covenant is ordered in all things in diverse respects. For: {1} the *occasion* of this royal Covenant touching God's building David a house, was when Israel's governors were now changed from judges into kings, and God's first king, David, had it in his heart to build God a house.[590] {2} The *federates*: God, on the one hand; David and his seed, especially Christ, on the other hand.[591] {3} The *impulsive causes*: not any at all from David or his house, but inwardly, God's own heart and good pleasure; outwardly, Christ the Lord's Word and servant.[592] {4} The

---

[585] 2 Samuel 7:14, Psalm 89:30-32
[586] Psalm 132:12
[587] Psalm 132:13-14; 2 Chronicles 7:19-22
[588] 2 Samuel 23:5
[589] Book 2 Chapter 2 Aphorism 1 Section 5
[590] 2 Samuel 7:1-2, etc.
[591] Psalm 89:3, etc.
[592] 2 Samuel 7:18, 21; 1 Chronicles 17:19

blessings promised were orderly directed, firstly to David himself, and then to his seed – ordinary and extraordinary, And lastly, to his and his seed's subjects, and in like sort, orderly, performed first to David, then to his ordinary seed and subjects, and lastly and chiefly to Christ and his kingdom. {5} The *conditions required*, are also orderly annexed to the completion of this covenant constitution. {6} The *form and dispensation* of it is so ordered, that it is subordinate to and comprised under the Sinai covenant administration, and yet the great mystery of Christ and his kingly office is displayed with a clearer revelation. {7} The *scope* of it also: immediate and remote, subordinate and ultimate, as has been explained, is all well ordered. Thus this whole Covenant has an excellent order, disposal, preparation, symmetry, and proportion throughout.

[5] **Sure and faithful.** This David also acknowledged: a covenant ordered in all things and sure.[593] The Hebrew שְׁמֻרָה *shmurah*, properly signifies, *kept, observed, performed* – and that, with care, solicitude and diligence. God made it every way sure to David and his seed, as: {1} By his name **Jehovah**, denoting God's giving subsistence actually to his Covenant and promises.[594] {2} By his immutable promises whereupon this Covenant is established. Yea by promises of special ratification annexed (Psalm 89:33, etc). {3} By the sacred, inviolable oath of God, of which he will not repent, and from which he will not turn. This is often mentioned – Psalm 89:2-3, 35, and 132:11, Acts 2:30. {4} By frequent recitals, allegations, expositions, enlargements of this Covenant in other Scriptures. See 2 Samuel 7, 1 Chronicles 17, 2 Samuel 23:1-10, Psalm 89 throughout, Psalm 132 throughout, Jeremiah 33:20-21, Luke 1:32-33, and Acts 2:30-31. {5} By gradual accomplishments thereof from time to time. {6} By ascertaining and ensuring illustrations. That this Covenant shall be as inviolable, sure, and unalterable, as the heavens themselves (Psalm 89:2, 29), as

---

[593] 2 Samuel 23:5
[594] 2 Samuel 7:5, 8; 1 Chronicles 17:4, 7, 10 with Exodus 6:3

the moon (Psalm 89:37), as the sun (Psalm 89:36), as the course of day and nigh (Jeremiah 33:20-21) – yea, as God himself (Psalm 89:35).

[6] **Everlasting**. This property also David expresses: *Although my house be not so with God, yet he hath made with me an everlasting covenant.*[595] But of this enough has been spoken formerly in opening the matter of this Covenant, in the second and third covenant mercies promised to David's seed. There see. And in the first mercy to David's subjects.

[7] Finally, this Covenant with David was a **comfortable** Covenant. This property necessarily results from all the former. For, in that this Covenant was gratuitous, depending merely upon God, evangelical, mixed, having promises absolute as well as conditional, ordered in all things, sure, and everlasting – in all these regards, it was exceeding comfortable. And upon these considerations, David in his last words notably raised up his consolations upon this Covenant, placing all his salvation, and all his delight thereupon, although at present his house was not so with God as the Covenant promised.[596] And this Covenant was his comfort to his last breath, to his dying day. Oh! The Covenant and promises of God in Jesus Christ are the safest, surest, sweetest, and most immovable comforts of believers, both in life and death. Let our last words, and last thoughts be all fixed upon God's Covenant, as David's were.

(4) Fourthly, hence see what agreement and disagreement this Covenant with David has, with or from all former Covenants.

For this Covenant, being an additional Covenant, annexed to, and comprised in the Sinai Covenant, and in some respects expounding and enlarging the same, has a sweet agreement with the Sinai Covenant, and very little difference from it. And consequently, as the Sinai Covenant, so this Covenant agrees with, or from the former Covenants:

---

[595] 2 Samuel 23:5
[596] 2 Samuel 23:4-5

[1] It **agrees with** the Sinai Covenant, and so with former Covenants: {1} In the *kind or sort of covenant*. This, as all the former being Covenants of Faith, not of Works; and Covenants of Promise, not of Performance. {2} In the *efficient and impulsive cause* – God being the author of all; God's mere grace being the inward impulsive, and Christ's merit the outward impulsive, cause of them all. {3} In the *general consideration of the federates*: the LORD God being the one party promising; Jesus Christ and his spiritual seed being the other party restipulating in all. {4} In the *general sum and substance of the Covenants* – the recovery and happiness of lapsed and lost sinners by Christ being the mercy promised; True fruitful obediential faith in Christ being the duty restipulated in all. All other covenant mercies and duties may be reduced to these two. {5} In the *mystery of sinners' justification revealed in them all*, which is by faith in Christ alone. David under this Covenant thus describes it.[597] {6} In the *common foundation and establishment of the Covenants* – they all being founded upon Jesus Christ alone, and the inviolable promises of God in him. {7} In the *general sameness of end*: the revealing of Jesus Christ, in order to lapsed sinners' recovery and happiness, and God's glory, being the intention of them all.

[2] It **disagrees from** the former Covenants, in such sort and accidental respects as the Sinai Covenant (comprising this Covenant) differs from them – which differences of the Sinai Covenant from them have been already explained.[598]

And it somewhat disagrees from the very Sinai Covenant itself. As,

{1} In the peculiar notion of the federates, for in that, God covenanted, as ***Jehovah***, their Covenant-God, Redeemer, Lawgiver, and husband. In this, God covenanted as the *LORD of Hosts*, the *God* and *Rock of Israel*, a *Father to David and his seed*, *the God of David*, and *Rock of his salvation*. Again, in that, Israel restipulated, as Abraham's *covenant seed*, The Lord's *redeemed*, his

---

[597] Psalm 32:1-2 with Romans 4:6-8
[598] In Book 3, Chapter 4, Aphorism 7, Corollary 5

espoused people, his *heirs under age*, and as his own commonwealth and National *church in the wilderness*. But in this, David himself restipulated as: a *mighty one*, God's *chosen*, God's *servant*, God's *anointed king*, and God's *firstborn, higher than the kings of the earth*. And David's seed restipulated as God's Son and God's King forevermore.

{2} In the individual mercies promised and duties restipulated, as may easily be discerned by making a parallel between them. But especially, the mercies promised in this Covenant have their chief tendency to the advancement and establishment of the kingly power and glory of David, of his seed, and chiefly of Jesus Christ forevermore. And the duties herein more peculiarly restipulated were the religious and righteous rule of David, his seed, and of Jesus Christ the primary seed of David.

{3} In the peculiar manner of manifestation and confirmation. *That* was manifested to all Israel immediately by God, in most dreadful sort, at Mount Sinai, God speaking to them out of the midst of the fire with a great voice:[599] *this* to David mediately by the prophet Nathan, according to the vision which he had from God. *That* being solemnly confirmed by sacrifices at the skirt of Mount Sinai;[600] *this* by God's sacred and immutable oath especially.[601]

{4} In the peculiarity of ends: *that* tending to reveal Jesus Christ the mediator of the Covenant, partly as a prophet, under the type of Moses; partly and principally as a priest, under the types of the Levitical priesthood, and the whole Levitical service of God. But *this* chiefly aiming to set Christ forth as a king (under the type of David and his royal seed) that should rule over the house of Jacob – the church – forevermore.

(5) Fifthly and lastly, hence it is evident that in this Covenant, much of Christ was revealed to David and his seed – yea, so much, that both

---

[599] Exodus 20:1, etc., Deuteronomy 5:1, etc.
[600] Exodus 24
[601] Psalm 89:3, 35 & 132:11

David and Solomon knew and spoke much of Christ in their sacred writings. Take a brief taste hereof:

David knew and prophesied much of *Jesus Christ*, namely: of his [1] person, [2] office, [3] states, and [4] effects of his offices.

[1] **Of his person:** {1} that he is God (Psalm 45:6, 11 with Hebrews 1:8), the Son of God (Psalm 2:7 with Hebrews 1:5), the Word of God (2 Samuel 7:21, 1 Chronicles 17:19), {2}. that he should be man, lower than angels (Psalm 8:4-6 with Hebrews 2:6-10), of the seed of David, the fruit of his loins, (Psalm 132:11. with Acts 2:30 & Luke 1:32-33).

[2] **Of his mediatory office**, as the LORD's Servant therein (1 Chronicles 17:19 with 2 Samuel 7:21).

{1} A *prophet*. Preaching God's righteousness, loving kindness and truth in the great church (Psalm 40:8-10).

{2} A *priest*. An everlasting priest of Melchizedek's order, above Aaron's (Psalm 110:4 with Hebrews 5:6-7. and 7:17; see also Psalm 2:7 with Hebrews 2:9) (i) Of his satisfaction for us by his offering up himself (Psalm 40:6-8 with Hebrews 10:5-15). (ii) Of his intercession for his people, (Psalm 2:8).

{3} A *king*. God's king in Zion, in his church (Psalm 2:6 and 132:11 with Acts 2:30, Luke 1:32-33). (i) That as God's Messiah (Psalm 2:2), he should be anointed with the Holy Spirit, that *oil of gladness above all his fellows* (Psalm 45:7 with Hebrews 1:8-9,. Acts 10:38, John 3:34, Ephesians 4:7). (ii) That he should rule his subjects religiously, and righteously, and gloriously (2 Samuel 23:3-4, Psalm 45:3-7 with Hebrews 1:8-9). (iii) That he should subdue his enemies powerfully (Psalm 45:5) – (a) by converting them to be his subjects (Psalm 110:2-3 & 2:8). (b) By confounding incurable rebels (Psalm 2:9 & 110:5-6). (iv) That he should be a universal king over the nations (Psalm 2:8-9, 22:27-30 & 72:8-11). (v) That he should be an everlasting king upon the throne of David for evermore (Psalm 45:6, 89:4, 36-37 with Luke 1:32-33).

[3] Of his **state of humiliation and exaltation**, wherein he should execute this his mediatory office.

{1} **Of his humiliation**, especially in four degrees, namely:

(i) In his *incarnation*; being made man, lower than the angels, (Psalm 8:5 with Hebrews 2:7-9).

(ii) In his *passion and sufferings*: (a) that he should be betrayed by his own familiar friend, one of his own family (Psalm 41:9 with John 13:18), namely: Judas the apostle. (b) That heathen and people of the Jews, with the kings and rulers of the earth; that is, both Herod and Pontius Pilate, with the Gentiles and people of Israel, should gather together, and confederate to destroy him (Psalm 2:1-3 with Acts 4:25-28). (c) That he should be crucified, his hands and feet pierced, his body so stretched that all his bones might be told, and by-standers should look and stare upon him (Psalm 22:16-17 with Matthew 27:35, Mark 15:24, Luke 23:33, John 19:23, 27). (d) That his garments should be parted, and lots cast upon his vesture (Psalm 22:18 with Luke 23:34, John 19:24). (e) That he should be derided by his enemies shooting out the lip, and shaking the head at him, for trusting in the Lord (Psalm 22:6-8 with Matthew 27:39, 43). (f) That, they should give him gall and vinegar to drink (Psalm 69:21 with Matthew 27:48, Mark 15:23 & John 19:29). (g) That he should be under a heavy desertion upon the cross, his God in some sense forsaking him (Psalm 22:1 with Matthew 27:46 and Mark 15:34).

(iii) In his *death* (Psalm 22:15).

(iv) In his *burial* (Psalm 16:8-10 with Acts 2:31 and 13:35).

{2} **Of his exaltation**, especially in three degrees. namely:

(i) In his *reviving and resurrection from the dead* (Psalm 2:7 with Acts 13:33, Hebrews 1:5; compare also Psalm 16:8-11 with Acts 2:25, 31, and 13:35).

(ii) In his *ascension into heaven*, leading captivity captive, and giving gifts to men (Psalm 68:18. with Ephesians 4:8-9).

(iii) In his *session at God's right hand*, until all his foes become his footstool (Psalm 110:1 with Matthew 22:44, Mark 12:36, Luke 20:42, Acts 2:34, 1 Corinthians 15:25 & Hebrews 1:13).

[4] Of the **happy fruits and effects of his offices**, such as:

{1} The captivating of our spiritual captivity (Psalm 68:18. with Ephesians 4:8).

{2} The receiving and giving gifts for men, even for the rebellious, that the LORD God might dwell among them (Psalm 68:18 with Ephesians 4:8-11, etc).

{3} The converting of a numerous company (like the morning dew) even of the Gentiles unto himself, as his seed that shall serve him, and be his willing people, his spiritual volunteers (Psalm 22:27-31 and 110:2-3).

{4} The true and saving blessedness of all believers that truly trust in him (Psalm 2:12 with Romans 9:33, 10:11 & 1 Peter 2:6).

These things spoke *David* of *Christ*, having an eminent prophetical knowledge of him, and that particularly by means of this excellent Covenant with him (Acts 2:29-31). So that in David's writings much of Christ is revealed: and out of them an excellent **gospel** may be extracted.

Solomon also – the immediate seed and son of David – knew much, and prophesied much of *Jesus Christ* in his writings which he penned by inspiration of the Holy Spirit, as:

[1] Of his Godhead: that he is the everlasting Wisdom of God, that makes wise to salvation, etc. (Proverbs 8 throughout).

[2] Of his manhood: fervently desired and longed for by his church (Song of Solomon 1:1 & 8:1).

[3] Of his sufficient plentiful gospel provisions which he hath made, that sinners may have life and refreshment by him, Prov. 9. 1. to 7.

[4] Of his holy, endeared, rich, ravishing, and saving communion with his church under the continued metaphor or allegory of two lovers under contract, and not yet married. In the whole Song of Songs.

[5] Of his calling and conversion of the little sister of the Gentiles; that she should be in his eyes as one that finds favor: and therefore, As on a wall, he would build upon her a palace of silver; and as a door, he would enclose her

with boards of cedar. That is, in spirituals she should be precious, fragrant and acceptable to God, and durable, as silver, or cedar of which the temple was built (Song of Solomon 8:8-10).

[6] Finally, of Christ's hastening to complete his church's sweetest glory with himself in heaven, She longing for his second coming, *Make haste my beloved, and be thou like to a roe, or to a young hart upon the mountains of spices* (Song of Solomon 8:14).

Hitherto of God's royal Covenant with **David** and his **seed**.

Chapter 6

Of the Discovery, Nature and Administration of God's Covenants of Promise, in the sixth and last noted Period of Time, namely:
From the Babylonian Captivity, Until the Death of the Blessed Messiah JESUS CHRIST.

The preface to this Covenant's explanation, namely, of this Covenant's: (1) duration, (2) difference from David's, and (3) order of handling it.

(1) The sixth and last observable period of time, wherein God renewed with several sweet spiritual enlargements, the *Covenant of Faith in Christ promised for sinners' restoration and salvation* (which is the last of the *Covenants of Promise*)[602] was from the Babylonian captivity until the death and cutting off of the Messiah, our Lord and only Savior Jesus Christ.

This is evident chiefly upon two considerations, namely:

[1] The first manifestation, and [2] the expiration of this Covenant, as to that which was vanishing therein.

[1] **This Covenant was first and most especially revealed to three holy prophets from the Lord, and by them to the Jews**, namely:

{1} To the prophet Isaiah long before the captivity of the Jews in Babylon came to pass, yet with reference to that captivity, see Isaiah 42:6, etc, & 49:8, etc; also 54:9-10 & 59:21 with 61:8, etc, 55:3-4 & 56:3-9, in which passages, express mention is made of this Covenant.[603] He foretold the captivity: and also foretold this comfortable Covenant to the captives.

{2} To Ezekiel in the twelfth year of their captivity, for the support and comfort of God's captives. This Covenant prepared them for the captivity, and supported them under it. In Ezekiel, this Covenant is laid down most pathetically [poignantly] and sweetly.[604]

---

[602] Ephesians 2:12
[603] See afterwards in Aphorism 1, §.1 – Author of this Covenant.
[604] Compare Ezekiel 33:21 with 34:22 to the end & 37:21

{3} To the prophet Jeremiah in the eighteenth year of King Nebuchadnezzar, and tenth year of Zedekiah, when the King of Babylon's army besieged Jerusalem, and Jeremiah the prophet was shut up in the court of the prison, in the King of Judah's house. Now this was in the eighteenth year of the captivity, or thereabouts.[605] For clearing this, note that Judah and Jerusalem were captivated by the Babylonians four several times, namely:

(i) In the third year of Jehoiakim, King of Judah, which was parallel to Nebuchadnezzar's first year.[606]

(ii) In the seventh year of Nebuchadnezzar (Jeremiah 52:28) and in the eighth year of Nebuchadnezzar (2 Kings 24:12). That is, in the latter end of his seventh, and beginning of his eighth year. At this time he carried to Babylon ten thousand captives (2 Kings 24:12-14), of which number, 3,023 were Jews properly so called, of the tribe of Judah (Jeremiah 52:28), and the remainder were of the tribe of Benjamin – and thus that twofold difference about the computation in Jeremiah and the Kings is easily reconciled. Now under this captivity, in the twelfth year, God revealed this Covenant to Ezekiel.[607]

(iii) In the eighteenth year of Nebuchadnezzar, when he carried captive from Jerusalem 832 persons.[608] At this time, this Covenant of God with the captives was revealed to Jeremiah, which seems formerly to be revealed to Ezekiel.[609]

(iv) In the 23rd year of Nebuchadnezzar, when Nebuzaradan carried captive 745 Jews.[610] Thus this Covenant was revealed first to Isaiah, then to Ezekiel, then to Jeremiah, and to all before and under the Babylonish captivity, so that it was *a Covenant to the captivity*, or *the uncaptivating Covenant*. This was the season of this Covenant's commencing.

---

[605] See Jeremiah 32:1-3, etc, with verse 36 to the end
[606] 2 Kings 24:1-3, Daniel 1:1-3
[607] Ezekiel 33:21 with 2 Chronicles 34, 36 & 37
[608] Jeremiah 52:29
[609] Jeremiah 32:1-2, 37, etc.
[610] Jeremiah 52:30

[2] This Covenant dispensation did not expire until the death of Jesus Christ, which put a period both to this, and the Sinai Covenant together, in regard to that which was waxing old, and vanishing therein.[611] So that the interval, or space of time allotted to this Covenant of God with the captives in Babylon, was above the whole seventy years of their captivity, and after that, the seventy weeks of years revealed to Daniel, until Messiah should be cut off, which seem to begin when the 70-years captivity ended (Daniel 9:25).[612]

(2) By this covenant expressure, the Sinai Covenant (remaining still in force) was eminently enlarged, as well as by God's former Covenant with David.

This has been formerly cleared.[613] And therefore this Covenant ran parallel with the Sinai Covenant, from the captivity until the death of Christ: when they both, according to what was vanishing in them, expired together – the *New Covenant* obtaining and commencing instead of the Old.[614] Both of these Covenants – namely: with David and the Jews – were additional explanations and enlargements of the Sinai Covenant, but differently.

[1] *That* was peculiarly directed to David's family; *this*, to the whole people of the Jews.

[2] *That* to David's family in prosperity; *this*, to the Jews in great adversity.

[3] *That* when the civil rulers were changed from judges to kings; *this* when they were changed from kings to governors.

[4] *That* establishing the kingdom of David and his seed forever, especially in the everlasting kingdom of Jesus Christ; *this* assuring the Jews of their

---

[611] See Book 3, Chapter 4, Introduction
[612] Daniel 9:24, etc.
[613] Book 3, Chapter 5, in the General Introduction
[614] See Book 3, Chapter 4, Introduction

restoration from Babylonian captivity into their own land, especially that Jesus Christ the true David might be a prince over them.

[5] *That* was more peculiarly a royal Covenant; this, more specially an un-captivating Covenant.

[6] *That* Covenant brought forth the magnifical and glorious temple of Solomon; *this* Covenant, the more glorious temple of Zerubbabel, into which Jesus Christ himself came in person, who is the desire of all nations.[615]

[7] By *that* Covenant, God promised to raise up Christ of the seed of David to sit upon his throne; by *this* Covenant, God not only promised, but also performed and exhibited Jesus Christ, the chief seed of David, sitting upon his throne forevermore. Thus both of these Covenants agree in substance with the Sinai Covenant. Both of them confirm, explain and enlarge the Sinai Covenant, but in different ways. And both of them tender Christ to the Jews: *that* promising him at a great distance, but *this* bringing Christ into the world as it were in its arms, who is *the salvation of God, the light of the Gentiles, and the glory of the people Israel.*[616]

This Covenant is represented in many heavenly and spiritual promises in the **Messiah** approaching, and particularly defines the time of the Messiah's being cut off, but not for himself; which no former Covenant had done.[617] This Covenant performs Christ, which foregoing Covenants only promised. This Covenant revealed him to the very bodily eyes of God's people, whom all former Covenants revealed only to the spiritual eye of their faith.[618] This Covenant peculiarly sets forth *the LORD, whom they sought, even the Messenger of the covenant, whom they delighted in, coming to his temple.*[619] Now therefore let us raise up our contemplations and attentions to a further height of spirituality and attentiveness, and let our hearts soar aloft to a higher

---

[615] Haggai 2:7-9
[616] Luke 2:30-32
[617] Daniel 9:24-26
[618] Luke 2:30
[619] Malachi 3:1

pitch of enflamed spiritual heavenly desires, joys, and affections towards **Christ**, in the consideration of this Covenant. Let our spirits rise, as the Covenant rises.

(3) **More particularly, for the better unfolding of this Covenant, consider: [1] the author, occasion, impulsive cause, federates, and nature of this Covenant; [2] the subject matter or substance of it; [3] the form of it; [4] the scope and end of it; and [5] such general inferences as may result from the whole.**

Aphorism 1

The Author, Occasion, Impulsive Cause, Federates & Nature of this Covenant.

Upon occasion of God's own people's sad captivity in Babylon, the Lord graciously renewed his Covenant with them, even his Covenant of Faith in the Promised **Messiah**. In this aphorism are comprised: (1) the author of this Covenant: God; (2) the occasion of it: his people's sad captivity in Babylon; (3) the impulsive cause of it: mere grace in Jesus Christ; (4) the federates: God and the afflicted captives; and (5) the nature of it: a Covenant of Faith and a Covenant of Promise in Christ promised. For brevity's sake, I couch all these particulars in this one short aphorism, and explain them as follows, namely:

(1) The author of this Covenant was the LORD God.

This is plain, for:

[1] God revealed and foretold by his Prophet Isaiah that he would make such a Covenant with his people, that should be captives in Babylon, long before the captivity came to pass.

This is very observable in the fourth and last part of his prophecy which is promissory, from chapter 40:1, etc, to the end of his book, which is especially directed to his people, with reference to their captivity in Babylon, which should certainly come to pass. Most, if not all his sermons after that, observably insisting upon their Babylonian captivity, their comforts under it, their certain deliverance out of it, and the happy restoration of their church and commonwealth, their temple, city Jerusalem, etc, when they should be brought again into their own land. And under this type leading them on further, to the great spiritual deliverance of God's people out of the woeful and more than Babylonian bondage under sin, Satan, wrath, etc, by the Messiah; as also to the advancement and enlargement of his spiritual kingdom, by subduing and bringing in such as had been enemies and aliens thereunto, even the Gentiles. Now in this evangelical part of his prophecy, Isaiah makes often mention of God's Covenant, with a special tendency to their consolation against their future captivity, such as: {1} Of his Covenant, upon which all that should lay hold, should have an everlasting name that should not be cut off, should be brought to God's holy mountain, etc.[620] {2} Of the Covenant of his peace, more immovable than the very hills and mountains.[621] {3} Of his everlasting Covenant with them, in Christ the Redeemer, *the sure mercies of David*, etc.[622] {4} Of the Messiah himself, as a *covenant of the people*.[623] Christ is so called by a metonymy, because he is the foundation, chief matter, and an eminent end or scope of God's Covenant with them. *Thus saith the LORD, In an acceptable time have I heard thee, and in a day of salvation have I helped thee: and I will preserve thee, and give thee for a **covenant** of the people, to establish the earth, to cause to inherit the desolate heritages; That thou mayest say to the prisoners, go forth; To them that are in darkness, show yourselves*, etc. Diligently consult those places here noted in the margin. Thus Isaiah spoke of this Covenant aforehand, and treasured it up in store against the time of their captivity.

[2] God revealed this Covenant to his prophet Ezekiel: *Thus saith the Lord GOD – I will set up one shepherd over them, and he shall feed them, even my servant David: He shall feed them, and he shall be their shepherd. And I the LORD will be their God, and my servant David a prince among them, I the LORD have spoken it. And I will make with them a **covenant** of peace*, etc. His covenant promises are also sweetly laid down, in chapter 36:22, etc, *covenant of the people*. And afterwards, God, having brought him in the Spirit into the valley full of bones, representing the dead and hopeless condition of the captives in Babylon, among many other sweet expressions, has these words:

---

[620] Isaiah 56:3-9
[621] Isaiah 54:9-10
[622] Isaiah 59:21, 61:8, etc, & 55:3-4
[623] Ezekiel 34:20, 23-25

Thus saith the Lord GOD, Behold I will take the children of Israel from among the heathen whither they be gone, etc. – *Moreover I will make a covenant of peace with them, it shall be an everlasting covenant with them, and I will place them, and multiply them, and will set my sanctuary in the midst of them for evermore. My tabernacle also shall be with them: yea, I will be their God, and they shall be my people,* etc.[624] In these 36th and 37th chapters, this Covenant is most sweetly described: especially in chapter 36:22 to the end and in chapter 37:21 to the end, as hereafter will more fully appear in unfolding the matter of this Covenant.

[3] God revealed this Covenant also to Jeremiah in the court of the prison, in the eighteenth year of the captivity, when Jerusalem was besieged: *Thus saith the LORD, the God of Israel, concerning this city – Behold I will gather them out of all countries –And they shall be my people, and I will be their God. And I will give them one heart, and one way, that they may fear me forever, for the good of them, and of their children after them. And I will make an everlasting covenant with them, that I will not turn away from them to do them good; but I will put my fear in their hearts, that they shall not depart from me,* etc.[625]

There are sundry other passages in the prophets setting forth the excellent blessings promised in this Covenant; but this Covenant is most eminently and peculiarly described by Isaiah, Ezekiel, and Jeremiah in the places forealleged, and unto these I shall have special reference in opening the matter of this Covenant.

Thus the LORD God was sole author and efficient cause of this Covenant, and the prophets Isaiah, Ezekiel, and Jeremiah were the instrumental revealers and publishers thereof to them of the captivity.

---

[624] Ezekiel 37:1, 21 to the end of the chapter
[625] Jeremiah 32:1-3, 36 to the end

(2) The occasion of this Covenant was the sad captivity of God's people of Judah and Jerusalem in Babylon.

For clearing this, I shall briefly open these particulars, namely: [1] what Babylon this was wherein they were captivated, [2] when and how long they were captivated there, [3] what were the causes why God left them to be so captivated, and [4] that whilst they were under this captivity, God took occasion to reveal to them this Covenant – and why?

[1] *What Babylon this was wherein they were captivated?*
Answer: The Scripture mentions a twofold Babylon, some think a threefold Babylon, namely:

{1} Proper Babylon, or literal Babylon: anciently called *Babel*, that is, *confusion comes*, or *confusion in it*, so called from the event, namely: the confusion of languages, in the first building thereof.[626] This was a very ancient city in Assyria, or rather in Chaldea, built by Nimrod the great hunter before the LORD; so called, not from his hunting of wild beasts, but from his hunting of men by tyranny, oppression, persecution, cruelty, and that openly, audaciously, impudently, without any fear of the Lord, etc. *Nimrod was mighty in hunting before the LORD:*[627] *and the beginning of his kingdom was Babylon.*[628] This city and tower was begun to be built in a plain in the land of Shinar, that is, *that-which-scattered-out-of-it*, namely: the inhabitants thereof upon the confusion of languages.[629] This Shinar was also called *Chaldea* and *Babylon* by the Chaldee paraphrase, and was *the land of Nimrod* (Micah 5:6). Targum Jerusalem calls it *Foytus*.[630] But it is usually called Shinar (Genesis 1:2, 9, 14, Isaiah 11:1, Daniel 1:2). And it is especially noted for the habitation and receptacle of wickedness (Zechariah 5:11). Nebuchadnezzar bragged of his

---

[626] Genesis 11:9
[627] Genesis 10:9-10
[628] Genesis 11:3-4, etc.
[629] Genesis 11:7-9
[630] Genesis 11:28, Jeremiah 51:24, 35, Ezekiel 23:16

building of Babylon: but he was rather the repairer and enlarger, than the first builder or founder thereof.[631] This seems to have been the metropolis and chief royal city and seat of the Babylonian empire, compared in Nebuchadnezzar's dream to the head of gold. To this Babylon, Judah and Jerusalem were carried captive for seventy years.[632] And after Christ, in this Babylon in Asia was the head of the dispersion of the Jews which were Christianized, among whom especially Peter (as minister of the circumcision) dwelt, and from which place he wrote his epistle.[633]

{2} Mystical Babylon, that is, Rome, the seat of Antichrist, the great whore (Revelation 14:8, 16:19 & 18:2, 10, 21). It is called *Babylon* from the great similitude and resemblance between Rome and the Chaldean Babylon. This, Tertullian,[634] Jerome,[635] and Augustine[636] all acknowledge, thus Augustine calls Babylon *the first Rome*, and Rome *the second Babylon*. Yea some of the papists acknowledge that Babylon mentioned in Peter's epistle to be Rome, that thereby they may prove Peter to have been at Rome. Surely they are in great straits for arguments, when they are forced to confess Rome to be Babylon. However they grossly mistake that passage in Peter, which imports the Chaldean, not the Roman Babylon: the Babylon where the Christian Jews of the dispersion had their primary residence.

{3} An Egyptian Babylon is mentioned by some, built (as is thought) by such as fled out of the ancient Chaldean Babylon, whereupon it was called *Babylon*, but now *Cayer*. Of this Cayer, or *Cayrus*, historians and profane writers make mention. Some interpret that of Peter (1 Peter 5:12-13) to intend this Babylon, but as groundlessly as the papists interpret it of the Roman Babylon. Here understand not the Roman or Egyptian, but the Chaldean

---

[631] Daniel 4:28-30
[632] Daniel 2:36-38, Genesis 10:10, Jeremiah 50:12, Isaiah 13:19, Daniel 4:30
[633] 1 Peter 5:12-13
[634] Tertul. de Coron. mil. Advers. Iud. & de probat. Nat. Christi.
[635] Hieron. in Epist. Paulae & Eustoch. ad Marcellan. Lib. 2. contra Iovinian. in fin. & Com. in Isa. 47.
[636] August. de Civit. Dei. lib. 18. c. 22.

Babylon: this was the lady of kingdoms; the hammer of the whole earth (Jeremiah 51:25) – hither the people of Judah and Jerusalem were carried into captivity.[637]

[2] *When, and how long they were captivated there?*
Answer:

{1} The time when they were carried captives into Babylon, was fourfold, namely: in the 1st, 7th, 18th, and 23rd years of Nebuchadnezzar, as I have formerly manifested.[638]

{2} Their continuance under this Babylonian captivity was, from their first captivity, until their delivery thence by Cyrus the Persian, 70 years. For: {1} This captivity was at first threatened to continue so long, and no longer (Jeremiah 25:11-12 & 29:10; herewith compare Daniel 9:2). {2} Their inflicted captivity did also continue seventy years, from their first going into captivity (Zechariah 1:12).[639] So long the land was to enjoy her sabbaths. So long the Jews were as people buried in their graves, and their deliverance thence as hopeless to human apprehensions, as the raising of dead and dry bones out of their graves.[640]

[3] *What were the Causes, why the Lord left his people of Judah and Jerusalem to be thus sadly and tediously captivated in Babylon?*

Answer: The causes why God left them to this captivity, were of two sorts, namely:

{1} **Moving and provoking causes** were his people's many and great sins provoking the Lord to this dreadful indignation. But these especially, namely:

(i) Their inveterate and long continued wickedness from generation to generation (Jeremiah 32:28-31). (ii) The general wickedness of all sorts and

---

[637] Isaiah 47:5, 17
[638] In the preface to this covenant-explanation.
[639] 2 Chronicles 36:21-22, Ezra 1:1.
[640] Ezekiel 37

degrees amongst them, both kings, prophets, priests, and people (Jeremiah 32:28-29, 32; 2 Chronicles 36:11-22, Daniel 9:11). (iii) Their obstinate impenitence under their sins, notwithstanding all the preachings, exhortations and warnings of the prophets (Jeremiah 25:2-13 & 32:28-29, 32-33, Daniel 9:5-7). (iv) Their contemptuous slighting of God's Word, mocking and abusing God's messengers, until there was no remedy (2 Chronincles 36:15-16). (v) The many horrid and prodigious sins of King Manasseh, once a very monster for wickedness (2 Kings 24:2-4). (vi) Peculiarly, the great abundance of innocent blood which Manasseh shed in Jerusalem: *For he filled Jerusalem with innocent blood, which the LORD would not pardon* (2 Kings 24:4). (vii) But especially, their desperate God-provoking sin of idolatry (Jeremiah 25:6-13 & 32:28-29, 34-35, Ezekiel 36:17-19). These were some of their special sins for which God sent them away into Babylon's captivity. And for these and many other our abominations here in England, it were just with God to deliver us into captivity under the mystical Romish Babylon, which the Romish emissaries have long endeavored, and at this day are in great hopes to accomplish through the extremity of our present spiritual apostasies, distractions, and confusions. *Quod omen avertat Deus in saecula saeculorum.*

{2} **Final**. The **final cause** or end which God propounded in sending his people into Chaldea, was their good (Jeremiah 24:5): their spiritual and eternal good especially – that they might be purged from their idols and other abominations,[641] and be reduced to true repentance and reformation for their salvation.[642] God is so good that he will not bring evil of affliction upon his people but for their good. Their captivity in Babylon, and their being buried in their graves there, shall be for their spiritual good, as well as their deliverance thence, and the opening of their graves and bringing them out of their graves there. Thus as God afflicts in severity, so he afflicts of fidelity: he remembers mercy in midst of judgment (Psalm 119:75).

---

[641] Ezekiel 36:23, 37:23, Jeremiah 33:8
[642] Jeremiah 24:7 & 50:5.

[4] ***Whilst they were under this captivity, God took occasion to reveal to them this Covenant. Why did God take such an occasion to reveal it?***

This particular has two branches.

{1} The former, that God took occasion to reveal this Covenant to his people being under Babylonian captivity is evident, by what has been formerly noted.[643] For: (i) this Covenant was made known to Ezekiel the prophet for them, in the 12th year of their captivity, or thereabouts.[644] (ii) And it was again revealed to Jeremiah the prophet, in or about the 18th year of Nebuchadnezzar, which was also the 18th year of their captivity.[645] The promises which God made to them at both these times, are expressly called *a covenant* (Ezekiel 34:15, 37:26-27, Jeremiah 32:37-41).

{2} The latter – why God took occasion to reveal this Covenant to them, even under this sad captivity – may be thus also briefly resolved. The Lord did this:

(i) So that his Covenant might make the deeper impression upon them, in that their deepest affliction; and so that they might more tractably [in a docile manner] set their hearts to believe his covenant promises and perform their covenant duties. The ear and heart that were close shut against God and his will in prosperity, are ofttimes wide opened in adversity. Manasseh himself, when *bound with fetters and carried to Babylon, in his affliction besought the LORD his God, and humbled himself greatly before the God of his fathers, and prayed unto him,* etc.[646] Before this, as the tenth verse notes, Manasseh and his people would not hearken to God, but now he hearkens and wonderfully reforms according to God's Covenant. So true is that of Elihu: *If they be bound in fetters, and holden in cords of affliction: then he showeth them their work and their transgressions that they have exceeded. He openeth also their ear to*

---

[643] In the preface to this Covenant.
[644] Ezekiel 33:21 & chapters 34, 36, & 37
[645] Jeremiah 32:1-2, 37, etc.
[646] 2 Chronicles 33:10-18

discipline, and commandeth that they return from iniquity.[647] No covenant dispensation so thoroughly cured God's people of Judah and Benjamin of their idolatry, of their stony-hardness of heart, and other evils; as did this covenant dispensation under their captivity.[648] And after their return from Babylon, what an excellent Covenant did they renew most solemnly with God![649]

(ii) So that the Lord might the more endear himself and his covenant mercies unto them. The Lord and his covenant mercy should be always sweet and precious to poor sinners, but when sinners are under distress for their sins, then they are wont to be double dear and precious. God loves to have himself and his mercies highly esteemed and dearly affected, and therefore sometimes he involves his people in miseries, so that thence they may learn the due estimate of his mercies. Mercy is always sweet, but mercy in midst of misery is doubly sweet. Light is always pleasant, but light shining out in darkness is doubly pleasant. Life is always delightful, but life in the shadow of death, life out of the grave, is doubly delightful. God and his covenant mercies are always precious: but God offering himself to be their God, and his mercies to be their mercies, and both by covenant, and this in Babylon, in captivity, in their graves – oh how incomparably precious![650]

(iii) To declare hereby his all-sufficiency, goodness, and fidelity to his people in their extremities. (a) His all-sufficiency: in that he could bring them out of Babylon into their own land, against all seeming improbabilities and impossibilities. Though they were as dead and dry bones, though buried in their graves, etc, yet God could open their graves and bring them out of their graves.[651] He could give them a resurrection in Babylon. (b) His goodness and faithfulness: in that he *would* deliver them as he easily *could* deliver them.[652]

---

[647] Job 36:8-10
[648] Ezkeiel 37:23 & 36:25-26, etc.
[649] See Nehemiah chapters 9-10 throughout
[650] Rediisse a morte [ae] vitam, [viae] gratiam duplicat.
[651] Ezekiel 37:1-15
[652] Ezekiel 37:12-14

And accordingly, when the time came, he *did* deliver them, and bring them out of their graves according to his promises beyond their expectation, and to their great admiration. They said: *Our bones are dried, and our Hope is lost, we are cut off for our parts.* But God said: *Behold, O my people, I will open your graves, and cause you to come up out of your graves, and bring you into the land of Israel.*[653] Whereupon when this great work was done, the captives could scarce believe it to be done: but thought they had been in a deluding dream: *When the LORD turned again the captivity of Zion: we were like them that dream,* etc.[654]

(iv) To demonstrate hereby more clearly his tender compassions to his distressed people, not for any of their deserts, but merely for his own holy name's sake. As for them, they transgressed exceedingly against God before their captivity: and they profaned God's name before the heathen under their captivity. Therefore God prefixes this preface to his covenant promises, saying; *But I had pity for mine holy name, which the house of Israel had profaned among the heathen, whither they went. Therefore say to the house of Israel, Thus saith the Lord GOD, I do not this for your sakes, oh house of Israel, but for mine holy name's sake,* etc.[655] So that God had compassion upon them, because he would have compassion upon them. And the riches of these his compassions are notably displayed in this Covenant.

(v) To support and comfort them under such great and long afflictions, lest they should faint under them, and be swallowed up by despair. They had at this time very disconsolate and despairing thoughts of their captivity. They said: *Our bones are dried, and our hope is lost, we are cut off for our parts.* But God replies comfortably: *O my people, I will open your graves, and cause you to come up out of your graves. – And ye shall know that I am the LORD, when I have opened your graves, O my people, and brought you up out of your graves.*[656]

---

[653] Ezekiel 37:11-14
[654] Psalm 126:1-3, etc.
[655] Ezekiel 36:20 to the end of the chapter
[656] Ezekiel 37:11-13

Oh how welcome are God's consolations to his afflicted! As the shadow against the heat, as the shelter against the storm, and as the seasonable showers to the parched ground. How sweet was it when, in reference to this captivity, the LORD answered with good words and comfortable words![657]

(vi) That God might assure his people by this Covenant, that though God had deeply afflicted, yet he did not utterly reject the two families which he had chosen, as their enemies imagined. This the prophet Jeremiah intimates to have been one reason of God's declaring the promises of this Covenant unto his captive people: *Considerest thou not what this people have spoken, saying, The two families which the LORD hath chosen, he hath even cast them off? Thus they have despised my people, that they should be no more a nation before them. Thus saith the LORD, if my covenant be not with day and night, and if I have not appointed the ordinances of heaven and earth: then will I cast away the seed of Jacob, and David my servant, so that I will not take any of his seed to be rulers over the seed of Abraham, Isaac and Jacob: for I will cause their captivity to return, and have mercy on them.*[658] That is, though God had cast the two chosen families into captivity: yet he had not utterly cast them away from himself. They should be his as certainly and immovably according to his Covenant, Jacob's family as his kingdom, and David's family and seed as his rulers in this kingdom; as the revelation of day and night, and courses of sun, moon, and stars were constant and immovable according to his Covenant, for their captivity should return. This I take to be the evident intent of the words. For by {*the two families which the LORD hath chosen*}, I see no just cause why we should understand the families of David and Aaron, the kingly and priestly family, as some do from verses 17-18,[659] nor the families of Judah and Benjamin, as others from Jeremiah 32:44, nor the families of Judah and Israel, as most from Jeremiah 33:14, but rather, the families of Jacob and David,

---

[657] Zechariah 1:12-13, etc.
[658] Jeremiah 33:23-26
[659] As in the Large London Annotations on this place, is noted to be the sense of interpreters.

which are here expressed in this very context itself in verse 26 – *that* as God's church and kingdom; *this* as his rulers in and over them, especially Christ therein. And this interpretation, as it is most apposite and fit, so it is most full and comprehensive.

(vii) To assure the captives that this their great captivity, whatever sad aspect it might have at present, should not destroy or make void God's former Covenant with David, touching the perpetual kingdom of his seed, especially in **Jesus Christ**, that branch of righteousness that should grow up unto David. The prophet therefore – expressing many promises to the captives touching their return out of captivity, etc. – intermingles this promise of the righteous kingdom of Christ the chief Seed of David over Judah and Jerusalem forevermore.[660] See the words: they are very pathetic [emotive]. But thus much of the occasion of this Covenant.

(3) The impulsive or moving cause of this Covenant was God's mere grace in Jesus Christ, not anything in the captivated People.

All motives in the people are excluded, when God lays down his covenant promises: *Thus saith the Lord GOD, I do not this for your sakes, O house of Israel. – Not for your sakes do I this, saith the Lord GOD, be it known unto you: Be ashamed and confounded for your own ways, O house of Israel.*[661] There was then no impulsive [cause] on their part moving God to make this Covenant with them: All the impulsives were on God's part, namely:

[1] The inward impulsive or moving cause in God was his mere grace to them in reference to his own holy name. *But I had pity for mine holy name, – I do not this for your sakes, O house of Israel, but for mine holy name's sake.*[662] This has reference to the mercies promised in this Covenant. People in distress are the proper object of divine pity.

---

[660] Jeremiah 33:1-23: especially note verses 15-17 & 20-22
[661] Ezekiel 36:22-32
[662] Ezekiel 36:21-22

[2] The outward impulsive or moving cause of this Covenant was Jesus Christ: the *branch of righteousness* that should grow up unto David, to *execute judgment, and righteousness in the land*; that true David that should *reign over Israel and Judah as their king forever*; in whose days *Judah shall be saved and Jerusalem shall dwell safely*, this being the name wherewith he shall be called, *the LORD our Righteousness*.[663] In this Jesus Christ, all the promises of this Covenant are evidently made: and he is laid as the base and foundation of this Covenant throughout, as in opening the matter of this Covenant will further appear. By virtue of his blood of the Covenant, they were brought out of this Babylonian pit wherein was no water.[664]

(4) The federates, or parties to this Covenant, were [1] God on the one hand, and [2] his captive people in Christ, on the other.

[1] God, as he was the sole author of this Covenant, so was he the chief federate party to this Covenant. See Jeremiah 32:36-40, etc, Ezekiel 34:24-25 and 37:26-28. God was the chief federate party to this Covenant in this notion and consideration, namely:

{1} As the Lord GOD, (Hebrew): *The Lord JEHOVAH*. Thus saith the Lord JEHOVAH – *Moreover I will make a covenant of peace with them, it shall be an everlasting covenant with them*, etc. (Ezekiel 37:19, 26 & 34:20, 24-25). Now what God's covenanting as **Jehovah** implies, has been formerly opened in the Sinai Covenant.[665]

{2} As the LORD, the God of Israel. *And now therefore thus saith the LORD, the God of Israel – And I will make an everlasting Covenant with them*, etc. And what this imports, that the Lord makes a covenant as the God of Israel; has also been already expounded in opening the Covenant with David – there see.[666]

---

[663] Jeremiah 33:15-16, 23:5-8, Hosea 3:5, Jeremiah 30:9, Ezekiel 34:23-24 & 37:24-25
[664] Zechariah 9:11
[665] In Book 3, Chapter 4, Aphorism 3
[666] In Book 3, Chapter 5, Aphorism 2

{3} As their redeemer that would gather them out of all countries whither they were driven and dispersed (Jeremiah 32:37, 40), and that would open their graves, and bring them out of their graves wherein they seemed to be buried as dead, dry and hopeless, and bring them into their own land (Ezekiel 37:11-26). And how God covenants as a redeemer, has been opened in the unfolding of the Sinai Covenant.[667] So that as to these particulars, there now needs no further explanation.

[2] The captives of Judah and Jerusalem under the power of the King of Babylon, were, in Christ, the other party to this Covenant. For it was made with them (as has been evidenced) during the time of their captivity. And they were federates with God in this notion, namely: as his people in captivity in heathen countries that should be thence redeemed by the Lord (Ezekiel 37:21-28, Jeremiah 32:36-37, 40). God's Sinai Covenant was made with Israel already redeemed from Egypt's bondage; this Covenant was made with them of Judah and Jerusalem, afterwards to be redeemed from Babylon's bondage. The substance of what was spoken there, is applicable here also.

(5) The nature of this Covenant of God with his afflicted captives is this: namely: [1] it is a Covenant of Faith in Christ, and [2] it is a Covenant of Promise in reference to Christ promised, and not as yet actually performed when this Covenant was revealed.

[1] This Covenant was a Covenant of Faith in **Christ**, and not a Covenant of Works, for:

{1} This Covenant was homogeneal, and of like nature, to the Sinai Covenant, being annexed as a sweet additional enlargement thereunto, and explanation thereof, as has been intimated.[668] Under this Covenant, the second temple at Jerusalem was built by Zerubbabel (Zechariah 4:9, Ezekiel 6:14-15). The Levitical priesthood was continued even till the death of Christ. The

---

[667] In Book 3, Chapter 4, Aphorism 3
[668] See Book 3, Chapter 5, General Introduction

ceremonial and typical worship at Jerusalem was in exercise until his days. Christ himself was made under the Law, in this, as in other regards (Galatians 4:4-5): being circumcised on the eighth day (Luke 2:21), and presented to the Lord at Jerusalem (Luke 2:22-24), going up to Jerusalem at the appointed feasts, as is noted by John in his evangelical history.[669] And keeping the ordinance of the passover in his season, till himself, as our true Passover, was sacrificed for us (Matthew 26:20, etc, 1 Corinthians 5:7). This Covenant therefore being of like nature with the Sinai Covenant, and the Sinai Covenant still remaining in force and use, even after the revealing of this Covenant, until the death of Jesus Christ, it must needs be concluded that this was a Covenant of Faith, as the Sinai Covenant has been proven to be.[670]

{2} The blessings promised in this covenant dispensation were not the blessings of the Covenant of Works, but the peculiar blessings of the Covenant of Faith, as: (i) sprinkling clean water upon them (Ezekiel 36:25), (ii) cleansing them from all their filthiness, iniquities and idols (Ezekiel 36:25, 33), (iii) oneness of heart and way to fear God forever (Jeremiah 32:39), (iv) newness of heart and spirit (Ezekiel 36:26), (v) God's putting his Spirit within them (Ezekiel 36:27), (vi) God's planting his fear in their hearts, that they shall not depart from him (Jeremiah 32:40), and (vii) making a Covenant of Peace and Reconciliation with them (Ezekiel 37:26), with various others which hereafter shall be explained in unfolding the subject matter of this Covenant.[671] And consequently, these pure evangelical blessings promised in this Covenant, plainly conclude it to be a pure evangelical Covenant of Faith.

{3} The duties conditioned and restipulated in this Covenant, are mere gospel duties peculiar to the Covenant of Faith. As: (i) True faith in Christ the promised Messiah (Isaiah 55:1-4 & 53:1-3, 11). Now the promissory part of this prophecy of Isaiah, from chapter 39 to the end of the book, does principally and especially insist upon promises of restoring the church of the

---

[669] See my *Key of the Bible*, upon John
[670] In Book 3, Chapter 4, Aphorism 2
[671] Isaiah 54:10

Jews from the misery that should befall them under the Babylonian captivity, and of completing the church's deliverance and glory at last by Christ himself, adding the Gentiles to the church.[672] And this necessarily implies faith touching these promises. (ii) The life of the just by faith, peculiarly directed to these Babylonian captives (Habakkuk 2:3-4). (iii) Repentance from former idolatries and iniquities (Isaiah 55:6-7, Jeremiah 24:7, Ezekiel 36:31-32). (iv) Obedient walking in God's judgments, and observing his statutes and doing them under David their king, namely: sincere obedience from faith in and under Christ their true David (Ezekiel 37:24-25). (v) Perseverance and constancy in covenant with God through strength of implanted and infused grace (Jeremiah 32:40). Therefore, as these covenant duties are merely evangelical, so this Covenant is merely evangelical: a Covenant of Faith and not of Works.

{4} Jesus Christ the sole foundation and Mediator of the Covenant of Faith in all ages, is notably revealed and declared in this Covenant to be the foundation and Mediator thereof; in and through whom God will confer his covenant blessings upon his people, and they shall perform their covenant duties to their God.[673] Now Christ is foundation and Mediator of no other Covenant but of the Covenant of Faith, namely: of the Covenants of Promise more typically and obscurely; of the New Covenant more clearly and truly.

Thus, this Covenant was plainly a Covenant of Faith in Christ.

[2] This Covenant was also a Covenant of Promise, having reference to Christ promised, and not as yet exhibited and performed.[674] For therein Christ is promised to be raised up afterwards (Isaiah 55:3-4, 59:20-21, Ezekiel 34:23-25 & 37:24-26) And is not represented as come already, or actually raised up already. Notwithstanding, towards the expiration and closing up of

---

[672] This I have evidently demonstrated in my *Key of the Bible*, on Isaiah §4. p.421, etc (London 1649).

[673] Isaiah 55:3-4 with Acts 13:34, Isaiah 59:20-21, Jeremiah 23:5-8, Ezekiel 34:22-25, 37:24-27, & 9:11

[674] Ephesians 2:12

this and the Sinai Covenant's administration, **Jesus Christ** was miraculously conceived and born of a virgin, and in human nature actually manifested unto Israel, as the salvation of God, the light of the Gentiles, and the glory of his people Israel.[675] So that, As it was the privilege of just and devout Simeon to have it revealed to him by the Holy Spirit that he should not see death, before he had seen the Lord's **Christ**, who, coming by the Spirit into the temple, when the parents brought in the Child **Jesus**, to do for him after the custom of the law, took him up in his arms, and blessed God with heavenly ravishment of spirit; so it was the high privilege of this covenant administration that it should not see death and be dissolved before it had seen the Lord's **Christ**, and triumphantly exalted God with this blessed babe Jesus Christ, the incarnate God, in its arms.[676]

Thus this Covenant was a Covenant of Faith in Christ, and one of the Covenants of Promise in Christ promised for time to come. This is the nature of this Covenant.

Inferences resulting from this aphorism thus unfolded, are various, namely:

(1) Hence, this Covenant is [1] divine, [2] gratuitous, [3] faithful, and [4] holy.

[1] **Divine, not human.** For God himself was the sole author, contriver, and revealer of it.[677] God alone made it, and God alone made it good. In this regard, God peculiarly appropriates this Covenant to himself as his Covenant, saying: *Neither shall the covenant of my peace be removed, saith the LORD,*

---

[675] Daniel 9:24-27, Matthew 3:1, etc. & 4:2-3, 5-6 with Luke 1:31-35 & 2:1-41
[676] Luke 2:25-28, etc.
[677] Isaiah 49:8, 54:10, 55:5, 59:21, Jeremiah 32:40, Ezekiel 34:25 & 37:26

that hath mercy on thee.[678] And elsewhere: *As for me, this is my covenant with them, saith the LORD, etc.*[679] This Covenant therefore is unquestionably of divine authority and excellency.

[2] **Gratuitous, and of God's mere free grace.** Yea therefore gratuitous: because divine. For all God's Covenants with his creatures are his gratuitous condescensions to his creatures. The Covenant of Works even in innocence was merely gratuitous, namely: *exgracia favoris*, from his grace of free favor. And every dispensation of the Covenant of Faith since the fall was merely gratuitous, namely: not only *exgracia favoris*, from his grace of favor undeserved, but also *exgracia commiserationis*, from his grace of commiseration to sinful creatures that had deserved the contrary. And such is this Covenant. God made it with them, of his own mere grace in Christ, not for any motive in or from them. *But I had pity for mine holy name, – Therefore say unto the house of Israel, Thus saith the LORD God, I do not this for your sakes, O house of Israel, but for mine holy name's sake, – Not for your sakes do I this, saith the LORD JEHOVAH, be it known unto you: Be ashamed and confounded for your own ways O house of Israel.*[680]

[3] **Faithful**. It's God's Covenant; all the promises of mercy therein are his, therefore it is most accurately faithful and sure. For God who promises cannot lie; neither can he deceive.[681] Yea, God's promise and oath are those *two immutable things, wherein it is impossible for God to lie.*[682] And this Covenant is established upon both these: not only upon his promises, but also upon his inviolable oath (Isaiah 54:9-10). How securely then might God's afflicted captives devolve themselves upon this faithful Covenant in all their extremities! Oh they too much dishonored God, and forgot this his faithful Covenant, when they spoke so despairingly: *Our bones are dried, and our*

---

[678] Isaiah 54:10
[679] Isaiah 59:21
[680] Ezekiel 36:21-22, 32
[681] Titus 1:2
[682] Hebrews 6:13, 17-18

Hope is lost, we are cut off for our parts. But what said the LORD? *Behold, O my people, I will open your graves* (namely: your Babylonian graves) *and cause you to come up out of your graves, and bring you into the land of Israel.*[683] He would open their graves, and raise up their dead and dry bones, rather than his faithful Covenant should fail, and not be performed.

[4] **Holy.** It is God's Covenant, therefore it is holy. In what sense God's Covenant and promise are holy, I have formerly explained; there see.[684] Oh what enlarged praises were due from the captive Jews to this blessed God, for so divine, gratuitous, faithful, and holy a Covenant with them in their abject state and low condition!

(2) Hence, how great was the condescension of the Creator, how high the exaltation of the creature; when the God of heaven and his captives in Babylon became confederates in one Covenant!

The people of the Jews were very low in condition, when God revealed to them this covenant dispensation. Their diadem was removed;[685] their *holy and beautiful house*, the temple, destroyed;[686] their public worship and solemn feasts overthrown;[687] their king, priests, and people of all sorts slain or carried into captivity, out of their own land of Canaan, into a foreign and pagan country, with greatest reproach;[688] they were wholly covered with shame and confusion in Babylon, as dead and dry bones buried in their graves.[689] And will the Most High God, possessor of heaven and earth cast an eye upon such dry bones, and despised captives? Yes then, even then, he looks upon them; he smiles upon them with sweetest aspects of grace; he stoops to them, he condescends to them so low; and he makes them ascend towards him so high;

---

[683] Ezekiel 37:11-12
[684] In opening God's Covenant with Abraham, Book 3, Chapter 3, Aphorism 6
[685] Ezekiel 21:26
[686] Isaiah 64:11; 2 Chronicles 36:19
[687] Lamentations 1:4 & 2:6
[688] 2 Chronicles 36:17-21
[689] Ezekiel 37

as to bring them into this blessed Covenant with himself, and to embrace these dry bones in his dearest arms of love. And all this, though they so heinously provoked him before their captivity, and so profaned his name before the heathen under their captivity.[690] Oh! Who can sufficiently admire such condescension of God, such exaltation of his people? The distance between them was infinite, yet they are brought near together in this Covenant of Peace.

And this is God's usual covenant season with his people, when they are very mean and low, such as with David when he cried out: *Who am I, and what mine house?* etc.;[691] with Israel when they were loathsome and in their blood;[692] with Abraham himself when he was in Chaldea in and ungodly an idolatrous family;[693] with Noah, when the earth was filled with violence, and wickedness abounding round about him, provoked God to sweep the whole world away with a dreadful deluge;[694] yea, with Adam himself, when by his fall he had newly ruined himself and all his posterity, without any visible possibility of relief or remedy.[695] Oh! Who would not love this God of love, that makes his creatures low estate, his very time of covenant-love?

(3) Hence, Jesus Christ – and the gospel of sinners' salvation through faith in him – was preached to the Jews in their captivity.

For this, being a Covenant of Faith in Christ, it represented and tendered Christ, and the gospel in him, unto the captives to whom it was revealed. Every dispensation of the Covenant of Faith since the fall preached Christ and the gospel in him, but the latter dispensations do this still much more clearly and fully than the former, and this last most fully and clearly of all, as hereafter will appear. And indeed Jesus Christ, and the gospel, are so preached in the

---

[690] Ezekiel 36:17-23, etc.
[691] 2 Samuel 7:18; 1 Chronicles 17
[692] Ezekiel 16:1-15
[693] Genesis 12:1-3, Joshua 24:2, Romans 4:3, 5
[694] Genesis 6:17-18, etc.
[695] Genesis 3:15

Covenant of Faith and promises dependent thereupon, that they are preached and revealed in them only.

(4) Hence, God neither forsakes nor forgets his covenant people in their deepest distresses.

How low were the Jews brought in this captivity – as low as even death and the grave to visible appearance![696] Hence they despairingly sighed out: *Our bones are dry, our hope is lost, we are cut off for our parts*, and captive Zion, most disconsolately lamented: *The LORD hath forsaken me, and my Lord hath forgotten me.* But what does the answer of God say to Zion? *Can a woman forget her sucking child, from having compassion on the son of her womb? Yea they may forget, yet will I not forget thee. Behold, I have graven thee upon the palms of my hands, thy walls are continually before me*, etc.[697] Oh, how pathetically! How sweetly! Here the Lord promises not to forget Zion, namely: his captive-people that once belonged to Zion. This promise is amplified:

[1] **By an emphatic illustration.** God's compassionate remembering of Zion far transcends the most compassionate remembrance of the tenderest mother to her dearest sucking babe. This is laid down: {1} **Interrogatively.** *Can a woman* (the more affectionate sex) *forget her sucking child, from having compassion on the son of her womb?* Can a woman, can a mother so forget, as not to compassionate, a child, which she naturally inclines to pity; a sucking child, which she usually more tenders than elder children; her sucking child, which together with the milk from the breast, draws love from her heart; her sucking child of her own womb, which her bowels more yearn upon, than upon any sucking nurse-child of another; and this, the son of her womb, which the mother usually embraces with warmer affections than the daughter of her womb: Can a woman, a mother forget her pity to such a babe? How

---

[696] Ezekiel 37:1-15
[697] Isaiah 49:13-18

unusual! {2} **Affirmatively.** Yea they may forget. It's possible a woman may be so unwomanly, yea a mother so unmotherly in some extremities, as to forget and be hard-hearted to the fruit of their own wombs. Extremity of hunger overmastered natural affection: the pitiful women did boil and eat their own children in the siege of Samaria and Jerusalem.[698] {3} **Negatively.** *Yet will I not forget thee.* God will be more constantly, immovably, unchangeably mindful of Zion, and compassionate to Zion. God will be more motherly to his captives, than any mother to her male sucking babe.

[2] **By a convincing argumentation:** {1} partly, from his engraving of them upon the palms of his hands, namely: their portraiture, their memorial was like a signet graven upon his hand. God will as soon blot out of mind and forget his own hands, as his Zion. {2} Partly, from his placing their walls still in his sight. Their ruined walls of Jerusalem were still before him, as to their commiseration,[699] as to their reparation.[700] Or, their intended walls of their new city, **Jehovah Shammah,**[701] or of the New Jerusalem,[702] are still in my thoughts as to the happy model of them, which I intend in after time.

Thus God remembers and pities his afflicted, in their low estate, because his loving kindness is forevermore.[703] Yea if there be any condition wherein God expresses more tender yearning bowels to his people than others, it is in their afflictions.[704]

(5) Hence, in the greatest extremities of tribulation, God's Covenant of Faith in Christ yields sweetest consolation.

This is evident here, by the course which God took for comforting and supporting his afflicted and disconsolate captives in Babylon, namely: by

---

[698] 2 Kings 6:24-30, Lamentations 4:10
[699] Lamentations 2:7-8
[700] Psalm 102:14
[701] Ezekiel 48:35
[702] Revelation 21:1, etc.
[703] Psalm 136:23
[704] See Isaiah 63:9, Lamentations 3:31-33, Zechariah 1:14-15 & 2:7-8

revealing to them his Covenant of Faith in Jesus Christ, by his prophets. This he peculiarly propounds, as his great antidote against all their afflictions and miseries in Babylon, and against all their diffidence, despondencies, and despair. This Covenant, full of good works and comfortable words, was propounded as their chief cordial. This held up their heads and hearts above waters. This opened a door of hope for them, even in the valley of Achor. This Covenant even revived them in their very graves.

And no wonder, for: [1] this Covenant assured them of their return from Babylon to Zion, from captivity to liberty, and under that as a type of the everlasting redemption of God's elect by Christ, out of their spiritual bondage under sin, and Satan.[705] [2] This Covenant assured them of the rebuilding of Jerusalem and the temple with greater glory than formerly, and therein typically of the building of his new city, and new spiritual temple, of both Jews and Gentiles, with surpassing spiritual glory.[706] [3] This Covenant assured them of pardon and cleansing, of justification and sanctification from all their idols and former uncleannesses.[707] [4] This Covenant assured them of a rich confluence of choicest spiritual blessings, from the saving influence of his Holy Spirit.[708] [5] This Covenant assured them, That **David**, namely: **Jesus Christ**, the true David of God, should be their prince and king forevermore.[709] [6] This Covenant assured them that the LORD would be their God, and they should be his people, and that his tabernacle should be with them, yea he would set his sanctuary in the midst of them forevermore.[710] God filled this Covenant with these choicest comforts, and made up this composition with these precious cordials, so that this Covenant made with them might be fuller of comfort to them, than all Babylon's bondage of disconsolation.

---

[705] Jeremiah 32:37-40, Isaiah chapters 42-44
[706] Isaiah 44:26-28 & 61 throughout, Haggai 2:7-9, Ezekiel 40:1 to the end of the book.
[707] Ezekiel 37:23, 26 & 36:25, 29
[708] Ezekiel 37:21 to the end, 36:25-32, Jeremiah 32:38-41
[709] Ezekiel 37:24-25
[710] Jeremiah 32:38, Ezekiel 37:26-28

When therefore we shall fall into extremity of tribulation: let us chiefly have recourse to this blessed fountain of consolation, God's Covenant of Faith in Jesus Christ, especially to the New Covenant. [1] Herein are most suitable comforts against all sorts of distresses. [2] Herein are most sufficient comforts against all degrees of distresses. [3] Herein our comforts are laid upon the surest rock and most impregnable foundation, namely: upon free grace, faith, divine truth, the Spirit of grace, Jesus Christ, and on God himself, *who is over all blessed forever, Amen*. [4] Herein are compendiously comprised and concentered all the comforts of the Bible, far surpassing all the comforts and discomforts of the world. Run hither therefore, O all ye afflicted, tempest-tossed souls, lay your mouth of faith to the Covenant's breasts, then suck and be satisfied with its blessed consolations.

(6) Hence, though God's people by their sins turn their mercies into miseries: yet God alone of his wisdom and goodness turns those miseries into mercies.

The sins of these Jews turned their mercies into miseries, namely: their glory into shame, their prosperity into penury, their liberty into captivity, their Zion into Babylon, etc. *A fruitful land turneth he into barrenness, for the wickedness of them that dwell therein.*[711] Oh what havoc was made of Canaan, Jerusalem, temple, of all their precious and pleasant things – yea of all sexes and degrees amongst them, through their iniquities! But it is only the infinite wisdom and goodness of God, that according to this his Covenant, turns their miseries again into mercies, their water into wine, their darkness into light, their bondage into liberty, and their Babylon into Zion. They could destroy their temple and holy city; God alone could cause them both to be rebuilt: They could cast themselves out of Canaan; God alone brings them back again into Canaan. They could bring themselves into Babylonian bondage and graves; God alone can break their bonds and bring them out of their graves:

---

[711] Psalm 107:34

etc. How often would God's people undo themselves, if God himself did not prevent them! And how long should they remain undone, if God himself did not restore them! From ourselves is our judgment; from our God is our salvation.

(7) Hence, God's Covenant with his captive Jews, so far as it is a Covenant of Faith, without peculiar restriction to the Jews, is applicable and useful unto the people of God now under the New Testament.

The faithful in all after-ages have this advantage of all that went before them, that they may extract much spiritual advantage to themselves, not only from God's present covenant dispensation to them, but from all that went before. And we under the New Testament have in this regard advantages surpassing all other ages. We may improve to ourselves all the mysteries of the New Testament fully: and all the benefits, comforts, promises and mysteries of the Covenants of Promise from Adam to this day, so far as they are of common concernment to the faithful, and not particularly restrained to such persons or times alone. Let us therefore accordingly consider them wisely, apply them believingly, improve them advantageously. The Covenants of Promise, were the New Covenant veiled and in its minority; the New Covenant, is the Covenants of Promise revealed in their maturity.

Thus of the author, occasion, impulsives, federates, and nature of this Covenant.

Aphorism 2

The Subject Matter or Substance Of God's Covenant with the Captive Jews.

The subject matter or substance of God's Covenant with his captive people in Babylon, consisted:

(1) In many excellent covenant mercies or blessings promised to them, on God's part, such as: [1] his raising up of **Christ** to them; [2] redeeming and returning them from Babylonian captivity into their own land; [3] cleansing them from all their spiritual defilements; [4] putting his Spirit within them, for new framing and spiritualizing their heart; [5] his presence in his sanctuary and tabernacle among them by his Spirit and Word forever; [6] the greatest covenant relation between him and them, that he would be their God, and they should be his people; [7] the mutual covenant constancy between God and them in this everlasting covenant: he would not turn from them, and they should not depart from him.

(2) In sundry covenant duties required and restipulated from them to God, on their part, such as: [1] faith in the Messiah promised; [2] repentance from all their former iniquities; [3] true obedience unto God; [4] becoming God's covenant people; [5] enquiring of God, for doing all his promised mercies to them.

To these particulars especially, we may refer and reduce the chief substance and subject matter of this Covenant: whether mercies promised or duties restipulated. And, here it is very observable that, as this Covenant with the captive Jews was the last of all the **Covenants of Promise**, immediately preceding the **New Covenant**, and at last exhibiting the **Messiah** to the world, according to the tenure of all foregoing Covenants, so it was the nearest and most like to the New Covenant of all others in [1] spiritualness, [2] clearness, and [3] fulness. And therefore now we are come to the very borders and suburbs of the New Covenant. Now Christ is near at hand indeed, and therefore now, let our thoughts be proportionably elevated to suitable spiritualness of contemplation. The matter of this Covenant, I shall unfold in two distinct sections.

Section 1

The Subject Matter of this Covenant on God's Part.

(1) **The subject matter or substance of this Covenant on God's part consisted in many excellent covenant mercies promised therein to his afflicted captives.**

God's promises and promised mercies under this covenant dispensation are exceedingly abundant. But I shall only insist upon such promised blessings as are laid down in Isaiah, Jeremiah, and Ezekiel, where mention is made of this Covenant, or where there is a more evident and eminent tendency thereunto. All of this may be comprised in those seven particulars in the aphorism, which I explain briefly as follows:

---

[1] His raising up the *Messiah*, namely: *Jesus Christ* unto them.

This is a primary and fundamental mercy; a fountain mercy whence the rest spring, and therefore deservedly challenges [requires] the first place and consideration. Now the Messiah is promised to them under a manifold notion and capacity, namely:

{1} **As their covenant-redeemer that should deliver them both from their corporal bondage in Babylon and from their spiritual bondage under sin, death, Satan, and so on, typified by that Babylonian bondage.** *Thus saith the LORD, In an acceptable time have I heard thee, and in a day of salvation have I helped thee; and I will preserve thee, and give thee for a* **covenant of the people,** *to establish the earth, to cause to inherit the desolate heritages; That thou mayest say to the prisoners, go forth: To them that are in* *darkness, shew yourselves: They shall feed in the ways, and their pastures shall be in all high places. They shall not hunger nor thirst, neither shall the heat nor sun smite them: For, he that hath mercy on them shall lead them, even by the springs of water shall he guide them. And I will make all my mountains away, and my high-ways shall be exalted. Behold, these shall come from far: and lo these from the north, and from the west, and these from the land of Sinim. Sing O heavens, and be joyful O earth, and break forth into singing oh mountains: for God hath comforted his people, and will have mercy upon his afflicted. But Zion said, The LORD hath forsaken me, and my Lord hath forgotten me. Can a woman forget her sucking child, that she should not have compassion on the son of her womb? Yea, they may forget, yet will I not forget thee. Behold I have graven thee upon the palms of my hands, thy walls are continually before me. Thy children shall make haste: Thy destroyers, and they that made thee waste shall go forth of thee.*[712]

In this sweet paragraph, for the clearing of it briefly, note these particulars. namely:

(i) God's acceptance of Christ, and assistance to Christ, in his mediatory office. *In an acceptable time*, etc (verse 8).

(ii) God's promise of Christ as a covenant to his captives, and afflicted in Babylon, and under them to all his spiritual captives: *And I will give thee for a* **covenant** *of the people* (verse 8). Christ is not properly but figuratively, and by a manifold metonymy *a covenant of the people,* namely: partly, as he is a foundation of the Covenant, in whom all the promises are made, and made good, being *yea and amen in him*.[713] Partly, as he is the peculiar mediator of the Covenant of Faith, in all ages: of the Covenants of Promise veiled under types; of the New Covenant revealed in truth of his humanity: partly, as he is a very considerable part of the matter of the Covenant promised; partly, as he is

---

[712] Isaiah 49:8-18, etc.
[713] 2 Peter 1:3-4; 2 Corinthians 1:20

one special end and scope of the Covenant, every Covenant tending more and more clearly to reveal him.

(iii) God's end and intent in this his promising of Christ as a Covenant, namely: the restoration of his people from corporal captivity in Babylon,[714] and from spiritual captivity under sin, etc.[715] Christ must effect and bring to pass both these: whatever be the instruments, he alone is author of both. (a) Christ should restore their land, and reinvest them in their desolate heritages (verse 8). (b) Christ should send both his corporal and spiritual captives out of their darksome bondage (verse 9). (c) Christ should supply them with all necessities in the way from Babylon to Zion, from sin to glory, such as food against hunger, water against thirst, shelter against scorching heat of the sun – as sometimes he dealt with Israel going from Egypt to Canaan, through the wilderness. (d) Christ should facilitate and level their way for them, depressing mountains, elevating valleys. All impediments and difficulties he should remove (verse 11). (e) Christ should fetch his exiles and captives from places most remote; both far remote from Canaan, and from one another; namely: from far, that is, from the Persian land eastward, as some; from the north, that is, from Babylon; from the west, that is, from the Philistines' land (see Isaiah 9:12); or, from the western transmarine islands such as Macedonia, Candia, Cyprus, etc.[716] {*From the land of Sinim*} – that is, from Egypt southward, a chief city whereof is called Sin, *the strength of Egypt* (Ezekiel 30:15-16). Thus Christ should gather them from all the four quarters of their dispersion (verse 12) – a notable type of Christ's gathering up his spiritual captives from all the four corners of the world.[717]

(iv) The amplification of Christ's restoration of his captives, corporal, and spiritual, namely: (a) By the joy of heaven and earth hereupon (verse 13). (b)

---

[714] Ezra 1:1-4, Isaiah 43:14], 44:28, 45:13, 51:14, Psalm 107:10-14
[715] Luke 13:16, John 8:31-32, 34, Acts 26:18, Colossians 1:13; 2 Timothy 2:16, Hebrews 2:14-15; 1 John 3:8, Isaiah 42:7, 61:1-2, Luke 1:71, 74-75
[716] See the late London Annotations also expounding this place to this effect.
[717] Luke 13:29

By the constancy of God's love to his, and of his care of their redemption, even then, when they thought themselves quite forgotten and forsaken of God. This is urged most pathetically: as I have formerly noted (verses 14-18). (c) By the numerous confluence of children from all parts, flowing to them, as to the mother church (verses 18-24). O what sweet promised blessings are these in Jesus Christ, if diligently considered!

{2} **As the sure mercies of David whereon God's everlasting Covenant is founded and built.** *Ho everyone that thirsteth, come ye to the waters, etc. – And I will make an everlasting covenant with you, even the sure mercies of David. Behold I have given him for a witness of the people, a leader and commander to the people.*[718] This sweet bundle of promises seems to be directed immediately to the captive Jews and mediately and in them to all such spiritual captives as need refreshment and comfort. And here Christ is offered as an all-sufficient supply and support of them both. In him, God will make them an everlasting Covenant: even the *sure mercies of David.*[719] As if he had said: "Though David's royal seed seems to fail and be cut off by your Babylonian captivity, and though this covenant mercy which I have covenanted with David touching the perpetual throne and kingdom of his seed, seem to be made void: yet know ye that in Christ it shall certainly and infallibly be performed, he chiefly is the sure mercies of David, the sure foundation, root, and mercy of mercies promised to David, and he shall be performed and made good to them."[720]

This interpretation helps us also well to understand the apostle's argumentation from this Scripture. For hence he proves Christ's resurrection from the dead, saying: *And as concerning that he raised him up from the dead, now no more to return to corruption, he said on this wise, I will give you the sure mercies of David.*[721] The argument is by a consequence to this effect:

---

[718] Isaiah 55:1-4 compared with Acts 13:34
[719] Isaiah 49:8; 2 Corinthians 1:20; 2 Peter 1:3-4
[720] 2 Samuel 7:11-18, 23:3-5, Psalm 89:2-4, 28-29, 35-37 & 132:11-12, Luke 1:32-33
[721] Acts 13:34 with Isaiah 55:3

- God promised or covenanted to give them the sure mercies of David, namely: especially his everlasting kingdom, chiefly to be accomplished in Christ, the chief seed of David.[722]
- Consequently, Christ could not be swallowed up by death, But must needs rise again. For if Christ should be swallowed up by death, David's kingdom and Christ's kingdom too, would be utterly swallowed up. Thus it is a very cogent argument.

Further, I offer this consideration upon this promise of Christ here: Christ seems therein to be promised as a complete Mediator, by whom their soul should live; if they would come to him believe and delight in him (verses 1-3). And the three great branches of his mediatory office are, not obscurely, insinuated. namely: (i) His **priesthood**, and the eternity thereof, in that he was *the sure mercies of David* who, though he died and was buried to make satisfaction for our sins – one act or part of his priesthood – yet he would rise again and ascend to make constant intercession for us, which is the other great act of his Priesthood. (ii) His **prophecy**, in that he is promised as a witness to the people, namely: a witness, testifier, or teacher of God's will touching sinners' salvation,[723] whereupon he is called, *Amen, the true and faithful witness.*[724] As also, a witness or testifier of the truth of God's promises, which are all yea, and amen, in him, and in him alone.[725] (iii) His **kingship**. In that he is promised, as a *leader and commander to the people.* A leader, as the word is sometimes translated (2 Chronicles 32:21) or a *ruler*, as 1 Chronicles 9:20 & 11:2, or a *prince*, as Ezekiel 28:2. This style is also given to Christ in the New Testament, namely: a *leader* or *archduke* (Hebrews 2:10 & 12:2), a *ruler* (Matthew 2:6 from Micah 5:2) and a *prince* (Revelation 1:5); a *commander of*

---

[722] See Beza, Drusium, Ludovic De Dieu in this place.
[723] John 7:16-17, 12:49-50, 17:6 & 18:37
[724] Revelation 3:14
[725] Isaiah 43:10, Hebrews 7:22; 2 Corinthians 1:20

the people, a supreme commander, whose commands all are bound to obey in all things, under pain of eternal death (Acts 3:22-23, 2 Thessalonians 1:8, Hebrews 5:9). These denominations therefore do plainly point out his kingship.

{3} **As a branch of righteousness growing up to David, and as a plant of renown raised up unto them.** Ezekiel – revealing many promises for the comfort of the Babylonian captives – said: *And I will make with them a covenant of peace, and I will cause the evil beasts to cease out of the land*, etc. – *And I will raise up for them a plant of renown*, etc.[726] Who this plant of renown was, Jeremiah sets forth, in some such like promises directed to the said captives. *In those days, and at that time, will I cause the* **branch** *of* **righteousness** *to grow up unto David, and he shall execute judgement and righteousness in the land. In those days shall Judah be saved, and Jerusalem shall dwell safely: And this is the name wherewith she shall be called the LORD our Righteousness.*[727]

In this promise of Christ, note four things especially. namely:

(i) **The time of the promise**: *In those days, and at that time*. Which days? What time? namely: In the days and time when God should cause his people's captivity to return, and bring them from Babylon. The context before and after plainly point out this time.[728] So that this promise has special reference to God's Covenant with his captives, and that in performance of his Covenant with David.[729]

(ii) **The description of the person of Christ promised**: the branch of righteousness growing up to David. He is called: (a) *The* **branch**:[730] metaphorically, in regard to his resemblance of a branch according to his human nature, sprouting or budding out of a stock or root. And in allusion to

---

[726] Ezekiel 34:25, etc, 29
[727] Jeremiah 33:15-17
[728] Jeremiah 33:6-8 to the end, particularly see verse 26
[729] Jeremiah 33:17-23
[730] Zechariah 3:8, 6:12, Isaiah 11:1, Jeremiah 23:5, 33:15, Isaiah 53:2

these Scriptures; from נֵצֶר *netzer, a branch*, it is thought by some that Christ is elsewhere called *a Nazarene*.[731] *And he came and dwelt in a city called Nazareth, that it might be fulfilled which was spoken by the prophets, He shall be called a Nazarene*. Not that he was a Nazarite by vow, as the antitype of Samson. Nor that he was so called from the city Nazareth, where he was educated, for where do the prophets intimate this his denomination from that city?[732] But from allusion to the word נֵצֶר *netzer, a branch*, which name is often given to Christ by the *prophets*.[733] (b) *The branch growing up to David*. Because he should bud, sprout and spring from David's root or stock according to the flesh (Isaiah 11:1). (c) *The branch of righteousness*, namely: *formally*, as being most righteous in himself, the very righteousness of God (Isaiah 53:9, 11, Hebrews 4:15 and 7:26, Psalm 45:7). *Materially*, as being made of God the very substance and matter of our righteousness, imputed to us through faith (1 Corinthians 1:30, 2 Corinthians 5:21, Jeremiah 23:5-6), and *efficiently*, as being the author of righteousness to his [people], both in justifying and sanctifying them (Isaiah 53:11, 1 Corinthians 1:30). And also in acting and executing righteousness for them in the land (Jeremiah 33:15), as the true Melchizedek, or King of Righteousness in and over the church (Hebrews 7:2, Isaiah 11:4-5, Revelation 19:11). From all this, Christ may well be called *a plant of renown*.

(iii) **The office of Christ thus described**: execution of judgment and righteousness in the land.

(iv) **The effect of this office of Christ**. Partly, the salvation and secure condition of Judah and Jerusalem, namely: of the church shadowed out by Judah and Jerusalem. Partly, his communication of his righteousness to Jerusalem, to his Church so effectually, that she may glory in that very name of Christ: *And this is the name wherewith she shall be called, The LORD our*

---

[731] Matthew 2:23
[732] Judges 13:5
[733] See Salomo Glassius in *Philologia Sacra*, l.2 Part 1 Tract 2, Section 4, page 423; John Piscator on Matthew 2:23

righteousness.[734] This name is formerly ascribed to Christ himself, where mention is made of God's bringing them out of the north country, namely: Babylon, a greater deliverance than that of old from Egypt. But here it's attributed to the church. Calvin has a good note hereupon: "Before, the prophet testified that Christ was the true **Jehovah** whence our righteousness flows; now he declares the church so truly to perceive the same, that she may glory in the very name. In the former place is put the fountain and cause of righteousness; in this latter, the effect of righteousness."[735]

{4} **As David their shepherd, prince, and king forever.** Christ is the true David: of whom David himself was but a type, as I have formerly manifested. Thus Ezekiel comforting the people against their unfaithful shepherds, and against their dispersion into heathen countries, Babylon, etc, says: *And I will set up one shepherd over them, and he shall feed them, even my servant* **David** (namely: Jesus Christ the true David), *he shall feed them, and he shall be their shepherd. And I the LORD will be their God, and my servant David a prince among them, I the LORD have spoken it. And I will make with them a covenant of peace, and will cause the evil beasts to cease out of the land: and they shall dwell safely in the wilderness, and sleep in the woods,* etc.[736] And elsewhere, this is one clause in his Covenant with his captives, and one of their covenant mercies after their return from Babylon: *And David my servant shall be king over them: and they all shall have one shepherd, – And my servant David shall be their prince forever. Moreover I will make a covenant of peace with them, it shall be an everlasting covenant with them,* etc.[737] Jeremiah also upon like occasion testifies: *Thus saith the LORD, David shall never want a man to sit upon the throne of the house of Israel. – If you can break my covenant of the day, and my covenant of the night, and that there should not be day and night in their season; then may also my covenant be broken with* **David** *my*

---

[734] Jeremiah 23:6-8
[735] John Calvin, *Institutes of the Christian Religion*, 1.13.9
[736] Ezekiel 34:23-25, etc.
[737] Ezekiel 37:24-26

servant, that he should not have a son to reign upon his throne. – Thus saith the LORD, If my covenant be not with day and night, and if I have not appointed the ordinances of heaven and earth: Then will I cast away the seed of Jacob, and David my servant, so that I will not take any of his seed to be rulers over the seed of Abraham, Isaac and Jacob: for I will cause their captivity to return, and have mercy on them.[738]

In these paragraphs, note: (i) That God has reference therein to his Covenant with his captives, styling it a {*Covenant of Peace*}: partly, because it reveals peace and reconciliation between God and them; partly, because it assures of peace and prosperity on every side after their return from Babylon; And also {*an everlasting Covenant*}, that is, everlasting *absolutely*, in respect to Christ the true David; everlasting *respectively*, namely: long-lasting in respect of David's ordinary seed that should rule over the house of Jacob.[739] (ii) That one blessing of this Covenant should be a continued succession of David's seed to feed and govern Israel: yea **David** himself (not the typical David, dead long before, but the true **David**, Jesus Christ) should be their shepherd, prince, and king forever – and he alone. (iii) That this constant succession of David's seed upon his throne, covenanted to David, should be as inviolable as the covenanted course and revolution of day and night in their season. (iv) That in order to the performance of this mercy, God would cause their captivity to return. For in that sad and long captivity, God's Covenant with David lay as dead, and David's seed as buried and cut off; but God would deliver them thence, and revive them out of their graves.

Thus of God's promise to raise up the Messiah unto them.

---

[738] Jeremiah 33:17, 20-22, 25-26
[739] Jeremiah 33:6, 9-15

[2] His redeeming them out of Babylon's captivity, and bringing them into their own land.

As he had promised them the Redeemer, so he promises them redemption by him. This mercy is much insisted upon in this Covenant – by Isaiah: testifying that Christ should therefore redeem them, as I have noted;[740] by Ezekiel, as: *Thus saith the Lord GOD, behold I will take the children of Israel from among the heathen whither they be gone, and will gather them on every side, and will bring them into their own land.* – *Moreover I will make a covenant of peace with them, it shall be an everlasting covenant with them, and I will place them, and multiply them, etc.*[741] And elsewhere: *For I will take you from among the heathen, and gather you out of all countries, and will bring you into your own land.*[742]

And again: *Thus saith the Lord GOD: Behold I, even I will both search my sheep, and seek them out. As a shepherd seeketh out his flock in the day that he is among his sheep that are scattered: so will I seek out my sheep, and will deliver them out of all places, where they have been scattered in the cloudy and dark day. And I will bring them out from the people, and gather them from the countries: and will bring them to their own land, and feed them upon the mountains of Israel by the rivers, and in all the inhabited places in the country. I will feed them in a good pasture, and upon the high mountains of Israel shall their fold be: there they shall lie in a good fold, and in a fat pasture shall they feed upon the mountains of Israel. I will feed my flock, and cause them to lie down, saith the Lord GOD, I will seek that which was lost, and bring again that which was driven away, and will bind up that which was broken, and will strengthen that which was sick*; etc. *And I will set up one shepherd over them, and he shall feed them, Even my servant* **David**; *he shall feed them, and he*

---

[740] Isaiah 49:8-24
[741] Ezekiel 37:21, 25-26
[742] Ezekiel 36:24

shall be their shepherd. *And I the LORD will be their God, and my servant David a prince among them. I the LORD have spoken it. And I will make with them a covenant of peace, and will cause the evil beasts to cease out of the land: and they shall dwell safely in the wilderness, and sleep in the woods*, etc.[743]

Here, under the metaphor of a good shepherd seeking and restoring his flock that was dispersed and driven away and torn by wild beasts, and bringing them again into their own folds and pastures, God sets forth his seeking of his dispersed, captivated and distressed people, scattered and torn by those wild-beasts, the Chaldeans, and his bringing them from Babylon and all places of their dispersion into the land of Israel.

By Jeremiah, also this blessing is promised: *Thus saith the LORD the God of Israel, – Behold, I will gather them out of all countries, whither I have driven them in mine anger, and in my fury, and in great wrath; and I will bring them again unto this place, and I will cause them to dwell safely. – And I will make an everlasting covenant with them, – And fields shall be bought in this land, whereof ye say, It is desolate without man or beast, it is given into the hand of the Chaldeans. Men shall buy fields for money, and subscribe evidences and seal them, and take witnesses in the land of Benjamin, and in the places about Jerusalem, and in the cities of Judah, and in the cities of the mountains, and in the cities of the valley, and in the cities of the south: for I will cause their captivity to return, saith the LORD.*[744]

And elsewhere under the type of good figs, he foretells their return from captivity: *Thus saith the LORD the God of Israel, like these good figs, so will I acknowledge them that are carried away captive of Judah, whom I have sent out of this place into the land of the Chaldeans for their good. For I will set mine eyes upon them for good, and I will bring them again to this land, and I will build them, and not pull them down: and I will plant them, and not pluck them up*, etc.[745] *– Behold the days come saith the LORD, that they shall no more*

---

[743] Ezekiel 34:11-19, 23-25, etc.
[744] Jeremiah 32:36-37, 40, 43-44; see also Jeremiah 33:5-7, 8-15
[745] Jeremiah 24:5-7

say, The LORD liveth which brought up the children of Israel out of the land of Egypt: But the LORD liveth which brought up, and which led the seed of the house of Israel out of the north country (namely: Chaldea and Babylon, which lay northward from Canaan)[746] *and from all countries whither I had driven them, and they shall dwell in their own land.*[747]

Now because this blessing of their redemption and return from Babylon into their own land is so often repeated and urged in this Covenant, so that the drooping and broken spirits of the captives might be raised up and comforted, after their long heavy and wasting captivity, it may be very useful to consider a little, these few things for the further illustrating of this great covenant redemption promised; namely: {1} the variety of promised mercies appertaining to this eminent mercy, {2} the emphatical arguments whereby God labors to persuade his captives of their return, {3} the accomplishment of this mercy in its season, and {4} the spiritual mystery of this their redemption from Babylonian bondage, typifying the spiritual redemption of God's elect from the greater bondage of sin, death, Satan, etc.

{1} **Firstly, the mercies promised, with relation and subordination to their redemption and return from Babylon, were very many. Take a taste of a few. The Lord promised:**

(i) **To remove such impediments out of the way as might hinder their Return from Babylon.** As: (a) Their brutish Babylonian oppressors, that like evil beasts did drive and keep them out of their land. *And I will make with them a covenant of peace, and will cause the evil beasts* (the cruel Chaldeans) *to cease out of the land, and they shall dwell safely in the wilderness, and sleep in the woods.* (b) Their strong bondage which they were under in Babylon; — *And they shall be safe in their land, and shall know that I am the LORD, when I have broken the bands of their yoke, and delivered them out of the hand of*

---

[746] Jeremiah 23:7-8, 16:14-15
[747] Jeremiah 6:1, 22

those that served themselves of them.[748] (c) The deadness and hopelessness of their condition in Babylon, they being as helpless and hopeless as dead dry bones, yea as the dead in their graves. Whereupon they despaired of deliverance, saying: *Our bones are dried, and our hope is lost, we are cut off for our parts.*[749] But God assures them that even this, that they were as dry bones or dead bodies laid low and fast in their Babylonian graves, should not at all hinder their return from Babylon. And this he does partly by a vision of dry bones clothed with sinews, flesh and skin, and reviving, represented to Ezekiel, and partly, by Ezekiel's explaining and applying this vision to the captives at God's appointment.[750] *Then he said unto me, Son of man, These bones are the whole house of Israel: Behold they say, Our bones are dried, and our hope is lost, we are cut off for our parts. Therefore prophesy and say unto them, thus saith the Lord GOD; Behold O my people, I will open your graves, and cause you to come up out of your graves, and bring you into the land of Israel. And ye shall know that I am the LORD, when I have opened your graves, O my people, and brought you up out of your graves, And shall put my Spirit in you, and ye shall live, and I shall place you in your own land: Then shall ye know, that I the LORD have spoken it, and performed it, saith the LORD.*[751] All this was fulfilled when Cyrus by his decree delivered the Jews from Babylon.[752]

(ii) **To plant them firmly in their own land, and to rejoice in doing them good most affectionately and entirely.** *And I will make an everlasting covenant with them, – yea I will rejoice over them to do them good, and I will plant them in this land assuredly* (Hebrew: *in truth*, or *in firm-stability*) *with my whole heart, and with my whole soul. For thus saith the LORD, like as I have brought all this great evil upon this people, so will I bring upon them all the good that I have promised them, etc.*[753]

---

[748] Ezekiel 34:27
[749] Ezekiel 37:11
[750] Ezekiel 37:1-11
[751] Ezekiel 37:11-14
[752] Ezra 1:1-2, etc.
[753] Jeremiah 32:40-44

(iii) **To make them dwell safely and securely in their own land.** *Behold I will gather them out of all countries whither I have driven them;*[754] – *And I will bring them again unto this place, and I will cause them to dwell safely. And I will make with them a covenant of peace, and will cause the evil beasts to cease out of the land, and they shall dwell safely in the wilderness, and sleep in the woods.* – *And they shall be safe in their land.* – *And they shall no more be a prey to the heathen, neither shall the beasts of the land devour them; but they shall dwell safely, and none shall make them afraid.*[755]

(iv) **To unite them into one nation and kingdom in their land after their return.** This is set forth: (a) *Parabolically*, under the parable of two sticks,[756] namely: the stick of Joseph, and the stick of Judah, both joined together and becoming one in the prophet's hands. (b) *Plainly*, by the Lord's explaining the meaning of this parable, namely: that these two sticks should be one in God's hand.[757] And yet more clearly: *Thus saith the LORD, behold I will take the children of Israel from among the heathen whither they be gone, and gather them on every side, and bring them into their own land. And I will make them one nation in the land upon the Mountains of Israel, and one king shall be king to them all: And they shall be no more two nations, neither shall they be divided into two kingdoms anymore at all. Neither shall they defile themselves anymore with their idols, nor with their detestable things,* – *And* **David** *my servant shall be king over them: And they all shall have one shepherd, etc.*[758]

Here the two sticks did signify two rods or two scepters, namely: the one stick for Judah and for the children of Israel his companions (Ezekiel 37:16)[759] signifying the scepter of Judah in the house of David, whereunto the tribe of Judah and Benjamin, with the city Jerusalem and many of the Levites still

---

[754] Jeremiah 32:37, 40
[755] Ezekiel 34:25, 27-28
[756] Ezekiel 37:15-17
[757] Ezekiel 37:18-19
[758] Ezekiel 37:21-24, 26
[759] See Ludwig Lavater, Homily 160 in Ezekiel

faithfully adhered; the other stick for Joseph, the stick of Ephraim, and for all the house of Israel, his companions (Ezekiel 37:16). This is called {*the stick of Joseph*} because Jeroboam – who was the first king of Israel after the division of the kingdom – was of the tribe of Ephraim, which *Ephraim* was one of the sons of Joseph. These two sticks of Judah and Israel joined together, and – becoming one in the prophet's hands – shadowed out the two scepters or kingdoms of Judah and Israel, which should after their return from captivity become one nation and one kingdom in God's hand (namely: by God's mighty power), and this under one shepherd and one king: Jesus Christ the true **David**.[760] And to this end, their idolatry (which at first divided them into two kingdoms, through God's just judgment) should now wholly be removed away from them. For clearing this great blessing of the union of these two kingdoms, consider briefly: (a) a narrative of their division, and (b) the accomplishment of this union.

(a) Israel – weary of their government by judges – desired a king. God gave them their first king, Saul, in his anger, and took him away in his wrath – thus chastising their inordinate desire.[761] After him, God made David king, and by covenant, established the kingdom upon him and his seed forever: *absolutely* upon his extraordinary seed Jesus Christ, and *conditionally* upon his ordinary seed, if they should keep his Covenant and testimonies. Solomon, David's immediate seed, forsook God and his Covenant by idolatry, through the enticements of his many strange wives. God forsook him and raised up adversaries against him, one whereof was his own servant Jeroboam the son of Nebat. And when Solomon was dead, the kingdom – which was united and one, as the nation one under David and Solomon – was divided into two in the days of Rehoboam: Jeroboam obtaining ten tribes of the twelve. This division occasioned constant enmity between Judah and Israel – especially by reason of their different religions. For Jeroboam – fearing that the ten tribes would

---

[760] Ezekiel 37:17-19
[761] Hosea 13:11

revolt from him to their ancient crown of David's house by going to worship God at Jerusalem – in carnal policy erected an idolatrous false worship in the two calves at Dan and Bethel, which turned to the ruin of his house, and of the house of Israel cleaving to his idolatry, so that at last, they were carried captive into Assyria by Shalmaneser, taking Samaria, and killing Hoshea their last king, and dispersing most of Israel into Media, Persia and other countries. Now in this Covenant, God promises to unite this divided nation and kingdom into one, under one King David, and to take away all their idolatry, which was the foundation of their former division, so that thereby, the miseries of their divided state should be removed; and the ancient happiness of their united state, as in the time of David and Solomon, should be restored.

(b) This covenanted union of these two sticks, these two kingdoms into one, has a twofold accomplishment: (1) literal and (2) mystical. (1) *Literally*, this was fulfilled when Judah was returned from their captivity in Babylon after seventy years, upon Cyrus' decree after he had taken Babylon – at which time, many of Judah returned into Canaan, rebuilt Jerusalem and the temple, etc, but some of them (types of carnal men preferring earth before heaven, and temporals before spirituals) stayed behind. And it is very probable that about the same time, many of the dispersed of Israel came back from Media, Persia, and other places of dispersion (through the indulgence of Cyrus and Darius) and joined themselves to them of Judah under the government of Zerubbabel, and other rulers of David's race. But these rulers were not called *kings* as formerly, lest the monarchs, from whom they had received so great favors, and to whom as their lords they paid tributes (1 Esdras 9) should be offended. Thus they – according to the letter of this Covenant – became one nation and one kingdom under David, under the seed of David, types of Christ; nor were they divided into two kingdoms as formerly anymore. (2) *Mystically and typically*, this union of these two kingdoms has its accomplishment: [1] partly, in the uniting of the Gentiles (typified by the kingdom of the ten tribes dispersed into pagan countries) to the church of the Jews under one shepherd,

Jesus Christ, by his death *breaking down the middle wall of partition, and destroying the enmity between them*,[762] namely: the ceremonial worship, that *law of commandments contained in ordinances, for to make in himself of twain* (namely: of Jews and Gentiles) *one new man, so making peace*, etc. And thus that of our Savior was fulfilled: *As the Father knoweth me, even so know I the Father: and I lay down my life for the sheep.* (namely: of the Jews) *And other sheep* (namely: of the Gentiles) *I have, which are not of this fold: Them also I must bring, and they shall hear my voice; and there shall be one fold, and one shepherd,* namely: of both Jews and Gentiles, incorporated into one church.[763] [2] Partly, in the gathering together, uniting, and perfecting all the elect in one mystical body of Christ: when they all shall *come in the unity of the faith, and of the knowledge of the Son of God, unto a perfect man, unto the measure of the stature of the fullness of Christ.*[764] [3] Partly, in the day of judgment, when Christ shall gather corporally all his elect from the four winds, whether dead or living; and shall set them, both in soul and body, as his sheep, at his right hand, pronouncing the final blessed sentence upon them, and shall accordingly afterwards take them all up into his heavenly kingdom with himself to be ever with the Lord.[765]

(v) **To multiply them in the land of Canaan, wherein he would place them.** *Moreover I will make a covenant of peace with them, it shall be an everlasting covenant with them, and I will place them, and multiply them.*[766] Multiplying of mankind was one of the first blessings conferred by God upon mankind: and it is the strength and glory of a nation to grow and multiply.[767] But this blessing and glory is then doubled and heightened, when by the multiplying of a nation the church is also multiplied, as in this case, this whole nation being God's church. This promise was fulfilled upon them according to

---

[762] Ephesians 2:13 to the end
[763] John 10:15-16
[764] Ephesians 4:12-13
[765] Matthew 24:30-31 & 25:31 to the end; 1 Thessalonians 4:14 to the end
[766] Ezekiel 37:26
[767] Genesis 1:28

the letter; as appears, if the small number that returned out of Babylon, namely: 42,360 – and 7,337 servants – should be compared with their great number afterwards, and particularly when the Romans destroyed Jerusalem.[768] For Jerusalem was besieged by Titus when the people from all parts were come thither at a solemn feast, and were shut up in Jerusalem as in a prison. And the authors of the *Magdeburg Centuries* note out of Hegesippus that of citizens and others, from other parts come thither, during the six months siege 1,000,000 were slain.[769] And out of Josephus, that of captives which were taken and carried in triumph or cast to the beasts or put to punishments, through all the cities in the way that Titus went, there were 97,000. And lest these numbers should be thought incredible, or impossible, Josephus reports that there were numbered at one passover in Jerusalem (besides leprous and unclean persons which might not eat the passover) 2,070,000 – so wonderfully did God multiply this people.[770]

(vi) **To bless and crown them with a confluence of prosperity and glory, both temporal and spiritual.**

(a) With temporal prosperity and matter of joy on every side. To this effect the Lord said: *And I will make with them a covenant of peace – And I will make them and the places round about my hill, a blessing; and I will cause the shower to come down in his season; There shall be showers of blessing. And the tree of the field shall yield her fruit, and the earth shall yield her increase, and they shall be safe in their land, and shall know that I am the LORD, when I have broken the bands of their yoke, and delivered them out of the hands of them that served themselves of them. And they shall no more be a prey to the heathen, neither shall the beasts of the land devour them: but they shall dwell safely, and none shall make them afraid. And I will raise up for them a plant of renown*[771] (so that in Christ, this *plant of renown*, all these outward blessings

---

[768] Ezra 2:64-65, Nehemiah 7:66-67
[769] Histor. Ecclesiastic. Magdeb. Cent. 1. lib. 2. cap. 14. pag. 520. Basil. 1624.
[770] Ibid.
[771] Ezekiel 34:25 to the end

are promised them, in whom all earthly blessings are added to believers)[772] *and they shall be no more consumed with hunger in the land, neither bear the shame of the heathen anymore. Thus shall they know that I the LORD their God am with them; and that they, even the House of Israel, are my people, saith the Lord GOD.* And afterwards he adds: *And I will call for the corn* (corn and all blessings are at God's call and command) *and will increase it, and lay no famine upon you. And I will multiply the fruit of the tree, and the increase of the field, that ye shall receive no more reproach of famine among the heathen.*[773]

By the prophet Isaiah also, God promised in Christ to these captives after their return many temporal mercies intermixed among spirituals.[774] And by Jeremiah how sweetly and pathetically [poignantly] does the Lord say: *And it shall be to me a name of joy, a praise and an honor before all the nations of the earth, which shall hear all the good that I do unto them: and they shall fear and tremble for all the goodness, and for all the prosperity that I procure unto it. Thus saith the LORD, Again there shall be heard in this place (which ye say are desolate without man and without beast, even in the cities of Judah and in the streets of Jerusalem, that are desolate without man, and without inhabitant, and without beast) The voice of joy, and the voice of gladness, the voice of the bridegroom, and the voice of the bride, the voice of them that shall say, Praise the LORD of hosts, for the LORD is good, for his mercy endureth forever, And of them that shall bring the sacrifice of praise into the house of the LORD; For I will cause to return the captivity of the land, as at the first, saith the LORD,* etc.[775]

(b) With spiritual prosperity and glory. Therefore, the Lord speaking comfortably to his captives that had been for a while as a woman forsaken and grieved in spirit, and as a wife of youth refused, tells her he had forsaken her for a small moment, and hid his face from her in a little wrath, but with

---

[772] 2 Corinthians 1:20; 1 Timothy 4:8, Matthew 6:33
[773] Ezekiel 36:29-30
[774] Isaiah 61:4 to the end
[775] Jeremiah 33:9-15

everlasting kindness he would have mercy upon her, and gather her. And the mountains and hills should sooner be removed out of their places, then his Covenant of Peace with them should be removed.[776] And further he adds: *Oh, thou afflicted, tossed with tempest and not comforted, Behold I will lay thy stones with fair colours, and lay thy foundations with sapphires, and I will make thy windows of agates, and thy gates of carbuncles, and all thy borders of pleasant stones. And all thy children shall be taught of the LORD, and great shall be the peace of thy children.*[777]

In these words, note:

(1) His church's misery under captivity, she being [1] afflicted (Isaiah 51:21), [2] tossed with tempest (Hebrew: *stormed*), even stormed like Jonah ship: the same word being used of both (Jonah 1:11, 13). As a vessel at sea in an extreme tempest, without anchor, rudder, mast, sail, or tacklings, violently driven. [3] And not comforted by God or man, but as it were wholly deserted and disconsolate.

(2) His church's spiritual glory after her captivity. This is set forth three ways, namely: [1] in her glorious, costly and stately spiritual structure, set forth even to admiration. Her *pavement of stones* curiously painted or colored. Her *foundations of sapphires*, which are precious stones of a sky color, and emblems of divine favor and peace, as I have formerly noted from Exodus 24:10.[778] Her *windows of agates*: the Hebrew word here translated *agates*, is by some rendered *a pearl*, by some a *chrysoprase*, by some *amber*, and by some *crystal*, which being most clear, pellucid, and transparent, suits most fitly to windows, for letting in the light. *Her gates of carbuncles*: the carbuncle is a precious stone of a fiery flame-like color, oriently [glowingly] sparkling. *All her borders pleasant stones*, namely: say some all her cities round about, called {*Jerusalem's cities*} in Jeremiah 33:1, richly built as well as Jerusalem. Others say better: All her walls round about pleasantly and delightfully built. Here are

---

[776] Isaiah 54:6, etc.
[777] Isaiah 54:11-13, etc.
[778] In Book 3, Chapter 4, Aphorism 5, Section 1

most magnificent and high expressions of the church's excellent spiritual frame which she shall have after her return from captivity under Christ – and this under an hyperbolical allusion to some city thus curiously and gloriously built. That interpretation of some – that this foundation should be Christ our Savior (1 Corinthians 3:11), the windows, the teachers who let in light to the people (Daniel 12:3), the gates and walls God's protection (Isaiah 26:2 & 60:2) – seems more witty than solid. [2] In the general and effectual instruction of her children by the Lord, namely: to salvation. The Lord's teaching is effectual teaching: when by the inward efficacy of his Spirit, he co-operates with the outward ministry of his Word.[779] All God's elect are thus taught, and thereupon come unto Christ by believing. [3] In the greatness of her children's peace, which may refer, not only to their temporal quiet and prosperity, but also to their spiritual peace, prosperity and tranquility in Jesus Christ (Romans 5:1, Philippians 4:7, Ephesians 2:14, etc).

(vii) **To cause them to dwell in their own land, under David their prince forever.** *And they shall dwell in the land that I have given unto Jacob my servant, wherein your fathers have dwelt, and they shall dwell therein, even they and their children, and their children's children forever: And my servant* **David** *shall be their prince forever. Moreover I will make a covenant of peace with them, it shall be an everlasting covenant with them, and I will place them,* etc.[780] To have a habitation on earth, is a comfort: such an outward comfort as Christ denied to himself, though he was heir of all things: *But the son of man hath not where to lay his head.*[781] But to have a constant habitation to them and their posterity forever; this was a double, yea a continual comfort.

Question: But how was this fulfilled, when Titus at last, after Christ's death, destroyed Jerusalem and the temple, and carried the people out of Canaan into foreign countries, as I have formerly shown?

---

[779] Jeremiah 31:34, John 6:45; 1 Corinthians 2:20; 2 Corinthians 13:3, Ephesians 4:20-21; 1 John 2:20, 27
[780] Ezekiel 37:25-26 & 36:28
[781] Matthew 8:20

Answer: This promise has a twofold accomplishment; namely: (a) Literal. So the Jews dwelt in their own land under David their prince forever, that is: for a long time (as the Hebrew phrase *forever* is sometimes used)[782] – even so long as the seed of David governed there, which was until the days of Christ; yea, so long as Christ himself the true **David** lived, and many years after. (b) Mystical. So all the true people of God, (typified by the Jews) dwell in the church militant or triumphant (typified by Canaan) under the spiritual kingdom of Jesus Christ the true **David** forevermore.

These, and like mercies were promised, as depending upon and subservient to this great mercy of the Jews' return from Babylon into their own land of Canaan.

{2} **Secondly, the arguments whereby God endeavors to persuade his captives of the certainty of their return from Babylon were many, and those very emphatically urged.**

Their condition in Babylon was so low, All ways and means of their deliverance thence so unlikely, and their spirits so overwhelmed with discomfort and despair; that they needed many arguments, many cordials, to raise them up to believe so improbable promises, and such an impossible deliverance. Therefore God strengthens this promise with many reasons or arguments. Take a taste or a few.

God endeavors to persuade and assure them of their return from Babylon:

(i) From the gratuitousness and freeness of God's redeeming his people, without money (Isaiah 52:1-7 & 48:9-16).

(ii) From the mutual interest, love and dearness between God and his people – he being theirs and they his, therefore he will deliver them (Isaiah 43:1-4, 48:14-15 & 49:13-18).

(iii) From God's inviolable constancy and faithfulness in his Covenant and promises to his people. His Covenant with David touching the perpetual rule of his seed, shall be as sure as the Covenant of day and night: therefore their

---

[782] See Exodus 21:6 with Leviticus 25:13, 28, 40-41; 1 Samuel 1:22

captivity should return. And the vision of their return, at the appointed time should speak and not lie (Jeremiah 33:19-26, Habakkuk 2:1-4, Jeremiah 33:14).

(iv) From God's removal of the grand impediment of their deliverance, namely: their sins, which he would freely and fully pardon (Isaiah 44:21-23, etc.) All the chains, fetters, and dungeons in Babylon could not hold God's people so fast in their bondage as their sins could.

(v) From God's omnipotence and matchless excellencies, showing that he is every way able and all-sufficient against all difficulties, to redeem his people and ruin their enemies (Isaiah 40:9 to the end & 52:9-10, Ezekiel 37:1-15). And therefore he names Cyrus long beforehand, who should be his instrument in their deliverance, and for rebuilding Jerusalem and the temple, before whom all difficulties should be removed (Isaiah 44:24-28 & 45:1-14).

(vi) From God's special presence with his afflicted captives in all their afflictions and extremities of distresses (Isaiah 43:2, 5-6), and God's presence is an excellent foundation of his people's preservation and speedy relief (Psalm 46:5).

(vii) From God's tender and vigilant providence over them continually. He still bears and carries them as in his arms, from the womb to their hoary hairs: and therefore will carry and deliver them (Isaiah 46:3-4). And when they go forth, God will be both their vanguard and rearward (Isaiah 52:11-12).

(viii) From their former experiences of God's redeeming and delivering them, especially Egypt's bondage of old (Isaiah 43:2-4 & 52:4-5).

(ix) From their conformity to the Messiah, Jesus Christ himself, in this their affliction and restoration out of it. Forasmuch as Christ himself should first be deeply humbled, and then highly exalted and magnified; and therefore they should patiently wait until their deliverance should approach (Isaiah 52:11-15 with chapter 53 throughout).

(x) From God's singular intent and aim of glorifying himself, and of sanctifying himself before the heathen, by their deliverance out of Babylon:

that this might be to him a name of joy, a praise and an honor before all the nations of the earth, which should hear all the good that he should do unto them, etc. (Jeremiah 33:6-15, Ezekiel 36:21-25).

By these, and various such like arguments most emphatically urged, the Lord endeavors to comfort his afflicted captives and raise up their hope, expectation, and assurance of their seasonable redemption out of Babylon. Consult the words of the Lord in those Scriptures, alleged only for brevity's sake.

{3} **Thirdly, this great mercy, the redemption of God's captive people from Babylon, was exactly accomplished in its season.** For clearing this, note:

(i) That the captivity of the Jews in Babylon was to last just 70 years, according as God foretold them by his prophet Jeremiah,[783] during all of which time, the land enjoyed her sabbaths.[784] These 70 years were to continue until the expiration of the Babylonian, and inchoation [beginning] of the Persian kingdom (2 Chronicles 36:20-21), so that the destruction of the Babylonian kingdom and the redemption of the Jews out of Babylon were contemporary.

(ii) That at the end of the Jews' 70 years captivity in Babylon, the prophet Daniel in Babylon, in subservience to God's promises, set himself by fasting and prayer most earnestly to entreat the Lord for their restoration.[785] His prayer is heard, and beyond his prayer, a further mystery is revealed to him, namely: that from the going forth of the commandment to restore and build Jerusalem until the Messiah should be 70 weeks of years, and then the Messiah should be cut off. So that when the 70 years of their captivity should end, the 70 weeks should begin. Both these fell out in the first year of Darius' reign over Babylon. And in the second year of Darius (after the Jews had received some degree of their deliverance) The Angel of the LORD (namely: the Angel of the

---

[783] Jeremiah 25:8-15 & 29:10, etc.
[784] 2 Chronicles 36:20-21
[785] Daniel 9:1 to the end of the chapter. See Broughton's *Consent of the Scripture* in the preface, and *Sacred Chronology* by Roger Drake.

Covenant, Jesus Christ our Mediator, interceding with his Father for the accomplishment of this their deliverance begun) said: *O LORD of hosts, how long wilt thou not have mercy on Jerusalem, and on the cities of Judah, against which thou hast had indignation this threescore and ten years?*[786]

(iii) That when the 70 years of captivity were now expired, the singular providence of God so ordered things that Babylon was taken by Darius the Mede and Cyrus the Persian, and so the Babylonian kingdom was given to the Persians.[787] Daniel briefly touches upon this history; others explain it to this effect,[788] namely:

(a) The 70 years of captivity were now expired.

(b) At this very time (God's vigilant providence so ordering and overruling all affairs), Darius and Cyrus had besieged Babylon now a good while together: wherein, as is reported, enough corn was laid up for ten years.

(c) During their siege against Babylon, Belshazzar King of Babylon made a great feast to a thousand of his lords, and drank wine before the thousand (Daniel 5:1-2, etc). Thus God infatuated him to his destruction: that in the midst of his danger he should be so secure and licentious, when he had need to have been taking care of his besieged city, especially Cyrus being so potent and active an adversary. At this feast, God miraculously sent a hand, writing Belshazzar his doom on the wall over against the candlestick: *Mene, mene, tekel, peres.* That he was weighed in the balances and found too light, and his kingdom should be given to the Medes and Persians; for expounding whereof, Daniel was clothed in scarlet, having a chain of gold put about his neck.

(d) On that very night, when they were drowned in wine, sleep and security, Babylon was taken by Darius and Cyrus, and King Belshazzar slain. It is noted out of historians – Xenophon and others – that Gobria and Gabatha betrayed the city to Cyrus by way of revenge against Belshazzar, who had ignominiously gelded [castrated] one of them, and slayed the son of the other.

---

[786] Zechariah 1:7, 12, etc.
[787] Daniel 5:24 to the end
[788] Daniel 5:1 to the end

And that Cyrus with his army having many sluices and trenches, suddenly on that night turned the River Euphrates into those sluices, and so entered the city, and possessed the kingdom of Babylon for his own.[789]

(e) In the very first year of Darius and Cyrus, proclamation is made by Cyrus to all the Captive Jews in Babylon, that they should be set at liberty to go build Jerusalem and the temple, and he restored to them the vessels of the temple.[790] And accordingly, many thousands of Jews went up to Jerusalem, and (though in troubled times) built, prospered in, and completed their work.[791] Thus their deliverance from Babylon was brought about most wonderfully and unexpectedly, insomuch that the very captives themselves [who were] released were amazed at it, and as people in a dream rather than in a real deliverance. *When the LORD turned again the captivity of Zion, we were like them that dream. Then was our mouth filled with laughter, and our tongue with singing: Then said they among the heathen, The LORD hath done great things for them. The LORD hath done great things for us whereof we are glad.*[792]

{4} Fourthly, this wonderful redemption of the captive Jews from Babylon had a spirit of mystery in it, shadowing out the greatest and spiritual redemption of God's elect from the bondage of sin, Satan, death, hell, and so on, into which they were implunged by the fall of the first Adam, and out of which they should be restored by Jesus Christ the last Adam. For evincing of this, ponder diligently these few ensuing considerations, namely:

(i) That the promises of God touching his people's deliverance from Babylon's captivity are jointly proposed and intermixed with his promises of restoring his elect from spiritual captivity, as Isaiah 49 throughout, Daniel 9:2, etc, 9:24, etc. – which notably insinuates thus much to us: that in their

---

[789] See Calvin's commentary on Daniel 5:1, etc.
[790] 2 Chronicles 36:22-23, Ezra 1:1-4
[791] Ezra 2 throughout & 6
[792] Psalm 126:1-3

redemption from Babylon's thralldom, God typed out their redemption from spiritual thralldom: and in that, they were especially to lift up their eyes to this.

(ii) That it is the primary scope and intention of the prophet Isaiah in the fourth part of his prophecy, which is promissory, namely: from chapter 40:1 to the end of the book, to comfort his spiritual captives under sin, Satan, death, and so on, with promises of their deliverance by Christ; all along under-laying as a foundation, handsel, and shadow thereof, the restoration of his captives from the bondage of Babylon. And therefore: (a) he assures the Jews of their deliverance by Cyrus (named about 200 years beforehand) out of their sad Babylonian captivity threatened, as also of Babylon's utter destruction – compare Isaiah 39 with chapter 40-49. (b) He carries and raises them hereupon to behold and expect a far greater deliverance by Jesus Christ the Messiah, from spiritual captivity under sin, Satan, wrath, and so on, which should be as the high accomplishment, perfection and glory of their return from Babylon to Zion – especially when Christ the blessed Redeemer should subdue and annex the Gentiles far and near unto his church, that mother church of the Jews (Isaiah 49 to the end of his prophecy).

And this will more fully appear: partly, by a diligent and judicious consideration of the whole series, order, connection, and intent of the prophecy from chapter 40 to the end of the book, as I have elsewhere clearly unfolded the same;[793] partly, by the concurrent judgment and interpretation of the godly learned, familiarly acquainted with the Scriptures, as Calvin, etc, and especially by those accurate and elaborate annotations, or large commentary upon Isaiah, digested into the large London Annotations upon the whole Bible.[794]

---

[793] In my *Key of the Bible* on Isaiah §4, p.421 (London, 1649)

[794] {*Comfort ye, comfort ye my people, saith your God.*} "In the foregoing chapter, a hint was given of the Babylonian captivity. And by the subject matter of the ensuing prophecies, it may appear, how fitly the story therein related, was here inserted. For, the subsequent sermons are generally most, if not all of them, concerning that their captivity, their delivery out of it, and the restitution of their state and church in after-times: but so, that they rest

(iii) That the Lord comforts his captives in Babylon by their conformity to the Messiah, the Lord's Servant, both in their deep affliction in it, and ensuing restoration out of it – forasmuch as even Christ himself should first be deeply afflicted and abased before he should be highly advanced and exalted.

(iv) That unto God's Covenant of promises for return of his people the Jews from Babylonian captivity, there are immediately annexed precious promises of the Messiah for effecting and full completing thereof. And therefore, after the Lord had largely expressed his Covenant touching their return from Babylon (Jeremiah 32:26-44 & 33:1-15). He presently adds: *In those days, and at that time* (namely: even in the days and time of this Covenant with the captives, and before the expiration thereof) *will I cause the branch of righteousness to grow up unto David, and he shall execute judgment and righteousness in the land. In those days shall Judah be saved, and Jerusalem shall dwell safely, and this is the name wherewith she shall be called, The LORD our righteousness. For thus saith the LORD, David shall never want a man to sit upon the throne of the house of Israel*, etc.[795] In these expressions, the restoration of Israel, both from the Babylonian and spiritual captivity, is ascribed to Christ, as to be accomplished by him fully and finally. And elsewhere Scriptures testify that, as Christ redeems from spiritual captivity by his death and blood, so the same Jesus Christ tells the church that by the blood of her Covenant (namely: by his own blood typified in the blood

---

not in that, but reach still farther, unto the spiritual delivery of God's people, from the far more direful thraldom under sin, and Satan, by the Messiah therein typified, the advancement of his kingdom and enlargement thereof, by the subduing and bringing in of those nations, that had formerly been enemies thereunto."
London Annotation on Isaiah 40:1.
{*Listen O isles, unto me; and hearken O people, from far*} "The prophecy delivered and recorded in this chapter, runs on in the same strain with the former, relating the restoration and enlargement of God's Church, consisting both of Jews and Gentiles, under a type of the Jews' release from the Babylonian deportation, and the re-establishment of them in their former estate, with much honor and increase, by accession of other nations unto them, both effected by the mighty power of the Lord Jesus, the Messiah."
London Annotation on Isaiah 49:1.
[795] Jeremiah 33:15-17, etc.

of sacrifices used in confirming his Covenant, as Exodus 24:5-8, which is God's Covenant, as author of it; her Covenant, as the federate party in it with God)[796] he had sent forth her prisoners out of the uncomfortable Babylonian pit: *As for them also, by the blood of thy covenant, I have sent forth thy prisoners out of the pit, wherein is no water.*[797]

(v) That God promises to his divided and dispersed people that when their dispersion should be gathered from Babylon and other countries into their own land, they should be united into one nation and one kingdom in their own land, under one king, even David (namely: Jesus Christ the true **David**) their king forever.[798] *Literally*, they were thus united at their return under Zerubbabel, a son of David and type of Christ; *spiritually*, they were thus united under Christ himself, as has been formerly explained: that being a type and shadow of this.

(vi) That Israel's redemption of old from Egyptian bondage was a plain type of the elect's redemption by Christ from spiritual bondage, as the mystery or sacrament of the passover then, and upon occasion of that deliverance, celebrated, does unquestionably evince;[799] proportionably, yea and much more, this greater redemption of the Jews from Babylonian bondage[800] (in comparison whereof that deliverance from Egypt should, as it were, be forgotten) was a type also of the elect's restoration by Christ from spiritual captivity.[801] And therefore it is very observable, that when the Lord had promised to gather his dispersed flock out of all countries, and to raise up to David a righteous branch for saving Judah and Jerusalem, even **the LORD our Righteousness**.[802] He presently adds: *Therefore behold the days come saith the LORD, that they shall no more say, The LORD liveth which brought up the*

---

[796] Isaiah 61:1-3, Luke 4:18, etc, Hebrews 9:12, 14; 1 Peter 1:18-19
[797] Zechariah 9:9-12, etc.
[798] Ezekiel 37:21 to the end of the chapter
[799] Exodus 12 with 1 Corinthians 5:7-8, Exodus 20:2, etc.
[800] Jeremiah 23:7-8
[801] Jeremiah 23:7-8
[802] Jeremiah 23:1-6

children of Israel out of the Land of Egypt: But, The LORD liveth which brought up, and which led the seed of the house of Israel out of the north country, and from all countries whither I had driven them, and they shall dwell in their own land.[803] By which he gives us to understand: (a) that the same Lord – namely: the Lord Jesus Christ – brought Israel out of Egypt and out of Babylon into Canaan, whatever the instruments were. (b) That the deliverance from Babylon should so far surpass that from Egypt that the transcendent greatness of that should eclipse, and as it were, obliterate the memory of this. (c) That consequently, as Canaan – whither they were to be brought – was a type of heaven, the eternal rest, so both Egypt and Babylon – whence they were delivered – were types of their spiritual bondage and misery under sin, Satan, death, and so on. And their redemption from Babylon was a type of their spiritual redemption by Christ, as well as their redemption from Egypt, and in some regards a more eminent type.

(vii) Finally, that there is a notable analogy or proportion between the Jews' deliverance out of the Babylonian captivity, and the elect's deliverance from their spiritual captivity. For:

(a) The term whence the Jews were delivered – namely: Babylon – was a place of wickedness, and a place of extreme misery and wretchedness to the captives.[804] There they were sadly oppressed for seventy years together as slaves and vassals to the pagans; there they were in as helpless and hopeless a condition, in reference to their deliverance, as dead bodies and dry bones in a grave.[805] So the term from which the elect were delivered by Christ, is a state of sin, and a state of misery, under curse, wrath, death, Satan, and so on; they being dead in trespasses and sins, under the power of Satan, and children of wrath, even as others.[806]

---

[803] Jeremiah 23:7-8
[804] Zechariah 5:8, 11 with Genesis 11:2-5, Psalm 137:3
[805] Ezekiel 37:1, etc.
[806] Ephesians 2:1, etc, Acts 26:18, Titus 3:3, Ephesians 2:3

(b) The Jews' deliverance from Babylon was a reviving of their dead bones, an opening of their graves, and a bringing them as it were out of their graves in Babylon. So the elect's deliverance from their spiritual bondage is their spiritual reviving and resurrection.[807] *God who is rich in mercy, for his great love wherewith he loved us, even when we were dead in sins, hath quickened us together with Christ, – and hath raised us up together.*[808] And elsewhere: *If ye then be risen with Christ, seek those things which are above.*[809]

(c) The Jews were delivered from Babylon by Cyrus when the appointed time of seventy years was fully come; so the elect were redeemed and delivered from their spiritual bondage in the fullness of time by Jesus Christ when the seventy weeks of years were come.[810]

(d) The Jews were so delivered from Babylon, as that they were cleansed from their idols, detestable things and transgressions. And the elect are so delivered from their spiritual thralldom,[811] that they are washed, sanctified, justified in the name of the Lord Jesus, and by the Spirit of our God.[812]

(e) The Jews delivered from Babylon were called to build the temple of God (Ezra 1:1-3, etc.); so the elect – being redeemed and actually delivered from their spiritual thralldom by Christ – are *built up a spiritual house, as living stones, upon the foundation of the prophets and apostles, Jesus Christ himself being the chief cornerstone. In whom all the building fitly framed together, groweth unto an holy temple in the Lord.*[813]

(f) The Jews delivered from Babylon, came into their own land, the land of Canaan, their typical rest. So the elect are redeemed by Christ out of their spiritual bondage,[814] that at last they might return into the true Canaan,

---

[807] Ezekiel 37:1, etc.
[808] Ephesians 2:1, 4-6
[809] Colossians 3:1
[810] Galatians 4:4-6, Daniel 9:24, etc.
[811] Ezekiel 37:21-23
[812] 1 Corinthians 6:11, Acts 26:18, Romans 6:4, etc.
[813] 1 Peter 2:5, Ephesians 2:20-22
[814] Ezekiel 37:21, Ezra 2:1, etc.

heaven itself, the eternal rest promised to God's people, where they shall sit together with Christ in heavenly places.[815]

Thus of God's promise to redeem the Jews out of Babylon, and to return them into their own land of Canaan.

---

[815] 1 Peter 2:5, Acts 26:18-19, Ephesians 2:4-6

[3] God's cleansing of his people the Jews, when redeemed out of Babylon from all their spiritual defilements, from all their idols, from all their detestable things, and from all their transgressions.

To this effect, the prophet Ezekiel laying down the substance of this Covenant to the captives,[816] and having promised firstly their return from captivity; secondly, the union and oneness of their nation under one king in their own land; and thirdly, he adds as a third covenant blessing, the cleansing, expiation, and pardon of their transgressions, saying: *Neither shall they defile themselves anymore with their idols, nor with their detestable things, nor with any of their transgressions: but I will save them out of all their dwelling-places, wherein they have sinned, and will cleanse them; so shall they be my people, and I will be their God. – Moreover I will make a covenant of peace with them*, etc.[817] And in the former chapter, reciting the promised blessings of this Covenant, he promises this mercy of their spiritual cleansing three several times, as Lavater observes, for the greater certainty that all sins shall be remitted to the penitent.[818]

God speaks it once twice, thrice: because he was peremptorily resolved and determined to confer this blessing upon them. *Then will I sprinkle clean water upon you, and ye shall be clean: from all your filthiness, and from all your idols will I cleanse you*[819] – *I will also save you from all your uncleannesses*, etc.[820] – *Thus saith the Lord GOD: In the day that I shall have cleansed you from all your iniquities, I will also cause you to dwell in the cities*, etc.[821] By Jeremiah also the Lord said: *And I will cause the captivity of Judah, and the captivity of*

---

[816] Ezekiel 37:22-23
[817] Ezekiel 37:23, 26 & 11:17-18
[818] Lavater, Homily 157 in Ezekiel 36:33
[819] Ezekiel 36:25
[820] Ezekiel 36:26
[821] Ezekiel 36:29

Israel to return, and will build them as at the first. And I will cleanse them from all their iniquity, whereby they have sinned against me, and I will pardon all their iniquities whereby they have sinned, and whereby they have transgressed against me.[822] Calvin thinks these two phrases, I will cleanse them, and I will pardon, do signify one and the same thing: because the Hebrew טָהֵר or *taher*, here rendered *cleanse*, properly signifies, *to expiate*.[823] And therefore cleansing here denotes not regeneration, or sanctification. And he further notes that the prophet by changing the number, iniquity, to iniquities, shows the company and variety of their wickednesses: As if he had said, there was a manifold heap of their wickednesses, standing in need of God's singular mercies.

In these sweet and comfortable promises of their cleansing, compared together, these things are very observable, namely:

{1} How the grievousness and sinfulness of their sins and idolatries are described. For the expressions are very emphatic, by which God would convince them and shame them. As (i) **idols**, גִּלּוּלִים, *gillulim*, properly, *dunghills, dung heaps*, etc. (Ezekiel 37:23 & 36:25). It's derived from גָּלַל *galal*: *to roll away, tumble*, etc. Thence גָּלַל *galal* signifies *dung* or *excrement* because it is rolled out, and carried out of sight; or because that which is rolled therein is defiled. Hence it's used to signify idols, as being dunghill-gods, dungheaps, vile excrements, and stinking filth. (ii) **Detestable things**. Hebrew: שִׁקּוּצִים *shikkutsim*, which properly signifies *execrable, accursed, loathsome, abominable things* (Ezekiel 37:23) – such abominable things as a man shuts his eyes, or stops his nose against. (iii) **Transgressions**. Hebrew: פְּשָׁעִים *peshagnim*, properly, *defections, rebellions, prevarications*, Ezekiel 37:23. (iv) **Filthinesses, uncleannesses, pollutions, or defilements, etc.** טֻמְאוֹתָם *tumothim*, properly, *defiling filthinesses* (Ezekiel 36:25, 29). It imports not only one, but rather, their manifold pollutions and spiritual filthiness, whereby themselves and

---

[822] Jeremiah 33:7-8
[823] John Calvin commentary on Jeremiah 33:7-8

their ways were so defiled, that they stood in need of God's cleansing. (v) **Iniquities.** Hebrew: עֲוֹנֹת *gnavonoth*, properly it signifies *perverseness, perverse iniquities, crookednesses*, etc. (Ezekiel 36:33). A thing is crooked, and warped awry, when it will not be brought to agree with that which is straight, but warps and starts from it. Such were their thoughts, words and ways, in reference to the straight rule of God's will in his Word. This same word also Jeremiah uses twice in the fore-cited promise,[824] namely: once in the singular number, and afterwards, in the plural, as intimating that they were guilty not only of one sin, or one sort of sins: but of a heap of sins and crooked carriages against God, as I formerly noted out of Calvin. Thus by all these aggravating expressions God endeavors to humble and shame them for the heinousness of their iniquities. God humbles sinners first under the true sense of their sinfulnesses, before he lifts them up with the pardon of their sins.

{2} **How exceeding graciously the healing and removing of all their sinfulnesses is by the Lord promised.** This is laid down also in a variety of expressions, such as:

(i) That he will sprinkle clean water upon them, and they shall be clean (Ezekiel 36:25). Sin had made them foul and filthy: God would sprinkle clean water upon them, to purge and wash off their filthiness. In this phrase is a plain allusion to the Levitical sprinklings, washings, and purifications, purging away the ceremonial uncleanness; without which cleansings, the unclean could not be admitted into the camp or congregation: all of which were evident types of the blood of Jesus Christ that blood of sprinkling speaking better things than the blood of Abel, purging the conscience from dead works, to serve the living God (Hebrews 9:13-14 and 12:24).[825] Christ's blood is this clean water sprinkled by faith upon the soul, that fountain opened for sin and for uncleanness (Zechariah 13:1, Psalm 51:2, 7).

---

[824] Jeremiah 33:8
[825] Hebrews 9:13-14 with Leviticus 16:14, Numbers 19:17, etc. & 5:2, 4 & 12:15 & 19:11-20, Leviticus 13:46 & 14:3, 7-8

(ii) That he will cleanse them (Ezekiel 37:23), will cleanse them from all their iniquity (Jeremiah 33:7-8), yea, from all their iniquities (Ezekiel 36:33), yea he will cleanse them from all their filthiness, and from all their idols (Ezekiel 36:25). This shows God's determinate resolvedness thus to cleanse them by the blood of Jesus Christ from all their sinful defilements fully and completely, so that they might be pure and spotless. Here's the freeness, fulness, and resoluteness of this mercy intimated.

(iii) That he will pardon (Hebrew: *will spare, remit, be propitious to*) all their iniquities whereby they have sinned, and whereby they have transgressed against him (Jeremiah 33:8).[826] This free and full pardon of iniquities, oh how sweet a privilege and consolation is it to the sinner! Herein David places a man's blessednesses.[827]

(iv) That they shall not anymore *defile themselves with their idols, nor with their detestable things, nor with any of their transgressions* (Ezekiel 37:23). This has reference to God's cleansing them by regeneration and sanctification from the power and stain of sin, especially of idolatry, set forth here in three words: *idols, detestable-things, transgressions*. Though formerly they were extremely addicted to idolatry, yet after their return from captivity, they should be thoroughly reformed from that sin, they should be given to idolatry no more.

(v) That he will save them from all their uncleannesses (Ezekiel 36:29). Yea, That he will save them out of all their dwelling-places wherein they have sinned (Ezekiel 37:23). That is, (a) he will save them from their sins, both from the guilt, and from the power and pollution thereof. He will justify and sanctify them: especially from their idolatries. (b) He will save them also from the punishment of their sins, out of all their dwelling places, whether Babylon, Egypt, or elsewhere, in which they are captives, wherein they have willingly, or compulsorily been partakers in pagan idolatries.[828]

---

[826] Fagnin, Thesaur. in ver.
[827] Psalm 32:1-2, Romans 4:6-8
[828] Ezekiel 14:3 & 20:30, 39, Jeremiah 44:8

{3} How these promises were performed and made good to the captive Jews. These promises had their accomplishment (i) upon the elect Jews which were carried captive. When they were effectually called, converted, sanctified, and justified, then clean water was poured upon them; then they were fully cleansed from all their defilements and idolatries, and so on, and analogically, upon all the elect in after-ages. (ii) Upon the whole body of the captives in some sense. Forasmuch as they were fully divorced, and thoroughly reformed from all their idolatries, detestable things, and prevarications, after their return from Babylon.

Before that time, they and their fathers were extremely prone to idolatry, and ready to run into it upon all occasions, and could not be divorced from it. The family of Terah, Abraham's father, beyond the flood, worshiped other gods in Chaldea before Abram was called into Canaan.[829] The family of Jacob, whilst with Laban, and afterwards, tainted with idolatry.[830] The Israelites served strange gods in Egypt, even the idols of the Egyptians.[831] When they were newly brought out of Egypt, and had solemnly covenanted with God against idolatry, while Moses was in the mount with God, they idolatrously trespassed in the golden calf which Aaron made, sitting down to eat and drink, and rising up to play.[832] When they came into the land of Moab in Shittim, they went to the sacrifices of the Moabite gods, and did eat, and bowed down to their gods, so that 24,000 of them thereupon died of the plague, and by the hand of justice.[833] In the days of the judges they served the gods of the heathens, Baalim and the groves, and Ashtaroth, and the gods of Syria, of Zidon, of Moab, of Ammon, and of the Philistines.[834]

In the days of the kings, Solomon encouraged and shared in the idolatry of all his strange wives (1 Kings 11:6-8). Jeroboam set up the idolatrous calves in

---

[829] Joshua 24:2
[830] Genesis 31:19, 34-35 & 35:2-4
[831] Joshua 24:14
[832] Exodus 32:1, etc.; 1 Corinthians 10:7, Acts 7:40-41
[833] Numbers 25:1-10 & 33:49; 1 Corinthians 10:8
[834] Judges 2:11-13; 3:5-7; 10:6; 17:5, etc. & 18:30

Dan and Bethel, whereby he made Israel to sin (1 Kings 12:28-33). And what shall I say? Time would fail me to tell of their idolatry, in the days of Ahab, Jehu, Hoshea, Manasseh, Amon, and of others till the very Babylonian captivity.[835] Yea, they were very idolatrous even under their captivity.[836] But now after they were brought out of Babylonish Captivity, how did God wean them from their idolatry, detestable-things, and prevarications!

I read not, that I remember, of any their idolatries afterwards, they after that defiled themselves with their idols no more. Yea I read in other writings, that after this the Jews extremely abhorred idols and idolatry. Cassius Dio reports that at that time when Jerusalem was taken by Pompey, there was no image found in the temple, and that the Jews did account their god to be ineffable and invisible.[837] Yea they so far loathed idols and idolatry that when some rash young men called *doritae* had, in a show of religion, put Caesar's statue in one of the Jews' synagogues, Petronius (then Claudius Caesar's legate) writes sharply to the Doriensian magistrates to send them to him to give an account of their fact, whereby they had profaned the synagogue of the Jews, by bringing in Caesar's statue, which their religion did not allow of, whereby the piety of the Jews was offended, etc, as Josephus recites the story.[838] And the authors of the *Magdeburg Centuries* declare that Herod Ascalonita – being made king in Judaea by Augustus Caesar – placed with great cost a golden eagle over the gates of the temple for the honor of Caesar.[839] But forty young scholars of eminent families and their two masters, Judas and Matthias, in their pious zeal – being grieved at such profanation of the temple – demolished by force the said structure at bright noonday. Thus this promise in this Covenant, of healing the Jews' idolatry was performed most eminently. Thus, of God's cleansing the captives from all their spiritual defilements.

---

[835] See at large in 1 & 2 Kings.
[836] See Ezekiel 8 throughout.
[837] Cassius Dio, *Roman History*, lib. 37
[838] Josephus, *Jewish Antiquities*, lib. 19 cap. 5 & 6
[839] Hist. Ecclesiast. Magdeburg. Cent. 1. lib. 1. cap. 3. p. 16. Basil. 1624.

[4] God's putting his Spirit within them, for new framing and spiritualizing their heart.

God promises his Spirit to them, and the blessed influences of his Spirit upon them. His promises to this purpose were very sweet, evangelical, and spiritual: *A new heart also will I give you, and a new Spirit will I put within you, and I will take away the stony heart out of your flesh, and I will give you an heart of flesh. And I will put my Spirit within you, and cause you to walk in my statutes, and ye shall keep my judgements and do them.*[840] – *And I will give them one heart, and I will put a new Spirit within you: And I will take the stony heart out of their flesh, and will give them an heart of flesh: That they may walk in my statutes, and keep mine ordinances and do them: and they shall be my people, and I will be their God.*[841] – *And I will give them an heart to know me, that I am the LORD; and they shall be my people, and I will be their God: for they shall return unto me with their whole heart.*[842] – *And I will give them one heart, and one way, that they may fear me forever, for the good of them, and of their children after them. And I will make an everlasting covenant with them,* etc.[843]

And the prophet Isaiah, promising to the exiled and captivated Jews deliverance from Babylon, especially under that from spiritual bondage by Jesus Christ the Redeemer, assures them of their constant enjoyment of his Spirit and Word for their constant direction and consolation, saying: *And the Redeemer shall come to Zion, and unto them that turn from transgression in Jacob, saith the LORD: As for me, this is my covenant with them, saith the LORD: My Spirit that is upon thee, and my words which I have put into thy mouth, shall not depart out of thy mouth, nor out of the mouth of thy seed, nor*

---

[840] Ezekiel 36:25-27
[841] Ezekiel 11:17-20
[842] Jeremiah 24:7
[843] Jeremiah 32:37-40

out of the mouth of thy Seeds Seed, saith the LORD, from henceforth and forever.[844]

The Spirit, with these effects, fruits, and influences of the Spirit of God, are promised and covenanted to be performed to the Captive Jews after their Return from Babylon. Let us view them a little: {1} more generally and {2} more particularly.

{1} **More generally**, here God promises his own Spirit to his captive people, after their return from Babylon (Ezekiel 36:27, Isaiah 59:20-21). Here several queries must be resolved for the sake of explanation, such as:

(i) **What is meant by the LORD's Spirit here promised?**

Answer: The word {*Spirit*} is used in a manifold sense in Scripture, as it is attributed to God. Here it is attributed to God: *I will put my Spirit within you*, etc. This word {*Spirit*} is attributed to God essentially and personally. (a) Essentially: so *God is a Spirit* (John 4:24); an *eternal Spirit* (Hebrews 9:14). Christ is said to be *justified in the Spirit,* i.e. in the Godhead, here opposed to his flesh (1 Timothy 3:16). Thus it is not to be understood here. (b) Personally, to the third person in Trinity peculiarly, namely: the Holy Spirit. To him this name {*Spirit*} is given properly and improperly. (1) Properly, as denoting the third personal subsistence in the Godhead, proceeding from the Father and the Son, and equal in essence or substance to them both (Luke 1:68, 70 compared with 2 Peter 1:21, Acts 5:3-4).[845] Nor is it here used in this sense. (2) Improperly and metonymically for the effects, fruits, works, gifts, endowments, and so on, of the Holy Spirit, whether ordinary or extraordinary, whether more common, or more special and peculiar to the elect. Thus Christ is said to be anointed with the Holy Ghost (Acts 10:38). God gave not the Spirit to him by measure (John 3:34). John was filled with the Holy Ghost (Luke 1:15), Stephen full of the Holy Ghost (Acts 7:55); *Be filled with the Spirit* (Ephesians 5:18); *sensual, having not the Spirit* (Jude 19) – give the

---

[844] Isaiah 59:20-21. See John Calvin's commentary on the place & D. Pareus adversus. Ibid.
[845] John 14:26 & 15:26; 1 John 5:7

Spirit to them that ask him (Luke 11:13 with Matthew 7:11); *If the Spirit of God dwell in you* (Romans 8:9); *Now we have received not the Spirit of the world, but the Spirit which is of God* (1 Corinthians 2:12). In this sense it is most frequently used in the Scripture. And in this notion the Spirit is promised here: that is, the effects, gifts, fruits, influences, etc, of the Spirit of God.

(ii) **Was not the Spirit, in this sense, bestowed upon the Jews, until after their return from Babylon?**

Answer: The Socinians hold that there were two promises, namely: of eternal life, and of the Holy Spirit, peculiar to the New Testament, never promised under the Old Testament – such excellent promises being deferred until Christ himself came. And therefore according to their opinion, the Holy Spirit, being not so much as promised, was not given till after Christ's coming.[846] But this Socinian error I have formerly refelled [refuted] in opening the Sinai Covenant, and it is so gross; I need not now add much more.[847] Thus in brief resolve: the Holy Spirit, taken metonymically for the fruits and effects of the Holy Spirit, ordinary or extraordinary, was promised and given before the death of Jesus Christ, yea and before the Jews' return from the Babylonian Captivity.

(a) The extraordinary gifts and effects of the Spirit were promised and given: to Moses and the seventy elders of Israel (Numbers 11:17, 25, 26, 29), to Elijah and Elisha (2 Kings 2:9, 15), to the prophets (Nehemiah 9:30, Zechariah 7:12 and 2 Peter 1:21), to David prophesying of Christ, and calling him Lord (Psalm 110:1 with Matthew 22:43), to John the Baptist, having the Spirit and power of Elijah (Luke 1:17), and to Simeon (Luke 2:27, etc).

(b) The ordinary endowments, gifts, and effects of the Spirit were also promised and given before the said times, such as to Adam (Genesis 3:15), to Abel (Genesis 4:4), to Enoch (Genesis 5:22, 24), to Noah (Genesis 6:9), to

---

[846] Catechis. Racoviens. in Q. X. de V. & N. Test. apud H. Alsted. in Theol. Polem. p. 322.
[847] Book 3, Chapter 4, Aphorism 4, Section 1.3

Abraham (Genesis 15:6, 18:19 & 22:12), to Isaac (Genesis 31:53), to Jacob (Genesis 32:24-26, etc, Hosea 12:4), to the Israelites, in the explaining of the Sinai Covenant (Deuteronomy 30:6, 8), to David: *Take not thy Holy Spirit from me*: he therefore had the Holy Spirit. *Restore unto me the joy of thy salvation, and stablish me with thy free Spirit* (Psalm 51:10-12), to all the faithful in the apostle's catalog: faith being a peculiar gift and grace of the Spirit (Hebrews 11 throughout and Galatians 5:22), to the captive Jews here: *I will put my Spirit within* you, etc. (Ezekiel 36:27, Isaiah 59:20-21). Therefore, the Socinians most impudently slander God's people before Christ, and belie the dispensations of God's grace, when they assert that the Holy Spirit was not promised until the coming of Christ. The elect in all ages had their measure of the Spirit of God, but before Christ, the Spirit was given very sparingly; after Christ very plentifully and bountifully. And usually, God dispensed his Spirit still more and more largely and liberally, according as he more and more enlarged his Covenant expressures in Jesus Christ. These captive Jews had the Spirit of God before and under their captivity, but God promised a more plenary endowment of them therewith, after their return from Babylon (Ezekiel 36:27).

More particularly, here God promised many precious influences and effects of the Spirit unto his captives after their return, which are laid down in these sweet promises forementioned, such as: (1) newness of heart and spirit, (2) a heart knowing the LORD, (3) fleshiness of heart instead of stoniness, (4) penitentialness of heart, (5) oneness of heart and way, (6) the constant fear of God, and (7) obedientialness towards God. These are the blessed fruits of God's Spirit which should be put within them. Here is a sweet garden and paradise of spiritual delights. Here let us dwell a while, and solace ourselves abundantly.

(Influence & Effect 1):
Newness of heart and spirit.

This is an eminent effect of God's Spirit promised to the captive Jews, after they should be cleansed from their spiritual defilement: *A new heart also will I give you, and a new spirit will I put within you.*[848] That paragraph in chapter 36:21-38, has evident reference to this Covenant with the captive Jews, if compared with Jeremiah 32 and Ezekiel 37 – the promises running in the same strain, and the performances thereof appropriated to the Jews' return from Babylon, in all these places. In these words, the Lord promises them a new spiritual frame and constitution of soul. Their old frame was so wholly corrupt and naught, that no less than a new frame would serve turn.

For unfolding this, let these questions be briefly discussed and determined, namely: {1} What is meant here by *heart* and *spirit*? {2} What is meant by a *new* heart and spirit, and wherein the new heart and new spirit consist? {3} Whether God alone gives this new heart, and puts this new spirit into his people? {4} Why does God give them a new heart and spirit? {5} How may this new heart and new Spirit which God gives may be known and discovered?

{Question 1} What is here meant by *heart* and *spirit*?

Answer: These two words, {*heart*} and {*spirit*} when they are mentioned distinctly and separately one from the other, are both of them of very various acceptations in Scripture, which we need not here so much as to point at. But when they are mentioned jointly and applied to man, as they are several times in this prophet, then (as Calvin has well noted) they are put for man's whole soul and all the faculties thereof,[849] namely: *the spirit* for the more sublime, high and spirit-full part of the soul, the mind and understanding, which is

---

[848] Ezekiel 36:25-26 & 11:9
[849] Ezekiel 11:19, 18:31 & 36:26

endowed with reason and judgment.⁸⁵⁰ This is the upper story, or tower of the soul: the heart, being the seat of the affections is put for the inferior parts or faculties of the soul, the will, and affections, whereby a man does will or nill, elect or reject, according to the proposal of the understanding. By *spirit*, therefore I understand here all the upper faculties, the intellectuals, chiefly seated in the head; by *heart*, all the lower faculties of the will and affections, chiefly seated in the heart; by both *heart* and *spirit*, the whole soul rational, with all its faculties and powers.

{Question 2} What is meant by a new heart and spirit, and wherein the new heart and new spirit consist?

Answer: For clearing this question, I shall show firstly, what the word {*new*} imports, then what the newness of the spirit and heart implies.

(i) First, a thing is styled {*new*} in Scripture, in several regards, such as:

(a) When it is fresh, or lately done, or lately begun, it's *new*. So it's opposed to that which is stale and old. Thus: *Old things are passed away, behold all things are become new.*⁸⁵¹ – The name above every name in heaven and earth, which Christ has obtained by his passion, is called his *new name*.⁸⁵² The Lord's mercies and compassions are *new every morning*.⁸⁵³ In this sense, {*new*} is used most properly and frequently.

(b) When it is another thing, or at least distinct from the former. Another in substance; or multiple in circumstance or accidents, then it is called {*new*}, such as {*new tongues*}, namely: other tongues than the mother tongue, or than

---

⁸⁵⁰ "Sicuti per nomen Cordis intelligit affectus, Ita etiam per Spiritum mentem ipsam, & omnes cogitationes designat. Spiritus hominis saepe capitur pro tota anima, & tunc comprehendit etiam omnes affectus. Sed ubi haec duo simul junguntur, Cor & Spiritus, Cor vocatur Sedes omnium affectuum, denique est ipsa voluntas hominis: Spiritus autem est facultas intelligendi. Scimus enim duas esse praecipuas animae Dotes, prior est quod Ratione polleat, Deinde, quod praedita sit Judicio & Electione.—Sed hoc principium tenendum est Animam hominis excellere primum intelligentia vel Ratione, Deinde Judicio, unde pendet electio & voluntas." – John Calvin, *Praelect.* in Ezekiel 11:19

⁸⁵¹ 2 Corinthians 5:17

⁸⁵² Revelation 3:12 with Philippians 2:9

⁸⁵³ Lamentations 3:23

were formerly used.[854] A *new king*, namely: βασιλεὺς ἕτερος, *another king*, as the Septuagint renders it.[855] *A new commandment, to love one another.*[856] This commandment, John calls both an *old commandment* and a *new* (1 John 2:7-8. and 2 John 5). This is an old commandment for the substance of it, and was enjoined from the beginning. But in regard to some accidents and circumstances of it, Christ has made it a new commandment: namely: partly, in propounding a new pattern of brotherly love. He says not only, *Love thy neighbor as thyself*, but, *love one another as I have loved you* (John 13:34) – partly, by writing this commandment in new tables of mind and heart, not as formerly in old tables of stone (Hebrews 8:8-10 with 2 Corinthians 3:3); partly, by his new reviving and vehement pressing of this commandment, as if it were a new commandment: new laws and statutes being more vehemently and forcibly urged than old laws that are wearing away. This commandment is still to continue, and never to be antiquated as to the use and exercise of it. Thus Christ says: *I will not drink henceforth of this fruit of the vine until that day when I drink it new with you in my Father's kingdom*,[857] namely: until I drink other manner of wine with you in heavenly glory, the wine of refreshing endless joys and ravishing delights (see Luke 22:29-30, Psalm 16:11, Revelation 3:21).

(c) When it is strange, unusual, unheard of, extraordinary, etc, then a thing is called {*new*}, such as Paul's preaching Christ Jesus and the resurrection to the Athenians, is called {*new doctrine*}.[858] *The LORD hath created a new thing in the earth, a woman shall compass a man.*[859] Thus the people wondering at the strangeness and unusualness of Christ's doctrine, said: *What*

---

[854] Mark 16:17 with Acts 2:4
[855] Exodus 1:8
[856] John 13:34
[857] Matthew 26:29, Mark 14:25
[858] Acts 17:19
[859] Jeremiah 31:22

thing is this? What new doctrine is this? For with authority commandeth he even the unclean spirits, and they obey him.[860]

(d) When a thing is not common, vulgar, etc. but singular, eminent, excellent, then it is called {*new*}, as a new song (Psalm 96:1 & 98:1). The church's new name (Isaiah 62:2), the faithful's new name (Revelation 2:17), Christ's new name (Revelation 3:12).

(e) When a thing is still to continue fresh in force, without waxing old or vanishing away, it is called {*new*}, as *the New Covenant*, opposed to *the Old*, wearing away (Hebrews 8:8, 13) – this New Covenant dispensation being to continue in force to the end of the world. These are the chief acceptations of the word {*new*} in Scripture – most of which may have fit place here.

(ii) Secondly, newness of heart and spirit may be considered in two ways:

(a) More generally considered, it has some answerableness in it to all these acceptations of {*new*}. For: (1) It is a fresh and late effect upon the soul, in reference to the old man of corruption, which was therein before. (2) It is a quite other and different frame of spirit and heart, than ever was therein formerly. Not sinful, but holy; not natural, but supernatural; not contrary, but conform to God, etc. (3) It is a strange and extraordinary work upon the heart and spirit. As strange, as the quickening and raising up of the dead,[861] as a regeneration, or being born again a second time,[862] or as a new creation itself, which is God's making something out of nothing[863] – so strange and wonderful that carnal men wonder at it: *They think it strange that ye run not with them to the same excess of riot.*[864] That Nicodemus, a teacher in Israel, wondered at it: *How can these things be!*[865] etc, that those who are thus renewed even wonder at themselves, *being called out of darkness into his*

---

[860] Mark 1:27
[861] Ephesians 2:1, 5-6
[862] John 3:3-5
[863] 2 Corinthians 5:17
[864] 1 Peter 4:1, 3-4
[865] John 3:3-11

marvelous light.[866] (4) It is not a vulgar communion or mean work, but a rare, singular, and most eminent effect upon the heart and spirit – so rare and singular that very few obtain it, especially of the *wise, mighty, and noble of the world*,[867] that they whose beauty and spirits are made new, are by God's eminent grace and power advanced from a most base to a most excellent condition above all other people in the world (Titus 3:3-7, Ephesians 2:1-14, etc, Acts 26:18, 1 Peter 2:9-10). (5) Finally, this newness of heart and spirit is such as shall never wax old and vanish away: but shall still be fresh and new, continually increasing more and more in luster vigor and strength till it come to full perfection (1 Peter 1:22-23, 2 Peter 1:5-12, 1 John 3:9, Ephesians 4:11-13, Philippians 3:13-15). Thus this newness of heart and spirit is: [1] A fresh or late work in regard to the former old man with his deeds, old sins. [2] Another and quite different work in the soul, from what was there before. [3] A strange and marvelous work; both in itself, to the renewed, and to others. [4] A rare and singular endowment, conferred but upon a very few. [5] As also a lasting and continuing effect, not waxing old, but still remaining new, yea being more and more renewed day by day. This is the newness of heart and spirit more generally considered.

(b) More particularly, this newness of heart and spirit is the new creation[868] or new supernatural frame of the whole soul,[869] heart, and spirit in part,[870] wrought by the Holy Spirit,[871] according to the image of God.[872] The nature of it is a new creation or new supernatural frame. The subject of this newness is the whole soul. The degree of it is imperfect, but in part. The author of it is the Holy Spirit. The pattern according to which this great new

---

[866] 1 Peter 2:9
[867] 1 Corinthians 1:26-29
[868] 2 Corinthians 5:17, Colossians 3:10, Romans 12:1-2, Psalm 51:10
[869] 1 Thessalonians 5:23, John 3:3, 5
[870] 1 Corinthians 13:9-10, Philippians 3:12-14
[871] Titus 3:5, John 3:5
[872] Colossians 3:1, 10, Ephesians 4:22-24

work is fashioned, is the image of God. So that if this newness of heart and spirit be duly considered, it implies these things especially, namely:

(1) That new qualities, accidents, or endowments are put into the soul and faculties thereof, not a new substance of soul. The natural essence or substance of the soul is not destroyed, but still remains, yet it's divested of the old and invested with new qualifications and properties – see 1 Thessalonians 5:23, Romans 12:2, and Ephesians 4:22-24. Grace does not destroy and ruin nature, but only refines and reforms it. The understanding still remains; but becomes renewed understanding; the will remains; but becomes renewed will, and so on. The new moon is one and the same in substance with the old, but it has a new and increasing endowment of light from the sun which it had lost; so the new heart and new spirit is one and the same in substance-with the old, but it has obtained new endowments from the Sun of Righteousness, Jesus Christ.

(2) That these new qualities or endowments upon the new heart and spirit are not natural or acquired, but merely supernatural and spiritual. Not natural; arising from any natural principle or ability of natural light of mind, or freedom of will, etc,[873] nor acquired by any works of righteousness which carnal man can do, for without Christ and supernatural grace he can do nothing.[874] But merely supernatural and gratuitous, by the saving operation of the Holy Spirit, who *worketh in us both to will and to do of his good pleasure* (Titus 3:4-6, Ephesians 2:8, Romans 9:15-16, Philippians 2:13, Titus 3:4-6, Ephesians 2:8, Romans 9:15-16, Philippians 2:13). Naturally, the soul can understand, but it is only supernaturally that it can understand God and the things of God savingly. Naturally, the soul can will, but it's only supernaturally, that the soul can will well, and so on.

(3) That these new supernatural qualities or endowments upon the new heart and spirit are the image of God in knowledge, righteousness, and true

---

[873] Romans 8:7-8; 2 Corinthians 3:5, Ephesians 2:8, Genesis 6:5, John 6:44
[874] Titus 3:4-6, 1:15-16, John 15:5

holiness renewed and repaired therein. This is a transforming renovation from the corrupt image of Adam to the pure image of God; from the Old to the New man. *And be not conformed to this world, but be ye transformed by the renewing of your mind.*[875] – *Ye have put off the old man with his deeds, and have put on the new man, which is renewed in knowledge, after the image of him that created him.*[876] – *That ye put off concerning the former conversation, the old man, which is corrupt according to the deceitful lusts: And be renewed in the spirit of your mind: and that ye put on the new man, which after God is created in righteousness and true holiness* (Greek: *holiness of truth*).[877] These supernatural qualifications are styled {*the image of God*}: partly, because they are a beam of God's glory, a print and character of the divine nature (2 Peter 1:4); partly, because they make such as enjoy them sweetly resemble God, and become like unto God (1 Peter 1:4-16) as the wax bears the image of the seal, or as the glass bears the image of the face. Now this image of God, what is it else but the knot, cluster, or treasury of inward spiritual infused habits or principles, enabling and disposing us to walk in newness of life (Romans 12:1-2 & 6:3-6).

(4) That these **new supernatural qualities** are universal, extended to the whole soul, not limited or restrained to this or that part, faculty, or affection thereof. There's [1] a **new mind** to know God and Jesus Christ savingly (John 17:3), and to be subject to the law of God willingly (Romans 8:6-7); [2] **new thoughts and imaginations**: not evil, only evil, universally evil continually evil, (Genesis 6:5), but holy, heavenly, spiritual, divine, humble, mortified, self-denying, etc. (Psalm 63:6, 1:2); [3] **new conscience**: not defiled (Titus 1:5), senseless, and seared (1 Timothy 4:2), etc, but purged from dead works (Hebrews 9:14), good, and void of offense (1 Timothy 1:5, Acts 23:1, 24:16), and full of peace (Romans 5:1); [4] **new will**: not carnal, crooked, rebellious, etc, against God and his will (Ephesians 2:3, Jeremiah 44:16-17, Ezekiel 18:31,

---

[875] Romans 12:2
[876] Colossians 3:9-10
[877] Ephesians 4:22-24

Matthew 23:37, John 5:40 & 8:44), but spiritual, regular, self-denying, and conform to the will of God in all things; [5] **new affections**, namely: new desires, as after righteousness, more than riches (Matthew 5:6), after the kingdom of God, more than earthly contentments (Matthew 6:33), after the light of God's countenance more than after corn, wine, or any earthly good, (Psalm 4:6-7); [6] **new loves and delights**, as to God more than to any in heaven or earth (Psalm 73:25) to Jesus Christ, more than to father, mother, sister, brother, husband, wife, or a man's own life (Matthew 10:37), etc, new joys and griefs – formerly joy was carnal, sensual, etc. but now holy, spiritual, in the Lord, in the Holy Ghost, etc. (Romans 5:2-4 & 15:13, Philippians 4:4, 1 Thessalonians 5:17, Romans 14:17). Formerly, grief was worldly, for affliction, etc.; now godly, for corruption, etc. (2 Corinthians 7:10-11). In a word: *If any man be in Christ he is a new creature* (an entirely new creature all over) *old things are past away, behold all things are become new. And all things are of God*, etc.[878] Therefore as corruption, by reason of its general extensiveness over the whole man, is called {*the old man*}, so the image of God and these new endowments, by reason of their general diffusion throughout, are styled {*the new man*}.[879] This the apostle also insinuates in his prayer for the Thessalonians: *And the very God of peace sanctify you wholly*; (ολοτελεις *wholly-perfect*) *and let your whole spirit* (Greek: ολοκληρον υμων το πνευμα και η ψυχη – *your whole, entire, or complete spirit*) *soul, and body be preserved blameless unto the coming of our Lord Jesus Christ.*[880] Hypocrites and castaways may have some new endowments in some faculties, but not throughout; their mind may be illuminated, their conscience convinced, etc, but their heart, and will not softened, etc.

(5) That though these new supernatural principles and qualities are implanted in the whole soul and every part thereof, yet they are not gradually complete, but incomplete in every part. As an infant has all the parts of a man,

---

[878] 2 Corinthians 5:17-18
[879] Ephesians 4:22-24, Colossians 3:9-10
[880] 1 Thessalonians 5:23

but none of them gradually perfect, *we know in part*, etc, *but when that which is perfect is come, then that which is in part shall be done away.*[881] Paul himself said: *Not as though I had already attained, or were already perfect*, etc.[882] Perfection of sincerity, and perfection of parts, the saints enjoy in this world (Job 1:1, Philippians 3:12-14), but perfection of degrees is reserved for the world to come. There, *the spirits of just men are made perfect.*[883] They that talk of their gradual and complete perfection in this life, are in a dream or fond delusion.

(6) Finally, though these new endowments of the new heart and spirit be gradually imperfect and incomplete, yet are they growing and increasing daily towards perfection. *Our inward man is renewed day by day.*[884] – *Your faith groweth exceedingly, and the charity of everyone of you all towards each other aboundeth.*[885] Living trees grow and increase, when dead trunks decay and rot. *From Christ the whole body* (of his church) *fitly joined together, and compacted by that which every joint supplies, according to the effectual working in the measure of every part, maketh increase of the body, unto the edifying of itself in love.*[886]

In these things especially the nature of the new heart and spirit consists.

{Question 3} Whether God alone gives this new heart, and puts this new spirit into his people?

The reason for this question is this: though here God promises to do this great work himself – *A new heart also will I give you, and a new spirit will I put within you*[887] – yet elsewhere, God says: *Cast away from you all your transgressions, whereby ye have transgressed, and make you a new heart, and a*

---

[881] 1 Corinthians 13:9-10
[882] Philippians 3:12-15
[883] Hebrews 12:23
[884] 2 Corinthians 4:16
[885] 2 Thessalonians 1:3
[886] Ephesians 4:16
[887] Ezekiel 36:25-26 & 11:19

new spirit, for why will ye die, O house of Israel?[888] In these words, God seems to devolve this work of making a new heart and a new spirit upon the people themselves. If they could not do it, this exhortation would be in vain.

Answer: This question (did I intend a polemic discourse) would presently lead us into those three great controversies about (i) universal sufficient grace, (ii) liberty or freedom of will, and (iii) the manner of a sinner's conversion unto God, which have a near alliance to, and mutual dependence upon one another; and which are corruptly held and maintained against the truth, by Pelagians, papists, Arminians, Socinians, and the present disguised spawn of all these, the Quakers.[889] But because I chiefly intend positively to assert doctrinal truths, and practically to instruct in answerable duties, I purposely wave polemical dissertations: and therefore to this present question, I briefly offer these few things, namely:

(i) **Firstly, that a mere carnal, unregenerate person cannot at all make to himself, or furnish himself with a new heart or a new spirit, such as is here intended.** By reason of his extreme (a) impotency, (b) pravity [depravity], and (c) enmity thereunto.

(a) Because of his extreme impotency and weakness to this and all such spiritual actions. For, The carnal man (1) is *mere darkness, and receiveth not the things of God: they are foolishness to him, neither can he know them, because they are spiritually discerned*;[890] (2) is mere hardness: a very stone, wholly unable to break, melt or move itself;[891] and (3) is wholly fully enthralled under the absolute dominion of sin and Satan, so captivated under sin, that he is *in the gall of bitterness and bond of iniquity*;[892] that sin fully *reigns over him, obeying it in the lusts thereof, and yielding his members weapons of*

---

[888] Ezekiel 18:31
[889] See D. Prideaux. Lect. 3. De Gracia Universali. & Lect. 4. De Modo Conversionis. & G. Ames. Coron. Art. 4. & P. Moulin's *Anatomy of Arminianism*, chapter 32 to the end of the Book.
[890] Ephesians 5:8; 1 Corinthians 2:14
[891] Ezekiel 36:26
[892] Acts 8:23

unrighteousness unto sin;[893] that he can do nothing but sin, his prayer is abomination, his very eating, drinking, plowing, etc. is sin.[894] He is still fulfilling the wills of the flesh (Ephesians 2:2-3) so captivated under Satan, that he is his prince and God, ruling in him as in a child of disobedience;[895] that *Satan carries him captive* (Greek: *takes him alive*) at his will;[896] that he is *of his father the devil, and the works of his father he will do*;[897] (4) is *wholly dead in sins and trespasses* (Ephesians 2:1, 5) no more able to revive himself spiritually, than a dead man can quicken himself in, and raise himself out of the grave naturally; (5) is wholly without strength in spirituals,[898] cannot of himself believe in Christ and come to him (Ephesians 2:8, John 6:44), cannot of himself think anything as of himself (2 Corinthians 3:5), and without Christ can do nothing (John 15:5).

(b) Because of carnal man's extreme pravity and corruptness, wholly depriving him of all habits, principles, seeds, dispositions, and inclinations to all true spiritual good, especially to this newness of heart and spirit. (1) Not only man's actions and words, but his very thoughts of heart: not only his thoughts, but his purposes, desires, imaginations of his thoughts, not only some; but all and every imagination of his thoughts, are evil, only evil, and continually evil.[899] The whole unregenerate man is wholly and only flesh. *That which is born of the flesh, is flesh*: and nothing else.[900] Every like begets his like. Both Jews and Gentiles are proved by the apostle to be universally and wholly under sin, so that they have not the least propensity or velleity [inclination]

---

[893] Romans 6:12-13
[894] Proverbs 15:8-9, 26 & 21:4
[895] Ephesians 2:2-3; 2 Corinthians 4:4
[896] 2 Timothy 2:25
[897] John 8:44
[898] Romans 5:6
[899] Genesis 6:5
[900] John 3:6

towards this new heart and new spirit.[901] (2) Yea they are willfully set upon evil, against good.[902]

(c) Because of carnal man's utter antipathy and enmity against God and all his laws and ways. The carnal mind (φρονημα της σαρκος),[903] the mind or wisdom of the flesh, namely: The highest excellency of the carnal spirit) is enmity (not only an enemy in the concrete, but very enmity itself in the abstract) against God: for it is not subject to the Law of God, neither indeed can be. A carnal man is wholly flesh (John 3:6), and the flesh only *lusteth against the spirit*.[904] He hates God (Romans 1:30), hates the very godly for God's image in them (1 John 3:12), etc, and hates instruction and reformation (Proverbs 1:25, 29, Psalm 50:17). He is as extremely and irreconcilably opposite to this new heart and spirit, as fire to water, light to darkness, life to death, and heaven to hell.

(ii) **Secondly, that this blessed work of a new heart and new spirit is the proper peculiar, and only work of God in man.** This is plainly evident, for:

(a) The Lord God alone has an absolute freedom and power, much more than a potter of the same lump of clay, to make one vessel to honor, another to dishonor.[905] *So that it is not of him that willeth, nor of him that runneth, but of God that sheweth mercy. – Therefore he hath mercy, on whom he will have mercy: and whom he will, he hardeneth.*[906] If God softens, man cannot harden; if God hardens, man cannot soften.

(b) This effect of a new heart and new spirit in man is so peculiarly appropriated to God alone, that man is wholly excluded from any efficiency or causality therein. Scriptures speak fully to this purpose. *Of his own will begat*

---

[901] Romans 3:9-19
[902] Jeremiah 44:16-17, John 8:44
[903] Romans 8:7
[904] Galatians 5:17
[905] Romans 9:20-24
[906] Romans 9:16, 18

he us with the word of truth.[907] – *Not by works of righteousness which we have done, but according to his mercy he saved us, by the washing of regeneration, and renewing of the Holy Ghost*[908] – *To them that believe on his name: which were born, not of bloods, nor of the will of the flesh, nor of the will of man, but of God.* Thus that eminent grace of faith in Christ, an eminent ingredient in the new heart and spirit, is appropriated to God, as cause thereof: *By grace are ye saved, through faith, and that not of yourselves, it is the gift of God.*[909] To this effect our Savior speaks plainly: *No man can come to me except my Father which hath sent me draw him.*[910]

(c) The nature of this new heart and new spirit is so great, sublime and difficult, that it utterly transcends all ability and activity of carnal men to produce it, and can only be effected by the omnipotent God. For, it is styled: (1) {*regeneration*}, or being born from above.[911] Man cannot generate himself naturally; much less regenerate himself supernaturally. This is God's proper work.[912] (2) Transplanting out of the natural wild olive tree, and ingrafting contrary to nature into a good olive tree.[913] Out of the first Adam, into the second Adam. Can the scions transplant, or engraft itself? The Jews indeed broke themselves off from Christ by unbelief, but it is God alone who is able to graft them in again.[914] (3) Quickening and raising up from the very dead.[915] Can the dead bodies revive or raise themselves from their graves? No more can dead souls quicken or raise themselves from sin. It is only God that raises the dead by his own power.[916] (4) New creation. *If any man is in Christ, he is a new creature* (Greek: *a new creation*).[917] To create properly is to produce

---

[907] James 1:18
[908] Titus 3:5
[909] Ephesians 2:8, Philippians 1:29
[910] John 6:44
[911] Titus 3:5, John 3:3, 5
[912] John 1:13, 3:5, Titus 3:5
[913] Romans 11:24
[914] Romans 11:20, 23
[915] John 5:24-25, Ephesians 2:1, 4-6; 1 John 3:14
[916] 2 Corinthians 1:9
[917] 2 Corinthians 5:17

something out of nothing, and that's God's sole prerogative.[918] David casts this only upon God: *Create in me a clean heart, O God, and renew a right spirit within me.*[919]

(d) The experimental acknowledgement of those (or of others on their behalf) that through grace were partakers of a new heart and new spirit, testifies that it is only from God, and not at all from themselves. As, of Ephraim converted by God, and repenting;[920] of Paul, called by the rich mercy and exceeding abundant grace of our Lord, acknowledging his own utter insufficiency, and that his sufficiency was of God;[921] of Paul and Titus, and other believers, saved, not by works of righteousness which they had done, but *according to his mercy, by the washing of regeneration, and renewing of the Holy Ghost*;[922] of the Ephesians, quickened and saved by God's mere grace, rich mercy, etc, as God's *workmanship, created in Christ unto good works*;[923] of the scattered strangers, the believing Jews, *begotten again by God, according to his abundant mercy, unto a lively hope, called by the holy God out of darkness into his marvelous light.*[924]

(e) Finally, God's exhortations in his word to people, to believe, to repent, to turn themselves, to make themselves a new heart and a new spirit, to work out their own salvation with fear and trembling, etc, are usually allayed and qualified in the same places or in some other Scriptures, with certain cautions, corrections, restrictions and interpretations, giving them to understand, that though God require such things from them, yet they are utterly beyond their ability to effect them as of themselves, being the proper and peculiar work of God himself alone. Thus, it is God's command that we believe on the name of his Son Jesus Christ.[925] But yet elsewhere it is signified that *faith is not of*

---

[918] Hebrews 11:3
[919] Psalm 51:10
[920] Jeremiah 31:18-20
[921] 1 Timothy 1:13-18; 2 Corinthians 3:5
[922] Titus 3:3-8
[923] Ephesians 2:1-11, etc.
[924] 1 Peter 1:1-5, 15 & 2:9-10
[925] 1 John 3:23

ourselves, it is the gift of God; and that *no man can come unto Christ, except the Father draw him.*[926] Again, the Lord requires: *Repent, and turn yourselves from all your transgressions, So iniquity shall not be your ruin; cast away from you all your transgressions, whereby ye have transgressed; – For I have no pleasure in the death of him that dieth, saith the Lord God, wherefore turn yourselves, and live ye.*[927] And yet elsewhere, repentance and conversion are declared to be the mere gifts of God's grace.[928] And Ephraim acknowledges: *Thou hast chastized me, and I was chastized, as a bullock unaccustomed to the yoke; Turn thou me and I shall be turned, for thou art the LORD my God. Surely after that I was turned, I repented; and after I was instructed, I smote upon my thigh*; etc.[929] So they in the Lamentations pray: *Turn thou us unto thee O LORD, and we shall be turned.*[930] Moreover, Israel is exhorted: *Circumcise therefore the foreskin of your heart, and be no more stiffnecked.*[931] Yet elsewhere, lest they should assume any such ability to themselves, God promises to do this work for them: *And the LORD thy God will circumcise thine heart, and the heart of thy Seed, to love the LORD thy God with all thine heart, and with all thy soul, that thou mayest live.*[932] Furthermore the Philippians are exhorted: *Work out your own salvation with fear and trembling*; but there also they are presently instructed: *For it is God which worketh in you both to will and to do of his good pleasure.*[933] In a word, God says by Ezekiel to his people "Make yourself a new heart and a new spirit,"[934] yet lest they should imagine this was within their own power, by the same

---

[926] Ephesians 2:8, Philippians 1:29, John 6:44
[927] Ezekiel 18:30-32, Joel 2:12-13
[928] Acts 11:18; 2 Timothy 2:25
[929] Jeremiah 31:18-20
[930] Lamentations 5:21
[931] Deuteronomy 10:16
[932] Deuteronomy 30:6
[933] Philippians 2:12-13
[934] Ezekiel 18:31

Ezekiel he promises: *A new heart also will I give you, and a new spirit will I put within you.*[935]

(iii) **Thirdly, that though a mere carnal man cannot at all furnish himself with, or make to himself, a new heart and a new spirit, but only God can do it, whose peculiar work it is: yet it is not in vain, that God exhorts carnal men to make them a new heart, and spirit, etc, as Ezekiel 18:30-32.** For such exhortations and commands are in several ways useful and advantageous, such as:

(a) To convince carnal man of the extremity of his present sinfulness, and corrupt frame of heart. The old heart and spirit are so bad, that no less than a new heart and spirit, a new frame, a new creation, will serve turn to cure it.

(b) To inform carnal man, wherein the cure of his Old sinful heart and spirit will chiefly consist, namely: in an absolute and total new frame of heart and spirit.

(c) To assure carnal man of the utter necessity of this new heart and new spirit unto salvation. Without this there being nothing to be expected but death (Ezekiel 18:30-32). Though therefore carnal man cannot renew his own heart and spirit, repent, and so on, yet God's exhortations, commands, and threats to this effect are thus of great consequence.

(d) To be a means of a new heart and spirit to carnal man. For ofttimes God commands man to do that which is indeed beyond his ability, that by that command (accompanied with the efficacy of his Spirit) he may enable him to perform what is commanded, for the glory of his own name. It was not in vain for God in creating to command light, etc. *Let there be light*: when by that effectual command he made light to be.[936] It was but a word, and a work. It was not in vain for Jesus Christ to command Lazarus, four days dead and buried, bound hand and foot with grave clothes, *Lazarus come forth*, when that command by the efficacy of the divine power brought him forth of his

---

[935] Ezekiel 36:26
[936] Genesis 1:3

grave.[937] It was not in vain for Peter and John to bid the cripple, *Rise up and walk*;[938] or for Ananias to say to Saul, *Brother Saul receive thy sight*, etc,[939] when by such words limbs were restored to the lame, and eyes to the blind. In like sort, sometimes God, commanding men to repent, to turn themselves from their iniquities, to make themselves a new heart, and a new spirit, etc. makes his commands effectual instrumental means to work in them the repentance and renovation required.

(e) Finally, to leave carnal men without excuse before the tribunal of God, if after such commands of repentance, and so on, they persist still in carnality and impenitency, not thoroughly performing in order to God's command, what they can do. For hereupon they shall be at last condemned, not only or chiefly for their weakness, that they cannot; but for their wickedness and willfulness, that they will not do what God requires. To this effect said Augustine appositely, "God does not command impossibilities, but by commanding he admonishes both to do what you are able, and to ask what you are not able to do."[940]

{Question 4} Why the Lord promises and gives a new heart and new spirit to his professed people?

Answer: The LORD promises and bestows a new heart and spirit upon his professed people, such as belong to his election, for these reasons, namely:

(i) Because the purpose of God according to election must stand inviolable. All God's visible and professed people are not within the election; some are, and in due time they must be called and renewed, so that they may be justified and glorified according to that chain of the causes of salvation in Romans 8:29-30.

---

[937] John 11:43
[938] Acts 3:6
[939] Acts 9:17
[940] Non igitur Deus impossibilia jubet, sed jubendo admonet, & facere quod possis, & petere quod non possis. Aug. *de Natur. & Grac. contra Pelagianos.* c. 43. Tom. 7.

(ii) Because of his own mere kindness, pity, and mercy towards them, not any their desert [merit] or goodness at all (Ezekiel 36:21, etc, 31-32). Notable is that of Paul to this effect in Titus 3:3-8.

(iii) Because, without this newness of heart and spirit, there is no escaping of death, or obtaining of justification and life eternal (Ezekiel 18:30-32, Hebrews 12:14) Renovation and regeneration are the very highway to justification and eternal salvation (Romans 8:29-30, Titus 3:5-7).

(iv) That from this new frame of heart and spirit, they might be enabled and inclined to walk in God's statutes and keep his ordinances and do them, as becomes God's covenant people (Ezekiel 11:19-20 & 36:26-27; see also Ephesians 2:10).

{Question 5} How may this new heart and spirit which God gives, be evidenced and discovered to them that have it?

Answer: This new heart and spirit may be evidenced to them that have it, according to that which has been already laid down – and that in many ways, such as:

(i) By the original fountain whence the new heart and spirit does spring, namely: not from anything in impotent carnal man, but only from the omnipotent God. If it be his peculiar work, it is right work (Ezekiel 36:26, Titus 3:5-7). Carnal man may make in himself many alterations, especially if helped by common grace and gifts, but can never reach to this heart renovation savingly.

(ii) By that new operation of God upon the heart and spirit to make them new. This is not an ordinary and common, but an extraordinary and special work of his saving grace. His new, his excellent work indeed (Ephesians 2:10), called in the Scriptures: (a) regeneration; (b) transplanting out of the olive tree wild by nature, and engrafting contrary to nature in the good olive tree; (c) quickening and raising from the dead; and (d) new creation. If therefore the heart and spirit be thus regenerated,[941] transplanted,[942] ingrafted, quickened, raised,[943] and newly created,[944] then without question, this is indeed the new heart and new spirit of God's own framing.

(iii) By the new supernatural qualities and endowments upon the heart and spirit. This newness of heart and spirit consists not in the newness of their essence or substance, but of their qualities, endowments, etc. and those qualities not natural, or acquired; but supernatural, and spiritually infused (John 1:12-13; 2 Corinthians 3:5, Ephesians 2:8, John 6:44, Genesis 6:5, Romans 8:7-8, John 15:5, Titus 3:5-8). Naturals cannot evidence supernaturals.

(iv) By the image of God, consisting in knowledge, righteousness, and true holiness, which comprises in it the substance of these supernatural qualities and endowments. This newness of heart and spirit being nothing else but the new man put on, which is created according to this image of God.

(v) By the universal extensiveness of these new supernatural qualities and endowments unto the whole heart and spirit, and to all the principles, faculties and affections there. Not only some things, but all things become new when the spirit and heart are made new. See formerly in Question 2. Every part is in some measure renewed, though none completely.

(vi) By the continual growth of the new man in all these new supernatural qualities and endowments, until they come gradually to their complete perfection (2 Corinthians 4:16; 2 Thessalonians 1:3; 2 Peter 3:18).

(vii) Finally, by the new acts, works, conversation, and course of life, resulting as fruits and effects from this new heart and spirit.[945] New principles and habits must needs produce new acts, and new causes new effects – even a holy, heavenly, gracious, conscientious newness of life. They therefore that are

---

[941] Titus 3:5, John 3:3, 5
[942] Romans 11:24
[943] Ephesians 2:1, 4-6, John 5:24-25; 1 John 3:14
[944] 2 Corinthians 5:17
[945] Ephesians 2:10, Romans 6:4-7; 2 Corinthians 5:14-17, Titus 3:4-9

not divorced from their old, sinful, corrupt, ungodly, unrighteous and intemperate conversation, do thereby declare themselves to be mere strangers to this new heart and spirit here promised.

Thus of this first effect and influence of God's Spirit promised: newness of heart and spirit.

(Influence & Effect 2):
A heart knowing the LORD.

A heart knowing the LORD, or, a heart to know God, that he is the LORD: This a second influence or effect of God's Spirit promised in this Covenant. *Thus saith the LORD, the God of Israel, like these good figs, so will I acknowledge them that are carried away captive of Judah, whom I have sent out of this place into the land of the Chaldeans for their good. For I will set mine eyes upon them for good, and I will bring them again to this land, and I will build them, and not pull them down; and I will plant them, and not pluck them up. And I will give them an heart to know me, that I am the LORD, and they shall be my people, and I will be their God: for they shall return unto me with their whole heart.*[946] In these words two sorts of blessings are promised, namely: [1] firstly, temporals, as: {1} God's acknowledging and setting his eyes upon his captives for good, {2} returning them into Canaan, and {3} setting or establishing them there (verses 5-6); secondly, spirituals, as: {1} an understanding heart, {2} a dear covenant relationship to God, and {3} a sincere and entire conversion unto God (verse 7). This last, of returning to the LORD with their whole heart, gives us to understand that these spirituals of knowledge and covenant relation here promised, are saving blessings tending indeed to their everlasting happiness.

Here only I shall speak to the first: *And I will give them an heart to know me, that I am LORD* (verse 7), wherein note: [1] the author, and [2] the nature of this spiritual influence.

[1] **The author of this spiritual influence or effect is only God.** *I will give them an heart to know me* – not themselves, nor any others but only I myself will give them this heart. This implies various things, such as: {1} that naturally they lacked this knowing and understanding heart, were blind in discerning spirituals, in knowing God savingly – this is one sad fruit of man's

---

[946] Jeremiah 24:5-7

first fall.⁹⁴⁷ {2} That this knowing heart cannot be supplied to them by any, but by God himself. *I will give them an heart*, etc. Now God gives such a knowing heart: partly by the ministration of his Word and gospel, by the light whereof God and the things of God are revealed and manifested to the soul; partly by the operation of his Spirit:⁹⁴⁸ (i) taking the veil of ignorance and unbelief from off the heart,⁹⁴⁹ and (ii) shining into the heart with such supernatural illumination, as savingly gives the light of the knowledge of God, and of the things of God, in the face of Jesus Christ.⁹⁵⁰

[2] **The nature of this spiritual influence or fruit of God's Spirit:** *An heart to know me, that I am JEHOVAH.* Herein consider: the habit, the act flowing from that habit, and the object of that act.

{1} **The habit or principle:** *a heart.* {*Heart*} in Scripture is variously taken: (i) sometimes for the intellectual part only: the understanding, mind, judgment, conscience, etc. *Yet the LORD hath not given you an heart to perceive, nor eyes to see, and ears to hear unto this day*;⁹⁵¹ and: *If our heart condemn us, God is greater than our heart, and knoweth all things*, etc.⁹⁵² (ii) Sometimes for the affective part only: the will and affections, such as: *I will put my laws into their mind, and write them in their heart*;⁹⁵³ *Whosoever looketh on a woman to lust after her, hath committed adultery with her already in his heart*;⁹⁵⁴ *Sorrow hath filled your heart*; *Your heart shall rejoice.*⁹⁵⁵ (iii) Sometimes for both the intellectual and affective part, even for the whole soul: *When thou shalt enlarge my heart*;⁹⁵⁶ *With my whole heart.*⁹⁵⁷ This is often used. Now here, {*I will give them an heart*} has reference not only to the

---

⁹⁴⁷ Ephesians 4:17-18; 1 Corinthians 2:11, 14
⁹⁴⁸ 2 Corinthians 4:2, 4, 6, Acts 26:18
⁹⁴⁹ 2 Corinthians 3:16-18
⁹⁵⁰ Hebrews 6:4; 1 Corinthians 2:11-13; 2 Corinthians 4:6
⁹⁵¹ Deuteronomy 29:4
⁹⁵² 1 John 3:19-21
⁹⁵³ Hebrews 8:10
⁹⁵⁴ Matthew 5:28
⁹⁵⁵ John 16:6, 22
⁹⁵⁶ Psalm 119:32
⁹⁵⁷ Psalm 9:1, 111:1, 119:2, 10, 34, 58, 69, 145 & 138:1

intellectual, but also to the affective part of the soul, and implies not barely and nakedly the whole heart, understanding, will, and affections – these they had naturally – but such an understanding, such a will and affections, so principled, so qualified, so sanctified, so habituated and furnished, as *to know me, that I am JEHOVAH*: these they have only supernaturally. This the habit, or habitual ability promised.

{2} **The act, which should particularly result from this habit: to know God.** Knowledge is twofold, namely: (i) **Of simple intelligence**: merely intellectual, speculative, or imaginative. This is either natural (Romans 1:19-21) or supernatural in Christ (2 Corinthians 4:6). (ii) **Of approbation** also; when we so know as to approve, affect, love, desire, esteem, delight in, etc. Here may be implied both, as it is very usual with the Hebrew phrase, according to that known maxim: *Verba sensus & Intellectus includunt voluntatem & affectus*. They shall so know and understand God, as to acknowledge, accept, own, love, desire, delight and acquiesce in God, as the only true God, and their only God in Christ, etc. This knowledge is a notable inlet and foundation to faith,[958] confidence,[959] repentance,[960] holy obedience,[961] and eternal life.[962] And therefore it is a great and most desirable blessing.

{3} **The object of this act, of this knowledge, is God, that he is Jehovah**. God is the supreme and most perfect object knowable, infinitely transcending the reach and capacity of all created understandings. God can perfectly be known by none, but himself. The creature may in Christ supernaturally know God unto salvation and life eternal sufficiently; and the more the creature does so know God, the more it attains to be like unto God.[963] To know God, that he is **Jehovah**, implies (according to the

---

[958] Hebrews 11:2, Isaiah 53:11
[959] Psalm 9:10
[960] Jeremiah 31:19
[961] John 13:17
[962] John 17:3
[963] John 17:3; 2 Corinthians 4:6

signification of the word **Jehovah** formerly explained):[964] (i) A God having eternal independent unchangeable being in and of himself (Revelation 1:8). (ii) A God giving being to all things that are, that have being (Isaiah 44:24-25, Amos 5:8, Romans 11:36, Acts 17:28). (iii) A God that gives being and actual subsistence to his decrees, words, covenants, and promises in Christ (Exodus 6:3). (iv) A God that chose Abraham, and entered into covenant with him and his seed, to give them Canaan, "renewed this my Covenant to Isaac, Jacob, and at Mount Sinai to the seed of Israel, and afterwards gave them the promised land in my truth and faithfulness."[965] In sum, "They shall know me, that I am the only true God, and the God of their fathers, and of them, and consequently, how heinously they have offended in departing from me their only true God, and bringing themselves into Babylonian bondage, that so they may sincerely and thoroughly repent, and return to me as their God, with their whole heart." For (as Calvin here well observes)[966] then the sinner has the gate of repentance opened to him, when he begins truly to know God, and looks up to him and his tribunal, etc. (Jeremiah 24:5-7).

Now this true saving supernatural knowledge of God and his ways, has these special properties, whereby it may be discovered, namely: it is (i) experimental (Philippians 1:9, Hebrews 5:14, Psalm 34:8; 1 Peter 2:3); (ii) heart-humbling and soul-abasing (Job 42:5-6, Romans 7:18, 24, Galatians 2:20, Philippians 3:7-8; 1 Corinthians 15:9, Ephesians 3:8; 1 Timothy 1:13, 15); (iii) communicative, in order to others' edification (Proverbs 15:7, Psalm 51:12-13); (iv) growing and prospering (Philippians 1:9, Colossians 1:10; 2 Peter 3:18); (v) affectionate, or heart-affecting (1 John 4:7-8; Philippians 1:9 & 3:8; 1 Corinthians 2:2); (vi) spiritualized, 2 Corinthians 5:16; 1 Corinthians 2:14, 7, Matthew 13:11); (vii) pure and sin-purging (James 3:17; 1 John 3:6); (viii) practical, obediential, and fruitful in all good works (James 3:17; 1 John 2:3-4, John 10:4, 13:17, Psalm 119:98-100). By these characteristics, a man

---

[964] Book 3 Chapter 4
[965] Genesis 12:1-3 & 17:2-4, etc.
[966] John Calvin on Jeremiah 24:6-7

may discern whether his knowledge of God, and the things of God, be true saving knowledge or not. All these particulars I do but here point at, because elsewhere I have more largely explained them. Thither I refer the reader for his fuller satisfaction.[967]

Thus of the second fruit of the Spirit here promised, namely: a heart knowing God, that he is **Jehovah**.

---

[967] In my *Communicant Instructed*, pp.99-109 (London, 1651)

(Influence & Effect 3):
Fleshiness or tenderness of heart,
instead of stoniness of heart.

(3) Fleshiness or tenderness of heart, instead of stoniness of heart. This is a third excellent fruit or influence of the Spirit promised to these captive Jews, after their return from Babylon. *A new heart also will I give you, and a new spirit will I put within you: And I will take away the stony heart out of your flesh, and I will give you an heart of flesh.*[968] And elsewhere: *And I will take the stony heart out of their flesh, and will give them an heart of flesh: That they may walk in my statutes, and keep mine ordinances, and do them: And they shall be my people, and I will be their God.*[969] This is a very sweet blessing, and precious promise. Touching this, note:

[1] The connection that it has with the former promise and blessing of a new heart and spirit (Ezekiel 36:26). Whence it's evident that as the new heart and new spirit are the fruit of God's Spirit, so this heart of flesh is a result of this new heart, is one of those gracious qualifications, dispositions, endowments, etc. of this new heart and new spirit. Fleshiness of heart is one excellent ingredient in that newness of heart, but both are the fruits of the Spirit of God.

[2] The description of the blessing, or fruit of the Spirit here promised: {1} Partly, by the author or efficient thereof, God and his free grace: *And I will take away – and I will give*, etc. It is God alone that must do all, in this matter; they could do nothing. God the sole agent; they merely passive in this first infusion of holy habits and principles into the soul. And thus it is also with all carnal men in the first work of renovation upon them, they are mere patients; but afterwards, *acti agunt*, being acted by God, they act together with God. {2} Partly, by the the twofold act of grace which God would put forth upon

---

[968] Ezekiel 36:26 compared with verses 24-25
[969] Ezekiel 11:19-20

them: (i) Firstly, removing or taking away the stony heart cut of their flesh. *Flesh* in this phrase denotes their body, unto which *heart* or *soul* is here opposed. Stony heart, (Hebrew: לֵב הָאֶבֶן *leb heeben, a heart of stone*) denotes their natural, habitual, and complete stoniness of heart. Their heart is not only stony, but stoniness; not only a stony heart, but a heart of stone; a mere stone; a heart constituted, compacted, and made up of nothing but stone. He does not say *a heart of clay* that, though very hard, may be softened with water; nor a heart of brass, iron, steel, etc. which though extreme obdurate, and intractable, may be made malleable, yea may be melted with fire, to take any form from the hammer, and to run into any mold, but *an heart of stone*, wherein (as Zanchi has well observed)[970] there is no softness nor disposition thereunto, it will break, rather than bend; no moisture that can be pressed out of it, no life at all: but only hardness, dryness, and deadness. God's taking-away or removing this stony heart, is emphatic. God does not say "I will heal it" or "I will transform it" or "I will soften it," etc, but: *I will take away their heart of stone*. It is so extremely hard, and past mending, that it must be abolished, taken away, etc, and a whole new frame of heart erected and substituted in its place. There is nothing in our nature that has any affinity with the divine nature, so that *old things must wholly pass away, and all things become new* (2 Corinthians 5:17). (ii) Secondly, giving them a heart of flesh. *Flesh* here is

---

[970] Cor hominis non renati vocatur Lapidcum, Ezek 11. & 36. [...] [Here some text is unclear in the copy of the original work that I accessed – Ed.], ut mani bus flecti non possit, versarique sicut cera: habet tamen quandam Qualitatem, licet exiguam, ad mollitiem nempe, ut si igni admoveatur, molle fieri] queat, & malleo in omnem formam [flucti], quanquam remaneat ferrum. At lapis nullam habet mollitiem, neque ad mollitiem aptitudinem, ut scilicet adjutus igne mollescere malleoque flecti possit, permanens lapis: Sic Cor nostrum nulla ratione ductile aut flexibile est ad recti obedientiam, ideeque opus est ut totum Cor auseratur, & aliud in ejus locum reponatur. 2. Ex lapide nullus unquam liquor exprimi poterit, unde Miraculum illud fuit maximum, cum è petra in deserto fluxerunt aquae: Sic è corde nostro nihil penitus exprimi potest boni, nisi aliud fiat, i. e. Elapideo Carneum. 3. Lapis non vivit ut Caro Nec in Corde est aliquid vitae spiritualis. 4. Non ait Deus, se transformaturum Cor lapideum in Cor Carneum: Sed ablaturum lapideum & daturum Carneum. Significans in nostra Natura nihil esse quod Affinitatem habeat cum Natura Dei, sed opus est ut tota vetus Natura toliatur, & nova reponatur. Hier. Zanch. *De Lib. Arbitr.* Thes. 9.

opposed to *stone*, and denotes softness, tenderness, tractableness, etc, of heart and soul to God in spirituals. But yet this is God's mere gift: *I will give them a heart of flesh*. This is God's second act of grace. {3} Partly, by the end and scope intended by God in this his double act of grace upon them: that they might walk in his statutes, and keep his ordinances, and do them. Formerly, their hearts were so stony, that they were wholly rebellious, contumacious, and refractory against him, and all his ordinances, etc, contemning, profaning, polluting, violating them, etc. But now their hearts should be so fleshy, tender, etc, that their course and conversation should be quite altered, and become most obediential and conform to the statutes and ordinances of God, they should be capable of any divine impression.

Thus we have the meaning of the Holy Spirit in this promise more generally. But because the heart of stone was not only the malady of the carnal Jews, but is the universal disease of all carnal men since the fall; and because, the heart of flesh, is a supernatural remedy and mercy, as necessary to us, as to the Jews; And because, the heart of stone cannot be removed, nor the heart of flesh conferred by any, but only by God alone, etc, therefore let us look a little more inwardly and accurately into these things, and discuss these few questions, namely: [1] What is the heart of stone? [2] What is the heart of flesh? [3] Can any besides God alone take away the heart of stone and give the heart of flesh? [4] How does God take away the heart of stone and give the heart of flesh? [5] How a man may know, whether this heart of stone be removed, and the heart of flesh bestowed upon him?

[Question 1] What is the heart of stone?

Answer: The heart of stone is such a heart, spirit, or soul as is most like a stone. A metaphorical expression, yet very emphatic. It's more to say {*a heart of stone*} than {*a stony heart*}. A heart of stone implies the whole heart to be a mere stone, having nothing else in it but stoniness, a mere stony composition.

Such the hearts of all men by nature; such the hearts of these Jews, mere stones. More particularly thus take the resemblance.

{1} **A stone is inanimate, dead, without life, and incapable of life.** Yea, even the most choice precious stones are dead things, so the heart of stone is a dead heart, as dead as a very stone unto all spirituals can act and move therein of itself no more than a very stone.[971] There is some deadness, dullness, etc, remaining in the most lively hearts of the saints, hence David so often prays for quickening; but the carnal heart is wholly dead in sin, there's not any the least principle of spiritual life there.[972]

{2} **A stone is exceedingly cold; dead and cold** – so a heart of stone is by nature quite cold in reference to spirituals, having no warmth, heat or sanctuary fire of true love, zeal, fervency, etc, towards God, Christ, and religion; or at most has but a counterfeit hypocritical lukewarmness, which is nauseous to God. Irreligion is stone-cold; true religion is fervent, hot as fire. Hypocrisy is lukewarm: neither hot nor cold.[973]

{3} **A stone is drossy, lumpish, heavy, naturally only descends downward, and never ascends upward.** *Lapis est terra condensata*, A stone is condensed earth, and earth the grossest, coarsest, drossiest, heaviest of all the four elements; so a heart of stone is a lumpish, heavy, drossy heart that by nature never tends upwards,[974] but only downwards, namely: from God, from Christ, from religion, from all spirituals, to Satan, sin, and all wickedness;[975] or if ever this heart of stone tends upwards towards God, etc. that is not from any true inward principle, but merely from some outward force or violence of fear, restraining grace, etc. and therefore when such force is over; it returns again to its natural course, falls down again.[976]

---

[971] Ephesians 2:1, 5, John 5:25
[972] Psalm 119:25, 37, 40, 88, 107, 149, 154, 156, 159
[973] Revelation 3:15-16, 19
[974] Acts 28:27
[975] Job 21:14-15 & 22:17 with Genesis 6:5, Psalm 14:1-3, 36:1-4, Romans 3:9-10
[976] Mark 6:20; 2 Kings 17:25-26, etc.

{4} A stone is very obdurate and hard; it is condensed earth, and the more condensed any body is, the harder it is; so the heart of stone is an obdurate hard heart. It has in it, not an iron-hardness or steel-hardness or metal-hardness, but a stone hardness; a flinty adamantine hardness. In regard to this hardness in a special manner, the carnal heart is here called {*an heart of stone*}. Let us inquire therefore a little further into the nature of this hardness of heart. Hardness of heart generally implies the heart's confirmedness, contumacy, rebellion, stubbornness, stiffness, settledness, etc, in any sinful evil. This hardness of heart is opposed sometimes to faith, as in Acts 19:9 and Hebrews 3:12-13. And so it is, the heart's hardness in unbelief: sometimes to understanding, judgment, wisdom, etc, such as Mark 6:51-52 and 8:17-22. And so it is hardness in ignorance, inapprehensiveness, dullness, and so on: sometimes to repentance, as Romans 2:5. So it is, the heart's hardness in impenitency: sometimes to obedience; as in Exodus 8:15, 32, and often; and also Psalm 95:8. So it is, the heart's hardness in disobedience: sometimes to humility, as Daniel 5:20. So it is, the heart's hardness in pride: sometimes to the fear of God, and the whole way of God's service, etc, as Isaiah 63:17. So it implies the heart's hardness in any fearless, godless, irreligious courses, etc.

But still *hardness of heart* imports the heart's obfirmation [obduracy] in some sin or other. Hardness of heart is either reigning or not reigning: *that* in the unregenerate; *this* in the regenerate.

(i) ***Hardness of heart reigning in the unregenerate*** is chiefly threefold, namely: natural, acquired, and judicial.

(a) **Natural** hardness of heart is that wherein every man is naturally involved during the time of his carnal ignorance, unbelief, impenitency, disobedience, and so on.[977] The heart of all men, as of the carnal Jews, is naturally a very heart of stone until Christ supernaturally vouchsafes his

---

[977] Romans 2:5

softening grace.⁹⁷⁸ This malady of the stone in the heart is hereditary to all the mere posterity of Adam.

(b) **Acquired** or **contracted** hardness of heart is that sinful improvement and increase of natural hardness, so that it becomes more fixed, rooted, habitual and predominant over the soul. This hardness gradually, and deceitfully, and insensibly steals upon the heart. *Nemo repent fit pessimus*: none becomes worst at first dash. *Lest any of you be hardened through the deceitfulness of sin.*⁹⁷⁹ James excellently discovers the deceit of sin creeping by little and little upon the soul, till it be hardened in it, and ruined by it. *Every man is tempted, when he is drawn away of his own lust, and enticed: then, when lust has conceived, it brings forth sin: and sin, when it is finished, bringeth forth death.*⁹⁸⁰ Here are these degrees of sins deceit in order to hardening therein, namely: (1) lust within; the foment of sin, and fuel of temptation. (2) *Withdrawing*, or *drawing away*, by that lust; namely: from God and goodness.⁹⁸¹ (3) *Enticement, allurement*, etc, properly, as the fish is enticed by the bait to swallow the hook; enticement to evil.⁹⁸² (4) Conception of lust; namely: a delightful accepting of the enticement by the consent of heart and will thereunto. (5) The birth, or bringing forth of sin conceived, namely: into act and execution. (6) Finishing or completing of sin brought forth and acted, namely: going on in an habitual course and custom of sinning, whereby the heart is more and more hardened therein.⁹⁸³ (7) Death, the wages of sin. Bernard also notably sets forth sin's subtlety and deceitfulness, gradually emboldening and hardening the heart in sin. "See," (he says), "the lapse, yea, fall of an evil conscience, how by little and little, step by

---

⁹⁷⁸ Ezekiel 36:26, 11:19, Psalm 95:7-8, Hebrews 3:7-8 & 4:7
⁹⁷⁹ Hebrews 3:13
⁹⁸⁰ James 1:14-15
⁹⁸¹ εξελκομενος
⁹⁸² δελεαζομενος
⁹⁸³ "By perfected sin, therefore, I understand, not any one act of sin perpetrated, but the completed course of sinning." John Calvin on James 1:15
<https://www.studylight.org/commentaries/eng/cal/james-1.html>
[Accessed 3/1/2024]

step it declines from God: and so descends into the deep, that the pit shuts her mouth upon it." [1] When a man accustomed to good sins grievously, it seems so importable [unbearable] to him, that he seems to go down into hell alive. [2] In the process of time, it does not seem not importable, but heavy: and between *importable* and *heavy*, there is no small descent. [3] A little afterwards, he judges it light; and when he is beaten with frequent stripes, he feels not the wounds, heeds not the stripes, etc. [4] In a short space of time, he not only does not feel it, but that which was bitter, both pleases and becomes sweet, and that which was sharp is turned into sweet. [5] Then it is brought into custom, that now it not only pleases, but it daily pleases, and he cannot contain himself. [6] And at last it cannot be pulled away, because custom is turned into nature, and what was at first impossible to be done, is now impossible to be refrained. Thus he descends, yea falls from Jerusalem to Jericho; thus he passes unto aversion and hardness of heart; here the sinner stinks; here he is four days dead. Here the stone put upon the sepulcher admits not those merciful divine rays of light, etc. unless at any time the merciful God converts the stony into a fleshy heart."[984] So he. Thus the acquired hardness of heart creeps upon the heart deceitfully and insensibly by degrees.

(c) **Judicial** hardness of heart is when God in his just judgment gives up hardened impenitent sinners unto their own hardness, leaves them to themselves and to Satan to be hardened in sin more and more. This God does, not by infusing any hardness, impenitency, or wickedness into the heart (James 1:13), but: (1) partly by withholding of his softening grace, renewing grace, which God is not bound to give unto his creature, whereupon the sinner falls by his own corruption, as a ruinous house, when a prop is withheld, falls by its own weight. (2) Partly, by giving men up to the sway and swing of their own lusts.[985] Then God takes off the chain from these mad corruptions: and seeing they will be vile and hard-hearted, they shall be so. (3)

---

[984] Bernard, Book of the Conscience, p.1109 (Antwerp, 1616)
[985] Psalm 81:11-12, Romans 1:26-28, etc.; 1 Kings 22:22-23, John 13:26-27

Partly by laying before men thus forsaken of God such means of restraints, as extremely irritated and exasperated corruption, as the damming up of a torrent makes it swell more outrageously, as a lion or tiger rages so much more in chains.[986] (4) Partly by denying them even those means of restraint (Hosea 4:14, Isaiah 1:5). (5) Partly by blasting to them the very means of grace (whereby others are softened) to their obduration. The very self-same doctrine and miracles of Christ that softened and saved the rest of the apostles, hardened and damned Judas. The same sun which softens wax, hardens clay: The same beams and showers which make a garden smell more fragrantly, make a dunghill stink more odiously. This natural, acquired, and judicial hardness of heart, is reigning hardness, proper to carnal men. This is taken away, when the stony heart is removed, and the heart of flesh conferred.

(ii) *Hardness of heart not reigning, but arising from relics of sin, and infirmity of grace, may be in the best and most tender hearted penitents.* The Lord Christ once and again reproves his apostles for the hardness of their hearts.[987] Such feel the stone in their own hearts, and lament and mourn under the sense of their hardness, which is a great evidence of softness and tenderness of heart, for sense of hardness cannot come from a principle of hardness, but of tenderness, no more than a stone can feel itself to be a stone, or a dead man perceive himself to be dead. There is some true sense where there is a complaint of numbness; some true life where there is a complaint of deadness. The heart of stone, all reigning hardness, may be removed, and yet some relics of hardness may remain even where there is a heart of flesh.

{5} **A stone is very impenetrable**, especially some sorts of stones, as the iron-stone, pebble, flint, marble, adamant: they will hardly receive any stamp or impression. Hammers and instruments of steel will hardly pierce them. So the heart of stone is a very impenetrable heart, and will not easily be pierced or wounded – no not with the hammer of God's threats and judgments, will not

---

[986] Romans 7:8, Isaiah 6:9-10 with 28:26-27
[987] Mark 6:52 & 8:17

easily receive any sacred impression from God and his Spirit. How many dreadful blows did God strike upon Pharaoh's heart of stone by all his judgments?[988] Yet his heart remained an impenetrable stone notwithstanding all. Neither promises, nor threats, nor mercies, nor judgments will work upon a hard heart.

{6} **A stone is inflexible**, will break to powder rather than bow or bend; iron or steel or brass, though hard and strong, yet by fire they may be made to bend as the workman pleases, and capable of any form or impression, still remaining iron, steel or brass; so the heart of stone is a froward, perverse, crooked, inflexible heart; a willful, stubborn, rebellious, intractable heart. Pharaoh's hard heart would not be bowed or inclined to let Israel go, and when he was forced to release them, in his hardness of heart he pursued after them, to his own destruction.[989]

{7} **Finally, a stone is a dry, sapless piece of condensed earth**. It affords little or no juice, or moisture; hence the proverb of squeezing water out of a flint or pumice, insomuch that it was a very great miracle which God wrought for Israel, when he turned the rock into a standing water, the flint into a fountain of waters;[990] so the heart of stone is a dry, sapless heart, no drop of the oil of grace is there, no drop of penitential water can spring thence: *But after thine hardness and impenitent heart, treasurest up unto thyself wrath against the day of wrath*.[991]

This is the heart of stone which God promises to take away; and these are the properties or characters of it. So that when God takes away this heart of stone and gives a heart of flesh, converts a man from hardness to tenderness of heart, he may then be said, even of stones to raise up children unto Abraham.[992]

---

[988] Exodus 7:13, 9:12, 10:1, 20, 27 & 11:10 & 14:8
[989] Exodus 11:10 & 14:8
[990] Psalm 114:8
[991] Romans 2:5
[992] Matthew 3:9

[Question 2] What is the heart of flesh?

Answer: A heart of flesh: {1} does not here imply a carnal sinful heart or soul, that is in a state of sin and flesh, as the word {*flesh*} is frequently used in the New Testament, for the corruption of nature, in which sense {*flesh*} is opposed to {*spirit*};[993] but {2} it implies a soft tender flexible tractable heart or soul, in reference to God and spirituals – the word {*flesh*} being here opposed to {*stone*}. So that by the heart of stone already described, we may easily discern what the heart of flesh is, namely:

{1} **Flesh is naturally a living substance.** Flesh is the fittest receptacle of life, sense, motion, etc. So the heart of flesh is spiritually, a living heart, not a dead heart. It has in it the true supernatural principle of spiritual life, sense, motion, activity, etc. towards God and all the ways of godliness. It is informed, animated and quickened by the Spirit of God, and accordingly led by him.[994]

{2} **Flesh, living flesh, has warmth and heat in it**: a natural heat wherein life doth partly consist; so the heart of flesh has holy warmth and heat in it, a spiritual flame of zeal and fervency, required in God's people.[995] David, who shed so many tears for his own and others sins (Psalm 6:6-7 & 38:3-6; 51; 119:136) was so warm-hearted towards religion that the zeal of God's house did even eat him up (Psalm 69:9). Among all the kings of Israel and Judah, none was so intensively zealous and fervent in spirit for a thorough reformation of the church according to God's will, as was that phoenix king, the melting tender-hearted Josiah. Compare 2 Chronicles 34:19, 27 with verse 29 to the end, and chapter 35:1-20.

{3} **Flesh, living flesh, is of a more noble and excellent constitution than any inanimate body** – it does not only move downwards like a stone, but can move upwards, forwards, and in every way. So the heart of flesh that is spiritually softened has a more excellent heavenly constitution than the heart of stone, and tends upwards towards God, notably pressing forward in all

---

[993] Romans 7:25 & 8:1, 4-6, 9, 12-14; Galatians 5:17
[994] Romans 8:9-11, 13-14
[995] Romans 12:11, Revelation 3:19

heavenly ways. How vehemently did the fleshy-hearted David thirst after God, his ordinances, and all his ways![996] How did he soar aloft in high celestial contemplations, affections, and devotions! Holy Paul after his heart of stone was removed, and the heart of flesh conferred upon him – how did he *press towards the mark*, etc.[997] Yea, he *labored more abundantly than all the apostles*,[998] yea he attained to such visions and revelations that he was *caught up into the third heaven, which is paradise (in the body or out of the body he could not tell) where he heard things which were not possible for him to utter*.[999]

{4} **Flesh is a soft and tender substance; so the heart of flesh is a soft and tender heart** – not a close compacted obdurate spirit, but an open spirit, quickly wounded and pained. But here, to avoid mistakes, consider that fleshiness, softness, or tenderness of heart is twofold: carnal and spiritual.

(i) *Carnal softness, tenderness, or fleshiness of heart*, is that which may be in a mere carnal man, in whom the heart of stone still remains. And this is threefold especially, namely: natural, worldly, and hypocritical. (a) **Natural fleshiness and softness of heart**, is nothing else but a mere natural disposition or inclination unto softness, tenderness and relenting of soul, arising from the natural frame, temper or constitution of the bodily heart, eyes, etc. which is in some more, in others less tender. This natural tenderness discovers itself upon occasion of any pathetic object; such a softly-composed heart, is among women rather than men, etc. quickly receives impressions of grief, and utters itself in expressions of tears. Such can weep at a pathetic sermon, and weep at a pathetic tragedy. (b) **Worldly fleshiness and softness of heart**, is that which takes its rise from some worldly ground, or occasion, etc. This may be in the godly and in the wicked. *Esau sought for repentance carefully with tears*,[1000] that is: by tears he sought to move his father Isaac to

---

[996] Psalm 42:1-3, 63:1-3, etc, & 84 & 119:32
[997] Philippians 3:13-14
[998] 1 Corinthians 15:10
[999] 2 Corinthians 12:2-4, etc.
[1000] Hebrews 12:16-17 with Genesis 27:38

repentance, and change of his mind, about the blessing.[1001] Jacob bitterly mourned for Joseph, supposing him to be torn in pieces and devoured by some wild beast.[1002] David's heart did bleed for Absalom.[1003] Rachel *wept for her children, and would not be comforted*.[1004] But all these were worldly sorrows, and *worldly sorrow worketh death*.[1005] (c) **Hypocritical fleshiness or softness of heart**, is nothing else but a counterfeit tenderness of heart pretended for religion, as in Ahab[1006] and the Pharisees.[1007] Now all these expressions of fleshiness and tenderness, merely arising from natural principles, were only natural, as the waters in the pipe cannot rise higher than the head of the spring. These are not here understood.

(ii) *Spiritual fleshliness, softness, or tenderness of heart*, is that supernatural fruit of the Spirit of Grace upon the hearts of true converts, wounding and melting their souls kindly for sin, especially as being against so good a God, so that they can find no satisfactory rest or refreshment in themselves or any other creature, but only in the favor of God pardoning and reconciling them to himself in Jesus Christ.[1008] This is the right *pricking in the heart*.[1009] This is the true *godly sorrow working repentance never to be repented of*.[1010] This is the true brokenness and contrition of spirit, which is the sacrifices of God, which God will not despise.[1011] Now this is: (a) habitual and (b) actual. (a) Habitual softness or tenderness is that holy habit or principle of contrition or tender-heartedness for sin, which at first conversion is wrought in the heart by the Spirit of God, whereby the soul is disposed deeply to mourn and be in bitterness for offending God, and is wrought up unto

---

[1001] Hebrews 12:16-17 with Genesis 27:38
[1002] Genesis 37:33-35
[1003] 2 Samuel 18:33
[1004] Matthew 2:18
[1005] 2 Corinthians 7:10
[1006] 1 Kings 21:27-29
[1007] Matthew 6:16
[1008] Zechariah 12:10-12, Acts 2:35-37, Matthew 26:75
[1009] Acts 2:36
[1010] 2 Corinthians 7:10
[1011] Psalm 51:17

unfeigned repentance (Zechariah 12:10-12, Acts 2:35-37, 2 Corinthians 7:10). (b) Actual softness or tenderheartedness is the actual exerting, putting forth, or expressing of this softness of heart in relenting for sin upon particular occasions,[1012] as did David for his fall,[1013] Josiah for the sins of the land, Peter for denying of his Master,[1014] etc. This spiritual tender frame of heart; this habitual tenderness, disposed to express itself penitentially upon all just occasions, is the heart of flesh here promised.

This softness, tenderness, fleshiness of heart is a most excellent qualification of the heart. For: (a) This is the sacrifices of God, to him instead of all, and beyond all ceremonial sacrifices. A broken heart is more pleasing to God than all burnt offerings, sin offerings, meat offerings, drink offerings, etc. (Psalm 51:16-17). (b) This broken and contrite spirit, God will not despise (Psalm 51:17). That is, the Lord will highly prize and make great reckoning of a contrite spirit: a meiosis [litotes]. (c) This broken spirit is preferred by God before all mere moral performances and pharisaical perfections whatsoever, (Luke 18:10-15). (d) God has a special eye and peculiar respect to a tender heart, to a poor and contrite Spirit (Isaiah 66:1-2; 2 Chronicles 34:27-28, 33:12-13, Luke 7:36 to the end). (e) God ranks this tender fleshy heart amongst his choicest spiritual blessings promised in his Covenant (Ezekiel 11:16-21 & 36:24-26, etc, Zechariah 12:10, etc.) (f) God himself is so affected with tenderness and brokenness of heart, that he peculiarly undertakes the healing, binding up, reviving and comforting of broken hearts and bleeding souls (Psalm 147:3, Isaiah 57:15 & 61:1-3 with Luke 4:18). (g) The blessed God is so taken with the humble and contrite spirit that he selects and singles it out for his peculiar habitation, and the place of his rest (Isaiah 66:1-2 & 57:15). But of these particulars I now speak no farther, having elsewhere opened them more at large.[1015]

[1012] 2 Chronicles 34:19, 27
[1013] Psalm 51 throughout
[1014] Matthew 26:75
[1015] In my sermon entitled: *A Broken Spirit, God's Sacrifices* – pp.8-13 (London, 1647)

{5} Flesh, being very soft, tender and porous, is easily pierced and wounded, is exceedingly penetrable. Not only swords and spears; but the least prick with a thorn or scratch with a briar makes it bleed. So the heart of flesh is very penetrable, quickly pierced with godly sorrow and contrition, and bleeds in penitential tears. Good Josiah melted at hearing the threats and curses of the law read,[1016] while Pharaoh melted not under all God's plagues inflicted on him.[1017] Yea Christ's very look upon Peter after his denial of him wounded Peter's heart, so that *he went out and wept bitterly*.[1018] Yea more than that, David's heart was so quickly pierced, that having numbered the people, his own heart smote him.[1019] A fleshy heart has a relenting principle within itself, that makes it quickly bleed at the least wound of sin and temptation.

{6} Flesh is soft and flexible. So the heart of flesh is a soft pliant flexible heart, will take any impression from God, will bend and bow as God shall please. Peter's hearers when they were pricked in their hearts, they presently cry out, to the apostles, *Men and brethren what shall we do?*[1020] As if they had said, we are ready to be, and do anything that the Lord would have us, that we may be delivered from our sin-guiltiness: oh direct us what way to take. The like see in Paul's conversion,[1021] and in the jailor's renovation.[1022]

{7} Finally, flesh has moisture in it, blood and other humors in it, which are apt to flow forth when it is pierced and wounded. So the heart of flesh has a moisture in it – when it is pierced for sin, how does it bleed and melt into tears of repentance! As in the instances aforementioned – David, Josiah, Peter, etc. – is evident.

This is the *heart of flesh* which here God promises to give his people.

[1016] 2 Chronicles 34:19, 27
[1017] Exodus 7:13, 9:12, 10:1, 20, 27 & 11:10 & 14:8
[1018] Luke 22:61-62
[1019] 2 Samuel 24:10
[1020] Acts 2:35-37
[1021] Acts 9:6
[1022] Acts 16:30

[Question 3] Can any besides God alone take away the heart of stone, and give the heart of flesh?

Answer: This question is for substance the same with that 3rd question at large formerly handled, namely: whether God alone gives a new heart, and puts a new spirit within his people. Thither therefore I refer the reader for his satisfaction – especially considering that this heart of flesh is one property or perfection in this new heart and new spirit.

[Question 4] How does God take away the heart of stone and give the heart of flesh?

Answer: God takes away the heart of stone, and gives the heart of flesh, in various ways, and usually by sundry gradual acts.

{1} Several ways, namely: (i) efficaciously, by his own Spirit, that Spirit of Grace; destroying stoniness, and infusing softness of heart in the great work of renovation and conversion (Ezekiel 36:26-27, Titus 3:5, Zechariah 12:10-14). (ii) Instrumentally, (a) sometimes by the furnace of afflictions, thawing and melting their obdurate stony hearts. The furnace melts and dissolves even Stones of iron and steel. Manasseh himself was softened, and humbled himself greatly under his affliction (2 Chronicles 33:12-13), so the prodigal (Luke 15:11-20). The convert thief upon the cross, had his cross so sanctified to him, that of a reviler of Christ, he became a justifier of Christ, and a condemner of himself (Matthew 27:44 with Luke 23:39-43). (b) Sometimes, by the overcoming streams of love and mercy: suppling insinuating oil in some cases pierces deeper than the keenest vinegar. *Then shall ye remember your own evil ways, and your doings which were not good, and shall loathe yourselves in your own sight, for your iniquities, and for your abominations.*[1023] *Then*! When? When God should have poured upon them the streams of promised mercies, spiritual and temporal: *then they should loathe themselves*, etc.[1024] (iii) Most

---

[1023] Ezekiel 36:31
[1024] Ezekiel 36:25-31

ordinarily, by the word preached (Acts 2:37-38, etc. & 9:4-6). This is as fire to melt, a hammer to break, and a sword to penetrate the most obdurate heart of stone.[1025]

{2} By sundry gradual acts, God could in a moment remove the heart of stone and give a heart of flesh, but ordinarily, working by means, he proceeds gradually, step by step. As, (i) God smites the heart of stone with sharp rebukes, with word rebukes (2 Chronicles 33:10, etc, Acts 2:33, 36, etc. & 9:4, etc.), and with rod rebukes (2 Chronicles 33:11-13, Acts 9:4, 8-9). As Moses with his rod smote the rock thrice before the waters gushed out, so God smites the rocky heart before it relents or bleeds – not only once or twice, but frequently. (ii) Having smitten the heart, he awakens and opens it by conviction. He convinces it of its own sinfulness and vileness (John 16:9, Acts 2:23, 36, etc, Job 36:8-9). This conviction was in some sort upon Judas (Matthew 27:3-5). And it notably awakens and opens the impenitent brawny and stony heart. (iii) Having awakened the heart by conviction, he wounds the heart with compunction, remorse and contrition. Thus Peter's hearers, after conviction were pricked in their hearts (Acts 2:37). They were punctually wounded as it were in every part and point of their hearts, as with so many swords or daggers. Yet this contrition reached not up to true repentance, the apostle afterwards putting them upon repentance (Acts 2:38). These three degrees may be in carnal men and hypocrites as well as in true believers. (iv) Having wounded the heart of stone by contrition, he newly-principles the heart with the Spirit of Grace and Renovation, and so lays a foundation of softening and suppling [making supple] the heart of stone. This is a supernatural principle of softness peculiar only to the elect: by this, the heart of flesh is created, and the heart of stone removed fundamentally (Zechariah 12:10, etc, Titus 3:5). (v) Having principled the heart with a Spirit of Grace, the root of softness of heart, he directs the eye of the heart and soul affectingly to look upon its sins peculiarly as against Christ (Zechariah 12:10, etc. John

---

[1025] Jeremiah 23:29, Ephesians 6:17

16:8-9, Acts 2:35-37). Now to look upon sin, as peculiarly against such a Savior, as neglecting and contemning Christ the only remedy against sin, yea, as piercing and wounding Christ with all his sufferings (Isaiah 53:4-6). This must needs deeply affect and wound the heart, and overcome the Spirit by the love of Jesus Christ. (vi) Having turned the eye of the soul to look upon him whom it has pierced, he kindly thaws and melts the heart into a flood of sincere godly sorrow and mourning for all sin, as against such a Savior (Zechariah 12:10-14, 2 Corinthians 7:9-11). (vii) Having drenched the soul in godly sorrow for sin, he works up the heart to a sincere and through repentance from sin, abhorring sin, and itself for sin, and for time to come declining all evil, and all appearance of evil, with all fear, care, vigilance, and tenderness of heart (2 Corinthians 7:9-11, Ezekiel 36:31). Thus God removes the heart of stone and gives a heart of flesh.

[Question 5] Lastly, how may a man know whether God has removed this heart of stone, and bestowed upon him this heart of flesh?

Answer: A man may discover this in several ways, such as:

{1} By the removal of the properties of the heart of stone. If they are removed, the heart of stone is taken away. These properties are described already in Question 1 about this particular.

{2} By the presence of the properties of the heart of flesh, laid down also in Question 2. Where the true properties and characteristics of the heart of flesh are, there the heart of flesh is.

{3} By God's way of proceeding with a man in removing the heart of stone, and conferring the heart of flesh. This is also described in Question 4. Try whether God has proceeded in such gradual acts and steps with you to mollify your heart, and this efficaciously by his Spirit; instrumentally by his afflictions, mercies, and Word.

{4} By the associates and companions of a heart of flesh or broken spirit,[1026] such as: (i) a spirit of prayer and supplication familiarly accompanies an heart of flesh (Zechariah 12:10, etc, Luke 15:17-18, Acts 9:11, Luke 22:44 with Hebrews 5:7). A broken spirit is a praying spirit. (ii) Humility and poverty of spirit. A broken heart of flesh is a humble heart (Isaiah 57:15 & 66:2). (iii) Love to Jesus Christ. A heart of flesh is tenderly affectionate, and entirely loving to Jesus Christ, who was broken and bruised for our iniquities (Zechariah 12:10-14, Luke 7:37-38, 44-49). Yea Christ binds up the broken-hearted (Isaiah 61:1-2, etc, with Luke 4:18-19). (iv) Obedience. A heart of flesh is a tractable, obediential heart (Ezekiel 11:19-20, 36:26-27, Acts 9:6 & 2:37." It can say as Augustine, "Enable me to do what you command, and command me to do what you will."[1027] But all these particulars, I have elsewhere more fully opened; there see.[1028] Now a heart of stone may be discovered by its contrary companions, namely: prayerlessness, pride, disaffection to Christ, and disobedience to God.

{5} Finally, by the adjuncts of a broken contrite heart of flesh. (i) A tender fleshy heart grieves and mourns for the sins of others, especially for the public sins of the times abounding, as David (Psalm 119:158, 53, 136), Josiah (2 Chronicles 34:19-21, 27), and those marked mourners in Ezekiel 9:4. (ii) A tender fleshy heart has clearest and saddest apprehensions of its own sinfulnesses, as those in Zechariah 12:10-14, David (Psalm 51:3-5, 8), and Paul (Romans 7:24, 9-11; 1 Timothy 1:13, 15). (iii) A tender contrite fleshy heart is most perplexed at sin, as against God, as against Jesus Christ (Psalm 51:4, Zechariah 12:10-12, etc). (iv) A tender fleshy heart trembles at God's Word (Isaiah 66:2) and at God's rod (Ezra 10:9; 2 Chronicles 34:27). (e) A tender fleshy heart kindly wounded for sin, sets speedily and seriously about a real reformation, as Peter (Matthew 29:75 with Luke 22:62), Paul (Acts 9:20), Ezra (Ezra 9:1-3 with 10:1-3, etc.), Josiah (2 Chronicles 34:27, 29 to the end), and

---

[1026] See my sermon entitled: *A Broken Spirit God's Sacrifices*, pp. 25-27 (London, 1647)

[1027] "Da quod jubes, & jube quod vis." August. *Confessions*. lib. 1. cap. 13. Tom. 1.

[1028] In my said sermon

Manasseh himself (2 Chronicles 32:12, 15-16). These things I do but briefly point at, because elsewhere in a sermon I have more fully insisted upon them: and yet I do mention them, because that sermon may perhaps be very scarce.[1029] Now a heart of stone has quite contrary adjuncts and properties: it rejoiceth in, rather than mourns for, the sins of others (Romans 1:32), grieves least at its own sinfulness, is not troubled at sin as against God and Jesus Christ, hardens itself against both God's Word and rod, and hates to be reformed. By these particulars we may discover notably whether the heart of stone be taken from us, and the heart of flesh conferred upon us.

Thus of the third fruit of God's Spirit here promised, namely: the taking away of the heart of stone, and giving the heart of flesh.

[1029] In my sermon entitled: *A Broken Spirit God's Sacrifices*, pp. 28-35 (London, 1647)

(Influence & Effect 4):
Penientialness of Heart.

This is intimated in various expressions having reference to this Covenant: *Then shall ye remember your own evil ways, and your doings that were not good, and shall loathe yourselves in your own sight, for your iniquities, and for your abominations.*[1030] *Neither shall they defile themselves anymore with their Idols, nor with their detestable things, nor with any of their transgressions: For I will save them out of all their dwelling-places, wherein they have sinned, and will cleanse them; so shall they be my people, and I will be their God.*[1031] *For they shall return unto me with their whole heart.*[1032] In these passages, compared together, note how their hearty repentance is described:

[1] **By the occasional ground and rise of it**, namely: the manifold acts of divine grace and mercy towards them, in bringing them from Babylon to Zion, in enriching them with many spiritual and temporal blessings: *Then shall ye remember*, etc. (Ezekiel 36:24-32), as if he had said, "When I shall thus have redeemed you, and furnished you with such and such streams of mercies on every side, then your hearts shall be so convinced and overcome with my expressions of kindnesses towards you, that you cannot choose but have kindly impressions of Repentance for your sins upon your hearts." Nothing in the world so kindly and effectually wounds and melts the heart for sin, as the loving-kindnesses and mercies of that God towards us against whom we have sinned.

[2] **By certain gradual acts of repentance**, such as:

{1} Remembrance of their own evil ways and doings. Impenitency forgets, but repentance remembers and calls to mind iniquities, lays them afresh before

---

[1030] Ezekiel 36:31
[1031] Ezekiel 37:23
[1032] Jeremiah 24:6-7

the open view of the conscience, though acted long ago; and lays them to heart.[1033]

{2} Self-loathing and self-abhorring for their iniquities and abominations. The Hebrew phrase is very emphatic: *And ye shall-cuttingly-loathe-yourselves in your faces for your iniquities, and for your abominations.* The word נְקֹטֹתֶם *nekotothem, ye-shall-cuttingly-loathe-yourselves,* is variously rendered. By Junius: *ye shall be a loathing to yourselves.*[1034] By Pagnin: *And ye shall judge yourselves in your sight worthy to be cut off, for,* etc.[1035] By Montanus: *And ye shall reprobate yourselves in your faces.*[1036] The word קוט *koot,* which is the root of it, properly signifies, To cast away, to abominate, or to be cut in pieces with trouble, offense, tediousness, etc. Hence our English word {*cut*} may be well derived. And in the New Testament (as Mercerus has well noted) it is rendered, Sometimes προσωχθισα, I was offended, or I was grieved (Hebrews 3:10 from Psalm 95:10); sometimes ετροποφορησεν – *He suffered-their-manners in the wilderness* (our translation has in the margin, perhaps for ετροποφορησεν, *As a nurse bears, or feeds her child* – Acts 13:18 from Psalm 95:10).[1037] Sometimes by διεπριοντο, *dissecari, to be cut asunder* (Acts 5:33 & 7:54), so that by this word, God intimates how his people should be cut and wounded for their sins, to the utter loathing and abhorring of themselves for them. True godly sorrow and repentance for sin, makes the sinner very despicable and abominable in his own sight. The penitent soul, most exactly knowing his own sinfulness, hath more mean and abject thoughts of himself than of any other, or than any other can have of him. The penitent publican *would not lift up his eyes to heaven, but stood afar off, smote his breast, and said, God be merciful to me a sinner.*[1038] Job repenting *abhorred*

[1033] Genesis 42:21-22, Psalm 51:3-5
[1034] Fastidio eritis verbis ipsis. Junius
[1035] Et quod succisione digni essetis, judicabitis in conspectu vestro. Pagnin
[1036] Et reprobabitis vos In faciebus vestris. Montanus
[1037] Mercer in Pagnin *Thesaur. ad verb.* קוט
[1038] Luke 18:13

himself as in dust and ashes.[1039] The penitent woman applies herself with her tears, her hair, her kisses, her ointment, to the very feet of Christ.[1040] The prodigal repenting, confessed to his father, *I am no more worthy to be called thy son, make me as one of thine hired servants.*[1041] Penitent Paul confessed himself to be *less than the least of all saints,*[1042] but *chief of sinners.*[1043] That pious, holy, and penitent martyr Mr. John Bradford did so extremely loathe himself for his own sinfulness, that in the close of his epistles to his Christian friends he was wont to style himself: *the sinful John Bradford; Miserimus peccator John Bradford; A very hypocrite John Bradford; A very painted hypocrite John Bradford; The most miserable hard-hearted unthankful sinner John Bradford.*[1044]

{3} Utter aversion from all their sins. Neither shall they defile themselves anymore with their idols, nor with their detestable things, nor with any of their transgressions (Ezekiel 37:23) Then sin is truly repented of, when it is forsaken: and never until then.

{4} Cordial conversion to God. For, they shall return unto me with their whole heart (Jeremiah 24:7). This is the completing act of repentance, to turn even unto God.[1045]

[3] **The integrity or entireness of their repentance:** {1} In aversion from sin: *That they shall not defile themselves anymore* – with any of their transgressions. {2} In conversion to God: that they shall return to him with their whole heart *heartily*, without dissimulation, and *entirely*, with the whole heart, without reservation.

This is that penitential frame of heart and course, which God here promised to his captive-people. And it is a great blessing from God,

---

[1039] Job 42:3-6
[1040] Luke 7:37 to the end
[1041] Luke 15:18-19
[1042] Ephesians 3:7-8
[1043] 1 Timothy 1:15
[1044] John Foxe, *Acts & Monuments of the Church*, Volume 3.
[1045] Acts 26:18, Jeremiah 4:1, Hosea 7:16

wheresoever he pleases to bestow it,[1046] and a special purchase of Jesus Christ.[1047] I shall not here need to add anything further, touching the {1} nature of repentance, wherein it consists; {2} notes of true repentance, whereby it may be tried and discovered to be in a man; having elsewhere handled both these particulars.[1048]

[1046] Acts 11:18; 2 Timothy 2:25
[1047] Acts 5:31
[1048] In my *Communicant Instructed*, pp.127-138 (London, 1651)

(Influence & Effect 5):
Oneness of heart and way.

This is a fifth notable influence or fruit of the Spirit promised in this Covenant to the captive Jews: *And I will give them one heart, And I will put a new spirit within you,* etc.[1049] *And they shall be my people, and I will be their God. And I will give them one heart, and one way, that they may fear me forever, for the good of them, and of their children after them. And I will make an everlasting covenant with them,* etc.[1050]

This oneness of heart and way here promised in this Covenant is described in these Scriptures:

[1] By the efficient cause, or author thereof, namely: God and his Spirit: *I will give them one heart and one way, – I will put a new spirit within you.* This oneness of heart and way therefore is not at all of ourselves; it is merely of God. For (as Calvin notes), it would be a needless and absurd promise for God to say he would give that which is our own already, and which everyone can confer upon himself. God takes to himself the sole glory of bestowing it.[1051]

[2] By the nature of it, which is, {1} partly inward: one heart, and {2} partly outward: one way. Calvin thinks that from this place Paul borrowed that expression: *It is God that worketh in you both to will and to do, of his good pleasure* (Philippians 2:13). One heart: there is to will; and because the heart is the seat of the affections, it implies also the affections consenting. One way: there is the outward execution, and effect of the will reduced to act. Oneness of heart without oneness of way, is fruitless; oneness of way without oneness of heart, is but hypocritical.

[1049] Ezekiel 11:17-20

[1050] Jeremiah 32:38-40, etc.

[1051] "Nam supervacua esset imo absurda Promissio, si diceret Deus se nobis daturum, quod jam nostrum esset, & quod quisque sibi potest conferre" John Calvin, commentary on Jeremiah 32:39

[3] By the end of it, which is twofold, namely: {1} immediate: *that they may fear me forever*. This end specifies the former oneness of heart and way, and declares what kind or sort it is. Not any sinful confederacy or combination in evil, not any mere natural, moral, or civil oneness of heart and way, but a religious, spiritual, supernatural oneness of heart and way. {2} Mediate: for the good of them and their children after them. Oneness in heart and way in matters of religion, brings welfare both upon parents and their posterity.

The chief thing here to be opened is the nature of this oneness of heart and way, which is the blessing here promised. To this purpose consider: [1] What is here meant by *heart* and *way*? [2] What the oneness of heart and way is: and wherein it consists? [3] How choice and excellent a blessing this oneness of heart and way is? [4] What helps and directions may best further the obtaining and maintaining of this Oneness of heart and way among God's people?

[Question 1] What is here meant by *heart* and *way*?

Answer: Not to mention the various uses and acceptations of *heart* and *way* in Scripture, thus I conceive: *heart* and *way* are here mentioned both of them in reference to religion and the fear of God (Jeremiah 32:39). Therefore we must understand them to be a *heart* and *way* religiously qualified. Again, *heart* and *way* are here opposed one to another. Therefore, by *heart*, I understand the whole soul, with all the faculties thereof: mind, conscience, will, and affections, graciously qualified. For *heart*, thus taken in its latitude, is most directly opposed to *way*, and it seems to import all the inward habits, principles, qualifications, and elicit acts of grace in the whole soul and all the faculties thereof. By *way*, I understand all the outward imperate [imperative] acts and expressions of religion in the whole course of life, in public or in private, but especially in the worship of God. By *heart*, understand all inward principles and religious dispositions in the whole soul: By *way*, all outward expressions and practices flowing from those principles. Thus they are very comprehensive.

[Question 2] What is this oneness of *heart* and *way*, and wherein does it especially consist?

Answer: There is a twofold oneness of heart and way, namely: {1} **personal and individual**, and {2} **ecclesiastical**, and in reference to Christian and church society.

{1} **Firstly, personal oneness of heart and way in affairs of religion, is such an oneness as peculiarly concerns a man's own individual person only towards God.** And this oneness of heart and way implies:

(i) The unfeignedness and uprightness of any person in religion. For his heart and way are not divided, but united; they are not two, but one. They are not repugnant, but sweetly correspond to one another in matters of religion. Hypocrisy and feignedness of religion appears in this: that the heart and way are not one; the principle and practice contradict one another. Their way holy, heavenly, saint-like, and so on, but their heart wicked, hellish, and devilish. Such the Pharisees: *outwardly fair and beautiful, like green graves, or painted sepulchers; inwardly full of dead men's bones and all filthiness.*[1052] They washed the outside of the cup and platter: but the inside remained full of ravening and excess. Such, like the boatman, look one way and row another.

(ii) The determinate and resolved simplicity or singleness of a person's religion, both in inward principle, and outward practice. He has not a double heart, and a double way in religion, but one heart and one way. He does not halt between two opinions, doubting which is right, between the worship of God and of Baal, between Christianity and Antichristianism, and between Christ and Belial.[1053] He does not equally love God and the world,[1054] and serve

---

[1052] Matthew 23:26-28
[1053] 1 Kings 18:21
[1054] 1 John 2:15

God and mammon,[1055] but he is determinedly resolved both in heart and way, as Joshua, to love and serve the Lord only.[1056] This is the true religious oneness and singleness of heart and way (2 Corinthians 1:12). Opposite unto this single *resolved heart*, is a *divided heart* (Hosea 10:2) – a heart and a heart, which is perfect neither towards God nor man (Psalm 12:2; 1 Chronicles 12:33 with 38). *A double-minded man*, δίψυχος, a wavering man, that wavers hither and thither, like an unsettled wave of the sea (James 1:8). Such a man is a sceptic in religion, has his religion to choose; is one day of one religion, another day of another religion, until at last he becomes of no religion. But this seems not to be that oneness here chiefly intended, and therefore I pass it.

{2} **Secondly, ecclesiastical oneness of heart and way in reference to a Christian and church society, is such an oneness in the inward principles**[1057] **and outward practice or exercise of religion,**[1058] **as concerns the people of God jointly and reciprocally in their church capacity as joint members of Christ and one of another.**[1059] Of this oneness of heart and way, the prophet seems here especially to speak, in my judgment: (i) Partly, because the promise of one heart and way is not directed to any particular persons of the Jews in their single capacity, but to the whole body of the Jews in their joint church capacity. *And I will give them one heart and one way*, etc. (Jeremiah 32:38-40, etc.) (ii) Partly, because the Jews had formerly been a very divided people in heart and way, both from God, and from one another in the matters of religion: *Their heart is divided.*[1060] The ten tribes under Jeroboam were divided from God and his true worship, and from the two tribes, by their idolatry in the two calves. And afterwards in the days of Elijah and Ahab, how did they halt between two opinions: between the worship of God and Baal, etc. The sin and misery of this division God promises now to cure by giving

---

[1055] Matthew 6:24
[1056] Joshua 24:14-15
[1057] 1 Corinthians 1:10, Ephesians 4:[25, 32] etc.
[1058] 1 Corinthians 1:10, Philippians 3:16
[1059] Ephesians 5:30; 1 Corinthians 12:13-28, Ephesians 4:13, 16
[1060] Hosea 10:2

them one heart and one way. (iii) Partly, because in this Covenant, God had promised to unite them, that they should be no more two nations or two kingdoms, but one under David their prince, namely: under Christ the only true David. And this their oneness in and under Christ for substance agreeing with their oneness of heart and way, is especially an ecclesiastical oneness. Now in this notion, consider we: (a) of oneness of heart, and (b) of oneness of way.

(a) **Oneness of heart** is an inward oneness and sameness of soul amongst them, whence their outward oneness of way should flow. This inward oneness of heart and soul, consists not in the natural identity or sameness of the soul amongst them, according to the fond dream of Averroes, that there was but one and the same numerical soul that informed all men's bodies; but in the spiritual oneness or sameness of principles, endowments, qualifications, etc, in their whole souls, namely: in their minds, wills and affections, in reference to God, Christ, and religion. Not that the people of God have all of them either an identity of gifts or a gradual equality of graces, for the Scripture plainly declares the contrary.[1061] But that there should be in the hearts of all God's people, notwithstanding all the variety of their gifts and graces, a sweet consent, concord, symmetry, harmony, agreement, compliance, and correspondence, as if their hearts and principles were but one and the same towards God and one another in the affairs of religion. This oneness of heart the apostle notably describes to the Philippians: ινα το αυτο φρονητε την αυτην αγαπην εχοντες συμψυχοι το εν φρονουντες – *Fulfill ye my joy, that ye be like-minded, having the same love, being of one accord, of one mind.*[1062] In these words, oneness of heart is excellently set forth, and that (as those two learned authors, Zanchi and Beza think)[1063] more generally and more particularly.

(1) **In general**, by those words: ινα το εν φρονουντες, *That ye mind the same thing*; our translation, *That ye be like minded*, not so exactly to the

---

[1061] 1 Corinthians 12:4-13, Ephesians 4:6-7
[1062] Philippians 2:1-2
[1063] See Zanchi's commentary on Philippians 2:2, and Beza's annotation on this place.

Greek. This is the genus or general nature of oneness of heart: those three that follow the species thereof. For, says Beza, otherwise there would be a vain tautology in the last phrase {το εν φρονουντες}.[1064] And the word {φρονητε} is referred sometimes to the acts of the will, sometimes of the understanding. Compare Romans 12:16 and 15:5 and Colossians 3:2 with Romans 12:3. This, by Zanchi, is fitly styled [αυτοφρονηοις], same-mindedness, same-affectionedness, etc. Our English can hardly reach the emphasis of this Greek word. This is that oneness of heart in general, when there is a sameness of mind, will, and affections among God's people towards religion.

(2) **In particular**, by the several species, sorts, or branches of this same-heartedness, which are here all expressed by participles, as the genus was expressed by the verb. These branches are three: oneness of affection, will, and mind ascending upwards from the lowest to the highest, from the affection to the will, and from the will to the mind – oneness of the mind in matters of religion being the cause and springhead of both the rest.

[1] **Oneness of mind and judgment.** το εν φρονουντες: *Minding that one thing*. This is not a tautology with the former expression of minding the same thing, but rather an explication of it, as one special branch of the general. For, they that mind that one thing, cannot but mind that same thing, for in one there is no variety, but in several.

But many may profess [το αυτοφρονηοις]: to mind the same thing, who do not altogether mind that one thing. When we recede from minding that one thing, we can never mind the same thing, as Zanchi well notes.[1065] So that this oneness of mind consists in minding that one thing, namely: in a joint consent of mind and judgment about the truth or doctrine of Christ touching all matters of religion, whether faith, practice, worship, or government and discipline, Christ's truth and doctrine extends to all these.

[1064] Beza's annotation on Philippians 2:2
[1065] Zanchi's commentary on Philippians 2:2

False teachers and seducers among the Philippians had begun to add other doctrines to the doctrine of Christ preached by the apostle, as touching the keeping of the law, observing circumcision, etc, to justification. This was not now to mind that one thing, that one truth and doctrine of Christ, but to have their minds divided and distracted about several doctrines and several things. As there is but one Christian truth, faith, or doctrine, so all the professed members of Christ ought (so far as is possible) to have an unanimous consent of mind and judgment touching that one truth of Christ in all affairs of religion.[1066] This should be their daily study and endeavor with all diligence. How vehemently does Paul urge this: *Now I beseech you brethren by the name of our Lord Jesus Christ, that ye all speak the same thing, and that there be no divisions among you: but that ye be perfectly joined together in the same mind, and in the same judgement.*[1067] Here note:

{1} **The matter exhorted to.** The apostle here ascends (thinks Beza)[1068] in a retrograde course, from speech to will, and from will to the fountain of all, the judgment of the mind: and therefore by *mind* {νοι} he understands the will; and by *judgment* {γνωμη} the understanding. Calvin contrariwise, by {*mind*}, the understanding; and by {*judgment*}, the will.[1069] What if we refer both these expressions to the understanding, interpreting {*mind*} of the theoretical or contemplative understanding, and {*judgment*} of the practical understanding? Or expounding {*mind*} of the intellectual or apprehensive act of the understanding, and {*judgment*} of the decisive, determinative, and conclusive act? Yea that whatsoever is in the mind or understanding, namely: thinking, apprehending, discoursing, judging, etc. all might be (as it were) one and the same amongst them touching the matters of religion. This the oneness of mind and judgment here exhorted to, which is Emphatically amplified by the closeness and compactedness of this union: *But that ye be perfectly joined*

[1066] John 18:37-38, Ephesians 4:5, Hebrews 6:1; 2 John 9-10
[1067] 1 Corinthians 1:10
[1068] Beza's annotation on 1 Corinthians 1:10
[1069] John Calvin's commentary on 1 Corinthians 1:10

together in the same mind, etc. ητε δε κατηρτισμενοι, properly: but that ye be perfectly-jointed-together. For the word is a metaphor from bones in joint. When the bones are in their place they are strong, active, etc. but when they are out of joint they are weak, useless, painful: thus in the mystical body, the church, they must be careful to keep all the members and bones well-jointed. A dislocation in judgment disturbs the whole body.

The other matter or duty exhorted to, is sameness of speech about matters of religion: *That ye speak the same thing*. Sameness of mind and judgment causes sameness of speech, but different speeches in new terms, new notions, new distinctions, new descriptions, etc, in singularity, strangeness, and quaintness of expressions, ministers have great cause of suspicion that there are differences of opinions. Some refuse to speak with others in the church's plain usual and received expressions, that they may be thought more wise than others, and that so they may the more plausibly vent their errors to others. This was the manner of heretical persons of old, and is too much taken up amongst us in these days.

{2} **The mischief or sin dehorted from**: *That there be no divisions* (Greek: *schisms*) *among you*. *Schism* signifies dissection, dilaceration, etc, from [σχιζω] to cut asunder, divide, etc. In the general, it implies any division, dissection, or dilaceration in the church, whereby the unity thereof is dissolved. (3) The arguments whereby he both dehorts and exhorts, namely: His sweet compellation of them: *brethren*. His earnest exoration: *I beseech you*. The cogent authority of Christ's name: by the name of our Lord Jesus Christ, as you love, respect, reverence, and honor this blessed name, avoid divisions, and pursue unity in speech, and in judgment. They that are *carried away with every wind of doctrine*;[1070] that *turn away from the truth unto fables, that use all cunning craftiness to deceive*,[1071] being more ambitious to be doctors of

---

[1070] Ephesians 4:14
[1071] 2 Timothy 4:4

error than disciples of truth, etc. These show little love, reverence or respect to this great blessed sweet and glorious name of our Lord Jesus Christ.

[2] **Oneness of will.** Συμψυχοι – being-same-souled.[1072] Zanchi refers this to the oneness and sameness of will. And the distribution here used by the apostle plainly evinces thus much. *Having the same love, being same-souled, minding that one thing.* Here is oneness of affection, will, and mind. This same-souledness, this oneness of will in matters of religion, consists not in the natural sameness of soul for substance, but in the supernatural consent and harmony of their souls and wills about all the things of God; when they so comply, conform, and sweetly correspond one with another therein, as if they were informed and acted only by one and the same soul. This oneness of will is highly commended in the primitive believers: *And the multitude of them that believed, were of one heart and of one soul.*[1073] There was a sweet and pleasant consent among them, their wills answered one to another in all religious matters, and in all church affairs (Acts 2:44 to the end). There was no discord nor jarring string among them; they were all sweetly in unison. Hereupon Calvin has a good note: "He says, *and the multitude were of one heart,* for this was much more excellent than if there had been consent among a few. For beforehand, he had declared that the church was increased to 5,000. Therefore it was not a little difficult to have concord reign among so great a number; and surely where faith reigns, it so reconciles men's minds that they all will and nill the same thing. For hence are discords, that we are not governed by one and the same Spirit of Christ. By the names of *heart* and *soul*, it is sufficiently known that the will is indicated."[1074] So he.

Now this oneness of will does especially comprise in it these three things; namely: {1} A conformity of their wills to the will of God, they being principled and acted by the Spirit of God. This the only foundation of all

---

[1072] Philippians 2:2
[1073] Acts 4:32 & 2:44 to the end
[1074] "Dicit *Cor unum* fuisse in multitudine: quia hoc longe praestantius suit," etc. John Calvin's commentary on Acts 4:32.

union and oneness of heart and will: when first they are united in God. {2} A consequential compliance and sameness of wills one with another: willing and nilling, electing and rejecting the same things (Acts 2:44, etc). {3} A humble estimation of others above themselves, having respect to others' affairs as well as their own. True sameness of will produces these two effects, yea and it is preserved and increased by them (Philippians 2:2-4). Thus of oneness of will.

[3] **Oneness of affection.** την αυτην αγαπην εχοντες: *Having the same love*.[1075] How could they have the same love? Not the same numerically, for that could not be, since they were divers Subjects. Nor the same in quantity and measure, seeing one hath this, another hath that degree of love, according to the measure of the gift of Christ. But this {*same love*} may here imply: {1} A like love, an answerable proportionable love one towards another, in sincerity and integrity of affection. Calvin and Beza incline this way. {2} A love of the same objects. When their hearts were distracted and divided after contrary objects – some loving Paul's doctrine, others the false apostles; some loving error and novelty, others truth, etc – then they did not have the same love, Their love was not united in the object. But when all their hearts should love the same God, the same Christ, the same gospel, the same faith, the same ordinances, etc, now they have the same love indeed. This is Zanchi's exposition.[1076]

Thus of the oneness of heart.

(b) *Oneness of way*, is an outward oneness flowing from the former oneness of heart – even that oneness of their whole course together in all the affairs and visible exercise of religion, in the outward practice of the fear of the Lord (Jeremiah 32:39). As their heart had been formerly divided, so their way had been divided: some hearkening to God's true prophets, some to false prophets; some following the LORD, others hankering after idols, etc. But

---

[1075] Philippians 2:2-3
[1076] Jerome Zanchi's commentary on Philippians 2:2-3

now God assures them, as he would give them one heart, so he would give them one way: and they should walk sweetly and harmoniously together in that one way. By this metaphor of {*way*}, it is ordinary with the Holy Spirit in Scripture to express the whole course and exercise of religion by churches or particular persons.[1077] More particularly, this oneness of way implies many things:

(1) One and the same way of expressions and speeches about religion. *Now I beseech you brethren, – that ye all speak the same thing.*[1078] Newly-coined expressions are shrewd arguments of newly-coined opinions. Confusion of tongues was Babel's calamity, and much more the church's misery. It is a high point of wisdom in the church for preserving truth and peace, and preventing division and error, to take singular care that all speak the same thing in common, known, plain and usual expressions.

(2) One and the same way of professing or confessing the true Christian faith unto salvation. *With the heart man believeth unto righteousness, and with the mouth confession is made unto salvation.*[1079] Hence it is evident that not only faith, but also the confession of faith is of use unto salvation. By confession of faith: [1] the purity and unity of faith is declared and preserved; [2] the contrary errors to truth are prevented; [3] Christ's truth and doctrine is to his singular glory solemnly avouched before all the world; [4] and others are allured to embrace the same faith and truth. Hence all the Reformed churches of late, and the ancient churches long before, have had their confessions of faith which they have published. Among which, that judicious and elaborate confession for the churches in England, Scotland, and Ireland does easily excel.[1080] It is most worthy to be particularly avouched by all the particular churches.

[1077] 1 Corinthians 4:17, Jeremiah 6:16
[1078] 1 Corinthians 1:10
[1079] Romans 10:10
[1080] The [Westminster] Confession of Faith presented to the Parliament: April 29th 1647.

(3) One way of worshiping God in all the public acts and ordinances of his worship, as preaching and hearing the Word, administration of sacraments, prayer, etc. – that they all be performed and managed not according to any private fancies, but the clear direction of the holy Scripture.[1081]

(4) One and the same way of church order, and that according to the Word (Colossians 2:5; 1 Timothy 3:1-11, Titus 1:5-10; 1 Timothy 4:24, Matthew 18:15-16, etc; 1 Corinthians 5 throughout; 2 Corinthians 2:6-12).

(5) One and the same way of holy and blameless conversation.[1082] O how sweet and comely it is to behold God's people all walking together holily and unblameably! This honors Christ highly; this adorns the gospel exceedingly.

(6) One and the same guide in this one way, namely: the word and Spirit of Christ. *The word is that more sure word of prophecy, as a light shining in a dark place* (2 Peter 1:19, etc). The Spirit leads the children of God (Romans 8:14).

(7) One and the same chief companion in this one way, namely: God. They that herein walk aright, do walk with God.[1083]

(8) Finally, one and the same journey's end, of this one way, namely: the same eternal glory (John 17:24). Such oneness of way, God covenants to bestow upon his people.

Thus, what this oneness of heart and way is, and wherein it consists.

[Question 3]: How choice and excellent a blessing this oneness of heart and way is.

Answer: The singular excellency of this oneness of heart and way among God's people in the matters of religion, may be briefly represented in these particulars.

[1081] 2 Timothy 4:2, 5, Matthew 28:18-19; 1 Corinthians 11:23, etc; 1 Timothy 2:1-2
[1082] Philippians 2:15; 1 Thessalonians 5:23; 2 Peter 3:14
[1083] Genesis 5:22 & 6:9

{1} ***Firstly, by the importunity of our Savior's prayer for this blessing upon all that should believe in him through the apostle's word.*** His importunity for this blessing implies the excellency of the blessing. *Neither pray I for these alone, but for them also which shall believe on me through their word. That they all may be one, as thou Father art in me, and I in thee, that they also may be one in us: that the world may believe that thou hast sent me. And the glory which thou gavest me, I have given them; that they may be one, even as we are one. I in them, and thou in me, that they may be made perfect in one, and that the world may know that thou hast sent me, and hast loved them as thou hast loved me,* etc.[1084] From verse 20 to the end, Christ prays for all his that should believe on him through the apostle's doctrine.

He begs for them two chief blessings, namely: (i) Spiritual unity, here (verses 21-24). (ii) Celestial glory, hereafter, (verse 24, etc). Spiritual unity: *That they all may be one,* – one in us, namely: by the Spirit, faith, love, etc. (verse 21). Sin dissipates, dissolves, and divides all things; Christ, the sinner's Savior, unites and reconciles all.[1085] He is the α and the ω; he is the author, continuer, and perfecter of all reconciliation and union. In Christ, God and man are united in one person, so that God and man might be united in one Christ. Christ died to destroy sin, the only matter of enmity between God and man.[1086] Christ gave all his New Testament ministers of all sorts for the final perfecting and completing of this unity.[1087]

For the more clear understanding of our Savior's meaning in this his earnest prayer for the unity of his apostles and members. Consider well the words of that acute Rainolds in his *Learned Conference with Hart*. He says: "The unity which the Scriptures do note in God and us, is of three sorts: the first of persons in one nature, the second of natures in one person, and the third of sundry natures and persons in one quality. In the first is one God,

---

[1084] John 17:20-23
[1085] Colossians 1:20
[1086] Romans 8:3
[1087] Ephesians 4:11-13

(Deuteronomy 6:4), in the second is one Christ (1 Corinthians 8:6). In the third is one church (Song of Solomon 6:4). The Lord did not receive Peter into the first unity, wherein the Father, Son, and Holy Spirit are one God; nor into the second, wherein he himself consisting of two natures (God and man) is one Christ. Into the third, wherein the church is one with Christ her head, and the church's members are one amongst themselves, he did receive Peter – but in society with his brethren, not without them in singularity. The multitude of the believers were of one heart, and of one soul (Acts 4:32). They all are one body, sanctified by one Spirit, through the sacrament of one baptism, knit to Christ by one faith, to themselves in one love, to serve together one Lord, in one hope and expectation of one eternal bliss and glory (Ephesians 4:4-5)."[1088] So he.

Now Christ presses his Father for this spiritual unity by many arguments, as:

(i) Partly, from some answerable resemblance it will have to the union between the Father and Christ (verse 21), as the Father and Christ are one divine essence, one by personal union of the human nature to the second person in the divine essence, one in consent of will – divine and human – in Christ, one in purpose and intention of saving all the elect in such a way. So they mystically and spiritually might be one with Christ their head, and with one another in heart and way as members.

(ii) Partly, From the glory that hence would redound to Christ. By this union of believers, the world should be effectually convinced of Christ's authoritative mission from the Father, thus powerfully gathering and uniting all his elect (verses 21, 23).

(iii) Partly, from Christ's giving or promising that glory to them in order to this union, which the Father had given him (verse 22), namely: that glory[1089] of his image,[1090] grace, Sonship, and all spiritual accomplishments, according

---

[1088] Dr. John Rainolds in his *Conference With Hart*, pp.15-16 (London, 1609)
[1089] So John Calvin on John 17:32
[1090] 2 Corinthians 3:17-18, John 1:12-16, Colossians 1:19

to their capacity, which were plenarily heaped upon Christ. All of these are notably and effectually uniting. That by *glory* here should be meant either this *unity*, as some;[1091] or *eternal glory*, as others, seems not so apposite nor agreeable.[1092]

(iv) Partly, from the foundation of this unity in Christ. That as God is in Christ essentially, etc. so Christ may be in them spiritually, knitting them to God, and one to another (verse 23).

(v) Partly, from the renown of the elect, that the world may be convinced that the Father loves them with the same love wherewith he loved Christ (verse 23). What importunity is here? What arguments here? And all for this oneness of believers, as if this oneness had in it all other spiritual blessings, and were beyond all other of greatest importance. Who can duly consider this, and not conclude that this oneness, this one only mercy which Christ so importunately begs for his elect in this world, is most excellent?

{2} *Secondly, by the sweet pattern of this oneness of heart and way in the purest primitive church at Jerusalem.*

(i) Oneness of heart among them was admirable. *And the multitude of them that believed* (namely: 3,000 in Acts 2:41 and 5,000 men in Acts 4:4) *were of one heart, and of one soul: neither said any of them, that ought of the things which he possessed was his own, but they had all things in common.*[1093] *And all that believed were together, and had all things common*, etc.[1094] Here was the power of God's Spirit and grace, that there should be oneness of heart among so many thousands; and that oneness so one, as if they had all lived but by one soul, and so demonstrated by community of goods, declaring the intensive integrity of their reciprocal affections, prizing one another's persons beyond all their outward possessions. This community was occasioned by the

---

[1091] Ierh. Harm. in Joh. 17:22. Late Large London Annotations on John 17:22.
[1092] See Beza's Annotations and Piscator on this place.
[1093] Acts 4:32
[1094] Acts 2:44-45

present pressing poverty and necessities of many of those believers, which at that time could not otherwise be relieved: which particular obliges not us or any to imitate, until the church of God be redacted into the like necessitous condition.

(ii) Oneness of way, wherein they walked, was singular. *And they continued steadfastly in the apostles' doctrine, and fellowship, and breaking of bread, and prayer.*[1095] *And they continuing daily with one accord in the temple, and breaking bread from house to house, did eat their meat with gladness and singleness of heart, praising God.*[1096] Their oneness of way, wherein they continued steadfastly and unanimously, is here ranked under four heads (which Calvin very fitly styles "four notes or marks of a true and well-constituted visible church"),[1097] namely, oneness: (a) In doctrine, in the true apostolic doctrine – this the foundation of all the rest. Herein was their oneness of faith. (b) In communion of saints: partly, with the apostles themselves (verse 42), and partly with one another (verses 46-47). This communion seems to be of a more private nature, and oneness of fellowship sweetly flows from oneness of faith. (c) In breaking of bread, namely: in receiving the Lord's Supper:[1098] that sweet token of oneness with Christ, and one with another, and that excellent seal of the New Testament, and of the doctrine thereof.[1099] How sweetly and purely did they break bread with the apostles, who heard and saw Christ's institution of this ordinance! (d) In prayers, namely: public prayers made by the apostles in the public assemblies of the church. Herein was their oneness of heart and way. There was no dissent in opinion, no discord in affection, no dissonance of expressions, no discrepancy in their religious worship and actions – but in all a sweet

---

[1095] Acts 2:41-42
[1096] Acts 2:46-47
[1097] John Calvin's commentary on Acts 2:42
[1098] Acts 20:7
[1099] 1 Corinthians 10:16-17

harmony, sameness, and oneness every way. Oh! Methinks it was the very suburbs of heaven thus to live in this primitive church at Jerusalem!

{3} *Thirdly, by the many and great mischiefs of the opposite divisions in heart and way, in matters of religion.* For:

(i) Hereby, various pernicious and damnable works of the flesh, as variance, emulations, envyings, wrath, strife, separations, heresies, and so on, are brought forth and nourished,[1100] and professed Christians maintaining or approving such division, walk as babes, yea as carnal men.[1101]

(ii) Hereby the temple of God which is holy (whose temple Christians are) is sinfully defiled, to the endangering of everlasting destruction.[1102] For the Spirit of God dwelling in these temples, being a Holy Spirit of unity, peace, love, and so on, cannot endure the aforementioned filthy fruits of the flesh.

(iii) Hereby, men walk most unworthy of the calling wherewith they are called, whilst they keep not the unity of the Spirit in the bond of peace.[1103] Unbelief divides, breaks, and scatters all; faith in Christ unites knits and gathers all the elect to Christ.

(iv) Hereby Christianity is so ill-managed, as if Christ were divided, and each different division of Christians had a different christ.[1104] Or as if some men, some ministers, etc, were very christs, or had been crucified for them; whilst they more eagerly pursue after the doctrines and ways of those men than after the naked doctrines and ways of Christ, prizing and gospel ordinances, etc. not so much for Christ's sake as for theirs.

(v) Hereby, men discover their lack of oneness with Christ which is the foundation of oneness with his mystical body and members.[1105] First we are one with Christ by the Spirit and faith, and then in Christ, we are one with his

---

[1100] Galatians 5:19-21; 1 Corinthians 3:3, Jude 19
[1101] 1 Corinthians 3:1-5
[1102] 1 Corinthians 3:16-17 compared with verses 3-5 & 21-22
[1103] Ephesians 4:1-3
[1104] 1 Corinthians 1:12-13
[1105] John 17:23; 1 Corinthians 10:16-17, Ephesians 4:15-16

body and members. When therefore we divide from them, we discover we are divided from Christ, and are no better than Christ-less formalists.

(vi) Hereby, men cast themselves out of the society of the church, service of the Lord Christ, and fellowship with God.[1106] *Mark them which cause divisions and offences, contrary to the doctrine which ye have learned, and avoid them. For they that are such serve not our Lord Jesus Christ, but their own belly: and by good words and fair speeches deceive the hearts of the simple.*[1107] They pretend Christ, intend themselves, like boatmen looking one way, but rowing another. Nor can such retain fellowship with God. For, God's habitation are they, that are built together through the Spirit, not they that are divided and torn asunder through the flesh. *In whom you also are built together for an habitation of God through the Spirit.*[1108] Fitly to this effect said Cyprian: "Whosoever is separated from the church, and joined to an adulterous one, he is severed from the church's promises. Nor shall he come to the rewards of Christ, who forsakes the church of Christ. He is an alien, he is a profane one, he is an enemy. He cannot now have God for his Father who has not the church for his mother," etc.[1109]

(vii) Hereby, the sweet communion of saints both public and private, that Eden of spiritual delights, and feast of fat things, is miserably destroyed. Union is the foundation of all communion; division therefore must needs be a destruction and desolation to all communion. What life, sap, growth, or fruitfulness has the branch, when cut off from the tree? Or what strength, life, sense, or motion has the limb, when cut off from the body? What quickening, comfort, edification, etc. in the society of saints can such have, as are separated from them? The sweet union of the primitive believers was that which so

---

[1106] Jude 19; 1 John 2:19, Ephesians 4:16

[1107] Romans 16:17-18

[1108] Ephesians 2:21-22

[1109] k. Quisquis ab Ecelesia segregatus adulterae jungitur a Promissis Ecclesiae separatur. Nec pervenit ad Christi praemia, qui rel inquit Ecclesiam Christi. Alienus est, profanus est, Hostis est. Habere jam non potest Deum patrem, qui Ecclesiam non habet matrem, &c. Cypr de Unitat. Eccles. Cathol. §. 5. p. 297. Edit. 1593.

heightened and improved their spiritual communion together (Acts 4:32, 34-35 & 2:42, 44-47). Now to be deprived of the manifold benefit of communion of saints, is a loss incomparable.

(viii) Hereby, that peculiar and excellent blessing of oneness of his elect in him, so earnestly begged of the Father by Jesus Christ, is apparently slighted and despised.[1110] And as Cyprian well: "They cannot come to the reward of peace, who by the fury of discord break asunder the Lord's peace."[1111]

(ix) Hereby, the great end of Christ's death for his church, and of his donation of his New Testament ministry to his church, is (so far as divisions prevail) un-Christianly crossed and undermined. For Christ died so that he might gather into one the children of God that were scattered abroad;[1112] that so at last he might bring all his sheep – both of Jews and Gentiles – into one fold; that there might be one fold, as one shepherd.[1113] *And Christ gave some, apostles; and some, prophets; and some, evangelists; and some, pastors and teachers, for the perfecting of the saints, for the work of the ministry, for the edifying of the body of Christ: till we all come in the unity of the faith, and of the knowledge of the Son of God, unto a perfect man, unto the measure of the stature of the fullness of Christ.*[1114] So that one special aim of Christ in giving all his New Testament ministry was, under Christ, the gathering of all his elect into one, and bringing them into unity.

(x) Hereby, finally, the truth of the gospel is perverted;[1115] Christians' minds and hearts are troubled, distracted, offended and subverted;[1116] Christianity is exposed to the contempt and scorn of all that hate it – of profane atheists, papists, Turks, and Jews, as daily experience evidences – the enemies of the church, Satan and his instruments singularly gratified; and the

---

[1110] John 17:20-24
[1111] Cyprian, *The Unity of the Catholic Church*, §. 10.
[1112] John 11:50-52
[1113] John 10:15-18
[1114] Ephesians 4:11-13
[1115] Galatians 1:6-7
[1116] Acts 15:24, Galatians 1:7 & 3:1

church of Christ herself exposed to, yea overwhelmed with all manner of error, heresy, blasphemy, profaneness, looseness, envyings, contentions, revilings, clamor, bitterness, distraction, and confusion. The woeful divisions in England about matters of religion for these few years last past, afford a lamentable experimental attestation to all these particulars. By these few mischiefs of divisions in heart and way about religion, we may judge of the rest, which are innumerable.

{4} *Fourthly, by the many precious advantages and benefits attending this religious oneness of heart and way here on earth.* For:

(i) This is the due fulfilling of the many commands of Christ in his word.[1117] And it is not only our duty, but our dignity to be obedient unto Christ. And this oneness of heart is Christ's new commandment: urged in a new manner, and still to continue new.

(ii) This is a blessed return of Christ's prayer upon his members.[1118] And that may comfortably assure us of his acceptance with the Father, and of the prevalence of his intercession.

(iii) This is an evident badge or character of Christ's disciples. *By this shall all men know that ye are my disciples, if ye have love one to another.*[1119] This character was eminent in the primitive Christians at Jerusalem. Contrariwise, by the opposite divisions, contentions, strife, and so on, men discover themselves too much to be the devil's disciples.

(iv) This is both *good and pleasant for brethren to dwell together in unity.*[1120] Some things are good, but not pleasant, such as repentance, affliction, and so on. Some things are pleasant, but not good, such as variety of sins and corruptions: Some neither good nor pleasant, as envy, the torture of the soul; but this oneness of brethren is both good and pleasant: doubly

---

[1117] John 13:34; 1 Corinthians 1:10, Ephesians 4:1-7, Philippians 2:1-4
[1118] John 17:20-24
[1119] John 23:35
[1120] Psalm 133:1, etc.

excellent, like Aaron's holy ointment, full of delicious fragrancy. As that ran from his head to the skirt of his garment, so this oneness flows from Christ our head to his meanest member. Yea, like the fruitful drops and dew upon Hermon and Zion, two very dry and barren mountains, yet their small and little grass is nourished and increased by dew and showers; so by unity, the smallest things grow and are preserved, by discord the greatest things are wasted and brought to naught.[1121] A threefold cord, a bundle of rods, is not easily broken: an untwisted cord, a single rod, is quickly broken.

(v) This is a special means whereby we may *walk worthy of that high and holy calling wherewith we are called*.[1122] We are called to be children of peace, love, unity, etc, to be sons and daughters of one heavenly Father (2 Corinthians 6:18, Ephesians 4:6, 1 Peter 1:15-17), to be brethren of one Christ (Hebrews 2:11), to be temples of one Holy Spirit (1 Corinthians 3:16-17, Ephesians 2:21-22), to be members of one mystical body of Christ the church, (Ephesians 5:30, 32; 1 Corinthians 12:12-28), to be professors and possessors of one faith (Ephesians 4:5), to be washed with one baptism (Ephesians 4:5), to be nourished with one Lord's Supper (1 Corinthians 11:20, 23, etc. & 10:16), to be taught and instructed to salvation by one gospel (Titus 2:11-12, etc), to be heirs by one hope of one and the same celestial kingdom (Ephesians 4:4, Matthew 25:33-34). This is a high and holy calling, and strongly engaging all the called unto unity among themselves. And this is a special ornament and honor to this our calling, that we are in heart and way united. Thus we shall walk worthily, suitably, answerably, to our calling.[1123] Oneness adorns; dividedness shames it. What honor is it to Christ, the fountain of unity, to have a company of wranglers, janglers, brawlers and contentious persons to be his disciples?

(vi) This promotes spiritual growth and fruitfulness in the church and members of Christ. They are first *fitly jointed and compacted together in*

[1121] Concordia res parvae crescunt; discordia res magnae dilabuntur
[1122] Ephesians 4:1-3
[1123] Ephesians 4:1-3, etc.

Christ,[1124] and then they grow up into Christ towards complete perfection, and mutual edification: but a limb severed from the body, a branch severed from the tree grows no more, but withers.

(vii) This is the sacred cement of the saints, consolidating them in one. The strength of the feeble church, whereby united weak ones are made invincibly strong; the admiration of the carnal world, that knows not the uniting force and efficacy of true grace; the orient [radiant] ornament of the gospel, that can produce such singular effects; the spiritual chariot of Christianity, carrying it on to its perfection with greatest delight; the vexation and envy of the devil, whose great endeavor hath still been to destroy the church of God by cursed divisions; and the delight of God blessed forevermore, who carries on his church by unity unto perfection.

(viii) This oneness of heart and way is that unity of the Spirit in the bond of peace, which is founded upon the sacred mount of unities. Happy are they that shall ascend into, and dwell in this holy mountain, where unities are the foundation, and unity and peace the superstructure! *Endeavouring to keep the unity of the Spirit in the bond of peace. There is one body, and one Spirit, even as ye are called in one hope of your calling, one Lord, one faith, one baptism; One God, and Father of all, who is above all, and through all, and in you all.*[1125]

(ix) This, in a word, is that sacred qualification whereby believers being one in God and Jesus Christ, do in some measure resemble that supreme unity of unities in God, between Father, Son, and Holy Spirit.[1126] Now the more we can aspire to be like God, the more we ascend to the perfection of godliness.

{5} *Fifthly, by the many sacred unities urged by the apostle as cogent arguments and motives to the maintaining of this spiritual unity.* All of these ones should strongly incline all the saints to be one. *Endeavouring to*

[1124] Ephesians 4:15-16
[1125] Ephesians 4:3-6
[1126] John 17:20-24; 1 John 5:7

keep the unity of the Spirit in the bond of peace. There is one body, and one Spirit, even as ye are called in one hope of your calling, one Lord, one faith, one baptism; One God, and Father of all, who is above all, and through all, and in you all.[1127] What? So many ones, to incite to oneness of the Spirit? Then doubtless this oneness of Spirit is a most excellent oneness. Consider them briefly:

(i) **One body**, namely: there is but one mystical body of Christ, the general church – visible or invisible – and all believers fellow-members of that one body.[1128] Now it would be monstrous for members of the same body to fight one against another, the hand against the eye, one hand against another, one foot against another, etc. but it would be mortal for the members to divide and separate one from another. Union preserves them; division destroys them. Fellow members mutually serve, and take care of one another.[1129]

(ii) **One Spirit**, namely: one and the same enlivening Spirit of Christ the head, supernaturally animating and acting this one body and all the members thereof.[1130] Every member of Christ has not a different spirit, as every man has a different soul, but as all the natural members of one man's body have but one and the same soul, though manifesting itself more eminently in some than in other members; so it is with the mystical members of Christ. Christ gives not many spirits, but one Spirit with many operations. And shall not they who live spiritually by one and the same Spirit, have one and the same heart and way?

(iii) **One hope of our calling**, namely: there is but one hoped-for heavenly glory and inheritance unto which we are all called in this life. We shall all agree in one eternal glory; can we not now agree in one principle, and way of grace? One heaven shall hold us all then; cannot one church hold us all now?

(iv) **One Lord**, namely: Jesus Christ our only Lord and Master, whom we serve and attend upon. Though servants of several masters may fall at variance,

---

[1127] Ephesians 4:1-7
[1128] 1 Corinthians 12:12 to the end; Ephesians 5
[1129] 1 Corinthians 12:12
[1130] 1 Corinthians 12:12-13

yet it is a great shame for fellow-servants of one and the same Lord and Master to be at strife.

(v) **One faith**, namely: one doctrine of faith, touching God's saving of sinners by Jesus Christ through faith alone. Thus it takes in the whole body of Christian doctrine. Now if there be but one faith, why are we not united therein in one judgment? Shall lesser differences be of more force to make division and separation than the body of faith and truth to make conjunction?

(vi) **One baptism, namely: one sacrament of baptism.** This is the first visible Christian cognisance or badge, whereby we are distinguished from all pagan, Jewish, and Turkish people, and incorporated into the visible body and society of Christians.[1131] This is Christ's livery. Shall there be strife, discord and division among men of one badge and livery? Shall we unbaptize ourselves by separating from that body into which we were baptized? Or tearing asunder that body whereunto by baptism we were united?

(vii) Finally one God and Father of all, who is above all, etc. namely: one true God in essence, though subsisting in three distinct persons.[1132] He is Father of all, and all are his generation and issue by creation and providence. Above all: by his special sovereignty and authority. Through all: by his special providence. In all: by his peculiar grace and Spirit. For (as Calvin well observes)[1133] all these are here to be restrained to the church, whose unity he persuades hereby. And shall not this one God and Father who is thus over us, through us, and in us, keep us in unity?

{6} *Sixthly and lastly, the excellency of this oneness in heart and way may be further demonstrated by the full perfection and exact accomplishment thereof in heaven.*

Many spiritual gifts and graces shall cease, as prophecy, tongues, and so on. Faith, hope, repentance, etc. – there shall be no need of these in heaven;

[1131] 1 Corinthians 12:12-13
[1132] 1 John 5:7
[1133] John Calvin's commentary on Ephesians 4:6

but this spiritual oneness, for the substance of it, shall go with us to heaven, and be a great part of the saints' glory and felicity there. Now those spirituals which shall accompany us both in earth and heaven, in this and the world to come, do in excellency far transcend those which shall only remain and be of use to us here on earth. Unity on earth is but in part; unity in heaven shall be perfect and complete, as all our spirituals that shall remain there shall be perfect.[1134] And the more our spiritual oneness attains to perfection on earth, the more it approaches the perfect oneness in heaven.

The oneness which is and shall be in heaven is manifold:

(i) The oneness of the three persons – Father, Son, and Holy Spirit (over all blessed forever) – in the unity of essence.[1135] The Father is not the Son, neither Father nor Son are the Holy Spirit, but Father, Son, and Holy Spirit are one God. This is the highest, happiest, and most perfect uncreated unity in heaven.

(ii) The oneness of Christ and his glorious mystical body made perfect.[1136] They are now one flesh (Ephesians 5:30-32), one body (1 Corinthians 12:12-13), one Spirit (1 Corinthians 6:17). Yea one **Christ** (1 Corinthians 12:12). Are Christ and his church thus one on earth? How accurate then shall be their oneness in heaven, where they shall be fully like him, where they shall beatifically see him as he is, where they shall immediately and eternally enjoy him – he in them, and they in him forevermore?[1137]

(iii) The oneness of all the glorious and triumphant saints of Christ, one with another. Then all causes, occasions and fuel of division – whether Satan's temptations, human seductions, or their own sins and corruptions – shall utterly cease. Then their minds shall not be divided by the least dissent of opinion, because all weakness and error shall be wholly removed by the perfection of glorious light and truth. Then their wills and hearts shall not be

---

[1134] 1 Corinthians 13:9-10, 12-13, Hebrews 12:23
[1135] 1 John 5:7
[1136] Hebrews 12:23
[1137] Philippians 3:21; 1 John 3:2; John 17:24

divided by the least disaffection or defect of love; because everyone shall fully rejoice in another's happiness as in his own, and all of them be ravished with the glory of Christ.

Then their way shall not be divided by any the least repugnant practises, because they shall all walk in the same white robes with palms in their hands, they shall all perfectly fulfill Christ's will with unanimous delight, they shall all triumph with the same hallelujahs to God and to the Lamb before his throne forevermore.

Then their names shall no more be divided by opprobrious denominations, as Hussites, Huguenots, Lutherans, Calvinists, etc, but still all glory in that blessed uniting name of **Christian**. Christ promises to him that overcometh: *And I will write upon him the name of my God, and the name of the city of my God (New Jerusalem which cometh down from my God), and my new name* (Revelation 3:12). There shall be (as Augustine notes)[1138] no envy amongst them; (as the angels do not envy the archangels, and in the body natural the hand desires not to be the eye, nor the foot to be the hand, no member envies another), because everyone shall have enough. No contempt, because everyone shall be perfectly glorious: no discontent, because everyone shall be satisfied with pleasures at God's right hand forevermore. But all shall most sweetly and fully acquiesce in God, in Christ, and in one another, as lacking nothing that can be desired; as having nothing that can be disesteemed. They shall all think, and will, and love, and desire, and do, as one man, what Christ God-man shall require. Yea, they shall all be so entranced, ravished, overcome, and even swallowed up with the blissful presence vision and fruition of God in Christ, who then shall be all in all, that they shall have no

---

[1138] "And in that blessed city there shall be this great blessing, that no inferior shall envy any superior, as now the archangels are not envied by the angels, because no one will wish to be what he has not received, though bound in strictest concord with him who has received; as in the body the finger does not seek to be the eye, though both members are harmoniously included in the complete structure of the body. And thus, along with his gift, greater or less, each shall receive this further gift of contentment to desire no more than he has."
<https://www.newadvent.org/fathers/120122.htm>
[Accessed 3/2/2024]

list nor liberty for division or distempers amongst themselves (could such defilements possibly have any place in heaven): But shall rather by the influences of that Glory be transformed into unity, peace, love, and joy most gloriously. Sweet and apposite is that of Augustine's in his close of his Books of the City of God: "There we shall rest and see, we shall see and love, and we shall love, and praise. Behold what shall be in the end, without end. For what else is our end than to come to the kingdom whereof there is no end?"[1139] O sweet consort, wherein there is not the least jarring! O delicious melody, when all the strings are so exactly tuned and unisone! Oh happy harmony, wherein there is not the least discrepancy! O glorious unity, wherein is no shadow of division, but all unity! How should we contend and aspire after gracious oneness now, that we may attain this glorious oneness forever? If so much of heavenly glory be comprised in perfect unity, how excellent is the very inchoate unity of the saints now that is the first-fruits and earnest of this perfection!

[Question 4] Lastly, what directions and helps may best further the obtaining and maintaining of this oneness of heart and way among God's people?

For as Jerome well notes, upon that of the apostle: *Endeavouring to keep the unity of the Spirit in the bond of peace* (Ephesians 4:3). He that has it, to him a care of keeping is appointed; but he that has it not, to him a studiousness that he may have it, is commanded.[1140]

Answer: This is a most necessary and seasonable question, especially in these sad days of our spiritual divisions and confusions, wherein God hath so left us to the folly and vanity of our own hearts that still dividing, subdividing, crumbling, rending, tearing the church of God among us into parties, sects, fragments, and separate heaps of backsliders, as dangerously threaten the subversion of religion and confusion of the church amongst us.

[1139] Augustine, *City of God*.
[1140] "Qui enim habet, servandi illi sollcitudo praecipitur; Qui autem non habet, studium illi ut habere valeat imperatur." Hieronym. Com. in Ep. ad Eph. 4. 3. Tom. 9.

For the gaining therefore and retaining of this excellent oneness of heart and way among Christ's members, seriously ponder and sincerely put in actual execution these few brief directions ensuing, namely:

{1} **First, meditate frequently and seriously, of the excellencies of this union in heart and way amongst the saints, and of the mischiefs of the contrary division.** Those may strongly allure any ingenuous spirit unto that; these may deter any judicious heart from this. A small taste of both, I have given already. Why do most so easily burst asunder all bonds of spiritual union and embark themselves in divisions and subdivisions, but because they never advisedly and deliberately weighed and considered the good of unity which they are rejecting, and the evil of division which they are embracing?

{2} **Secondly, piously consider and be thoroughly convinced in your own conscience what an excellent and important duty union is; what an abominable and dangerous sin division is.** Of both I have given some brief touch already.

(i) *How excellent and important a duty is this unity*! Being: (a) Frequently commanded by the Spirit of God (1 Corinthians 1:10, Ephesians 4:3, Philippians 2:2-4): *Be of one mind, live in peace* (2 Corinthians 13:11). (b) Pathetically pressed upon the churches and saints by the apostle. He speaks not so much words as affections; not so much arguments as forcible compulsions, not so much suasions [exhortations] as persuasions, when he comes upon this subject. As, to the saints at Corinth: *Now I beseech you brethren, by the name of our Lord Jesus Christ, that ye all speak the same thing, and that there be no divisions among you, but that ye be perfectly joined together in the same mind, and in the same judgement.*[1141] He *beseeches* – he beseeches them as brethren; he beseeches by the name of our Lord Jesus Christ. *To the saints at Ephesus; I therefore the prisoner of the Lord, beseech you that ye walk worthy of the vocation wherewith ye are called, with all lowliness and meekness, with longsuffering, forbearing one another in love;*

[1141] 1 Corinthians 1:10

Endeavouring to keep the unity of the Spirit in the bond of peace.[1142] He beseeches them; he beseeches them as the Lord's prisoner. As if he had said: "If ye will not hear Paul, yet hear his prison, hear his chains for the Lord Christ, speaking unity to you." *To the saints at Philippi: If there be therefore any consolation in Christ, if any comfort of love, if any fellowship of the Spirit, if any bowels and mercies; fulfill ye my joy, that ye be likeminded, having the same love, being of one accord, of one mind.*[1143] "See here," (says Chrysostom) "how copiously, how vehemently, how sympathetically he speaks."[1144] But for what is the apostle thus earnest? Is it for supply of necessaries; or deliverance out of dangers, bonds, prisons; or relief against persecutions, etc? No, no, not a word of this kind for himself, but all for them, their concord and unity. (c) Strongly urged by many unities and other cogent arguments.[1145] (d) Highly commended by the Holy Spirit, in the practice of the primitive church at Jerusalem.[1146] (e) Peculiarly intended by Christ in the whole work of all the New Testament ministry: extraordinary and ordinary.[1147] (f) Earnestly begged by Christ in his solemn prayer before his passion.[1148] (g) Dearly purchased by Christ, at the price of his own precious and invaluable blood.[1149] (h) And is clearly assured of the special presence of the God of love, and peace, by his faithful promise: *Be of one mind, live in peace, and the God of love and peace shall be with you.*[1150] What? will the God of love and peace be with them? Then, the sweetest love will be with them: the God of love. The most perfect peace will be with them: the God of peace. The highest happiness will be with them: the blessed God. This shall be the reward of them, that are of one mind and live in peace, and that in this present life.

[1142] Ephesians 4:1-6
[1143] Philippians 2:1-4
[1144] Chrysostom, Homily 5 in Philippians 2
[1145] Ephesians 4:1-6, Philippians 2:1-4
[1146] Acts 1:14, 2:42-46 & 4:32
[1147] Ephesians 4:11-13
[1148] John 17:20-24
[1149] John 10:15-17
[1150] 2 Corinthians 13:12

(ii) ***How abominable and dangerous a sin is division!*** For as much as: (a) It is ranked among the filthiest and most detestable works of the flesh.[1151] (b) It renders the sanctified members of the church that cherish strife, schism, etc. in a sort carnal and babes in Christ.[1152] (c) It denominates such as cause division, servants, not of Jesus Christ, but of their own bellies, and deceivers of the simple: to be noted and avoided by the saints.[1153] (d) It is a vehement and suspicious sign of the hypocrisy of such persons' whole religion, that they go out from the church, because they are not of the church really, but only formally and feignedly.[1154] (e) It disturbs the church of God, and tends to subvert the souls of the members thereof, which Christ has bought with his most precious blood.[1155] (f) In a word, it is so damnable that they who act and walk in division, strife, heresies, etc. shall not (without sincere repentance) inherit the kingdom of God.[1156] They are not in Christ true heirs of the kingdom of grace now, nor ever shall be co-heirs with him of the kingdom of glory hereafter.

{3} **Thirdly, pluck up the very roots, and cut off all the occasions of division.** While the roots thereof remain, though it be never so much topped, it will sprout again; whilst the causes and occasions thereof continue, the ill effect must needs continue. Remove therefore all the causes and roots of this mischievous evil out of your own breast and heart; for in your heart chiefly the roots of strife, contention, and division are fixed. Corrupt principles and lusts within are the fountains of these wretched divisions without. As James said of worldly, so may I say of this spiritual contention: *From whence come wars and brawlings among you? Come they not hence, even of your lusts, that war in your*

[1151] Galatians 5:19-21
[1152] 1 Corinthians 1:2 with 3:1-5
[1153] Romans 16:17-18
[1154] 1 John 2:19
[1155] Acts 15:24
[1156] Galatians 5:19-20

members?[1157] Especially, extirpate out of your heart these principles and bitter roots of division, namely:

(i) ***Ignorance, childishness and babishness about the great affairs of Christian religion.*** They that are children in religion are (through their good affections and weak judgments) apt to be *tossed to and fro, and carried about with every wind of doctrine, by the sleight and cunning craftiness of men.*[1158] And no wonder, for as yet *they have not their senses exercised to discern between good and evil*, nor can they digest the strong meat, but only the milk of Christianity.[1159] Hereupon the apostle taxes the Corinthians for their carnality and babishness in their divisions:[1160] one being for Paul, another for Apollo, another for Cephas, etc, which argued their lack of solid understanding and judgment, to consider: that one and the same spirit wrought in them all their variety of gifts, that they and all their gifts were given to the church and to them for their spiritual good, and that they all were but ministers by whom God works, not efficients but instruments. All efficacy upon their gifts and ministrations was only from God. *I have planted, Apollo watered, but God gave the increase.* So that he that planted, and he that watered – the ministers – were nothing; but God that gave the increase, he was all, and on him they should principally have an eye and dependence for spiritual fruit and success. *Therefore be no longer children, but men in understanding.* Let our senses be exercised to discern things that differ, etc.

(ii) ***Error of opinion.*** This is a bitter root of division, as experience sadly testifies: And error proceeds from ignorance in matters of religion. Now there are especially these two grand errors about divisions, which abundantly patronize and cherish divisions in those that pretend to religion.

[1157] James 4:1
[1158] Ephesians 4:14
[1159] Hebrews 5:12-14
[1160] 1 Corinthians 3:1-8, etc.

(Error 1): That divisions are not sinful, but warrantable, yea gainful and needful to the church: for *there must even be heresies therein*, which are worse.[1161]

Answer: (a) That divisions are dangerous and damnable sins, I have already proved here, in the second direction. (b) That the church of God properly and directly can neither need nor gain by any divisions or heresies, but loses extremely, as did the church at Corinth, etc. Properly, poison does good to no patient. (c) That when any good comes by division or heresy to the church, that is merely by accident as to those evils, through the mighty overpowering providence and goodness God, who brings light out of darkness, good out of evil, medicines out of poisons, etc, but this gives no countenance at all to divisions. The expert physician can digest the viper into a treacle; is this any encouragement to any one to eat vipers?

(Error 2) That all men should be left at liberty, to the liberty of their own conscience in matters of religion, without any force, restraint, or control.

Answer: (a) Conscience is either natural and unsanctified, as in carnal men, and in pagans,[1162] or spiritual and sanctified, as in true believers,[1163] who have a good conscience purged from dead works by the blood of Christ, and purified by faith to serve the living God. Do they mean that both sanctified and unsanctified conscience must be left at liberty? Then hereby, unsanctified conscience is made a man's guide and rule for his religion; a goodly guide; a goodly religion, of the mind and conscience which is defiled, and polluted with dead works.[1164] A blind and corrupt guide. Then hereby, the unsanctified conscience is made equal in matters of religion to the sanctified conscience, which extremely debases the grace of God in the purified conscience. Then hereby, the corrupt conscience may freely break out in all prodigious corruptions of heresy, scandal, etc. (for a defiled conscience can act and

---

[1161] 1 Corinthians 11:18-19
[1162] Romans 2:14-16
[1163] Acts 23:1, 24:16, Hebrews 9:14, Acts 15:9
[1164] Titus 1:15, Hebrews 9:14

produce nothing but defilements; being corrupt, it can only act corruptly) and yet not be restrained. How then shall they that ought to restrain them clear themselves from fellowship with the unfruitful works of darkness?[1165] Do they intend that only the sanctified conscience must be left at liberty? Who can certainly tell, what conscience, or whose conscience is sanctified, to whom this liberty may be left? Or why should a sanctified conscience be left to the liberty of sinning without remedy? What has the sanctified conscience done to deserve this mischief?

(b) Conscience has two sorts of acts, namely: elicit and inward, in the soul, as to accuse or excuse, etc, imperate and outward, in the life;[1166] as to live in all good conscience before God continually, exercising a man's self herein to have a conscience void of offense towards God and man;[1167] or to walk in defilements of conscience, putting away a good conscience, etc.[1168] Now which of these acts do they mean should be left at liberty: the inward or outward acts of conscience? If the inward acts only, then they grant that the outward acts should in some cases be restrained and forced. Then, they erroneously suppose that the inward elicit acts of conscience may be compelled, etc. which is utterly impossible, and destroys the very nature of conscience. A man may be compelled and forced in his outward act to be present at Mass, to bow towards an idol, etc, but the inward act and consent of his conscience cannot be forced. Conscience may be enlightened and convinced by the truth, may be seduced and deceived with error, and so persuaded one way or another: but cannot be forced in its inward acts. If the outward acts also are to be left at liberty, then by what clear solid and unwrested warrant of the holy Scriptures? Then, what sort of outward acts are they wherein conscience is to be left at liberty? All sorts of outward acts about religion are: necessary, arbitrary, or sinful: *necessary*, as prescribed duties, which God has limited, and with which none

---

[1165] Zechariah 13:3 with Deuteronomy 13:1-6, Ephesians 5:11
[1166] Romans 2:14-16
[1167] Acts 23:1 & 24:16
[1168] Titus 1:5, Hebrews 9:14; 1 Timothy 1:19

but God can dispense. And where God restrains, no creature may grant liberty. *Arbitrary and indifferent*: as many circumstances and accidents about God's worship, which God has not particularly determined, but left to our choice, such as calling the church together by a bell or trumpet or otherwise.

The churches coming to public worship precisely at such or such an hour; The performing acts of worship in this or that order, etc. Herein the church is free to take that course which best agrees with the general rule, that *all things be done decently, in order, and to edification*[1169] – and herein the church should not be restrained to the prejudice of herself or members, but be left at liberty. *Sinful and in themselves unlawful*: such as all things prohibited and condemned in the table of religion, containing the four first commandments: atheism, heresy, schism, idolatry, superstition, witchcraft, blasphemy, etc. Now if men's consciences are so corrupt and depraved, as to allow them in these or like abominations, shall such sins be tolerated under pretense of liberty of conscience? If men suppose (as once Paul did)[1170] that they are bound in conscience to persecute Christ in his members to death,[1171] etc. must they therefore have liberty, and be tolerated so to do? God forbid! This is not properly a liberty of conscience, but licentiousness of corrupt unconscionable practises against a good conscience. Not liberty of conscience, but liberty of lusts and corruptions.

(c) Why should conscience be more left at liberty in matters of religion immediately relating to God, than in matters of righteousness immediately relating to man? Is not religion far above civil righteousness? Is not God's glory, more to be tendered, endeavored and provided for, than man's outward right? Or is man more dear to us than God?

(d) Has not God both in Old and New Testament abundantly declared himself against such liberty of conscience, and toleration of evils in religion?

[1169] 1 Corinthians 14:40, 26
[1170] Acts 26:9-10
[1171] John 16:2

Partly, by commanding idolatry,[1172] false prophets,[1173] witches,[1174] blasphemers,[1175] etc. to be punished with death; partly, by dispraising and condemning such as tolerated and suffered such sinful acts about religion upon whatever pretense (Revelation 2:20); partly, by commending those that could not tolerate false apostles, and them that were evil (Revelation 2:2).

(e) Has it not been the subtle practice of seducers and seduced persons in all ages to cloak and nurse up all their abominable errors, heresies, blasphemies, divisions, scandals, etc. under the specious pretenses of conscience, liberty of conscience, toleration of tender consciences, etc. Oh what spiritual miseries, distractions and confusions, is religion and the Church of God in England hereby involved into in these days!

(f) Among the members of Christ, some are babes, some men in understanding and spiritual exercise; some are weak, others strong, etc. Hereupon may arise diversity of apprehensions and difference of opinions about some particulars in religion, but this should not make a division among them in such case, They that have any singular or different opinion should keep it to themselves before God,[1176] endeavoring after satisfaction, and not publish it to the disturbance of the church's peace, and they that are strong, should bear and forbear the weak in love, maintaining communion with them, wherein they agree, and being ready to help and satisfy them wherein they disagree.[1177] This toleration is not only tolerable, but warrantable and comfortable.

(iii) ***Spiritual pride and vain-glory, in regard of men's own, or others' spiritual gifts whom they admire.*** The more gifts, graces, and mercies we have from God – temporal or spiritual – the more humble we should be, as being greater debtors to God, and under deeper obligations. But

---

[1172] Numbers 25:4-5 & Deuteronomy 13:6 to the end
[1173] Deuteronomy 13:1-6, Zechariah 13:3
[1174] Exodus 22:18
[1175] Leviticus 24:11-17
[1176] Romans 14:22
[1177] Ephesians 4:2-3, Romans 14:1, etc.

alas, how hard is it to have spiritual gifts, and not to be puffed up? How hard to admire men's persons, and not carnally and vainly to glory in them? *Knowledge puffeth up.*[1178]

The Corinthians excelled in gifts,[1179] and their ministers (which were many) excelled in gifts:[1180] therefore they were vainly puffed up one against another, and carnally gloried one in this, another in that teacher – for which vanity and carnality the apostle justly and sharply rebukes them (1 Corinthians chapters 1-4) *Who maketh thee to differ from another? and what hast thou that thou didst not receive? Now if thou didst receive it, why didst thou glory as if thou hadst not received it?*[1181] And again: *Who is Paul, or who is Apollo but ministers by whom ye believed, as the Lord gave to every man? I have planted, Apollo watered: but God gave the increase. – Therefore let no man glory in men, for all things are yours, whether Paul, or Apollo, or Cephas,* etc.[1182]

Now this spiritual pride and vainglory of the Corinthians in their own and teachers' gifts caused many divisions, parties and factions amongst them. *I am of Paul, and I of Apollo, and I of Cephas, and I of Christ.*[1183] Pride makes a man think himself singular; and puts a man upon such singularities of way, that others may think him singular, and somebody also. Hence so many singularities, of odd unsound opinions, of unjustifiable practises in the church, etc, which will not abide the exact trial of the Word. Many count it a greater honor to be masters and doctors of error than disciples of truth: to be ringleaders in separation and division than followers of peace and union. The apostle therefore – wisely prescribing a means of union and antidote against division – says: *Let nothing be done in vain-glory,*[1184] and so on, as intimating

---

[1178] 1 Corinthians 8:1-2
[1179] 1 Corinthians 1:7
[1180] 1 Corinthians 12 & 14
[1181] 1 Corinthians 4:7
[1182] 1 Corinthians 3:5-7, 21-22
[1183] 1 Corinthians 1:10-12
[1184] Philippians 2:1-3

that pride and vain-glory were great enemies to unity, but notorious foundations of division.

(iv) *Contentious, peevish, quarrelsome dispositions of some, who are never well but when they are perversely disputing, jangling, wrangling, galling and reviling their brethren and the truth.* The apostle styles such: *gainsayers, unruly, and vain-talkers, and mind-deceivers, – whose mouths must be stopped, who subvert whole houses, teaching things which they ought not for filthy lucre sake.*[1185] *– These resist the truth, men of corrupt minds, reprobate* (or *void-of-judgment*: αδοκιμοι) *concerning the faith.*[1186] Such as these are like salamanders, whose delight (as writers say) is to lie and live in the fire. They are the devil's blacksmiths, still blowing up the flames of strife and contention. One such brawling unpeaceable and fiery spirit is enough to set a whole church on fire, and tear the bond of their sweetest union in pieces. How severely does the apostle brand such for church *makebates [false accusers]*? *If any man – consent not to wholesome words, the words of our Lord Jesus Christ, and to the doctrine which is according to godliness: he is proud* (or *he is fanatic*)[1187] *knowing nothing, but doting about questions and strifes of words, whereof cometh envy, strife, railings, evil surmisings, perverse disputings* (properly: *preposterous studies, preposterous exercises,* or *mutual gallings*)[1188] *of men of corrupt minds, and destitute of the truth.*[1189] And how strictly does he charge Timothy (and in him, us) to shun the contentious practises of such persons? — *But shun profane and vain-babblings, for they will increase unto more ungodliness: And their word will eat as doth a gangrene; of whom is Hymenaeus and Philetus.*[1190] Such like also are the skeptics of our times, that question and dispute everything about religion: insomuch that many in this

---

[1185] Titus 1:9-11 φρεναπαται
[1186] 2 Timothy 3:8
[1187] τετυφωται
[1188] 1 Timothy 6:3-5
[1189] λογομαχιας
[1190] 2 Timothy 2:16-17

[way] have disputed away a good conscience, and wrangled away all their religion.

(v) ***The itch of the ear.*** This is an evil disease, an itching humor inclining many most intemperately to lust after novelty of doctrines, heaps of teachers new-fangled ways, courses, and crotchets in religion, to the great detriment of the church's peace and unity. This is an itch that deserves to be soundly scratched with wholesome reproof. The apostle prophesied of this malady long ago: saying: *The time will come when they will not endure sound doctrine, but after their own lusts shall they heap to themselves teachers, having itching ears. And they shall turn away their ears from the truth, and shall be turned unto fables.*[1191] This time is already come upon us with a witness in this church. How many are infected, not only with itching but with leprous ears? Not only will not endure sound doctrine, but endeavor to corrupt and make all doctrine unsound? Not only heap to themselves teachers, but heap up themselves as teachers, though they understand not the very principles of Christ's doctrine? Not only turn their ears from the truth to fables; but to heresies, but to blasphemies also; yea counting God's truths fables, and fables truth? This is a pestilent root of division and distraction in the church.

(vi) ***Admiration of some men's persons for the difference of their gifts.*** Jude gives this for one character of the separatists crept in in his days, that as they were *sensual, having not the Spirit,* so they *had men's persons in admiration because of advantage.*[1192] Let truths be preached by the persons admired. Oh how sweet, how precious, how choice, etc. are they accounted! (It is well if they value not truth for their sakes, more than for Christ's). But let the same truths be as lively, faithfully and judiciously preached by others, alas they are but dry vulgar ordinary things. Is not this to *have the faith of Christ with respect of persons?*[1193] This was the error of the Corinthian church. One was for Paul: he was a deep man; another for Apollo: he was an eloquent man;

[1191] 2 Timothy 4:3-4
[1192] Jude 16, 19
[1193] James 2:1

another for Cephas: he was a zealous and solid man, etc.[1194] Here was a weak and childish admiring of men's persons, and this fomented strongly those hot contentions and mischievous divisions amongst them. Truth is to be accepted and esteemed for Christ's sake, the author of it; and for its own sake and the precious nature of it. The preachers of truth are to be esteemed for the truth they preach, for the work they do; not the truth and work for them.

(vii) *Causeless prejudice against Jesus Christ, his church, his members, or ordinances.* Prejudicating opinions and hard thoughts without just ground or cause against these, extremely obstruct union, and promote division. The Jews' prejudice against Christ kept them from union with him by faith, yea, occasioned their opposition and persecution of him to the death.[1195] Saints' prejudice against the church, members, and ordinances of Christ, set him at such a distance from them, that he thought with himself that he ought to do many things against Jesus Christ in them, which also he did, with much insolence and cruelty.[1196] And how far such prejudice has estranged the hearts of people in this nation from a sweet closing together in heart and way in matters of religion, every judicious and observing Christian amongst us knows very well. Oh therefore bury all causeless prejudice: do not fore-judge or fore-condemn any person or thing until, after due examination, there be found just cause. How many divide from the church of Christ among us with the Anabaptists, merely out of prejudice against infant baptism disgraced by them: who never duly examined nor understood the just grounds of infant baptism? How many depart from us upon prejudice against our church constitution: who understand not at all solidly what a true visible church constitution means, or wherein it consists? How many make divisions and distractions among us about church government out of mere causeless prejudice: never duly considering what that government is, which Christ has left to his visible church? etc. Now this is a most un-Christian, inhumane, and irrational-way,

---

[1194] 1 Corinthians 1:10-12
[1195] John 1:11, Matthew 13:55-57, Mark 6:3, etc, Matthew 21:46, John 18:35
[1196] Acts 26:9-10, etc.

to prejudge and pre-condemn any person or cause before a just hearing and deliberate examination.

(viii) *Finally, sordid and filthy covetousness, especially in seducers and false teachers, is another common and notorious cause of divisions in the church.* Many devise and publish new opinions, new ways in the Church, yea new ordinances of their own, not of Christ's, that under specious pretenses of singularity, and more than ordinary purity, they may draw disciples after them, especially such as are great and rich in this world, by whom they may increase in worldly wealth. He is blind that cannot behold these devices of many in this land in these days, to the rending of the church in pieces – and thus it was in the apostles' times. *There are many unruly ones, and vain-talkers, and deceivers, – who subvert whole houses, teaching things which they ought not for filthy lucre's sake.*[1197] Paul tells the Philippians with tears that the false teachers which went about to pervert them, were *enemies to the cross of Christ, whose end is destruction, whose God is their belly, and whose glory is in their shame, who mind earthly things.*[1198] And he beseeches the saints at Rome to *mark them which cause divisions and offences, contrary to the doctrine which they had learned, and avoid them. For they that are such, serve not our Lord Jesus Christ, but their own belly, and by good words and fair speeches deceive the hearts of the simple.*[1199] Jude also describing such persons, styles them {*men crept in unawares*},[1200] and says: *Woe unto them, for they have gone in the way of Cain* (namely: by their cruelty against the saints) *and ran greedily after the error of Balaam for reward* (namely: by their filthy covetousness, and self-seeking) *and perished in the gain-saying of Core*; who with his confederates, were ancient separationists from the church of God: but to their own destruction, for a warning to all that should afterwards make like separation. Yea this evil was common and abounding among all false teachers

---

[1197] Titus 1:10-11
[1198] Philippians 3:18-19
[1199] Romans 16:17-18
[1200] Jude 4 with 2 Peter 2:15-16

in the very primitive apostolic times, that of such especially Paul complains: *All seek their own, not the things which are Jesus Christ's.*[1201] And Peter prophecies that the church shall be troubled in after times with such covetous self-seeking seducers: *But there were false prophets also among the people, even as there shall be false teachers among you who privily shall bring in damnable heresies, even denying the Lord that bought them, and bring upon themselves swift destruction. – And through covetousness shall they with feigned words make merchandise of you; whose judgment now of a long time lingereth not, and their damnation slumbereth not.*[1202]

These are some of the chief bitter roots of division and confusion in the church of God, to be utterly extirpated, in order to oneness in heart and way among believers.

{4} **Fourthly, cherish all the foundations, supporters, preferrers, and friends of unity.** Hereby, unity shall be maintained and improved. Especially labor that yourselves and others may abound with these eminent cementing and uniting graces, namely:

(i) **With solid and judicious knowledge of Jesus Christ, and of the great mystery of sinners' salvation by him.**[1203] This knowledge of the Son of God (as Paul notes) has a uniting property in it, and tends to the saint's highest perfection: and when the saints thus become men in understanding, they shall *not be anymore like children tossed to and fro with every wind of doctrine,* etc. There are many that have a smattering of knowledge, a few swimming notions, some ungrounded and infant apprehensions of Christ, but being not well bottomed, ripened, and fixed, they prove but fuel for seducements. But labor so that you are thoroughly instructed in the very mystery of Christ. Dive deeply into this blessed secret, so as to be rooted and grounded herein.

[1201] Philippians 2:21
[1202] 2 Peter 2:1-3
[1203] Ephesians 4:13-15; 1 Corinthians 1:10-11

(ii) **With unfeigned faith.** There's a feigned faith, as in temporaries,[1204] and as in Simon Magus.[1205] This no more unites to Christ or to Christians, than a thread or a piece of clay unites a branch or scions to the stock of a tree. There's also a *faith unfeigned*,[1206] peculiar to God's elect. This faith in Christ has an eminent uniting faculty to knit us to Christ the head, and to make us one with him, which is the foundation of oneness with his members.[1207] Especially considering that this unfeigned faith *works by love*, both towards Christ and towards his body the church and all his members, inclining sweetly to close with them and embrace them in dearest sincere affections.[1208]

(iii) **With sincere love.** Love (as Zanchi has well evidenced)[1209] has in it as it were three degrees, or three primary acts which it exercises towards any beloved object, namely: (a) Benevolence, or wellwilling to the object beloved, for its loveliness, though not possessed or enjoyed. (b) Desire of union to it, or enjoyment of it. Amiableness attracts and snatches the heart's desires after it (c) Complacency and acquiescence in the enjoyment of, and union to, the object desired. So that true love, in the very intrinsic nature of it, has an uniting property, knitting the heart and object together affectionately, and inclining strongly unto union of them actually. Paul therefore exhorting the Ephesians unto this spiritual unity, he commends love firstly to them as a special help thereunto: *I beseech you that ye walk worthy of the vocation wherewith ye are called, – forbearing one another in love, endeavoring to keep the unity of the Spirit in the bond of peace.*[1210] And in like sort to the Philippians: *Fulfill ye my joy, that ye be like minded, having the same love, being of one accord, of one mind*, etc.[1211] Love was the sacred solder and glue which so strongly united the primitive Christians, that *the whole multitude,*

[1204] Luke 8:13
[1205] Acts 8:13
[1206] 1 Timothy 1:5
[1207] Ephesians 4:13-15 & 3:17
[1208] Galatians 5:6
[1209] Zanch. *De Natur. Dei*. lib. 4. cap. 3. Quest. 1. §. 2.
[1210] Ephesians 4:1-3
[1211] Philippians 2:2-3

even many thousands, *were of one heart and of one soul*.[1212] Where love decays, union decays. We want sincere and fervent love to Christ, to his church, to one another as his members, to his truth, ways, and ordinances, etc and therefore it is, that we have so little union and so much division amongst us. *Love or charity suffereth long, and is kind: Charity envieth not: charity vaunteth not itself; is not puffed up; doth not behave itself unseemly; seeketh not her own; is not easily provoked; thinketh no evil; rejoiceth not in iniquity, but rejoiceth in the truth; beareth all things; believeth all things; hopeth all things; endureth all things*.[1213] O precious love! How it treads underfoot all occasions of discord and division! How does it frame itself every way to gain and maintain unity! Love is the *bond of perfectness*;[1214] the most perfect bond of unity.

(iv) **With peace, and peaceable dispositions.** Persons of a peaceable and quiet Spirit towards the church and members of Christ are of an excellent Spirit, especially in order to this spiritual unity. *Endeavouring to keep the unity of the Spirit in the bond of peace* (Ephesians 4:1-3, etc). Peace is not only a friend of this unity; but even a bond of unity. How vehemently is peace urged upon us by God? *Be at peace among yourselves*,[1215] – *Follow peace with all men, and holiness*.[1216] – *If it be possible, as much as in you lies, live peaceably with all men*.[1217] – *Be of one mind, live in peace, and the God of love and peace shall be with you*.[1218] How extremely therefore are all unquiet, turbulent, contentious, quarrelsome dispositions and practices offensive to God? They that love war with the church, can never maintain peace with Christ. Paul said of such: *I would they were even cut off that trouble you*.[1219] David lamented his dwelling

---

[1212] Acts 4:32
[1213] 1 Corinthians 13:4-8
[1214] Colossians 3:14 Claromontanus codex legit [ενοτητος], Unitatis: Quod nusquam alibi inveni, sed mihi accommodatissimum videtur. Bez. Annotatan loc.
[1215] 1 Thessalonians 5:13
[1216] Hebrews 12:14
[1217] Romans 12:18
[1218] 2 Corinthians 13:11
[1219] Galatians 5:12

in Meshech, hating peace.[1220] We have many Meshechs and Meshechites, in this nation; woe is him that has his tabernacle amongst them. *Let us therefore follow after the things which make for peace, and things wherewith one may edify another.*[1221]

(v) **With all humility or lowliness of heart and mind.** Humility is a sanctifying grace, repressing (a) pride, and disposing a person, both inwardly and outwardly towards (b) God and (c) man, to all acts of lowliness in (d) thoughts, (e) words, and (f) works. (a) Psalm 131:1; 1 Samuel 9:21. (b) 2 Samuel 7:18. and 6:14, 20-21, etc. (c) John 13:5. (d) Isaiah 57:15, Philippians 2:3. (e) Gen. 18. 2. Ruth 2. 20. (f) Psalm 131:2. Faith is the captain grace[1222] and the buckler grace,[1223] but humility is the decking and adorning grace: *Be ye clothed with humility,*[1224] ταπεινοφροσυνην εγκομβωσασθε, *for God resisteth the proud, but giveth grace unto the humble.* The word εγκομβωσασθε, *be ye clothed,* properly signifies, *Be ye knotted,* from κομβος, a knot – an allusion to the custom of curious women who deck their heads and adorn their garments with comely knots. Humility is the knot of virtue, the excellent ornament of grace. *Only by pride comes contention;*[1225] shall I say on the contrary: only by humility comes peace and unity? Sure, eminently, by humility, comes unity. See how the apostle directs: *Walk worthy of the vocation wherewith ye are called with all lowliness – Endeavouring to keep the unity of the Spirit in the bond of peace.*[1226] And elsewhere: *Let nothing be done through strife or vainglory, but in lowliness of mind let each esteem others better than themselves,* etc.[1227] The humble soul is of a sweet, peaceable, tractable, persuadable disposition – and that is a wonderful, uniting disposition.

[1220] Psalm 120:5-7
[1221] Romans 14:19
[1222] 2 Peter 1:5, etc.
[1223] Ephesians 6:16
[1224] 1 Peter 5:5
[1225] Proverbs 13:10
[1226] Ephesians 4:1-3
[1227] Philippians 2:3-4

(vi) **With meekness.** Humility, and meekness are inseparable companions in the soul, and are often joined together in Scripture.[1228] Some say, humility is the mother, meekness the daughter; humility the root, meekness the fruit. None can be meek that is not first humble. As humility represses pride and disposes to lowliness, so meekness represses anger and disposes to a gentle quietness. Meekness is a sanctifying grace, repressing anger, revenge, etc. and disposing to quietness, gentleness, towards God and man (Matthew 11:28-29, Job 1:21; 1 Peter 2:23; 1 Peter 3:4). Meekness therefore in the nature of it, is a singular furtherance to unity. *In all lowliness and meekness, – endeavoring to keep the unity of the Spirit in the bond of peace.*[1229] Meekness, like oil, pierces deeper than the vinegar of wrath. Meekness is an excellent quench-fire to strife and contention, and is not easily disturbed, no, not with many provocations. Therefore learn we of Christ, who was *meek and lowly of heart.*[1230] For *a meek and quiet spirit is an ornament in the sight of God of great price.*[1231]

(vii) **Finally, abound with long-suffering one towards another.** There will arise, even in the church, and among the members of Christ, offenses, provocations, vexations, discontents, etc. sometimes from the weak, sometimes from the strong: In such cases it is the excellency of long-suffering not to be soon inflamed with every spark, but to endure and pass by much, with a long forbearance. And this conduces much to unity: *With long-suffering forbearing one another in love, endeavoring to keep the unity of the Spirit in the bond of peace.*[1232] Mutual forbearance in love seems here to be pointed at as a primary act of long-suffering for furthering of unity. Now we are in love to forbear one another: (a) In instructing against error of opinion, if the error is not very dangerous, using strength of arguments, but forbearing passion and harshness of words.[1233] (b) In case of weakness of conscience, forbearing to

---

[1228] Matthew 11:29, Ephesians 4:2, Colossians 3:12, Matthew 21:5
[1229] Ephesians 4:2-3; 2 Timothy 2:25, Galatians 6:1
[1230] Matthew 11:29
[1231] 1 Peter 3:4
[1232] Ephesians 4:1-3
[1233] 2 Timothy 2:24-25

urge to the practice of anything, wherein conscience is doubtful and unsatisfied, yet exhorting to the diligent use of all means of satisfaction.[1234] (c) In case of lapses into sin against God. When a man does not so much overtake sin, as sin overtake him, he is to be restored with a spirit of meekness, considering ourselves, lest we also be tempted. In such cases we are to bear one another's burdens: not to countenance one another in sin, but to encourage, comfort and strengthen one another against sin. (d) In case of private wrongs, or personal injuries. Forbearing sometimes strictness of right, always extremities of revenge; being *kind one to another, tender-hearted, forgiving one another, Even as God for Christ's sake hath forgiven us.*

{5} **Fifthly, note them that cause divisions and offenses contrary to the true doctrine of Christ, and avoid them; go not forth after them.** *Such serve not Christ, but their own lusts and belly; deceive the simple; subvert whole houses; through covetousness make merchandise of souls; draw away disciples after them*; and hereby endeavor to cut as under the sinews and bands by which Christ's mystical body is knit together.[1235] These the apostle calls Satan's *deacons* or *ministers*.[1236] Satan the envious one sows the tares of dissension in the field of the church, and these are his seedsmen. These are his subtle foxes with fire-brands. These are his factors, and agents, who act with all possible *subtlety and cunning craftiness to deceive the weak and simple*, and to destroy the purity, peace and unity of the church. Oh flee such, as holy John fled from that heretical Cerinthus in the bath at Ephesus, leaping out of it unwashed, and saying, "Let us flee, lest the bath fall, because Cerinthus the enemy of the truth is in it."[1237] And cleave close to the rule of Christ recorded by John: *If there come any unto you, and bring not this doctrine* (namely: the doctrine of Christ – verse 9 – not in pretense, but in reality), *Receive him not into your*

[1234] Romans 14:1, etc.
[1235] Romans 16:17-18, Matthew 24:26, Titus 1:10-11; 2 Peter 2:1-3, Acts 20:30, Colossians 2:19, Ephesians 4:16
[1236] διακονοι αυτου 2 Corinthians 11:14-15
[1237] Irenaeus, *Against Heresies*, Book 3 Chapter 3

house, neither bid him Godspeed. For he that biddeth him Godspeed, is partaker of his evil deeds.[1238] And if they who bring not Christ's doctrine but false doctrine must neither be entertained in our houses, nor bidden God-speed, then much less must their doctrine be heard or entertained, seeing that their persons are to be rejected for their doctrine.

{6} Sixthly, if it come to pass, that you shall at any time be otherwise minded, and have a faith or opinion different from the church of God and generality of the saints, then trouble not the church or the members thereof with your divulging of it, but keep it to yourself, using means of information, and expecting until God shall reveal even this unto you. Thus the apostle directs: *Hast thou faith? Have it to thyself before God.*[1239] And elsewhere: *And if in anything ye be otherwise minded, God shall reveal even this unto you.*[1240] Having of different opinions, is unavoidable; by reason of different light in the saints, some being babes, weak and unexercised, others by reason of use having their spiritual senses exercised, being strong and men in understanding; but divulging, publishing, spreading of different opinions is intolerable.[1241] Hereby the strong are grieved, the weak and unstable staggered and endangered, error is countenanced, truth called in question, and a great disturbance made against the peace and unity of the church. Therefore do not pride yourself on your own private conceptions, Idolize not, dote not upon your own opinions so far, as to prefer them above the general judgment of the church and saints of God, or to disquiet them therewith. A multitude may err, but a single person is in much more danger and suspicion of erring. True piety will not in matters of religion build upon man's judgment, but on the Word of God. And yet true humility dare not ascribe more to a man's own single judgment, than to the unanimous judgment of God's ministers and people. *For if a man thinks himself to be something, when he is nothing, he deceiveth*

[1238] 2 John 9
[1239] Romans 14:22
[1240] Philippians 3:15
[1241] Hebrews 5:12-14; 1 Corinthians 3:1-2

himself.[1242] Had this wisdom, sobriety and humility been amongst us in this nation, we should never have so profusely vented such swarms of private unsound opinions, (the fruit of wanton minds, the froth of empty corrupt hearts, and the spawn of old rotten heresies and errors) to the distracting of the church, and dividing of the people of God. The press is so oppressed daily with the devil's libels against God, Christ, gospel, ordinances of Christ, and the whole truth; and they are so dispersed throughout the nation that the whole land stinks because of them in the nostrils of the churches of Christ round about us; much more than the land of Egypt stank by reason of the dead frogs, in the nostrils of the Israelites.

{7} **Seventhly, let all the people of God be careful to avoid newly-minted words and notions in matters of religion, especially in matters of faith; speaking the same thing unanimously.** When Paul prescribed his remedies against the divisions in the church of Corinth, this was the very first of all: *Now I beseech you brethren, by the name of our Lord Jesus Christ, That ye all speak the same thing, and that there be no divisions among you.*[1243] They speak different things: *One said, I am of Paul: another, I of Apollo: another, I of Cephas: another, I of Christ.*[1244] Here were different speakings, whereby divisions were produced, as Babel's different languages occasioned their dispersion and scattering upon the face of the earth. Likewise when men devise new fashioned words and phrases, it is a shrewd sign and ground of suspicion that they intend to broach some newly-devised doctrines and opinions. Let all sober-minded Christians speak the same thing with the church, and with each other, and the same thing in the common usual known expressions.

{8} **Eighthly, whereunto the faithful have attained already, let them mind the same thing, walk by the same rule:** according to the apostle's

---

[1242] Galatians 6:3
[1243] 1 Corinthians 1:10
[1244] 1 Corinthians 1:12

excellent advice.[1245] This one golden rule fully and faithfully observed, would wonderfully unite all the true members of Christ in faith, worship, and government in some comfortable measure. For, though there may be among them some difference of opinions, according to their different degrees of light; yet there are some, yea many things wherein they all agree, both in doctrine, worship, and church government. So far therefore as they have attained to the same concord and consent in any of these, let them unanimously walk together and maintain church communion by one and the same rule. And so far as they have not attained, but dissent in some things one from another, let them endeavor in a way of love and sweetness to satisfy one another, bearing one with another, until satisfaction and consent are obtained. But let them take heed of separating from communion for every difference. Separation and abscission is the last remedy. There are especially two clear cases wherein separation from a visible church is warrantable and necessary, namely:

(i) When the whole frame of religion therein, both in doctrine, worship and discipline, is so generally corrupted and depraved, that a man cannot hold communion therewith, but he must necessarily drink poison, partake of her corruptions, and infringe his communion with the head Jesus Christ himself. For, there were some corruptions in government and tolerations of scandals, some schisms and divisions, yea there was some heresy in the church of Corinth in Paul's time, and yet it was a true church of Christ, and such a church as from which none could separate without great sin, notwithstanding all those corruptions.

(ii) When a pure and thorough reformation of such general corruptions according to the Scriptures has been desired by the godly from a church so corrupted, and yet is refused by such a church. When a church is thus sick, and will not be cured; thus polluted and will not be cleansed, as the church of Rome was before the Reformation was attempted, then in such a case, the faithful may depart and separate from her communion, as our first Protestant

---

[1245] Philippians 3:16

Reformers did from Rome. Except in these two cases, and they both concurring, it will hardly be proved warrantable to divide and separate.

{9} **Ninthly, let everyone look not only on his own things, but on the things of others.**[1246] This (as the apostle intimates) will conduce much to church unity. As the members of the same body have a mutual love, tenderness and care one of another; *if one member suffer, all the members suffer with it; if one member be honored, all the members rejoice with it* – so it ought to be among the members of the body of Christ, for so is that intended.[1247] The hand is ready to defend the head or heart, though to its own hazard; the eye is ready to help the foot, never objecting the distance; the foot is ready to convey the body from place to place, not repining at the burden, etc. Why then should not Christians take like mutual care one for another, wisely considering what may be most suitable and comfortable to one another's Condition? Mind therefore not only what may please yourselves: but may profit others. Mind the things of the weak: to bear with them and strengthen them. Mind the things of the doubtful and staggering: to settle, resolve and establish them. Mind the things of the tempted: to advise and encourage them. Mind the things of the lapsed: to recover and restore them, etc. This will sweetly link the people of God together.

{10} **Tenthly, let all seek the things of Christ, before their own concernments.** Christ's kingdom, not their own dominion; Christ's honor, not their own glory; Christ's truth and gospel, not their own private opinions; Christ's ordinances, not their own inventions; Christ's worship, not their own superstitions; the prosperity and unity of Christ's house, temple, and mystical body the church, not the carnal prosperity of your own houses, much less of the synagogues of Satan, etc. The want of this made Paul complain: *All men seek their own things, and not the things that are Jesus Christ's.*[1248] The neglect of this made God complain, *Is it time for you, O ye, to dwell in cieled houses:*

[1246] Philippians 2:1-4
[1247] 1 Corinthians 12:12 to the end
[1248] Philippians 2:21

and my house lie waste?[1249] The Christ-neglecting and self-seeking dispositions of men in this land, aiming only or principally at their own power, profit, glory, greatness, carnal liberty, and so on, have wretchedly undone this Church, and torn it all to pieces. But alas what are all our things, our nothings; to the things of Christ? Did not Christ seek our things, before his own: our redemption, our reconciliation to God, our righteousness, our adoption, our salvation and eternal happiness; before his own liberty, reputation among men, livelihood in this world, natural relations, precious blood, or dearest life itself? Shall not we deny ourselves for him, and chiefly seek the things of Christ, who thus denied himself for us, and sought every way our felicity; especially if ever we tasted how pleasant and gracious the Lord Christ is; in his person, in his office, in his blood, in his graces, in his smiles, in his comforts, in his Spirit, and in his promises?

By these and like directions, sincerely walk, and this excellent oneness in heart and way will be successfully both obtained and maintained.

Thus of this oneness of heart and way: the Spirit's fifth notable influence promised. Wherein I have the more enlarged, because this is a matter of so high importance to the saints, and the manifold divisions in heart and way have been long, and still are most predominant and pernicious to the church of God in this land.

[1249] Haggai 1:2-4

(Influence & Effect 6):
The constant fear of God.

This is a sixth influence or fruit of the Spirit here promised, as an effect or consequent ensuing upon oneness of heart and way. *And I will give them one heart, and one way, that they may fear me forever* (Hebrew: *all days*) *for the good of them and of their children after them. And I will make an everlasting covenant with them*, etc.[1250]

This fear of God is here described: [1] By the root or principle of it, namely: one heart. That is, That holy frame of heart within, by the principles and habits of grace infused, which should be harmoniously one in them; this should produce the actual fear of God. Their inward habits should not be idle, but should break forth into the outward acts of religious fear. [2] By the constancy of it. *All days.* Constancy and perseverance in grace is of God's gift, as well as grace itself – he is both author and finisher thereof.[1251] And constancy is one eminent distinctive character between true and counterfeit grace. [3] By the commodity of it, namely: partly their own; partly their children's good after them. {*Good*} may extend to temporals, spirituals, and eternals – all the results of the fear of God; but temporal welfare and prosperity seems here specially to be intended. All outward good upon ourselves and posterity depends upon our true fear of the Lord. The fear of God procures all welfare and prosperity both to parents and posterity.

Fear has many various acceptations in Scripture (as I have elsewhere evidenced, and whereto I refer the reader),[1252] but here it seems peculiarly to denote the actual exercise of that gracious habit of religious fear, planted in the sanctified heart, whereby the saints are afraid to offend God their heavenly Father for his goodness, mercy, etc, and are careful to do those things which

---

[1250] Jeremiah 32:39-41
[1251] Hebrews 12:2
[1252] In my *Believers' Evidences for Eternal Life*. Ch. 6. §. II. p. 203, &c.

are well pleasing in his sight (Psalm 130:4, Job 1:1, Deuteronomy 6:13-14, Ecclesiastes 12:13, Acts 10:8).

Now God, in promising this fear – this constant fear of God to them – did promise them an excellent blessing indeed, a very rich spiritual jewel. As may briefly appear by these few considerations. For:

[1] The fear of the Lord makes men truly blessed (Proverbs 28:14, Psalm 112 throughout & 128 throughout).

[2] The fearers of the Lord are in high account and much set by with God (Acts 10:8). God sets so much store by them that fear him, that: {1} he dwells with them (Isaiah 66:2); {2} he imparts his secrets to them (Psalm 25:14); {3} his goodness is great towards them, even to admiration (Psalm 31:19); {4} his vigilant eye and protection is over them (Psalm 33:18 & 60:4), and his salvation is near them (Psalm 85:9); they shall never want any good thing which the wisest God knows to be good for them (Psalm 34:9); {6} the mercy and pity of the Lord is most fatherly, most tenderly upon them from everlasting to everlasting, and his righteousness to children's children (Psalm 103:13, 17); {7} the Lord has placed his delight and pleasure upon them peculiarly (Psalm 147:11); and finally, {8} they that fear the Lord are his *segullah*, his peculiar treasure, his jewels (Malachi 3:16-17).

[3] Many great and precious promises are made to them that fear God. The Lord has promised these things to them that fear him: {1} to reveal to them his Covenant, which is the marrow and mystery of the whole Scriptures (Psalm 25:14), {2} to let them want no good thing (Psalm 34:9-10); {3} to bless them, both small and great (Psalm 115:13); {4} to fulfill their desire, hear their cry, and save them (Psalm 145:19); and {5} to take and acknowledge them for his own, in the day, when he makes up his jewels (Malachi 3:16-17), and to record them in his Book of Remembrance for that end. And is it a small matter to be invested with these promises?

[4] The true fear of God springs from an excellent root, namely: partly, the true and saving knowledge of God, which fills the heart with a reverential

awe of him (Deuteronomy 31:11-13); partly, unfeigned repentance. The bitterness of repenting for sins past, makes fearful of offending for time to come (2 Corinthians 7:11).

[5] The true fear of God produces many blessed effects. The fruit thereof is most sweet and pleasant to the right spiritual taste, the effects and fruits thereof are these, and such like, namely: {1} it possesses the heart with a most awful reverence of God for his mercy and goodness, as well as for his majesty and greatness (Psalm 130:4, Hosea 3:5, Psalm 76:7). {2} It makes a man use the glorious and fearful name of God with dread and reverence (Deuteronomy 28:58). {3} It causes a man continually to set himself before God, as in his eye and presence. *That fear God, that fear before him* (Ecclesiastes 8:12). {4} It forceth a man even to tremble at God's Word, because of the infinite purity, wisdom, majesty, etc. of God resplendent therein (Isaiah 66:2). {5} It diverts a man mightily from evil, from evil of sin, and wickedness. The fear of God is as walls and bars against sin (Proverbs 3:7, 14:16, 16:6, Job 1:1). {6} It effectually inclines a man to all good, to all sincere obedience towards God (Deuteronomy 6:13-14, Ecclesiastes 12:13). {7} Finally, to add no more, it makes a man constant with God, and persevering in all his ways (Jeremiah 32:40).

[6] Finally, the companions which Scripture associates with the fear of God, are very eminent: and make the fear of the Lord very illustrious, as: {1} hope and affiance in God's mercy (Psalm 33:18); {2} vehement desires after more and more grace (Psalm 86:11); {3} Sincere and entire love to God, with all the heart, and with all the soul (Deuteronomy 10:12, etc); {4} entire and unfeigned serving of God, walking in all his ways (Deuteronomy 10:12); {5} great delight and pleasure in God's commandments – the true fearers of the Lord, not only do his commandments, but delight in them, greatly delight in them (Psalm 112:1); humility – the special ornament of the saints: *Be ye clothed with humility* (Proverbs 22:4); {7} sincerity, uprightness, and integrity (Proverbs 14:2, Job 1:1) – the very crown of all the graces; {8} the comforts of the Holy Spirit, which are the very fore-tastes and suburbs of heaven (Acts

14:22). With these choice associates, is the fear of God ranked by the Holy Scripture, whence we may easily discern what an admirable grace the fear of the Lord is, that consorts with such illustrious companions.

By all this it's apparent that this fruit of the Spirit – the constant fear of the Lord, promised in this Covenant – was a singular blessing and mercy to be highly accounted of.

Hereby also, as by so many marks or characteristics, we may try and discover, whether we ourselves do truly fear the Lord or not.

(Influence & Effect 7):
Obedience towards God.

Finally, the last influence or fruit of the Spirit, which I shall here mention; as promised in this Covenant, was obedience, or, obedientialness towards God. This is plain by the prophet Ezekiel: *And I will put my Spirit within you, and cause you to walk in my statutes, and ye shall keep my judgments and do them.*[1253] And elsewhere: *And I will give them one heart, and I will put a new Spirit within you; and I will take the stony heart out of their flesh, and I will give them an heart of flesh: That they may walk in my statutes and keep mine ordinances and do them: and they shall be my people, and I will be their God.*[1254] Here we may see that God's Spirit causes obedience to God, and the inward habits of grace, those sacred effects and influences of his Spirit, are therefore promised and bestowed upon God's covenant people, that they thereby might become really dutiful, and practically obedient to God.

If there is never so much grace within, and yet no works of obedience; if never so much profession without, and yet no practice; all this is not satisfactory to God – he must have obedience, practice, doing. [1] Obedience is that, which God has so frequently called for and commanded.[1255] [2] Obedience is that, which God has so highly commended and approved (1 Samuel 15:22). *Behold, to obey is better than sacrifice*, etc. Christ commends the obedient doer of the word to a wise man that builds on the rock.[1256] [3] The obedient are Christ's special friends (John 15:14), and Christ is the author of eternal salvation to them all (Hebrews 5:9). [4] Heaps of sweet and excellent promises are made to the obedient, See Deuteronomy 28:1-15 & 5:10 with Exodus 20:6, Deuteronomy 4:40 & 5:29, 233 & 6:2-3, Leviticus 26:3-5, etc, and Exodus 19:5-6. [5] Obedient persons are happy persons. *O the blessednesses*

[1253] Ezekiel 36:27
[1254] Ezekiel 11:19-20
[1255] Deuteronomy 27:10 & 30:2, 8, 20
[1256] Matthew 7:24-25

of the perfect in the way, walking in the law of the LORD! O the blessedness of them that keep his testimonies, and that seek him with the whole heart.[1257] – *If ye know these things, happy are ye if ye do them.*[1258] – *Blessed are they that do his commandments, that they may have right to the tree of life, and may enter in through the gates into the city.*[1259]

Therefore, in covenanting to make them obedient, God promised a Great mercy to them. But touching the nature of obedience to God, I shall here need to enlarge no further, having more fully insisted upon this subject heretofore, both in opening Abraham's walking before God in obedience,[1260] and in unfolding Israel's obedience to God's commands which they so solemnly restipulated to God.[1261] Let the reader diligently consult those two places.

Hitherto, of God's putting his Spirit within them, for newly framing and spiritualizing their hearts, and of the sacred influences of his Spirit here covenanted to that end – wherein I have been the more full, because of the spirituality, usefulness and comfortableness of these sublime spiritual mysteries. This is the fourth covenant mercy.

[1257] Psalm 119:1-2
[1258] John 13:17
[1259] Revelation 22:14
[1260] In Book 3, Chapter 3, Aphorism 3, Section 2
[1261] Book 3, Chapter 4, Aphorism 4, Section 2

[5] God's presence and residence in his sanctuary and tabernacle among his people, by his Spirit, Word, and public ministry forever.

This is a fifth covenant mercy here promised: *Moreover, I will make a covenant of peace with them, it shall be an everlasting covenant with them, and I will place them and multiply them, and will set my sanctuary in the midst of them for evermore. My tabernacle also shall be with them: yea, I will be their God, and they shall be my people. And the heathen shall know, that I the LORD do sanctify Israel,*[1262] *when my sanctuary shall be in the midst of them for evermore.*[1263]

Here God assures the captives of his everlasting Covenant of Peace with them; And in this passage promises these blessings, namely: {1} placing them in Canaan. {2} Multiplying them there. Of both these I have spoken formerly, in opening the second covenant mercy. {3} Setting his sanctuary in the midst of them forever, and his tabernacle with them: that the heathen might know that the LORD sanctifies Israel – this the blessing now to be unfolded. {4} His being their God, and they his people – of which hereafter.

And by Isaiah it is said: *And the Redeemer shall come to Zion, and unto them that turn from transgression in Jacob, saith the LORD. As for me, this is my covenant with them, saith the LORD, My Spirit that is upon thee, and my words which I have put in thy mouth, shall not depart out of thy mouth, nor out of the mouth of thy seed, nor out of the mouth of thy seed's seed (saith the LORD) from henceforth and forever.*[1264] In these words, there is some obscurity and difficulty. But it is plain, God therein covenants to give his Zion, his church, these three blessings, namely: {1} the redeemer, to all that turn

---

[1262] Book 3, Chapter 4, Aphorism 4, Section 2
[1263] {*do sanctify Israel*} "That is, do take it, and consecrate it to myself, and by my presence do keep it holy and invincible against all manner of injuries and offenses." Large London Annotations on Ezekiel 37:28.
[1264] Psalm 59:20-21

from transgression. – **Question:** *What redeemer?* – **Answer:** Typically, Cyrus to redeem and deliver the penitent Jews out of Babylon; truly or anti-typically, Christ, who redeems sinners from sin and death, and turns away ungodliness from Jacob – as Paul interprets and applies this text, touching Christ's restoring the Jews after the Gentiles' fullness;[1265] {2} the Spirit of God; and {3} the Word of God, which was now conferred upon the church, to be both of them continued still to the church from generation to generation. This interpretation I prefer before any other. Now in this sense, this Covenant assures of the continuance of God's ordinance his word among his redeemed people, and the continuance of his Spirit, whereby the word becomes effectual. Add hereunto in the prophet Jeremiah, the continuance of the public ministry, under the notion of the priests the Levites is also covenanted and promised very pathetically [poignantly] by God to these his captive people.[1266]

Thus the Lord has promised in this Covenant to the captive Jews after their redemption: {1} his tabernacle and sanctuary to be among them, in the midst of them; {2} his Spirit to remain upon them and their seed; {3} his Word, not to depart from them, etc.; {4} his public ministry to be successively continued to them, for the managing of his word and ordinances in his tabernacle and sanctuary – and all these forever.

Now here consider: {1} the greatness and excellency of this promised mercy; {2} how this promise may be conceived to be fulfilled to the captive Jews, when he has long since taken away both his tabernacle, sanctuary, Spirit, Word, and public ministry from them to this day.

{1} **The greatness and excellency of this promised mercy of God's setting his sanctuary in the midst of them, etc, is evident:**[1267]

(i) By the excellency of God's tabernacle, and the manifold advantages of God's special presence and residence therein amongst them – as I have already

---

[1265] Romans 11:26-27; see Large London Annotations here.
[1266] Jeremiah 33:17-23
[1267] Book 3, Chapter 4, Aphorism 4, §. 1. N. 5. & 6

shown in seven particulars implied in this presence and residence of God among them.

(ii) By the singular benefit of God's Spirit remaining upon and in his church, for: (a) Hereby the ordinances of God are made lively and effectual unto God's people, in order to their salvation, which without God's Spirit are but as a dead letter; or as a body without a soul.[1268] (b) Hereby, the understandings of men in the church are notably illuminated in divine mysteries, and have them plentifully revealed to them (Ephesians 1:17-19, 1 Corinthians 2:8 to the end). (c) Hereby, the hearts and souls of God's elected are newly framed, sanctified, and spiritualized, being furnished with many admirable fruits and influences of the Spirit of God, as I have at large demonstrated.[1269] (d) Hereby, the saints and sons of God art supernaturally acted, led and guided in all the ways of God (Romans 8:14). (e) Hereby, a variety of gifts and spiritual endowments are bestowed upon the several members of Christ for the good of his whole mystical body (1 Corinthians 12:4-14). (f) Hereby, the church is comforted continually in the ways of well-doing (John 14:16-17, Acts 14:22). (g) Hereby, finally the members of Christ's body are knit fast together to Christ and to one another in holy unity (1 Corinthians 12:12, Ephesians 4:1-5).

(iii) By the great advantage of the enjoyment of the word. This Paul counts a chief privilege of the Jews, that *the oracles of God were committed of trust to them.*[1270] And no wonder, for: (a) the word of God is all *inspired of God,*[1271] therefore it is of unquestionable authority, verity, and infallibility. (b) The word is *a light shining in a dark place; a light to our feet, a lantern to our paths,* in the darkness of this world.[1272] (c) The word is that *fundamentum quo*: that secondary foundation[1273] whereby we are founded upon Christ: the

---

[1268] John 16:8-11 with Acts 2:2, etc, 35-36; 1 Corinthians 14:24-25, Romans 8:2
[1269] In this chapter, in opening the fourth covenant-mercy
[1270] Romans 3:1-2
[1271] 2 Timothy 3:16
[1272] 2 Peter 1:19, Psalm 119:105
[1273] Ephesians 2:20-21

Word converting the sinner, and working faith in him.[1274] (d) The word is an edifying means of grace, *able to build us up, and to give us an inheritance among all them which are sanctified.*[1275] (e) The word is most useful and profitable, *for doctrine of the truth, for conviction of error, for correction of ill doing, for instruction in righteousness,* and for *consolation of the disconsolate; that the man of God may be perfect, thoroughly furnished to all good works.*[1276] (f) The word is the *sword of the Spirit,* whereby we not only defend ourselves, but offend Satan in our spiritual conflict with his temptations.[1277] (g) The word is a singular purifier and preserver from sin and corruption.[1278] (h) And what shall I say? The word is able to make a foolish sinner *wise unto salvation.*[1279] And these are eminent advantages.

(iv) By the commodity and privilege of enjoying the public ministry of the Word and ordinances of God. Paul – reckoning up the privileges of the Corinthians – makes the first of all in his catalog, the ministry, *all things are yours, whether Paul, or Apollo, or Cephas, or the world,* etc.[1280] The ministers of the gospel are a great privilege to any people: For: (a) they are seers, as anciently they were called.[1281] And as Moses said to Jethro in the wilderness: *Thou mayest be to us instead of eyes*;[1282] so ministers are instead of eyes to the mystical body of Christ in the wilderness of this world,[1283] to guide it in the right way: spiritual guides to happiness.[1284] (b) They are the Lord's angels and ambassadors to his churches and elect, beseeching them in Christ's stead to be reconciled to God – this the intent of their embassy, peace, and unity with

---

[1274] Acts 26:18 with Romans 10:17
[1275] Acts 20:32
[1276] 2 Timothy 3:16-17, Romans 15:4
[1277] Ephesians 6:17
[1278] John 15:3, Psalm 119:9, 11
[1279] 2 Timothy 3:15
[1280] 1 Corinthians 3:21-23
[1281] 1 Samuel 9:9, 11
[1282] Numbers 10:31
[1283] 1 Corinthians 12:17, 21
[1284] Hebrews 13:17

God forevermore in Christ.[1285] (c) They are *co-workers, laborers together with God*, in the spiritual husbandry and building of the church of God.[1286] (d) They are stewards of the mysteries of God.[1287] These mysteries are rich *treasures, though in earthy vessels*.[1288] (e) They are God's *watchmen to the house of Israel*, to warn them from God, of their sins and the judgments of God thereby deserved, of their duties and the rewards of God thereunto promised.[1289] (f) They are *instruments* whereby God enables his elect to believe and be converted, to be built and perfected till the day of Christ.[1290] They are *fathers* begetting spiritual children to God, and espousing them as a chaste virgin unto Christ,[1291] and they are *nurses* that bring them up and educate them in Christ, cherishing them with all affectionate tenderness.[1292] (vii) They are, in a word, eminent evidences of the presence of God and Christ with a people. Christ has promised to *be with them all days till the end of the world*,[1293] therefore while Christ continues his ministers to a people, he continues his own presence among that people; but when he takes his ministers away, he also removes himself away.

{2} **How may we conceive that God's promise of continuing his tabernacle, sanctuary, Spirit, Word, and ministry to the captive Jews, should be accomplished, when all these have been long since taken away from them?** Yea and Jesus Christ the great Shepherd of the sheep, did by his prophet Zechariah threaten prophetically to cast off this flock of the Jews, and to cease his pastoral care over them, cutting asunder his two pastoral staves (called **Beauty** and **Bands**) thereby symbolically representing his utter

---

[1285] Revelation 1:20 & 2:1; 2 Corinthians 5:20
[1286] 1 Corinthians 3:9-10
[1287] 1 Corinthians 4:1
[1288] 2 Corinthians 4:7
[1289] Ezekiel 33:7-8, etc.
[1290] 1 Corinthians 3:5, Acts 26:18, Ephesians 4:11-13
[1291] 1 Corinthians 4:15; 1 Thessalonians 2:11
[1292] 1 Thessalonians 2:7
[1293] Matthew 28:19-20

rejection of them, that he would feed them no longer, but would break his Covenant which he had made with all the people.[1294]

Answer: This has some difficulty in it, because the history of these Jews sad condition after Christ, deprived of all these blessings, is quite repugnant to these promises. But, may we not thus resolve?

(i) These promises were not absolute but conditional, upon condition of their walking worthy of such blessings and enjoyments, by faith, obedience, fruitfulness, etc, therefore in after ages their posterity becoming enemies to the prophets and messengers of God – yea to Christ himself. And waxing barren under all these means of grace, Christ tells them that the kingdom of God should be taken from them, and given to a nation bringing forth the fruits thereof.[1295] And this is in substance that which was intended by Christ in the prophet Zechariah (Zechariah 11:7-15), in which paragraph, the scope or intent of the Holy Spirit is to show, how Christ would utterly reject and cast off his covenant people the Jews, and break his Covenant with them judicially, because they would at last utterly reject Christ for a base price of thirty pieces of silver, and so broke covenant with him most perfidiously.

More particularly in the words consider: (a) The description of Christ's pastoral office over the Jews, his spiritual flock, by his taking of two staves. By *staff*, understand his shepherd's staff or crook. Every shepherd has one staff, but Christ had two, to show (as Calvin well notes)[1296] that he did not ply his pastoral office in a vulgar manner, but herein excelled all shepherds, in feeding and guiding that people. One staff he called **Beauty**, as denoting the beauty and comeliness of his ordinances whereby he ordered them. The other **Bands**, as implying the union between Judah and Israel by this Covenant (Zechariah 11:7, 14). (b) Christ's removal of three, that is, many false shepherds, from over that people, among whom Pharisees, Sadducees and Essenes were principal (Zechariah 11:8). (c) Christ's casting off at last his own pastoral care

---

[1294] Zechariah 1:6-15
[1295] Matthew 21:33-45
[1296] John Calvin's commentary on Zechariah 11:7

of them, and as it were breaking his Covenant with them (Zechariah 11:9-10, etc). This is amplified: (1) by the sign or token thereof, symbolically, namely: his cutting asunder his two staves of **Beauty** and **Bands**, denoting their full rejection (Zechariah 11:10-11, 14). (2) By the cause thereof, their wicked contempt and rejection of Christ, for a base price of thirty pieces of silver (Zechariah 11:12-13;. compare herewith Matthew 26:15 & 27:5-11).

(ii) When these blessings were taken away from the Jews, they were more spiritually conferred upon the Gentiles, who became fellow-heirs with the Jews, and of the same body.[1297] The Gentiles then – being incorporated into one church body with the Jews (though the Jews afterwards broke themselves off by unbelief) – these blessings being still continued to the Gentiles, of the same body, may in a sort be said to be continued unto the Jews.

(iii) The Jews' captivity and dead, hopeless condition in Babylon, as also their strange resurrection out of their graves there by a wonderful deliverance;[1298] seem to shadow out the spiritual bondage and misery of the Jews during all the time of their breaking off from Christ by unbelief, and also of their restoration and reimplantation of them again into Christ by faith, which shall be as life from the dead.[1299] And Paul – alleging that of Isaiah, which had immediate reference to the captive Jews in Babylon (Isaiah 59:20-21) – interprets and applies it mediately to the Jews' calling and reingrafting into Christ, after the Gentiles' fullness will have come in (Romans 11:25-27). This notably insinuates to us that the Jews' misery in and recovery out of Babylon were types of their future misery in being broken off from Christ by unbelief, and of their happy reviving and being reingraffed into Christ by faith. After this restoration of the Jews by their conversion, all these promised blessings of God's tabernacle, Spirit, Word and public ministry shall be continued unto them – but much more spiritually until the end of the world.

[1297] Matthew 21:41, Acts 13:46-47 with Ephesians 3:6
[1298] Ezekiel 37:1-35
[1299] Romans 11:15, etc.

Thus of God's presence and residence amongst them by his Spirit, Word and ministry in his tabernacle and sanctuary forever.

[6] God's greatest covenant relation between himself and them, namely: that he would be their God, and they should be his people.

This is a sixth great covenant mercy often inculcated to the captives, as by Jeremiah: *Behold I will gather them out of all countries, and they shall be my people, and I will be their God. – And I will make an everlasting covenant with them, etc.*[1300] By Ezekiel also again and again: *Moreover I will make a covenant of peace with them, it shall be an everlasting covenant with them – My tabernacle also shall be with them; yea I will be their God, and they shall be my people.*[1301]

This covenant mercy is the chief excellency and glory of all covenant mercies. This covenant relation is the most perfect and transcendent of all relations. With this sweetest promise, God supports his captives in Babylon – and it is the best and richest cordial in the world.

But touching this relation, I have already in various places insisted largely in the unfolding of it,[1302] having shown, {1} concerning the Lord's being a covenant God: (i) in whom, or through what means the Lord becomes a covenant God to a people; (ii) what the Lord promised, in promising to be a God in covenant; (iii) why the Lord covenanted to be such a God to his people; and (iv) many inferences from the whole. {2} Concerning a people's being God's covenant people, I have also explained:[1303] (i) what it implies, to be a covenant people to God – and this in many particulars; (ii) why it is requisite that all who enter into covenant with God, should so be his covenant people; (iii) inferences hence. Among the rest, many directions and motives, for becoming God's covenant people, and twelve discoveries whereby we may try

---

[1300] Jeremiah 32:37-40 & 24:5-7
[1301] Ezekiel 37:26-27 & 34:25, 30-31 & 36:28
[1302] *God's Covenant with Abraham*, Book 3, Chapter 3, Aphorism 3, Section 1; and the Sinai Covenant with Israel, Book 3, Chapter 4, Aphorism 4, Section 1.
[1303] Book 3, Chapter 3, Aphorism 3, Section 1 & Chapter 4, Aphorism 4, Section 2.

whether we are God's covenant people or not? To all this, I refer the diligent reader hereof, for his fuller satisfaction.

Thus of the greatest covenant relation between God and the captives – he becoming their God, and they his people in covenant.

[7] Finally, the seventh and last covenant blessing, which the Lord in this Covenant promised to his captives, was: the mutual covenant constancy between God and them in this everlasting Covenant – He would not turn from them, and they should not depart from him.

This is very clearly expressed by the Lord in the prophet Jeremiah, saying: *And I will make an everlasting covenant with them; that I will not turn away from them* (Hebrew: *from after them*) *to do them good: And I will put my fear in their hearts, that they shall not depart from me*, etc.[1304]

Here note:

{1} **The perpetuity of this Covenant promised**: an everlasting covenant, which also is elsewhere pathetically assured them: *For the mountains shall depart, and the hills be removed, but my kindness shall not depart from thee; neither shall the covenant of my peace be removed, saith the LORD that hath mercy on thee.* This Covenant shall be more constant, firm and immovable than the very hills and hugest mountains.

{2} **The ground or foundation of this Covenant's perpetuity, which is twofold: (i) On God's part.** His covenant constancy towards them. He will not turn away from them to do them good. Why? Because he will not. His own mere grace and good pleasure of his will is the sole motive inclining him hereunto; not anything at all in them. And if God will not turn away from them, then his love, his grace, his assistance, his protection, etc. shall not turn away from them. Yea, if God does not turn away from them, then God will be with them; and if God is with them, who shall be prevailingly against them?[1305] Not sin, death, hell, Satan, nor all the powers of darkness. They can never want any requisites for their establishment, constancy, and perseverance in his Covenant, that enjoy God with them and for them, according to his

---

[1304] Jeremiah 32:40, etc.
[1305] Romans 8:31

Covenant. (ii) **On their part.** Their covenant constancy towards God – and that arising from God's fear, which he promises to put into their hearts. The true religious fear of God (which here in this chapter is formerly opened),[1306] comprising much of true religion in it, when once savingly planted in the heart, is a prevalent antidote against apostasy, and strong preservative in constancy (Job 1:1, Jeremiah 32:40). But this fear is not of themselves, it is the gift of God: God puts it into their heart spiritually; it does not grow in their hearts naturally. And from this fear of God's implanting there, they shall be so confirmed, as they shall not depart from him. O what unquestionable security is here, by God's own promises, for God's constancy with them, their perseverance with him, and the perpetuity of this Covenant between both! He will not forsake them; they shall not forsake him. He will so secure their hearts by his fear implanted there. God undertakes for both parties, for himself and them: he will not; they shall not.

How inviolable this Covenant – though they could undertake for no side at all! In the very marriage relation, the man and woman do not either of them undertake for both parties, though their love is never so entire and affectionate; but the husband only can undertake for himself, and the wife for herself. Yet here this covenant relation between God and his people, is so far beyond the marriage relation that therein God undertakes for both sides, for both parties: for himself, that he will not depart from them; for them, that they shall not depart from him. And then, what shall separate between God and them? What shall change or overthrow this Covenant wherein all is undertaken by the unchangeable and omnipotent God? O happy! Thrice happy are God's covenant people, whose constancy, perseverance, and performances towards God, are thus undertaken by God! How may this raise and revive them against all their own infirmities? They can perform nothing, but their God will perform all for them and in them.

[1306] See in this 6th Chapter, Aphorism 2, Section 1, *The 6th Influence of the Spirit*.

Thus of the mutual covenant constancy between the federates, namely: God and his captives in Babylon.

Hitherto, the subject matter of this Covenant, on God's part, consisting in many choice covenant mercies, has been at large unfolded in this first section. Next, the covenant duties required and restipulated from the captive Jews on their part towards God, come under consideration in the second section. And the inferences (for brevity's sake) will conveniently be drawn from them both together.

Section 2

The subject matter or substance of this Covenant, on the part of God's captive people, consisted in sundry covenant duties required and restipulated from them to God.

Such federal duties were especially these, namely: (1) faith in the Messiah promised; (2) repentance from all their former iniquities; (3) true obedience unto God; (4) becoming God's covenant people; (5) enquiring of God for doing all his promised mercies unto them. I shall speak a little to them very briefly: having had occasion more fully to insist upon most of them heretofore.

(1) **Faith in the Messiah promised.** The blessed Messiah was not only promised in all the foregoing, but also even in this present Covenant: and that very eminently, namely: [1] as their complete covenant redeemer, that should ransom them not only from Babylon, but chiefly from all their spiritual, and more than Babylonian bondage; [2] as the sure mercies of David, whereon God's everlasting Covenant is founded and built; [3] as a branch of righteousness growing up to David, and as a plant of renown raised up unto them; [4] As **David** their shepherd, prince, and king forever.

Now the Messiah – that peculiar object of saving faith – being in this Covenant so notably promised and tendered on God's part to them, they on their part were consequently obliged, in the nature of the thing: [1] to embrace these promises, and accept this tender of the Messiah by faith, and [2] to live by this faith:

[1] **To embrace these promises, and accept this tender of the Messiah in this Covenant by faith.** God's federal tender of Christ, and of many benefits in him to his people, implies and consequentially requires their answerable acceptance of Christ by believing, and of all other blessings

tendered with him. Besides (remembering still that the prophecy of Isaiah from chapter 49 to the end of the book has very remarkable reference to this present Covenant with the Babylonian captives, as has been noted), it is evident: {1} that God required all thirsty souls to come to Christ, as to waters, wine, milk, bread and fatness[1307] – which coming to Christ, is believing in him;[1308] {2} that God promised justification by faith in Jesus Christ, unto many. *By his knowledge* (namely: by the knowledge of him through faith, for faith has in it knowledge, assent, and affiance) *shall my righteous servant justify many, for he shall bear their iniquities*, etc.;[1309] and {3} that the not-believing in Christ is sharply blamed: *Who hath believed our report? And to whom hath the arm of the LORD been revealed? For he shall grow up before him as a tender plant*, etc.[1310] Thus faith is here required. And when this Covenant had at last exhibited the Messiah unto the world (before the New Covenant began to commence), how often did Jesus Christ invite and importune his own people the Jews, the posterity of the captives redeemed from Babylon, to come unto him and believe in him for life and salvation?[1311]

But touching true faith in Christ Jesus the Messiah, I have already shown at large: (i) what justifying or saving faith in Christ is, and (ii) how we are justified by believing.[1312]

[2] **To live by this faith.** The righteous under their captivity are required to live by faith, though their bondage was heavy, and their deliverance delayed, because at last (when the vision's appointed time should come) they should certainly be delivered by the Messiah. *The vision is yet for an appointed time, but at the end it shall speak and not lie: though it tarry, wait for it; because it will surely come, it will not tarry. Behold his soul which is lifted up, is not*

[1307] Isaiah 55:1, 3, 24
[1308] John 6:35
[1309] Isaiah 53:11
[1310] Isaiah 53:1-4
[1311] Matthew 11:28-30 & 23:37, John 3:14-18, 36 & 6:35, 37, 47-59
[1312] In Book 3, Chapter 3, Aphorism 5, Questions 1-7

upright in him: but the just shall live by his faith.[1313] This last sentence is famously alleged in the New Testament, by the apostle Paul in order to prove life and justification by faith.[1314] The words may be considered:

{1} Partly, as a promise. And so, they may be again understood two ways; for the word {*by his faith*} in the Hebrew – standing in the midst between the subject and the predicate here – may be referred either: (i) to the subject, thus: *The just by his faith* – and so it declares the instrumental mean whereby a man is justified, namely: by his faith; or (ii) to the predicate, thus: *By his faith shall live* – and so it implies to the captives in Babylon, that the just among them should by faith live, and out-live their captivity, and be delivered according to God's Covenant, yea live eternally and spiritually – their redemption from Babylon being a type of their eternal redemption.

{2} Partly, as a precept or command to the righteous which were in Babylon, that in the midst their affliction there they should wait upon God for deliverance, and by faith live upon God, upon Christ, upon his Covenant, and upon his promises, until the appointed time of the vision should come, although they were as dead and buried in their graves in Babylon. For God's elect should by the Messiah be certainly delivered both from Babylonian and from hellish bondage.

More generally, how they that are justified by faith do live by faith, especially in five chief acts of faith, I have already shown.[1315]

More particularly, how the just should live by faith, in times of affliction, and misery upon themselves and the church of God, may in part appear by these acts of true faith, which in such cases are to be exerted and exercised. For in such sort believers of old have lived by faith, upon God, Christ, Covenant and promises in troublous and afflicting times.

(i) Faith – being forewarned of affliction – forearms against it. Faith puts upon providing an ark, before the flood comes (Hebrews 11:7).

[1313] Habbakuk 2:2-4
[1314] Romans 1:17, Galatians 3:11, Hebrews 10:38
[1315] In Book 3, Chapter 3, Aphorism 3, Section 2

(ii) Faith encourages against all visible fears and troubles by beholding him that is invisible (Hebrews 11:27).

(iii) Faith leans and rests upon God in Christ in the saddest wilderness of woe and distress, as on the only rock of support and safety (Song of Solomon 8:5, Isaiah 50:10, Psalm 73:25-26). Faith enables to trust in God, though he slay us (Job 13:15).

(iv) Faith puts upon fervent prayer unto God in afflictions (Psalm 116:10).

(v) Faith accounts the afflictions of God's people, the reproach of Christ, and prefers that reproach of Christ beyond all earthly treasures, having respect to the recompense of reward (Hebrews 11:24-26).

(vi) Faith – eyeing the promises (though afar off) – is so persuaded of them, and so embraces them as to enable God's people to live as afflicted pilgrims and strangers in this world, denying earthly comforts, and enduring much hardness, because they look for *a city that hath foundations*, and for *a better, that is an heavenly country* (Hebrews 11:8-10, 13-17).

(vii) Faith lightens the heaviest and sweetens the most bitter distresses and tribulations (Romans 5:1-4). Faithful Paul gloried in the cross of Christ (Galatians 5:14, 17), and took pleasure in reproaches, in necessities, in persecutions, in distresses for Christ's sake (2 Corinthians 12:10).

(viii) Faith supports and bears up the heart under all sorts of afflictions with spiritual consolations, which are not small (2 Corinthians 1:4-6; 1 Samuel 30:6). Especially upon these and like grounds of comfort, namely: (a) by former experiences (2 Corinthians 1:10; 2 Timothy 4:17-18); (b) by God's promises (Hebrews 13:5-6, Luke 21:15, 18, Matthew 10:19, 32, Mark 10:29-30, Revelation 2:10); (c) by God's presence with us in affliction, and sympathizing (Isaiah 43:1-3, Acts 18:9-10, Isaiah 63:9); (d) by the nature of affliction: a Father's cup (John 18:11) wholly for our profit (Hebrews 12:5-12). The reproach and afflictions of Christ (Hebrews 11:26, Colossians 1:24) are the lot of Christians (1 Corinthians 10:13; 2 Timothy 3:12, John 16:33) –

cannot separate from God's love in Christ (Romans 8:35-37) and the highway to glory (Romans 8:17).

(ix) Faith enables patiently to undergo all varieties and extremities of miseries for obtaining of the promises (Hebrews 11:35-40), and to refuse deliverance from tortures in hope of a better resurrection (Hebrews 11:35).

(x) Faith makes the saints rejoice under sufferings, through assurance of their future reward (Hebrews 10:32-36 & 12:2, Romans 5:1-3).

(xi) Faith looks upon all afflictions, as inflicted for good (Job 23:10, Jeremiah 24:5, Hebrews 12:10; 2 Corinthians 4:16-18).

(xii) Faith waits for God's time of deliverance, as fittest, and makes not haste out of trouble by indirect means (Job 14:14, Isaiah 28:16, Habakkuk 2:2-4).

(2) **Repentance from all their former sins and iniquities.** Its very observable that after the Lord promised his people's deliverance out of captivity, planting in their own land, with many excellent spiritual mercies, he declares how his people shall be affected with deep self-abhorring, and sincere penitential dispositions at the consideration of God's overcoming love and kindnesses. *And I will give them an heart to know me, that I am the LORD; and they shall be my people and I will be their God: For, they shall return unto me with their whole heart.*[1316] Not formally, feignedly, or hypocritically; but cordially, entirely, with their heart, and with their whole heart. Notable is that in Ezekiel: *Then* – that is, when God had redeemed them from Babylon, restored them to Zion, sprinkled clean water upon them, and heaped all those fore-promised blessings upon them – *Then shall ye remember your own evil ways, and your doings that were not Good, and shall loathe yourselves in your own sight, for your iniquities, and for your abominations.*[1317] Nothing more kindly and thoroughly melts the heart of a sinner into penitential tears,

---

[1316] Jeremiah 24:5-7
[1317] Ezekiel 36:23-33

self-loathings, and self-debasings, than the infinite flames of God's gratuitous love and bowels of mercy once savingly felt, and influences thereof *shed abroad upon the heart*.[1318] Love breeds love, as naturally as fire breeds fire. *We love God, because he hath loved us first*.[1319] And love to God makes us hate and loathe whatsoever is contrary to that blessed God whom we entirely love. Hence it is, that we cannot choose but hate and loathe our sins and ourselves for them, when we come to a true sense, and apprehension of them, as being against God, who is all purity, all goodness, and all love.[1320]

But having formerly spoken of the nature of repentance in sundry particulars, I need not here to superadd further.[1321]

(3) **True obedience unto God.** This covenant duty is mentioned several times: *And David my servant shall be king over them: and they all shall have one shepherd: They shall also walk in my judgments and observe my statutes and do them. – Moreover I will make a covenant of peace with them*, etc.[1322] Here, their obedience shall arise from their enjoying Christ the true **David** to be their king and shepherd. *And I will put my Spirit within you, and cause you to walk in my statutes: and ye shall keep my judgments and do them*.[1323] *– And I will give them one heart, And I will put a new spirit within you; And I will take the stony heart out of their flesh, and will give them an heart of flesh: That they may walk in my statutes, and keep mine ordinances and do them: and they shall be my people and I will be their God*.[1324] Here their obedience shall also spring from God's Spirit of renovation and sanctification in them. In these passages, Their obedience is spoken of in a double notion, namely: [1] as a mercy promised from God to them. God promises to give them Christ, his

---

[1318] Romans 5:5
[1319] 1 John 4:19
[1320] 1 John 1:5, Matthew 19:17; 1 John 4:16
[1321] Book 3, Chapter 4, Aphorism 4, Section 2
[1322] Ezekiel 37:24, 26
[1323] Ezekiel 37:27
[1324] Ezekiel 11:19-20

Spirit, newness of heart, tenderness of heart, etc, and all to work them up to sincere universal obedience. He will furnish them with these excellent inward principles and abilities for obedience. [2] As a duty required from them by God. Being thus principled and enabled, they are to return true and upright obedience unto God, as their covenant duty.

But touching this covenant duty of obedience, I shall here need to enlarge no further, having largely opened this particular duty, both in God's Covenant with Abraham, and with Israel at Mount Sinai.[1325]

(4) Becoming God's covenant people. It is their covenant privilege that they may be his people; it is their covenant duty also to become his people and behave themselves towards him accordingly. Shall the Lord covenant to be their God, which is the greatest and fullest of all mercies promisable, and shall not they restipulate to be his people, which is the greatest and fullest duty repromisable? Relatives do mutually infer and remove one another.[1326] *Moreover I will make a covenant of peace with them, it shall be an everlasting covenant with them. – My tabernacle also shall be with them: Yea, I will be their God, and they shall be my people.*[1327] This is also elsewhere often inculcated; whereby they may see that God insists much upon it.[1328]

This covenant duty of being God's people; is a sweet and ample theme, and here I should have contentedly paused a while, had I not unfolded touching this covenant duty already, these things, namely: [1] what it implies – to be a covenant people to God; [2] why God makes us his covenant people, and [3] certain inferences, among which are twelve characteristics whereby we may discover whether we are God's covenant-people or not – and all in

---

[1325] Book 3, Chapter 3, Aphorism 2 & Chapter 4, Aphorism 4
[1326] Relata mutuo se ponunt & tollunt.
[1327] Ezekiel 37:26-27
[1328] Ezekiel 11:20, 36:28 & 37:23

opening the Sinai Covenant.[1329] Let the diligent reader return thither for his satisfaction.

(5) Lastly, enquiring of God, for doing all his covenanted mercies unto them. God will do much for his people of his own mere grace – yea, he is not only *able* but *wont* to do *exceeding abundantly above all that we ask or think*.[1330] But yet he loves to be sought unto by his people, that he may stream his blessings upon them. Hereupon, after he had made many promises to his captives of high concernment, he subjoined: *Thus saith the Lord GOD, I will yet for this be inquired of by the house of Israel, to do it for them*.[1331] As a great king proffers many royal favors to his subjects, but yet they that mean to partake them, must petition for them; or as a rich possessioner holds a manner *in libero soccagio*, in free socage,[1332] but yet he must perform to such a court, or he must pay a pound of pepper, A red rose in rose time, etc. as a chief rent; so here God will be honored by petitions, in his court of requests; he will have his rent and his homage from his people in order to the performance of his promised mercies to his people. God does not give his blessings for their prayers, though he will not give them without their prayers.

[1329] Book 3, Chapter 4, Aphorism 4, § 2
[1330] Ephesians 3:20
[1331] Ezekiel 36:37 with what went before, from verse 24, etc.
[1332] "Socage, in feudal English property law, form of land tenure in which the tenant lived on his lord's land and in return rendered to the lord a certain agricultural service or money rent. At the death of a tenant in socage (or socager), the land went to his heir after a payment to the lord of a sum of money (known as a relief), which in time became fixed at an amount equal to a year's rent on the land. Socage is to be distinguished from tenure by knight service, in which the service rendered was of a military nature, although, by statute in 1660, all knight-service tenure became socage tenure. In time, most of the land in England came to be held in socage tenure. In the United States, lands in the early colonies were given in socage, particularly in Pennsylvania, where the royal charter given to William Penn created a socage tenure with an annual rent of two beaver skins for the land. After the American Revolution, lands held in socage tenure from the crown were deemed to be held by the state as sovereign, and several states passed statutes or enacted constitutional provisions abolishing tenure." *Encyclopedia Britannica*
<https://www.britannica.com/topic/socage>
[Accessed 3/4/2024]

When our hearts are fervently put upon prayer for covenant blessings, it is a good argument we are not far from enjoying such covenant blessings. And what we reap by prayer: [1] is best discerned whence it comes; [2] is doubly sweet when it comes; [3] is more carefully retained and improved, as not obtained without many wrestlings, prayers and tears; and [4] does most redound to the glory of the Giver, enlarging our hearts by many thanksgivings unto God.

Thus of the matter of this Covenant on the captives' part, namely: their covenant duties required from them towards God.

Section 3

Inferences from the whole matter of this Covenant.

We now conclude this whole subject matter of this Covenant – both on God's part, and on the part of his captive people – with some brief inferences, thence offering themselves to us, such as:

(1) Hence, *Jesus Christ* **was promised in this Covenant with special reference to** *David***, and to the performance of God's former Covenant made with him in Christ.** For, **Christ** is herein promised: [1] as *the sure mercies of David*, whereupon God's everlasting Covenant is founded and built;[1333] [2] as a Branch of Righteousness growing up to **David**, and a Plant of Renown raised up to them;[1334] [3] as **David** their Shepherd, Prince, and King forever. **Christ** is a second **David**; yea, the only true **David**.[1335] All of these particulars have been here already explained. Now why is Christ thus promised with such reference unto **David**, but because God would thereby let us see that God's Covenant with David and his seed was not forgotten – no, not in his seed's woeful captivity and seeming rejection, but should certainly be fulfilled. And that it should have its chief accomplishment in Jesus Christ? For indeed, under this covenant dispensation, Jesus Christ was not only further promised than in the Covenant with David, but also actually performed and exhibited in human flesh of the seed of David, according to all the former promises that went of Christ.

(2) Hence, *Christ* **alone was the covenant redeemer of God's captives from Babylon to Zion – whoever or whatever were the instruments employed in that their redemption.** Cyrus the Persian and Darius the Mede with their armies were their instrumental redeemers. They took Babylon,

---

[1333] Isaiah 55:1-4 with Acts 13:34
[1334] Ezekiel 34:25, etc. & chapter 29; Jeremiah 33:15-17
[1335] Ezekiel 34:23, etc. & 37:24-26; Jeremiah 33:17, 20-22, 25-26

destroyed their king Belshazzar, proclaimed liberty for the captive Jews, both to depart out of Babylon, and to return into Canaan, to build the house of God, etc.[1336] But Jesus Christ, who ordered and over-ruled all these things was their principal redeemer, as that prophecy in Isaiah, formerly opened, does especially manifest.[1337] As he of old was the principal redeemer of his people out of Egypt's bondage, witness the type of the paschal lamb, although Moses and Aaron were therein very instrumental to him.[1338] Hereupon the ransomed captives owe all the praise of the return of their captivity to the LORD alone.[1339] Oh how vehemently is Christ pleased with the office of a redeemer that redeems from Egypt, redeems from Babylon, and redeems from hell.

(3) **Hence, the great and wonderful redemption of captive Jews from Babylon to Canaan, was an eminent type of Christ's greater and more wonderful redemption of captive sinners from sin to grace, from Satan to God, from death to life, from hell to heaven.** This typicalness has been already proven, and the parallel made between these two redemptions.[1340] The Jews of old might notably spell out their spiritual redemption from sin and misery, in their corporal redemptions from Egypt and Babylon. These were to them not only mercies, but mysteries: not only restorations for the present, but instructions also for the future. And when we read this great work of God in redeeming his captives from Babylon's graves, we remember and admire much more Christ's stupendous work in redeeming his elect from the grave of Sin and gulf of hell.

(4) **Hence, no difficulties whatsoever or seeming impossibilites can hinder the accomplishment of God's Covenants and promises.** God in this Covenant promised to bring his people out of Babylon into Canaan, and to place them there, etc. Alas! How hard and impossible a thing might this seem

---

[1336] Daniel 5:30-31; 2 Chronicles 36:22-23, Ezra 1:1, etc.
[1337] Isaiah 49:8-18, etc.
[1338] Exodus 12
[1339] Psalm 126:1-3, etc.
[1340] See in this Aphorism, Section 1, Covenant-Mercy 2

unto them? Canaan was wasted and depopulated; the holy city and temple destroyed and laid on heaps; the Jews carried captive into Babylon and there entombed like dead persons in their graves[1341] – the Babylonian kingdom being at that time the great and potent empire over the world, unlikely to be subdued by any visible power; and Babylon itself the royal seat of the empire being so strongly fortified, naturally by the great River Euphrates, artificially by walls extraordinarily thick and high; etc. Yet notwithstanding all these difficulties and visible impossibilities, God's Covenant and promises for the Jews' deliverance were exactly performed when the seventy years were accomplished: Cyrus and Darius taking Babylon in that night after Belshazzar and his lords had sensually feasted and quaffed in the silver and golden vessels of the temple;[1342] immediately after which, Cyrus proclaims liberty to the captives to return into Canaan for rebuilding of the temple and Jerusalem.[1343] So they were placed in their own land, and (though they had troubled times, and many subtle malicious and potent adversaries, whereby the work was long obstructed and retarded, yet) they built, prospered and finished. Zerubbabel laid the foundation, and the topstone.[1344]

When therefore any difficulties or seeming impossibilities stand in the way between the promises of God and his performances thereof, let not our faith stagger or be discomfited [utterly defeated]; God will engage his omniscience and his omnipotence, rather than there shall be the least violation of his fidelity. So that even against reason, and sense, and hope, in hope, we may most confidently rely upon him.

(5) Hence, Christ's redeemed people become his cleansed people. Sin is the sinner's only spiritual defilement. When Christ redeems any sinner, he cleanses him from his sins: partly by his own blood, unto justification;[1345]

[1341] Ezekiel 37:1, etc.
[1342] Daniel 5:30
[1343] 2 Chronicles 36:22-23, Ezra 1:1-3, etc.
[1344] Zechariah 4:6-10, Ezra 6:14-15
[1345] Revelation 1:5

partly by his Spirit unto sanctification.[1346] Christ redeemed these Jews so from their misery, as also to cleanse them from all their iniquities.[1347] Christ redeems the sinner, so as to renew the sinner. He purchases us, not to protect us in sin, but to purge us from sin. Jesus Christ *gave himself for us, that he might redeem us from all iniquity: and purify unto himself a peculiar people zealous of good works.*[1348] And Christ's redemption is actually applied to none but only to such as are effectually called and cleansed. Redeemed Jews, must abandon their Idols. Redeemed Sinners must forsake their sins. To pretend to be redeemed by Christ, and yet to allow ourselves in sin is great hypocrisy in us, and brings great infamy upon Christ, as if he were a patron of sin and wickedness.

(6) **Hence, that the Jews (who extremely doted upon idolatry) were weaned from idolatry, is merely to be ascribed to the grace and Covenant of God.** Not the loss of Canaan, Jerusalem, and the temple; not the miseries of their Chaldean bondage; not the good example of the Chaldeans, who were extremely addicted to idolatry and superstition; but only God's free grace and Covenant, promising this mercy, did accordingly divorce them from their idolatry.[1349] When nothing else can do it, the grace and promise of God can estrange us utterly from our iniquities. Wait we therefore upon his grace, and Covenant for attainment of this blessing to ourselves and others.

(7) **Hence, God's Spirit, or the Spirit of Christ, was not only promised, but also performed to God's redeemed under the Old Testament.** For besides what has been evidenced to this effect in opening of former Covenants, it is plain that this Spirit of God and Christ was promised and performed under this Covenant. This is diligently to be noted against the Socinians, who falsely assert that the Spirit was not promised under the Old

---

[1346] 1 Peter 1:18-19, 22, Titus 3:4-6
[1347] See before in the 3rd Promised Mercy
[1348] Titus 2:13-14
[1349] Daniel 3:1-2, etc.

Testament.[1350] What could be more express than this? *A new heart also will I give you, and a new spirit will I put within you; and I will take away the stony heart out of your flesh, and I will give you an heart of flesh. And I will put my Spirit within you, and cause you to walk in my statutes,* etc.[1351] See the fourth covenant mercy.

(8) **Hence, when God's Spirit is put within the heart, he brings many sacred endowments and blessed influences with himself into that heart.** I have here in this Covenant noted and opened seven such holy influences introduced into the soul by the Spirit of God; and all of very precious consequence.[1352] The Spirit is the spring and immediate author of all gifts and graces.[1353] He that once is possessed of this spring has all the streams of grace thence flowing. It is therefore a very great and complexive mercy, to enjoy the Spirit of God according to God's Covenant. Our Savior intimates that God's giving of his Spirit to them that ask him, is the great attainment by prayer.[1354] He that can pray down this blessing upon his heart, may have anything of God. And Paul sums up the whole blessing of Abraham that was to come upon the Gentiles through Christ, his most blessed seed, in this one: the receiving of the promise of the Spirit (i.e. the promised Spirit) through faith. The promised Spirit enjoyed, instates believers in the whole blessing of Abraham, and makes them every way blessed with Abraham.

(9) **Hence, the Lord delights to afford his special presence among his covenant people.** His tabernacle shall be with them, and his *sanctuary in the midst of them forevermore.*[1355] And hereby God affords his special presence with his covenant people, as has been explained.[1356] Now God's presence is his people's protection (Psalm 46:5). their encouragement, and consolation

---

[1350] Racovian Catechism, Question 10
[1351] Ezekiel 36:26-27
[1352] In the 4th Covenant-Mercy
[1353] 1 Corinthians 12:4-12, Galatians 5:22-23, Ephesians 5:9
[1354] Matthew 7:11 with Luke 11:13
[1355] Ezekiel 37:26-28
[1356] In the 5th Covenant-Mercy

against all evils, even in the valley of the shadow of death (Psalm 23:4), and a special token of God's discriminating favor to them, separating them from all the people on the face of the earth (Exodus 33:16). Moses set so much store by this presence of God, that he was not willing to go out of the wilderness towards Canaan itself without it: *If thy presence go not up with me, carry us not up hence.*[1357] Ezekiel – having described the new temple, new worship and ministry, new land, and new city (as elsewhere I have shown)[1358] shuts up his description of the new city with the blessed denomination given to it: *And the name of the city from that day, shall be, JEHOVAH-SHAMMAH* – i.e. *the LORD is there.*[1359] Hereby intimating, that God's presence and residence in this city, should be the high excellence and chief glory of this city, instead [in the place] of all blessings.

(10) **Hence, God's Covenant with a people, advances them to the highest covenant relation with God**. For what relation can any people have towards God, or with God, like this: that he should be their Covenant-God, and they his covenant people?[1360] And this relationship between God and his captives is sweetly established in this Covenant (Ezekiel 37:23, 26-27, 36:28 & 34:30-31). Oh how comfortable, sweet and blessed is this relation! What a miracle of mercy is it, that the most holy, holy, holy Lord God, should ever admit sinful dust and ashes into such a relationship to himself? How excellent is God's Covenant, that is the mysterious foundation in Christ of this relation between God and man! Surely, to be effectually called and savingly brought into covenant, and covenant relation with God indeed, is so complexive a mercy that it comprises all other saving blessings in its bosom, and is the very gate of heaven itself.

(11) **Hence, God so requires covenant duties from us, that he undertakes all our covenant performances for us**. As God on his part will

---

[1357] Exodus 33:15
[1358] In my *Key of the Bible* on Ezekiel, §5
[1359] Ezekiel 48:35
[1360] See formerly in the 6th Covenant-Mercy.

bestow covenant mercies, so his covenant people on their part must return covenant duties. The obligation must be mutual and reciprocal. But here's the mystery: God undertakes for both sides. He will be their God, and they shall be his people;[1361] he will not turn away from them to do them good, and they (his fear being put into their hearts) shall not depart from him.[1362] O happy Covenant! Wherein God undertakes the covenant performances on his people's part, as well as on his own. In this point, no covenant in the world can compare with this Covenant of God. In all covenants between man and man, no man undertakes for his confederate, but only for himself. In all covenants between man and wife, no husband undertakes for his wife, and no wife undertakes for her husband, but the husband only for himself, and the wife only for herself. But in God's Covenant, he undertakes for himself and for us also. Though our sins are never so many, our infirmities and weaknesses never so pressing, our temptations never so violent, our duties never so great and difficult; yet he will so furnish us with his fear and grace, that we shall do what he requires, and not depart from him. Oh what a comfort and stay may this be to our hearts! Let us depend upon this Covenant faithfully, and let us urge the Lord upon this his Covenant importunately, so that he will honor himself and his truth in performing all things for us. Let him enable us to do what he requires, and let him require us to do what he pleases.

(12) **Hence, God's Covenant in Christ is an everlasting Covenant, and cannot be disannulled.** The outward form or manner of ministration may be changed and annulled, but the essence and substance of it cannot be violated. God will not turn from them; they shall not depart from God.[1363] All other things in the world cannot divide between God and his people, or destroy his Covenant. This perpetuity of God's Covenant with his captives, exceedingly augments the sweetness, comfortableness and benefit of all the covenant mercies.

[1361] Ezekiel 37:23, 26-27
[1362] Jeremiah 32:40
[1363] Jeremiah 32:40, Ezekiel 37:26-28

(13) Hence, finally, we may clearly take notice of many eminent points of Christian religion which are revealed in and under this Covenant. Consider well the covenant mercies promised, and see if they don't amount to a considerable gospel, and brief abstract of Christianity. It shall suffice only to mention these points now, because I have, in opening this Covenant's mercies, and in sundry other Covenants, explained them already.

In and under this Covenant, these points of Christian religion are disclosed:

[1] **The person and office of Jesus Christ the Messiah.**

{1} *His person*: that he should be true man, of the Seed of David: *A branch of righteousness growing up to **David***;[1364] *the sure mercies of David*,[1365] etc.

{2} *His office of mediatorship*. For, he is called: **The Lord Our Righteousness** (Jeremiah 33:16-17). And he is the covenant redeemer of his captives from spiritual thralldom (Isaiah 49:8-18). More particularly, that he should be: (i) a prophet. *Behold I have given him for a witness to the people* (Isaiah 55:1-4, John 7:16-17 & 12:49, 56). (ii) A priest. This is implied in that denomination given him: *the sure mercies of David*, which implies his resurrection from the dead (Isaiah 55:1-4 with Acts 13:34). And this consequently presupposes his death. Christ died to satisfy for our sins (Romans 4:25 & 8:3 Hebrews 9:14 & 10:10, 12, 14). Christ rose again from the dead, that he might ever live to make intercession for us (Hebrews 7:25 & 9:24). Now Christ's satisfaction for sin, and intercession for sinners, are the two grand parts or acts of his priesthood.

{3} *A king*. A leader and commander of the people (Isaiah 55:1-4). Yea he is promised, as another **David**, their shepherd, prince, and king forever (Ezekiel 34:23-25, etc, 37:24-26, Jeremiah 33:17, 20-22, 25-26).

[1364] Jeremiah 33:15-17
[1365] Isaiah 55:1-4 with Acts 13:34

[2] **The great work of redemption.** That God's elect should be redeemed from their spiritual bondage by Christ, is primarily intended to be revealed to the Jews, under Christ's promised redeeming of the captive Jews from Babylon, the type thereof (Isaiah 49:8-24, Ezekiel 37:21, 25-26 & 34:11-19, 23, etc, Jeremiah 23:7-8 & 16:14-15).[1366]

[3] **The donation of the Spirit of God.** *And I will put my Spirit within you*, etc.[1367] And with the Spirit, many fruits and influences.

[4] **Renovation or renewing of Spirit and heart** (Ezekiel 36:25-26). This in substance is one with regeneration, and effectual calling (Titus 3:4-6).

[5] **Justification**: that all their iniquities should be cleansed and pardoned (Jeremiah 33:7-8). And that Christ's righteousness should so effectually be made theirs, that Christ himself should be the **Lord** their **Righteousness** (Jeremiah 33:16-17). And justification does especially consist in these two things, namely: non-imputing of our sins to us, but to Christ; and imputing of Christ's righteousness unto us, as the matter of our righteousness before God.

[6] **Sanctification, and spiritual cleansing from their sinful uncleannesses**[1368] – not to defile themselves any longer therewith, but to walk in newness of life and obedience (Ezekiel 36:27). More particularly, they should be so sanctified, as: {1} to know God, that he is the LORD (Jeremiah 24:5-7); {2} to believe in Jesus Christ, and to live by that faith (Isaiah 55:1-4 & 53:1-3, 11, Habakkuk 2:3-4); {3} to be of tender fleshy, not of heard stony hearts (Ezekiel 36:26); {4} to have and exercise sincere repentance (Ezekiel 36:31); {5} to have one heart and one way in matters of religion (Jeremiah 32:38-40); and {6} to be constant in the fear of God (Jeremiah 32:39-41).

[7] **God's presence among his people in his ordinances** (Ezekiel 37:26-28).

[8] **Dearest union to, and communion with God, as a covenant people with a Covenant-God** (Ezekiel 37:26-27, and often).

[1366] See the 2nd Covenant-Mercy here.
[1367] Ezekiel 36:25-27
[1368] Ezekiel 37:23-26 & 11:17-18

[9] Perseverance with God in his Covenant (Jeremiah 32:40, etc.).

These, among other points of Christian doctrine, are revealed in this Covenant. And therefore it may very justly be accounted and made use of as an evangelical and Christian Covenant.

But hitherto of the substance, or subject matter of this Covenant.

Aphorism 3

The Form of God's Covenant with his captive people.

The form of God's Covenant with his captive-people the Jews, was inwardly, the mutual obligation of the federates one to another; outwardly, the manner of this Covenant's manifestation, confirmation, and administration. This aphorism I explain as follows.

Concerning this form of God's Covenant with his captive people the Jews, I need not say much. It is (1) inward and (2) outward.

(1) **Inward.** The more inward and essential form of this Covenant, consisted in the mutual obligation of the federates one to another: of God to the captive Jews by stipulation of mercies, and of the captive Jews to God by restipulation of duties. These mercies and duties, have both of them been already explained. The high excellency and glory of all these mercies and duties, is set forth in that clause, often recited in this Covenant: *I will be their God, and they shall be my people.*[1369]

(2). **Outward.** The more outward and accidental Form of this Covenant, stood in the manner of God's [1] manifestation, [2] confirmation, and [3] administration of this Covenant to the captive Jews.

[1] *God's manifestation of this Covenant* to the captive Jews was not immediate by his own immediate revelation or voice to them, as to Adam, Noah, Abraham, and to Israel at Mount Sinai; but mediate, by the ministry of his prophets, especially Isaiah, Jeremiah, and Ezekiel, as has been already evidenced.[1370] As God first made known the former Covenant to his prophet Nathan, and then by him to David; so here God first revealed this Covenant to these his prophets, and then by them to the captive Jews. God delights to impart his covenant mysteries unto his people by the ministry of his prophets,

---

[1369] Ezekiel 37:26-27, 23 & 11:20 & 14:11 & 36:28
[1370] Book 3, Chapter 6, in the preface to this Covenant's explanation

unto men by men: {1} partly, that they may not be dashed, terrified and amazed, at the terrible majesty of the Lord, as once Israel was;[1371] {2} partly, that the Lord may condescend more familiarly unto his people in his covenant dealings with them, as he did with David (2 Samuel 7:19); {3} partly, to teach his people to prize, love, and hearken to his prophets, by whom the richest treasures of gospel truth and covenant assurances of their salvation in Christ, are revealed to them. Who would not highly value those ambassadors, that shall come from God with a Covenant of Faith, purposely to assure them of their eternal happiness by Christ through believing?

[2] *God's confirmation of this Covenant* to his people the captive Jews, was various: chiefly fourfold: {1} by exegetical repetitions of it, {2} by various illustrating symbols and similitudes, {3} by sundry ratifying promises, and {4} By God's sacred and inviolable oath.

{1} By exegetical repetitions of it. God made known this Covenant by his prophets to his people, not only once, but often. He spoke it frequently so that he might confirm it to them firmly. And his following repetitions were not only confirmations, but also explanations of the foregoing discoveries of this Covenant. God made known this Covenant, especially to three prophets: (i) to Isaiah before the captivity, often repeating it by him, (ii) to Ezekiel, and (iii) to Jeremiah, both during the captivity – often ingeminating [reiterating] it to them all, which I have particularly shown in the beginning of this sixth chapter, in the preface there. Now why should God thus often ingeminate and repeat this Covenant, but to put his people out of doubt of the certainty of it?

{2} By various illustrating symbols and similitudes. Parables or similitudes illustrate much, and consequently obtain some kind of force for confirmation of things illustrated, and for persuasion of our hearts thereunto. God used especially these parables, symbols, or similitudes for confirming and assuring of several covenant mercies to the captive Jews, namely: (i) the symbol of two

---

[1371] Exodus 20:18-21, Deuteronomy 5:22 to the end

baskets of figs set before the temple: the one very good, the other very bad[1372] – the good figs representing the captives in Babylon, towards whom God had thoughts and purposes of much good, to redeem them from Babylon, to bring them into their own land, etc.; the bad figs representing Zedekiah and his princes, and the residue of Jerusalem, which remained still in the land, etc, whom God would consume and make fit for nothing. (ii) The symbol of two sticks, written on, the one for Judah, the other for Ephraim: both of them becoming one in the prophet Ezekiel's hand[1373] – hereby God assuring them that Judah and Israel should no longer remain two kingdoms or two nations, but they should both become one in the hand of God under the true **David**, Jesus Christ their prince. This was another eminent mercy promised in this Covenant. (iii) The symbol of dry bones in the valley, reviving at Ezekiel's prophesying, and standing up an exceeding great army[1374] – hereby the Lord assuring the captive Jews that though they were as it were dead and buried in their graves in Babylon, and their condition visibly as helpless and hopeless as of these dead dry bones; yet God would open their graves, bring them out of their graves, make their dead and dry bones live, and redeem them from Babylon. This was another grand covenant mercy promised.

{3} By sundry ratifying promises. I mean such promises as were annexed to, or inserted in this Covenant, purposely to ratify, confirm and assure them of the certainty and inviolable stability of this Covenant. As, when God promised the perpetuity of this Covenant and the covenant mercies in Christ, the true **David**: *And they shall dwell in the land that I have given unto Jacob my servant, wherein your fathers have dwelt, and they shall dwell therein, even they and their children, and their children's children forever, and my servant* ***David*** *shall be their prince forever. Moreover I will make a covenant of peace with them, it shall be an everlasting covenant with them, etc.*[1375] And again: *I*

[1372] Jeremiah 24:1 to the end of the chapter
[1373] Ezekiel 37:15 to the end of the chapter
[1374] Ezekiel 37:1-15
[1375] Ezekiel 37:25-26

will make an everlasting covenant with you, even the sure mercies of David (Isaiah 55:3). And elsewhere God ratifies this Covenant by promising greater and more immovable stability to it, than to the very mountains and hills: *For the mountains shall depart, and the hills be removed: but my kindness shall not depart from thee, neither shall the covenant of my peace be removed, saith the LORD, that hath mercy on thee.*[1376] How sweet are these promises!

{4} By God's sacred and inviolable oath. For God – comforting his people by his Covenant and promises against the Babylonian captivity, confirms that his Covenant and the promises thereof by his holy oath, saying: *For this is as the waters of Noah unto me: for as I have sworn that the waters of Noah shall no more go over the earth; so have I sworn that I would not be wroth with thee, nor rebuke thee. For the mountains shall depart, and the hills be removed,* etc.[1377] Now God, interposing himself by these two immutable things, his promise and his oath, intended his people's strong consolation in this Covenant.[1378]

[3] **God's administration of this Covenant with the captive Jews (as well as of his former Covenant with David) was for substance the same with that of the Sinai Covenant, which determined not until Christ's death, when the New Covenant began to commence.** For both these Covenants were, as it were, Under-Covenants to the Sinai Covenant. This Covenant then was administered: {1} with a typical and outward sanctuary, {2} with a Levitical priesthood ordinarily, and many prophets extraordinarily, {3} with Levitical ordinances of divine worship, and ceremonies, etc, {4} with temporal and typical promises touching Canaan, their rest there, etc, {5} with ordinary covenant tokens, circumcision, and the passover. All of these (except the prophets) remained still in use until the incarnation and death of **Jesus Christ**.

[1376] Isaiah 54:10
[1377] Isaiah 54:5-11
[1378] Hebrews 6:17-18

Nevertheless, this Covenant's administration was greatly raised and heightened by some perfective alterations and additionals, above all foregoing covenant administrations. For under this Covenant:

{1} The people, priests. and worship of God were more fully cleansed from idolatry than ever since their redemption from Egypt.[1379]

{2} The temple of Zerubbabel wherein they had their solemn worship, was far more glorious than the temple of Solomon under the former Covenant. Not in regard of fabric and structure, therein Solomon's excelled; but in regard of use, the most glorious Son of God Jesus Christ glorifying this latter temple with his own blessed presence and ministry in it: *And I will shake all nations, and **the desire of all nations** shall come, and I will fill this house with Glory, saith the LORD of Hosts. The silver is mine, and the gold is mine, saith the LORD of Hosts. The glory of this latter house shall be greater than of the former, saith the LORD of Hosts: And in this place will I give peace, saith the LORD of Hosts.*[1380]

{3} The promises of this Covenant (which is the very next door to the New Covenant) do run in a far more spiritual strain touching spiritual blessings in heavenly things in Christ, than did the promises of any former Covenant whatsoever.[1381] And do determinately point out the very time of the Messiah's suffering, which in no other covenant administration was done before.[1382]

{4} The chief passover that ever was sacrificed since the institution of the passover, was offered up under this Covenant. For under it Christ our passover was sacrificed for us.[1383] Never passover like this passover. All they were but types and shadows; this alone was the truth and substance of them all.

[1379] Ezekiel 37:23, etc.
[1380] Haggai 2:7-9
[1381] Read diligently Ezekiel 36 & 37, Jeremiah 32 & Isaiah 49 to the end of his prophecy.
[1382] Daniel 9:24-27
[1383] 1 Corinthians 5:7

{5} Finally, under this Covenant, the political government of the commonwealth of Israel was transmitted to the true **David**, namely: **Jesus Christ**, Lord of Lords and King of Kings, in whose spiritual, heavenly, and everlasting kingdom, the outward kingdom and government of Judah and Israel determined, and was swallowed up forevermore.[1384]

Inferences

(1) **Hence, the bounty of God's grace was very illustrious towards his people in this Covenant, which he so often revealed to them.** Here is not a seldom, but a frequent covenant manifestation, whereby God's covenant grace obtained not a penurious, but a bounteous demonstration. God's often tenders of his grace, do eminently imply the riches and bounty of that grace. He often offered what he was most willing to bestow.

(2) **Hence, the truth and certainty of this Covenant was altogether infallible and unquestionable** – being revealed by three several prophets, repeated several times, and confirmed sundry ways, by symbolic tokens, ratifying promises, and the oath of God himself. How could they doubt of its faithful accomplishment?

(3) **Hence, the Lord in this Covenant abundantly provided for his captives support and consolation.** Not only the matter of it was exceeding comfortable to them, in regard both of the rich mercies promised, and of God's undertaking for their constancy in covenant. But the very form of this Covenant was most comfortable also, being so importunately manifested, so strongly confirmed, and so sweetly administered. What people could more need consolation?[1385] And what way could be more effectual than this Covenant way which God took for their consolation?

[1384] Ezekiel 37:22 to the end with Matthew 2:2, 11, John 18:36-37, Revelation 19:16
[1385] Isaiah 54:6-8

(4) Hence, this Covenant with the captives did not only explain, but also highly improve the Sinai Covenant unto much evangelical spirituality. As the former Covenant with David, so this with the captives was explanatory to the Sinai Covenant. But this Covenant has highly advanced and raised up the Sinai Covenant with many sublime spiritual promises, so that when that Old Covenant was to wear away, and to be swallowed up by the new, it had become very spiritual.

(5) Hence, the subsequent Covenants still had their special excellencies above those that were foregoing. *That* with David surpassed all that went before, which also still excelled one another; but *this* transcends *that* Covenant with David, as appears in those five forementioned particulars. The substance of the Covenant of Faith is still the same: but yet it still more and more excels itself in gradual perfections, until it attains to the most perfect of all dispensations: the New Covenant.

(6) Hence, finally, when the mutual tie and obligation between the federates was broken, the very essence of this Covenant was violated and overthrown. For in this mutual obligation of federates, the essential form and being of this and of all Covenants consists. When therefore the Jews rejected the Messiah actually exhibited, sold him for a base price of thirty pieces of silver, set him at naught, and cruelly murdered him with wicked hands (so far were they from believing in him). No wonder that God cut asunder his two staves of Beauty and Bands, broke his Covenant with them, and utterly cast them off until the fullness of the Gentiles be accomplished.[1386]

[1386] Zechariah 11:7-15, Romans 11:25-26

Aphorism 4

The End or Scope of God's Covenant with his captive people in Babylon.

God's end and intended scope in this Covenant with his captives in Babylon was: more immediately, a further discovery of the promised Messiah Jesus Christ; more mediately, the promoting of their present consolation and future salvation, and the advancement of God's glory in all. This aphorism I thus in brief explicate:

(1) **The more immediate end intended by God in this Covenant was: a further discovery of the promised Messiah Jesus Christ**. Every Covenant tends to improve and advance in some regard or other, the further revelation of Christ, as I have shown in the ends of the several Covenants; and especially in God's Covenant with David, which the reader may consult. **Christ**, and sinners' happiness by him, is the great mystery of all discoveries of the Covenant of Faith.[1387]

This Covenant, together with the promises reducible and appertaining to it, tends to make a further discovery of Christ, in regard to his [1] person, [2] office, and [3] actual appearing in human flesh.

[1] *In regard to Christ's person according to the flesh*, this Covenant and the promises thereunto belonging do discover: {1} his descent: that he shall not only, as a Branch of Righteousness, grow up to David,[1388] but also that he should descend from David by Zerubbabel, a special type, and forefather of Christ: as that passage of Haggai, being solidly understood, does intimate,[1389] for it is chiefly applicable to, and intended of Christ the true

---

[1387] Book 3, Chapter 5, Aphorism 6
[1388] Jermeiah 33:15-17
[1389] Haggai 2:21-23

Zerubbabel. {2} His properties: righteous, having salvation, lowly, speaking peace to the heathen, being wounded for our iniquities, etc.[1390]

[2] ***In regard to Christ's office***, this Covenant and the promises annexed thereunto do reveal: {1} more generally, that Christ should be a Redeemer, not only of his people the Jews from Babylonian bondage, but also of all his elect from sinful and hellish thralldom, by the blood of the Covenant;[1391] {2} more particularly, that Jesus Christ the Messiah should be: (i) a prophet: a witness to the people,[1392] the messenger, or angel of the Covenant, delighted in;[1393] (ii) a priest forever: becoming an offering for sin, and making intercession for the transgressors (which are the two grand acts of his priesthood),[1394] whence he is said to *send prisoners out of the pit wherein there is no water by the blood of the covenant*,[1395] and to be *the sure mercies of David*;[1396] (iii) *a king, a leader, and commander to the people*[1397] – yea that he as a true **David** should be their shepherd, prince, and king forever,[1398] under whose dominion the divided kingdoms of Judah and Israel should be united and made one, as at first they were under David. Thus, though the Sinai Covenant discovered Christ as a prophet and priest, under the types of Moses and Aaron; and the Covenant with David reveal Christ as an everlasting king; yet this Covenant does as much as both, and sets him forth as prophet, priest, and king forever. Herein therefore, Christ is revealed more fully than in either of those Covenants.

[3] ***In regard to Christ's actual appearing in human flesh***, this Covenant and the promises thereto belonging, discover: {1} that *from the going forth of the commandments to restore and to build Jerusalem unto the Messiah the Prince, shall be seven weeks* (that is thinks Calvin from the second

---

[1390] Zechariah 9:9-10, Isaiah 53:11, 4-6, etc.
[1391] Isaiah 49:8-11, etc, Zechariah 9:11
[1392] Isaiah 55:4
[1393] Malachi 3:1
[1394] Isaiah 53:10, 12
[1395] Zechariah 9:11
[1396] Isaiah 55:3 with Acts 13:4
[1397] Isaiah 55:4
[1398] Ezekiel 34:23-24, etc. & 37:24-26

year of Cyrus until the baptism of Christ, when he began publicly to appear in his mediatory office)[1399] *and threescore and two weeks the street shall be built again, and the wall, even in troublous times. And after threescore and two weeks shall Messiah be cut off, but not for himself,* etc.[1400] Here, the determinate time of the Messiah's appearing and Suffering for sin, is revealed to Daniel about the time of the Jews release from Babylon: which was never done before under any former Covenant. {2} That Christ, the **Desire of All Nations**, should come, and by his presence fill the later temple built by Zerubbabel with more glory than ever the first temple had which was built by Solomon.[1401] {3} That Christ, Zion's king, should come to Jerusalem, being just, having salvation, lowly, and riding upon an ass, and upon a colt the foal of an ass.[1402] {4} That *the LORD whom they sought; even the angel of the covenant, whom they delighted in, should suddenly come to his temple.*[1403] Malachi, the last prophet of the Old Testament, tells them that now Christ's coming was nigh at hand, he would come suddenly without delay. And Elijah the prophet (that is, John the Baptist in the Spirit and power of Elijah – Luke 1:17, Matthew 11:10-15) as Christ's herald or harbinger, should come to prepare Christ's way before him.[1404] And the next tidings which the Scripture brings in the history of the four evangelists is, the manifestation of John the Baptist, the second Elijah, and shortly after him the incarnation and nativity, etc, of **Jesus Christ**. These, besides other discoveries this Covenant made of Christ, beyond all foregoing Covenants.

(2) **The more mediate end intended by God in this Covenant, was twofold**, namely: [1] subordinate and [2] ultimate.

[1399] John Calvin's commentary on Daniel 9:25
[1400] Daniel 9:24-27
[1401] Haggai 2:6-9
[1402] Zechariah 9:9 with Matthew 21:5, John 12:15, Isaiah 62:11
[1403] Malachi 3:1
[1404] Malachi 3:1 & 4:5-6

[1] *Subordinate*: the captives' {1} present consolation, and {2} future salvation of them and their posterity.

{1} **The present consolation of God's captives in Babylon.** As they were there greatly afflicted: so they were deeply dejected. They were then, *as a woman forsaken and grieved in spirit, and as a wife of youth refused; yea forsaken of God, who in wrath for that season hid his face from them.*[1405] So that *when they sat down by the rivers of Babylon, they wept when they remembered Zion. They hanged their harps upon the willows in the midst thereof.*[1406] – *They could not sing the LORD's song in a strange land. They said, Our bones are dried and our hope is lost, we are cut off for our parts.*[1407] Thus they were even drowned in sorrow, and swallowed up in discomfort. Therefore God purposely sets himself to comfort them with good words, and comfortable words in this Covenant. See Isaiah 54 throughout, and Zechariah 1:12 to the end of the chapter, and Isaiah 49:8-18, where Christ is promised as *a covenant of the people, to establish the land, to cause to inherit the desolate heritages' to say to the prisoners, go forth; to them that are in darkness, show yourselves*, etc. and at last this triumphant close is added: *Sing, O heavens; and be joyful, O earth; and break forth into singing, O mountains; For God hath comforted his people, and will have mercy on his afflicted* (verse 13). Seriously consider all the covenant mercies formerly unfolded, how suitable and full remedies they were against all their Babylonian distresses, and then it must needs be confessed that in this Covenant, God singularly intended his afflicted people's consolation.

{2} **The future salvation of the captives and their posterity.** God in this Covenant aimed at a higher end and advantage to his people then their present consolation – even their and their seed's eternal salvation. And therefore, under their corporal redemption from Babylonian bondage to Canaan's liberty and rest, he represents typically their spiritual redemption

---

[1405] Isaiah 54:6-8
[1406] Psalm 137:1-4, etc.
[1407] Ezekiel 37:11

from sinful and hellish bondage to heaven by Jesus Christ,[1408] as I have already manifested. And this is extended to them, and to their children, and to their children's children (Ezekiel 37:25-26, Isaiah 59:20-21). And if the spirituality of the promises of this Covenant be well weighed, then half an eye may see that in this Covenant, God intended much more their spiritual redemption by Christ than their corporal deliverance by Cyrus, and that he had a far greater desire to lead his people and their seed unto, and place them in the heavenly rather than the earthly Canaan.

[2] ***Ultimate***: God's highest and last end in this, as in all Covenants, was the advancement of his own glory. Therefore, when the Lord was about to propound the sweet promises of this Covenant touching the Jews' redemption from Babylon to Zion; from Chaldea and other countries to Canaan, he tells them that herein he had principal respect to his own holy name and glory, which through them was profaned among the heathen: *But I had pity for mine holy name, which the house of Israel had profaned among the heathen whither they went. Therefore say unto the house of Israel, Thus saith the Lord GOD, I do not this for your sakes O house of Israel, but for mine holy name's sake which ye have profaned among the heathen whither ye went. And I will sanctify my great name which was profaned among the heathen, which ye have profaned in the midst of them: and the heathen shall know that I am the LORD, saith the Lord GOD, when I shall be sanctified in you before their eyes. For I will take you from among the heathen, etc.*[1409] So that God made this Covenant, and made it good: that he might sanctify, exalt and glorify his own great name.

More particularly by this Covenant, God intended: {1} the glory of his free grace without – yea, contrary – to their deserts [merits] (Ezekiel 36:22, 31-32); {2} the glory of his rich mercy, compassion, and lovingkindness (Isaiah 49:13, 15-16, Zechariah 1:12-17) – all the covenanted blessings demonstrate

---

[1408] Isaiah 49:8-18, Zechariah 9:11, Ezekiel 36 & 37:15 to the end
[1409] Ezekiel 36:21-24, etc, 32

this; {3} the glory of his power: that he would open their graves, and bring them out of their graves (Ezekiel 37:1-15); {4} the glory of his faithfulness: not only in the sight of his own people (Ezekiel 37:14), but also in the sight of the very heathen (Ezekiel 36:33-37); and {5} the glory of his justice and severity, in that for their contempt of Christ at last, God would cut asunder his two staves of **Beauty** and **Bands**, and break his Covenant which he made with all the people (Zechariah 11:6-15).

Inferences

(1) **Hence, see how this Covenant answers, yea excels the foregoing Covenants in the immediate end thereof.** It answers and agrees with them, in that it tends to reveal Christ to the Jews. It excels them, in that it tends to make a higher and further revelation of Christ than ever any did before; yea and at last before its expiration, actually exhibits Christ incarnate according to all the faithful's expectation. So that in the perusal of this Covenant, you must not only look at Christ promised, but at Christ promised as near at hand, and *suddenly to come into his temple.*[1410] Yea in this Covenant are the last promises of Christ to come in the flesh. Under this Covenant, Christ was so promised that he was actually performed. Therefore under this Covenant you may with good old Simeon take Jesus Christ in your arms, and bless the Lord for his salvation.

(2) **Hence, this Covenant was the captives' cordial, and great matter of rejoicing.**[1411] Herein God peculiarly intended their comfort and their joy over all their afflictions. And if they fainted after the publication of this Covenant, that must needs be a great reproach unto their faith and spiritual courage. This Covenant also – primarily intending spirituals in that corporal

---

[1410] Malachi 3:1
[1411] Isaiah 49:8-10, etc, 13

redemption from Babylon, the return of the captives to Canaan, etc. – may be improved by us as a singular cordial to ourselves in reference to our all-sufficient redemption by Christ from spiritual thralldom, and our investiture into all spiritual privileges by him.

(3) **Hence, though God in his Covenants and promises has a tender care of his people's present consolation, yet therein he principally provides for their future and eternal salvation.**

(4) **Hence, when we read and ponder upon this Covenant, let us ascribe to God the glory due unto his great name, from his excellent contrivance and revelation of this Covenant, and the mysteries thereof.**

Thus of God's intended scope and end in this Covenant.

Aphorism 5

Fifthly, General Inferences from the whole of this Covenant with the captive Jews.

Having thus at large unfolded this Covenant of God with his captive Jews in Babylon, in regard to the (1) author, (2) occasion, (3) impulsive cause, (4) federates to it, (5) nature of it, (6) subject matter on God's part and on theirs, (7) form, and (8) end thereof, I shall now briefly conclude my discourse about this covenant discovery with certain general inferences resulting from the whole that has been spoken, wrapping them up in this ensuing aphorism, namely:

Hence, from all that has been proved concerning this Covenant with the captive Jews these things are evident: (1) that this was a Covenant of Faith; (2) that the substance of God's Covenants of Faith was but one, though the circumstances various; (3) that God may change the outward condition of his people, and yet not change the substance of his Covenant with his people; (4) that David's royal seed and diadem were continued in Christ; (5) that as God's Covenant with David was the royal, so this was the redeeming, un-captivating Covenant; (6) that God's sweetest consolations are showered on his people in their sharpest tribulations; (7) what the properties of this Covenant are; (8) what agreement or disagreement this Covenant has with or from all foregoing Covenants; (9) what pre-eminences this Covenant had beyond the former Covenants; and (10) that this Covenant and the promises thereof approach most near to the New Covenant, and the promises thereof. These I briefly thus explain:

(1) **That this Covenant with the captives was a Covenant of Faith in Christ, purely evangelical, and not a Covenant of Works – yea, and the**

last of the Covenants of Promise, under which Christ promised was exhibited. This I have already sufficiently cleared.[1412]

(2) **That the substance of God's Covenants of Faith was but one, though the circumstances of the several discoveries were various.** The several covenant discoveries of God's Covenant of Faith, were in several times, to several persons, in several places, upon several occasions, in several ways of manifestation, confirmation, and administration according to the wise pleasure of the Lord for his people's best advantage. The circumstances were very various, but the essence and substance of them all was one and the same, namely: The revealing and tendering of one and the same Messiah Jesus Christ to his people, as their only all-sufficient Savior through faith. Herein this present Covenant with the captives was one and the same with all former covenant dispensations, though in some circumstances differing from them. And it was meet that the covenant discoveries should be still more and more full, perfect, clear and glorious as the incarnation of the Messiah approached nearer and nearer, who is the perfection and glory of them all. It is but one sun that shines in the sky from the shortest to the longest day in the year, yet this one sun rises every morning earlier and earlier, climbs up in the heavens still higher and higher, shines still hotter and hotter, and runs his race still longer and longer; like here conceive of Christ the Sun of Righteousness in the several covenant expressures.

(3) **That God may change the outward condition of his people, and yet not change the substance of his Covenant with his people.** When God made covenant with Israel at Sinai, they were a newly redeemed people; when he covenanted with David, they were a people advanced to high prosperity and peace under a royal government: But when he covenanted with these captives, they were in an afflicted and enthralled condition. Then at Sinai, afterwards at Zion, and now in Babylon. Then, in an anarchy without any settled government; afterwards, under a monarchy under kingly government; but

---

[1412] In this 6th Chapter, Aphorism 1.5

now, under tyranny, even the cruel Babylonian government. Yet though thus God had changed their outward condition, he did not change the substance of his Covenant with them. In all varieties of their state, he still reveals the same Messiah and the same salvation by him through faith. To let all know, that in reference to God and happiness, the outward condition is as nothing; it's only Christ and enjoyment of him through faith according to his Covenant that makes people happy in any condition, and makes every condition sweet and comfortable.

(4) **That David's royal seed and diadem chiefly had their continuance and perpetuity in Christ.** From the captivity until Christ's incarnation, David's throne was thrown down,[1413] his diadem removed,[1414] and his seed (as a royal seed) seemed to cease, being only governors not kings, over that people of Judah[1415] – by all which, God seemed in outward appearance to make void his Covenant with David and his seed, in regard to the perpetuity of his royal seed and kingdom (Psalm 89:39), etc. But David's ruined throne was exalted, his removed diadem and crown was restored, and his royal seed revived; at the appearing of Jesus Christ (his primary seed) in the flesh; and in Jesus Christ, the perpetuity of David's seed, throne, crown, and Covenant, had its chiefest and fullest accomplishment, according to the tenor of this Covenant.[1416] So faithful is God in his promises, that he cannot suffer his Covenant to fail.

(5) **That as God's Covenant with *David* was peculiarly the Royal Covenant (as has been manifested). so this Covenant with the captives was the redeeming or un-captivating Covenant.** The main stream of promises in that Covenant did run upon the kingdom of David and of his seed, and a chief burden of the promises in this Covenant was upon the captives' redemption and return from Babylon to Zion, from Chaldea to Canaan, etc. And as they were seventy years in Babylon, and then corporally redeemed thence by Cyrus,

---

[1413] Psalm 89:44
[1414] Psalm 89:39, Ezekiel 21:26-27
[1415] Haggai 2:21
[1416] Jeremiah 33:15 to the end with Jeremiah 32:37 to the end, Ezekiel 21:26-27

especially by the Messiah; so from their redemption out of Babylon until Christ were seventy weeks of years accomplished, and then all the elect of Jews and Gentiles were spiritually redeemed from sin and death by Jesus Christ.[1417] That was as a type of this, and whilst Daniel was praying for performance of the former, he received from God a punctual promise of the latter.

(6) **That God's sweetest consolations are usually showered on his people in their sharpest tribulations.** This most consolatory Covenant was then revealed to God's people the Jews, when they were most disconsolate captives in their graves in Babylon. When Abraham's seed should become as a smoking furnace,[1418] then God assures Abraham that he would be to them a burning lamp. When the church in the wilderness and afterwards, should become as a bush burning with the fire of affliction, then God assures Moses that the Lord himself would be in the midst of the burning bush that it should not be consumed.[1419] Tender parents are most affectionately compassionate and comforting to their children in sicknesses and distresses; so the heavenly Father then yearns over his people with tenderest bowels when they are involved and wracked up in deepest sufferings and sorrows. God thus spoke to the nations that spoiled his people in Chaldea, etc.[1420] *He that toucheth you, toucheth the apple of his eye* – and that's a most tender part.[1421]

The afflictions of God's people go very near the heart of God. While they smart, he bleeds.[1422] While they suffer, he cries out.[1423] When they sigh, he binds up their hearts with sweetest consolations. And no wonder, for: [1] then is the time when his consolations are most needful; [2] then is the time when his consolations will be most effectual; [3] then is the season when his consolations will be most welcome to the tossed and wearied soul. Therefore,

---

[1417] Daniel 9:20 to the end
[1418] Genesis 15:13, 17
[1419] Exodus 3:2-3
[1420] 2 Corinthians 1:3-5
[1421] Zechariah 2:8
[1422] Isaiah 63:9
[1423] Acts 9:2, 4-5

when our troubles are most pressing upon us, let us conclude that God's comforts are most hastening to us as the night is of times darkest towards the break of day. *Light is sown for the righteous, and gladness for the upright in heart.*[1424] The light of joy and comfort is as seed sown for the just and upright: it may be hidden and buried a while under the clods, but at last it will sprout and spring up. When? Even under the very showers of affliction. For, *unto the upright there ariseth light in the darkness.*[1425] Our darkness is the very season for God's light to shine out in.

(7) **That hence it is very evident what the properties and excellent perfections of this Covenant are** – namely, it is: [1] divine, [2] gratuitous, [3] evangelical, [4] holy, [5] sure and faithful, [6] spiritual, [7] reconciliatory, [8] redemptive, [9] consolatory, and [10] everlasting. I need but briefly to touch on these and pass, because much has been already spoken to this effect.

[1] ***Divine, of divine authority***. For God himself was the sole author and revealer of it to his captives by his prophets – as has been evidenced.[1426] Therefore the promises thereof were to be believed and depended upon without staggering.

[2] ***Gratuitous***. Not at all from any desert, motive, or impulsive cause in them: but merely from his own gracious inclination (Ezekiel 36:31-32).

[3] ***Evangelical not legal; of faith not of works***. It has been already proven that this Covenant was a Covenant of Faith in Christ promised, and not as then exhibited, when this Covenant was revealed[1427] – and therefore it is merely evangelical, and pure gospel in Christ to come afterwards.

[4] ***Holy***. The author, federates, matter, form, end, and even the whole of this Covenant being holy,[1428] how can it [be anything] but be holy?

[1424] Psalm 97:11
[1425] Psalm 112:4
[1426] In Aphorism 1 of this Chapter
[1427] In this Chapter, Aphorism 1.5
[1428] See Book 3, Chapter 3, Aphorism 6, Inference 1

[5] ***Sure and faithful***. For: {1} God that cannot lie has made it, and is the sole author of it. See Aphorism 1 of this chapter (Titus 1:2). {2} God, that cannot change, hath sworn it (Isaiah 54:9-10). {3} Christ as the *sure mercies of David*, is the foundation and matter of it (Isaiah 55:3).

[6] ***Spiritual***. The greatest number of the promises in this Covenant are about sublime spiritual things.[1429] And those promises about deliverance from captivity in the earthly Babylon, and restoration of the captive Jews to their earthly Canaan, did chiefly intend spiritual mysteries: namely: Christ's redemption of his spiritual captives from the bondage of sin and death, to life and heavenly glory: as has been formerly manifested.

[7] ***Reconciliatory***. God intended this as a Covenant of Reconciliation between himself and the captives who had deeply offended him before their captivity.[1430] For herein he promises to sprinkle clean water upon them, and to cleanse them from all their idols and filthiness (Ezekiel 16:25 & 37:23), and styles this a {*Covenant of Peace*} with them (Ezekiel 37:26, 34:25 & Isaiah 54:10).

[8] ***Redemptive***. In this Covenant God assures the captives often (as has been shown already)[1431] of their deliverance and redemption from Babylon, and under the type of that, of their spiritual redemption by Christ. Between these two redemptions, there is great similitude and resemblance. How fitly is this redeeming Covenant placed last of all the Covenants of Promise, which brings the great Redeemer of sinners Jesus Christ into the world as in its arms!

[9] ***Consolatory***. This Covenant is full of consolation: partly, against the outward earthly discomforts of the Jews' Babylonian captivity; partly, against the inward spiritual disconsolations of God's elect, whether Jews or Gentiles,

---

[1429] Isaiah 55:3-4, etc, Jeremiah 32:38-40, Ezekiel 36:25-27 & 37:22 to the end

[1430] 2 Kings 24:2-3, etc.; 2 Chronicles 36:11-22

[1431] In this Chapter, Aphorism 2, Section 1, Covenant-Mercies 1 & 2

under the bondage of sin and death. Duly read and consider the promises of this Covenant, and you will find them all very rich cordials.[1432]

[10] ***Finally, everlasting.*** God several times styles this Covenant {*an everlasting Covenant*} (Ezekiel 37:26, Isaiah 55:3-4, Jeremiah 32:40). This Covenant for the substance of it, is so strongly confirmed and established by God's repetitions of it, symbols, or similitudes, ratifying promises, and his inviolable oath:[1433] that the waters of Noah shall sooner return a second time to drown the whole world:, the mountains and hills shall sooner be removed out of their places (Isaiah 54:9-10), God's Covenant of day and night – that there should not be day and night in their season, shall sooner be broken (Jeremiah 33:17-23) and his ordinances of heaven and earth shall sooner fail (Jeremiah 33:25-26) than this Covenant with the captives and people of God, for the substance of it, shall fail, be broken, or removed.

(8) **What agreement or disagreement this Covenant has with or from all foregoing Covenants.** This Covenant, being an additional and explanatory Covenant to the Sinai Covenant (as was also the former Covenant with David)[1434] and under the same administration, must needs have in effect the same agreements and disagreements with and from all foregoing Covenants, which the Sinai Covenant has with and from them. Therefore, judiciously consult the Sinai Covenant and the Covenant with David as to this point, and there will be found sufficient satisfaction.[1435] I must avoid repetition of things spoken already, and contract what is possible.

(9) **What pre-eminences this Covenant had beyond the former Covenants:** this – being the last expressure of the Covenants of Promise[1436] – had some special excellencies in it, above all that went before it. For:

[1432] See Isaiah 54 throughout & 55:1-6 & 49:8-18; Jeremiah 32:36 to the end of the chapter & 33 throughout; Ezekiel 36:21 to the end of the chapter & 37 throughout.
[1433] See Aphorism 3 in this Chapter
[1434] See Book 3, Chapter 5, the general introduction, etc.
[1435] Book 3, Chapter 4, Aphorism 7, Corollary 5 & Chapter 5, Aphorism 7, Inference 4
[1436] Ephesians 2:12

[1] The promised mercies in the body of this Covenant, and which under this covenant dispensation are revealed as appertaining thereunto, are far more plentiful and abundant than in or under any foregoing covenant expressure. As: {1} promises comprised in the body of this Covenant – see in Isaiah 49:8-18, 54:7 to the end, 55:1-6, Jeremiah 32:36 to the end, 33 throughout, and Ezekiel chapters 34, 36, and 37 throughout; {2} promises revealed under this covenant dispensation: and which are to be ranked and referred thereunto – see in Isaiah from chapter 49 to the end of his prophecy, which has a special eye all along to the matters of this Covenant: and also in the whole books of those prophets which prophesied near-upon, under, or after the Babylonian captivity, as Jeremiah, Ezekiel, Daniel, Obadiah, Haggai, Zachariah and Malachi.[1437]

[2] The promises of this Covenant are far more spiritual, than in former Covenants: as the former places, containing promises in the body of this Covenant, abundantly evidence.

[3] The redemption and deliverance of God's people from Babylonian bondage under this Covenant, far surpassed all their former deliverances, yea even that miraculous one from the Egyptian yoke (Jeremiah 16:14-15 & 23:7-8).

[4] The place of God's public worship, namely: the temple built by Zerubbabel, did far excel in glory (through Christ's personal presence therein) all former places of worship, even the magnificent temple of Solomon itself (Haggai 2:6-9).

[5] The great mystery of Christ and sinners' salvation by him through faith is more fully and clearly laid open, in and under this, than in any former Covenant, as the promises in the places fore-alleged in the first particular will easily evince.

[1437] See my *Key of the Bible*, in the chronological table before Isaiah.

[6] The punctual time and end of the Messiah's manifestation and death is more determinately declared under this Covenant than ever before (Daniel 9:1-2, etc.; 20 to the end).

[7] Finally, **Jesus Christ**, the soul of this, and all foregoing Covenants of Promise, was under this Covenant actually performed and exhibited, and thereby all former Covenants had their great accomplishment in him.[1438] So that under this Covenant, the seed of the woman came, to bruise the serpent's head; the true Noah came into the ark of his church to save his elect remnant; the seed of Abraham came, to bless all the nations and kindreds of the earth; the great prophet, like Moses, came, to reveal completely all the blessed counsels and contrivances of God, necessary to be known unto salvation; the primary seed of David came, to sit upon his throne forever; yea, now **Christ**, the true **David**, the Son of the Highest came, to possess the kingdom of his father David, and to reign over the house of Jacob, the church, forevermore.[1439]

These were the pre-eminences of this Covenant, above all foregoing: in which regard, this Covenant must needs be confessed to be a Covenant far excelling.

(10) **That finally, this Covenant and the Promises thereof, approach most near (as in time, so in their excellent, clear, full, heavenly, spiritual nature) to the New Covenant and the promises thereof.** This is most apparent by all that has been said. This is as the very brink, borders, or suburbs of the New Covenant. This is almost the bright noontide of God's covenant expressures. This exhibits Christ under the Old Covenant, that he might bring all his people under the New Covenant – yea represents Christ as abrogating the Old, and instituting the New Covenant by his death. This Covenant shakes hands with the New Covenant – and so shall I invite my reader now to shake hands with, salute, and embrace the completest and sweetest New Covenant administration, to turn his eyes from Hagar the bondwoman, to

---

[1438] See all four evangelists testifying this much.
[1439] Luke 1:32-33

Sarah the freewoman, and to pass on from Mount Sinai, to Mount Zion.[1440] And it is our eminent happiness that we are not under the Old but New Covenant; that we are not children of the bondwoman, but of the free.[1441]

Thus far of God's Covenant with his Captives in Babylon.

Hitherto of all the expressures of God's **Covenants of Promise** in Christ promised; next of the **New Covenant** in Christ already exhibited and actually performed.

[1440] Galatians 4:22 to the end
[1441] Galatians 4:31

(BOOK IV)

OF

God's Covenant

OF

PERFORMANCE,

made and confirmed in JESUS CHRIST actually performed and exhibited in our flesh, according to the Covenants of Promise, namely*:*

THE

New Covenant:

BEING

The last and most excellent covenant expressure, which shall continue NEW, *from Christ's death, until the world's end.*

Chapter 1

Of the discovery and administration of the **New Covenant,** *in the seventh and last period of time most remarkable, namely: from the death of Jesus Christ, until the end of the world.*

The Covenants of Promise in Christ promised,[1442] being unfolded at large in the former book, according to the most observable expressures and discoveries thereof, we come now in the last place to the **Covenant of Performance**, or **New Covenant** in Christ exhibited and performed,[1443] far surpassing all former covenant expressures in many regards – especially in (1) clearness, (2) spiritualness, (3) spiritual liberty, (4) fullness, (5) extensiveness, (6) efficacy, (7) comfortableness, (8) durableness, and (9) glory; as shall hereafter in due place be manifested.

Now, the types and shadows of future good things are gone, and the antitype, truth, and substance of them all, **Jesus Christ**, is come.[1444] Now the church's non-age and minority is over, her full age and maturity takes place.[1445] Therefore consequently, now the Lord discloses to his church the brightest noontide of his **Covenant**; conducts her from Mount Sinai dark and terrible to Mount Zion clear and comfortable;[1446] takes away the veil from before her eyes, that with open face she may behold the transforming glory of the Lord **Christ**;[1447] and exalts her most sweetly, from the Old Covenant's servile dispensation, to the **New Covenant's** filial administration.[1448] Now therefore let us proportionably bring new apprehensions, new heart and affections, new

---

[1442] Ephesians 2:12
[1443] Jeremiah 31:31-35, Hebrews 8:6 to the end & 9:15-17, etc. & 10:16-18, Matthew 26:27-29; 1 Corinthians 11:24-26
[1444] Hebrews 10:1, Colossians 2:16-17, John 1:17
[1445] Galatians 4:1-8
[1446] Galatians 4:24-26, etc., Hebrews 12:18 to the end
[1447] 2 Corinthians 3:14-18
[1448] Galatians 4:24-26; 2 Corinthians 3:6, etc.

dispositions and inclinations for embracing and entertaining of this **New Covenant**. Let old things pass away, and all things in us become new.[1449]

This **New Covenant** is often mentioned in the holy Scriptures, but it is purposely revealed from the Lord: (1) by the prophet Jeremiah, fore-promising it;[1450] (2) by the apostle Paul explaining it.[1451] Both of them together will singularly direct in the opening of it.

Jeremiah does prophetically fore-promise the **New Covenant**, saying:	Paul does exegetically explain this **New Covenant**, saying:
	6 But now hath he obtained a more excellent ministry, by how much also he is the mediator of a better covenant, which was established upon better promises.
	7 For if that first covenant had been faultless, then should no place have been sought for the second. **8** For finding fault with them, he saith,
31 Behold, the days come,	Behold, the days come,
saith the LORD, that I will make a **new covenant** with the house of Israel, and with the house of Judah:	saith the Lord, when I will make a **new covenant** with the house of Israel and with the house of Judah:

[1449] 2 Corinthians 5:17
[1450] Jeremiah 31:31-35
[1451] Hebrews 8:6 to the end

32 not according to the covenant that I made with their fathers in the day that I took them by the hand to bring them out of the land of Egypt; which my covenant they brake, although I was an husband unto them, saith the LORD:	9 not according to the covenant that I made with their fathers in the day when I took them by the hand to lead them out of the land of Egypt; because they continued not in my covenant, and I regarded them not, saith the Lord.
33 but **this** shall be the covenant that I will make with the house of Israel; After those days, saith the Lord, I will put my law in their inward parts, and write it in their hearts; and will be their God, and they shall be my people.	10 For **this** is the **covenant** that I will make with the house of Israel after those days, saith the Lord; I will put my laws into their mind, and write them in their hearts: and I will be to them a God, and they shall be to me a people:
34 And they shall teach no more every man his neighbour, and every man his brother, saying, Know the Lord: for they shall all know me, from the least of them unto the greatest of them, saith the Lord: for I will forgive their iniquity, and I will remember their sin no more.	11 and they shall not teach every man his neighbour, and every man his brother, saying, Know the Lord: for all shall know me, from the least to the greatest. 12 For I will be merciful to their unrighteousness, and their sins and their iniquities will I remember no more.
	13 In that he saith, A new covenant, he hath made the first

	old. Now that which decayeth and waxeth old is ready to vanish away.

This is the substance of this **New Covenant**, and thus the Lord did fore-promise it by Jeremiah; and after-expound it by Paul. Some small difference there is in their words, as this parallel shows, but the sense is one and the same, as hereafter will appear. The words of Paul, and in them the words of Jeremiah, I have 1 elsewhere analytically explained; whither for brevity sake, I refer the reader.[1452] And upon these words especially, I shall ground my ensuing discourse about the New Covenant, though not precisely insisting in the very method of the apostle's laying them down.

Now from Paul's expository recital and narrative of the **New Covenant**, for the more clear and orderly unfolding of this last and highest covenant expressure, I shall insist upon, (1) the terms, (2) the names and general nature, (3) the author, or efficient cause, together with the occasion and impulsive causes, (4) the federates, (5) the matter, (6) the mediator, surety, or testator, (7) the form, (8) the end of this most precious **New Covenant**, and lastly, (9) certain general inferences from the whole of this New Covenant, shall close up this book, and this whole treatise of God's holy Covenants.

In this chapter, I shall begin with the first of these, namely: the terms or bounds of time peculiar to the New Covenant, and here I shall show: [1] what these terms or limits of time – peculiar to the New Testament – are: [2] that these terms of time for the New Covenant are of all other revolutions of time most remarkable – and those in two distinct aphorisms.

[1452] In my *Key of the Bible* on the Epistle to the Hebrews, Section 4, p.951 (London 1649)

Aphorism 1

The **terms, bounds,** *or* **limits of time** *for and during which the New Covenant became and remains of force, are especially from the death of our Lord and only Savior Jesus Christ, until the end of the world.*

These *terms, bounds,* or *limits of time* for the New Covenant are hinted both by the prophet Jeremiah and the apostle Paul, reporting the New Covenant, namely:

(1) The *terminus à quo,* or *term of time,* whence it takes its beginning, in these words: *Behold the days come saith the LORD, that I will make a **new covenant**, etc.*[1453] What days were here intended?[1454] Peculiarly, the days of Christ's manifestation in the flesh, when he should dedicate and establish his New Covenant or Testament in his own blood, which in fullness of time, Christ has performed.

(2) The *terminus ad quem,* or term of time unto which it will be continued, and when it will end: is intimated in those words: *That I will make a new covenant with*[1455] – that is, a covenant that shall still continue new, and never wax old or wear away, as the former did (Hebrews 8:13). And such a Covenant, always remaining new, must needs be continued until the world's end. As also in those words: *And their sins and their iniquities will I remember no more,*[1456] that is, though in the sacrifices of the Old Covenant there was a remembrance again made of sins every year, those sacrifices being unable to

---

[1453] Jeremiah 31:31, Hebrews 8:8

[1454] "Now, by the *days* which the prophet mentions, all agree that Christ's kingdom is signified" John Calvin, commentary on Hebrews 8:8 [https://www.studylight.org/commentaries/eng/cal/hebrews-8.html] <Accessed 3/28/2024>

[1455] Jeremiah 31:31, Hebrews 8:8

[1456] Jeremiah 31:34, Hebrews 8:12

take away sin (Hebrews 10:3-4). Yet by the New Covenants one sacrifice for sins forever, even by the offering of the body of Jesus Christ once for all, Christ shall *perfect forever them that are sanctified*, that there shall be no more need of an expiatory offering for sin (Hebrews 10:10-19). So then, this New Covenant bringing in everlasting remission of sins, by the everlasting efficacy and virtue of Christ's one sacrifice of himself once for all; this New Covenant must needs, for the substance of it, continue forever; and for the administration of it, endure until the end of the world, without any other succeeding Covenant to antiquate the same.

Let me now a little explain, and then confirm this aphorism.

(1) **For explanation hereof**, consider:

[1] That when I fetch the date or beginning of the New Covenant from the death of Christ, I understand the death of Jesus Christ (in the same latitude as I have formerly expressed in defining the terms and bounds of the Old Testament),[1457] as comprising also his resurrection, ascension, session at the right hand of God, and his pouring forth his Spirit on the feast of pentecost – all of which were within a few days after Christ's death. So that, at, or near upon Christ's death, this New Covenant commenced and began to be of force – as I have formerly said.

[2] That the beginning of this New Covenant, or the *terminus à quo*, The term of time from which this New Covenant became authentic and of force, was (as I have formerly noted)[1458] either: {1} More incomplete: partly, from the beginning of John the Baptist's ministry, who by his doctrine and baptism made way for Christ and his New Testament kingdom, as a middle prophet between those of the Old and of the New Covenant. Partly, from the beginning of Christ's own ministry, and of his disciples, who by doctrine, miracles, and baptism (the initiating token of the New Covenant) began to lay a foundation for the New Covenant administration. {2} Or more complete,

---

[1457] In Book 3, Chapter 4, Introduction
[1458] See Book 3, Chapter 4, Introduction, etc.

namely: from the death of Jesus Christ, and from his actions near thereunto: As in the fore-cited place I have already proved.

Or thus more briefly: the term of the New Covenant's beginning, comprises in it three things, namely: {1} the preparation to it: which was by the ministry of John the Baptist, of Jesus Christ, and of his disciples; {2} the dedication or sanction of it, which was properly by the death and blood of Jesus Christ, the great New Covenant's sacrifice; {3} the solemn publication of it, which was on the solemn feast day of Pentecost (fifty days after Christ our passover was sacrificed, as the Old Covenant was given at Sinai fifty days after the typical passover was offered) when the Holy Spirit fell upon the apostles in shape of fiery cloven tongues, enabling them in all languages to preach the doctrine and mysteries of the New Covenant to Jews – devout men then assembled at Jerusalem out of every nation under heaven.[1459] Then this New Covenant (which was to take in all nations) was solemnly published unto a very great assembly gathered together out of all nations.

[3] That, the *terminus ad quem*, the term of time until which this New Covenant shall continue and remain in force, is the end of this world, and Christ's coming to the general judgment.

(2) **For confirmation of this,** these two terms of the New Covenant's continuance, namely: [1] the term from which it takes its beginning; [2] the term to which it shall be still carried on; are to be proven.

[1] ***The term of time from which*** the New Covenant properly took its beginning from the death of our blessed Lord and Savior **Jesus Christ**, and near thereunto. For,

{1} The New Covenant administration began when the Old Covenant administration ended and was abrogated, for the New Covenant immediately succeeds the Old, and vacates the Old.[1460] But the Old Covenant

---

[1459] Acts 2:1-6, etc., to the end of the chapter
[1460] Hebrews 8:7-8, etc, 13 & 10:9-10

administration ended and was abrogated at and near upon the death of Jesus Christ, for:

(i) Then Christ said, *It is finished*,[1461] namely: the redemption of God's elect by Christ's death is finished; and the Old Covenant dispensation is finished; all the typical sacrifices thereof being fulfilled, vacated, and disannulled by the antitype of them all the true sacrifice of Jesus Christ himself offered once for all – there being no more use of shadows, when Christ crucified the body and substance of all those adumbrations was come. (ii) Then the veil of the temple was rent in twain from the top to the bottom,[1462] importing: partly, the abrogation of all the Levitical administrations of the Old Covenant – holy things should now no longer be under a veil, but be openly manifested to all people by the unveiled New Covenant expressure;[1463] partly, Christ's removing the veil of ignorance and infidelity from the hearts of Jews and all others that should believe in him;[1464] partly, Christ's entering by his death, and opening a way also for us by the veil of his flesh, rent, into the true holiest of holies, heaven itself.[1465] (iii) Then Christ abrogated the Passover, the token of the Old Covenant, instituting instead thereof the Lord's Supper as a token of the New Covenant, as the New Testament in his blood.[1466] (iv) Then God would no longer have sacrifice and offering – in burnt-offerings and sacrifices for sin he could take no pleasure; but in the body of Christ prepared.[1467] He takes away the first (namely: the sacrifices of the Old Covenant) so that he may establish the second (that is, Christ's sacrifice of himself, the only propitiatory sacrifice of the New Covenant) – *by the which will we are sanctified, through the offering of the body of Jesus Christ once for all*.

[1461] John 19:30 – see John Calvin's commentary on this place.
[1462] Matthew 27:51, Mark 15:38
[1463] 2 Corinthians 3 throughout
[1464] 2 Corinthians 3:13 to the end
[1465] Hebrews 10:19-20
[1466] Matthew 26:17-31
[1467] Hebrews 10:7-11

{2} The New Covenant most properly then began, when it had its dedication and solemn sanction by blood and sacrifice.[1468] For both Old and New Covenant are established by blood and sacrifice: the Old by typical blood and sacrifices of slain beasts; the New, by the better blood and sacrifice of Christ himself. But the New Covenant had its solemn sanction and establishment only at Christ's death by the effusion of his blood (called *the blood of the new covenant*) and by the sacrifice of himself (Hebrews 10:18, etc).[1469]

{3} The New Covenant is testamentary: it's so a Covenant, that it is also a testament – Christ's last will and New Testament – as after will appear: Christ himself being Testator.[1470] Therefore as a man's last will and testament *is of no force while the testator liveth, but begins to be of force as soon as he is dead*, so that there can be no addition to it, detraction from it, nor alteration of it; so Christ's last will, the New Testament, began to be of force as soon as Christ the testator was dead. His death has irrevocably and unalterably established it forever, until the end of the world.

{4} Lastly, Jesus Christ – immediately upon his death – gave commission to his apostles to preach the gospel of the New Covenant, and to administer the tokens thereof, baptism and the Lord's Supper, to all nations;[1471] instructed them and gave commandments to them concerning the kingdom of God;[1472] gave gifts to men, even all sorts of his New Covenant officers;[1473] and poured forth the promised Spirit upon his ministers and members in most eminent and extraordinary manner[1474] – all of which being peculiar to the New Covenant, demonstrate clearly the commencing and date of the New Covenant to be from the death of Jesus Christ.

[1468] Hebrews 9:18 to the end
[1469] Matthew 27:28
[1470] Hebrews 9:15-17
[1471] Matthew 28:16-20
[1472] Acts 1:2-3
[1473] Ephesians 4:8-13
[1474] Acts 2:1, etc. & 10

This is the *terminus à quo*: the term of time from which the New Covenant takes its beginning, namely: most properly from the death of Jesus Christ.

[2] **The term of time to which** the New Covenant shall remain and continue of force and full efficacy without revocation or repeal until the end of the world. This is the *terminus ad quem*, the term of time to which this New Covenant shall be continued. For:

{1} The denominations of this Covenant intimate the perpetuity of its nature. The Lord is wont to signify the natures of spiritual mysteries in their very names. Now this Covenant is styled: (i) the {*New Covenant*}[1475] and {*New Testament*}.[1476] Why? For this reason especially among others: because it is still to continue **new**, and never to wax old or wear away so long as this world shall continue – nor does the Holy Scripture anywhere reveal another Covenant or Testament which shall succeed this New Covenant to antiquate the same; (ii) {*the Everlasting Covenant or Testament*} – *Now the God of peace that brought again from the dead our Lord Jesus, that great shepherd of the sheep, through the blood of the everlasting covenant, etc.*[1477] The substance of this Covenant shall be, *a parte post*, absolutely everlasting, and shall continue forever in heaven in the world to come; and the administration of it shall be respectively everlasting, and shall endure so long on earth as this present world shall continue.

{2} The mediator or surety of this New Covenant, Jesus Christ, is not mortal or mutable as was Moses the typical mediator of the Old Covenant; but he is everlasting and everliving in his mediation, or mediatory office. – *Thou art a priest forever after the order of Melchizedek.*[1478] – *But this man, because he continueth ever, hath an unchangeable priesthood.* – *He ever liveth to make*

[1475] Jeremiah 31:31, Hebrews 8:8, 10
[1476] Matthew 28:16-20
[1477] Hebrews 13:20
[1478] Psalm 110:4, Hebrews 7:15-17, 21

intercession for us. – But the word of the oath, which was since the law, maketh the Son, who is consecrated for evermore.[1479]

In like sort, his mediatory kingship is everlasting. – *He shall be called the Son of the Highest, and the Lord God shall give unto him the throne of his father David. And he shall reign over the house of Jacob forever; and of his kingdom there shall be no end.*[1480] His mediatory kingdom as to the essence and substance of it shall be endless and absolutely everlasting: but as to the manner of administration thereof by his New Covenant ordinances, the Word preached, sacraments and censures dispensed, by his effusion of his Spirit, etc., so he shall only reign until he has put death and all his enemies under his feet, until the end of the world; and then he shall deliver up this his dispensatory kingdom to the Father, and there shall be an end thereof at the end of the world as to the present manner of administration.[1481] Now if Jesus Christ, the Mediator of this New Covenant, is immortal, immutable, and everlasting, and his mediation according to the present manner of New Covenant administrations, shall continue until the end of the world; consequently, this New Covenant must needs continue forever until the end of the world.

{3} The doctrine and sacramental tokens of the New Covenant are still to be dispensed to all nations until Christ come: until the end of the world.[1482] And whilst the New Covenant doctrine shall be preached, the New Covenant tokens administered; so long the New Covenant itself must needs be of force and continue.

{4} The New Covenant ministry: *extraordinary*, as apostles, prophets, evangelists; and *ordinary*, as pastors and teachers were given of Christ to his church, *for the perfecting of the saints, for the work of the ministry, for the edifying of the Body of Christ: till we all come in the unity of the faith, and of the knowledge of the Son of God, unto a perfect man, unto the measure of the*

[1479] Hebrews 7:23-25, 28
[1480] Luke 1:30-33
[1481] 1 Corinthians 15:24-26
[1482] Matthew 28:19-20 with 1 Corinthians 11:26

stature of the fullness of Christ.[1483] This building up of Christ's mystical body, perfecting of saints, and bringing all the elect to the measure of the stature of the fullness of Christ, was inchoate by the extraordinary ministry, shall be consummate by the ordinary; but it shall not be fully completed until the world's end, until when all the elect shall not be fully called and brought in to Christ. Consequently, the New Covenant administration shall last so long – even until the end of the world.

{5} Finally, Jesus Christ has promised to be with his New Covenant ministry – namely: by his special presence, grace, assistance, blessing, protection, etc., *always* (Greek: *all days*) *even unto the end of the world, Amen.*[1484] And therefore, as there must be a constant succession of his New Covenant ministry, and a constant administration of the New Covenant ordinances by that ministry, and a continued presence of Jesus Christ himself with this his ministry; so there shall be a like continuance of this New Covenant itself, until the end of the world.

Inferences

Does the New Covenant take place from the death of Jesus Christ, and remain of force until the end of the world? Then:

(1) Hence, the inchoation, duration, and determination of the New Covenant, was, is and shall be, of all other most excellent and illustrious.

[1] ***The inchoation of the New Covenant*** was most excellent and illustrious above the rise and beginning of all former Covenants. This is evident by the three degrees of its inchoation: namely:

[1483] Ephesians 4:8, 11-13
[1484] Matthew 28:19-20

{1} By the preparation for it, by the ministry of John the Baptist, and of Jesus Christ himself:[1485] both of them preaching the doctrine of the New Covenant and kingdom of God approaching;[1486] and both of them administering by themselves or their disciples, the first federal token of the New Covenant: baptism with water.[1487] And these preparations were transacted for about the space of three and a half years, until the death of Christ. Now how great were these two! And how eminent their preparations for this New Covenant!

John the Baptist was, by Christ's own testimony, more than a prophet, and *among them that are born of women there arose not a greater than John the Baptist: notwithstanding he that is least in the kingdom of heaven is greater than he.*[1488] That is, John the Baptist was greater than all the prophets of the Old Covenant, because he came as a minister and messenger to prepare Christ's way before him, pointing out the Messiah the Lamb of God with his finger, and as an harbinger and herald of the New Covenant, So that he is ranked as in a sort between the Old and New Covenant in his ministration; but the least minister of the New Covenant is greater than John the Baptist.

Jesus Christ also was the great prophet of prophets, the fountain of all prophecy under Old and New Testament, in comparison with whom, all other prophets were but as shadows and ciphers.[1489] John's administration was lively and powerful (Matthew 3:1, etc.), but **Christ's** was with divine authority and majesty, to his hearers' astonishment,[1490] insomuch that his very adversaries that went to apprehend him, confessed: *Never man spake like this man.*[1491] The preparations therefore for this New Covenant by such a ministry of two such persons as John the Baptist and Jesus Christ, and that for so long time

---

[1485] Matthew 3:1-3
[1486] Matthew 3:1-2 with 4:17
[1487] Matthew 3:5-6, 11, John 1:33 with John 3:16 & 4:1-2
[1488] Matthew 11:7-11
[1489] John 3:29 to the end of the chapter
[1490] Matthew 7:28-29
[1491] John 7:46

excels all preparations for all former covenant dispensations. Only the Sinai Covenant, of all that went before, had a preparation preceding, but that preparation was managed only by Moses, and that only for about three days' space.[1492] That three-day preparation of the people by Moses showed the great glory of the Old Covenant's dispensation; but this three-year preparation of the people by John the Baptist and Jesus Christ, evidenced the far greater and more excelling glory of the New Covenant's administration.[1493]

{2} By the sanction, dedication, or establishment of it,[1494] in and by the blood and death of **Jesus Chirst** himself, God-man in one person, whereupon his blood is accounted the blood of God.[1495] Several of the Covenants of Promise foregoing, but chiefly the Old Covenant at Sinai, were established by blood and sacrifices of slain beasts;[1496] but alas how mean and despicable that blood, those sacrifices! At best, they were but types, and shadows of good things to come in Jesus Christ.[1497] But this New Covenant was established by the most precious blood of the most perfect sacrifice Jesus Christ himself crucified. Never blood like this blood; never sacrifice like this sacrifice; never covenant sanction like this New Covenant sanction.

{3} By the solemn publication of it, by the apostles' preaching it to people assembled at Jerusalem out of all nations under heaven on the solemn feast of Pentecost, after the Holy Spirit had been miraculously and abundantly poured forth upon the apostles.[1498] The Sinai Covenant, or Old Covenant had an eminent publication; but this of the New Covenant did far transcend [that],[1499] for, (i) That publication was in the wilderness; this in Canaan, in Jerusalem itself. (ii) That was fifty days after the typical passover; this fifty days after the sacrificing of Jesus Christ the true passover. (iii) That was only to one

---

[1492] Exodus 19 throughout
[1493] 2 Corinthians 3:7-11
[1494] Matthew 26:28, Hebrews 9:14 to the end
[1495] Acts 20:28
[1496] Genesis 3:15, 20-21 & 15:9 to the end, Exodus 24 throughout.
[1497] Hebrews 10:1, etc.
[1498] Acts 2:1-2, etc., to the end
[1499] Exodus 20

nation of the Jews newly come out of Egypt; this was to devout men out of all nations under heaven, So that it was in a sort published to all nations of the world at once. (iv) That was with terror; this with familiar sweetness. (v) That affrighted the hearts of the hearers even unto aversion and flight from God;[1500] this pricked the hearts of the hearers unto conversion to God, so that on that day, three thousand souls were added to the church (Acts 2:37, 41). Thus the inchoation of this New Covenant was most illustrious.

[2] *The duration of the New Covenant* is also most excellent and illustrious, surpassing every other covenant expressure. All other covenant administrations have waxed old and worn away; only this covenant administration remains still fresh and new, and shall not vanish away until the world's end. This New Covenant succeeds and supersedes them all, but no other shall succeed or supercede this New Covenant. Yea, the New Covenant has already obtained a longer continuance than any former covenant administration, for {1} God's covenant administration from Adam until Noah, which was longest of them all, lasted but about 1536 years;[1501] {2} from Noah until Abram, about 542 years; {3} from Abram until the Old Covenant at Mount Sinai, precisely 430 years (Genesis 3:16-17); {4} From the Old Covenant at Mount Sinai until the death of Jesus Christ, when the New Covenant commenced, about 1444 years; {5} but from the date of the New Covenant at the death of **Christ** to this present year, 1656, it already has continued about 1623 years. And how many years longer it may continue, till the world's end, who can tell?

[3] *The determination of the New Covenant administration* will likewise be transcendently excellent and illustrious. For it shall not expire and determine until the world's end. The world and it shall end together. Now the world shall end: {1} with Christ's second coming to judge the whole world, descending from heaven, in his own and his Father's glory and all the holy

---

[1500] Exodus 20, Deuteronomy 5
[1501] See Book 3 Chapters 1-4 at the beginning

angels with him;[1502] {2} with a shout of the Lord Christ himself, with the voice of the archangel and the trumpet of God;[1503] {3} with the resurrection of the dead;[1504] {4} with the change of the living, from corruptible to incorruptibility;[1505] {5} with the catching up of all the elect, both raised, and changed, to meet the Lord in the air, and to attend upon him, to his dreadful tribunal;[1506] {6} with Christ's convention of all, both elect and reprobate, as well angels as men, before his judgment seat, the elect being set at his right hand, the reprobate at his left;[1507] {7} with Christ's final doom and sentence upon them all, either to everlasting punishment, or to life eternal, which shall then be executed accordingly;[1508] {8} with the passing away of the heavens with a great noise, melting of the elements with fervent heat, conflagration of the earth and works therein with fire, and dissolution of the whole frame of the present creation.[1509] O therefore what a glorious time, what a dreadful day will that be, when this world shall be dissolved, and when this New Covenant administration shall determine!

(2) **Hence, none can certainly define or punctually determine how long the interval or space of time for the New Covenant's duration shall be.** We know when it began, at Christ's death, but cannot know when it shall end. For it shall last till the end of the world, and who, besides God alone, can tell when the world shall end? Christ said: *But of that day and hour knoweth no man, no not the angels in heaven, but my Father only.*[1510] We find that even in the apostles' times that there were some temerarious and bold assertors, upon pretense of the Spirit, Word, or letter as from the apostle, that affirmed

---

[1502] Matthew 25:31
[1503] 1 Thessalonians 4:16
[1504] 1 Thessalonians 4:16; 1 Corinthians 15:52
[1505] 1 Corinthians 15:51-52
[1506] 1 Thessalonians 4:17
[1507] Matthew 25:32-33
[1508] Matthew 25:34 to the end of the chapter
[1509] 2 Peter 3:10-11
[1510] Matthew 24:36

that the day of Christ was at hand: and thereby did shake the minds and trouble the spirits of the Thessalonians. But Paul assures them: *that day should not come, Except there come a falling away first* (namely: a general apostasy of the greatest part of the Christian world from faith, purity of worship, and obedience towards God, in Jesus Christ) *and that man of sin be revealed, the son of perdition* (namely: the Roman Antichrist).[1511]

And after the apostles' days, it went for an oracle among the profane Pagans, that the Christian religion should last but 365 years; whence some Christians concluded that the world also should then end. This fond conceit Augustine reports, refutes, and derides; and time has discovered the falsehood of it.[1512] In the days of Cyprian, the opinion was that the world should continue but a while, and the last judgment hastened.[1513] In the days of Lactantius Firmianus, which were about 317 years after Christ, it was supposed that the world should last after that but about 200 years.[1514] These and many like groundless guesses and uncertain conjectures we find in ancient and modern writers touching the time of the world's end and Day of Judgment, but God having kept this under the seal of his own secret counsels, it is not for us curiously to inquire into the times and seasons which the Father has put in his own power.[1515] *Secret things belong to God; things revealed, unto us and to our children*, etc.[1516] But until this world ends, we shall see no end of this New Covenant.

(3) Hence, the New Covenant is a far better Covenant than the Old, as in other respects, so in regard to the date, duration and determination thereof. This New Covenant is better than the Old, in other regards: for it is

---

[1511] 2 Thessalonians 2:1-3, etc.
[1512] Augustine, *City of God*, Book 18, chapters 52 & 53, Tom. 5
[1513] Cyprian in Epist. 56. §. 1. & 58. §. 2. & 67. §. 8.
[1514] Lactan-Firmian. *De Divin. Praemio* lib. 7. cap. 25
[1515] Acts 1:7
[1516] Deuteronomy 29:29

called, A better Covenant; as being established upon better promises;[1517] as being more strong, profitable and perfect than the Old Covenant, which was weak, unprofitable, and made nothing perfect, etc.[1518] This New Covenant also is better in this respect, that it continues forever, from the death of Christ until the end of the world: forasmuch as Christ Jesus the surety of this Covenant, was made an everlasting priest with an oath, whereof God will never repent: *The Lord sware and will not repent, thou art a priest forever after the order of Melchizedek. By so much was Jesus made a surety of a better testament.*[1519] Christ's New Testament priesthood is everlasting and unchangeable; consequently, the New Testament itself is everlasting and unchangeable. The administration of it shall still last till the end of the world: but the substance of it shall continue even in heaven for evermore. Therefore this covenant administration is far better in regard to its continuance, than any that went before. It began when Jesus Christ, at his first coming, was judged by the world; and it shall end when Jesus Christ at his second Coming, shall be the judge of all the world.

(4) Hence, believers under the New Covenant are, in regard of the terms and continuance thereof, much more happy than the believers that lived under any former covenant dispensations. For: [1] the sanction and foundation of this Covenant was in the precious blood of Jesus Christ himself, infinitely beyond all the typical blood of all former Covenants. And how much happier are they that have the true blood of Christ himself, than they that had only the typical blood of slain beasts? [2] The duration of this Covenant is longer than in any other, as has been shown. And duration of mercies enjoyed, still augments the happiness of the enjoyer. [3] The termination of the New Covenant shall not be until the world terminates. And that termination shall be swallowed up in the final consummation of the happiness of all God's true

---

[1517] Hebrews 8:6
[1518] Hebrews 7:18-20, 22
[1519] Hebrews 7:20, 22

covenant people. Where this New Covenant shall end, there their new kingdom shall begin.

(5) Hence, how comfortable may this be, both to ourselves and all our Christian posterity, that both we and they from generation to generation shall still live under the administration of the New Covenant. For, this New Covenant under which we live, shall live and last from Christ's death until the world's end. Therefore: [1] we and they shall live under the self-same Covenant, under which the blessed apostles, the purest primitive churches, and the holy martyrs of Jesus Christ themselves lived; who are now triumphant in glory. Now what a comfort is it, to be made to sit down with such blessed society in Christ's New Covenant kingdom? [2] We and they shall live under the highest, clearest, fullest, sweetest, and in every way the most excellent covenant administration. For all other administrations give way to this of the New Covenant, but the New Covenant administration gives way to none; shall be last and most complete of all. And how comfortable is it, that we and ours shall still be under the guidance, blessing, grace, and influence of the best and most complete Covenant?

(6) Hence in these last times of the world, no doctrine should be taught, no worship or practice should be entertained, no future events, occurrences, or change of things should be expected, in the church of God, which are inconsistent with the New Covenant administration. Why? Because this New Covenant or New Testament administration, is the only administration of these last times, from Christ's death until his second coming. Therefore, all doctrine, worship, practice and future events in the church, during this New Covenant, must be conformed and agreeable to this New Covenant or New Testament, and to the explanations thereof in the books of the New Testament.

[1] No other doctrine should be taught in the church until the world's end, but the New Covenant doctrine and truth, in Christ exhibited. If any does not teach according to this rule, it is because they have no light in them. Such doctrine as is not homogeneal to, and founded upon the New Testament, but repugnant thereunto: is but wood, hay, and stubble, instead of gold, silver and precious stones, and shall be consumed.[1520] Hence the doctrines of Judaism, Mahometanism, popery, Pelagianism, Arminianism, Socinianism, Quakerism, and so on, are justly to be rejected whenever they shall be obtruded upon the Church, because they are inconsistent with the New Covenant of Christ, the rule of all true Christian doctrine.

[2] No other worship or practice should be used in the church until the world's end, but the New Covenant worship and practice. {1} The New Covenant worship, is the worshiping of the only true God in Jesus Christ in spirit and truth in every place according to the tenor of the New Testament.[1521] Therefore it is not lawful to exercise any Jewish, Mohametan, Antichristian, popish, idolatrous, superstitious, pagan, or false worship, in the church of God, or to tolerate the same to be done in the church.[1522] {2} The New Testament practice required is to cast away the works of darkness, and put on the armor of light, to walk honestly as in the day, and as children of the light, putting on the Lord Jesus, etc,[1523] to repent, believe in Christ exhibited, live by faith in him, walk in love and all upright obedience as the workmanship of God, created in Christ Jesus unto good works, etc., to walk as Christ walked,[1524] to walk worthy of God, of his gospel and kingdom, etc,[1525] and in a word, to keep truly the feast (even all this spiritual festival time of the New Testament) with the unleavened bread of sincerity and truth, purging out the

---

[1520] 1 Corinthians 3:11-12, etc.
[1521] John 17:3 & 4:21-23, Hebrews 7 & 9 & 10; 1 Timothy 2:8
[1522] Revelation 2:14, 20
[1523] Romans 13:12-14, Ephesians 5:8, Acts 17:30-31; 1 John 3:23, Romans 1:17, Ephesians 5:2, 10
[1524] 1 John 2:6
[1525] 1 Thessalonians 2:12, Ephesians 4:1, Colossians 1:27; 2 Thessalonians 1:5

old leaven of malice and wickedness (as the Jews typically kept, after their passover, the feast of unleavened bread), forasmuch as Christ our passover is sacrificed for us.[1526]

[3] No future events or occurrences in or to the church of God are to be expected until the world's end, but what are according to the prophecies, predictions, revelations, and nature of the New Testament, continuing in force until the world's end. Hence, {1} the Jewish expectation of the Messiah to be hereafter revealed in the flesh, being utterly inconsistent with the New Covenant established by Christ's death and blood already revealed, is altogether unwarrantable. Christ Jesus came in fullness of time to his own people the Jews, and they received him not.[1527] Christ was incarnate and cut off precisely at the time prefixed by Daniel's prophecy.[1528] Therefore the Jews – rejecting Christ – rejected, or at least understood not, Daniel's weeks. And whatsoever christ shall rise up hereafter under the New Testament established by the blood of the only true Christ, must needs be a false christ and an Antichrist. {2} The chiliasts or millenaries' expectation of Christ's personal reign on earth in his human nature and present glory, with all his martyrs and many saints, for a thousand years together, from the year 1647 or 1650 or 1694, or at furthest, 1695, etc, being inconsistent with the doctrine, prophecies, and nature of the New Testament (as several authors, especially these here mentioned in the margin, have already manifested) is wholly groundless. For what solid foundation can we have for this thousand years personal reign of Christ on earth with his martyrs and saints (which is counted as the fifth monarchy) during this term of the New Testament or New Covenant, but from the New Testament itself?

Thus I have shown what the terms or limits of time proper and peculiar to the New Testament are: namely: from the death of Jesus Christ until the very end of the world. Next I shall show that this interval or space of time during

---

[1526] 1 Corinthians 5:7-8
[1527] John 1:11, Galatians 4:4-5
[1528] Daniel 9:23-24, etc.

which the New Covenant or New Testament administration remains of force, is the most remarkable revolution of time of all other allotted to any covenant administration foregoing.

Aphorism 2

The interval, space, or revolution of time, from the death of Jesus Christ until the end of the world, during which the New Covenant administration continues, is of all other revolutions or intervals of time, during which any other fore-going covenant administration continued, most considerable and remarkable.

For, this interval or space of time during which the New Covenant continues, from Christ's death until the world's end, over and beyond all other: (1) has most eminent terms and bounds for its beginning and ending, (2) has already had the largest prolongation, (3) does comprise in its circuit or compass the most admirable events and occurrences by divine dispensation, in and to the church of God, (4) approaches most near, as in contiguity of time, so in excellency of covenant administration, and the church's condition under it, even unto the supreme celestial perfection of the church triumphant in glory.

(1) **This New Covenant time has most eminent terms and bounds for its beginning and ending.** No foregoing Covenant ever had such terms, such a beginning, and such an ending.

[1] *This New Covenant began from the death of Jesus Christ, and had its sanction in his blood*, as has been manifested. Now, how eminent was this death and blood of Christ, and that, in solemnity, dignity, and efficacy!

{1} **In solemnity.** Great was the solemnity of the death of sacrifices, when God made Covenant with Abram.[1529] Greater was the solemnity of killing sacrifices and sprinkling their blood, at the dedication of the Old Covenant at

---

[1529] Genesis 15 throughout

Mount Sinai[1530] – as I have at large explained in opening that Covenant. But greatest of all was the solemnity of Christ's death and bloodshed, at the sanction and establishment of the New Covenant, who did hang upon the cursed cross, at least six hours together, dying.[1531] For:

(i) Then Christ miraculously converted one of the thieves that were crucified with him, assuring him: *This day shalt thou be with me in paradise.*[1532] One, that none might despair; but one, that none might presume. (ii) Then there was an unusual and preternatural darkness over all the earth from the sixth until the ninth hour:[1533] from our midday until about our three o'clock in the afternoon. The sun itself puts on sables and as it were mourns, to see his maker so shamefully abused. At this darkness, Dionysius was so astonished, that he said: "Either the God of nature suffers, or the whole fabric of the world will be dissolved."[1534] (iii) Then Christ *with a loud cry yielded up the ghost*, to the centurion's conviction (Mark 15:37, 39). (iv) Then *the veil of the temple was rent in twain from the top to the bottom* (Matthew 27:51), denoting Christ's opening a way into the holiest of all, heaven itself for us by his flesh rent; and Christ's accomplishing and abrogating the types and ceremonies by his death. (v) Then the earth did quake. (vi) Then the rocks did rend. (vii) Then the graves were opened, to show that Jesus Christ had the keys of the grave and death,[1535] and *many bodies of saints which slept arose, and came out of the graves after his resurrection, and went into the holy city and appeared unto many.*[1536] These were trophies of Christ's miraculous resurrection. Thus, both Jews and Gentiles; both godly and wicked, both the living and the dead: both heaven and earth, were shaken, moved and as it were passionately affected, yea astonished: when **Jesus Christ** died. What solemnity

---

[1530] Exodus 24 throughout
[1531] Mark 15:25, 34, 37, Hebrews 9:14-15, etc.
[1532] Luke 23:40-44
[1533] Luke 23:44-45
[1534] Aut Deus Naturae [paritur]: aut tota Mundi Machina dissolvetur. Io. Gerh. Harm. Evangel de Passione, &c. c. 16. p. 190. a. Edit. Geneva 1628.
[1535] Revelation 1:18
[1536] Matthew 27:51-53

of death and sacrificing, was ever like this of Christ's dying and sacrificing of himself for the establishment of his New Covenant!

{2} **In dignity.** The sacrifices by whose death and blood former Covenants were established, were only brute beasts or fowls, etc., and therefore, as themselves, so their death and blood, were but very mean and despicable;[1537] but this sacrifice of Jesus Christ himself, by whose death and blood the New Covenant was dedicated and confirmed, was the supreme sacrifice of the Son of God.[1538] Christ is God as well as man, therefore the infinite dignity of his person, made his sacrifice and blood of infinite worth and value, so that it is accounted God's own blood.[1539] In this regard, if all the fowls of the air, and all the beasts of the field, had been put into one sacrifice, and the blood of them all put together: all this would have been as nothing to this incomparable sacrifice and blood of Christ. Yea, if all the men on earth from Adam, until the judgment day, and all the angels in heaven, should suffer death forever, yet this is as nothing to Christ's suffering of death for a time – Christ's person being the infinite God, and they but finite creature. Now between God and the creature, between finite and infinite, there is no proportion.

{3} **In efficacy.** The death and blood of Jesus Christ incomparably excels the death and blood of all other sacrifices whatsoever in all kinds of virtue and degrees of efficacy. The ceremonial commandment was disannulled because it was weak, unprofitable, and made nothing perfect: but the bringing in of a better hope did, by which we draw nigh to God.[1540] The ceremonial washings, purifications, blood, sacrifices, etc., could not make them thereunto perfect; could not purge the conscience of the worshippers from sin;[1541] did only sanctify to the purifying of the flesh;[1542] did renew a remembrance of sins

---

[1537] Genesis 15 with Exodus 24
[1538] Hebrews 9:11 to the end & 10:1-19
[1539] Acts 20:28
[1540] Hebrews 7:18-19, etc.
[1541] Hebrews 10:1-4
[1542] Hebrews 9:13

every year;[1543] did but make way into the typical holiest of all on earth;[1544] but the death and blood of Jesus Christ contrariwise was very efficacious, for:

(i) Hereby God was most abundantly satisfied and well-pleased: having no delight at all in any Levitical sacrifices in comparison of this sacrifice.[1545] (ii) Hereby he has obtained for us eternal redemption.[1546] (iii) Hereby he has wrought the atonement, having reconciled us to God, though enemies, by his own death.[1547] (iv) Hereby we are justified, our consciences purged from dead works to serve the living God, and we, being sanctified, are forever perfected, so that our sins shall be remembered to us no more, nor shall there need be any more offering for sin.[1548] (v) Hereby he mortifies and subdues our sins and corruptions daily; our old man is crucified with him, that the body of sin might be destroyed, that henceforth we should not serve sin. For *he that is dead is freed from sin.*[1549] (vi) Hereby, Christ subdued death, and him that had the power of death, that is the devil, having spoiled principalities and powers, and triumphed over them openly upon the cross. (vii) Hereby, Christ entered, not into *the holy places made with hands, which were figures of the true; but into heaven itself, now to appear in the presence of God for us,*[1550] as our ever-living intercessor and advocate: as also to make way for us, *even a new and living way which he hath consecrated for us through the veil, that is to say, his flesh,*[1551] into the holiest of all, heaven itself, there to serve and glorify God triumphantly forever. Here is saving efficacy indeed in the blood and death of Christ, whereby the New Covenant was established. Never a covenant besides this one had such a sanction, such an inchoation.

[1543] Hebrews 10:3
[1544] Hebrews 9:7
[1545] Ephesians 5:2, Hebrews 10:5-22
[1546] Hebrews 9:12
[1547] Romans 5:10-11
[1548] Romans 5:9, Hebrews 9:14 & 10:12, 14, 17-18
[1549] Romans 6:6-7
[1550] Hebrews 9:24 & 7:25; 1 John 2:1-2
[1551] Hebrews 10:19-20

[2] ***This New Covenant administration shall not end till the end of the world, which will be at the judgment of the great day, the general assize of the world.*** And that shall be a day of days, a most famous day indeed, as I have already intimated in eight particulars in the first aphorism. Never a covenant administration had such an ending; such a determination. It began with Christ's humiliation, but it shall end with Christ's exaltation. It began with Christ's being judged by the world, but it shall end with Christ's general judging of the world. It began when Christ *was once offered to bear the sins of many*; but it shall end when unto them that look for him, he shall appear the second time without sin unto salvation.[1552]

Thus this New Covenant time has most eminent terms and bounds for its beginning and ending, beyond all other covenants.

(2) This New Covenant time has already had (as has been shown) the largest prolongation. And how far further it may yet be extended until the world's end; who knows but he alone that knows and has determined when the world shall end?[1553]

(3) This New Covenant time does comprise within its circuit and compass the most admirable events and occurrences by divine dispensation in and to the church of God. During the time of former Covenants, many rare events appeared even under every covenant dispensation, as has been manifested. But the admirable and excellent events under this New Covenant far transcend them all, from Christ's death until the world's end. Shall I briefly point out some particulars? Under and during the New Covenant administration, these among other occurrences come to pass, namely:

[1552] Hebrews 9:28
[1553] Matthew 24:36

[1] The resurrection of Jesus Christ on the third day from the dead by his divine power, as the first fruits of them that slept:[1554] showing himself alive after his passion, to many witnesses, but especially to his apostles, by many infallible proofs, being seen of them forty days, and speaking of the things pertaining to the kingdom of God.[1555] Many bodies of the saints also which slept arose, coming out of their graves after his resurrection, and appearing unto many in the holy city, were the first fruits, experiments, and trophies of Christ's resurrection.[1556]

[2] The ascension of Jesus Christ up into heaven forty days after his resurrection from Mount Olivet in the sight of his apostles. For while they beheld he was taken up, and a cloud received him out of their sight, and while they were steadfastly looking after him, two angels said to them: *Ye men of Galilee, why stand ye gazing up into heaven? This same Jesus which is taken up from you into heaven, shall so come in like manner as ye have seen him go into heaven.*[1557]

[3] Christ's sitting down on the right hand of the throne of the majesty in the heavens.[1558] For *God by his mighty power, having raised him from the dead, set him at his own right hand in heavenly places, far above all principality, and power, and might, and dominion, and every name that is named, not only in this world, but also in that which is to come. And hath put all things under his feet, and gave him to be the head over all things to the church, which is his body, the fullness of him that filleth all in all.*[1559]

[4] Christ's effusion or shedding forth most plenteously and miraculously fifty days after his death, on the feast of Pentecost, the promised Holy Spirit, received of the Father, upon the apostles, in the shape of *cloven tongues like as of fire, sitting upon each of them; so that they were all filled with the Holy*

[1554] 1 Corinthians 15:4, Romans 1:4; 1 Corinthians 15:20-21
[1555] Acts 1:3, John 20:14-15, 19-20, 26-27; 1 Corinthians 15:5-8
[1556] Matthew 27:52-53
[1557] Acts 1:9-12
[1558] Hebrews 1:3-4, etc. & 8:1, etc.
[1559] Ephesians 1:19-23

Ghost, and began to speak with other tongues, as the Spirit gave them utterance. Whereupon the Jews then at Jerusalem that had come from every nation under heaven, were all amazed, hearing them speak every man in his own language wherein they were born the wonderful works of God.[1560]

[5] The solemn publication of the doctrine of the New Covenant in the blood and death of Jesus Christ, by the apostles, to devout Jews out of every nation under heaven, met together by special providence at Jerusalem, on the feast of Pentecost. Peter in his sermon – preaching Jesus of Nazareth's life, death, resurrection, exaltation on God's right hand, receiving from the Father, and shedding forth the promise of the Holy Spirit – assures them that God had made that *same Jesus, whom they had crucified, both Lord and Christ*: and therefore exhorts them to *repent and be baptized, because the promise*, or *Covenant, was to them and to their children, as also to the Gentiles afar off, as many as the Lord our God shall call*; and consequently to their children.[1561]

[6] The wonderful conversion of three thousand souls, at the first preaching and publication of the doctrine of the New Covenant in Christ crucified, as also of many thousands more afterwards by the disciples preaching and miracles,[1562] which converts – professing their faith in Jesus Christ – were visibly implanted into his mystical body the church by baptism, the initiating token of the New Covenant.[1563]

[7] The admirable and exemplary piety, unity, and community of goods (because of the present pressing necessities of many believers) amongst the primitive Christians.[1564]

[8] Christ's giving of gifts to men, as the rich fruits of his ascension,[1565] namely: his bestowing upon his church all his New Testament officers for the guiding of his church – extraordinary: apostles, prophets, evangelists;

[1560] Acts 2:1-37
[1561] Acts 2:1-40
[1562] Acts 2:37 to the end & 4:4 & 5:14
[1563] Acts 2:41 & 8:12-13
[1564] Acts 2:42 to the end & 4:32 to the end
[1565] Ephesians 4:7-11, etc.; 1 Corinthians 12:28, etc.

ordinary: pastors and teachers and governments.[1566] And for ministering to the necessities of poor and distressed church members: deacons; called also *helps*.

[9] The celestial vision of Stephen the proto-martyr, one of the first deacons, full of the Holy Ghost; who, when the Jews were now ready to stone him to death for his most zealous seraphical sermon, looking up steadfastly into heaven, saw the glory of God, and **Jesus** standing on the right hand of God. And said: *Behold, I see the heavens opened, and the Son of man standing on the right hand of God*. This blessed vision supported him against that shower of stones by which he fell on sleep.[1567]

[10] Saul's miraculous conversion, as he was in his circuit and career of persecution, making havoc of the church of God, by Christ's own appearing to him from heaven, by a sudden light above the light of the Sun striking him down to the ground, and making him three days blind, and by his speaking to him from his throne of heavenly glory. Christ gave him an extraordinary call, whom he had intended for an extraordinary work of the ministry among the Gentiles, wherein he labored more abundantly than all the apostles.[1568] So that (as Augustine notes well): "He was sent to the Gentiles, of a thief, a shepherd; and of a wolf, a sheep," etc.[1569]

[11] The Lord's rejection of the Jews upon their contempt of Jesus Christ and his gospel, and his conversion of the Gentiles, of the world;[1570] which is one great branch of the great mystery of godliness (1 Timothy 3:16). Yea, Paul, the teacher of the Gentiles, highly magnifies this mystery of Christ, which is other ages was not made known unto the sons of men, as it is now revealed by his holy apostles and prophets by the Spirit; that the Gentiles should be fellow heirs and of the same body, and partakers of his promise in Christ, by the

---

[1566] Acts 6:1-9; 1 Corinthians 12:28
[1567] Acts 7:55, etc.
[1568] Acts 9:1-32
[1569] "Missus est ad Gentes, ex latrone, Pastor; ex lupo, ovis." Augustine, *De Tempore*, Serm. 47. Tom. 10.
[1570] Acts 13:45-48 with chapter 10 throughout & 11:1, etc. & 15:7 to the end, Romans 11:15 to the end

gospel, etc, calls it: *The mystery which from the beginning of the world, hath been hid in God* (Ephesians 3:1-13). Now the manchild, Christ mystical, began to be born in the Roman world (Revelation 12:2, 5).

[12] The utter destruction of Jerusalem (so highly commended in Scripture) by the Roman armies, about forty years after Christ's passion, for the Jews' horrid contempt of Jesus Christ and his gospel, according to our Savior's severe minatory prediction.[1571] *When he was come near, he beheld the city, and wept over it, saying; If thou hadst known, even thou at least in this thy day, the things which belong unto thy peace! but now they are hid from thine eyes. For the days shall come upon thee, that thine enemies shall cast a trench about thee, and compass thee round, and keep thee in on every side, and shall lay thee even with the ground, and thy children within thee; and they shall not leave in thee one stone upon another, because thou knowest not the time of thy visitation.*[1572] The Lord had affixed his worship to the temple at Jerusalem, having put his name there, and had ordained that there the manifestation of the Messiah, and his death should be accomplished, for reconciling man to God – which done, and the Son of God being returned into heaven, according to the prophecies, at last that most large and famous city (as the authors of the *Magdeburg Centuries* note)[1573] was by the dreadful judgment of God leveled to the ground, and the whole Jewish nation dissipated, that it might be evident to all posterity that {1} the Messiah was exhibited; {2} the Mosaical state of religion had ceased; {3} the church of God from among the Gentiles was called; {4} nor should any sin be more severely punished by God than the contempt of his Son and gospel.

[13] The more pure and regular state of the primitive church and of religion therein, for the first 300 years after the death of Christ, represented by the measuring of the temple of God, the altar, and the worshippers therein.[1574]

[1571] Psalm 87 throughout & 122:1-2 to the end
[1572] Luke 19:41-44 with Matthew 24:2, 15-23
[1573] *Magdeburg Centuries*, Book 1 cap. 2
[1574] Revelation 11:1

In this time, everything was more exactly according to sanctuary measure, and Scripture rule. But yet the church, during this time, was grievously afflicted, especially with ten cruel persecutions of the heathen Roman emperors, then under the dominion of the dragon the devil, who endeavored to devour the manchild, Christ mystical, as soon as he should be born and brought forth into the Roman world.[1575] This the church's more pure state, but persecuted under heathen tyranny.

[14] The more impure irregular state of the successive church and of religion therein, for 42 months, or 1260 days of years, after the first three hundred years, revealed under the type of the court without the temple left unmeasured,[1576] for so long time trodden underfoot and profaned by the Gentiles, and those profanations so long also lamented by the two witnesses prophesying in sackcloth until the seventh trumpet, under which the mystery of God should be finished.[1577] During all this time, the church was in her wilderness condition, though freed from heathen tyranny, yet afresh exercised with Antichristian cruelty; the ten-horned and two-horned beast instigated by the dragon, persecuting her under pretenses of Christianity,[1578] until the beast should kill the two witnesses who should lie dead for three and a half days, and then revive immediately before the sounding of the seventh and last trumpet. And then the tenth part of the city should fall (that is, Rome which then was but the tenth part to what it was formerly), even in the same hour wherein the two witnesses revived. During this state of the church, the two witnesses (namely: a small but sufficient number of witnesses to the truth of Christ, both ministers and other Christians), shall carry on and finish their testimony, be slain, and revive again.[1579]

[1575] Revelation 12:1 to the end
[1576] Revelation 11:2-3
[1577] Revelation 11:3 to the end
[1578] Revelation 12:24 to the end & 13 throughout
[1579] Revelation 11:7 to the end

[15] The Lord's wonderful preserving and reserving to himself a certain select number of 144,000, his true church, his virgin-company, in their purity of doctrine, worship, etc., and spirituality of condition: notwithstanding the impurity of these idolatrous, and cruelty of these persecuting times, so sadly lamented by the two witnesses in sackcloth.[1580]

[16] Christ's deliverance of his church at last out of all these doleful distresses and calamities, by destroying all her enemies with seven vials of the wrath of God and other judgments poured forth upon them, for their persecuting cruelties[1581] – especially these grand enemies: {1} the great whore of Babylon, namely: Rome (Revelation 17-18); {2} the beast and the false prophet with him (Revelation 19), namely: the Roman empire and the papacy; {3} the dragon himself, that old serpent: the devil and Satan, with his Gog and Magog (Revelation 20:1 to the end).

[17] The first resurrection, during the Lord's carrying on of the dragon's destruction, namely: the corporal resurrection of two sorts of Christ's peculiar favorites – his martyrs and pure worshippers – to reign with Christ a thousand years, whilst the dragon is under the chain and judgment of Christ.[1582] But understand not here Christ's personal reign on earth – as I have formerly intimated in Aphorism 1.

[18] The church's happy condition, after her full deliverance from all these her enemies, and their destruction – in the new heavens, new earth, New Jerusalem coming down from God out of heaven, and the new condition of all the citizens inhabiting that New Jerusalem.[1583]

[19] The calling of the Jews and reimplanting them by faith in their own olive tree, the church, *when once the fullness of the Gentiles is come in, that all the elect Israel may be saved. – Their fall and diminution was the riches of us Gentiles; how much more their fullness? – Their casting away, was the*

[1580] Revelation 14:1, etc.
[1581] Revelation 15:1, etc. to 21:1
[1582] Revelation 20:4-7
[1583] Revelation 21:1-22:6

reconciling of the world: what then shall their receiving be, but life from the dead? – We have obtained mercy, through their unbelief: That through our mercy, they also may obtain mercy.[1584]

[20] The finishing of the mystery of God, at the sounding of the seventh trumpet, *the kingdoms of this world becoming our Lord's and his Christ's, and he shall reign forever and ever.*[1585] And his whole church, in all her elect members, shall be completed *when we shall all come in the unity of the faith, and of the knowledge of the Son of God unto a perfect man, unto the measure of the stature of the fullness of Christ.*[1586]

[21] The dreadful signs of Christ's coming to judgment, and of the end of the world,[1587] namely: {1} more mediately: (i) the darkening of the sun, (ii) the not shining of the moon, (iii) the falling of the stars from heaven, (iv) the shaking of the powers of heaven – the strong firmament itself – which at last shall vanish like a scroll, etc,[1588] (v) the sea and the waves roaring,[1589] (vi) and upon the earth distress of nations, with perplexity, men's hearts failing them for fear, and for looking after those things which are coming on the earth; and {2} more immediately: *the sign of the son of man in heaven shall appear.*[1590] What sign, that day will discover. After this sign, this immediate harbinger of the great judge, the Son of man himself, shall be seen coming in the clouds of heaven with power and great glory.

These admirable and unparalleled occurrences shall come to pass during this New Covenant's administration. The like are not to be found in any or all the foregoing Covenants.

[1584] Romans 11:11 to the end
[1585] Revelation 10:7 with 11:15
[1586] Ephesians 4:11-13
[1587] Matthew 24:29
[1588] 2 Peter 3:10
[1589] Luke 21:25-26
[1590] Matthew 24:30

(4) Finally, this revolution or period of the New Covenant's continuance, approaches nearest, as in contiguity of time, so in excellency of covenant administration, and of the church's condition under it, unto the supreme celestial perfection of the church triumphant in glory.

[1] In contiguity of time, this New Covenant season approaches nearest to the heavenly perfection of the triumphant church in glory. For at the end of the world, when this New Covenant administration shall cease, the complete perfection of the whole church in glory both of soul and body shall begin, so that *this* shall immediately succeed *that*.[1591]

[2] In excellency of covenant administration, this of the New Covenant comes nearest to celestial perfection. For this Covenant (as hereafter in the General Inferences will appear) far excels all that went before, in: {1} clarity, {2} spirituality, {3} spiritual liberty, {4} completeness, {5} extensiveness, {6} efficaciousness, {7} comfortableness, {8} durableness, and {9} gloriousness. And all these are celestial ingredients, which (among others) do eminently make up the heavenly happiness and perfection of the triumphant church in paradise.

[3] In excellency of the church's condition under this New Covenant dispensation, it comes nearest to heavenly perfection. For God, in his covenant expressures, still proceeded from the more imperfect to the more perfect, until he at last had brought his church to this New Covenant the highest and most perfect federal expressure in this world. And in all this, he had special respect to his church's capacity and condition, which under the three first Covenants was only domestic: a family church; under the Old Covenant at Sinai, etc., was only national: a national church only of the Jewish nation; but under this New Covenant became ecumenical: a universal church throughout all the nations of the world. The church of God in her family-state under the first three Covenants was but in her infancy; in her national-state was but in her youth; in both but in her minority, like an heir under-age, *under tutors and*

[1591] Matthew 25:31 to the end; 1 Thessalonians 4:14-17

governors;[1592] but in her ecumenical state, she is come to maturity and fullness of age under this New Covenant.

In her non-age she received a spirit of bondage; in her full-age a *Spirit of adoption whereby we cry Abba Father.*[1593] Now this ripe age, this full age of the church under the New Covenant, evidently approaches nearest to her most complete fullness and perfection which she shall have in glory. The apostle, not obscurely, signifies thus much to the New Testament church, saying: *For ye are not come unto the mount that might be touched, and that burned with fire, nor unto blackness, and darkness, and tempest, and the sound of a Trumpet, and the voice of words, which words they that heard, entreated that the word should not be spoken to them anymore, etc. – But ye are come unto Mount Zion; and unto the city of the living God, the heavenly Jerusalem: and to an innumerable company of angels; To the general assembly and church of the firstborn, which are written in heaven; and to God the judge of all; and to the spirits of just men made perfect; and to **Jesus** the mediator of the new covenant; And to the blood of sprinkling that speaketh better things than that of Abel.*[1594] So that the church's condition under this New Covenant not only far transcends her former condition under the Old Covenant, and consequently under all former Covenants, in liberty, spirituality, etc; but also becomes very celestial: she having communion with such persons and things as are most celestial.

Inferences

(1) **Hence behold the wisdom and goodness of God in his covenant dispensations**: every covenant discovery of the Covenants of Faith from first to last, rising up to a higher degree of excellence and perfection, but this New

---
[1592] Galatians 4:1-6
[1593] Galatians 4:3-5, 22 to the end, Romans 8:15
[1594] Hebrews 12:18-25; See in my *Key of the Bible* these words expounded.

Covenant being most perfect and far excelling them all. The Lord has reserved his good wine until now: his admirable New Covenant until these latter days; until our days. Oh, how great goodness has God kept in store for his people in this last age of the world, that Christ – promised in all former ages – should be performed only in this, and all those admirable occurrences should ensue upon his performance! The saints of old obtained a good report through faith, but received not the promise (namely: especially, not Christ promised; Christ was not exhibited in flesh unto them, as unto us); God having provided some better thing for us, that they without us should not be made perfect.

(2) **Hence all God's people that live under and in these New Covenant times, should set their hearts exceedingly upon this New Covenant administration, highly to admire and esteem it, judiciously and seriously to consider it.** Forasmuch, as of all other Covenants it is most admirable and considerable; not only in regard to the nature, matter, form, and end thereof (as after will in due place appear), but also in regard of the Revolution or Space of time during which it doth continue, as has been now explained. The *magnalia Dei, mysteria Christi, miraculosa evangelii, & gloriosa ecclesiae*, that is: the great things of God, the mysteries of Christ, the miraculous effects of the gospel, and the glorious events prepared for the church, have been, are, and hereafter shall be most eminently transacted and brought to pass in these times of the New Covenant. This New Covenant time, therefore, is unto the church, an extraordinary time: before it, there never was since the foundation of the world, such a time. Have deep and fixed thoughts upon it. Pry diligently into the bowels and heavenly secrets of it. Suck oil and honey out of this rock. Be transformed as it were, into the beauteous image of it. It is the liveliest portraiture of Christ; it is the sweetest breathing of the Spirit; it is the top-turret of the gospel; it is the richest treasury of better promises; it is the very center of choicest privileges; it is the last and best discovery of spiritual ordinances; it is the very suburbs of heaven, and it conducts the church

immediately to the glorious presence of Jesus Christ, and celestial gates of glory.

Thus far of the New Covenant's terms and period of time, from Christ's death until the end of the world, most remarkable.

Chapter 2

Of the Names and General Nature of the New Covenant.

Having thus disclosed the terms and bounds of the New Covenant's administration – when it began, and when it shall end – next, we consider: (1) the names given in Scripture to this covenant expressure, and (2) the general nature of it. The names will not a little conduce to describe the nature of it, and the general nature of it laid open, will afford much light unto all the particular mysteries in it. I offer both in these two succinct aphorisms ensuing, with all possible brevity.

Aphorism 1

In various respects and considerations, this Covenant is represented to us in holy Scriptures under a variety of names.

In various respects and considerations, this Covenant is represented to us in holy Scriptures under a variety of names, being denominated: (1) a New Covenant, (2) a New Testament, (3) the Second Covenant or Testament, (4) a Better Covenant, (5) the Everlasting Covenant, and (6) the ministration far surpassing the ministration of the Old Testament.

The four first of these denominations are expressed in the narrative of this Covenant by Jeremiah and Paul, and give us occasion to add the two last from other Scriptures.[1595] Now because names fitly given do singularly denote and signify to us the very natures of things, and are as the shell, which being opened discovers to us the kernel therein comprised, let me a little explain and open these names in order.

(1) **A New Covenant**. Jeremiah calls it בְּרִית חֲדָשָׁה *berith chadasha*;[1596] the apostle also styles it διαθηκην καινην.[1597] The English translators in both places render it {*a new covenant*}.

[1] **It is a *covenant***: that's more than a bare naked promise, for a promise may be the act of one alone. A covenant properly is the act and agreement of more than one. A promise may be absolute, binding only the promiser, but a covenant properly is conditional, containing in it the mutual and reciprocal terms and conditions upon which the federates contract and agree. The true

---

[1595] Jeremiah 31:31, Hebrews 8:6-8
[1596] Jeremiah 31:31
[1597] Hebrews 8:8

meaning of this Hebrew and Greek word for *covenant*, I have already declared – there see.[1598]

[2] **It is a *new covenant*.** Now I am especially to speak to the newness of it. This Covenant is already over 1600 years old, and yet it is still **new**. It is called {*a new covenant*}:

{1} **Because it is a recent and lately established Covenant – a Covenant lately, last of all other Covenants dedicated.** In Scripture, late, fresh, recent things, lately done or made, or lately begun, are called *new*. So fruit lately brought forth, is called {*new fruit*};[1599] Joseph of Arimathea's tomb lately made, is called {*a new tomb*};[1600] a house lately built is called {*a new house*};[1601] a wife lately married, is styled {*a new wife*},[1602] etc. So this Covenant, being in comparison of all other Covenants of God with man, but lately made and confirmed in the blood of the Mediator Jesus Christ, and the last Covenant that ever God made, (though over 1600 years ago) is justly called {*a new covenant*}.

{2} **Because it succeeds and antiquates or makes old the former Covenant, which was given at Mount Sinai.** The apostle intimates this reason, in these words: *In that he saith, a new covenant, he hath made the first old. Now that which decayeth and waxeth old, is ready to vanish away.*[1603] As the Sinai Covenant is counted old, because it gives place to this Covenant to succeed: So this Covenant is called *new*, because it supersedes and comes in place of the Sinai Covenant.

{3} **Because, this Covenant is another and very distinct from that Sinai Covenant which it succeeds, supersedes, and antiquates.** In Scripture's phrase, that which is another, distinct, or any way different from what was before, is called {*new*}. So other tongues (Acts 2:4) are called {*new*

[1598] In Book 1, Chapter 2, Aphorism 1, Section 1
[1599] Ezekiel 47:12
[1600] Matthew 27:60
[1601] Deuteronomy 20:5 & 22:8
[1602] Deuteronomy 24:5
[1603] Hebrews 8:13

tongues};[1604] another king in Egypt, as the Septuagint has it βασιλεὺς ἕτερος, is called {*a new king*};[1605] the command of mutual brotherly love urged by our Savior in another way, not only to love one another as themselves, but to love one another as Christ has loved them, is called {*a new commandment*}.[1606] And elsewhere, John calls this both an old commandment and a new: old, for the matter and substance – new, for the manner and circumstance of urging it upon them, etc. In this sense, this Covenant, being another and a very distinct Covenant, both from the Old Covenant and from all that went before; not in substance, but in circumstance; not in essence, but in accidents; not in inward constitution, but in outward administration; is called {*a new covenant*}. For, this New Covenant:

(i) Is established upon new promises, better promises, than those of the Old Covenant.[1607] (a) Those promises of the Old Covenant were more carnal and temporal, principally running upon visible outward earthly blessings, as the earthly land of Canaan, the outward rest, peace, settlement, and prosperity which they should have there, the visible place of worship in Canaan, etc. These promises of the New Covenant are more spiritual and heavenly, chiefly running in a spiritual strain, about spiritual blessings in heavenly things in Christ, the spiritual beauty and glory of his church, and the eternal rest and bliss of the elect in heaven. As in those there was very little mention of spirituals, so in these there is very sparing mention of temporals. (b) Those were made in Christ to be exhibited afterwards; these in Christ actually exhibited in human flesh already. (c) Those were more restrictively directed to that one nation of the Jews; these are more amply and universally extended to all nations of the Gentiles also.

(ii) Is dedicated with new blood and death of a new sacrifice, even with the most precious blood and death of Jesus Christ, the Mediator and Testator, the

---

[1604] Mark 16:17
[1605] Exodus 1:8
[1606] John 13:34
[1607] Hebrews 8:6

Sacrifice of Sacrifices, once offered up to God to bear the sins of many.[1608] Hence Christ said: {*This is my blood of the new testament*},[1609] and the apostle calls Christ's blood: {*the blood of the everlasting covenant*}.[1610]

(iii) Is written upon new tables. Not (as the Old Covenant) in tables of stone, denoting the people's obdurate, stony, hard hearts: but in the soft, pliant, yielding, fleshy tables of the mind and heart: *I will put my laws into their mind and write them in their hearts*.[1611]

(iv) Is published and tendered to a new people, to the house of Israel, and to the house of Judah.[1612] By these two houses, we are to understand both the people of the Jews and the people of the Gentiles, which should be reduced into one body, and coalesce into one church, under this New Covenant. For these two houses of Israel and Judah, were divided one from the other in the days of Rehoboam, ten tribes revolting from David's house, called {*the house of Israel*}: two tribes remaining, Judah and Benjamin, called {*the house of Judah*}. Judah still continued God's people, before, under, and after the Babylonian captivity until the days of Christ and his apostles. Israel for their great defection from God, and his Covenant, were as it were cast off comparatively (though God did somewhat acknowledge them), and were dispersed among the Gentiles in Assyria, Media, etc, so that, under {*the house of Israel*}, God seems to design and intend the nations of the Gentiles: as, under the house of Judah, the nation of the Jews, or, by {*house of Israel*} and {*house of Judah*}, he understands the whole church under the New Testament, because anciently the whole church was contained in these two houses of Israel and Judah, and the church is called now {*the Israel of God*} (Galatians 6:10). To this effect this is also interpreted by others.[1613] Now this is a new people: not Israel after the

---

[1608] Hebrews 9:12, 14-17, 26, 28 & 10:10
[1609] Matthew 26:28
[1610] Hebrews 13:20
[1611] Jeremiah 31:33, Hebrews 8:10
[1612] Jeremiah 31:31, Hebrews 8:8
[1613] {*With the house of Israel, and with the house of Judah*}. With the main body of my church, consisting of Jews and Gentiles (Romans 11:25-26). Thus the large London Annotations on Jeremiah 31:31.

flesh, but spiritual Israel of Jews and Gentiles incorporated together into one church under this one Covenant, and therefore in this regard it may well be called a {*New Covenant*}.

(v) Is taught to this new people in a new way and manner. Not obscurely, darkly, typically, and under a veil of ceremonial types, shadows, etc, as Moses spoke the Old Covenant doctrine to the old Israel, having his face all the while covered with a veil: But clearly, plainly, familiarly, and as with open face is this New Covenant doctrine manifested in the face of Christ. *We use great plainness of speech. And not as Moses, which put a veil over his face, that the children of Israel could not steadfastly look to the end of that which is abolished. But their minds were blinded: for until this day remaineth the same veil untaken away, in the reading of the Old Testament: Which veil is done away in Christ. But we all with open face, beholding as in a glass the glory of the Lord, are changed into the same image, from glory to glory, even as by the Spirit of the Lord.*[1614]

(vi) Is applied and confirmed to the heart by a new Spirit of God, namely: by new degrees and new effects of the same Spirit's manifestation and operation. Under the Old Covenant, the Spirit of God was given but so sparingly, so restrictively, to a handful of people the Jews, and in such small

---

{*House of Israel*}, etc. Under these terms, we are to understand all the faithful, not only the Jew, but also the Gentile, who was to be engrafted into the true olive tree. See Romans 11:17, etc. The same London Annotations on Hebrews 8:8.

Domum Israel & Domum Iudah nominat, quod posteri Abrahae in duo regna divisi erant. Ita promissio est de omnibus electis in unum Corpus iterum colligendis, utcumque prius segregati fuerant. Ioan. Calvin. Com. ad Heb. 8. 8. videatur etiam Ioan Calvin. Comment. in Ier. 31:31.

{*Cum Domo Israel & cum Domo Iudah*} An vero ad solos Israelitas & Iudaeos Pactum Novum Pertinet? Nequaquam. Alibi enim ad omnes Gentes extendit. Ies. 49 22. & 66. 18. Ioel 2. Hag. 2. 8. Christus quoque Novi Testamenti Gratiam extendit ad omnes Gentes; Docete omnes Gentes,—Praedicate omni creature, &c. Nomine igitur Domus Israel & Domus Iudah universa Ecclesia Novi Testamenti insignitur: qula olim duobus illis Regnis seu Familiis tota Ecclesia continebatur. Cui quia Gentes inseri debuerunt, idem nomen in Prophetarum Scriptis obtinent, & fideles Novi Testamenti non rato Spiritualis Israel appellantur in Apostolorum Scriptis. David Pareus' commentary on Hebrews 8:8

[1614] 2 Corinthians 3:6 to the end with Exodus 34:29 to the end.

measure, and producing so few and small effects; that it is said, not to be given: *for the Holy Ghost was not yet given, because Jesus was not yet glorified.*[1615] But under the New Covenant, the Spirit was shed forth abundantly, in great variety of graces and gifts, both upon Jews and Gentiles, beginning at Pentecost to be poured forth upon the apostles, and afterwards falling upon private believers.[1616] Nor is it *a spirit of bondage to fear,* as under the Old Covenant, but *a Spirit of adoption whereby we cry, Abba Father,* with filial confidence and boldness, which is given now under the New Covenant: *witnessing with our spirits that we are the sons of God,* and sealing us, being *the earnest of our inheritance until the possession of the purchased redemption* (Romans 8:15-16, Galatians 4:5-6, Ephesians 1:13-14).

(vii) Finally, this New Covenant is visibly ratified by New Covenant tokens, namely: not circumcision and the passover, dark shadows of Christ to come afterwards; but baptism and the Lord's Supper: clear representations of Christ exhibited and come in the flesh already.[1617] That of Augustine's is very apposite here: "But the first sacraments observed and celebrated by the law, were pronunciative [declarative] of Christ to come: which, when Christ had fulfilled by his coming, they are taken away; and therefore taken away, because fulfilled; for he came not to destroy, but to fulfill the law; and others are instituted – in virtue, greater; in utility, better; in act, easier; in number, fewer; etc." And elsewhere: "But in this time after the most manifest judgment of our liberty has shone out by the resurrection of our Lord Jesus Christ, we are not burdened with the grievous operation of those signs which we now understand. But the Lord and apostolic doctrine has delivered some few, for many – and those: in doing, most easy; in understanding, most stately; in

---

[1615] John 7:39
[1616] John 7:38-39, Isaiah 44:3, Joel 2:28, Acts 2:1-2 to the end & 10:44-45; 1 Corinthians 12:7-12
[1617] Matthew 28:18-20, Colossians 2:10-12, Matthew 26:26-31; 1 Corinthians 11:20, 23 to the end & 12:13

observing, most chaste; as is the sacrament of baptism, and the celebration of the body and blood of the Lord."[1618]

Thus, this Covenant, being quite another Covenant, not in essence and inward constitution, but in accidents and outward administration having wholly a new form and manner of dispensation; is justly called a {*New Covenant*}.

{4} Because this Covenant advances the Church of God and members of Christ to a new state and condition. Under this Covenant, the church is so reformed, refined, renewed, and the whole face of all things in the church made new: that effectively it may well be called a {*New Covenant*}.[1619] As the gracious image of God infused into us is called {*the new man*}: because it renews the whole man.[1620] To this effect, this time of the New Covenant is called {*the time of reformation*}.[1621] This reformation not only corrects and redresses the weakness, infirmities and insufficiencies of the Levitical priesthood, sacrifices, etc., by the better and most perfect priesthood, sacrifice, and ministration of Christ, in the church;[1622] but also much more efficaciously reforms and renews everything in the elect, so that they more fully partake of new natures, new minds, new spirits, new hearts, new principles, etc, become

---

[1618] "Proinde prima Sacramenta, quae observabantur & celebrabantur ex lege praenunciativa erant Christi venturi; Quae cum suo adventu Christus implevisset, ablata sunt; & ideo ablata, quia impleta. Non enim venit solvere legem, sed adimplere. Et alia sunt Instituta, Virtute Majora, utilitate meliora, actu faciliora, numero pauciora, &c. Aug. contra Faust. Manichaeum. lib. 19 ch. 13. Tom. 6. Hoc vero tempore posteaquam resurrectione Domini nostri Iesu Christi manifestissimum judicium nostrae libertatis illuxit, nec eorum quidem signorum quae jam intelligimus operatione gravi onerati sumus; Sed quaedam pauca pro multis, eadem{que} factu facillima, & intellectu augustissima, & observatione Castissima, ipse Dominus & Apostolica tradidit disciplina; Sicuti est Baptismi Sacramentum; & Celebratio corporis & Sanguinis Domini." Augustine, *De Doctrin. Christian.* lib. 3. cap. 9. Tom. 3.

[1619] Ephesians 2:15
[1620] Ephesians 4:22-24
[1621] Hebrews 9:10
[1622] Hebrews 7:18 to the end & 10:1-19

new creatures, walk in newness of life, old things pass away, and all things become new.[1623]

{5} Because this Covenant was a very unknown Covenant, and wholly unheard of by the church of the Jews till the days of Jeremiah, who first mentions the same prophetically.[1624] Now things unknown and unheard-of, are called {*new*}: as the Athenians and strangers *spent their time in nothing else but to tell or hear some new thing;*[1625] so the apostles' doctrine of Jesus and the resurrection – unknown and unheard of by the Athenians – is called {*new doctrine*}.[1626] Thus, the New Covenant doctrine, which was to be published both to Jew and Gentile in order to reduce them all into one body of the church – is called *a mystery; the mystery of Christ, which in other ages was not made known unto the sons of men, as it is now revealed to his holy Apostles and prophets by the Spirit; that the Gentiles should be fellow-heirs, and of the same body, and partakers of his **promise** in Christ by the gospel.*[1627]

{6} Because this Covenant is eminent, excellent, admirable, far surpassing all former covenant expressures, therefore it may fitly be called a {*New Covenant*}. In Scriptural language, choice, rare, eminent, excellent, and admirable things, are called {*new*}. So *a new name*, and *my new name*, that is, an excellent name; my excellent name.[1628] *A new song*, that is a choice, eminent song.[1629] New wine (Psalm 4:7). As Christ said: *I will not drink henceforth of this fruit of the vine, until that day when I drink it new with you in my Father's kingdom;*[1630] that is: most excellent, admirable wine indeed. See also the word {*new*} used in this sense in Jeremiah 31:32 and Isaiah 48:6, 9. Now this covenant administration is beyond all foregoing, most eminent,

---

[1623] 2 Corinthians 5:17, Romans 6:4
[1624] Jeremiah 31:31, etc.
[1625] Acts 17:21
[1626] Acts 17:19
[1627] Ephesians 3:3-6
[1628] Revelation 2:17 & 3:12
[1629] Psalm 33:1 and often; 40:3
[1630] Matthew 26:29

excellent, illustrious, and that in many regards; as hereafter in the general inferences will appear – and therefore it is a new covenant in this sense.

{7} **Finally, because this Covenant is still to continue recent, fresh, vigorous, new, and never to wax old or wear away while this world lasts.** Therefore in a special manner, it is called {*new*}, as the former by reason of its waxing old, and wearing away, is called {*old*}. Mark the apostle's words: *In that he saith, a new covenant, he hath made the first old: now that which decayeth and waxeth old, is ready to vanish away.*[1631] Nor is it unusual with Scripture, to style things {*new*} in this sense. As {*the new heavens and new earth*}, which the Lord has promised to create are so called, not only because of their admirable excellency, and the perfection of their renewed state; but also in regard of their constant continuance, they shall still remain before the Lord; as it were fresh, vigorous, new, etc. (Isaiah 66:22).[1632]

For these reasons, this Covenant may fitly be styled {*a **New Covenant***}. And unto these reasons, certain others may be annexed, out of the learned and

---

[1631] Hebrews 8:13
[1632] Isaiah 65:17 & 66:22; 2 Peter 3:13, Revelation 21:1

judicious annotator upon the prophet Jeremiah,[1633] which, because they are

---

[1633] "A New Covenant not simply in regard of the substance of it: for the main matter and substance of the former was as here, ver. 33. So Genesis 17:7, Deuteronomy 26:17-18 & 29:13. And this Old Covenant was ratified, as well as the new by the blood of the Messiah (who was ever the same – Hebrews 13:8; 2 Corinthians 1. 19, 20), that blood of his being in those times, as well as typified by the blood of the sacrifice, as by another element is in these days obsigned [confirmed]. See the same words in a manner to this effect of either in Exodus 24:8 compared with Matthew 26:28, Luke 22:20; 1 Corinthians 11:25, and Hebrews 9:20. But it is in various respects called a {*New Covenant*}: as the commandment of love is in some respects called a new commandment, though in nature and substance the same still that it was ever (Leviticus 19:18, Matthew 22:39, Luke 10:27, John 13:34; 1 John 2:7-8). And so is it with this Covenant, though in nature and essence it continue the same, to wit, of remission of sin and eternal salvation by the messias, upon condition of faith in him, repentance and newness of life; yet is it in various regards said to be new:

(1) In that it is ratified by the death of our Savior exhibited, which was but in expectation before: the faith of God's people being then fixed on the Messiah to come, and to be sacrificed for their sins (Isaiah 53:10, 12, John 8:36, Acts 15:11); the faith of Christians now resting on Christ already come in the flesh, having been sacrificed for them, and being ascended up into heaven (John 1:14. Acts 13:31-34, Romans 10:9; 1 Corinthians 5:7; 1 Timothy 3:16, Hebrews 9:11-14 & 11:13, 39–40; 1 John 4:2).

(2) In that the doctrine of the gospel is now more fully, distinctly, and clearly revealed than formerly it had been; when it was more darkly, confusedly, and in generalities only by that dimmer candle-light which then they enjoyed, with most that then lived, apprehended and discerned (Malachi 4:2, John 3:19; 2 Corinthians 3:18; 2 Peter 1:19).

(3) In that the former Covenant comprehended together with those spiritual promises, which yet were the principal part of it, many temporal blessings, as the possession of the land of Canaan, and multiplicity of issue, and outward prosperity (Genesis 15:5, 7-8 & 17:2, 7-8, Psalm 105:8, 11, Deuteronomy 28:1, 14); whereas this latter runs wholly upon the spiritual and celestial blessings (Romans 3. 24-25 & 5:1-2, Ephesians 1:3, Hebrews 8:6).

(4) In regard of those manifold ceremonies and shadows, to the observation whereof they that lived under that Covenant were thereby strictly obliged: whereas in this latter they are all taken away, and a service of God more spiritual substituted in the room of them, chapter 3:26, John 1:14, 17 & 4:21, 23, Galatians 3:24-25 & 4:1-9 & 5:1-5, Hebrews 9:1-12 & 10:1-10.

(5) In regard to the dilatation and enlargement of it, it being in those days confined to the Jewish nation and state, and some few proselytes that adjoined themselves thereunto, (Deuteronomy 33:4, Psalm 76:1-2 & 147:19-20, Romans 3:1-2 & 9:4, Ephesians 4:12), whereas now it is propounded and extended without respect of persons or places unto all indifferently of all people and nations that shall embrace the faith of Christ (Isaiah 2:2 & 11:10 & 54:1 & 56:6-7, Jeremiah. 3:17, Micah 4:1-2, Malachi 1:11, Matthew 28:19, Mark 16:15, Luke 24:47, Romans 10:18 & 15:8-12, Ephesians 2:13-19, Colossians 1:23, Revelation 7:9).

(6) In regard to that large measure of spiritual endowments and variety of gifts, so plentifully exhibited after Christ's ascension, such as the like had never been known nor heard of before (Isaiah 11:6, Joel 2:28, John 7:38-39, Acts 2:4, 16, 17, 33; 1 Corinthians 12:4-10, 28).

solidly and succinctly laid down, and those annotations not in the hand of each one that may peruse this, I have here inserted in the margin.

(2) **A New Testament:** η καινη διαθηκη, as it is styled by Luke and Paul, reciting the institution of the Lord's Supper. *This cup is the **new testament** in my blood*; that is, "This wine in this cup is a sign, token, seal, etc., of my blood, by which the New Testament is established and confirmed."[1634] Matthew and Mark vary the phrase a little, but not the sense, in their recital of the institution: *This is my blood of the new testament.*[1635] And Paul elsewhere expresseth this denomination more clearly: *And for this cause he is the mediator of the **new testament**, that by means of death, for the redemption of the transgressions that were under the first testament, they which are called might receive the promise of the eternal inheritance.*[1636]

This Greek word διαθηκη, *diatheke*, properly signifies a disposition, or disposal of things: and that either: [1] federal, and so it is often translated, a covenant, As Hebrews 8:6-10, 9:1, 4 & 10:16 & 12:24 & 13:20, Ephesians 2:12, Colossians 3:15, 17 & 4:24; or [2] testamental, and so it is often rendered {*a testament*}, as 2 Corinthians 3:6, 14, Hebrews 7:22 & 9:15-18, Revelation 11:19, and in the places formerly alleged. By this Greek word, the Septuagint in the Old Testament, and also the penmen of the Holy Spirit in the New Testament, do still render the Hebrew word בְּרִית *berith*, *covenant* – as I have

---

(7) In regard to the efficacy of the spirit accompanying the use of these gifts, whereby so many millions have been out of all places converted unto Christ (Acts 2:41 & 4:4 & 8:6, 12 & 9:35 & 10:21, 24, 26 & 19:20 & 21:20).

(8) Lastly, in regard to continuance, the government of God's church by the evangelical ministry (succeeding in the room of the Levitical priesthood and ministry now abolished; and the worship of God settled in place of the Mosaical rites, now abandoned), being to continue without change in the church, end among the people of God, until the end of the world, and the consummation of all things at Christ's second coming (Matthew 28:18- 20; 1 Corinthians 11:26, Ephesians 4:11, 13)." See the large London Annotations on Jeremiah 31:31.

[1634] Luke 22:20 & 1 Corinthians 11:25
[1635] Matthew 26:28, Mark 14:24
[1636] Hebrews 9:15

formerly noted.[1637] And this New Covenant has in it the nature of a testament, as well as of a covenant – and is a testamental covenant, or a federal testament. It is called: [1] a *covenant*, in respect of God and his people in Christ, agreeing therein as federates upon terms; a *testament* in respect of Jesus Christ the testator of this testament. [2] a *covenant*, in regard to the federal manner of agreement; a *testament*, in regard to the testamental manner of confirmation by the testator's death. *Testamentum, a testament* is a law term originally. Lawyers say it is *testatio-mentis*, etc – a testification of the mind or will, which is made upon no fear of present peril, but only upon thought of mortality.[1638] Every testament is consummated by death, a testament is a man's last disposal or devising of his estate real or personal, according to his own will and pleasure, before competent witnesses, by word or writing – which testament becomes of force when he is dead. In allusion to, and in analogy or proportion with a man's testament, this New Covenant is called {*a testament*}. We now consider: [1] why it is called {*a testament*}, and [2] why it is styled {*a new testament*}.

[1] **Why this New Covenant is called {*a testament*}.** This is from the testamental nature of this Covenant, having such analogy, resemblance to, and agreement with a man's last will or testament, for:

{1} As in a human testament, there is a testator that makes his will or testament – testator and testament being relatives; so in this divine testament Jesus Christ himself is testator (Hebrews 9:15-16 & 7:22, Matthew 26:28, & Luke 22:20).

{2} As in human testament, the testator is presupposed to be vested with the possession or right of some estate in lands or goods which he does devise by will, for he that has nothing, can give and devise nothing; so in this New Testament, Jesus Christ the Testator is presupposed to be fully vested with

---

[1637] In Book 1, Chapter 2, Aphorism 1, Section 1

[1638] "Testamentum [vl.] testatio mētis, which is made [sic.] nullo presentis metu periculi, sed sola cogitatione mortalitatis. Omne Testamentum morte Consummatum."
Cook's *Institutes* 1 Part lib. 3 cap. 10. Sect. 586.

possession and right of all things, temporal, spiritual and eternal; devised, disposed and bequeathed in this New Testament. *God hath made him Lord and Christ.*[1639] – *He is Lord of all.*[1640] – *Him God hath appointed heir of all things.*[1641] – *He hath put all things under his feet, and gave him to be head over all things to the church.*[1642] – *It pleased the Father that in him should all fullness dwell.*[1643] – *The Father loveth the son, and hath given all things into his hand.*[1644] – *The Father judgeth no man, but hath committed all judgment to the Son.* And Christ after his resurrection testified: *All power* (or *authority*) *is given to me in heaven and in earth.*[1645]

{3} As in human testaments, the disposal of things is made according to the sole will and mere pleasure of the testator; no other can impose a testament upon him; so this New Testament was made of the mere grace, good will, and pleasure of Jesus Christ the Testator. He, of his mere good pleasure, preached the doctrine of this New Testament (Mark 1:14-15 & 16:16, John 3:16, etc.) He of his own will annexed baptism and the Lord's supper as seals to his New Testament (Matthew 28:18-20 & 26:26-31; 1 Corinthians 11:26-31, etc.) He voluntarily laid down his life (no man took it from him, he laid it down of himself; having power to lay it down, and power to take it up again – John 10:18) and shed his blood for the establishment of his New Testament to all that are called (Hebrews 9:15-17).

{4} As by human testaments, men set their houses in order, dispose and settle their inheritance, lands or goods upon wife, children, allies, friends, etc., to be possessed by them after the testator's decease; so Jesus Christ by this New Testament has disposed and settled upon his spiritual spouse, the church, his spiritual children, members, friends, and called ones all good things for the life

---

[1639] Acts 2:36
[1640] Acts 10:26
[1641] Hebrews 1:2
[1642] Ephesians 1:20-23
[1643] Colossians 1:19
[1644] John 3:35 & 5:22
[1645] Matthew 28:18

present and to come. So that as he is appointed heir of all things: so they are made heirs of God; co-heirs with Christ.[1646]

{5} As in men's testaments, there is usually before witnesses, a signification of their wills in writing, and an obsignation thereof under hand and seal; so Jesus Christ has signified his last will and testament in the sacred Scriptures of the New Testament;[1647] these books are his testamental tables, and he seals his New Testament inwardly and privately by his Spirit (Ephesians 1:13-14, Romans 8:15-16); outwardly and publicly by baptism and the Lord's supper (Mark 16:15-16, Matthew 28:19-20 & 26:26-31). And his apostles were undoubted witnesses of these things.

{6} As in men's testaments, they are *of no force while the testator liveth, but begin to be of force as soon as the testator is dead*, so this New Testament of Christ became of force by and after the death of Jesus Christ – hence it is called {*the new testament in his blood*}.[1648] The Old Testament had its consummation, and the New Testament its inchoation by the death of Jesus Christ. And this is a strong argument why this New Covenant should commence from Christ's death, because it is Christ's New Testament, and therefore began to be of force as soon as Christ the Testator was dead (Hebrews 9:15-18, etc).

{7} Finally, as in men's testaments, after the testator's death, there's first an authentic approbation, and then an execution of the testament; so in this testament of Jesus Christ, there was first a solemn demonstration and approbation of it at the feast of Pentecost, and afterwards an effectual execution of it by the Holy Spirit efficaciously applying to God's elect all the blessed legacies and bequests of Christ in this his last will and testament.[1649]

[1646] Hebrews 8:6 to the end; 2 Corinthians 1:20; 2 Peter 1:3-4; 1 Timothy 4:8, Romans 8:16-17

[1647] Hebrews 8:6 to the end; Matthew 26:26-31

[1648] Luke 22:20; 1 Corinthians 25-26

[1649] Acts 2 throughout. See also the ensuing history of the Acts of the Apostles.

[2] **Why this New Covenant is styled** {*a New Testament*}. Why it is styled {*a Testament*}, I have shown; now, why {*a New Testament*}, will briefly appear.

It is called a New Testament in opposition to the Old Testament, which was made at Mount Sinai: *even that first testament, not dedicated without blood. For when Moses had spoken every precept to all the people, according to the law, he took the blood of calves and of goats, with water and scarlet wool, and hyssop, and sprinkled both the book and all the people, saying, this is the blood of the testament which God hath enjoined unto you*, etc.[1650] Among all God's covenant expressures, these two only, namely: the Covenant given at Mount Sinai, called {*the Old Covenant*}, and this New Covenant, have the nature of a testament. These two are federal testaments, or testamental covenants. These two, being in substance the same, though in accidents distinct, had for substance one and the same Mediator, one and the same Testator, namely: Jesus Christ, but differently considered. Jesus Christ promised was Mediator and Testator of the Old Testament, typically and obscurely, under the types of Moses of the death of Levitical sacrifices, and of their blood sprinkled, etc;[1651] but Jesus Christ actually exhibited and performed in the flesh is the Mediator and Testator of this New Covenant, truly and clearly, without types or adumbrations, even by means of his own death and blood, that they which are called may receive the promise of the eternal inheritance.[1652]

Hence, as this is called {*a New Covenant*}, in opposition to this Old Covenant; so upon all the same grounds it may justly be styled {*a New Testament*}, in opposition to that Old Testament. For: {1} it is most lately, last of all established; {2} it antiquates and revokes the Old Testament, and {3} it is very distinct from that Old Testament revoked by it, being (i) established on better promises, (ii) dedicated with new death and blood of Christ, (iii)

[1650] Hebrews 9:15-20, etc.
[1651] Hebrews 9:11 to the end & 10:1, etc. 7:18-22, etc.
[1652] Hebrews 9:11-18

written upon new tables, (iv) tendered and published to a new people, (v) taught in a new manner, (vi) applied and confirmed to the heart by a new Spirit, and (vii) ratified visibly by New Testamental seals; {4} it advances the church and members of Christ to a new condition; {5} it was very strange and unknown until these later days; {6} it eminently excels in many regards the Old Testament; and {7} this testament is never to wax old, to be antiquated or revoked, but still to remain new until Christ's second coming. All these as they are grounds, why this Covenant is called {*New*}; so are as fit grounds why this Testament and last will of Jesus Christ is called {*New*}.

(3) **The Second Covenant.** This denomination the apostle signifies to us in his explanation of this New Covenant, saying: *For if that first covenant had been faultless, then should no place have been sought for the second*, etc.[1653] By the following expressions in verse 8-10, it is evident that he calls that Sinai Covenant {*the first Covenant*} and the New Covenant {*the second*}.

Question: But how can we understand this, seeing as the Sinai Covenant was not the first Covenant; God's Covenants with Adam, Noah, and Abram going before it? Nor is the New Covenant the Second after the Sinai Covenant; God's Covenants with David, and with his captives in Babylon, coming between them?

Answer: There are two things which may be fitly replied to this Objection, for clearing and removing this doubt:

[1] These two Covenants, namely: the Sinai Covenant and the New Covenant are the two most illustrious, famous and eminent covenant expressures among all the rest. For: {1} these were made with greatest solemnities; {2} these were tendered to the greatest number of people: the Old Covenant to the whole national church of Israel; the New Covenant, to the whole ecumenical or general church gathered out of all nations in the world Jewish and Gentile; whereas the Covenants with Adam, Noah, Abram, David,

---

[1653] Hebrews 8:7, etc.

were directed but to their particular persons, families and their seed. And the Covenant with the captives was tendered to a people comparatively very few in number, very mean, obscure, despicable and inconsiderable in condition; {3} these two Covenants, beyond all other, were managed with peculiar administrations most remarkably distinct and opposite to each other:[1654] the three Covenants preceding the Sinai Covenant being preparatory and homogeneal in their ministrations to it; the two Covenants next following the Sinai Covenant being additional explanations of it, and (as has been already manifested) under the same ministration. So that in these regards, these two Covenants may be called {*the First Covenant*} and {*the Second Covenant*} because they are the first and second most illustrious Covenants; although in regard of time, and order of discovery, the Old Covenant was not precisely the first; nor this new, the second.

[2] The Greek word διαθηκη, translated {*covenant*} in the said Scripture alleged for this denomination, may also as well be rendered {*testament*}. *For if that first testament had been faultless, then should no place have been sought for the second.*[1655] And thus the same Greek word is often translated {*testament*}, as Hebrews 9:15-20, Luke 22:40; 1 Corinthians 11:25-26 & Matthew 26:27. And then the difficulty is easily removed, for these two Covenants were the only testamental covenants. The Old Covenant was the first Testament, and the New Covenant, the second Testament.

(4) A Better Covenant, or a Better Testament. The Greek for this denomination is rendered both ways, as: *But now hath he obtained a more excellent ministry, by how much also he is the mediator of a better covenant, which was established upon better promises.*[1656] And elsewhere: *By so much was Jesus made surety of a better testament.*[1657]

[1654] Hebrews 12:18-25; 2 Corinthians 3
[1655] Hebrews 8:6-7
[1656] Hebrews 8:6
[1657] Hebrews 7:22

Now this New Covenant is called {*a better covenant*} and {*a better testament*} in opposition to the Old Covenant and Testament. And this, not in essence and substance, but in accidents and circumstances, namely:

[1] Because it is established upon better promises.[1658] The promises of the Old Covenant were: {1} more carnal and earthly; {2} more obscure, in Christ to come afterwards; {3} more restrained, to one nation of the Jews, as I have formerly noted.[1659] But the promises of this New Covenant are: {1} more spiritual and heavenly; {2} more clear and conspicuous in Christ come already; {3} more extensive and universal, to all nations.

[2] Because it is not an earthly, servile, slavish, terrible dispensation, bringing into communion only with things terrible and terrified, as the Old Covenant; but a heavenly, free, filial and comfortable dispensation, bringing into a more sweet and happy communion, as elsewhere I have explained that eminent passage of the apostle: Hebrews 12:18-25.[1660]

[3] Because it was dedicated with better sacrifice and blood than the Old Covenant: not with the typical sacrifices and blood of slain beasts, but with the true sacrifice and blood of Jesus Christ crucified, most acceptable to God, and most available for our redemption, reconciliation, and eternal salvation.[1661]

[4] Because it is administered by a better priesthood, even the perfect, everlasting, unchangeable Melchizedekian priesthood of Jesus Christ himself: made priest with the sacred oath of God, whereof he will never repent; not by the imperfect, mortal, mutable, Levitical priesthood consecrated without an oath.[1662] And therefore, hence this New Testament is called {*a better testament*} (Hebrews 7:20-22), and Christ's better priesthood which makes this a better testament, is called *the bringing in of a better hope, which perfects*

[1658] Hebrews 8:6
[1659] In this Book 4, Chapter 1, Aphorism 2, Particular 6
[1660] In my *Key of the Bible* on Hebrews 12:18, etc.
[1661] Hebrews 9:11 to the end & 10:1-22
[1662] Hebrews 7:20-23, etc.

us *(when the law made nothing perfect), and brings us nigh unto God* (Hebrews 7:19).

[5] Because upon all the grounds why it's called {*a new covenant*}, it may also deservedly be counted a better covenant.

[6] Because it has many excellencies, privileges, and prerogatives above the Old Covenant, as after will appear in the general inferences – and therefore in all those regards it must needs be a better covenant.

(5) **The everlasting Covenant, or everlasting Testament.** So the apostle Paul denominates this New Covenant: *Now the God of peace that brought again from the dead our Lord Jesus, that great shepherd of the sheep, through the blood of the everlasting covenant (or testament) make you perfect*, etc.[1663]

Question: But in what sense is this New Covenant Everlasting?

Answer: This New Covenant is everlasting in a double sense; namely: [1] absolutely everlasting, so as it shall never know any end, in regard of the primary essence and substance of it. The Lord will be their God, and they his people forever, even in glory: *They shall have his law in their hearts forever; Their sins shall be remembered to them no more forever*, etc.[1664] [2] Respectively everlasting, so as it shall last for a long time, even so long as this world shall last, and shall never have an end until this world has an end. And thus it is everlasting in respect of the very accidents, circumstances and administration of it: this New Testament ministration, by preaching Christ crucified, dead, buried, risen, ascended, sitting at God's right hand, and this to all nations – by dispensing the New Covenant tokens: baptism, and the Lord's Supper; by the New Covenant's spiritual way of worship, etc., shall continue until the world's end. The Old Testament ministration is called {*that which is done away*}; the New Testament's ministration is called {*that which doth remain*}.[1665]

[1663] Hebrews 13:20-21
[1664] Hebrews 8:10-12
[1665] 2 Corinthians 3:11

(6) The ministration far surpassing the ministration of the Old Testament. The apostle Paul in various places – entering a parallel between the Old Covenant given at Mount Sinai, and this New Covenant from Mount Zion – far prefers this ministration of the New Covenant or Testament, before that ministration of the Old.[1666] Let me briefly point at them particularly:

[1] This New Covenant ministration is ministration of the Spirit; that Old Covenant ministration was a ministration of the letter (2 Corinthians 3:6-8).[1667] {1} That being only written in dead letters upon dead stones had no spirit, life, and efficacy in it; this being engraven in the mind and heart by the Spirit of God, works many spiritual effects there, as faith, love, etc. {2} That literally declared what was to be done, but gave no spiritual ability for doing and performing of it; this, spiritually furnishes with ability for performance of what is required. {3} That afforded so much letter, so little Spirit, that it seemed to be no Spirit, but all letter; this affords so little letter, so much Spirit, that it seems to be no letter but all Spirit.

[2] This, a ministration of life; that of death (2 Corinthians 3:6-7).

[3] This, a ministration engraven in the heart and mind; that, engraven in stones; in two tables of stone (2 Corinthians 3:7).[1668]

[4] This, a ministration excelling in gloriousness, in inward unveiled and durable gloriousness; that comparatively inglorious, having only an outward, veiled, and perishable gloriousness, represented by the glory of Moses' face which was to be done away (2 Corinthians 3:7-11, 18).

[1666] 2 Corinthians 3:6 to the end, Galatians 4:21 to the end, Hebrews 12:18 to the end

[1667] "Paul does not mean there the simple and plain sense of the law; for he calls it the letter for another reason, because it only sets before the eyes of men what is right, and sounds it also in their ears. And the word letter refers to what is written, as though he had said, The law was written on stones, and was therefore a letter. But the gospel – what is it? It is spirit, that is, God not only addresses his word to the ears of men and sets it before their eyes, but he also inwardly teaches their hearts and minds."
John Calvin's commentary on Jeremiah 31:33
[https://biblehub.com/commentaries/calvin/jeremiah/31.htm]
<Accessed 3/30/2024>

[1668] Hebrews 8:10, Jeremiah 31:33

[5] This a ministration of righteousness and justification in the blood of Jesus Christ taking away sin forever, that it shall never be remembered or imputed to them any more;[1669] that a ministration of condemnation (2 Corinthians 3:9). Not only in detection of sin,[1670] and denunciation of the curse;[1671] but also in the repetition of the Levitical sacrifices, which were so far from taking away sin as pertaining to the conscience, that in those sacrifices, there was a remembrance again made of sins every year.[1672]

[6] This a ministration remaining; that abolished, and done away (2 Corinthians 3:11).

[7] This a ministration clear, perspicuous, with open face; that, dark, obscure, and under a veil of types and ceremonies, which veil is done away in Christ (2 Corinthians 3:12 to the end).

[8] This a ministration most Free, filial, gendering unto true spiritual liberty, freedom, and adoption in Jesus Christ: *If the Son shall make you free, ye shall be free indeed*;[1673] hence this Covenant is, in the Apostle's allegory, compared to Sarah the freewoman; that, a ministration most servile and slavish, gendering unto bondage, resembled unto Hagar the bondwoman (Galatians 4:21 to the end).

[9] This a ministration most sweet, comfortable and delectable; that a ministration most harsh, terrible and intolerable (Hebrews 12:18 to the end).

In all these respects this New Covenant ministration did far surpass and excel that of the Old, and under these various denominations, the holy Scriptures represent the New Covenant unto us.

Thus of the names given to this Covenant.

[1669] Hebrews 10 throughout
[1670] Romans 3:20
[1671] Galatians 3:10
[1672] Hebrews 10:1-4, etc.
[1673] John 8:36

Aphorism 2

Having thus considered the names, next we consider briefly the nature of this New Covenant more generally, in this aphorism.

The nature of this **New Covenant** considered more generally, may be comprised in this or the like description: namely: the **New Covenant** is God's last[1674] and most excellent[1675] expressure of the Covenant of Faith, as a New Testamental Covenant, antiquating the Old Testament administration, in **Jesus Christ** as Mediator, Surety, and Testator thereof,[1676] actually incarnate, crucified, dead, buried, risen from the dead, ascended into heaven, sitting at God's right hand, and shedding forth his Spirit upon his elect;[1677] to and with the houses of Israel and Judah, even the whole church in all nations of the world,[1678] from Christ's death until the world's end:[1679] wherein he promises to all that shall believe in Jesus Christ already exhibited, shall repent of their sins, and shall love and obey him in Christ as his New Covenant people; to write his laws in their hearts and inwards;[1680] to make them all small and great know the Lord; to be merciful to their unrighteousnesses, and remember their sins no more; yea to be to them a God, and make them be to him a people – all which he confirms visibly by the New Covenant's tokens, baptism, and the Lord's Supper;[1681] invisibly, by the operation of the Holy Spirit.[1682]

[1674] Jeremiah 31:31, Hebrews 8:8 & 13:20
[1675] Hebrews 8:8-10, Galatians 4:22 to the end; 2 Corinthians 3:6 to the end, Hebrews 12:18 to the end
[1676] Hebrews 9:14-17 & 8:13 & 7:22
[1677] Hebrews 9:14-15 & 10:9-22, Galatians 4:4-6 & 3:13-14; 1 Corinthians 15:3-4, etc, Ephesians 4:8-11, Acts 2:1-2, etc, 33
[1678] Hebrews 9:8, Jeremiah 31:31
[1679] As has already been evidenced in this Book 4, Chapter 1, Aphorism 1
[1680] Hebrews 8:10-12, Jeremiah 31:33-34
[1681] Matthew 28:19-20 & 26:26-31; 1 Corinthians 11:20, 23, etc.
[1682] Ephesians 1:13-14, Romans 8:15-16, Galatians 4:6, etc.

Now the nature of the New Covenant, according to this description thus confirmed by Scriptures, consists, especially in these few particulars following, namely:

(1) **In the order and time of manifestation** – the New Covenant being the last covenant expressure of all others.

(2) **In excellence of constitution and administration** – the New Covenant in many respects and degrees far transcending not only the Old Covenant, but all Covenants that went before: as has been intimated in part, and hereafter may more fully appear. It is an expressure of the Covenant of Faith, herein it agrees in the general nature of it, with all the Covenants of Promise foregoing, which were as so many distinct expressures of the Covenant of Faith.[1683] It is the most excellent expressure of the Covenant of Faith. Herein it transcends them all, and differs from them all, both in constitution and administration: [1] *in constitution*, for {1} it is a better Covenant, established upon better promises, in a better mediator;[1684] {2} it is a better Testament, even a New Testament – antiquating and revoking the Old in regard of its legal rigor, rites and gravaminous ceremonies, furnished with better bequests and legacies, and confirmed by the death and blood of the best testator in the world, Jesus Christ – a federal testament and a testamentary Covenant.[1685] [2] *In administration*; for this New Covenant beyond all other is administered {1} most clearly, {2} most spiritually, {3} most freely, with greatest spiritual liberty, {4} most fully and perfectly; {5} most extensively to all sorts of nations, {6} most efficaciously, under this Covenant, the Holy Spirit being most plentifully given, {7} most comfortably, in the fullest communication of the Comforter, {8} most durably, even until the world's end, and {9} most gloriously, in regard of true lasting inward spiritual glory – As hereafter will be evidenced more at large.

[1683] Ephesians 2:12
[1684] Hebrews 8:6
[1685] Hebrews 7:19-22 & 8:13 & 9:15-17, etc.

(3) **In the new kind or way of doctrine**: more open, plain, full, spiritual, evangelical, etc. touching God's gratuitous blessings in Jesus Christ the Messiah; not promised, but performed; not expected for future, But exhibited already; Not to come afterwards, But actually come in the flesh, crucified, dead, buried, risen, ascended, and set down on the right hand of the throne of the majesty in the heavens (Hebrews 8:1).

(4) **In the amplitude, extensiveness and enlargement of the federates**, namely: the New Testament church throughout all nations of the world.[1686] Whereas all former Covenants were limited to particular families, or to that one nation of the Jews alone, this is extended not only to the house of Judah, but also to the house of Israel – yea, to the universal church in all nations, (Hebrews 8:8, Jeremiah 31:31).

(5) **In the peculiar eminence of covenant blessings promised**,[1687] namely: [1] complete sanctification of their minds and inwards to be conformed to his Covenant fully; [2] eminent and general illumination of their understandings in the knowledge of the Lord; [3] full and final expiation and remission of their sins, and removal of the curse forever, even perfect justification, by the sacrifice of Christ offered once for all, so that they shall never more be remembered to us, as the sins of the Jews were again remembered to them every year; [4] the highest covenant relation possible between God and his creatures; [5] and the promise of the eternal inheritance, not in Canaan, but in heaven itself.[1688]

(6) **In the New ratification of this Covenant**; Outwardly by baptism and the Lord's supper; inwardly, by the new operations of the Holy Spirit.

(7) **Finally, in the peculiar duration of this New Covenant administration, namely: from Christ's death until the end of the world.** For in this, all former administrations are swallowed up forever.

[1686] Matthew 28:18, Mark 16:15-16
[1687] Hebrews 8:10-12, Jeremiah 31:33-34, Hebrews 9:14-15 & 10:1-21
[1688] Hebrews 9:14-15

In these especially, the nature of this New Covenant or New Testament consists, as the Scriptures, and particularly those annexed to the description of the New Covenant, do abundantly evince. And therefore, the restrictive limitation of the nature of this New Covenant, only to three of these particulars (as is done by David Pareus,[1689] and after him by Mr. Ball),[1690] is very prejudicial and derogatory to this excellent New Covenant.

What inferences might be drawn from these two aphorisms in this chapter, will more properly offer themselves hereafter in opening the matter, form, etc, of this Covenant, and therefore here they are wholly waved.

[1689] "Haec descriptio Novi Testamenti naturam perspicue explicat, tamque in tribus his potissimum consistere ostendit. I. In genere Doctrinae, aperto & plano, merè Evangelico de beneficiis gratuitis Messiae exhibiti. II. In immunitate à maledictione legis, & ab onere legalium rituum, & politiae Mosaicae. III. In Ecclesia Nova amplitudine seu dilatatione per totum orbem, unde Catholica dicitur." D. Pareus in Prolegom. General. ante Ep. ad Rom. pag. 42. a. (Frankfurt, 1647).

[1690] "The nature of this Testament stands principally in three things: (1) the kind of doctrine: plain, full, and merely evangelical; (2) in freedom from the curse of the law, and freedom from legal rites; (3) in the amplitude and enlargement of the new church, throughout all nations of the world." Mr. John Ball in his *Treatise of the New Covenant*, Chapter 1, page 198 (London, 1645).

Chapter 3

Of the Author or Efficient; the Occasion, and Impulsive Causes of this New Covenant.

Having thus viewed the (1) terms, (2) denominations, and (3) nature of this **New Covenant** more generally, we now descend to the opening of this New Covenant, more particularly, as touching: (1) the efficient cause, (2) the federates, or parties to this Covenant, (3) the matter, (4) the Mediator, surety, and testator, (5) the form, (6) the end, or intended scope of this **New Covenant**. These more general and remote considerations afford much light to this New Covenant; but these more particular and near considerations will yield much more.

The efficient cause of this New Covenant will best be discovered by notice-taking of these two things especially, namely: (1) who was the efficient cause or author of the New Covenant, and (2) upon what occasions and impulsives this New Covenant was authorized. These shall be briefly and plainly resolved in two distinct aphorisms, namely:

Aphorism 1

The LORD God – namely: God the Father, in the Son Jesus Christ, by the Holy Spirit – is the sole efficient Cause or Author of this New Covenant: promising it of old, establishing it in fullness of time, and applying it in due time to his called people.

The LORD God, namely: God the Father, in the Son Jesus Christ, by the Holy Ghost is the sole efficient cause or author of this New Covenant: promising it of old, establishing it in fullness of time, and applying it in due time to his called people.

In this aphorism (that I may a little explain and confirm it) two things are intimated to us: (1) that God – Father, Son, and Holy Spirit – is sole author of the New Covenant; (2) how God acts unto the effecting or authorizing of it. Both of these are to be cleared.

(1) **That the LORD God – namely: God the Father, in the Son Jesus Christ, by the Holy Spirit – is the sole efficient cause or author of the New Covenant, may be evinced in various ways.** As,

[1] *By the express testimony of holy Scriptures.* The Scriptures testify:

{1} That God promised to make this New Covenant, and peculiarly appropriates it to him as his work; *Behold the days come (saith the LORD) when I will make a New Covenant, with the house of Israel*, etc. – *This is the Covenant that I will make with the house of Israel, after those days saith the LORD*, etc.[1691] In that he says {*I will make a New Covenant*}, he excludes all others, and declares himself the only author of it. {2} That Jesus Christ, as Testator, is author of this his New Testament, confirmed and completed by his own death and blood. – *And for this cause he is the mediator of the new*

[1691] Jeremiah 31:31, 33, Hebrews 8:8-9

testament, *that by means of death for the redemption of the transgressions that were under the first testament, they which are called might receive the promise of eternal inheritance. For where a testament is, there must also of necessity be the death of the testator. For a testament is of force after men are dead: otherwise it is of no strength at all while the testator liveth.*[1692] Here the apostle shows that Jesus Christ the Mediator, is also Testator of the New Testament, making it of force (as men their testaments) by death. And who can be author of any testament, but the Testator himself? {3} That the Holy Spirit also made this New Covenant – and the benefits thereof in Christ – known to the church: *For by one offering he hath perfected forever them that are sanctified*; whereof the Holy Spirit also is a witness to us: *For after that he had said before, This is the covenant that I will make with them after those days, saith the Lord: I will put my laws into their hearts, and in their minds will I write them*, etc. And the Holy Spirit – making this New Covenant known, revealing it by his own authority to the prophet – must needs be the author of it.[1693]

[2] **By the plain current of the New Covenant itself.** For therein the promises are uttered by the Lord himself in the first person, as from himself, saying: *I will put my laws into their mind, – I will be to them a God, – I will be merciful to their unrighteousnesses, and their sins and their iniquities will I remember no more.*[1694] Now, the same Lord God, that promises to perform the New Covenant blessings himself, he must needs be sole author of the New Covenant.

[3] **By the form or name in which baptism, the first New Covenant token, is to be administered, by Christ's own appointment after his resurrection.** *Go ye therefore* (he says to the eleven apostles) *and disciple ye all nations, baptizing them in the name of the Father, and of the Son, and of the Holy Ghost: teaching them to observe all things whatsoever I have commanded*

[1692] Hebrews 9:15-17
[1693] Hebrews 10:14-17
[1694] Jeremiah 31:33-34, Hebrews 8:10-12 & 10:16-17

you, etc.[1695] Why {*in the name of Father, Son, and Holy Ghost*}? But partly because baptism is to be dispensed by warrant and authority of all these three; partly because all the New Covenant benefits signified, sealed, and conveyed by baptism are from all three. Partly, because the restipulation and federal obligation of the baptized, in regard of faith, repentance, and all other New Covenant duties conditioned, is to be made to all the three persons in the blessed Trinity. Now if the Lord God – Father, Son and Holy Spirit – is the sole author of baptism, and of the benefits thereof, which is the New Covenant token, consequently he is sole author of the New Covenant itself. Who can authorize the Covenant token, but the author of the Covenant?

[4] **By the joint undertakings of the three most sacred persons, Father, Son, and Holy Spirit in this New Covenant.** They jointly undertake to perform all New Covenant blessings to the federates, but yet in their own peculiar order and proper way of working, which is according to the order of their subsisting.[1696]

The Father eternally subsists, first in order, of himself (Matthew 28:19; 1 John 5:7) not begotten, nor proceeding; the Son eternally subsists from the Father, second in order, being eternally and ineffably begotten of the Father (Hebrews 1:5-6, John 1:18, 3:16 & 17:5); the Holy Spirit eternally subsists from the Father and the Son. The third in order, proceeding eternally and inconceivably from the Father and the Son (John 15:26 and 14:26). According to this order of their subsisting, is their order of working, as the apostle intimates: *To us there is but one God, the Father, of whom are all things, and we in* (or, *for*) *him; and one Lord Jesus Christ, through whom are all things*, and we through him; and proportionably, one Holy Spirit by whom are all things, and we by him.[1697] And elsewhere he shows that our access to God is

---

[1695] Matthew 28:18-20
[1696] See John Forbes' *Treatise of Justification*, chapter 10, more fully clearing this.
[1697] 1 Corinthians 8:6, Romans 11:36

answerable to this order: *For through him* (namely: the Son Jesus Christ) *we both have an access by one Spirit unto the Father.*[1698]

Now in this New Covenant:

{1} God the Father undertakes: (i) to be a Covenant-God and Father in Jesus Christ his only Son, unto all that shall truly believe, repent and obey him as his people; accepting them as his covenant people, and adopting them as his sons and daughters into his family;[1699] (ii) to bestow Jesus Christ upon them (who was given up freely for them, Romans 8:32) as their all-sufficient Savior and Redeemer, making him unto them wisdom and righteousness and sanctification and redemption (John 6:44, Ephesians 3:14-17; 1 Corinthians 1:30); (iii) to confer the Holy Spirit upon them (Luke 11:13, Ephesians 3:14-16); (iv) to be the justifier of him that believes in Jesus (Romans 3:24-26); and (v) to bless them with *all spiritual blessings in heavenly places* (or, *things*) in Christ (Ephesians 1:3, Titus 3:4-7, etc.)

{2} God the Son undertakes: (i) to redeem his elect sheep, and make them free indeed, from sin, curse, wrath, and condemnation, by the invaluable price of his own death and blood (John 10:11, 18, Hebrews 10:5-9, etc. & 9:14-15; 1 Peter 1:18-20, Ephesians 5:2, Acts 20:28, Titus 2:13-14, John 8:36); (ii) to rescue them actually and effectually from the power and tyranny of sin, Satan, etc. bringing them unto everlasting reconciliation to, and favor with God (Acts 26:17-18, Romans 5:1-2, 10-11; 2 Corinthians 5:20-21); (iii) to be the material means of their righteousness, justification, and spiritual cleansing from the guilt of their sins, that they may be the righteousness of God in him (2 Corinthians 5:21).[1700] (iv) To give them eternal life, and to preserve them so securely that they shall never perish, nor shall any pluck them out of his hand (John 10:27-29) (v) To be their way unto the Father, that now they may enjoy him graciously (John 14:6, Ephesians 2:18) being acceptable to God through him in all their spiritual sacrifices (1 Peter 2:5). And that hereafter they may

---

[1698] Ephesians 2:18
[1699] Hebrews 8:10; 2 Corinthians 6:16-18, Acts 8:35-39, Ephesians 1:5
[1700] Revelation 1:5, Romans 5:9; 1 Corinthians 1:30, Jeremiah 23:5-6 & 33:15-16

come by this new and living way to enjoy him gloriously in heaven itself (Hebrews 10:19-20, etc).

{3} The Holy Spirit undertakes for these redeemed of Christ Jesus: (i) to cleanse and sanctify them, by purging them from their sinful defilements, and repairing the image of God in them;[1701] (ii) to lead, act and guide them, as the children of God, into all truth, and in all the ways of God; that they may walk in, and after the Spirit (Romans 8:14, John 16:13, Romans 8:1, Galatians 5:25); (iii) to strengthen them with all might in the inner man (Ephesians 3:16), helping all their infirmities, especially their prayer infirmities, enabling them *with groans unutterable to cry Abba Father* (Romans 8:15, 26-27); (iv) to assure them, as a witness, seal, and earnest of their sonship and good spiritual estate towards God (Romans 8:16, Ephesians 1:13-14); and (v) to continue and abide in them, as their Comforter, supplying Christ's absence forever, until we come where he is to behold his glory (Job 14:16-18 & 17:24).

Those and such like New Covenant benefits, God – the Father, Son, and Holy Spirit – undertakes to perform to the federates with them in this New Covenant, and therefore God alone is author and primary efficient of this New Covenant. For who can perform or make good this Covenant's benefits, but he that made the Covenant?

[5] ***By the joint influence and concurrence of the whole Trinity unto all works ad extra, that are without the Trinity.*** According to that known maxim: "The works of the Trinity without are undivided."[1702] The works of the Trinity within themselves, as to beget, to be begotten, to proceed, are so proper and peculiar to one person, as they are not nor can be belonging to another; but the works of the Trinity without themselves, as decree, creation, providence, etc. (among which also covenant-making is one) are common to all the persons – they all act therein, but in their peculiar way of working proper to each person. The Father acts of himself through the Son by the Spirit; the

---

[1701] 1 Corinthians 6:11, John 3:3, 5, Titus 3:5, Galatians 5:22-25
[1702] Opera Trinitatis ad extra sunt indivisa.

Son from the Father by the Spirit; the Holy Spirit from the Father and the Son. *The Son can do nothing of himself, but what he seeth the Father do; for whatsoever he doeth, those also the Son doeth likewise.*[1703] Therefore if God the Father, or Son, etc., is author of this New Covenant, then all the three persons consequently must needs be authors of it; namely: God the Father, in and through his Son Jesus Christ, by the Holy Spirit.

(2) That the LORD God – Father, Son, and Holy Spirit – do act unto the effecting of this New Covenant, especially three ways: namely: [1] of old, promising it; [2] in fullness of time, establishing it; [3] in due time, applying it to his called people. All the three persons do jointly concur in every of these three acts. But yet so, as that the Father's influence and activity chiefly appears, in promising this Covenant of old; the Son's in establishing it in fullness of time; the Holy Spirit's, in applying it efficaciously to God's called in due time.

[1] God the Father promised this New Covenant of old by the prophet Jeremiah. *Behold the days come saith the LORD, that I will make a new covenant with the house of Israel, and with the house of Judah, etc.*[1704] Herein the LORD promised long beforehand that he would make a New Covenant with Israel and Judah. This promise was revealed by the Lord to Jeremiah, and by him to God's people when they were in their Babylonian captivity, as the context shows abundantly.[1705] The Old Covenant was not sufficiently comfortable and supporting to them in their deep distresses in Christ promised. God therefore promised to them in after times a New Covenant, more effectually comfortable in Christ exhibited. But this promise of making a New Covenant did not have its accomplishment until the death of Christ. So then, the Lord was the principal efficient or author of this New Covenant, contriving it by his infinite wisdom, and revealing the promise of it, to the prophet Jeremiah, and by him as his instrument unto his people.

[1703] John 5:19-20
[1704] Jeremiah 31:31, etc.
[1705] See Jeremiah chapters 29-33, etc.

[2] God the Son Jesus Christ established this New Covenant in fullness of time by his death and blood, and this he did as Mediator, Surety, and Testator of this New Testamental Covenant, or Federal Testament.[1706] Upon this account also, the same night wherein he was betrayed, he annexed the Lord's supper as a visible seal to this New Covenant, saying: *This is my blood of the New Testament which is shed for many for remission of sins*[1707] – hereby intimating that this New Covenant was dedicated and solemnly established in the blood of Jesus Christ himself, as the Old Testament formerly was dedicated and established with the typical blood of sacrifices, Moses saying: *Behold the blood of the covenant which the LORD hath made with you*, etc. or as Paul alleges it: *This is the blood of the testament, which God hath enjoined unto you.*[1708]

[3] God the Holy Spirit in due time actually and effectually applies unto the called of God this New Covenant, with all the benefits thereof.

{1} That the New Covenant and benefits thereof are effectually applied to them that are called; is evident – partly, by that of Paul's: *And for this cause he is the mediator of the new testament, that by means of death, for the redemption of the transgressions under the first testament, they which are called might receive the promise of eternal inheritance;*[1709] partly, be that of Peter's on the day of Pentecost: *Repent and be baptized everyone of you in the name of Jesus Christ, for the remission of sins, and ye shall receive the gift of the Holy Ghost: For the promise is to you and to your children, and to all that are afar off, even as many as the Lord our God shall call.*[1710] Here it is plain that the gift of the Holy Ghost, and the promise of the eternal inheritance, are the promised benefits of the New Covenant, forasmuch as both these promises, though made of old, yet are now confirmed by, accomplished in, and digested

---

[1706] Hebrews 7:22 & 9:15-17
[1707] Matthew 26:28
[1708] Exodus 24:8, Hebrews 9:20
[1709] Hebrews 9:15
[1710] Acts 2:1, 38-39

into the New Covenant, and that these benefits are actually received only by them that are actually called.

{2} That now they that are actually and effectually called, are so called by the Holy Spirit of God, and that ordinarily by the gospel truth and Word preached: is plain also. For, Paul tells the Thessalonians: *God hath from the beginning chosen you to salvation, through sanctification of the Spirit and belief of the truth, whereunto he called you by our gospel, to the obtaining of the glory of our Lord Jesus Christ.*[1711] Here the apostle evidences their election, by their effectual vocation: their effectual vocation is described: partly, by the causes whereby it is wrought; namely: (i) efficaciously and inwardly, by the sanctification of the Spirit; (ii) instrumentally and outwardly, by the gospel preached. Partly, by the last term, end or issue whereunto their calling tends, namely: obtaining the glory of Christ, that is, conformity to and communion with Christ in glory. The Holy Ghost then is the immediate efficient cause of effectual calling, and by effectual calling, the New Testament and the benefits thereof are applied actually and effectually. Therefore they are actually and effectually applied by the Holy Spirit.

Inferences from this, and the next aphorism, shall be laid down together.

[1711] 2 Thessalonians 2:13-14

Aphorism 2

The LORD God, Father, Son and Holy Spirit, took occasion, From his own people's afflicted condition, the Old Testament's insufficiency, and the greatness of man's misery, to promise, establish, and apply this New Covenant to them that are called of his mere grace, in and for the merit of Jesus Christ.

In this aphorism are expressed: (1) the occasion, and (2) the impulsive or moving causes inclining God to make this New Covenant.

(1) **The occasion which God took of promising, establishing, and applying this New Covenant, is threefold**: the first more peculiarly concerning his people the Jews, the second properly respecting the nature of the Old Covenant, and the third generally referring to mankind.

[1] *The afflicted condition of God's own people the Jews.* When God first revealed his purpose and promise to Jeremiah, of making a New Covenant in after times with Israel and Judah, at that time both Israel and Judah were under great affliction and distress. Judah was in sad captivity in Babylon where they were as dead dry bones in their graves, when this New Covenant was first promised (Jeremiah 31:31, etc, with the context before and after).[1712] And Israel, long before that, had been carried captive into Assyria by Shalmanesar, King of Assyria, and were placed in Halah and Habor and the cities of the Medes because they transgressed God's Covenant; and there they remained in thralldom among the Gentiles.[1713] Nor do we read of their return until Judah returned out of Babylon, when probably some of Israel returned also, as I have heretofore observed in opening God's Covenant with the captives in

---

[1712] See Jeremiah chapters 29-34, etc. & Ezekiel 37
[1713] 2 Kings 17:1-24 & 18:9-13

Babylon.[1714] This was the distressed condition of Israel and Judah, against which, the LORD – having propounded many promises of their deliverance thence, of their reduction into, and prosperity in their own land, of their union again as at first under David into one nation and one kingdom, etc., to which effect he at that time made a Covenant with his captives, for their support and comfort; at last, that he might advance their consolations beyond all their tribulations – he promises that the days should come, wherein he would make a New Covenant with the house of Israel, and the house of Judah (Jeremiah 31:31-34), hereby intimating to them that they were not only to look at the present Covenant and promises tendered to them for their comfort, but that they were to look further beyond this, to the New Covenant which should be made in after days with them in Jesus Christ exhibited, who should redeem them from the bondage of sin, Satan, death, wrath, curse, hell, etc. infinitely worse than the bondage of Babylon; and upon this Covenant, they should principally ground their comforts and hopes, in all their adversities.[1715] *That* Covenant assured them of their reduction from Babylon to Canaan; *this* of their reduction from sin, death, hell, etc., unto heaven. God would have his afflicted to be strongly and abundantly comforted: therefore over and beyond all other promises, he promised in after days to make with them a New Covenant. This was the first and most immediate occasion.

[2] *The Old Testament's, or Old Covenant's insufficiency, weakness, unprofitableness, and imperfection,* was another Occasion of the Lord's establishing this more sufficient profitable and perfect New Covenant. This the apostle notably declares to us, saying: *There is verily a disannulling of the commandment going before, for the weakness and unprofitableness thereof. For the law made nothing perfect: but the bringing in of a better hope did; by the which we draw nigh unto God.*[1716] And yet more fully afterwards: *He is the*

[1714] Ezekiel 37:15 to the end
[1715] To this effect, Calvin, in his commentary on Jeremiah 31:31, expounds this occasion of God's promising this New Covenant.
[1716] Hebrews 7:18-19

mediator of a better covenant, which was established upon better promises. For if the first covenant had been faultless, then should no place have been sought for the second. But finding fault with them, he saith; Behold the days come saith Lord, when I will make a new covenant with the house of Israel, and the House of Judah: Not according to the covenant that I made with their fathers, etc.[1717] God in covenant-making still proceeded from the more imperfect, to the more perfect; and at last to the most perfect. In the Old Testament, there was much imperfection and insufficiency: It made nothing perfect, as pertaining to the conscience, having but a shadow of good things to come.[1718] It required duty, but furnished not with ability for it. Hence the federates continued not in it, but broke it, thereby bringing God's displeasure upon themselves (2 Corinthians 3:6-9, Hebrews 8:7-9). Hereupon God took occasion to establish a better Covenant, even this perfect New Covenant in the blood of Christ (who by one offering perfected forever them that are sanctified),[1719] which Covenant not only requires duty, but also (being not engraven in stones, but written in the mind and heart)[1720] furnishes the federates with ability for performance; and at last gives entrance by Christ's new and living way into the holiest of all, heaven itself.[1721]

[3] **The greatness of man's misery under sin, death, and the wrath of God**, was another occasion of this New Covenant's establishment and application. The greatness of man's spiritual misery under sin, death, etc., is abundantly set forth in the Scriptures. See Romans 5:12-14 & 6:23 & 3:9-20, Ephesians 2:1-3; 2 Timothy 2:25, Acts 8:23, Galatians 3:10, and many like passages. This greatness of man's spiritual misery can be removed by no other remedy in the world, but only by the meritorious death and mediation of our Lord Jesus Christ, becoming sin, and being made a curse for his elect, that they

---

[1717] Hebrews 8:6 to the end
[1718] Hebrews 7:18-19 & 9:8-12 & 10:1, etc.
[1719] Hebrews 10:14
[1720] Hebrews 8:10-12
[1721] Hebrews 10:15-21

might become the righteousness of God in him, and be redeemed from the curse (Acts 4:11-12, Romans 8:3; 2 Corinthians 5:21, Galatians 3:13-14). No other Covenant represents Christ actually sacrificed, and his blood actually shed for us, but only this New Covenant, which was established in his blood; former Covenants representing Christ and his blood only in promises and types, as to come afterwards (Matthew 26:28, Hebrews 9:14-17 & 10:1-22), whereupon – all other former Covenants of Promise being herein imperfect and defective – God took occasion to bring in this New Covenant, swallowing up all former Covenants, and actually exhibiting a full and perfect remedy against man's sin and misery in Christ crucified. *And for this cause he is the mediator of the new testament, that by means of death, for the redemption of the transgressions that were under the first testament, they which are called might receive the promise of eternal inheritance.*[1722] Not only the sins under this New Covenant, but those also under the Old Covenant, that First Testament, are not purged away but only by the price of Christ's redemption performed in establishing this New Covenant.[1723] Thus man's deep sin and

---

[1722] Hebrews 9:14-15, etc.

[1723] "Prevaricationum sub [V]eteri Foedere. An vero patribus praevaricationes non fuerant remissae? & cur praevaricationum veteris Foederis potius meminit, quam Novi, cum Novi Foederis Mediator videatur potius Novi Foederis praevaricationes expiare debuisse? Respond. Non hoc vult, quasi praevacationes Novi Foederis non etiam expiarit. Id enim dubitatione vacat. Ad veteres vero praevaricationes mortem Christi extendit, ne ad novi duntaxat Testamenti tempus ejus vigorem adstrictum putemus. Dixerat, λατρειας veteres peccata eluere, Conscientias purgare non potuisse: Deus quoque sub Novo demum foedere praevaricationum remissionem promiserat. Hinc videbatur patribus negata peccatorum remissio. Non, inquit, negata fuit eis remissio, sed sub Novum Foedus suspensa fuit vera peccatorum expiatio. Quare patribus obtigit quidem promissa prepitiatio: non vero propter λατρειας, victimas, purgationes, lotiones typicas; sed propter mortem Mediatoris Novi Testamenti. Locus non absimilis est Apostoli, Rom. 3. 25.—per remissionem peccatorum praecedentium. id est, eorum, quae sub veteri Foedere remissi quidem, sed nondum expiata fuerant Mediatoris Sanguine," &c.

David Pareus' commentary on Hebrews 9:15

misery occasioned God's great New Covenant remedy.[1724] Had man not sinned, Christ would not have suffered. Had man not brought himself under the curse, Christ would not have been made a curse to redeem him from it, etc.

Thus of the occasion of this New Covenant.

(2) **The impulsive or moving causes, inclining the LORD to promise, establish, or apply this New Covenant, were not anything at all in the Jews or Gentiles, to whom this Covenant is extended, but only his own mere grace and good pleasure, and the meritorious mediation of Jesus Christ.**

This thing therefore may be cleared: [1] negatively, and [2] affirmatively.

[1] *Negatively*: that there was nothing at all in Jews or Gentiles, to whom this New Covenant is extended, moving or inclining God by way of causality, to promise, establish, or apply this New Covenant unto them, is very evident, for:

{1} **The Jews** – to whom the promise of God's future making of a New Covenant was first revealed by Jeremiah from the Lord (though they were at that time God's own and only covenant-people, yet) – had nothing at all in themselves of worth or dignity, that might move the Lord to reveal this promise to them, or afterwards to establish it for them. For: (i) Their fathers were, in God's first promise of making a New Covenant, found fault also as a

---

[1724] "There is nothing in man to move God to shew mercy, but only misery; which might be an occasion but can be no cause, either why mercy is promised, or salvation granted. If man had not fallen from grace and state of innocency, God would never have sent his Son to redeem him, nor shown mercy, reaching to the pardon and covering of his iniquity; If he had not lost himself, Christ would never have come to find and restore him; if he had not wounded himself, he would have not been healed and repaired of grace. Man then is a subject on whom God bestows grace, and in whom he works it; and his misery an occasion that the Lord took of manifesting his mercy, in succoring and lifting him up out of that distress; But the free grace and love of God is the sole cause of what the Lord has promised in this New Covenant, and does give according to promise." Mr. John Ball in his *Treatise of the New Covenant*, Chap. 1. p. 199, 200 (London, 1645).

covenant-breaking people, that continued not in God's Covenant, and therefore God regarded them not.[1725] And they themselves are taxed for being polluted with idolatry, like their fathers (Ezekiel 20:30-32 compared with verses 1-30; Daniel 9:4-20). So that neither their fathers nor they themselves had any worth in them, which might move the Lord to promise a New Covenant to them. (ii) These captive Jews had nothing in themselves inviting and inclining God to make his uncaptivating Covenant with them when they were in Babylon: *I do not this for your sakes O house of Israel, but for mine holy name's sake; – Not for your sakes do I this, saith the Lord GOD, be it known unto you; be ashamed and confounded for your own ways O house of Israel.*[1726] Much less could they have any motives or impulsive causes in themselves inclining God to promise the New Covenant, which is a far more perfect and excellent covenant expressure than that, or any that went before.

{2} **The Gentiles** – who at that time when this New Covenant was first promised, *were afar off from God, were not his people, had not obtained mercy, were dead in trespasses and sins, were without Christ, being aliens from the commonwealth of Israel, and strangers from the covenants of promise, having no hope, and without God in the world* – were much more destitute than the Jews of all worth and excellency in themselves, which might move God to promise or establish this New Covenant with them.[1727]

[2] *Affirmatively*: that the LORD's own mere grace, and the meritorious mediation of Jesus Christ, were the sole impulsive causes moving and inclining him to promise, establish, and apply this New Covenant to his called of Jews and Gentiles: is also very apparent, for:

{1} The mere grace and good-pleasure of God's will is evidently hinted in the tenor of this New Covenant to be the inward impulsive or moving cause of his promising and making of it. He says: *The days come when I will make a new covenant; – But this is the covenant that I will make with the house of Israel*

[1725] Jeremiah 31:32 with Hebrews 8:9
[1726] Ezekiel 36:21 to the end
[1727] Ephesians 2:17; 1 Peter 2:9-10, Ephesians 2:1, 5, 10

after those days; – I will put my laws into their hearts, and in their minds will I write them; – I will be to them a God; – I will be merciful to their unrighteousnesses, and their sins and iniquities will I remember no more.[1728] Here the Lord says {*I will*} seven several times in the tenor of the New Covenant, and gives this still as the ground or motive why he made this New Covenant, because so it is his mere will and pleasure. He fetches all impulsives from himself, from his own free love, rich grace, and mere good-pleasure of his will, for making this New Covenant. I have formerly shown that even his Covenant of Works with man before his fall was originally of grace, *ex gratia favoris*, of the grace of God's favor, which the innocent creature could not deserve; and that God's Covenant of Faith with man since his fall, in all the foregoing discoveries and periods of it, was originally of grace much more, namely: *ex gratia commiserationis*, of his mere grace of commiseration and pity, the sinful creature deserving the quite contrary. Now therefore consequently, this New Covenant – the height, perfection, and accomplishment of all Covenants – must needs be of grace, of favor, and commiseration most of all. In this fullest expressure of Covenant, is God's fullest expressure of grace, mercy, and love.

Under former Covenants, God made some discovery of his grace, mercy, love, lovingkindness, and so on: Adam had a promise of mercy in the seed of the woman against the serpent;[1729] Noah and his family found federal favor in God's sight, to be saved, when all the world was drowned;[1730] Abraham was taken into Covenant with God, and justified by faith without the works of the law; Israel, though the fewest of all people, were brought into Covenant with God, who loved them because he loved them, being merciful to whom he would be merciful, and proclaiming himself *gracious, merciful, longsuffering, abundant in goodness and truth, forgiving iniquity transgression and sin*

[1728] Hebrews 8:8, 10, 12 & 10:16-17
[1729] Genesis 3:15
[1730] Genesis 6:18 & 7:1

(Deuteronomy 7:6-8, Exodus 33:19 & 34:4-7);[1731] David – brought into special Covenant with God – confessed: *O LORD, for thy servants sake, and according to thine own heart, hast thou done all this greatness, in making known all these greatnesses;*[1732] and the captive Jews were brought into covenant with God and partakers of his promises, not for their sakes, but for his holy name's sake.[1733] Thus God expressed his grace, mercy, love, and so on, in all these former covenant administrations. But come now to this New Covenant, excelling the rest as far as the light of the sun excels the like of the moon, and then see what transcendent discoveries of divine grace, mercy, love, etc., are made there.

(i) When it speaks of God's free grace, how is grace exalted! Saving grace (Ephesians 2:5, 8) riches of grace (Ephesians 1:7), exceedingly abundant grace (1 Timothy 1:14). The exceeding riches of his grace, in his kindness towards us, through Christ Jesus (Ephesians 2:7), and the glory of his grace (Ephesians 1:6).

(ii) When it mentions God's mercy, how is mercy magnified! *It is not of him that willeth, nor of him that runneth, but of God that sheweth mercy. – Therefore he hath mercy on whom he will have mercy, and whom he will he hardeneth.*[1734] *– Not by works of righteousness which we have done, but according to his mercy he saved us,* etc.[1735] *– God, even the Father of our Lord Jesus Christ, is the father of mercies, and God of all comfort,* etc.[1736] *– But God, who is rich in mercy, for his great love wherewith he loved us, even when we were dead in sins, hath quickened us together with Christ (by grace ye are saved) and hath raised us up together, and made us sit together in heavenly places in Christ*

[1731] Genesis 12:1-3 & 15:18, Romans 4:1-5, 9-13
[1732] 1 Chronicles 17:19 with the context
[1733] Ezekiel 36:21 to the end
[1734] Romans 9:16, 18
[1735] Titus 3:5-6
[1736] 2 Corinthians 1:3

Jesus:[1737] – *He will be merciful to our unrighteousnesses, and our sins and iniquities will he remember no more.*[1738]

(iii) When it speaks of his and Christ's love to sinners, how is love omnified! *His great love wherewith he loved us.*[1739] – *God so loved the world, that he gave his only begotten Son, that whosoever believeth in him, should not perish, but have everlasting life.*[1740] – *He that spared not his own Son, but delivered him up for us all: how shall he not with him also freely give us all things?*[1741] And elsewhere, John admires God's familiar sweet fatherly love to us in Christ, saying: *Behold, what manner of love the Father hath bestowed upon us, that we should be called the sons of God,* etc.[1742] And of Christ's love, it is said: *Who loved us, and washed us from our sins in his own blood.*[1743] – *Greater love hath no man than this, that a man lay down his life for his friends. But – when we were without strength, in due time Christ died for the ungodly. For scarcely for a righteous man will one die: yet peradventure for a good man some would even dare to die. But God commendeth his love towards us, in that while we were yet sinners, Christ died for us.*[1744] – *I bow my knees unto the Father of our Lord Jesus Christ, – That Christ may dwell in your hearts by faith, that ye being rooted and grounded in love, may be able to comprehend with all saints, what is the breadth and length, and depth, and height: and to know the love of Christ which passeth knowledge, that ye might be filled with all the fullness of God.*[1745]

Philosophy has but three dimensions: length, breadth, and depth; but here Paul ascribes four dimensions to the love of Christ, adding height.[1746] He

---

[1737] Ephesians 2:4-6
[1738] Hebrews 8:12
[1739] Ephesians 2:4
[1740] John 3:16
[1741] Romans 8:32
[1742] 1 John 3:1-3
[1743] Revelation 1:5
[1744] John 15:13 with Romans 5:6-8
[1745] Ephesians 3:14-17, 18-19
[1746] To the like effect, Zanchi expounds this excellent Scripture out of Photius

would have us know that Christ's love is beyond all dimensions; as it is beyond all knowledge and comprehensions. Christ's love has length in it because he loves his elect from eternity to eternity. It has breadth in it because it is extended not only to the Jews, but also to all the nations of the Gentiles, far and near. It has depth in it because love brought him as low as earth, as low as grave, as low as hell, becoming a man of sorrows, a crucified dead and buried man, and a conflicter with the powers of darkness for our sakes, that we may be spiritually quickened, at last corporally raised and eternally redeemed. And beyond all these ordinary dimensions, Christ's love has in it a height also, because he has ascended up far above all heavens, that he might fill all things, be our everlasting advocate with the Father, prepare a place for us, and take us home at last to himself, that where he is we may be also, to behold his glory, and enjoy him forever gloriously. This the free grace, mercy, love, and goodness of God is displayed most oriently [clearly], magnificently, and illustriously in the New Covenant. And this rich grace and love of God to us, was the sole inward impulsive cause moving him to make this New Covenant.

{2} The meritorious mediation of Jesus Christ was the only, sole outward impulsive or moving cause of God's making this New Covenant, and making it good to his federates. For: (i) *All the promises of God in Christ are yea, and in him amen*. He speaks not of God's promises made to man before, but after his fall. All such promises, especially and principally the promises of the New Covenant, are *in Christ yea, and in him amen*. That is, they are in him certain truth, *yea*, not an uncertain, doubtful, *yea* and *nay*, and in him they are assurance, or firm ground of assured dependence, *Amen*. Or, according to the variant reading, the Greek, *wherefore also through him let them be amen* – that is, "Let us, let the church assent and subscribe to this truth and certainty of God's promises in Christ." Calvin, prefers this latter interpretation and reading.

Question: Now how are all the promises of God, yea, certain truth in Christ?

Answer: By various ways:

(i) Partly, in that Jesus Christ (*yesterday, today, and ever the same,* Hebrews 13:8) is the principal mystery and matter of the promises. One way or other they all tend to him, terminate in him, and center themselves upon him. He being still yea and amen; the promises in him are still *yea and amen* also.

(ii) Partly, in that Jesus Christ, as he is the chief matter, so he is the chief object to and with whom, and the great motive in and for whom he makes his promises and Covenant. The Covenant of Faith and the promises thereof, are first made with and to Christ, and then to all his spiritual seed in him and for his sake, as hath been formerly proved.

(iii) Partly, in that the Covenant of Faith, but especially this New Covenant and the promises thereof, have their assured foundation, firm establishment, and unalterable ratification or sanction, in the death and blood of Jesus Christ the Mediator, Surety and Testator thereof (Galatians 3:17, Hebrews 9:15-17 & 7:22).

(iv) Partly, in that none can have God's Covenant and promises savingly theirs indeed, effectually communicated to them and accomplished in them, till they actually become Christ's. *And if ye be Christ's, then are ye Abraham's seed, and heirs according to the promise.* That is a good note: "As Christ is the same in God's promises which are unchangeable, so are all such promises touching our salvation, *yea*, that is, truth; and *amen*, that is, assurance – for so much as God in the New Covenant makes no promises of salvation, nor fulfills any, but in Christ, and by Christ."

(b) Remission of sins forever, so as to have them remembered by God against us no more; and redemption from the curse due for sin – *that the blessing of Abraham might come upon the Gentiles through Jesus Christ, that we might receive the promise of the Spirit through faith* (all of which are the proper benefits of the New Covenant) – are meritoriously procured only by the death and mediation of Jesus Christ (Hebrews 10:10-19, Galatians

3:13-14). Consequently, Christ's meritorious mediation – procuring for us these New Covenant mercies from God – is also the moving and procuring cause of the New Covenant itself.

(c) Jesus Christ brings us to be God's New Covenant people and children by faith: *For ye are all the children of God by faith in Christ Jesus.* Consequently, Jesus Christ and his merit is the motive why God makes, and makes good this New Covenant to us, assuring us of this highest covenant relation to God.

Thus the efficient cause or author, the occasion, and impulsive causes of this New Covenant have been unfolded and cleared in these two aphorisms – now consider a few inferences from them both together.

Inferences

(1) Hence the New Covenant, thus authorized and erected, thus promised, established and applied by God – Father, Son, and Holy Spirit – must needs be an exceedingly wise, holy, faithful, gratuitous, and righteous Covenant.

[1] An exceedingly wise Covenant. For it is contrived by the only wise God,[1747] and by the joint counsel of the whole Trinity of the blessed persons in the Godhead. The Father of lights (even of all lights, natural, spiritual, and celestial) has clothed it with the beams of his light and brightness.[1748] The Son, the wisdom of God *in whom are hid all treasures of wisdom and knowledge,* has imprinted his wisdom upon it.[1749] The Holy Ghost, that Spirit of truth, wisdom and understanding, has secured it from all error and folly.[1750] Every

---

[1747] 1 Timothy 1:17
[1748] James 1:17
[1749] 1 Corinthians 1:24, Colossians 2:2-3
[1750] John 14:17, Isaiah 11:2

Covenant of God is wise, but this New Covenant is eminently wise, for: {1} the defects of all former Covenants are fully supplied in this. {2} The wisdom and perfections of all former Covenants are digested and molded into this. {3} Completeness of provision for sinners' salvation is comprised ultimately in this, both for Jews and Gentiles – no other being to succeed and vacate it until the world's end. {4} The brightest glory of divine wisdom in the face of Jesus Christ shines out most clearly in this.[1751] {5} By this New Covenant, the federates are assured of more saving wisdom and general knowledge of the Lord than in all former Covenants.[1752] {6} And by this New Covenant, the Lord has so fully provided for the peace and consolation of a poor bruised, wounded and broken-hearted sinner, that no temptations, scruples, or objections can assault him, but by the help of this New Covenant skillfully improved, they may be resisted and removed.

[2] An exceedingly holy Covenant. It is very pure, holy, and separate from all sinful pollution – not only in regard of the federates, matter, form, and end thereof, which are very holy, but especially with regard to the author and Mediator thereof which are most holy.[1753] The Lord is holy in all his works, especially in his spiritual works, such as are his covenant contrivances. The most holy God imprints a holy character upon every ordinance that comes out of his hand.[1754]

[3] An exceedingly firm and faithful Covenant. For: {1} the Author of it is the most faithful and unchangeable God, *who cannot lie, will not repent, and with whom is no variableness nor shadow of turning*;[1755] {2} the Surety, Mediator and Testator of it is Jesus Christ, who has established it by his own death and blood, past all revocation or alteration;[1756] {3} and the Applier of it

---

[1751] 2 Corinthians 3:18 & 4:6
[1752] Hebrews 8:11
[1753] Isaiah 6:3
[1754] Psalm 145:17
[1755] 2 Timothy 2:13, Titus 1:3, Hebrews 5:6-7 & 7:17, James 1:17
[1756] Hebrews 7:22 & 9:15-17

is the Spirit of Truth: abiding in the faithful forever (John 14:16-17; 2 Thessalonians 2:13-14, Acts 2:1, 38-39).

[4] An exceedingly gratuitous Covenant – being bottomed or grounded upon nothing, procured by nothing at all in man, Jew or Gentile; but wholly flowing from the fountain of God's rich free grace, according to the mere good pleasure of his will, as has been shown.[1757]

[5] And lastly, this New Covenant is most righteous and equal, forasmuch as it is established upon Christ's meritorious mediation – whereby God's justice is fully satisfied for man's sin by a full price paid;[1758] as well as the sinner redeemed from sin and misery, and restored to divine favor by Jesus Christ.[1759]

I only touch at these things now, and pass: because these, with many such like, will hereafter come under consideration in opening the properties and perfections of this New Covenant.

(2) Hence, the *New Covenant* is an excellent antidote against the greatest adversities and afflictions of God's covenant people. This inference flows clearly from the first occasion which God took of promising this New Covenant by the prophet Jeremiah to his covenant people the Jews.[1760] They were at that time in extreme distress in their Babylonian captivity, they saw no visible way or possibility of deliverance, they were even as helpless and hopeless as dead dry bones in their graves, saying: *Our bones are dried, and our hope is lost, we are cut off for our parts.*[1761] Now at that time, God had made an un-captivating Covenant with them, stored with many choice and comfortable promises for their support against their present pressing distresses; which Covenant and promises he did much inculcate and reiterate to them, as is evident in Jeremiah chapters 29-33. Notwithstanding, the Lord thought not

---

[1757] Hebrews 8:8, 10, 12 & 10:16-17
[1758] Hebrews 10:5-21, Ephesians 5:2
[1759] Hebrews 9:12-14; 1 Peter 1:18-19, Galatians 3:13-14, Romans 5:9-10
[1760] Jeremiah 31:31 with the context foregoing and following
[1761] Ezekiel 37:11

this enough for their consolation and support; and therefore over and above all (that he might advance their comforts eminently indeed), he promises that the days should come, wherein he would make a New Covenant with the house of Israel and Judah, far surpassing that Sinai Covenant, that Old Covenant, under which they were: upon this Covenant chiefly they should set their minds and hearts; hence they should extract their sweetest consolations, against all their present tribulations. As if the Lord had told them: "O mine afflicted captives, I have spread before you many consolations in the promises both of the Old Covenant made when I brought your fathers out of Egypt, and of my present Covenant made with you under your captivity: but further I tell you for your comfort, I have better promises, and a better Covenant, affording better comforts, in store for you hereafter; I will make a New Covenant with you in the after-days, I will keep my best wine until then, I have treasured up my choicest cordials therein, Come therefore to these wells of salvation and draw waters with joy. No covenant consolations against distresses can compare with my New Covenant consolations."

Question: But whence or whereupon is it, that this New Covenant is so eminently consolatory, such an excellent antidote, against the greatest afflictions of God's covenant people?

Answer: This comes to pass from the nature and perfections of the New Covenant, far excelling all foregoing covenants. The New Covenant is a very shop or treasury of richest cordials; of most sovereign antidotes. For:

[1] *The New Covenant most fully and sweetly removes all our transgressions, the procuring cause of all our afflictions*. Sin is the original cause and inlet of all sorrow,[1762] and of death itself, and is the very gall of bitterness, poison of trouble, and sting of death.[1763] If sin be removed, the soul and venom of all affliction is removed: and nothing but the bare carcass, name, and shadow of affliction remains. The removal of the cause of the disease

---

[1762] Romans 5:12 & 6:23
[1763] Acts 8:23; 1 Corinthians 15:56

makes the most perfect cure. Now this New Covenant removes all our transgressions, so fully, that there needs no more sacrifice for sins; so sweetly, that the Lord will remember them no more. *This is the covenant that I will make with them after those days, saith the Lord: I will put my laws into their hearts, and in their minds will I write them: And their sins and iniquities will I remember no more. Now where remission of these is, there is no more offering for sin.*[1764] The Old Covenant renewed sacrifices yearly, daily; and remembered their sins yearly and daily, and therefore could not so fully comfort against the fruit of sin, affliction; but this New Covenant admits no more sacrifice for sin, Christ's once offering up of himself being enough forever; and therefore blots out our sins forever.[1765] O how sweet is this to an afflicted soul in covenant! My Covenant-God and Father lays his chastisements upon me; but my comfort is that the bitterness of all sorrow and death is past – he will remember my sins no more unto me.

[2] *The New Covenant most spiritually represents to us, and assures us of our restoration from deepest miseries, to greatest mercies: and therefore of all others is most comfortable against miseries and distresses.* Other Covenants set forth man's restoration from miseries to mercies; as from the serpent's head,[1766] from the general deluge of waters,[1767] from the Egyptian servitude to Canaan,[1768] from the wilderness to the land of rest and place which God should choose,[1769] from Babylonian captivity to Canaan's liberty, and under these their restoration from spiritual miseries, to spiritual and heavenly mercies was obscurely adumbrated.[1770] But this New Covenant most spiritually and plainly describes our redemption and restoration, from darkness to light, from sin to grace, from the power of Satan to God,[1771] from

---

[1764] Hebrews 10:16-18 & 8:12
[1765] Hebrews 10:1-3, etc.
[1766] Genesis 3:15
[1767] Genesis 6:17-18, etc.
[1768] Genesis 15:13
[1769] Deuteronomy 12:9-10, etc.
[1770] Ezekiel 37 throughout
[1771] Acts 26:17-18

the wrath of God to his Fatherly love and favor;[1772] from the curse to the blessing of Abraham;[1773] yea, of Jesus Christ, from death to life,[1774] from condemnation to salvation,[1775] and from hell to the highest heaven itself. Now this New Covenant – affording most comfortable assurance of our recovery from deepest spiritual miseries to greatest heavenly and eternal mercies – it must needs be most comfortable of all other against all lesser and outward afflictions. That Covenant which is most comfortable against the wrath of God, torments of hell, etc., must needs be most comfortable against the wrath of man, Babylon's bondage, etc.

[3] *The New Covenant most fully displays and conveys Jesus Christ to us; who is our primary hope and rock of all consolation.* Christ was in former Covenants displayed obscurely under remote promises and types, and conveyed sparingly to that one select nation of the Jews, scarce an handful to the rest of the world; and accordingly their comforts were obscure and sparing: but in this New Covenant, Christ in all his spiritual glory is displayed openly with open face as exhibited already,[1776] and conveyed liberally even to people in all nations of the world.[1777] Now the more fully Christ is displayed and conveyed in any Covenant, the more fully is that Covenant comfortable in all cases of disconsolation, afflictions or others. For Jesus Christ is our hope, the very rock and root of all our consolation from God (Philippians 2:1; 2 Thessalonians 2:16-17).[1778] His comforts are applied and proportioned to our crosses, *for as the sufferings of Christ abound in us, so our consolation also aboundeth by Christ*.[1779] The sufferings of Christians are counted the sufferings of Christ – so near is his union and relation to them; so dear are his sympathizings with them. And for their abounding crosses, Christ has

---

[1772] Romans 5:9-10
[1773] Galatians 3:13-14
[1774] Ephesians 2:1, 5
[1775] Romans 8:1
[1776] 2 Corinthians 3:12 to the end
[1777] Matthew 28:19-20, Mark 16:15-16
[1778] 1 Timothy 1:1
[1779] 2 Corinthians 1:4-5

abounding comforts. What then, though our tribulations abound, whilst Christ's consolations under them do also equally abound or super-abound?

After holy Stephen, the proto-martyr, had seen heaven opened and Jesus standing at the right hand of God, this blessed glimpse of Christ in glory, upheld his Spirit victoriously and triumphantly against that cruel shower of stones by which he fell asleep.[1780] Yea, so strong and predominant are Christ's consolations, that being thoroughly shed abroad in the heart, they are able to make such an entranced soul follow Christ, not only through torments, and death, but (if it were possible) through hell itself. Hence, notably Ignatius – inflamed with the love, and upheld with the comforts of Christ – said: "Now begin I to be a disciple, being zealous after nothing of visibles or invisibles, that I may obtain Jesus Christ. Let fire and cross, and the joint insurrection of wild beasts, anatomies, dilacerations, dissipations of my bones, dissections of my members, dissolutions of my whole body, and the punishment of the devil, come upon me – that I may obtain Jesus Christ."[1781]

[4] *The New Covenant most plenteously confers upon the federates the Holy Spirit*. The former Covenants afforded, as it were, some drops and sprinklings of the Spirit, in some dark, sparing and seldom promises; but under this New Covenant, the Holy Spirit is plentifully shed forth, poured out abundantly in showers and rivers upon believers.[1782] Hence Christ said: *Whosoever drinketh of the water that I shall give him, shall never thirst: but the water that I shall give him shall be in him a well of water springing up into everlasting life*.[1783] And elsewhere more fully: *He that believeth on me, as the Scripture hath said; out of his belly shall flow rivers of living water. But this spake he of the Spirit, which they that believed on him should receive: for the Holy Ghost was not yet given, because Jesus was not yet glorified*.[1784] That is, the

---

[1780] Acts 7:55 to the end
[1781] Ignatius in Epist. ad Roman. p. 86. Oxon. 1644.
[1782] Acts 2:1, 4, 16-18, 33
[1783] John 4:14
[1784] John 7:37-39

Holy Spirit was not yet so plentifully and abundantly given until Christ's ascension, which was not to be till Christ had established his New Covenant by his death.

Now the Holy Spirit being most plenteously given under this New Covenant; consequently, this New Covenant must needs afford the most full and plenteous comforts against, not only the federates' afflictions, but also all other their disconsolate cases and conditions whatsoever. For: {1} The Holy Spirit is the comforter, by office, abiding in the hearts of Christ's disciples forever. They that have this Comforter in them forever must needs have a fountain; an inexhausted treasury of all saving comfort in them forever.[1785] {2} The Holy Spirit peculiarly enables to that work, which is most proper and useful to ease and support an afflicted soul; namely: prayer – *Is any afflicted? Let him pray*[1786] – for *the Spirit helps our infirmities*, and especially our prayer infirmities, enabling us with groans unutterable to cry *Abba Father.*[1787] {3} The Holy Spirit notably assures us of our good childlike condition and relation towards God, and of our everlasting inheritance in the highest heavens, being *a witness with our spirits that we are the children of God,*[1788] and a seal after our believing, and *an earnest of our inheritance until the possession of the purchased redemption.*[1789] Now when once these two grand privileges are clearly and strongly assured to us, namely: that we ourselves are the children of God, and that the everlasting heavenly inheritance is ours, what shocks of trouble shall we not abide? What extremities of distresses shall not we very easily overcome?

[5] ***The New Covenant most powerfully disposes and raiseth up the soul to a capacity of consolation in all conditions, and at last most effectually lays a foundation of sweet support and comfort therein.*** This is

---

[1785] John 14:16-17
[1786] James 5:13
[1787] Romans 8:15, 26
[1788] Romans 8:16
[1789] Ephesians 1:13-14

very evident in the whole body of the New Covenant mercies promised, which are all of them most admirable cordials to the federates. For, this New Covenant assures:

{1} That *from the greatest to the least, they shall all know the Lord.*[1790] Now the right knowledge of the Lord – of his perfections in himself, of his proceedings with his people in all regards, and particularly in their afflictions – makes them wisely consider that all is from his Fatherly hand in love, and faithfulness, and prudence for their spiritual and eternal good (Hebrews 12:5-12; 1 Corinthians 10:13, Psalm 119:75, 67, 71, Isaiah 28:24 to the end, Romans 5:3-5; 2 Corinthians 4:16-18). Now this disposes and raises up the soul exceedingly to a capacity of consolation.

{2} That God will put his laws into their minds and write them in their hearts. Their hearts shall have in them as it were a counterpane of God's laws; there shall be an harmonious consent between God's laws and their hearts, between his will & their wills, that they shall have an inward Principle of sanctification and grace inclining them readily and cheerfully to do and endure what the Lord shall please. Here is now an excellent disposition to, and foundation of contentment and consolation. For usually, it is the stubbornness, perverseness, frowardness, hardness and intractableness of our hearts that makes our conditions, especially our afflicted conditions so harsh, grievous and uncomfortable to us. Our vexing and chafing at the yoke, proves more afflicting than the very yoke itself. Christ himself first had the law of God in his heart, in the midst of his bowels: and then he delighted to do the will of his father, yea to endure his will also in that sharpest conflict of laying down his life and pouring out his blood for us.[1791]

{3} That *God will be merciful to our unrighteousnesses, and will remember our sins and transgressions no more.* Sin unpardoned, is the affliction of affliction. Nothing in the world is so bitter upon the Spirit, and lies so heavy

---

[1790] Hebrews 8:10-12, Jeremiah 31:31-34
[1791] Psalm 40:6-10 with Hebrews 10:5-11

upon the heart as this. When sin is pardoned, in heaven and in the heart, then the storm is over, though the waves of affliction dash never so impetuously.[1792] Then the tossed soul can lift up head and heart above water with this consolation: *I am troubled on every side, yet not distressed; perplexed, but not in despair; persecuted, but not forsaken; cast down, but not destroyed;*[1793] I am sore pained, but yet all my sins are pardoned; I am *chastened by the Lord*, but I *shall not be condemned with the world*.[1794]

{4} That the Lord will be to me a God, and I shall be to him one of his covenant people. O this affords, not only a spring, but even a sea of comfort against all afflictions and disconsolate conditions. If God is mine, what can I lack? If I am God's, what can hurt me? etc. But this ocean of comfort I shall not further sail in until I come to handle this particular covenant mercy in the matter of this New Covenant – there see.

[6] ***The New Covenant judiciously considered and improved, most satisfactorily answers all the perplexing scruples and objections of the afflicted.*** The doubts and objections of the afflicted under afflictions, are the sad aggravations of their afflictions, for these distress the heart, that should bear up all the rest above distress. If then this New Covenant is so sweetly contrived by the Lord, that it is sufficient to repel and remove all the troublesome doubts and scruples of the afflicted, how excellent an antidote and cordial it is against all afflictions!

Let us a little imagine and suppose what their doubts and objections may be, especially in extremity of long afflictions.

[1792] In foro poli et in foro soli.
[1793] 2 Corinthians 4:8-9
[1794] 1 Corinthians 11:32

{Objection 1}: The Lord has called my sins to remembrance, by this his severe rod.[1795] *He numbereth my steps, doth he not watch over my sin? My transgression is sealed up in a bag, and he soweth up mine iniquity.*[1796] – *He writeh bitter things against me, and maketh me to possess the iniquities of my youth.*[1797]

Answer: The New Covenant tells you: *The Lord will be merciful to thine unrighteousnesses, and thy sins and iniquities will he remember no more.*[1798] He has passed an act of oblivion upon them forever: and therefore in propriety of speech, he will never punish you for your iniquities. Your afflictions may be: (i) παιδειαι, *fatherly chastisements, teaching chastisements* (Hebrews 12:5, 7); (ii) δοκιμαι, *probations* or *trials* (2 Corinthians 8:2); (iii) πειρασμοι, *temptations* (1 Corinthians 10:13, James 1:2, 12, Revelation 3:10), but they shall not be properly (iv) τιμωριαι, the punishments of an angry sin-avenging God (Hebrews 10:29).

{Objection 2}: But I lack a gracious and sanctified heart, patiently, contentedly, and silently to bear the indignation of the Lord without murmuring, repining, fainting, etc.; my principles are very bad.

Answer: The New Covenant assures you that God will give his laws into your mind, and write them in your heart.[1799] And this brings the whole frame of sanctification, and all the treasures of grace into your soul. And of all others, these are the best principles.

{Objection 3}: I want wisdom and skill, to know why the Lord contends with me, and to improve mine afflictions for my spiritual and eternal advantage.

[1795] 1 Kings 17:18
[1796] Job 14:16-17
[1797] Job 13:26
[1798] Hebrews 8:12
[1799] Hebrews 8:10

Answer: This New Covenant promises: (i) that you shall know the Lord,[1800] and that will make you wise to discern the Lord's intendments [intentions], and skillful in the managing of all his chastisements advantageously (James 1:2-5); (ii) that he will give his laws into your heart and mind.[1801] And therefore his laws within, will instruct you as his rod without does correct you: *Blessed is the man whom thou chastenest, O LORD; and teachest him out of thy law* (Psalm 94:12). Oh it is a happy thing indeed when the Lord's instruction accompanies the Lord's correction!

{Objection 4}: Oh I shall never hold out under all this sore and long Trial: my heart will break, my spirit will fail, one day I shall perish in these extremities.[1802] *Oh that my grief were thoroughly weighed, and my calamity laid in the balances together! For now it would be heavier than the sand of the Sea, therefore my words are swallowed up.*[1803]

Answer: Yet this New Covenant affords you a rock of refreshment. He will be your God, and you shall be one of his covenant-people.[1804] What? Cannot your God contract and conclude your trials when he pleases? And cannot he meanwhile keep up your heart? Is not he *the Father of mercies and the God of all consolations*? (2 Corinthians 1:3). And *are the consolations of God small with thee*? (Job 15:11). If God is for you, who shall be against you? (Romans 8:32). If God upholds you, who shall cast you down? Say with David: *Mine heart and my strength faileth me, but God is the Rock of mine heart, and my portion forever* (Psalm 73:26).

{Objection 5}: Alas, now you touch me to the quick, now you wound me to the heart. Oh, if the Lord is with me, if he is my God, why then is all this

---

[1800] Hebrews 8:11
[1801] Hebrews 8
[1802] 1 Samuel 27:1
[1803] Job 6:2-3
[1804] Hebrews 8:10

befallen me?[1805] – *The LORD hath forsaken me, and my God hath forgotten me.*[1806] Oh, *Wherefore hidest thou thy face, and holdest me for thine enemy?*[1807]

Answer: This New Covenant is not a changeable or vanishing, but an Everlasting Covenant.[1808] And therefore, if ever you were persuaded upon good grounds that the Lord was your God according to this Covenant, then he is your God still, and will be your God forevermore. He may for a while hide his face, and suspend your sense of his wonted favors for a little moment: but *with everlasting kindness will he have mercy upon thee.*[1809] He cannot forsake you, nor forget you, nor count you for his enemy – any more than he can forget this his everlasting Covenant, no more than the blood of this Covenant can be shed a second time. Hearken not to your present sense, *consult not with flesh and blood*; but live by faith, and cleave close to this Covenant. Afflicted Zion said: *The LORD hath forsaken me, and my Lord hath forgotten me.* But what said the answer of the Lord? *Can a woman forget her sucking child, that she should not have compassion on the son of her womb? Yea, they may forget, yet will I not forget thee. Behold, I have graven thee upon the palms of my hands: thy walls are continually before me.*[1810] This was God's comfort to his afflicted Zion; let it be your consolation [also], O distressed soul.

---

[7] Finally, this New Covenant establishes the most constant and lasting consolation to its federates, because it shall not be broken and laid aside as the Old Covenant was, but shall still continue new, and remain until the end of the world (Matthew 28:18-20; 1 Corinthians 11:26, Hebrews 13:20). Now those consolations that are most continuing are most consolatory.

[1805] Judges 6:13
[1806] Isaiah 49:14
[1807] Job 13:24
[1808] Hebrews 13:20
[1809] Isaiah 54:7-8
[1810] Isaiah 49:14-16

(3) Hence, the New Covenant administration far excels that of the Old, and the good condition of the New Covenant people far surpasses that of the Jews under the Old Covenant. The divine influences of Father, Son, and Holy Spirit, unto the promising, establishing, and applying of this New Covenant, as also the riches of divine grace thereunto, being more clearly, plenarily and gloriously manifested than in reference to the Old. But I shall hereafter have more fit and full occasion to speak to this particular – and therefore now I add no more.

Thus far of the efficient, occasion, and impulsive causes of this New Covenant.

Chapter 4

Of the federates, or parties to this New Covenant.

After the particular handling of the efficient or author of this New Covenant, together with the occasion taken, and impulsives moving thereunto. In the next place, the federates or covenanting parties to this New Covenant are to come under Consideration. In every Covenant properly so called, and so in this New Covenant, these things are necessarily required: namely: (1) parties covenanting – a covenant is not of one alone, but of two at least, or of more than two; (2) the mutual consent and agreement of such parties upon certain matters, articles, points, terms or conditions propounded reciprocally; (3) the interposing or intervening of some fit middle person having interest in both parties to bring on and make up this agreement: when otherwise the parties are at too great a distance one from another, or either of them proves unable to perform the agreement without a surety undertaking for the impotent party. This is the case between God and man: the distance between them is extremely great.[1811] Man of himself is utterly unable to undertake and perform the covenant terms or conditions with God;[1812] Christ God-man a fit middle person having sufficient interest in both God and man interposes as Mediator to bring them together in a sweet covenant agreement, undertaking for man the impotent party that he shall perform,[1813] as a Surety of the Covenant.[1814] The first of these, the federates, shall be treated on in this fourth chapter; the second, the matters or terms agreed and consented to, in the fifth chapter; the third, namely: the Mediator and Surety of the Covenant, Christ Jesus, in the sixth chapter (the blessed Lord and Mediator of this New Covenant assisting).

[1811] Romans 5:10 & 8:7, Colossians 1:21
[1812] Romans 5:6, John 15:5, Ephesians 2:1-3, 5, Philippians 2:13
[1813] 1 Timothy 3:16, John 1:14; 1 Timothy 2:5-6, Hebrews 9:15 & 12:24
[1814] Hebrews 7:22

The federates or parties to this New Covenant, are expressed both by Jeremiah and Paul in their mentioning of the New Covenant: *Behold the days come, saith JEHOVAH, that I will make a new covenant with the house of Israel and the house of Judah: Not according to the covenant that I made with their fathers*, etc. – *saith JEHOVAH, but this shall be the covenant that I will make with the house of Israel, after those days, saith JEHOVAH; I will put my law in their inward parts*, etc.[1815] Here it is evident, who are the federates or parties to this New Covenant: namely:

(1) The first and principal party is God, as **Jehovah** – *saith Jehovah, I will make a new covenant, etc. Not according to the covenant, etc. saith Jehovah: – But this the covenant that I will make – saith Jehovah*. God makes; man accepts this Covenant – God therefore is the principal federate. He makes it as **Jehovah**, as the LORD – this is thrice expressed: {*saith Jehovah*}. I will not peremptorily aver that herein the Trinity of persons is intimated, every of which persons is **Jehovah**: but yet God **Jehovah** – Father, Son, and Holy Spirit (as has been shown) – do concur in making this New Covenant. This God the LORD is the primary party, touching which there is no difficulty.

(2) The second and less principal party is expressed two ways, namely: [1] the house of Israel and the house of Judah (Jeremiah 31:31, Hebrews 8:8). Both are mentioned as the joint covenanting party on the other hand, with God the LORD. [2] The house of Israel (Jeremiah 31:33, Hebrews 8:10). This alone is mentioned in the repetition of the phrase, without recital of the house of Judah. In the former expression, the house of Israel is discretive distinctly opposite to the house of Judah; in the latter, the house of Israel seems to be collective and complexive, as comprising in it the house of Judah also. So that for substance, both of these expressions amount to one and the same. We shall so understand the meaning of these phrases, in the explanation of this ensuing aphorism touching the federates or parties to this New Covenant.

[1815] Jeremiah 31:31-33 & Hebrews 8:8-10, etc.

Aphorism 1

The confederates, or federate parties to the New Covenant, are, on the one hand, God the LORD, or God as Jehovah, the principal party; on the other hand, the house of Israel, and the house of Judah, in Christ, the less principal party; that is, the Jews, Israel, and Judah united, and their seed; as also the Gentiles that shall be called and their seed.

This aphorism I explain and confirm, as follows.

(1) **The first and principal federate, is God the LORD; or, God as the LORD; or, as** *Jehovah*. [1] That God, as **Jehovah**, or as the LORD; in that precise notion and consideration here offers himself as the chief federate party, is plain in the words wherein he promised at first to make this New Covenant.[1816] [2] What this imports, that he is the chief federate, as the LORD; or, as **Jehovah**, has been heretofore sufficiently explained in the opening of the Old Covenant[1817] – the substance whereof is applicable here analogically.

(2) **The second and less principal federate party is the house of Israel and the house of Judah** (Jeremiah 31:31, 33, Hebrews 8:8, 10). The sense of these terms and phrases may be thus in brief represented:

[1] {*Israel*} – that is, *one-that-as-a-prince-has-power-with-God*. {1} It was first given by the Lord as a surname to Jacob, upon occasion of Jacob's wrestling in prayer with the angel, and prevailing for a blessing from him: and at the same time the interpretation of the name was annexed.[1818] {2} And it is

---

[1816] Jeremiah 31:31-33 & Hebrews 8:8-10
[1817] In Book 3, Chapter 4, Aphorism 3
[1818] Genesis 32:24-30

afterwards applied: (i) sometimes, more restrictively to all the natural seed or posterity of the patriarch Jacob, that is, Israel – and thus the people of God, the Jews, even the whole Jewish church under the Old Testament, are often styled Israel, because they descended of Israel, as Psalm 25:22 & 128:6, Isaiah 1:3 & 14:1, and often in the Old Testament. As also in the New Testament, Matthew 8:10 & 27:9, Luke 1:80, 2:34 & 7:9, John 1:31, 35 & 9:15, Romans 9:31, 10:1, 19, 21 & 11:1, 25-26. In this sense, they are called sometimes {*Israel and Judah*}, because the tribe of Judah (which was part of Israel) was a very potent tribe, wherein the royal line was settled in David and his seed, and whence Christ according to the flesh should come[1819] – as 2 Samuel 11:11 & 12:8 & 24:1; 1 Kings 1:35 & 4:20, 25, and Psalm 114:2. But especially they are called {*Israel and Judah*} after the rending of the kingdom in the days of Jeroboam, the ten tribes departing from Judah and from David's family, as Jeremiah 36:2 & 51:5, Hosea 1:11, Zechariah 1:9 & 11:14, and in this sense they are here styled {*Israel and Judah*} in this New Covenant (Jeremiah 31:31, 33, Hebrews 8:8, 10). God, having reference to their former division, promised in this Covenant again to reunite them as one covenant people. (ii) Sometimes, more comprehensively and largely, to the whole Christian church of God both of Jews and Gentiles. Thus the whole Christian church is called {*the Israel of God*} (Galatians 6:16) and {*the house of Jacob or Israel*} (Luke 1:33). Unto which is opposed, Israel according to the flesh, namely: the carnal posterity of Israel, who believed not, but rested in outward formalities of religion (1 Corinthians 10:18). And in this comprehensive sense, the word {*Israel*} seems here to be taken (Hebrews 8:8, 10, Jeremiah 31:31, 33), as hereafter I shall endeavor to make more fully appear.

[2] {**House of Israel, and house of Judah**} – {*House*} is taken in Scripture: {1} properly, for an edifice, structure, or building erected to dwell in, as Judges 16:26-27, 29-30; 2 Samuel 15:16 & 20:3; 2 Chronicles 8:15, Nehemiah 12:37, Psalm 132:3; {2} improperly, by a metonymy, for those who

---

[1819] Genesis 49:8-13, Judges 1:1-2, etc; 2 Samuel 2:4, etc. & 7:5-18, Hebrews 7:14

are contained and dwell in the house. The inhabitants, the family, are called {*the house*}, as in Genesis 7:1 & 18:19, John 24:15, John 4:53, Acts 10:2; 1 Corinthians 1:16, and Hebrews 11:7, thus it is used very frequently. According to this sense, {*house*} is put: (i) sometimes, for the family, stock, or ancestors whence one descends, as Genesis 12:1 & 20:13, Luke 15:17-18, and 16:27. (ii) Sometimes, for the posterity, seed, or issue of such ancestors, whether amounting only to a family, as Genesis 7:1, 7, Joshua 24:15, or to a tribe, as the house of Issachar, that is, the tribe of Issachar (1 Kings 15:27). {*The house of Judah*}, that is, the tribe of Judah (2 Samuel 2:7, 10-11, Hosea 1:7 & 5:12, 14, or {*the kingdom of Judah*} (as Isaiah 37:31, Ezekiel 4:6), and thus it is used here for the kingdom of Judah, distinct from Israel (Jeremiah 31:31, Hebrews 8:8). {*The house of Israel*}, that is, the ten tribes which descended from Israel, but fell off from the house of David (1 Kings 12:21 & 20:31, Isaiah 46:3), thus the house of Israel is opposed to the house of Judah (as Jeremiah 31:31 and Hebrews 8:8). Or {*the house of Israel*}, that is, the whole twelve tribes, Judah also being comprehended in the phrase (as Exodus 16:31, Joshua 21:45, and often). Thus largely also, the house of Israel is to be taken in the latter mention of the federates of this New Covenant (Jeremiah 31:33, Hebrews 8:10). This is the sense and use of these words and phrases {*Israel*}, {*Judah*}, {*house of Israel*}, and {*house of Judah*} in Scripture, which may more specially help us to understand here, whom God intends for his federates in this New Covenant by {*house of Israel*} and {*house of Judah*}.

Now therefore that I may more distinctly and clearly discover these New Covenant federates with God. Who they are, I shall lay down and make good these positions following, namely:

[1] That Israel and Judah, even the whole body of the Jews united in one, in Christ, were first and immediately intended to be federates with God in this New Covenant. [2] That the Gentiles, whom afterwards God should call and incorporate into one church body with the Jews in Christ, were next intended to be confederates with the Jews in this New Covenant. [3] That the house,

posterity, issue, or seed of Jews united, and Gentiles called, were with their parents or ancestors intended by God to be taken in as confederates, in this New Covenant. By {*house of Israel*} and {*house of Judah*}: (i) the Jews united; (ii) the Gentiles called, as well as Jews; (iii) the posterity and children of both such Jews and Gentiles; are intended to be federates with God in this New Covenant.

Position 1

That Israel and Judah, or the house of Israel and Judah, that is, the whole body of the Jews, or Jewish church, united in Christ, were first and immediately intended to be federates with God in this New Covenant: is evident upon these grounds.

(1) Because these phrases {*the house of Israel*} and {*the house of Judah*}., (under which God describes his New Covenant federates) do in their original, literal, and most usual acceptation in Scriptures denote the whole church and body of the Jews jointly together, as 2 Samuel 12:8, Jeremiah 31:27, Zechariah 8:13, Ezekiel 9:9, and therefore here in this promise of the New Covenant directed especially at first unto the Jews (Jeremiah 31:31, 33, Hebrews 8:8, 10), the whole church of the Jews, both of Israel and Judah, to be reduced again into one by Christ, must needs be immediately and primarily intended in these phrases, as federates with God in this New Covenant – and that in the first place before any other people. For it is but in a secondary place that these phrases denote the whole Christian church of Jews and Gentiles, in regard to the Gentiles' after-incorporation into the same body with the Jews (Galatians 6:16).[1820]

(2) Because the Lord God in his Covenant with his captives in Babylon, next preceding this New Covenant, promised this great mercy to them, under the parable of two sticks united in the prophet's hands, the collection and union of the dispersed of Judah and Israel into one nation and one kingdom under **David** their king and prince forever, and that they should no more be two nations, or two kingdoms.[1821] This cannot be understood literally of David, who was dead long before; nor does this promise have its full accomplishment but only in Christ Jesus the true **David** spiritually, who by his

---

[1820] Romans 11:17, 24, Ephesians 3:6 & 2:13 to the end
[1821] Ezekiel 37:15 to the end of the chapter

New Covenant gathered and united the scattered of Judah and Israel into one spiritual kingdom and church under himself – as I have formerly manifested in opening that Covenant. This great work began to be effected most notably on the feast of Pentecost.[1822]

(3) Because when this New Covenant was first promised to the captives of Judah in Babylon for their comfort; the then-divided houses of Israel and Judah are joined together in that promise, as those that hereafter should be joint federates in this New Covenant. That the houses of Israel and Judah were then divided, is plain, for from the time of Rehoboam when the ten tribes called Israel revolted, until that day they remained still actually divided: Israel being captivated and dispersed in Assyria, Media, etc., and Judah in Chaldea.[1823] That God promised that they should be joint federates united in this New Covenant, is also clear. *For behold the days come, saith the LORD, that I will make a new covenant with the house of Israel and the house of Judah.*[1824] Here they are expressed in two phrases, as united federates. And afterwards: *But this shall be the covenant that I will make with the house of Israel, after those days*, etc.[1825] Here they are both comprised in one phrase, though hitherto they have been two houses, two nations, two kingdoms – yet by my New Covenant after those days, they shall be one house of Israel in covenant with me.

(4) Because the doctrine and blessings of the New Covenant founded and established by Christ's death, were first solemnly published and effectually applied to a very considerable body of the Jews met at Jerusalem on the feast of Pentecost, not only out of Judea, but also out of every nation under heaven.[1826] This was a most solemn transaction, all things duly considered. For: [1] As the

---

[1822] Acts 2 throughout

[1823] "Erat vero tum (ut omnes norunt) in duas factiones scissum Davidis regnum, quas significat [proprieta] Novi pacti [interventii] [tuisus] conjunctum iri" Beza's Annotation on Hebrews 8:8

[1824] Jeremiah 31:31

[1825] Jeremiah 31:23

[1826] Acts 2:1 to the end

Lord God, fifty days after the sacrificing of the first passover, appeared to all Israel like devouring fire, and spoke his law – that Old Covenant – to them out of the midst of the fire, so the Holy Spirit, fifty days after the sacrificing of our great passover Jesus Christ for us, appeared to all this conflux of Jews in the shape of cloven tongues, as of fire sitting upon the heads of the apostles, speaking in all their languages the wonderful works of God, and mysteries of the New Covenant; as is especially evident in Peter's sermon, preaching Christ's life, passion, death, burial, resurrection, exaltation at God's right hand in highest glory as Lord and Christ, whence he had shed forth those admirable endowments of the Holy Spirit. [2] It was a singular and strange providence of God, that so great a body of Jews from all nations under heaven, not of Judah only, but of Israel, should meet at Jerusalem at that time, when this New Covenant doctrine in Christ should be so solemnly published after the establishment of it. Since the death of Jesus Christ, the like convention of Jews is not storied in all the New Testament. [3] The New Covenant doctrine was most effectually applied to them, to the conviction, contrition, and conversion of three thousand souls who were baptized and added to the Christian church under this New Covenant the self-same day, besides the many thousands which were added afterwards. This publication and application of New Covenant doctrine and mercies is first made to the Jews of Judah and Israel united in Christ before the tender thereof was made to any Gentiles.

(5) Because on that day of Pentecost, when the Jews pricked in their hearts, cried out to the apostles for a remedy – *Men and brethren what shall we do?*[1827] – Peter prescribed to them spiritual remedies: the New Covenant remedies: repentance and baptism, assuring them of those two great blessings of the New Covenant thereupon, namely: remission of sins, and the gift of the Holy Spirit. And this, because of the promise, namely: the covenant promise made to Abraham and his seed was first to them and to their children, and then to the Gentiles afar off whom God should call, and to their seed

---

[1827] Acts 2:36-39

proportionably: *Then Peter said unto them, Repent and be baptized everyone of you in the name of Jesus Christ, for remission of sins, and ye shall receive the gift of the Holy Ghost: For the promise is unto you and to your children; and to all that are afar off, even as many as the Lord our God shall call* (Acts 2:38-39).[1828] The words contain a spiritual remedy prescribed against a spiritual malady.

[1] The malady was trouble of heart and conscience for sin, and particularly for their guilt of Christ's blood in crucifying him (Acts 2:36-37).

[2] The spiritual New Covenant remedy against this malady is both propounded and proven.

{1} Propounded and directed, partly by commanding and imposing upon them a double New Covenant duty towards God, namely: to repent, and to be baptized in the name of Jesus Christ; partly by promising to them thereupon a double New Covenant blessing from God, namely: remission of sins, and the gift of the Holy Ghost (Acts 2:38).

{2} Proven and demonstrated, to be their New Covenant duty which they ought to perform to God, and to be their New Covenant blessing which they may expect from God, from the nature and large extent of the promise – first to them and their children, and then to the Gentiles afar off whom God shall call, and consequently to their children (verse 39). As if Peter had said: "O you Jews, pricked in heart for crucifying of Christ, here is your New Covenant remedy: repent and be baptized in the name of Christ, so your sins shall be remitted, and the gift of the Holy Ghost shall be conferred upon you, for God has intended and extended his covenant promise (requiring these duties, and assuring of these mercies) generally both to Jews and Gentiles, but first to you and your children, and then to all that are afar off, namely: the Gentiles whom the Lord shall call; and proportionably to their children." This I judge to be the clear genuine sense and intent of the words, without vexing or forcing of them. By {*promise*} I understand, not that particular promise in Joel precisely,

---

[1828] Genesis 12:2-3 & 17:8 & 22:16-18 & 26:3-4 & 28:12-14, etc.

which is fore-cited in this Chapter, but the ancient covenant promise made to Abraham, Isaac, and Jacob, and their seed, and to all nations in them.[1829] And my reasons are: (i) Because this promise is said to be to them and to their children, and to all afar off whom God shall call (this is the tenor of the Covenant with Abraham, Isaac and Jacob which is made with their seed, both of Jews and Gentiles). (ii) Because from their interest in this promise, they are exhorted and commanded to be baptized. Now no interest in any foregoing promise or Covenant, except those promises which are confirmed by Christ in the New Covenant, can be a sufficient warrant for partaking of baptism, which is peculiarly one of the tokens of the New Covenant only.[1830]

(6) Because the New Covenant doctrine in Christ exhibited was first preached, and the New Covenant tokens were first administered to the Jews – before they were tendered and dispensed to the Gentiles at all. For:

[1] The New Covenant doctrine was preached by John the Baptist, Jesus Christ, and his apostles more preparatorily before Christ's death to the Jews only, by John the Baptist (John 1:6-8, etc, verses 15-16, etc., verses 26-38; Matthew 3:1-3, 10-12, John 3:26 to the end), and by Jesus Christ (Matthew 4: 17, 23 & 5:2, etc.) See also the history of Christ throughout all the four evangelists testifying of Christ's New Covenant doctrine. By the apostles also, whom Christ sent forth and commanded them, saying: *Go not into the way of the Gentiles, and into any city of the Samaritans, enter ye not: But go rather to the lost sheep of the house of Israel. And as ye go, preach, saying: the kingdom of heaven is at hand*, etc.[1831]

[2] Although Christ had enlarged the apostles' commission after his resurrection to the discipling, baptizing and teaching all nations,[1832] yet notwithstanding the apostles preached the New Covenant doctrine more

---

[1829] Genesis 12:2-3 & 17:7-8 & 22:16-18 & 26:3-4 & 28:12-14, etc.
[1830] Romans 15:8-12
[1831] Matthew 10:5-7, etc.
[1832] Matthew 28:18-20

plenarily after Christ's ascension, to the Jews only at first.[1833] And afterwards to certain proselytes of the Greeks and Gentiles,[1834] and to the Samaritans.[1835] But they did not purposely and thoroughly set to the work of preaching the New Covenant doctrine to the Gentiles until Christ by special vision from heaven sent Peter to preach to Cornelius and his company, being Gentiles;[1836] and until the Jews began to reject the apostles' doctrine – contradicting and blaspheming it.[1837] *Then Paul and Barnabas waxed bold, and said, It was necessary that the word of God should first have been spoken to you, but seeing ye put it from you, and judge yourselves unworthy of everlasting life; lo, we turn to the Gentiles. For so hath the Lord commanded us, saying, I have set thee to be a light of the Gentiles, that thou shouldst be for salvation to the ends of the earth. And when the Gentiles heard this, they were glad, and glorified the word of the Lord: and as many as were ordained to eternal life believed.*

[3] The New Covenant tokens, namely: Baptism and the Lord's Supper, were first administered to the Jews only, before Christ's death;[1838] and for a good while also after his death to them and none other.[1839] Now by this preaching of the New Covenant doctrine, and dispensing baptism and the Lord's Supper, the New Covenant tokens, first unto the Jews only, it is plain that first and immediately God intended the Jews to be federates in this New Covenant with him. To this effect, that speech of Peter to the Jews is very observable: *Ye are the children of the prophets, and of the covenant which God made with our fathers, saying unto Abraham, and in thy seed shall all the kindreds of the earth be blessed. Unto you first, God having raised up his Son Jesus, sent him to bless you, in turning away everyone of you from his iniquities.*[1840]

[1833] Acts 2:5, etc.
[1834] Acts 6:1 & 8:35, etc.
[1835] Acts 8:1-26
[1836] Acts 10:1 to the end & 11:19-21
[1837] Acts 13:45-48
[1838] Matthew 3:5-6, John 4:1-2, Matthew 26:17-31
[1839] Acts 2:5, 41-42
[1840] Acts 3:25-26

(7) Because the Jews – the natural branches of the good olive tree – were some of them first broken off through unbelief;[1841] before the Gentiles, the branches of the olive tree wild by nature, were grafted in, in their stead by faith (their fall being the Gentiles' rise, their diminution the riches of the Gentiles, and their casting away the reconciling of the world).[1842] Nor were the Jews totally and finally broken off, but only *till the fullness of the Gentiles be come in*, that the salvation of the Gentiles may *provoke the Jews to jealousy*, and at last *all Israel may be saved*.[1843] Now the Jews being the natural branches, Gentiles wild branches; Jews first broken off, before Gentiles were grafted in, and after the Gentiles fullness, the Jews being to be grafted in again; it is evident that first and immediately God looked at the Jews as his federates in this New Covenant.

Consider all these six arguments together, and they fully prove the first position.

[1841] Romans 11:17-25
[1842] Romans 11:11-12, 15
[1843] Romans 11:12, 25-27

Position 2

That the Gentiles, whom afterwards God should call and incorporate into one church body with the Jews by Christ, were next intended to be joint federates with the Jews in this New Covenant with God.

This may be evinced by several arguments. For,

(1) The word {*Israel*} in God's Promise of the New Covenant, not only well may, but needs must comprise in it the Gentiles whom God should call, as well as the Jews.[1844] Forasmuch as:

[1] This word {*Israel*}: {1} Sometimes used in such latitude, as to comprehend the whole church of God both of Jews and Gentiles as Galatians 6:16, and why should it be restrained here, where God expresses who shall be his New Covenant federates? Does not God under these terms {*Israel*} and {*Judah*}, and then under one word {*Israel*} fully comprise all that should be federates with him? Certainly other Scriptures abundantly declare that God intended all the Gentiles which should be called to be federates as well as Jews in this New Covenant, as after will appear – and this many sufficiently expound to us, what God here intended by this word {*Israel*}, namely: all called Gentiles, as well as Jews in Christ. {2} The Gentiles were (according to God's frequent promises) to be Israelitized, to be made part of the Israel of God, by being engrafted into the good olive tree, to partake the root and fatness of the olive tree.[1845] That is, by being engrafted into the true church of Israel in covenant with God, to partake all church privileges with Israel. This the apostle excellently expresses, saying: *That the Gentiles should be fellow heirs, and of the same body, and partakers of his promise in Christ by the*

[1844] Jeremiah 31:31, 33, Hebrews 8:8, 10
[1845] Romans 11:17, 29

gospel.[1846] And some are of the opinion that Ephraim, [the ten] tribes, or Israel were in a sort, a type of the Gentiles. Nor does there lack a resemblance between them, for: (i) Israel were many more than Judah; so Gentiles many more than the church of God; (ii) Israel departed and separated themselves from under the rule of David's house; so Gentiles were actually severed from, and at enmity with the rule of Christ the true David (Ephesians 2:11-12); (iii) Israel was very idolatrous, not only worshiping the true God falsely in the two calves, but worshiping false gods, as Baal, Ashtaroth, etc; so Gentiles were carried away to these dumb idols even as they were led (1 Corinthians 12:2). (iv) Israel should at last be reunited to Judah (Ezekiel 37:16 to the end); so Gentiles should at last be incorporated into one body with the church of God (Romans 11:17, etc., Ephesians 3:6). Now God intending the Gentiles' union with Israel, that Jews and Gentiles should become one Israel, one church under the New Testament – how great cause have we to conclude that under this name {*Israel*}, God intended his whole church of Jews and Gentiles to be confederates with him in this New Covenant. {3} Learned and judicious

---

[1846] Ephesians 3:4-6; See Mr. [Beza] on this place.

writers, as Calvin,[1847] Pareus,[1848] and others[1849] understand by {*Israel and Judah*} (which then comprised the whole church of God), the whole church which should be made up after Christ's death, both of Jews and Gentiles.

[2] The calling and conversion of the Gentiles by the Gospel to partake with the Jews the grace, blessings, and benefits of the New Covenant in Jesus Christ, was from the beginning of the world intended by God, *the fellowship of this mystery from the beginning of the world being hid in God* (Ephesians 3:9 with verses 4-8). And accordingly it was by degrees (but very obscurely at the first) revealed and promised, until it came to be performed. As, *God shall enlarge Japheth* (or, *persuade Japheth*) *and he shall dwell in the tents of Shem*.[1850] Of Japheth came the Gentiles, especially the European Gentiles; in Shem's posterity especially true religion and the true church was continued. God himself should at last by his word and Spirit persuade Gentiles to embrace the true religion, and to dwell in the true church as members thereof.

[1847] "And he names the house of Israel and the house of Judah, because the posterity of Abraham had been divided into two kingdoms. So the promise is to gather again all the elect together into one body, however separated they may have been formerly." Calvin's commentary on Hebrews 8:8
[https://www.studylight.org/commentaries/eng/cal/hebrews-8.html]
<Accessed 4/1/2024>

[1848] "*Ecce dies venient*] Tempora Messiae exhibiti in carne designat, phrasi Prophetis Consueta. Tunc lgitur promittit se novum foedus pacturum cum Domo Israel & cum Domo Iudah. An vero ad solos Israelitas & Iudaeos pactum Novum pertinet? Nequaquam. Alibi enim ad omnes gentes extendit: Ies. 49. 22. & 66. 18. Ioel 2. Hag. 2. 8. Christus quoque Novi Testamenti graciam extendit ad omnes gentes: Docete omnes gentes. Praedicate omni creaturae, &c. Nomine igitur Domus Israel & Domuus Iudah universa Ecclesia Novi Testamenti insignitur: Quia olim duobus illis Regnis seu familils tota ecclesia continebatur. Cui, quia gentes inseri debuerunt, idem Nomen in Prophetarum Scriptis obtinent: & fideles Novi Testamenti non raro Spiritualis Israel Appellantur in Apostolorum Scriptis." David Pareus' commentary on Hebrews 8:8

[1849] "{*With the House of Israel, and with the House of Judah*} As verse 27, chapter 3:18. With the main body of my church consisting of Jews and Gentiles (Romans 11:25-26)." Large London Annotations on Jeremiah 31:31, 33.
"With my whole church of choice ones: {*with the House of Israel*} etc. Then, the party in the New Covenant is not all mankind, but the church of the New Testament: the spiritual Israel and Judah." David Dickson on Hebrews 8:8.

[1850] Genesis 9:27

So God told Abram: *In thee shall all the families of the earth be blessed.*[1851] Elsewhere: *In thy seed shall all the nations of the earth be blessed.*[1852] This the apostle applies to the Gentiles, saying: *And the Scripture foreseeing that God would justify the heathen through faith, preached before the gospel unto Abraham, saying, In thee shall all nations be blessed.*[1853] God said elsewhere to Christ: *Ask of me, and I will give thee the heathen for thine inheritance, and the uttermost parts of the earth for thy possession.*[1854] And again: *It is a light thing that thou shouldst be my servant, to raise up the tribes of Jacob, and to restore the preserved of Israel: I will also give thee for a light to the Gentiles that thou mayest be my salvation unto the end of the earth.*[1855] Christ also tells the Jews: *And other sheep I have, which are not of this fold* (namely: the Gentiles) *them also I must bring, and they shall hear my voice; and there shall be one fold, and one shepherd.*[1856] That of Paul's (to add no more) is pregnant: *Now I say that Christ was a minister of the circumcision for the truth of God, to confirm the promises made unto the fathers:*[1857] *And that the Gentiles might glorify God for his mercy, as it is written; for this cause I will confess to thee among the Gentiles, and sing unto thy name.*[1858] *And again he saith, Rejoice ye Gentiles with his people.*[1859] *And again: Praise the Lord all ye Gentiles and laud him all ye people.*[1860] And again Isaiah saith: *There shall be a Root of Jesse, and he that shall rise to reign over the Gentiles, in him shall the Gentiles trust.*[1861] The Scriptures abound with testimonies to this effect. Consequently, all such prophecies and promises touching the Gentiles' calling by Christ to partake of

---

[1851] Genesis 12:3
[1852] Genesis 22:18
[1853] Galatians 3:8
[1854] Psalm 2:8. See also Psalm 22:27-28 & 72:11 & 86:9 & 110:2-3
[1855] Isaiah 49:6 with Acts 13:46-47
[1856] John 10:16
[1857] Romans 15:8-13
[1858] Psalm 18:49
[1859] Deuteronomy 32:43
[1860] Psalm 117:1
[1861] Isaiah 11:10

the New Covenant's grace and mercies, must needs have their accomplishment in their becoming joint federates with the Jews in this New Covenant.

[3] Jesus Christ by his death, did meritoriously, virtually, and fundamentally incorporate the Gentiles into one church body with the Jews: of twain, making them one new man; of foreigners and strangers, making them *fellow-citizens with the saints, and of the household of God, fellow heirs and of the same body*.[1862] This great and blessed union of Jews and Gentiles, Christ Jesus meritoriously wrought by his death in various ways, namely: {1} by bringing the Gentiles nigh unto God, as the Jews were a people near unto him (Psalm 148:14) *Remember that ye being in time passed Gentiles in the flesh, – That at that time ye were without Christ*, etc. – *But now in Christ Jesus ye who sometimes were afar off, are made nigh by the blood of Christ for he is our peace who hath made both one*;[1863] {2} By redeeming the Gentiles as well as the Jews, from the curse, that they as well as Jews might share in the blessing of Abraham. *Christ hath redeemed us from the curse of the law: being made a curse for us: for it is written, cursed is everyone that hangeth on a tree: That the blessing of Abraham might come on the Gentiles through Christ; that we might receive the promise of the Spirit through faith.*[1864] {3} By reconciling the Gentiles as well as the Jews unto God: who were originally one as well as the other enemies to God. *And that he might reconcile both unto God in one body by the cross, having slain the enmity thereby, or, in himself*. Even the enmity between God and them, by reason of sin: and not only the enmity between Jews and Gentiles by reason of the ceremonial law.[1865] {4} By demolishing the partition wall of Levitical ordinances and ceremonies, which divided and distinguishing the Jews from all other nations, and set them at odds and enmity with all the Gentiles. *For he is our peace, who hath made both one, and hath broken down the middle wall of partition between us: Having abolished in*

[1862] Ephesians 2:13 to the end & 3:6
[1863] Ephesians 2:11-14
[1864] Galatians 3:13-14
[1865] Ephesians 2:16

his flesh the enmity, even the law of commandments contained in ordinances, for to make in himself of twain, one new man, so making peace.[1866] This was Christ's way: he takes away the partition and enmity that was between Jew and Gentile by reason of circumcision and other ceremonials, and so consolidates them in one – as a man that would make two rooms one, or two fields one; he pulls down the partition wall, and plucks up the hedge, and then it is done. {5} By vouchsafing unto the Gentile as well as the Jew a sweet access unto God as to a Father in all their suits and requests *For through him* (i.e. *Christ*) *we both* (namely: *Jew and Gentile*) *have an access by one Spirit unto the Father. Now therefore ye are no more strangers and foreigners, but fellow-citizens with the saints, and of the household of God*, etc.[1867] Thus, as Jesus Christ by his death established his New Covenant, founding it in his blood; so by his death he reduced Jews and Gentiles into one body mystical, that they might be equally joint federates in his New Covenant.

[4] Jesus Christ, having by his death, both actually established his New Covenant, and meritoriously united Jews and Gentiles into one body to be federates in his New Covenant; in the next place he proceeds to call the Gentiles by the preaching of his gospel, that they might formally and actually be united to the Jews by his New Covenant. And therefore being risen from the dead, before he ascended into heaven, he gave commission to his apostles, to disciple, baptize, and teach all nations. *Go ye into all the world, and preach the gospel to every creature*, etc.[1868] – *Go ye therefore and disciple ye all nations, baptizing them in the name of the Father, and of the Son, and of the Holy Ghost: Teaching them to observe all things whatsoever I have commanded you. And lo, I am with you all days, even unto the end of the world, Amen.*[1869] And speedily after his ascension, he caused his apostles actually to execute this his commission, as is evident in the history of their Acts. But more especially, he

---

[1866] Ephesians 2:14-16
[1867] Ephesians 2:18-22
[1868] Mark 16:15-16
[1869] Matthew 28:18-20

commanded Peter by vision from heaven to go preach his New Covenant doctrine to Cornelius and his company,[1870] and by extraordinary voice and apparition from heaven he called Paul to be the great teacher of the Gentiles: *Delivering thee from the people and from the Gentiles, unto whom now I send thee, to open their eyes, and to turn them from darkness to light: and from the power of Satan unto God; that they may receive forgiveness of sins, and inheritance among them that are sanctified through faith that is in me* (Acts 26:15-18).[1871] Accordingly, the apostles and disciples preached this New Covenant doctrine to the Gentiles far and near, and the Lord crowned their labors – especially Paul's – with wonderful success in converting the Gentiles most abundantly throughout the world (Romans 15:16-20).[1872] This their preaching of the New Covenant doctrine both to Jews and Gentiles, was so authorized, commanded, assisted, blessed, prospered, and owned by Christ, was so much Christ's: that in their going and preaching, Christ himself is said to come and preach: *And coming* (that is, Christ coming by his authority, Spirit, efficacy, and spiritual presence with his apostles and ministers) *he evangelized peace to you which were afar off, and to them which were nigh*.[1873] Why did Christ take all this care after his death speedily to have the Gentiles called by the preaching of the New Covenant doctrine to them: but that he might actually enstate them with the Jews in all his New Covenant privileges settled on them both by his death?

[5] The promise (that is, the promise made to Abraham, Isaac and Jacob, touching God's blessing all nations, in their seed, confirmed and fulfilled in the New Covenant), equally belongs and is extended to the Gentiles that should be called, and to the Jews; it is made to both. Therefore Gentiles as well as Jews are federates therein. Hence Peter – preaching on the feast of Pentecost to that great assembly of Jews, wherein also were some Gentile proselytes (Acts 2:1, 5,

---

[1870] Acts 10:1 to the end
[1871] Acts 9:15 & 26:20 & 22:21, Romans 15:15-16, Ephesians 3:8-9
[1872] See the history of Peter in Acts 10-12, and of Paul in Acts 13 to the end of the book.
[1873] Ephesians 2:17

9-11) said: *Repent and be baptized everyone of you in the name of Jesus Christ for the remission of sins, and ye shall receive the gift of the Holy Ghost: For, the promise is unto you, and to your children; and to all that are afar off, even as many as the Lord our God shall call.*[1874] This promise – confirmed, fulfilled in, and digested into the New Covenant – belongs both to Jews and called Gentiles and to their children, and this is here urged as a ground why they should be baptized, and so actually installed into the New Covenant.

[6] The Gentiles called by the gospel, actually partake of New Covenant graces, privileges and benefits of all sorts, as well as the Jews; therefore God made them federates therein with himself, equally with the Jews, putting no difference between Jew and Gentile.[1875] Gentiles believed as well as Jews (Acts 15:7, 13:48 with 2:41-44); Gentiles had their hearts purified by faith, and were justified by faith without the deeds of the law as well as Jews (Acts 15:9, Galatians 3:8 with 2:16); Gentiles received the Holy Spirit as well as Jews (Acts 10:44-48); Gentiles were baptized as well as Jews (Acts 10:47-48 & 16:14-15, 32-33 with Acts 2:41); Gentiles received the Lord's supper, therein maintaining communion with Christ and one with another as well as Jews (Acts 20:7 with 2:42) – and in a word, the Gentiles came behind the Jews in no New Covenant blessing. How then can any imagine but that Gentiles as well as Jews were federates in this New Covenant?

[7] Finally, Paul declares to us that Abraham had two sons, namely: Ishmael and Isaac: that by a bond-maid, Hagar, this by a free-woman Sarah; that after the flesh, this after the Spirit and by Promise; and that these things are an allegory: the two mothers are two covenants, or resemble to us God's two covenants, namely: Hagar the bondwoman typed out the servile Old Covenant from Mount Sinai; Sarah the freewoman figured out the free New Covenant from Mount Zion.[1876] The two sons shadowed out the two sorts of churches and their conditions under these two covenants: Ishmael, the Jewish

---

[1874] Acts 2:38-39
[1875] Acts 10:34-35 & 15:9
[1876] Galatians 4:22-31

Church, the Jerusalem below in a state of bondage under the Old Covenants servile dispensation; Isaac, the Christian Church, the Jerusalem above, which is free, the mother of us all, whether Jews or Gentiles. *The desolate hath many more children, than she that had an husband.*[1877] And at last he concludes: *So then brethren, we* (that is, Jews and Gentiles now since Christ) *are not children of the bondwoman, but of the free.*[1878] Exhorting the Gentile Galatians to stand fast in this New Covenant liberty wherewith Christ has made us free.[1879] Thus he makes Gentiles called as well as Jews, federates and parties to this New Covenant.

Put all these seven particulars together, and the second position is clear beyond contradiction.

[1877] Isaiah 54:1, etc.
[1878] Galatians 4:31
[1879] Galatians 5:1, etc.

Position 3

The posterity, seed, or children both of believing Jews and called Gentiles, are – with their parents – federates in this New Covenant.

As Jewish and Gentile parents believing are in this New Covenant with God; so their seed, their children with them are in the same New Covenant. Both parents and children, both root and branches, are federates with God in this New Covenant, and so accounted by him. Although some would fain [gladly] void this New Covenant charter as to their children, and blot their interest out of Christ's last will and Testament.

This position may briefly be confirmed by these ensuing arguments, drawn partly from the New Covenant itself; partly from other Scriptures.

(Argument 1) All sorts of persons which are necessarily comprised under those New Covenant phrases, {*I will make a New Covenant with the house of Israel and with the house of Judah*} (Jeremiah 31:31, 33, Hebrews 8:8, 10). must needs be federates with God in this New Covenant.

This proposition is evident. For, in these phrases {*the house of Israel*} and {*house of Judah*}, God expresses all his New Covenant federates. Consequently, all sorts of persons, which here are necessarily comprised in and under these phrases, must needs be his New Covenant federates. Who can better signify to us in fit [suitable], full, and comprehensive terms or phrases God's New Covenant federates, than God himself the Author of this Covenant?

But the seed, posterity, or children of believing Jews and called Gentiles are necessarily comprised under those New Covenant phrases {*the house of Israel*} and {*the house of Judah*}, for:

[1] *House* or *family* most properly consists of parents and their seed, posterity or children. God said to Noah: *Come thou and all thine House into the ark* – and who went in, but parents and children? *And Noah went in, and his sons, and his wife, and his sons' wives with him.*[1880] These were all. David said, *Although my house be not so with God*, etc,[1881] that is, although I and my posterity are not as yet in this excellent flourishing condition, etc., yet God's Covenant with me and my seed is sure. He by {*house*} understood himself and his seed. Scriptures abound with like instances. Parents and their children are the integral parts of the house; servants are but accidentals.

[2] Otherwise, when this New Covenant was made, it was made only with the present parents then in being: their posterity being wholly left out of the Covenant. But this is absurd, for then the children of the New Covenant federates were in nature and condition altogether Christ-less, covenant-less, church-less, hopeless, God-less, as the very children of heathens, which is abominable to assert.[1882]

[3] Otherwise also, the Christianized Jews should become great losers by exchanging their Old Covenant condition and interest with this New Covenant condition. For by this means, their children are shut out of covenant with God, and have no covenant state or privilege under this New Covenant, which yet the Old Covenant afforded to them (Deuteronomy 5:2, 22 & 29:10-13, etc., with Genesis 17:7-8). This would have been small encouragement to the Jew to have become a Christian. This would have been an intolerable stumbling block before the Jew against the New Covenant. But doubtless the New Covenant privileges and advantages must needs be every way greater and larger than those of any fore-going Covenant whatsoever – the New Covenant being the highest, fullest, perfectest, last and best of all covenant expressures. Therefore, the children of believing Jews and called Gentiles must needs be federates with God in this New Covenant.

[1880] Genesis 7:1 with verse 7
[1881] 2 Samuel 23:3-5
[1882] Ephesians 2:11-12

(Argument 2) **All such sorts of persons as God admitted federates in the more imperfect expressures of the Covenant of Faith, are intended by God to be federates still in this most perfect expressure of the Covenant of Faith, the New Covenant.**

[1] That this New Covenant is the most perfect expressure of the Covenant of Faith, and all covenant expressures that went before were comparatively more imperfect; has already been manifested, and will afterwards be more fully cleared, and is in itself so evident that I think no rational man that is acquainted with the Scripture can contradict it.

[2] That such sorts of persons as were admitted by God federates in Covenants more imperfect, are intended still to be federates in this most perfect New Covenant, is a sequel so clear and cogent, from the lesser to the greater affirmatively, that it cannot rationally be denied, for the most perfect in any kind must needs comprise in it all perfections of the less perfect, and some perfections further. If it lacks any perfections or excellencies of that which is less perfect, it cannot be any longer most perfect.

But the seed, posterity, or children of professed believing parents both Jewish and Gentile are a sort of persons which were with their parents admitted federates by God in the more imperfect expressures of the Covenant of Faith. This is evident:

{1} Of the seed and children of Abraham, Isaac, and Israel: (i) *In God's Covenant with Abraham*. God established it with him and with his seed after him in their generations.[1883] And in Isaac, his covenant seed was called.[1884] This is one limitation of the covenant seed of Abraham.[1885] Again, the Lord limited the covenant seed of Isaac unto Jacob, for when Rebekah had conceived by one, by our father Isaac: *It was said to her, the elder shall serve the younger; as*

[1883] Genesis 17:7-9
[1884] Genesis 17:19, 21 & 21:12, Romans 9:7
[1885] Romans 9:10-13

it is written, Jacob have I loved, but Esau have I hated.[1886] And so the Covenant was settled on Jacob and all his seed without limitation, till they should break themselves off by unbelief. Thus all the seed of Abraham by Isaac and Jacob (except such as should cast off God's Covenant by infidelity) until the time of the New Covenant were still admitted federates with their parents. (ii) *In God's Covenant with Israel at Mount Sinai*, which was made, not only with parents, but with their posterity and children: promising (as I have formerly shown)[1887] to be a God to them and their children – see Deuteronomy 5:2, 3-6, etc. The Covenant was made with the whole body of Israel, old and young, even with their captains of tribes, elders, officers, men, little ones, wives, and strangers (Deuteronomy 29:10-15, etc.). (iii) *In God's Covenant with David, which was made with him and his seed* (Psalm 89:3-4, 28, 29-38 & 132:11-12). (iv) *In God's Covenant with the captives in Babylon*, which was made with them and their children, and children's children (Ezekiel 37:25-27, Isaiah 59:20-21). Thus the children of Abraham, Isaac, Israel, and the Jews, were with their parents admitted federates in these four less perfect expressures of the Covenant of Faith.

{2} Of the seed of Gentile proselytes, joining themselves to the seed of Abraham, the church. This is also evident, that not only they themselves, but also their children were taken in by God into the same Covenant (as Mr.

[1886] Romans 9:10-13
[1887] In Book 3, Chapter 4, Aphorism 4, Section 1

William Lyford has well observed),[1888] their males being circumcised: *He that is*

[1888] "God took into the Covenant of Grace, not the parents only, but with them their infant seed. This is the express tenor of the Covenant (Genesis 17:7) between God and Abraham, between me and you, and your seed, to be a God unto you. What seed does he mean? His infant seed (verse 12): *He that is eight days old, whether it be a child of thy loins, or of a Stranger, a proselyte, which is not of thy seed*. This Covenant was first made with Abraham, (Genesis 12:3), wherein God promised that in his seed should all the nations of the earth be blessed, i.e. in Christ; and it was renewed with the sign of circumcision added unto it (Genesis 17:7, 12), wherein observe three things:

(1) That the Covenant made with Abraham, was the Gospel Covenant, wherein blessedness was promised in and through Christ the promised seed. For, God preached the gospel to Abraham when he said: *In thy seed shall all nations be blessed*, as St. Paul reasons in Galatians 3:8, which Covenant – seeing it was 430 years before the law, and not disannulled by the coming of the law – it was to endure till the seed should come to whom the promise was made (verses 17 & 19). and consequently to the end of the world, because Christ came to establish the Covenant made to the fathers (Romans 15:8) and after Christ no more changes to be expected.

(2) That the persons with whom that Gospel Covenant was made, were Abraham and his infant seed, and all nations, even us Englishmen and our infant seed, as appears from Genesis 17:4, 11: *My covenant is with thee and with thy seed in their generations, and with the stranger that is not thy seed, all of them must be circumcised*, compared with Romans 15:8, 15: *Now I say that Jesus Christ was a minister of the circumcision* (i. e. of the Jews) *for the truth of God, to confirm the promises* (of the Covenant) *made unto the fathers, and that the Gentiles might glorify God for his mercy, being made partakers with them of the same Promises, accord\ing as it is written, Rejoice ye Gentiles with his people*, etc. Now this Covenant of Promises made with the fathers, Christ should not confirm, but clip and curtail it, if so great a part as all our infants be left out and excluded. But if God [should] take our infants into covenant, then who shall dare to exclude them?

(3) When God at first gave that Covenant to Abraham and to the nations, he also gave a commandment that the initial mark of the Covenant should be set upon all whom he had taken into covenant, both Jews and Gentiles, and their infants. The Covenant itself and the mark of the Covenant are alike extended to all the same persons, whether young or old (Genesis 17:12). Note further, that when Christ renewed and established that Covenant in his own blood, though he changed the sign, yet he did not repeal that commandment – nay, he added a new commandment, enjoining the new sign of baptism to be given to all nations (Matthew 28:19), without exception of any persons formerly received into covenant. So that we are under a twofold commandment to baptize our infants: one, from God who first made the Covenant, and gave that commandment, which is still so of force, that if Christ the Lord of the house had not changed it, we would all be bound at this day to be circumcised. And seeing he has changed that sign into baptism, but not the Covenant it self, nor the commandment thereto annexed, it follows that, by the old commandment enjoining infants to be marked, and by Christ's new commandment enjoining baptism to be that mark, all, that are not excepted out of the Covenant, stand bound to receive it," etc. Mr. William Lyford in his *Apology for our Public Ministry and Infant Baptism*, Question 2. pp. 32-33.

eight days old shall be circumcised among you, every man-child in your generations, he that is born in the house, or bought with money of any stranger, which is not of thy seed. He that is born in thy house, and he that is bought with thy money must needs be circumcised, etc. (Genesis 17:10-14).[1889] This stranger, not of Abraham's seed, yet bought by Abraham's money must be circumcised, that is: if he accepted Abraham's God, religion and Covenant as a proselyte, otherwise they were not to be forced; and they being circumcised, all their males also were to be circumcised when they were eight days old, as the males of Abraham's seed (Exodus 12:48-49).

Therefore, the seed, posterity or children of professed believing parents, both Jewish and Gentile are intended by God to be federates, as well as their parents in this most perfect expressure of the Covenant of Faith, the New Covenant.

(Argument 3) All such sorts of persons as God has heretofore taken into the Covenant of Faith, and hath never since excluded or debarred them from it, are still intended by him to be federates in this New Covenant also. This proposition cannot rationally be denied:

[1] Because, the nature of the Covenant of Faith, as to the essence and Substance of it, is one and the same in this New Covenant expressure, and in all the foregoing expressures of the Covenants of Promise, though their accidentals and circumstantials are different. Therefore parents and their children being once admitted Federates in the Covenant of Faith, and never after debarred, are still intended to be Federates therein; in this New Covenant

---

[1889] "This is to be understood of the children of strangers, for none of them, if of age to consent or dissent, was to be compelled to be circumcised. For circumcision was to be used but as a token of the Covenant (verse 11). And he that was out of the Covenant (as all those who were not of Abraham's seed by the free-woman were, unless they were proselytes, and willingly betook themselves to the profession of the religion of Abraham, and then they were Abraham's spiritual, though not his carnal posterity) was kept out from circumcision also."
Large London Annotations on Genesis 17:13.

as well as in any other, yea rather than in any other, this being the top excellency of the Covenant of Faith.

[2] Because, God the Author of the Covenant of Faith has all and sole authority of admitting and excluding, what sorts of persons he pleases, into and from the Covenant of Faith in every gradual discovery thereof. It is his peculiar prerogative royal to appoint and declare, who shall, and who shall not, be federates with him in his Covenant. He admits and he debars whom he pleases without control. If therefore God has once admitted the seed and children of believing parents, Jewish or Gentile, into the Covenant of Faith as well as their parents, and after such admission has nowhere excluded or debarred them from the Covenant of Faith, then such seed and children are still intended by him to be federates within that Covenant of Faith in all the following dispensations thereof, and so in this New Covenant.

But the seed, posterity, or children of professed believing parents, whether Jews or proselyte Gentiles, are a sort of persons which God has heretofore taken into the Covenant of Faith, and has never since excluded or debarred them from it. This assumption also must needs be granted, for: {1} that, the seed, posterity or children of professed believers, Jews or Gentile proselytes, have been heretofore admitted or taken into the Covenant of Faith by God, is plain. For, God's Covenants with Abraham, with Israel, with David, with the captives, were all of them Covenants of Faith, into which God admitted heretofore the children of such parents, with their parents, as I have already proven.[1890] {2} That since such admission of children with their parents into the Covenant of Faith, he has never after excluded or debarred them from the Covenant of Faith, in all the Scripture, is also evident. For, where, or by what Scriptures has the Lord excluded and debarred children of believing parents from his Covenant of Faith. Has God anywhere said to this effect: "I have heretofore accepted all the infants of professed believers into Covenant, but now under the New Covenant, I will accept them no longer?" The adversaries

---

[1890] In the assumption of the second argument.

of infants' covenant state cannot solidly produce any such Scriptures, excluding or debarring them. God has once put such children into possession of this Covenant interest, and never since put them out of possession.

Therefore, the seed, posterity, or children of professed believing parents Jews or proselyte Gentiles, are still intended by God to be federates in this New Covenant.

(Argument 4) All such sorts of persons as God declares to be Covenant saints, or federally holy under the New Covenant, are accepted and accounted by God to be federates with him in his New Covenant.

For clearing of this proposition, I shall show: [1] What I intend by *covenant saints* or *federally holy*. [2] That all such as God declares to be covenant saints under the New Covenant, are accounted and accepted by him as federates in the New Covenant.

[1] **What I intend by *covenant saints*, or *federally holy*,** I shall the better discover, by noting briefly some various uses and acceptations of the word {*holy*} and {*sanctified*} in the Scriptures, as it is applied unto men or women. Men are *holy* or *sanctified*:

{1} By segregation, separation, or calling – and this: (i) Either when they are visibly and outwardly called and separated, from the profane, paganish, unbelieving, impure mass of the world, to the worship and service of the true God in Christ, to be a people near to God. So all within the church visible are holy and sanctified (Deuteronomy 7:6 & 14:2 & 26:19, Romans 1:6-7; 2 Timothy 1:9). (ii) Or when they are separated, set apart or dedicated from the common sort in the visible church, to some special service or peculiar office about holy things, as holy priests (Exodus 22:31, Leviticus 21:6-7, Numbers 16:5, 7, Psalm 106:16), holy prophets (Luke 1:70, Acts 3:21), and holy apostles (Ephesians 3:5, Revelation 18:20). (iii) Or when persons (as well as things) are segregated, separated, and allowed to the lawful and warrantable use of believers: so that they may use them purely, lawfully, conscientiously without sin, etc. thus, the unbelieving husband is sanctified by the believing wife, and the unbelieving wife is sanctified by the believing husband, namely: sanctified to cohabitation and propagation of an holy covenant seed, that the believers issue by the infidel should not be counted an infidel, but a Christian seed.[1891] Thus, every creature is said to be sanctified by the word and prayer, etc., to the pure.[1892]

{2} By profession: when men make a holy profession of faith, love, obedience, and religion towards God, Jesus Christ, etc, then they are called {*saints*}, {*holy*}, {*sanctified*}, etc. (Deuteronomy 26:17-19; 1 Corinthians 1:2 with 3:3, Hebrews 10:29).

{3} By federation with the most holy God, in his holy Covenant.[1893] They that are severed from the profane unbelieving world, unto God, by accepting his Covenant, are covenant saints, federally holy, yea though they want the true inward holiness. Thus all Israel were holy, God's saints (Exodus 19:4, 6, Psalm 50:5): *Gather my saints together unto me, those that have made a covenant with me by sacrifice.* So the children of parents, whereof one was a believer the other a pagan, are counted holy, because such children are taken into God's Covenant with the believing parent.[1894] *And if the root be holy, so are the branches;*[1895] that is: if Abraham, Isaac, Jacob and other fathers of the Jews were holy federates with God, so are their posterity the Jews federally holy also.

{4} By infusion and real participation of true inward holiness, part of the image of God, 1 Corinthians 6:1, 11, Ephesians 4:24; 2 Peter 1:4. Thus it is evident what I mean by {*covenant saints*} or {*federally holy*}: namely: those that become holy by federation, as in the third particular.

[1891] 1 Corinthians 7:14
[1892] Titus 1:15; 1 Timothy 4:4-5, [3]
[1893] Luke 1:72, Psalm 105:42
[1894] 1 Corinthians 7:14
[1895] Romans 11:16

[2] That all such as God declares to be *covenant saints* or *federally holy* under the New Covenant, are accounted by God federates in the New Covenant; is plain.

For, they are therefore accounted covenant saints, or federally holy, because they are brought within God's holy Covenant, and thereby separated from the unholiness of the covenantless world. Covenant holiness does not precede, but follow upon a covenant state. First men are in covenant, and then they are federate saints by that Covenant. The Covenant can denominate none holy that are out of covenant.

But the seed, posterity, or children of federate parents, professed believers – Jewish or Gentile – are a sort of persons declared by God to be *federally holy* or *covenant saints* now under the New Covenant. This assumption is evident. For God has declared such children {*covenant saints*} or {*federally holy*} in sundry passages of the New Testament.

{1} **In that to the Romans**: *For if the firstfruit be holy, the lump is also holy: and if the root be holy, so are the branches.*[1896] For understanding of this, Note:

(i) That these words are brought in as an argument, both proving that the Jews (though broken off from their root) shall again be grafted in and called; and also inciting the apostle to endeavor their calling.

This argument is couched in a double similitude: the one of the firstfruit, and the lump; the other, of the root and branches.

- Such as is the firstfruit, such is the lump; and such as is the root, such the branches.
- Therefore if the firstfruit and root of the church of the Jews were holy, that is federally holy, the whole lump and branches thereof must needs be holy in like manner, federally holy. And

---

[1896] Romans 11:16 compared with the context. See this Scripture solidly expounded and urged for maintaining of children's covenant holiness of federate parents, and ten exceptions to the contrary refelled, by my godly, judicious, and learned friend Mr. Thomas Blake in his *Vindiciae Foederis*. ch. 38.

consequently the Jews were not cut off from all hope, because the Covenant and promises made to their root belonged in some sort to them the branches; who therefore should in God's due time be grafted in again upon their root.

(ii) That this *firstfruit and lump*, this *root and branches*, are parents and their seed brought into Covenant with God, and making up his church. (a) The firstfruit and root of this olive tree, the parents, were Abraham, Isaac, and Jacob, especially and jointly considered, for Ishmael the son of Abraham, and Esau the son of Isaac, are excluded from this privilege.[1897] Why are these compared to the firstfruit and root? Because they are the general root of the church – the Covenant being made to them and to their seed (Genesis 17:8-13, 21:12 & 28:13-14). These were the parents. (b) The lump, the branches, the seed, were natural or grafted. The natural branches were the Jews or Israelites, naturally descending from the common root: Abraham, Isaac, and Jacob.[1898] These made up the church of the Jews. The grafted branches or spiritual seed are all the believing Gentiles, heirs of Abraham's faith, and so his children.[1899] These make up the church of the Gentiles, grafted into the good olive tree with the Jews, and of the same body. Now, as the root was holy, so all the branches – both natural of Jews, and grafted of Gentiles – were holy likewise with the root. Root and branches are alike.

(iii) That this holiness of root and branches, could not be any infused and inherent holiness; for, such holiness cannot be derived and propagated from the root to the branches, as this holiness is here implied to be, but must needs be a covenant holiness, belonging to all the branches, because the branches of that holy root are in covenant with God. Covenant holiness is conveyable and descendable from parents to children; inherent holiness is not. So then, as the parents are in church state and federally holy: so the children are with them in church-state and federally holy, whether among Jews or Gentiles.

[1897] Romans 9:7-14
[1898] Romans 11:17-19, 21, 23-24
[1899] Romans 11:17, 19, 24 & 4:11-13, Galatians 3:7, Ephesians 2:13 to the end & 3:6

{2} **In that passage to the Corinthians:** *The unbelieving husband is sanctified by the wife, and the unbelieving wife is sanctified by the husband; else were your children unclean, but now are they holy.*[1900] For clearing of this, consider:

(i) That these words, together with the context from verses 12-18 are the apostle's answer to a case of conscience put to him, touching continuance of marriage between a pagan unbeliever and a professed Christian believer. It was a frequent case in those times among the heathens, that after marriage one of the married parties was converted from paganism to Christianity, thence doubts and scruples did arise to the believing parties. Here now the question, or case of conscience put to the apostle (as appears by his answer) was this, or to this effect, namely:

Question: Whether such a marriage society between a believer and an unbeliever, that is, between a professed believing Christian and an infidel Pagan was to be continued or dissolved? There being some doubt and scruple – partly touching their issue in such marriage state, lest hereby they should be reckoned among the unclean sinners of the Gentiles, and not among the believing saints, as under the Old Testament it was in a much like case resolved (Ezra 9:1-3, etc., with 10:1-3); partly touching themselves, lest they should be perverted and seduced to idolatry by their idolatrous yoke-fellows respectively, as Nehemiah 13:26; see also Deuteronomy 7:13.

The apostle answers:[1901] (a) That they should dwell together as man and wife; because the infidel pagan in such case was thereunto sanctified by the believing Christian, as to the propagating of a holy covenant issue. The issue being reckoned with the better, not with the worse parent: becoming federally holy with the believer, not remaining paganishly unclean with the believer (1 Corinthians 7:12-14). Thus he removes their scruple about their children and issue. (b) That in case the infidel pagan voluntarily depart, the believing

---

[1900] 1 Corinthians 7:14

[1901] See the series of the context to this effect in my *Key of the Bible* on 1 Corinthians 7:12-18

Christian in such case is free (verse 15). (c) That there was great hope and probability of the infidel's conversion by the believer, which therefore was to be endeavored by their cohabitation (verse 16). Thus he removes their scruple, as to themselves.

(ii) That the children of such parents, whereof one was still an infidel pagan, the other a professed believing Christian, were not unclean as Gentiles out of Covenant, but clean and holy, that is, relatively and federally holy and in Covenant with God together with the believing parent. This is the plain and direct sense and intent of the apostle in these words: *Else were your children unclean, but now are they holy*.[1902] That is, now since one parent is a federate believer, such children are no longer unclean but holy; no longer pagans but Christians; no longer without, but within God's Covenant, although the other parent remains a pagan.

The great dispute here is about the word {*holy*}, in what sense it is to be taken, and how their children are here styled {*holy*}. There are three interpretations given, two extreme, one middle between the extremes. One, that they are holy *qualitatively*, by holiness infused and inherent; another, that they are holy *matrimonially*, by a kind of marriage holiness – *your children are holy*, that is, *legitimate*; another, that they are holy *relatively* or *federally* by being within covenant with their believing parent: that is, they are joined with God in Covenant, dedicated to his service, are visible church members, distinguished from pagans, Turks and all infidels. The first advances their children's holiness here too high, the second debases their holiness too low, and the third sets their holiness in its due place and state. For:

(a) Their children were not asserted by the apostle here to be holy *qualitatively*, by a true infused inherent holiness. (1) Firstly, because the true infused and inherent holiness of regeneration is wholly supernatural: and cannot be propagated or derived from parents to children by natural

---

[1902] See the Scripture judiciously vindicated from misinterpretations by my godly and learned friend Mr. Thomas Blake in his *Vindic. Foederis*, Chapter 39.

generation.[1903] True grace and regeneration is not universally, nor mostly, drawn through the loins of the elect. But here the apostle intends such a holiness as belongs to the children of a believer, because [they are] the children of a believer, and consequently to all the children of a believer. *A quatenus ad omne, valet argumentum.* (2) Secondly, because should the apostle here have intended their children's inherent holiness of regeneration, he had not answered their question so as to remove their scruple. Their scruple was not touching children of parents, professing one and the same religion, one of them really, the other only formally, whether such children were really or only formally holy, but it was touching children of parents of several religions, the one a pagan idolater, the other a professed Christian believer, whether such children were to be counted unclean pagan children out of covenant with God, or holy Christian children in covenant with God. The apostle resolves that, because one parent was a believer, the children were a holy seed of such a root, federally holy.

(b) Their children were not here on the other hand asserted or intended by the apostle to be *matrimonially holy*, that is, legitimate children, not spurious and bastards. (1) First, because thus, and in this sense their children had been holy, that is, matrimonially holy, legitimate, and not bastards, if both parents had remained infidel pagans, and neither of them had become a professed believing Christian – marriage being an ordinance of a civil not of a spiritual or ecclesiastical nature, common to heathens as well as to Christians; the children of parents lawfully married, whether pagans or Christians, are legitimate, and no bastards. (2) Secondly, because the apostle devolves and grounds the holiness of the children here peculiarly upon the privilege and interest of the believing parent only. It is the believer, the professed Christian by whom the unbeliever was sanctified to cohabitation and propagation of a holy covenant seed. It is the believer, upon whose interest the children are holy, and not unclean. *Else* (that is, otherwise, if it were not so, that one of the

---

[1903] John 1:12-13 & 3:3, 5-6

parents at least were a believer, a professed Christian) *your children should have been all unclean* – unholy, un-covenanted pagans – *but now* that one parent is a believer, they also are with their parent federally *holy*. Therefore the apostle could not intend legitimacy of the children here, the benefit of legitimation equally flowing from both parents, but this holiness peculiarly from the believer. (3) Thirdly, because the Scriptures do not anywhere, that I can remember, style the children {*holy*} because the parents are lawfully joined together in marriage, and may warrantably dwell together as man and wife. (4) Fourthly, because the uncleanness of children here opposed to their holiness, is not intended of a matrimonial or civil uncleanness, that all the children born at Corinth of infidel parents were an illegitimate impure spurious offspring of bastards, which were absurd to assert; but is meant of a pagan uncleanness, that they were not comprised within God's holy Covenant, but altogether strangers to it and to God. Consequently, the children's holiness here cannot be meant of their matrimonial or civil holiness, of their legitimacy. And the phrase {*but now are they holy*} is emphatic, and denotes a preeminence of all the children of believing Christians above those of infidel pagans – and what preeminence can be rationally imagined, but their holy interest in God's Covenant into which they are taken with their parents? (5) Fifthly, because should the apostle here have understood and intended matrimonial holiness, that their children were legitimate and not bastards, it had not at all satisfied the doubt or scruple of the Corinthians. For their doubt was not, whether if they continued in their marriage society their children should be bastards or legitimate, but whether they should be pagan sinners or Christian saints.

(c) Their children therefore were declared here by the apostle to be holy by covenant, covenant saints, and federally holy, with their believing and federate parent, for their holiness is here bottomed upon the peculiar privilege and interest of the believing parent, being in covenant. Again, their holiness is universally extended to all children of such a parent without exception or limitation: *else were your children unclean, but now are they holy* – even all of them. Both of these reasons agree only to federal holiness. Finally, their federal holiness here asserted, answers properly and fully to their proposed doubt and scruple, as Mr. Robert Baillie, my godly and learned friend, has well observed.[1904] And therefore by {*holy*}, the apostle here intends only *federally* holy, not *inherently* holy, nor *matrimonially* holy.

Thus the assumption is proven, namely: that the seed, posterity, or children of federal parents, professed believers – Jewish or Gentile – are a sort of persons declared by God to be covenant saints or federally holy now under the New Covenant. I conclude.

Therefore, the seed, posterity, or children of federate parents, professed believers – Jewish or Gentile – are accepted and accounted by God to be federates with him in the New Covenant.

(Argument 5) All sorts of persons to whom in the time of the New Covenant, that ancient covenant promise made to Abraham, Isaac, and Jacob and to their seed touching the blessing of all nations in their seed, and being a God to them and their seed, does appertain, are intended by God to be federates with him in his New Covenant.

This proposition is firm:

[1] *Because that ancient covenant promise made to Abraham, Isaac, and Jacob and to their seed touching the blessing of all nations, in their*

[1904] "The Corinthians had propounded to the apostle their doubt; If a believing husband might lawfully cohabit with his unbelieving wife. The apostle's answer is affirmative: And the reason for the answer is, because whatever the unbelieving parties may be in themselves, yet their cohabitation is sanctified to believers. And of this sanctification, the holiness of their children is brought for an evidence: since the Lord counted their children holy and in covenant with him, the believers might rest assured, that their abode with their companions (though unbelieving) was acceptable unto God.

The apostle here is speaking of husbands and wives, not of men and whores. - To have said, that children was lawful, was no more than that their marriage was lawful, which was not the question; but to say that the children of their lawful marriage were holy, did infer not only the lawfulness of the marriage, but the sanctified use of the marriage, and that now their cohabitation was without sin, and acceptable to God."

Mr. Robert Baillie in his *Anabaptism Unsealed*, chapter 5, p. 138.

seed, and being a God to them and to their seed in their generations, is ratified, confirmed and has its full accomplishment upon Jews and Gentiles by Jesus Christ under the New Covenant.[1905]

Yea, it is digested by Christ into the New Covenant, and is perpetuated in and with the New Covenant to the end of the world. *Now I say that Jesus Christ was a minister of the circumcision for the truth of God, to confirm the promises made unto the fathers; And that the Gentiles might glorify God for his mercy: as it is written, For this cause I will confess to thee among the Gentiles, and sing unto thy name. And again he saith, Rejoice ye Gentiles with his people. And again, Praise the Lord all ye Gentiles, and laud him all ye people. And again Isaiah saith: There shall be a Root of Jesse, and he that shall rise to reign over the Gentiles, in him shall the Gentiles trust,*[1906] where it is plain:

{1} That Jesus Christ was a minister of the circumcision for the truth of God: that is, a minister of the Jews by the discharge of his mediatory office in his prophecy, priesthood, and kingship both in state of humiliation and exaltation, that the Jews might be saved, and the truth of God in Christ be verified, by his confirming the promises made unto the fathers. What promise? Especially those promises made to Abraham, Isaac, Jacob and their seed touching his blessing of all nations therein, and his being a God to them, and to their seed in their generations.[1907] How did Christ confirm these promises? Especially by his death, resurrection, etc., whereby Jews and Gentiles were redeemed, and by the application of these effectually unto them, whereby they became actually partakers of the blessing of Abraham, compare Galatians 3:13-14 with Acts 3:25-26. Now this he does by establishing his New Covenant by his blood, by publishing his New Covenant by his ministers, by applying his New Covenant by his Spirit – in all which the promises made to the fathers were confirmed and ratified.

[1905] Genesis 12:2-3 & 17:7-8 & 22:16-17 & 26:3-4 & 28:12-14, etc.
[1906] Romans 15:8-13.
[1907] Compare Romans 15:8 with Acts 3:25-26 & Genesis 12:3 & 17:7-8 & 22:16-17 & 26:3-4 & 28:12-14

{2} That Christ's ministry to the Jews for confirming the promises made to the fathers had a special intent to the gaining also of the Gentiles, that they might partake the same promises and glorify God for his mercy as well as the Jews (Romans 15:9-12). This was fulfilled by his calling the Gentiles by his New Covenant to partake of the blessing of Abraham (Acts 3:25-26, Galatians 3:13-14). Seeing therefore the promises made to the fathers touching the blessing of all nations in their seed were confirmed to, and accomplished upon both Jews and Gentiles by Jesus Christ in his New Covenant; it is plain that those promises, and so the New Covenant, appertained to such Jews and Gentiles, and that God intended them to be federates in his New Covenant.

[2] *Because in and under the New Covenant, Peter exhorted his hearers to perform the New Covenant duty of repenting, and to partake of the New Covenant token of being baptized for remission of sins, promising thereupon the New Covenant blessing, the gift of the Holy Spirit* – and all this because the promise (namely: the covenant promise made to Abraham, Isaac, Jacob, and their seed touching the blessing of all nations in their seed, and being a God to them and to their seed in their generations),[1908] was to them and to their children, and to the Gentiles afar off, whom God should call, and proportionally to their children. *Then Peter said: Repent and be baptized every one of you in the name of Jesus Christ for the remission of sins, and ye shall receive the gift of the Holy Ghost: For, the promise is unto you and to your children, and to all that are afar off, even as many as the Lord our God shall call.*[1909] Because the promise made to the fathers, appertained to them, and was to them, therefore they are urged to receive the New Covenant token of baptism, and assured of the New Covenant benefit, the gift of the Holy Spirit, which peculiarly belonged to the federates of the New Covenant. Consequently, all such Jews or Gentiles under the New Testament to whom that promise was, were intended by God to be federates in his New Covenant.

[1908] To Abraham: Genesis 12:2-3 & 17:7-8, 22:16-17, to Isaac: Genesis 26:3-4, and to Jacob: Genesis 28:12-14, etc.
[1909] Acts 2:38-39

Otherwise, that promises being unto them, and so on, was not a sufficient ground for the apostle's exhortation of them to New Covenant duties, or for his assurance given them of New Covenant blessings.

But the seed, posterity, and children of Jews and called Gentiles are a sort of persons, to whom in the time of the New Covenant the promise made to Abraham, Isaac, Jacob, and their seed touching the blessing of all nations in their seed, and his being a God to them and their seed in their generation, does appertain. This is evident in the words of Peter to his hearers at Pentecost, both Jews and proselytes,[1910] saying; *Repent, etc., for the promise is to you and to your children, and to all that are afar off, even as many as the Lord our God shall call.*[1911] These words I have formerly explained according to the plain genuine sense of them – there see.[1912] Now I am to prove some points of that explanation in order to confirm this assumption – especially these, namely: {1} that the promise here spoken off was especially God's promise made of old to Abraham, Isaac, Jacob, and their seed; {2} that this promise belonged to the children of the Jews and of the called Gentiles, as well as to their parents; and {3} that this promise appertains to such children of Jews and Gentiles in this time of the New Testament.

{1} That the promise here spoken off, was especially God's ancient covenant promise to Abraham. Isaac, Jacob and their seed, touching his blessing of all nations in their seed, and his being a God to them and to their seed in their generations,[1913] I thus prove:

(i) Because of all foregoing promises mentioned in Scriptures, this covenant promise made to Abraham, Isaac, Jacob and to their seed touching the blessing of all nations in their seed, etc., is most congruous, apposite and suitable here to this passage, and to Peter's intent therein. For (a) this of all other foregoing promises was most eminent and famous among the Jews (the

---

[1910] Acts 2:10, etc.
[1911] Acts 2:38-39
[1912] In Position 1, Reason 5 – there see.
[1913] Genesis 12:2-3 & 17:7-8 & 22:16-17 & 26:3-4 & 28:12-14, etc.

chief hearers of Peter at that time)[1914] who greatly gloried in their being Abraham's children. See Galatians 3:8-9, 16-17. And here the apostle speaks not of any obscure, but of an eminent, famous and noted promise well known to them. (b) This of all other fore-going promises was most notably extended, both to Jews and Gentiles: in their seed all the nations of the earth – Jews or Gentiles – should be blessed; as also to parents – Jews or proselytes – and to their seed (Genesis 17:7-8, 12, Exodus 12:48-49). And this promise here mentioned is urged with this extensiveness to Jews and Gentiles; to parents and their children (c) This of all other foregoing promises was most observably confirmed and fulfilled by Jesus Christ under the New Covenant (Romans 15:8-13). Hence said Paul: *Christ hath redeemed us from the curse of the law, being made a curse for us: – That the blessing of Abraham might come on the Gentiles through Jesus Christ, that we might receive the promise of the Spirit through faith* (Galatians 3:8, 13-14). And the promise here mentioned is implied to be so confirmed by Christ and by his New Testament, yea so incorporated into his New Covenant, that from this promise to them and their children, they are exhorted to accept the first token of the New Covenant, namely: baptism. (d) This promise here urged, seems in the next chapter to be interpreted by Peter in his sermon of like nature, of God's promise with Abraham, whence the Jews are again urged to repentance and conversion: *Ye are the children of the prophets, and of the covenant which God made with our fathers, saying unto Abraham, and in thy seed shall all the kindreds of the earth be blessed. Unto you first, God having raised up his son Jesus, sent him to bless you, in turning away every one of you from his iniquities.*[1915]

(ii) Because this promise cannot be meant of that particular promise of the extraordinary gifts of the Holy Spirit, formerly alleged by Peter out of Joel – no, not although it be said in the verse immediately foregoing: *And ye shall*

[1914] Acts 2:5, 9-11, John 8:[33], 39
[1915] Acts 3:12-19, 25-26

receive the gift of the Holy Ghost.[1916] For: (a) this promise is to Jews and Gentiles, even to all Gentiles whom the Lord shall call until the world's end. Here is no limitation of time. But the extraordinary gifts of the Holy Spirit are here promised to be given and continued to Jews and Gentiles till the world's end. (b) This promise is to called parents and to all their children – even to infant children as well as to adult children. But children, especially infant children, are less capable of the extraordinary gifts of the Holy Spirit than of his ordinary gifts and graces. (c) This promise is here urged as a ground or reason why they should be baptized, and the gift of the Holy Spirit is assured to them upon such their baptism. But baptism is grounded upon, and annexed to only the doctrine and promises of the New Covenant, or on the promises made to the fathers confirmed by the New Covenant.[1917] And though the ordinary gifts of the Holy Spirit are sometimes imparted to the baptized upon their baptism, as Acts 2:41 to the end, 8:38-39 & 16:33-34. Yet where do we find in all the New Testament these extraordinary miraculous gifts of the Holy Spirit annexed to, or communicated with baptism? Sometimes they were poured forth at the preaching of the word, before baptism, as Acts 10:45-48; sometimes at or upon imposition of hands, after baptism, as Acts 8:16-17 & 19:6; sometimes upon occasion of fervent praying, as Acts 4:31. (d) These hearers of Peter here received upon their baptism the ordinary gifts of the Holy Spirit (Acts 2:41 to the end of the chapter). But the extraordinary, miraculous gifts of the Holy Spirit were not (that we read) conferred upon them: therefore not the extraordinary, but only the ordinary gifts of the Holy Spirit were here promised to them, for doubtless they received what was promised. (e) The promise here mentioned and made to them was such as was most pertinent and suitable to the comfort of Peter's hearers pricked in heart, and crying: *Men and brethren what shall we do?*[1918] Now, the promise of the extraordinary gifts of the Holy Ghost (which may possibly befall reprobates:

[1916] Acts 2:38-39 with verses 16-22
[1917] Mark 16:16, Matthew 28:19, Romans 15:8, etc.
[1918] Acts 2:37-39

Matthew 7:22-23; 1 Corinthians 13:1-2) could not be suitable to their comfort, but the promise of the ordinary were most suitable, and the covenant promise of blessedness by Christ, Abraham's seed to all nations, in remission of sins, sanctification, and assurance thereof by the Holy Spirit were most proper and comfortable. And this exceeding fitly agrees to the current of other Scriptures. Compare Isaiah 44:3, Ezekiel 11:19 & 36:27 with Galatians 3:13-14 & Acts 3:25-26. (f) That promise of the extraordinary gifts of the Spirit alleged out of Joel, is interpreted by Peter here to have been fulfilled by God's pouring forth his Spirit upon the apostles (Acts 2:15-34). And for these reasons it seems clear to me, that this promise was not the promise of extraordinary gifts of the Spirit alleged out of Joel, but especially the covenant promise to Abraham, Isaac, Jacob, and their seed, touching God's blessing of all nations in his seed, and being a God to them and their seed, etc.

{2} **That this promise belonged to the children of the Jews, and of the Gentiles that should be called, as well as to their parents.**

(i) That it belonged to the children of the Jews, as well as to the parents, is evident beyond all contradiction; partly by these express words directed by Peter here especially to the Jews: *the promise is to you and to your children*;[1919] partly by the tenor of God's Covenant with Abraham, which was with him and his seed in their generations.[1920]

(ii) That it belonged also to the children of the Gentiles (called here, as elsewhere, *afar off*, Ephesians 2:13, 17) as well as to their parents whom God should call, must needs consequently be granted. For (a) here Peter, as to that promise, puts the Gentiles that afterwards should be called, into an equality or sameness of covenant interest and covenant condition with the Jews, only giving the priority or precedence of covenant state to the Jews. Therefore as the promise was to the Jewish parents and their children; so it was to the Gentile parents afar off, when they should be called, and to their children. The

---

[1919] Acts 2:39
[1920] Genesis 17:7-8, etc.

Gentiles' children, though they be not here expressed, yet are they not here excluded, but must needs be here implied, as much reason being for the Covenant privilege of the one as of the other. (b) God's covenant promise with Abraham, etc., is extended to parents and their seed, both Jews and Gentiles.[1921] Hence all proselyte Gentiles and their seed were to be circumcised as well as the Jews (Genesis 17:12-13, Exodus 12:48-49). Thus the second thing is clear, that this promise belonged to the children of Jews and of Gentiles that should be called, as well as to their parents.

(iii) That This covenant promise belongs to the children of Jews and of called Gentiles now in this time of the New Covenant, is plain: (a) because Peter, in the time of the New Covenant already established by the blood and death of Jesus Christ, declares that this promise belongs to such children; (b) because Peter here urges his hearers, from their interest in this promise to accept baptism, the token of the New Covenant; (c) because Jesus Christ by his New Covenant confirms this promise both to Jew and Gentile, receiving them as his people (Romans 15:7-12). Thus the assumption is proved.

Therefore the seed, posterity, and children of Jews and called Gentiles are a sort of persons intended by God to be federates with him in the New Covenant.

(Argument 6) All sorts of persons since Christ, which are causelessly and absurdly denied to be in Covenant with God, ought to be acknowledged federates with God in his New Covenant. For:

[1] No sorts of persons under the New Testament since Christ can be justly denied their covenant state and interest, but upon some just cause or ground from Scripture, wherein God the Lord and sole Author of the Covenant has sufficiently declared, whom he accepts as federates in his New Covenant, whom he rejects. Whom God accepts in covenant, men are to acknowledge to be federates, whom God rejects and excludes from his

---

[1921] Genesis 17:7-8, 12 & 12:2-3 & 22:16-17

Covenant, men may deny to be federates. Men must not presume to admit or exclude declaratively, but only whom God admits or excludes authoritatively.

[2] God's proceedings in his New Covenant as to admission or exclusion of men in point of federation, though they are above reason, yet they are not against reason. Christianity does not admit, but condemns all absurdity and irrationality.[1922] Therefore Christians, as they must do and declare nothing causelessly, without just reason, so they must do and declare nothing absurdly, against just ground and reason, touching the New Covenant state of any sort of persons.

[3] The New Covenant is the only Covenant since Christ, wherein men are federates with God. But the seed, posterity, and children of professed believing parents – Jewish or Gentile – are a sort of persons since Christ which are causelessly and absurdly denied to be in covenant with God.

{1} *Causelessly* are the children of professed believers Jewish or Gentile denied to be in Covenant with God: there being no just and sufficient cause of their exclusion from covenant state either in regard of God, Christ, the Covenant, or such children themselves – and what other cause can be imagined or pretended?

(i) No cause in regard to God, the Lord and Author of the Covenant. For, (a) God has before Christ still admitted children from Abraham till the coming of Christ into Covenant as well as their parents, and since Christ, God hath never excluded or debarred children from his Covenant.[1923] (b) God has since Christ declared by his Spirit, that such children are holy, that is, federally holy;[1924] and that the covenant promise is to such children as well as to their parents.[1925]

(ii) No cause in regard to Jesus Christ the Mediator of the New Covenant. For, (a) Jesus Christ has not contracted, limited, or curtailed the Covenant of

---

[1922] 2 Thessalonians 3:1-2; 1 Corinthians 11:13-17
[1923] Genesis 17:7-8, etc, Luke 1:59 & 2:21
[1924] 1 Corinthians 7:14, Romans 11:36
[1925] Acts 2:38-39

God by his death, resurrection, and New Covenant administrations, which he should have done extremely if he had excluded so great a part of federates as all the children of federate parents, but he has confirmed and enlarged the same exceedingly, even to Gentiles and their children, as well as to Jews and theirs.[1926] (b) Jesus Christ has declared the infant children of federate parents to be such persons, as of whom is the kingdom of God, and therefore judged them capable of being brought to him, for his embracements, imposition of hands, and benediction.[1927] And can Christ be rationally imagined to seclude such from his Covenant, as he took up in his arms, put his hands upon, blessed, and declared to be within the kingdom of God?

(iii) No cause in regard to God's Covenant since Christ. For, (a) the New Covenant administration nowhere has excluded the children and seed of federate parents from covenant state. (b) The New Covenant of all other covenant administrations, being fullest, largest, most perfect, most extensive and comprehensive, must needs, in the nature of it, take in all sorts of federates and more than the Old Covenant or former Covenants. They took in the Jews and proselytes with their children; but this takes in both Jews and Gentiles called of all nations, and their children. The New Covenant is styled {*the better Covenant*} and {*the better Testament*} (Hebrews 7:22 & 8:6), whereupon my worthy friend Mr. Baillie says very pertinently and judiciously: "The Covenant of Grace for the substance was ever the same, but for the manner of its administration, it was the longer, the better, and after Christ's incarnation, best of all. But it would have been evidently worse after that time in a very great and main particular, if all Jewish infants which before were church members and partakers of the sacrifices and sacraments, as the elect ones of them were of the spiritual promises, should have lost these privileges after the coming of Christ; and have been so far then unchurched, that neither

---

[1926] Romans 15:7-8, etc to 13, Matthew 28:19-20
[1927] Mark 10:13-16

covenant, sacrament, promise, nor any such benefit could belong to them before their years of discretion." So he.[1928]

(iv) Finally, there is no just cause in regard to the children themselves of professed believing parents, why they should be discovenanted since Christ. For the children of professed believers since Christ under the New Covenant, are every whit as capable and receptive of the New Covenant – the initiating token, baptism, and the benefits thereof – as ever the children of Abraham, Isaac, Jacob, and of the Jews were of former Covenants, circumcision, and the benefits thereof. All objections against those, militate as strongly against these. Thus it is evident that the children of professed believers – Jewish or Gentile – are causelessly denied to be in Covenant with God in this New Covenant.

{2} *Absurdly* also are such children denied to be federates with God in his New Covenant. For:

(i) Hereby, the dispensations of divine grace since Christ, are made more strait and narrow than they were before Christ. But that is absurd: God having reserved his most large, liberal, extensive, and diffuse dispensations of his grace for the times of Christ.

(ii) Hereby Jesus Christ, by his coming and establishment of his New Covenant, is necessarily supposed to diminish, not to increase the privileges of his church. But that is absurd: Christ every way increasing his church's privileges by the New Covenant.

(iii) Hereby, a Jewish disciple of the Old Covenant, becoming a Christian Disciple of the New Covenant, shall wholly deprive his children and posterity (until they come of years of discretion to repent and believe) of their covenant state and privileges. Before he accepted the New Covenant, all his children as well as himself were in covenant with God, circumcised, and marked for God's people, dedicated to him, separated from the world, etc. But as soon as he had embraced the New Covenant, all his children are presently discovenanted both from the Old Covenant and New. But this is notoriously absurd, for thus the

---

[1928] Mr. Robert Baillie in his *Anabaptism Unsealed*, chapter 5, pp.134-135

Jew loses by Christ's coming; thus the New Covenant diminishes his privilege and comfort that he had in regard of his children under the Old Covenant; thus the Jew might justly be deterred and discouraged forever from embracing the Christian faith, or becoming a Christian under the New Covenant, because by so doing he should presently (for ought he knows) undo all his children, shutting them out of covenant state with God, out of church membership, and from all the benefits and advantages of both.

(iv) Hereby, the condition of children of federate parents – Jews or Gentiles – should be, not better under the New and Better Covenant, but much worse than the condition of the Jews under the Old Covenant. These were federates with God, but they are discovenanted – yea, they are reduced into as bad a condition as the covenant-less children of pagans and heathens, *without God in the world*. But this is abominably absurd. Shall Jews be Christianized, and shall their children thereby, or thereupon, be paganized?[1929] Shall parents become Christians, and their posterity remain heathens? The New Testament affords better tidings and comfort to the children of believers (Acts 2:38-39; 1 Corinthians 7:14, Romans 11:16).

Thus the children of federates are both causelessly and absurdly denied their covenant state since Christ.

Therefore, the seed, posterity, and children of professed believing parents – Jewish or Gentile – ought to be acknowledged as federates with God in his New Covenant.

And thus I hope it is sufficiently cleared to any sober judgment, That not only Jews, Judah and Israel united, but Gentiles that shall be called; Not only parents, Jewish and Gentile, but with them, their seed, posterity, and children

---

[1929] "It is," said one well, "God's great work to church the world; and the devil's counter-work is to heathenise the church. It troubles the devil much that children from their infancy should be under an engagement to receive nurture and admonition in the Lord, to frequent the ordinances, and to own Jesus Christ by an external profession. If he could but contrive to prevent their coming into that engagement, he might hope more easily to keep them out when they are grown up than to work them out (so grown up) to a renouncing of Christianity, which yet he has brought some unto." A treatise entitled, *A Blow at the Root; or, A Discovery of Satan's Devices*. p.154.

also – even their infant-children. All of this, those phrases {*the house of Israel*} and {*the house of Judah*} do comprehend, are intended by God, and ought to be acknowledged by man, to be federates with God in his New Covenant. This New Covenant state of the children of federate parents, I have insisted upon the more largely, and laid down my arguments for it the more formally, because that especially is opposed by catabaptistic and anabaptistic spirits. Yet I have purposely declined all polemic disputes against particular persons as being besides my intention in this work, wherein I have propounded to myself positively to assert the truth, without interesting myself in the frivolous janglings and fruitless wranglings of particular adversaries.

Inferences

Forasmuch then as the confederates or federate parties to the New Covenant are, on the one hand, God the **Lord**; or God as **Jehovah**, the principal party; on the other hand, the house of Israel and the house of Judah, in Christ – that is, the Jews: Israel and Judah united and their seed, as also the Gentiles that shall be called, and their seed, the spiritual Israel of God, the less principal party. Hence, various inferences of great consequence naturally result, which I shall comprise in this ensuing aphorism.

Aphorism 2

Hence, (1) the New Covenant is most sure and faithful; (2) most complete and comprehensive; (3) most uniting and consolidating to the church and people of God; (4) and is, beyond all other Covenant dispensations, greatest matter of consolation, joy, and thankfulness to the Gentiles. (5) In and under which, All the infant children of New Covenant federates, being in Covenant with their parents, ought to be signed and marked with the first New Covenant token, baptism, as well as their parents.

These five inferences in this aphorism I explain and evince as follows:

(1) Hence the New Covenant is most sure and faithful. Why? Because the chief federate party therein is God the LORD, or God as **Jehovah**. The nature of God is such, the nature of this **Jehovah** is such, actually fulfilling, giving being and subsistence to all his promises, that he can as soon lay aside his very nature, essence, and being, as break his New Covenant, or suffer the promises thereof to fail.[1930] Why does God in his promise of the New Covenant so often repeat that confirming and assuring phrase in his own great and glorious name – {*saith JEHOVAH*} or {*saith the LORD*} – even four times over, but to let us know that, because the Author and chief Federate of this New Covenant is **Jehovah**, therefore this Covenant should be certain, and all the promises thereof infallibly faithful and sure?[1931] There are many other grounds of this New Covenant's sureness and faithfulness, which I shall have cause hereafter to insist upon; but at present this is one eminent cause thereof: **Jehovah** himself has said it, has engaged himself as the chief federate in it,

---

[1930] Exodus 6:3, etc.
[1931] Jeremiah 31:31-34

therefore it cannot fail, we may certainly depend and rely upon it. But of the sureness of God's Covenant from the nature of God and his name **Jehovah**, I have spoken enough already, and it is applicable here.[1932]

(2) **Hence the New Covenant is, beyond all other Covenants, most complete, comprehensive, and extensive.** Why? Because this New Covenant is extended by God most comprehensively to the most ample and numerous multitude of federates. Former Covenants were more limited and restrained: some to particular families, as God's Covenants with Adam,[1933] with Noah,[1934] with Abraham,[1935] and with David;[1936] some to particular tribes, or a part of a nation, as God's Covenant with his captives of Judah and Jerusalem, etc., in Babylon;[1937] some to a particular nation singled out from among all the nations of the world, as God's Sinai Covenant made with the whole nation of Israel in the wilderness.[1938] But this New Covenant is to the utmost enlarged and extended to Jews and Gentiles – even to all sorts of people of all nations, tongues, and languages throughout the whole world, whom the Lord our God shall call to the faith, and profession of the gospel, from the death of Jesus Christ until the end of the world.[1939]

Some few Gentile proselytes, some gleanings of the Gentiles, that willingly came in and joined themselves to the God, religion, and people of Abraham, were taken into covenant, and enfranchised with the Jews heretofore; but the streams and floods of the Gentiles came not in until these New Covenant times.[1940] The proselytes offered themselves to God's former Covenants; but

---

[1932] See Book 2, Chapter 2, Aphorism 2, Section 5, p.139, etc. & Book 3, Chapter 4, Aphorism 3
[1933] Genesis 3:15
[1934] Genesis 6:18, etc.
[1935] Genesis 17:7-8, etc.
[1936] 2 Samuel 23:5
[1937] Ezekiel 37:26
[1938] Deuteronomy 5:2, etc.
[1939] Jeremiah 31:31, etc., Acts 2:38-38
[1940] Genesis 17:12-13, Exodus 12:48-49

this New Covenant is offered and preached by Christ's appointment to all nations, to all the world,[1941] according to that eminent promise of the Lord: *I will gather all nations and tongues, and they shall come and see my glory. And I will set a sign among them, and I will send these that escape of them, unto the nations, to Tarshish, Pul, and Lud, that draw the bow, to Tubal and Javan, To the isles afar off, that have not heard my fame, neither have seen my glory; and they shall declare my glory among the Gentiles. And they shall bring all your brethren for an offering unto the LORD, out of all nations, upon horses and in chariots, and in litters, and upon mules, and upon swift beasts, to my holy mountain Jerusalem, saith the LORD, as the children of Israel bring an offering in a clean vessel into the house of the LORD. And I will also take of them for priests and for Levites saith the LORD.*[1942] This promise had its eminent performance and accomplishment in the apostle's preaching the New Covenant doctrine to all nations – but first unto the Jews, and then unto the Gentiles.[1943]

(3) Hence the New Covenant is to God's church and people the most uniting and consolidating Covenant of all others. And this chiefly in two respects, namely:

[1] In respect of Israel and Judah. God rent ten tribes from Solomon for his idolatry, and gave them to Jeroboam, Solomon's servant – which ten tribes were usually called {*Israel*}, in opposition to the other two tribes continued to David's house, which were called {*Judah*}.[1944] These – Israel and Judah – continued as two distinct kingdoms, under two distinct sorts of kings, and two sorts of religions; never after united till they were both carried away into captivity out of Canaan: Israel into Assyria and the cities of the Medes;[1945]

[1941] Matthew 28:19-20, Mark 16:15-16
[1942] Isaiah 66:18-22; see also Isaiah 60 throughout.
[1943] Acts 3:25-26 & 13:46-47
[1944] 1 Kings 11:4-14, 26-37
[1945] 2 Kings 18:9-12

Judah into Babylon.[1946] During the Babylonian captivity, God made a Covenant with his captives wherein, among other blessings, the uniting of Israel and Judah, that they should no longer be two nations and two kingdoms, but one nation and one kingdom, under one Shepherd, Prince, and King **David** (that is, Jesus Christ the true David) forever.[1947] Perhaps many of Israel came in and joined themselves with Judah when they returned from Babylon, but the primary and most plenary accomplishment hereof was in the time of this New Covenant, when Jews from all nations under heaven were converted unto Christ, at the feast of Pentecost and afterwards; so that not only many thousands, but many myriads, namely: many ten thousands, accepted Jesus Christ as their Shepherd, Prince and King,[1948] and became one spiritual kingdom, one holy nation, one peculiar people under Jesus Christ **the David**.[1949] Thus Jesus Christ, by his New Covenant made an eminent union and consolidation of the house of Israel and of the house of Judah, that they became joint federates with God in his New Covenant: *Behold the days come saith the LORD, that I will make a new covenant with the house of Israel and with the house of Judah.*[1950] Thus the divided nations and kingdoms of Judah and Israel were united and consolidated in one under Christ **the David** by the New Covenant. And this consolidation will have its final consummation, when by the New Covenant doctrine, the broken-off unbelieving Jews, shall again be called and grafted into their own natural stock, *and so all Israel shall be saved.*[1951]

[2] In respect of Jews and Gentiles. There was an extreme division and distance between these, until the days of Jesus Christ and the time of the New Covenant, Jews were near to God; Gentiles afar off from him.[1952] Jews were the

---

[1946] 2 Kings 24-25
[1947] Ezekiel 37:15
[1948] Acts 2:5-14, 41 & 4:4-5 & 5:14 & 6:7 & 9:31 & 12:24 & 21:20
[1949] 1 Peter 2:9-10 with 1 Peter 1:1
[1950] Jeremiah 31:31, etc.
[1951] Romans 11:11 to the end
[1952] Psalm 148:14, Ephesians 2:17-18

children; Gentiles, dogs.[1953] Jews were saints; Gentiles, sinners.[1954] Jews were the church, *to whom pertained the adoption, and the glory, and the covenants, and the giving of the law, and the service of God, and the promises,* etc. Gentiles, the world, *without Christ, aliens from the commonwealth of Israel, and strangers from the covenants of promise, having no hope, and without God in the world.*[1955] And between Jews and Gentiles there was a middle wall of partition, that severed them: an enmity that hindered their unity, even the law of commandments contained in ordinances, circumcision, the ceremonial law, and the whole Levitical service;[1956] but Christ by his death and blood, not only broke down this middle wall of partition, and destroyed this enmity: all those ceremonies, types, and shadows receiving their plenary accomplishment in him;[1957] but also reconciled both Jews and Gentiles unto God in one body by the cross, established his New Covenant in his blood – whereby he *preached peace and union to them which were afar off, and to them which were nigh*;so that, *both have access by one Spirit, unto the Father; and Gentiles are no more strangers and foreigners, but fellow-citizens with the saints, and of the household of God; and are built upon the foundation of the prophets and apostles, Jesus Christ himself being the chief corner-stone.*[1958] Thus the Gentiles are through Christ, by his New Covenant incorporated, and consolidated with the Jews into one church body. This is the mystery, that *mystery of Christ, the mystery which from the beginning of the world hath been hid in God, which in other ages, was not made known unto the sons of men, as it is now revealed unto his holy apostles and prophets by the Spirit; that the Gentiles should be fellow-heirs, and of the same body, and partakers of his promise in Christ by the gospel.*[1959] O how Paul, the teacher of the Gentiles, admires and magnifies this

---

[1953] Matthew 15:26, Mark 7:26[-27]
[1954] Deuteronomy 14:2, Galatians 2:15
[1955] Acts 7:38, Romans 9:4-5 & 11:12, 15, Ephesians 2:12
[1956] Ephesians 2:13-16, etc.
[1957] Ephesians 2:14-16
[1958] Ephesians 2:16-19, etc, Hebrews 9:12-16
[1959] Ephesians 3:3-9, etc.

sweet mystery! And the whole New Covenant ministry – both extraordinary and ordinary – was given by Christ, for the completing of this union fully and finally: *And he gave some, apostles; and some, prophets; and some, evangelists; and some, pastors and teachers: for the perfecting of the saints, for the work of the ministry, for the edifying of the body of Christ; till we all come in the unity of the faith, and of the knowledge of the Son of God, unto a perfect man; unto the measure of the stature of the fullness of Christ.*[1960]

(4) Hence the New Covenant, beyond all other covenant dispensations, is the greatest matter of consolation, joy, and thankfulness to the Gentiles. For until the New Covenant came, the Gentiles (except some few gleanings of proselytes) were wholly destitute of Christ, God, church privileges, true religion, and hope of salvation.[1961] But by the New Covenant in and through Christ's death and blood, they are incorporated into one and the same mystical body of Christ, adopted into the same household of God, enfranchised in the same spiritual city and commonwealth of the saints, and partakers of all the promised mercies, privileges, and ordinances of the New Covenant[1962] – God putting no difference between Gentiles and Jews, purifying their hearts by faith, and giving them the great blessing of Abraham, the promised Spirit through faith, as well as to the Jews.[1963] Now therefore this New Covenant is the Gentiles' door of hope. Other Covenants left them out; the New Covenant takes them in. Other Covenants separated them from the Church; this New Covenant unites them to the church, etc. Therefore, this New Covenant ministers matter of unspeakable, everlasting spiritual consolation, joy, and thankfulness to the Gentiles, more than all other Covenants – as both the Scriptures abundantly intimate,[1964] and the

---

[1960] Ephesians 4:11-13
[1961] Ephesians 2:12
[1962] Ephesians 3:3-6, etc. & 2:19-21
[1963] Acts 15:8-9, Galatians 3:13-14
[1964] Romans 15:8-12

experience of called Gentiles do eminently testify.[1965] Oh! Then, let us Gentiles account this New Covenant, our cordial, our triumph, our jubilee: let us suck the honey and oil of true refreshing consolation out of this rock; let us triumphantly rejoice in this full sunshine of mercy; let us in heart word and life return all possible thanksgivings unto God for this Covenant of Covenants, the **New Covenant**.

(5) Hence all the infant children of New Covenant federates, being in Covenant with God, as their parents, ought to be signed and marked with the first New Covenant token, baptism, as well as their parents.

I have already proven[1966] that the confederates with God in this New Covenant were not only Jews, but Gentiles, *even all that are afar off, whom the Lord our God shall call.*[1967] And not only such Jewish and Gentile parents, but also all their children. Professed believing Jews and Gentiles, and the children of them both, come under the phrase of {*the house of Israel and the house of Judah*}, with whom God makes his New Covenant.[1968] And therefore, not only professed believing Jews and Gentiles, but all their children also ought to be signed and marked with the first New Covenant token, baptism. This inference I shall further evince briefly by these few arguments, namely:

[1965] Acts 13:46-48
[1966] In this 4th Chapter, Aphorism 1
[1967] Acts 2:38-39
[1968] Jeremiah 31:31-32, etc., Hebrews 8:8-10

[Argument 1] *All sorts of persons that are federates with God in the New Covenant, ought to be initiated, signed, marked, and distinguished by baptism: the first token of the New Covenant.*

This proposition I confirm: partly by showing that baptism is the first token of the New Covenant, and partly by proving that all sorts of federates with God in the New Covenant ought to be signed with that first token, the initiating token of the New Covenant.

{1} **That baptism – namely: baptism with water, in the name of Father, Son and Holy Spirit – is the first token, the initiating token of the New Covenant**, is evident in various ways, for:

(i) Baptism was first instituted before the Lord's Supper was instituted. Baptism was instituted in the beginning of John the Baptist's ministry. John himself said: *But he* (namely: God) *that sent me to baptize with water*.[1969] Christ's command therefore to his disciples after his resurrection, to disciple and baptize all nations, was not the first institution of baptism, but only an enlargement of their former commission.[1970] Now they should not only baptize Jews but all nations. Now the Lord's Supper was not instituted till the latter end of Christ's ministry, till the very night wherein he was betrayed.[1971]

(ii) Baptism was first accepted and sanctified by Christ in his own person, namely: at the beginning of his public ministry whereby he began to preach the New Covenant doctrine; the Lord's Supper, not until the latter end of his public ministry.[1972]

(iii) Baptism was first dispensed in order and time to God's New Covenant people, before the Lord's Supper was administered to them. See Matthew 3:5-6, etc. with Matthew 26:26-31. Thus Peter's converts first were

---

[1969] John 1:6, 33
[1970] Matthew 28:19
[1971] 1 Corinthians 11:23, etc, Matthew 26:26-31
[1972] Matthew 3:13, etc, with Chapter 4

baptized; and after admitted to the breaking of that sacramental bread (Acts 2: 41-42). Nor do we read in all the New Testament of any that first received the Lord's Supper and then were baptized.

(iv) Baptism in the nature of it precedes the Lord's Supper. Baptism signifies our implantation into Christ;[1973] the Lord's Supper our nourishment in and by Christ (1 Corinthians 11:20, 23-26). Baptism signifies our putting on Christ and union to him;[1974] the Lord's Supper our continued communion with him (1 Corinthians 10:16). Baptism signifies our regeneration and new birth in Christ; the Lord's Supper our continuation and augmentation in Christ (1 Corinthians 10:16-17. & 11:20, 24-26). Baptism denotes our admission into the mystical body of Christ the church; the Lord's Supper, our Spiritual maintenance and continuance in that body (1 Corinthians 12:13).[1975] Now our implantation into Christ, union to Christ, regeneration in Christ, and admission in Christ's mystical body, do in nature go before our nourishment by Christ, our communion with Christ, our augmentation in Christ, and our continuation in his mystical body. Consequently, baptism precedes as the first New Covenant token in order of nature, and the Lord's supper follows as the Second. Thus the first is so clear, that few adversaries (if any at all) will be found to oppose.

{2} That all sorts of persons who are federates with God in the New Covenant, ought to be signed, marked, and distinguished by baptism, this first token of the New Covenant, is also evident, for:

(i) When God brought Abraham and his seed into covenant with himself, he also appointed that all sorts of persons so brought into covenant, whether Abraham and his seed, or strangers, proselytes, and their seed, should be signed, marked and distinguished from all others by circumcision the first

---

[1973] Romans 6:3-5
[1974] Galatians 3:27
[1975] John 3:3-5, Titus 3:5

token of that Covenant.¹⁹⁷⁶ This was the initiating token of the Covenant. And this course was afterwards continued both with Abraham's covenant seed, and with proselytes and their seed until the days of Jesus Christ, under the Covenant with Abraham, Israel, and David and the captives.¹⁹⁷⁷ Consequently, as all sorts of federates in former Covenants were to be signed, marked, and distinguished by the first Covenant token before Christ, so all sorts of federates in the New Covenant are to be signed, marked, and distinguished by the first New Covenant token after Christ – the Covenant both before and after Christ being for substance one and the same, though the administration, and therein the federal tokens, were changed. And, although the federate women before Christ were not *actually* signed and marked with the first token of the Covenant, yet *virtually* they were marked and circumcised, in the males, and so reputed of God as circumcised, as is plain: partly, in that the whole house of Israel are intimated to be circumcised in the flesh;¹⁹⁷⁸ partly, in that the whole Jewish nation is called {*the circumcision*}, in opposition to the Gentiles called {*the uncircumcision*};¹⁹⁷⁹ partly, in that their females as well as males did eat the passover, which no uncircumcised person might do.¹⁹⁸⁰

(ii) When Jesus Christ commissionated and authorized his apostles to go and gather his New Covenant church out of all nations, even of Gentiles as well Jews, he commanded them to sign, mark, and distinguish all such sorts as they should make disciples with the first initiating token of the New Covenant Baptism — *Go therefore disciple ye all nations, baptizing them into the name of the Father, and of the Son, and of the Holy Ghost*, etc.¹⁹⁸¹ All that should be made Christ's disciples, and federates in his New Covenant – out of all nations, Jews or Gentiles, male or female, bond or free, young or old – all such

---
[1976] Genesis 17:7-14, Exodus 12:48-49
[1977] Luke 2:21
[1978] Jeremiah 9:25-26
[1979] Romans 4:9, etc. & 15:8
[1980] Exodus 12:3-4, 45-48
[1981] Matthew 28:19-20

must be marked with baptism: the first New Covenant token. Christ will have all his federates and disciples hereby dedicated to God and his service, matriculated and solemnly entered into his church, and distinguished from all covenantless persons which remain the devil's disciples and people.

(iii) Answerably, the apostle's practice in the gathering and planting of the New Covenant church was to mark, sign, initiate, and distinguish all sorts with baptism that were converted to the faith of the New Covenant in Christ: both particular persons and whole families, thereby separating them visibly from the world to God and Jesus Christ.[1982]

(iv) A New Covenant state or federation of any sorts of persons, is the primary, most direct, clear, proper and unquestionable ground for their initiation, signing, and obsignation [formal ratification] by baptism: the first New Covenant token. *Repent and be baptized – For the promise is to you and to your children, and to all that are afar off, even as many as the Lord our God shall call.*[1983] Whence I argue:

- If their interest in the ancient covenant promise made to Abraham, Isaac and Jacob (there intended as I have shown)[1984] confirmed and fulfilled by Christ in the New Covenant, and digested into the New Covenant, were a ground to them for their being baptized, then much more their interest in the New Covenant itself must needs be a plenary and sufficient ground for their baptism. It's an argument from the less to the greater, affirmatively. Thus the proposition is firm.
- But the seed, posterity, children – yea, infant children of professed believers Jews or Gentiles – are a sort of persons that are federates with God in his New Covenant. This assumption I

[1982] Acts 16:14-15 & verses 31-33; 1 Corinthians 1:16
[1983] Acts 2:38-39
[1984] In this 4th Chapter, Aphorism 3, Position 5

have already proved by many arguments, so that I need here to add no more.[1985]

- Therefore, the seed, posterity, children – yea, infant children of professed believers Jews or Gentiles – ought to be initiated, signed, marked, and distinguished from all others by baptism: the first token of the New Covenant.

[1985] See Position 3 of this 4th Chapter, Aphorism 1

[Argument 2] *All sorts of persons for whom Christ's enlarged New Covenant commission in Matthew 28:19-20 was intended, ought to be baptized.*

This proposition is clear in the text, and cannot be denied:

- *Go therefore, disciple ye all nations, baptizing them into the name of the Father and of the Son and Holy Ghost; teaching them to observe all things,* etc.[1986] Here, discipling and baptizing are of the same equal extent; and both alike commanded and jointly given in commission by Jesus Christ, to his ministers, namely: with intention and reference to all nations.
- But the children – yea, the infant-children of professed believers Jews or Gentiles are a sort of Persons for whom as well as for their parents Christ's enlarged New Covenant commission in Mat. 28. 19, 20. was intended.

This assumption I prove: partly, from the extent of the object of the ministerial work here intended {*all nations*}: partly from the first act or effect required from the ministers about this object, {*discipling them*}; and partly, from the order of proceeding directed to the ministers in this commission: first disciple them, then baptize them, then teach them.

{1} **The object for whom this enlarged commission of Christ was intended, is expressed so extensively and largely, as to comprehend in it children – infant children as well as their parents, whether Jews or Gentiles – {*all nations*}.**

He does not say "the parents in all nations," or "the adult grown or riper persons come to years of discretion in all nations." for then there would have

---

[1986] Matthew 28:19-20

been some color here for excluding children, especially infant children. But he says "all nations" without adding any restriction or limitation to these or those sorts of people in all those nations. Herein Christ seems to intend the whole body of those nations of the Gentiles respectively. Mr. Stephen Marshall has very well argued that as the whole nation of the Jews – male and female, parents and children, etc. – were visibly taken in as his covenant people heretofore under the Old Testament: so the whole nations of the Gentiles: children as well as parents, one as well as another, might be visibly taken in as his covenant people and disciples now under the New Testament.[1987] And this is rather so to be judged, because the Gentiles were to be grafted into the church of the Jews (Romans 11) and to be *fellow-heirs, and of the same body*, etc. (Ephesians 3:6). Certainly, children are a very considerable part – yea, usually the major part of nations. Why then should not children as well as parents be here intended and comprised in this complexive word {*nations*} – there being nothing here in Christ's commission to exclude them?

[1987] "Secondly, we have the persons to whom they were to do this, {*all nations*}, whereas before, the church was tied to one nation, one nation only were disciples. Now their commission was extended to make all nations disciples: every nation which should receive the faith should be to him now, as the peculiar nation of the Jews had been to him in time past. In a word, {*nations*} here are opposed to the one nation before. Now we know that when that one nation of the Jews were made disciples and circumcised, their infants were made disciples (made to belong to God's school) and circumcised with them. When that nation was made disciples in Abraham's loins, and circumcised, their seed also was the same; When that nation was taken out of Egypt, and actually made disciples, their children were also with them; and we know that in every nation the children make a great part of the nation, and are always included under every administration to the nation, whether promises or threatenings, privileges or burdens, mercies or judgments, unless they are exempted. So are they in cities, in families, it being the way of the Scripture, when speaking indefinitely of a people, nation, city, or family, to be either saved or damned, to receive mercies or punishments, expressly to exempt infants when they are to be exempted, as we see in the judgment that befell Israel in the wilderness, when all that rebellious company that came out of Egypt, was to perish by God's righteous doom, their little ones were expressly exempted (Numbers 14:31), and in the Covenant actually entered into by the body of the nation (Nehemiah 10:28), it is expressly limited to them who had knowledge and understanding," etc.

Mr. Stephen Marshall in his sermon *Of The Baptizing Of Infants*, p. 38, etc.

{2} The first act which Christ commands his apostles and ministers to perform towards or upon this object, {*all nations*}, is such, as may agree to children, yea to infant children, as well as to parents, πορευθεντες ουν μαθητευσατε παντα τα εθνη βαπτιζοντες αυτους, etc. *Therefore going, Disciple ye all nations, baptizing them*, etc.[1988]

Thus the word (as Beza has well noted) may properly be rendered.[1989] Our translation – *teach ye all nations*, etc. – interprets it not so fitly and exactly here; another word being used in the next verse for *teaching*: διδασκοντες. Hugo Grotius has noted that: "there is a twofold way of teaching: the one by way of initiation in the first elements or principles, the other by way of doctrine, and that the former seems to be indicated in the word μαθητευσατε, to initiate into discipline, and is set before baptism; the latter in the word διδασκοντες, which is here placed after baptism."[1990] The former word (thinks Beza)[1991] by proper and peculiar command belonged to the apostles, who by promulgation of the New Covenant were to lay the foundation of the catholic church in the whole world (1 Corinthians 3:10, Ephesians 2:22). Hence believers at first were called {*disciples*}, not of this or that apostle (1 Corinthians 3:4, Ephesians 2:20), but of Christ; and afterwards more significantly they were called {*Christians*}. The latter word διδασκοντες, he thinks to be more generally intended to pastors and teachers, yet the former word μαθητευσατε (in my judgment) ought secondarily to be extended to pastors and teachers, who sometimes lay foundations of churches among pagans; and the later word [διδασκοντες] well agrees to the whole New Testament ministry.

Now this first act here enjoined by Christ to his ministers towards all nations, is to disciple them, to make them Christ's disciples: *Disciple ye all nations*. He does not say, "Disciple ye all parents, all grown persons, all

---

[1988] Matthew 28:19-20
[1989] Beza's Annotations in Matthew 28:19
[1990] Hugo Grotius' Annotations in Mat. 28. 19.
[1991] Beza's Annotations in Matthew 28:19

intelligent persons, all of years of discretion, etc." but "all nations," which comprises children as well as parents. They all were to be discipled, to be brought in as disciples to Christ. But firstly, the parents and adult persons, actually, formally, etc. by initiating them in the principles and first elements of Christianity, of the New Covenant doctrine, and then their children, even their infant children, in and with their parents, virtually, fundamentally, etc., are made disciples. This is plain, for:

(i) The children of Christ's disciples are with their parents in the same school of Christ: to be trained up publicly and privately in the nurture and admonition of the Lord Christ (Ephesians 6:4).

(ii) Little children are accounted by Christ church members: *of such is the kingdom of God* (Mark 10:14). And are not all church members Christ's disciples?

(iii) The Scripture ranks children – even infant children – in the number of disciples: calling all them {*disciples*}, upon whose neck the men of Judea would have put the yoke of circumcision after the manner of Moses (Acts 15:1, 10), and we all know that infant children were to be circumcised as well as their parents (Genesis 17:7-15), and this yoke of circumcision lay most upon the infant children. Thus not only parents in all nations, but also their children, even their infant children, are capable of being made disciples. Therefore, the first ministerial act of discipling all nations is such, as whereof children are in a sort capable in and with their parents, and therefore we may conclude that this part of the commission took in the children with their parents in all nations, and was in part intended for them.

{3} The order of ministerial proceedings directed in this commission towards all nations (namely: first disciple them, then baptize them, then teach them) also further manifests that this commission of our Savior was intended for children, even infant children as well as for their parents and adult persons in all nations.

First, disciple them, initiating them into the elements of the Christian New Covenant doctrine, then baptize them, etc, upon their professing of the Christian faith according to those principles, that so they may be separated from the world, dedicated to God, entered into his church; then teach them to observe all things whatsoever I have commanded you; carry them on unto further perfection of knowledge by more complete and perfect instruction. Hence, Christ's intention in this commission is plain, namely:

(i) That all nations should be discipled, or made his disciples; therefore children, infant children as well as parents, children being parts of the nations, and capable of being made Christ's disciples in their kind as well as their parents.

(ii) That all the nations which should be discipled, and all the parts of nations (children as well as adult persons) which should become disciples, should be baptized, etc.

(iii) That all who should be so discipled, and baptized, should be afterwards more fully, completely & perfectly taught to observe all Christ's commands.

(iv) That this course should be observed (as occasion should require) until the end of the world: the Lord promising his continual presence with his apostles and his successive ministers, pastors and teachers to that effect, until the end of the world (Matthew 28:19-20),[1992] from all of which I conclude:

Therefore, the children – yea, the infant children of professed believers, Jews or Gentiles – are a sort of persons which ought to be baptized.

[1992] See Hugo Grotius' Annotation on Matthew 28:20

[Argument 3] *All sorts of persons to whom the promise is (which was anciently made to Abraham, Isaac, Jacob and to their seed, etc. and afterwards confirmed by Jesus Christ in his New Covenant) ought to be baptized.*

This proposition is in effect the apostle Peter's (Acts 2:38-39): *Repent and be baptized everyone of you, etc. for the promise is to you and to your children, and to all that are afar off, even as many as the Lord our God shall call.* Here Peter exhorts and commands them to be baptized, upon this ground, and for this very reason: because the promise was to them and to their children, etc. – *for the promise is to you and to your children*, etc. (namely: the promise made to the fathers, and confirmed by Christ, as I have formerly proven).[1993] If therefore they were to be baptized, because that promise was to them, then all sorts consequently ought to be baptized, to whom that promise is, and appertains.[1994]

But the children, infants as well as adult children of professed believers, Jews or Gentiles, are a sort of persons to whom the promise is (which was anciently made to Abraham, Isaac, Jacob and to their seed, etc. and afterwards confirmed by Jesus Christ in his New Covenant). This assumption also for substance is the apostle Peter's: *for the promise is to you and to your children*,[1995] etc. And I have formerly shown for the clearing of this particular:

{1} **That this promise belonged to the children of believers whether Jews or Gentiles, as well as to their parents.**

{2} **That this promise belongs to the children of believing Jews and Gentiles now under the New Testament as well as to their parents** – there see.[1996]

[1993] See in this 4th Chapter, Position 3, Argument 5
[1994] Argumentum a Quatenus – ad Omne
[1995] Acts 2:38-39
[1996] In this 4th Chapter, Position 3, Argument 5

Therefore, the children, infants as well as adult children, of professed believers, Jews or Gentiles, are a sort of persons which ought to be baptized.

[Argument 4] *All sorts of persons that were once admitted by God to the initiating sacrament or first Covenant token of the Covenant of Faith, and were never since by him debarred, ought still to be admitted to the first token of the Covenant of Faith, what ever it be, under all sorts of ensuing federal administrations.*

This proposition cannot well be denied, for:

{1} **God alone has supreme prerogative to admit and debar what sorts of persons he pleases both to, and from his Covenant of Faith, and all Covenant tokens thereof.** If he admits once, and never after debars, who shall exclude?

{2} **The Covenant of Faith, as it is substantially and essentially still one and the same in all ages since the fall, and in all the expressures thereof, though circumstantially and accidentally distinct.** So God has still raised and advanced the after-administrations of the Covenant of Faith to a higher degree of excellence and perfection than those that went before, until he brought forth his New Covenant – the most excellent and perfect of them all. This I have formerly manifested.[1997] Therefore the Covenant of Faith under all administrations being one and the same, and the latter still more perfect than the former, all sorts of persons once admitted to the first covenant token thereof must be admitted still to the first covenant token of that Covenant of Faith, whatever it be. The Covenant is still the same, though the federal token is changed. Yea that Covenant is still more and more perfect: and therefore the sacramental initiation of federates into it must not become defective and imperfect, but be answerably more and more perfect.

{3} **Though the first federal tokens of the Covenant of Faith are distinct under several administrations, yet the ground of God's admitting**

[1997] In Book 2, Chapter 2, Aphorism 2, Section 4.1

any sorts of persons thereunto is still the same, namely: God's accepting and accounting of such sorts of persons to be within his Covenant – therefore he will have them marked and distinguished by his first initiating covenant token. Federate persons do not lose their federate state or privileges when God changes his covenant administrations and tokens, but advance their covenant state and privileges of all sorts to a higher degree of perfection.

But the children, the infant children of professed believers, both Jews and Gentiles, are a sort of persons which were once admitted by God to the initiating sacrament or first covenant token of the Covenant of Faith, and were never since by him debarred. This assumption I prove in both the branches of it: namely:

(i) *That the infant children of professed believers, Jews and Gentiles, were once admitted by God to the first covenant token of the Covenant of Faith.* For: (a) God's Covenant with Abraham, and so the Sinai Covenant or old Covenant, were Covenants of Faith, as I have formerly proven.[1998] But God admitted infant children of professed believers Jews and Gentiles to circumcision, the first covenant token of those Covenants (Genesis 17:7-15, Exodus 12:48-49, Luke 2:21 & 1:59, Philippians 3:5). And from Abraham until Christ, this admission of children to the first federal token was continued. (b) When the Covenant of Faith came under a new administration, even that of the New Covenant after Christ, so that the first federal token was changed from circumcision to baptism, the apostles in the primitive churches admitted not only particular professed believers, but also their whole families (though their actual faith be not recorded) to the initiating sacrament of the New Covenant: baptism. When governors of families were converted, not only they, but their families were baptized also, as Cornelius and his company (Acts 10:1-2, 24, 44 to the end), Lydia and her household (Acts 16:14-15), the jailor and all his (Acts 16:33. Stephanas and his household, 1 Corinthians 1. 16.

[1998] In Book 3, Chapter 3, Aphorism 1, Proposition 3, etc. & Chapter 4, Aphorism 2, Particular 3

Now when, not only the governors of families, but their whole families with them were baptized, can we rationally imagine that none of their children – of their infant children – were baptized? Do not parents and their children most properly make up the family, servants being only as accidental foreigners thereunto? Take away children from the family, do not you usually take away the greatest part of the family? When their households are said to be baptized, of whom can we understand it but chiefly of their children?

(ii) *That children – yea infant-children of professed believers, Jews or Gentiles – were never, since their first admission, debarred by God from the initiating token of the Covenant of Faith*, may thus be cleared, for:

(a) When did God debar them? (1) Not in all the Old Testament, from Abraham until the days of Christ: infant children being all that while circumcised.[1999] (2) Not in all the New Testament, for where's the prohibition that can be pleaded in bar against them in all the New Testament? The adversaries of infant baptism cannot produce any divine inhibition of infant children from the first covenant token, either in express terms, or by any just and necessary consequence, in all the New Testament. They cry: "Where is infant baptism commanded?" Nay rather we say, "Infants are by God's command once put into possession of the initiating token of the Covenant of Faith, and where has God ever since dispossessed them? Why then should they not keep their possession still, without any new command?"[2000]

(b) How, wherewith, or whereby has God debarred them? (1) Not by straitening [narrowing] the successive covenant administrations or privileges thereof. For, they have been gradually still more and more enlarged. (2) Not by the discovenanting of infant children of believers, for the New Covenant still declares that they are federally holy,[2001] and that the promise is to them.[2002] (3) Not by withdrawing his covenant grace from them, for they are counted saints

---

[1999] Genesis 17:7-15, Exodus 12:48-49 with Luke 1:59 & 2:21, Philippians 3:5
[2000] Genesis 17:7-15
[2001] Romans 11:16; 1 Corinthians 7:14
[2002] Acts 2:38-39

(1 Corinthians 7:14), and Christ says: *of such is the kingdom of God* (Mark 10:14). (4) Not by prescribing any stricter qualifications of children for their baptism under the New Covenant than were required in children for their Circumcision under the Old Covenant. Children descended of federate parents, were, because children of such parents, sufficiently qualified for the initiating sacrament or first covenant token, both under Old and New Covenant. And though faith and repentance are pre-required unto baptism in the New Testament, yet these preparatory qualifications are only required in adult or grown persons that should be called from Judaism or paganism unto the communion of the Christian Church under the New Covenant, either at the first planting of the New Covenant church, or afterwards.[2003] But we nowhere read that faith and repentance are pre-required in infants of professed believing parents, as to fit them for their baptism: they being taken into covenant and admitted to the first token thereof with their parents, as the Jewish children were of old. And for strengthening this, I desire the reader further to observe that he shall not find one instance in all the New Testament, of any infant child of a baptized parent that was kept or debarred from baptism until years of discretion, and then upon actual profession of faith baptized. (5) Not by reason of infant children's in capacity for baptism, for they are every way as capable of baptism, as Jewish children were of circumcision; and the promise belongs to children, therefore baptism belongs to them.[2004] By none of these ways, nor by any other that can be justly alleged, are infant children of believers excluded or debarred by God from the initiating token or sacrament of the Covenant of Faith, since he first admitted them thereunto. We may justly conclude:

Therefore, the children, the infant children of professed believers, Jews and Gentiles, are a sort of persons that ought still to be admitted to the first

---

[2003] Mark 16:16, Matthew 3:2, 6, Acts 2:38-39 & 8:36-37, 12-13
[2004] Acts 2:38-39

token of the Covenant of Faith, whatever it be, under all sorts of ensuing federal administrations. And therefore to baptism under the New Covenant.

[Argument 5] *All sorts of persons that were Circumcised before and under the Old Covenant administration even until the days of Christ, ought to be baptized under the New Covenant Administration since the days of Christ.*

This proposition and the sequel thereof, may strongly be confirmed by several grounds from Scripture. For:

{1} The Covenant of God with Abraham, under which circumcision was first instituted;[2005] the Sinai Covenant or Old Covenant, under which it was after continued until the death of Christ;[2006] and the New Covenant under which circumcision was abrogated (Acts 15, Galatians 5:1-4) and baptism appointed (John 1:33, Matthew 28:19), are but all one Covenant of Faith substantially and essentially; though distinct administrations of that Covenant, differing circumstantially and accidentally (as I have often shown), but the latter administrations being still more complete and perfect than the former. Now:

(i) These Covenants being for substance the same, the Tokens of these Covenants consequently are for substance the same, and the admission of federates to the first federal tokens must be for substance the same. As therefore the infant children of federate Jews were circumcised, so the infant children of federate Jews and Gentiles are to be baptized.

(ii) Besides, the New Covenant being more complete and perfect in all covenant privileges, infant children under the New Covenant must needs as fully at least enjoy the initiating privilege of baptism as the infant children before and under the Old Covenant enjoyed the initiating privilege of circumcision. Otherwise the federal privileges of ensuing Covenants should not be enlarged, but contracted and abridged, which is utterly repugnant to God's order of federal administrations.

[2005] Genesis 17:7-15
[2006] Exodus 12:48-49, Luke 1:59 & 2:21, Philippians 3:5

{2} God's command, which did formally oblige Abraham to sign and seal his infant children with circumcision, the initiating token of the Covenant of Faith under that administration;[2007] does virtually oblige Christians to sign and seal their infants with baptism, the initiating token of the same Covenant of Faith under this New Covenant administration. And if Christ had not changed the initiating token from circumcision to baptism, we ought still to have circumcised our infants. Now though the token is changed, yet the Covenant is not substantially changed, nor is God's command of initiating the infants of federates substantially changed. Therefore God under the former Covenants commanding infants to be sacramentally signed and initially marked, and under the New Covenant appointing baptism to be that initial mark or sign, to all nations, without any exception at all of infants; the infants of believers ought now to be baptized by virtue of that first command, as well as infants of federates ought then to be circumcised; [just] as the fourth commandment requiring a sabbath to be sanctified – namely: any sabbath which God should appoint; and formally in express terms requiring the seventh day of every week to be that sabbath during the Old Testament administration[2008] – does virtually require and command us Christians since Christ to sanctify the first day of every week for the sabbath, Christ having changed the particular day from the seventh to the first upon a greater ground, but not abrogated the substance of the fourth commandment.

{3} Baptism clearly succeeds in the room and stead of circumcision: *In whom also ye are circumcised with the circumcision made without hands, in putting off the body of the sins of the flesh by the circumcision of Christ*; συνταφεντες αυτω εν τω βαπτισματι, etc. *being buried together with him in baptism, wherein also you are risen with him*, etc.[2009] Here (as I have elsewhere

---

[2007] Genesis 17:7-15
[2008] Exodus 20:8-11
[2009] Colossians 2:11-12, etc.

shown)[2010] Paul dissuades them from Mosaical ceremonies, especially from circumcision, as needless to Christians, because they have in Christ a circumcision far better, in respect of the (i) author: *Christ*; (ii) manner: *made without hands*; (iii) effect: *true sanctification, in putting off the body of the sins of the flesh*; (iv) visible sign, namely: baptism, wherein they are sacramentally buried with Christ, and raised with Christ. That phrase is much to be noted: *In whom ye are circumcised – being baptized*; whence he gives them to understand that baptism is our Christian circumcision; baptism is Christ's circumcision: Christ has appointed baptism instead of circumcision. And the analogy or similitude between them is clear and observable. (a) Circumcision was a token of the Covenant of Faith (Genesis 17:7-15); so baptism (Mark 16:15-16, Matthew 28:19-20, Acts 2:38-39). (b) Circumcision was the first token, the initiating token of the Covenant (Genesis 17:7-15, Exodus 12:48-49). They must first be circumcised before they might eat the passover; so baptism is the first token, the initiating token of the Covenant (as I have already proven):[2011] they must first be baptized, before they may eat the Lord's supper (Acts 2:41-42). (c) Circumcision signified and sealed regeneration and sanctification (Deuteronomy 30:6, Colossians 2:11). Baptism also signifies and seals the same (John 3:3, 5, Colossians 2:12, Titus 3:5; 1 Peter 3:21). (d) Circumcision was only once applied to particular persons; so baptism. (e) Circumcision signified and sealed the righteousness of faith in Christ's blood (Romans 4:11); so baptism (Matthew 28:19, Romans 6:3-6, Galatians 3:26-27; 1 Peter 3:21) – so that the analogy and answerable resemblance between them is very great and palpable. Thus the proposition is confirmed.

But the infant children of all federate parents Jews or Gentile proselytes are a sort of persons that were circumcised before and under the Old Covenant

---

[2010] In my *Key of the Bible* on Colossians 4, and in this treatise of *God's Covenants*, Book 3, Chapter 3, Aphorism 2, Question 1

[2011] In this 4th Chapter, Inference 5, Argument 1

administration, even until the days of Christ. This assumption is undeniably evident in many Scriptures.[2012]

Therefore, the infant children of all federate parents Jews or Gentiles are a sort of persons that ought to be baptized under the New Covenant administration since the days of Christ.

[2012] Genesis 17:7-15, Exodus 12:48-49, Luke 1:59 & 2:21, Philippians 3:15

[Argument 6] *All sorts of persons to whom the mercies, benefits, and blessings promised in the New Covenant and signified in this first New Covenant token of baptism, appertain, and are communicated, ought to be baptized.*

This proposition is firm, for:

{1} The apostle Peter argues that Cornelius and his company were to be baptized because they had received the New Covenant mercy promised: *Can any man forbid water, that these should not be baptized, who have received the Holy Ghost as well as we?*[2013] And elsewhere; *Forasmuch as God gave them the like gifts as he did unto us, what was I that I could withstand God?*[2014] And in another place: *If thou believest with all thine heart, thou mayest.*[2015] That is, "if you have the faith of the New Covenant, you may have the baptism of the New Covenant."

{2} Where God gives the blessings signified, will he not allow the signs thereof? Shall God give the inward, spiritual, heavenly, and most excellent part of baptism to any: and shall the outward, earthly, and meanest part of baptism be withheld from such? It is an argument (*à majori ad minus*) from the greater to the lesser. If God admits to the greater, he will not exclude from the lesser.

{3} Some of the most learned Anabaptists confess that if they knew any infants to have received the inward grace, they durst not deny them the outward sign; and that those particular infants which Christ took up in his arms and blessed in Mark 10 might have been baptized.[2016]

But the infant children of federate parents, Jews or Gentiles, are a sort of persons to whom the mercies, benefits, and blessings promised in the New

---

[2013] Acts 10:47
[2014] Acts 11:17
[2015] Acts 8:36-38
[2016] See Mr. Marshall's sermon *Of Baptizing Infants*, p.41.

Covenant, and signified in this first New Covenant token, baptism, appertain and are communicated. This assumption is also firm, for:

(i) The promise, confirmed and accomplished by Christ under the New Covenant, is to such children, as well as to their parents, therefore the promised blessings therein belong to them.[2017]

(ii) Children, even infant children of federate parents are covenant saints, federally holy.[2018] And federal holiness is one benefit of the New Covenant as well as of the Old.

(iii) Little children, infant children may partake all such spiritual blessings and benefits belonging to the initiation and being of Christians, as are signified and sealed in baptism; whether regeneration and sanctification (John 3:5, Titus 3:5, Colossians 2:12), remission of sins and justification (Acts 2:38), union to, and communion with Christ (Galatians 3:27, Romans 6:2-5), or, the great blessing of the Holy Spirit (John 3:5, Titus 3:5, Acts 2:38), or eternal life and salvation, Mark 16. 16. 1 Peter 3:21. These and such like Spiritual blessings are signified and sealed (as these Scriptures show) by baptism. Now of all these, little children may be partakers, for as much as Christ tells us: *Of such is the kingdom of God; of such is the kingdom of heaven; and therefore he put his hands upon them and blessed them.*[2019] But without regeneration, sanctification, etc., none can enter into, or be members of the kingdom of heaven (John 3:3, 5, Hebrews 12:14), therefore little children, of whom, as well as of grown persons the kingdom of heaven is, must needs partake these and all such like New Covenant benefits, fitting them for the kingdom of God.

(iv) Should not the saving benefits and blessings promised in New Covenant, and sealed in baptism, appertain and be communicated to the Infant children of federate parents, no such children dying in their infancy before years of discretion could be saved – which to assert or imagine, were very horrid, unscriptural, and uncharitable. I conclude:

[2017] Acts 2:38-39 with Romans 15:8, etc.
[2018] Romans 11:16; 1 Corinthians 7:14
[2019] Mark 10:13-16, Matthew 19:14-15

Therefore, the infant children of federate parents – Jews or Gentiles – are a sort of persons that ought to be baptized.

[Argument 7] *All sorts of persons, whom God has expressly or virtually commanded to be baptized, ought to be baptized.*

This proposition is evident, for:

{1} God's command in all parts of his worship ought to be obeyed, and observed as the rule of his worship. We can have no clearer warrant for any religious undertaking than God's command. Anabaptists will confess this.

{2} God's virtual commands by clear and necessary consequence, are to be observed and obeyed, as well as his express commands in so many words and syllables. Otherwise, what warrant do we have in the New Testament for sanctifying a weekly sabbath; for observing the first day of the week for our Christian sabbath; for ministers preaching twice, namely: morning and evening, on the Lord's day sabbath; for women's participation of the Lord's supper; for public collections of alms on the first day of the week; for observing the laws of forbidden degrees in marriage; for taking an oath before a magistrate or otherwise, for determining of strife, etc. For we have no express syllabical command for these and many like things in all the New Testament; and yet we hold them sufficiently warranted and authorized by God's virtual and implicit commands laid down in the New Testament by good and undeniable consequence.

{3} The apostle Paul and Barnabas held themselves obliged, by a mere virtual and implicit command to turn from the Jews and preach to the Gentiles: *Lo, we turn to the Gentiles. For so hath the Lord commanded us, saying, I have set thee to be a light of the Gentiles, that thou shouldst be for salvation to the ends of the earth.*[2020] Here is an express promise, no express [sic] but only an implicit and virtual command; yet this, they held themselves bound to obey.

[2020] Acts 13:46-47

But children, even the infant children of federate parents, or of professed believers Jews or Gentiles, are a sort of persons whom God has expressly or virtually commanded to be baptized. This assumption I prove by several implicit and virtual commands of God for baptizing of such infant children:

(i) *Go disciple ye all nations, baptizing them*, etc.[2021] Here is Christ's express formal command for discipling and baptizing of all nations: and here is Christ's implicit virtual command for baptizing the infant children of all professed believers in all nations. Unless we shall deny that their infants to be any parts of the nations, or in any capacity of being made Christ's disciples, of both which enough formerly.[2022]

(ii) *Repent and be baptized every one of you* (said Peter to his heart-pricked hearers), *for the promise is to you and to your children*, etc.[2023] Here is another implicit virtual command for baptizing of their infant children. The words I have analytically explained heretofore.[2024] Here's a command: *Repent and be baptized*, etc.; a promise: *and ye shall receive*, etc.; and the ground of both: *for the promise is to you and to your children*, etc. whence I note these three things: (a) that a right to baptism and a duty of being baptized are consequences resulting from a covenant state, and interest in the promise; (b) that children, even infant children, of professed believers as well as their parents, have now under the New Covenant a covenant state and interest in the promise; and (c) that the promise (which is here the ground of baptism) being to children as well as to their parents, the command of being baptized equally reaches to the children and to the parents.

(iii) Finally, God – commanding Abraham to sign or mark his covenant seed and infant children with the initiating token of the Covenant, circumcision[2025] – did implicitly and virtually command us under the New

---

[2021] Matthew 28:19-20
[2022] See in this 4th Chapter, Inference 5, Argument 2
[2023] Acts 2:38-39
[2024] In this 4th Chapter, Inference 5, Argument 3
[2025] Genesis 17:7-15

Covenant to sign our New Covenant seed and infant children with the initiating token of the New Covenant: baptism, for: (a) the Covenant is still for substance the same, but now under a more perfect administration; (b) the command for an initiating marking of federate children with the first covenant token still remains unrepealed, only Christ has changed the initiating covenant token from circumcision to baptism, from which he has nowhere excluded believers' infant children; (c) and baptism succeeds in place of circumcision, being most analogous thereunto, yet afar excelling it.[2026] From all of this, it is evident that God – expressly and formally commanding Abraham to circumcise his infant children – implicitly and virtually commands us Christians now to baptize our infant children also.

Therefore, children – infant children of professed believers: Jews or Gentiles – are a sort of persons that ought to be baptized.

By these seven arguments (to add no more) I hope it will be evidently clear to all sober un-pre-engaged judgments that: **as infant children of professed believers Jews or Gentiles are of the house of Israel and Judah, and federates as well as their parents in this New Covenant; so they ought to be signed, marked, and distinguished from all others by the first sacrament, or initiating. token of the New Covenant: baptism.**

Such objections, as may possibly be made against these or any of these arguments, may easily be removed and refelled by what has been said in explanation and confirmation of these arguments.

Hitherto of the federates, or parties to the New Covenant: namely: God the LORD, on the one hand; professed believers – Jews and Gentiles with their children – on the other.

[2026] Colossians 2:11-12

www.ingramcontent.com/pod-product-compliance
Lightning Source LLC
Chambersburg PA
CBHW021146060526
44107CB00146B/1343/J